RECONSIDERATIONS IN
SOUTHERN AFRICAN HISTORY

Jeffrey Butler and Richard Elphick, Editors

Milton Shain, *The Roots of Antisemitism in South Africa*

COLONIAL SOUTH AFRICA AND
THE ORIGINS OF THE RACIAL ORDER

COLONIAL SOUTH AFRICA AND THE ORIGINS OF THE RACIAL ORDER

Timothy Keegan

UNIVERSITY PRESS OF VIRGINIA
Charlottesville

First published 1996
in Southern Africa by David Philip Publishers (Pty) Ltd, 208 Werdmuller
Centre, Claremont, 7735, South Africa

in North America by the University Press of Virginia, Box 3608, University
Station, Charlottesville, Virginia 22903-0608, USA

in the United Kingdom and Europe by Leicester University Press, *A Cassell
Imprint*, Wellington House, 125 Strand, London WC2R 0BB, UK

ISBN 0-86486-308-X (David Philip)
ISBN 0-8139-1735-2 (University Press of Virginia, cloth)
ISBN 0-8139-1736-0 (University Press of Virginia, paper)
ISBN 0-7185-0133-0 (Leicester University Press, cloth)
ISBN 0-7185-0134-9 (Leicester University Press, paper)

British Library Cataloguing in Publication Data is available from the British
Library.

Library of Congress Cataloging-in-Publication Data

Keegan, Timothy J.
    Colonial South Africa & the origins of the racial order / Timothy
Keegan.
        p.   cm. -- (Reconsiderations in southern African history)
    Includes bibliographical references and index.
    ISBN 0-8139-1735-2. -- ISBN (invalid) 0-8135-1736-0 (pbk.)
    1. South Africa--Race relations. 2. South Africa--History--To 1836.
    3. South Africa--History--1836-1909. I. Title. II. Series.
    DT1756.K44   1997
    305.8'00968--dc20   96-35827
                                                              CIP

Printed in South Africa by Creda Press, Eliot Ave, Epping, Cape Town, South
Africa

Contents

Maps

Preface

This book has had a complex genesis. It grew out of an interest in the South African highveld in the later nineteenth century. But I was increasingly drawn back into the first half of the century, and to the original colony of settlement, the Cape Colony, as the continuities in colonial experience became clear, and as questions arose which awoke my curiosity. I have been constantly aware that I am intruding into territory which has been charted by others with far greater sensitivity and imagination than I possess; and in writing this book, I have been in a constant state of awe at the fecundity and quality of much of the mass of research that has appeared in recent times on early southern African history. It is probably true to say that the centre of gravity in South African historical research has shifted in the last decade away from the concentration on the industrial age that characterised the 1970s, to a much greater appreciation of the importance of earlier periods.

In the process, a large and impressive historiography of slavery and post-slave societies has emerged. At the same time the formative convulsions in African societies in the early nineteenth century have opened a rich and productive vein of research and debate. Post-structuralist perspectives, which have profoundly influenced the study of history everywhere, have been brought to bear in recent studies of the subcontinent; these have made original use of such sources as newspapers and artworks of the day to decode the hidden meanings of race and class.

The study of South African history has come full circle. Today's young scholars are more likely to be preoccupied with meaning and mentality, ideology and culture, than were their predecessors. The wellsprings of consciousness and perception are now in scholarly fashion. The contingent and the obscure have supplanted the mechanical workings of class struggle. The result is a world-view that is less deterministic and more complex, more interested in real lives and the hidden and unexpected conjunctures of history. Some of the new history is as prolix and obsessed with its own cleverness as was some of the old. But an amalgam of the cultural and the social, the economic and the political, is apparent in the best of it.

It is also true that the one period most in need of a new synthesis is the period that has produced much of the most exciting new research, the first half of the nineteenth century. This period was fundamental in the shaping of South African society as we know it. It was in part this realisation which provided the impetus for this book. Despite the rich vein of research and the exciting new ways of approaching the writing of history that have come out of the universities in recent years, the task of constructing a larger picture, an interpretation of the period as a whole, has not yet been attempted. Macro-analysis, then, is the task of this book. But at the same time, I have throughout sought to ground the study in a firm foundation of narrative.

This book, however, does not pretend to be an all-encompassing 'general history'. Rather I have pursued issues which seem to me to have been particularly significant. A general history would pay at least as much attention to the ruled as to the rulers, to women as to men. This book is preoccupied with structuring forces, with the forces of imperialism and colonialism, and less so with the peoples who experienced their effects. Thus it gives greater attention to the powerful than the powerless, the colonisers than the colonised, to men than to women. It might seem to some that the perspectives and world-views of dominant actors are given privileged status over the experiences and perceptions of the victims and the powerless. I offer no excuses, as the investigation of structuring forces is of profound significance. Without it, the history of society, community and culture can become an exercise in romanticism and obscurantism.

This book is offered not as a declaratory statement, but as a spur to further thinking and further research. This is much needed, particularly in South Africa, where all sorts of official assumptions about the past have been discarded in the wake of the collapse of the apartheid order, and where perceptions about the past are in a state of ferment and flux. Inevitably, much of the historical imagery that occupies the spaces opened up by the democratisation of cultural life in South Africa is concerned with heroics, with resistance and struggle. There is also a tendency to reduce South African history to a morality play, in which a long series of calamities and degradations is visited upon the local people by the evil forces of European colonialism. There is enough truth in this. But Africans were never passive victims, stripped of agency, and the invasive forces were never omnipotent. Conspiracy theories about the past make for good politics, but bad history. In the intellectual cauldron of contemporary South Africa, reconstructing our understandings of the past is a crucial and contested task.

❖

Some consideration of terminology is called for. Race is no longer regarded as a useful or meaningful scientific concept. Nonetheless, in a purely socio-political sense, race has been profoundly formative in the making of modern societies. Terms such as 'white' and 'coloured' are used here, but it should be understood that these are cultural constructions, and there was never any clear-cut dividing line, given the extent of genetic mixing. Physical appearance was often not a clear indicator of group belonging, which itself shifted with political or economic circumstances. But these categories had real social meaning in a period in which racial classification was becoming central in the perceptions and policies of dominant groups.

I have used the terms Khoi and Bushman to describe the Cape's indigenous peoples. They clearly were originally distinct peoples, although boundary lines became very fluid. 'Bushman' seems now to be regarded as acceptable terminology, and in some ways is less problematical than 'San', especially as the people so described were by the nineteenth century largely redefined by the experience of European colonisation. 'Khoisan' is a widely used blanket term which indicates the difficulties of distinguishing these peoples in historical contexts. Khoisan (many with an admixture of European or Xhosa ancestry) gradually merged, together with ex-slaves, into what by the middle of the nineteenth century was already being called the 'coloured' population. This term, too, has gained some respectability (not least among coloured people themselves) as a descriptive reality in post-apartheid South Africa, having acquired a degree of opprobrium as a result of the divisive policies of the apartheid regime. Coloured people have to be distinguished from the Bantu-speaking mixed farmers, living in settled chiefdoms, whose encounter with invasive colonial forces is a theme running through this book.

'Colonist' refers to those of putatively European origin who were defined as forming the dominant colonising population. The term 'burgher' refers to colonists of mainly Dutch–Afrikaner origin who were accepted as full members of the dominant group. I use 'settler' to refer to colonists of British origin, especially those who arrived in the eastern Cape or on other frontiers from 1820 onwards. 'Afrikaner' describes those of the putatively 'white' population who spoke Dutch (or local variants which were already distinct from the mother tongue), whereas 'Boer' (or 'trekboer') describes more narrowly those Afrikaners who lived off the land as stock farmers and hunters in the pastoralist stretches beyond the arable southwestern corner of the colony. In dominant usage, emergent Afrikaner identity was defined increasingly in racially exclusive ways, but it is true that in language and cultural terms, this identity was forged in the interaction between 'whites', Khoisan and slaves.

A book of this kind rests on a great deal of other people's labour. The first chapter below examines some of the literature that I take issue with. However, a more recent generation of writers has provided grist for my mill and helped form my views. They are honoured in the endnotes of this book, but mention needs to be made of some of them here. Historians at the University of Cape Town have been at the forefront of the new historiography of the pre-industrial Cape, under the auspices in particular of Nigel Worden. UCT graduates whose work has contributed substantially to my understanding include Andrew Bank, Wayne Dooling, Kirsten McKenzie, Elizabeth Elbourne, Lalou Meltzer, Digby Warren and many others. Richard Elphick and Hermann Giliomee have done much to breathe new life into the Dutch period in Cape history. Susan Newton-King and Nigel Penn among others have immeasurably enriched our understanding of the early Cape frontier and relations with Khoisan. Robert Ross at Leiden has contributed widely to debates on the early Cape. In the United States Mary Rayner, Robert Shell and John Mason have made important contributions to the study of Cape slavery. Jeffrey Peires and Clifton Crais have added to our understanding of the eastern Cape in diverse ways.

Other names need to be mentioned. Shula Marks, Richard Elphick, Christopher Saunders and Jeffrey Butler read the manuscript of this book. Rodney Davenport engaged me in debate on the liberal impact in South African history and tempered my less judicious conclusions. Martin Legassick lent me the enormous benefit of his incomparable insights into the South African past, with detailed and thought-provoking critiques. Russell Martin again proved to be a consummate editor. Needless to say, I remain solely responsible for all infelicities and downright errors that remain. My thanks go to Leonie Twentyman-Jones for her index and Susan Sayers for her maps. Finally, my wife, Margaret Kinsman Keegan, bore the brunt of this tiresome enterprise, while she herself was working long and unpredictable hours for the Constitutional Assembly and, later, as director of the African National Congress's parliamentary research department. Our children, Matthew, Brendan and Thomas More, have endured their parents' obsessions with remarkable equanimity and good humour. To them I am profoundly grateful.

CHAPTER ONE

Introduction

Mainstream liberal historians in the inter-war years developed the idea that South African history was characterised in the main by the emergence of an integrated, albeit radically unequal, multiracial society. They took as their starting point the fact of a common society in which black and white were irrevocably interdependent. Their stress on the growing intertwining and interaction of black and white in a new society contrasted with an earlier colonial school which had stressed the ubiquity and inevitability of racial conflict, growing out of the irreconcilable clash of 'civilisation' and 'barbarism'.

The liberals' concern was to chart the historical origins of the exclusionary and oppressive policies of white governments towards blacks, and the roots of the contemporary state of poverty and rightlessness under which black South Africans laboured in the twentieth century. These roots and origins they found in the irrational and anachronistic inheritance from Boer frontiersmen which sought to deny the growing reality of a common society. Inherent in this historiographical tradition was the assumption of continuity, the assumption that attitudes formed in the seventeenth- and eighteenth-century interior, attitudes that flew in the face of the reality of interdependence, remained the heritage of South African colonists, including many later British settlers, into the twentieth century, and explained the policies of racial supremacy of twentieth-century governments. Thus the inter-war liberals viewed South African history in terms of a battle between the liberal and benevolent tendencies which they associated with metropolitan influences, and the backward-looking and negrophobic tendencies of the isolated frontiers of white settlement.[1]

In this tradition, isolation was the essence of frontier experience, isolation from metropolitan civilisation, from ordered government and law, and from markets. But the frontier was also the meeting point of settlers of European origin with indigenous peoples.[2] Boer group identity and solidarity were forged out of the hostile and dangerous conditions on the frontier, faced as they were with the constant threat of attack, impoverishment and displacement at the hands of indigenous peoples, and with the daily struggle to tear from the barren environment the means of survival. Racial distinctions, set in concrete by the assumptions of their primitive Calvinism, became fundamental to their drive to overcome the forces which threatened their very existence. Racial exclusion and discrimination, coupled with a set of deeply ingrained racial attitudes, were born out of these conditions of peril, and explained the peculiar contours of twentieth-century South African economy and society. The natural development of a more inclusive society and economy had become distorted by the dysfunctional forces of Afrikaner–Boer republican–settler racism. The inevitable corollary was that the racial order grew out of the peculiar nature of South Africa's own colonial history, and hence was unique and not imported from elsewhere.

In this interpretation, the Boers' Great Trek of the 1830s had a very particular significance as the flight of the frontier from the intrusive and transformative forces of the Enlightenment, modernity, liberal values and the global market. It was the diehards of the Trek who carried the frontier of racial exclusion deep into the subcontinent, vastly expanding its reach deep within the lines of African settlement. There, beyond the dynamic impact of the modern world, the values of the frontier, of the Trek, were free to fester and spread, eventually to infect the entire South African body politic. It was beyond the Orange River that the future of South Africa was to be decided. In the words of W. M. Macmillan, a giant among South African historians who did more than anyone else to formulate the basic ingredients of this paradigm, the roots of the Great Trek

> were deeply laid in the past, and, being essentially a conservative movement, the Trek served to carry on into a later generation elements of the life of the eighteenth century that had better have died, accentuating and perpetuating the dispersal and the isolation of South African life ... In colour policy it meant in the end the substantial defeat of the enlightened liberalism that triumphed in the Cape in the emancipation of the Hottentots in 1828 and of the slaves in 1833 (even at the same time that the withdrawal of the die-hard Trekkers cleared the way for the legal and political equality which marked the Cape Constitution of 1853). The Trek was the direct means of bringing European colonists for the first time into direct contact with the great scattered mass of the Bantu tribes ... A large part of the South African Bantu thus began and continued to be dealt with, not in the spirit of liberalism, but on principles that looked backwards to the old days before 1828.[3]

Summing up in the second edition of his book, Macmillan described the Great Trek as the 'supreme disaster of the country's history'.[4]

The imagery of the frontier resurgent, sweeping back triumphantly through the reunited South Africa of the twentieth century, obliterating the liberal traditions of the British Cape in the name of a triumphant Afrikaner nationalism, pervades Macmillan's seminal two volumes of the late 1920s. And it was spelled out in explicit form in Eric Walker's Rhodes House lectures published as *The Frontier Tradition* in 1930, although Walker did not stress the element of racial interaction that characterised Macmillan's work. For Walker, the Great Trek was 'the central event in South African history'. North of the Orange 'the Trekkers and their sons gained ... a further lease of the rigid and circumscribed life that was fast passing in the colony'. In their republics, 'the tragedy of the Trek was deferred for a generation', but eventually their ideas, 'confined and invigorated during those fifty years of grace, have permeated the Union of South Africa and extended their influence as far north as Kenya'.[5]

Macmillan's student, C. W. de Kiewiet, took up the theme of the enduring influence of the frontier. The trekkers, he wrote, 'moved beyond range of the modifying influences of the thought and the swiftly changing mental climate of the mother colony … Thus were fixed those attitudes and habits of mind which later returned from exile profoundly to influence all South Africa.'[6] They took with them the 'non-literary and non-industrial habits of the eighteenth century'. The Trek was 'the eighteenth century fleeing before its more material, more active, and better organised successor'. De Kiewiet saw the frontier tradition, preserved and intensified in the republics, as extending its insidious influence right from the beginnings of industrial enterprise at the diamond fields in the 1870s:

> What had hitherto been a rural and even a frontier problem now was fast becoming an urban problem as well. It was a new social disease that was destined to become chronic. Into the new urban and industrial communities the native policy of the frontier farmers intruded itself. In a South Africa that the British Government hoped would soon be a self-governing federation, able in its strength and security to develop a calm and liberal native policy, it was actually the attitude of the frontier that was everywhere to the fore. In very truth the Great Trek was coming out of exile and avenging itself. The old Cape liberalism was losing ground on all sides.[7]

The 'attitude of the frontier … called for the reduction of native power and looked upon even the very hesitant and timid humanitarianism of the British Government as ignorant, wrongheaded and dangerous interference'. The equality which had been denied blacks in church and state was 'again denied them in the temples of labour'. For De Kiewiet, the principles of the frontier were inscribed in the constitution of the united South Africa itself: 'the Union Constitution, in native policy at all events, represented the triumph of the frontier, and into the hands of the frontier was delivered the future of the native peoples. It was the conviction of the frontier that the foundations of society were race and the privileges of race.'[8]

The social psychologist I. D. MacCrone provided in 1937 the first detailed empirical attempt to define exactly what the 'frontier tradition' comprised. He saw a new society emerging in the harsh environment of the eighteenth-century interior, characterised by group consciousness and cohesion despite isolation and dispersion. Racial prejudices and beliefs which were already part of the European heritage were intensified in this environment, resulting in the development of an intense race consciousness and hostility to those outside the group.[9] Underlying such imagery of a cohesive and self-conscious people lay what André du Toit calls the Calvinist paradigm – the widespread belief among the liberal historians that a primitive seventeenth-century Calvinism survived and flourished in isolation from modernising tendencies in European Christianity, succoured by the patriarchal, Old Testament piety of the Boers. Crucial in this alleged religious tradition were the notions of predetermination and the elect, notions which, by analogy with the Old Testament Israelites, were transformed into a sense of national calling as a chosen people, with a mission to subdue the heathen. Thus, Afrikaner rejection of *gelykstelling* (equalisation) and assimilation is derived in the Calvinist paradigm from a divine mandate, legitimated by the dichotomy between elect and non-elect. In much of the historiography under review, this interpretation of the religious wellsprings of Afrikaner culture became the explanation of racial policies and social practices of the twentieth century.[10]

If the tradition of the frontier was the source of all evil in the eyes of these pioneering inter-war liberal scholars, the British imperial factor was over-whelmingly portrayed as on the side of the good. They equated all that was progressive and virtuous in the liberal tradition at the Cape with metropolitan influence. Their explicit or implicit assumption was that British imperialism in the early nineteenth century was propelled in part by the desire to protect indigenous societies from exploitative and rapacious impulses among local colonists. The spread of Christianity and civilisation was held to be funda-mental to the imperial mission, and this entailed the transformation of indigen-ous peoples into responsible and worthy citizens, their integration into colonial society albeit at the lower social levels, and the expansion of a culture of human rights irrespective of racial differences.

But imperial influence was not one-dimensional. In this perspective, imperi-al power was in reality a contested terrain between rival impulses. The British government had to be constantly persuaded to indulge its better nature, to recognise its mission in the world, against the petty constraints of economy. Britain's historical mission would have been realised if only parochial consid-erations of expense had been overcome. South Africa's tragedy ultimately lay in the failure of British policy-makers to carry through their imperial mission to stamp their philanthropic imprint irrevocably on the emergent colonial soci-ety, to counteract in other words the forces of the frontier.

Of course, there has always been an alternative historiographic tradition, represented by the settler historians George Theal and George Cory, and sub-sequently by the Afrikaner nationalists, who have seen philanthropic influences as the baneful product of meddling missionaries and do-gooders, intent on sub-verting and denigrating the social order of the colonists.[11] Colonial settlement and expansion were regarded in this view as positive and good, and the reduc-tion of indigenous peoples to a state of rightless servility was regarded as the inevitable lot of primitive and savage peoples. This tradition, which has its roots in the early settler polemicists such as Robert Godlonton, J. C. Chase and Donald Moodie in the first half of the nineteenth century,[12] was antagonistic to the philanthropic tendencies in British imperial policy, represented notably in the drive in the 1820s and 1830s to emancipate the coloured servile class and the slaves, and to extend legal equality to all persons of colour. Writers in this tradition considered the proper role of the imperial power to be supportive of the extension and entrenchment of settler enterprise, to protect and preserve the social hierarchy, and to exercise proper coercive control over indigenous peoples.

Indeed, in the colonial context, far removed from Whitehall, imperial power was commonly bent to such purposes. Rogue governors such as D'Urban or Smith became independent actors with priorities far closer to those of the settlers than those of the philanthropists; and they have always been remembered approvingly in settler and Afrikaner nationalist historiography. One episode which has always been seen in the settler–nationalist tradition as representing a crucial moment in the struggle for the heart and soul of the imperial power in southern Africa was the annexation of Queen Adelaide Province in the cisKei region of the eastern Cape in 1835, and its subsequent retrocession by the secretary of state, Lord Glenelg. Here were the rival faces of imperialism revealed – the governor, supporting with military power the forward march of white settlement and colonisation, seeking to destroy and incorporate centres of black resistance in the process, and the rival influence of humanitarianism, which at this juncture had the ear of the government in London, concerned to keep settler advance at bay.

However, the liberal historians were also supporters of imperial expansion, but imperial expansion of a very different kind. They approved of the annexation of territory in pursuit of the task of protecting, civilising and converting indigenous peoples. Thus their view of Glenelg's withdrawal from Queen Adelaide Province, in our paradigmatic case, was that it was a second-best option in protecting the Xhosa against settler-inspired depredations. Direct rule by the imperial power was always the liberal historians' preferred prescription. In this they were following the missionary leader John Philip, the leading liberal in the early-nineteenth-century Cape. The British government 'fought shy of taking responsibility and real control' in the eastern Cape in the 1830s, wrote Macmillan; it failed to realise that 'civil administration in Kafirland was a necessity'.[13]

Similarly, the liberal historians regarded the policy of treaties with indigenous chiefs, whereby the British sought to protect them from the encroaching forces of the frontier in the 1830s and 1840s, as at best an inadequate response and at worst a dereliction of duty. Macmillan expressed this more forcefully in the second edition of his book: 'Thus, beyond any doubt, "treaties" bulked so largely in the years that followed [the Great Trek] only because the British Government could never be brought to do more than flirt with the new responsibilities forced on its unwilling attention by the doings of its emigrant subjects.'[14] De Kiewiet wrote that 'by affecting to treat the tribes as sovereign and independent societies outside the pale of British rule', the treaty system 'maintained a dangerous fiction', and overlooked 'the truth that the natives were as much a direct responsibility of government as the colonists themselves'. British timidity 'prevented the extension of the rule of law to the interlocked elements on the frontier. What the frontier needed was government, and the authority of able administrators.'[15]

In summary, the liberal historiographical tradition, dating from the 1920s, saw the imperial factor in the nineteenth century as essentially and ideally driven by the philanthropic desire to protect and civilise indigenous peoples, although in practice that impulse was obstructed by parochial considerations of economy, and occasionally by rogue administrators on the spot who sought to use their position to further the colonists' cause. The settler–nationalist school, on the other hand, saw settler prosperity and expansionism as being the natural and beneficial cause which the imperial power was ideally meant to support and succour, but this was constantly undermined by meddling philanthropists who put the interests of 'heathens' and 'savages' before those of European colonists. The irony is that both the liberal historians and the settler–nationalist school were agreed that the independence of African peoples and the self-sufficiency of their economies and cultures were obstacles to the realisation of their respective ideals, whether those ideals were the protection and redemption of the natives, or the dominion of the colonists.

For the liberal historians, the British annexation of Transorangia, the whole region (including Lesotho) between the Orange and Vaal rivers, in 1848, and the subsequent withdrawal of sovereignty in 1852–4, constituted a moment of pivotal significance, second only perhaps to the Great Trek itself, in the long-term battle for hegemony between the forces of the frontier and the forces of humanitarian imperialism. It was in this context that the philanthropic impulses of the imperial mission most obviously came up against the pernicious obstacle of penny-pinching economy. De Kiewiet in particular emphasised the importance of this moment. Governor Smith's territorial annexations were 'the culmination of a tendency in British South African politics' towards the grudging realisation of Britain's humanitarian mission, rather than 'a rash and ill-considered act'. But a dramatic turning point was in the offing: 'Then in the 1850s, came the reaction. The rise to power of free trade ideas with their intolerance of unremunerative expenditure, coupled with the incidence of a number of expensive native wars in South Africa, caused the eclipse of humanitarian policy.'[16] By the Conventions of 1852 and 1854 recognising the independence of the post-trek Boer communities, the British government 'formally resolved to have no more to do in any form with natives and native problems' beyond colonial borders. It

> was at no time after 1854 prepared to sacrifice men or money in pursuit of purely native interests. In consequence a large proportion of South Africa's native population was subjected to the 'colonist' point of view. And that point of view was that the native held too much land; that the white man

was a superior being to whom the black man was by Providence ordained to be subject.[17]

The significance of the Conventions 'can scarcely be overestimated ... The pendulum had swung away from the former humanitarian policy with a vengeance.' South Africa was condemned to a future in which the Boer republican north would be 'the foundation on which all South Africa would build its political future'. In the struggle 'between ethics and politics, between right and expediency', ethics and right had succumbed. 'The Great Trek had conquered. South Africa was a land divided.'[18]

Other historians echoed the theme. In Eric Walker's opinion, the half-dozen years of British rule in Transorangia were 'among the most fateful in the history of South Africa'. The momentous question at issue for South Africa as a whole was whether relations with African peoples 'were to accord with the liberal rules already fairly established in the original colony, or with the ideas which the Trekkers had departed from the colony to preserve'. Walker regarded the abandonment of Transorangia as splitting South Africa into an illiberal north and a liberal south, 'as sharply divided from one another as were the North and the South of the United States'; but, unlike the United States, it was the illiberal section that eventually dictated the terms of reunification. To Walker, British abandonment of the far interior was the final consummation of the 'tragedy of the Great Trek'.[19]

But the liberals' enthusiasm for humanitarian imperialism contained a certain ambiguity. For while they regarded the complete transformation of indigenous peoples into productive and legally equal members of colonial society as a long-term goal of imperial intervention, they were also inclined to regard territorial segregation as essential to prevent the oppression and subjugation of indigenous peoples by the colonists. Eventual assimilation (inevitably mostly as a lower class) was the desired goal, but this within a common society on the humanitarians' terms, and not as rightless and exploited bondsmen on the terms of the rapacious colonists. And this required that their land rights be secured under imperial rule, while their essential political, social and cultural institutions were undermined and transformed by the agents of civilisation – missionaries, traders and administrators. Hence in Macmillan's early writings of the 1920s in particular there was a contradiction between the belief in the common society as being the true legacy of South African history, and the conviction that only protective segregation in adequate reserves could have saved Africans from the parlous state of propertylessness and poverty which was their lot by the early twentieth century. Macmillan's position was that

> their different standards make it desirable to keep the races apart as far as possible, that in unrestricted competition the backward race is at a hopeless disadvantage ... In the 1840s only the British Government was strong enough to carry out such a comprehensive policy. In the twentieth century

South African opinion is at last more and more inclined to accept these principles as sound ... that the characteristic malaise of White South Africa is due to over-expansion and to the superficial taking up of land that had far better have been left as Native Reserve – as it might have been if only these principles had been applied in the forties.[20]

The element of ambiguity in Macmillan's position was revealed in his attitude towards Governor Sir George Grey (1854–61), the 'great civiliser', pioneer of African education and founder of the first hospital for Africans: 'under him the Cape took its first serious steps towards civilising the natives; henceforth they were to be "inhabitants of one country" along with their European conquerors'. But Grey's land settlement plans drove the Xhosa to desperation. His active promotion of white settlement among the African reserves led to congestion. 'The crude "location" policy of the 1850s recklessly started that steadily accelerating process of soil-destruction which was to reduce tribal lands (it has been said officially) "to desert conditions."'[21]

The ambiguities of the liberal vision were accompanied by cultural absolutism. While applauding policies designed to protect Africans against subjugation and the loss of land, Macmillan and his followers nevertheless were blind to the cultural integrity of African societies, and implicitly assumed the absolute superiority of European civilisation. They often referred to precolonial African societies as barbarous and inferior (in the 1963 edition of *Bantu, Boer and Briton* the language was changed, although Macmillan still wrote of 'civilised races').[22] The breakdown of tribalism and the integration of Africans into a new society were beneficial and inevitable, and the European agents of transformation were the heroes of their texts, as were the modernisers in African societies, the educated elites and the agricultural innovators, who had broken free from the archaic inhibitions of African communalism. The fact that the 'advance of civilisation' inevitably entailed conquest, coercion and cultural suppression was never recognised by the liberals. They overlooked the means by which 'civilisation' was in practice imposed. And so the ubiquity of violence was ascribed to the ruder methods of negrophobe settlers or frontiersmen. Further, the enormous potential for class conflict implicit in the incorporation of the great majority as a subordinate proletariat was not addressed. In their determination to stress the inter-racial cooperation and harmony of the common society of their fond imaginings, the liberal historians overlooked the inherently conflictual form of African incorporation into the larger society and economy.

The liberal historians were, it must be said, not unconcerned with the economic dimensions of racial supremacy. Macmillan was preoccupied with the historical roots of rural poverty; and De Kiewiet saw the importance of the process of industrialisation and the onset of labour migrancy and urbanisation. But they certainly did not perceive that the industrial and urban economy arising in the latter part of the nineteenth century had any explanatory relevance for the policies of racial segregation and dominance in the twentieth century. Their assumption of frontier influences was so pervasive as to preclude any possibility that there could be a connection between the requirements of the capitalist economy and the racial structuring of the workforce and society at large. The common society, shorn of the racist legacy of the pre-industrial frontier, would be a place of harmony and mutual benefit.

These assumptions were still very strong in the *Oxford History of South Africa* (1969–71), which in its fundamentals did not deviate from the liberal paradigm of the inter-war years, although the strictly historical chapters largely avoided the confident polemics of the earlier historiography. The assumption of an innate, albeit adaptive, frontier mentality among Afrikaners as the driving force behind twentieth-century race policy was clear in the second volume especially. The forces making for racial conflict were seen as external to the economic system, dysfunctional and disruptive, while the modern capitalist economy was seen as innately harmonious, rational, beneficial and race-blind.[23]

One crucial new development in the 1960s, reflected in the *Oxford History*, was the rise of an Africanist tradition in historiography, commensurate with the emergence of new and self-conscious African nations. The liberal Africanists of the 1960s showed a respect for and sensitivity to African history that had been lacking hitherto. They helped pioneer new interdisciplinary approaches to uncovering the African past. Their focus tended to be on politics, leadership and state formation, themes appropriate to an age of decolonisation and nation building. But they still embraced the view that acculturation, Christianisation and integration into the common society of Western modernism were beneficial and progressive processes. Monica Wilson in particular brought an evangelical perspective strongly to bear on her interpretation of the past.[24] The liberal Africanists also shared the earlier liberals' positive view of imperial activism in the subcontinent, although this was tempered by the writings of new historians of imperialism generally and in southern Africa specifically, such as J. S. Galbraith, who questioned the view that philanthropy was ever much of a motive force in the official mind of nineteenth-century imperialism.[25]

The enduring influence of the early liberal paradigm was vividly revealed in Fredrickson's acclaimed comparative study of *White Supremacy* (1981), particularly in his emphasis on the frontier tradition as the root of the South African racial order. Fredrickson, a brilliant American historian of race, contrasted the American frontier with the frontier of the semi-subsistent Boer pastoralists. The former was seen as an extension and recapitulation of the metropolitan civilisation, tending towards permanent and denser settlement and economic diversification, and dependent on the establishment of towns. The Boers, in contrast, 'neither desired nor anticipated the kind of economic "progress" that was eagerly awaited on the American frontier'. The comparison with North America leads in Fredrickson's analysis to an emphasis on the alleged backwardness, isolation from metropolitan or capitalist impulses, and lack of commercial incentives or ambitions on the South African frontier. There was 'little sense on the South African frontier that white movement was part of a process of cultural and economic evolution that would culminate in the reproduction of a civilised society on the model of Europe or even of Cape Town'.[26]

The refusal of the Boers to compromise with the forces of change associated with metropolitan markets or metropolitan cultural influences was, for Fredrickson, in large part the explanation of the Great Trek – a flight of the frontier from 'progress'. He implies that no real market-related economic motive lay behind the urge to expropriate native land and labour, an urge which apparently was almost exclusively a phenomenon of the Boer frontier. 'The interest in further native dispossession or subjugation remained a local interest on the frontier, one which might involve the government in military actions but did not crucially concern the colony as a whole, to say nothing of the British Empire.'[27] Indeed, 'the further the Boers wandered the less access they had to a market and the more self-sufficient they became'.

Fredrickson clearly sees the forces of dispossession, subjugation, discrimination and exclusion in pre-industrial South Africa – the forces of the frontier – as having had no relation at all to the world of European imperial or commercial enterprise. As we shall see, this whole set of assumptions is profoundly questionable. Suffice it to point out here that Fredrickson nowhere mentions the existence of several thousand British settlers on the eastern Cape frontier who arrived in and after 1820. A self-consciously commercial and progressive fragment of metropolitan society, they were arguably far more involved than the Boers in 'native dispossession and subjugation', not only in the eastern Cape but on frontiers of settlement in Natal and north of the Orange. Nor does Fredrickson mention that the Great Trek took place at a time when much of the South African interior was being opened up by long-distance trade, in which Boers themselves played a not inconsiderable role; and that mercantile interests in Cape Town and, by extension, in London had an interest in all these developments.

Fredrickson also incorporated the belief that the heritage of primitive Calvinism in its local manifestation on the frontier explains much of the Boer world-view. An Old Testament Christianity 'of an attenuated Calvinist origin … constituted a prime source of group identity' among frontier Boers, who at the time of the trek 'already possessed a body of folk beliefs capable of dispelling any doubts about what role God had prescribed for the nonwhites in their midst'. They saw the 'humanitarian assault on their racial order as a denial of what they took to be firm biblical sanctions for dominating nonwhites by force and formally excluding them from citizenship'. They held the 'conviction that white men had an inherent right to rule despotically over people of a darker hue'. A fully blown self-image of the Boers as a chosen people arose out of the trek, contends Fredrickson. 'The idea that there was a divine plan to establish independent white Christian communities ... contained the seeds of an Afrikaner nationalism that would eventually lay claim to all of South Africa in the name of ethnic and racial supremacy.'[28]

Fredrickson thus also emphasises the group consciousness and the group cohesion of the Boers – at least those who went on the Great Trek – at an early date. He describes the Boer ideology as one of '*herrenvolk* egalitarianism', 'with equality for all whites and rigorous subordination for all nonwhites'. Land shortage and stratification, evident in the eastern Cape in the late eighteenth century, 'aroused strong desires to preserve or recapture an intra-racial egalitarianism that was in danger of being attenuated'. Fredrickson sees the *herrenvolk* principle of 'rough equality of social and economic status among white heads of families' as having been 'close to a literal reality' in the post-trek republics. He thus regards Boer republican state formation as a function of Boer classlessness and of the absence of any economic dynamism, and the drive to dominate and subjugate as the expression of an inchoate, pre-modern religious–social ideology.[29]

It is not surprising that Fredrickson shares quite explicitly the assumption of continuity in race relations from the pre-industrial frontier via the Great Trek right through to the industrial context of the twentieth century. Africans were incorporated into the industrial workforce 'without altering traditional patterns of white dominance and black servility'. The 'slaveholding mentality', which 'remained the wellspring of white-supremacist thought and action long after the institution that originally sustained it had been relegated to the dustbin of history', is invoked to explain the policies of twentieth-century governments.[30] Fredrickson endorses Blumer's thesis that industrialisation 'adapts' to pre-existing patterns of race relations rather than transforming them. After the Anglo-Boer War, Fredrickson writes, Britain 'found it expedient to give the white inhabitants of the ex-republics a free hand to rule over blacks more or less according to the settlers' own traditions' – as if the South African state after 1910 was simply the old Boer republican state *redivivus*.[31]

The republican tradition of 'native policy' that was thus confirmed in urban conditions was premised, in Fredrickson's interpretation, on permanent and complete subordination (a policy of *baasskap*), as opposed to the British policy of providing reserves, embodying an ideal of trusteeship. The assumption again is that British intentions were always basically benevolent, but that they betrayed their own best intentions in the interest of white unity, which took precedence over earlier commitments to the 'ideal of a nonracial citizenship'.[32] The characterisations of both republican 'native policy' and of British intentions are, to say the least, open to question. It would be more accurate to argue that the Transvaal Republic had neither the capacity nor the desire to rule over large, intact African societies; whereas the extension of imperial rule from the late nineteenth century was a function of both the capacity and the need to subjugate, dominate and ultimately to exploit.

L. M. Thompson's *Political Mythology of Apartheid* (1985) debunked some elements in the frontier tradition which were still prominent in Fredrickson's book. Drawing on work by Du Toit and Giliomee among others, Thompson showed that key myths of the twentieth-century Afrikaner nationalist movement (relating to the Slagtersnek rebellion of 1815 and the Covenant of 1838) were based on distortions and elaborations of the evidence. The elements of Afrikaner nationalist ideology that lay behind these particular myths were also elements in the frontier tradition of the earlier liberal historians, namely the notion that Boer society in the early nineteenth century was cohesive, classless and united by a powerful group consciousness, and that the main binding factor was an ideology of the chosen race based on a local elaboration of primitive Calvinism. Thompson reveals just how malleable and manipulable images of the past can be in providing tools for the attainment of more immediate concrete purposes.[33]

But fundamental elements of the older frontier tradition are not subjected to the same degree of dissection in Thompson's book. Thus here, too, the racial order of twentieth-century South Africa is treated solely in terms of inherited belief systems, as if it had no material or economic determinants, but grew out of mistaken assumptions and distortions of the past. In Thompson's chapter on 'unassimilable races' the emphasis is on ideas about race and racial attitudes, with very little on the content and context of race relations. The impression is created that the racial order was an ethnically based atavism, without any functional relationship to contemporary economic life. The economic context of urban industrialism and the formation of an industrial working class merit no more than a single incidental paragraph.[34] Although Thompson does not use the imagery of the frontier as the seedbed of racial attitudes, and concedes that Afrikaner attitudes were not out of line with those common in the European world until after World War Two, it seems from his book as if the forces of historically conditioned illusion and unreason lay behind the horrors of apartheid. The racial politics of South Africa have indeed been replete with myth, but the origins and nature of the twentieth-century racial state cannot be analysed in those terms alone.

There has thus been a long and enduring historiographical tradition that asserts a fundamental continuity in race attitudes and race practices having their origin in pre-industrial frontier conditions. Twentieth-century government policies of racial supremacy and discrimination are explained as an ethnic atavism, flying in the face of the countervailing influences of metropolitan culture and capitalist enterprise. In strong contrast to the forces of the frontier, the imperial factor is seen largely as a progressive and humanitarian force in racial matters, spawning a distinctive liberal tradition at the Cape in the nineteenth century. In the 1920s, Macmillan assumed the problem of the 'Cape Coloureds' or 'Eurafricans' had been solved in the first half of the nineteenth century. His book *Cape Colour Question* concerned the story of how the 'Hottentots' had 'come to achieve a measure of civilisation deemed sufficient to entitle them to a full share in European privileges'. The struggle for legal equality which began with the arrival of the British missionary factor 'resulted in the establishment in the old colony of that policy of equal rights for civilised men which is still known distinctively as "the Cape policy.'"[35] Similarly, Macmillan believed a policy of emancipation from legal and political restrictions could in the twentieth century free the African majority from the thraldom imposed by those forces inimical to the Cape's liberal tradition.

This narrow legalism conceals a lot more than it reveals about the racially hegemonic nature of the Cape Colony and its role in spawning the impulses of dispossession and subjugation which towards the end of the nineteenth century were to surge forth through the subcontinent as a whole. The contradictions inherent in the whole liberal humanitarian project of the first half of the nineteenth century are a theme running through my study. Early-nineteenth-century liberalism was profoundly ambiguous. Its rhetorical commitment to the legal formalities of equality and freedom was in sharp contrast to its fundamental compatibility with cultural imperialism, class domination and, ultimately, racial subjugation. And it could be argued that these were not just failings, but were a function, direct or indirect, of the role of liberal ideology in sustaining the hegemony of class and culture in the rapidly developing economic order of free-trade capitalism.[36]

The issue of race in South African history is at the centre of my concerns in this study. Here race is treated not simply as a derivative of relations of production or of economic class, but as an autonomous variable with a life of its own (though, in practice, race as a historical reality takes on meaning in the context of specific social and economic systems). For from the beginnings of settlement colonial society was built on a racial basis. It was unthinkable to the colonists in early South Africa, as it would be to those who exercised power and dominance in the industrially based state established in the early twentieth century, that the social order might be built on anything other than the foundations of racial or ethnic exclusiveness and hegemony. At first, cultural as much as economic considerations motivated the construction of a racial order. The legal status groups of the first century and a half of European settlement were racially based (slaves, Khoi, burghers), though they were not justified by explicit racial ideology.

However, over time the racial order went through very different phases. The ideology of racial supremacy in the industrial age sought to impose quite new forms of exploitation, extending beyond the colonial realm by incorporating indigenous societies intact, their economic and political systems still functioning, as suppliers of low-cost labour. This idea that colonial hegemony should be exercised over independent African farmers and intact African societies, rather than at the level solely of the individual colonial household or colonial enterprise, was something new. In the nineteenth century, the African societies that were subjected to racial oppression were mixed-farming societies which were too strong to be dismantled, unlike the less substantial Khoisan societies encountered earlier. Their incorporation took radically different forms, serving new capitalist purposes.

At the same time there was also a marked difference in the ethnic composition of the new dominant colonial class, although it was their economic interests rather than their ethnicity that was the salient variable. Increasingly in the nineteenth century the levers of economic power came to be exercised by a new British bourgeoisie. It was this bourgeoisie which embodied the ideal of white supremacy as a total system, rather than the descendants of the old slave-owners or the pioneers of the frontier.

Thus although the racial ordering of economy and society was a global given in the world conquered by Europeans right up to the latter half of the twentieth century, we must acknowledge as inadequate the idea that race was an archaism having its roots in a pre-modern past (the 'frontier' or the institution of slavery), even while imposing its stamp on the capitalist order of the nineteenth and twentieth centuries. The scope, the intensity, the ideological underpinnings of racial hegemony changed dramatically. The racial nature of the industrial order was not the invention in the first instance of mining magnates hungry for cheap labour and high profits; but neither was it purely a leftover of earlier social and economic relations. If crude economic reductionism is inadequate as an explanation, so too is the idea of racial prejudice and discrimination as cultural inertia. This book deals with the rise in the first half of the nineteenth century of those forces of development and modernisation which used racial categorisation in new ways to forge a new white-supremacist order appropriate to the modern world of capital and enterprise.

At this time racial subjugation within the realm of the African farming peoples beyond the old established colony at the Cape was as yet fitful, unsustained and reluctantly pursued by the wielders of state power. The state was still a weak instrument, resistant to the forward proddings of settler capitalism, which was itself embryonic and without much persuasive influence at the centres of power. Some recent revisionist historians, Clifton Crais for example, way overemphasise the strength and resolve of the state.[37] Contrary to the capitalist triumphalism of Crais's analysis, this study dwells on the very partial and incomplete capitalist transformation of the pre-mineral period. Nevertheless, the forces at work in the first half of the nineteenth century prefigured the transformations that were set in motion by the mineral discoveries in South Africa in the last third of the century.

CHAPTER TWO

Dutch Beginnings

The colonial society that emerged at the Cape in the seventeenth and eighteenth centuries was almost accidental. The Dutch East India Company (VOC) did not favour the establishment of settler communities in its trading empire. But the exigencies of providing sustenance for the garrison planted there in 1652 and the passing maritime traffic obliged the company to grant freeburgher status to certain of its employees, and to allow them to set up as independent farmers, first in the Cape Peninsula and, later, further afield in the rich soils of the Boland. Encouraged by the success of this experiment, the company granted free passages from 1685 to 1707 to Hollanders wishing to settle at the Cape, but lost interest once the supply of produce was adequate for its needs. In fact, the importation of European settlers was not particularly successful, the largest batch being a group of some 200 French Huguenot refugees in and after 1688. The original colonists were augmented by company employees returning from the East who stayed on at the Cape, and some women were sent out from Dutch orphanages as wives for colonists. From the start, settler women were heavily outnumbered by settler men.[1]

The company authorities also concluded that imported slave labour of African and Asian origin (present in the settlement since its beginnings) would be the basis of the burgher economy, and turned their backs on the option of encouraging immigration of European labourers. Thus early in the eighteenth century it became clear that the Cape would develop as a colonist-dominated multiracial society, in which labour was to be largely unfree and the preserve of people of non-European origin. As in the Americas, local natives could not easily be enslaved without posing an intolerable threat to the security and stability of the embryonic settlement. Nevertheless, the western Cape Khoi societies, whose period of grace as independent trading partners had been shortlived, quickly disintegrated, a process that was consummated by the 1713 smallpox epidemic. Khoi women were the first to be incorporated into the colonial household. Khoi men initially moved about in gangs of workers; eventually they also became bonded labourers on the farms.[2] By this time too, the frontier proper had already emerged. That is, the mountain escarpment separating the arable southwest from the drier reaches of the interior had been breached by colonists without the capital to succeed closer to Cape Town, and the trekboer frontier had been opened up.

Implicit in some of the earlier historical literature was the assumption that Cape Town and its immediate environs, in contrast to the frontier, formed in the seventeenth and eighteenth centuries a more open, tolerant society, where racial divisions were not harsh or stark or ultimately determinant of class status. Cape slavery, it was commonly asserted, was mild and benevolent in comparison with New World slave systems – an idea that has been decisively challenged in more recent historiography.[3] Equally questionable was the notion, to which George Theal lent his substantial authority, that Christian baptism in the seventeenth-century settlement was considered sufficient grounds for emancipation from slavery, that the baptism of slave children was a generally accepted duty, and that in consequence slaves born in the colony were usually granted their freedom. According to this line of argument, no distinctions on the grounds of colour or origin were made among those who professed Christianity. The rights and obligations of burgher status were open to all believers.[4]

This characterisation of early Cape society as fluid and open has proved remarkably resilient over the years. It formed the basis of I. D. MacCrone's influential analysis of race relations in the Dutch period, and indeed is still clearly evident in Fredrickson's sophisticated comparative study, as well as in the work of Robert Ross.[5] The issue of baptism, analogous to civil and legal enfranchisement in the Reformed tradition, was crucial in this reading. In Catholic tradition, baptism was unproblematical and universally imposed on subject and captive peoples. In the Dutch empire, however, it was a complex and disputed issue. The Synod of Dort of 1618, at which the Dutch Reformed Church established the doctrine that Christianity and chattel slavery were incompatible, foreclosed the pragmatic British North American path of justifying slavery by heathen descent rather than actual heathenism (thereby condemning all those of African descent in British North America to enslavement in perpetuity). Thus at the Cape there was always a degree of official uncertainty whether private owners had an obligation to baptise slaves, and about the legal status of the Christian slave. In practice the matter was left to the discretion of individual slave-owners. It was not until the British had taken over the Cape that official sanction was extended in the early nineteenth century to the practice of maintaining baptised slaves in servitude.[6]

There was never any policy at the Cape requiring that converts be manumitted, and baptised slaves in fact were rarely granted their freedom. Occasional ecclesiastical pronouncements suggested that baptised slaves should indeed be freed, such as instructions issued in 1683 by the church council at Batavia (the VOC's main administrative centre in the East Indies).[7] But these were of no avail, nor were instructions by Commissioners Goske in 1671 and Van Reede in 1685 that slave children of European fathers (mulattos) be freed. Van Reede instructed that they were to be freed at the age of 25 (males) or 22 (females), and trained in useful occupations, including agriculture, 'so that in time the whole country may be handed over to the same, together with its cultivation, for which they are better fitted than anyone else, since, born in these parts ... the Honourable Company would have no better subjects'. Van

Reede also instructed that foreign-born slaves become eligible for emancipation as a matter of favour after thirty years' service, and colonial-born slaves without any European parentage at the age of 40, provided they spoke Dutch and had been baptised. These prescriptions were permissive, and in any event applied only to company slaves, who were a small proportion of the slave population through the eighteenth century. Van Reede's vision of an essentially Eurasian colony coming into being should thus not be allowed to overwhelm the historical picture. It was in any event notable mainly for its being at variance with colonial realities. Such ritual pronouncements of the rights of slaves, particularly those of mixed race, to baptism and to manumission were largely ineffectual, and have been overstated by historians as representing some significant indicator of Cape practice.[8]

The company followed a policy of baptising and educating slave children at the company lodge in Cape Town. But the low fertility rates among company slaves meant that statistically theirs was a small number – especially since company slaves constituted a diminishing proportion of the total slave population (only 3 per cent by 1795). In 1685 the company established a slave school in the lodge that lasted to the end of the Dutch period. But in 1779 only 82 slave children attended school. However, the much larger privately owned slave population remained overwhelmingly innocent of either formal education or Christianity. The Dutch Reformed Church had no mission wing or orders. Although the Moravian station at Genadendal under Georg Schmidt met some limited success among Khoi between 1737 and 1744, the missionaries then left, returning only in the 1790s. By 1790 there were still fewer than ten Dutch Reformed ministers at the Cape, and they were all employees of the company.[9]

As far as private slave-owners were concerned, there seems to have been very little interest in the Christianisation of slaves. Religious zeal was never a characteristic of the burgher population: contrary to common assumptions, few burghers owned Bibles, according to inventory records, and many burghers were not full members of the church (although baptism remained the indispensable key to full civic status among colonists). Also, there seems to have been from early on a certain aversion to slave baptism, based on a perceived fear that Christian slaves might have some vague claim to rights that non-Christians did not have. Uncertainty over the issue was reinforced in 1770 when the Council of the Indies in Batavia ruled that slave-owners were bound to educate their slaves in Christianity, and to allow baptism to those who wished it; furthermore, baptised slaves could not be sold or otherwise alienated, and had to be freed when their owners either left the colony or died. However, the church council in Cape Town accurately reflected the situation at the Cape when, in response to a query from the church council in Stellenbosch in 1792, it declared that neither the law of the land nor that of the church prohibited retention of baptised persons in slavery, and that local custom strongly supported the practice of not freeing them.[10]

At the same time, the late-eighteenth-century evangelical revival, which saw the widespread proselytising of North American and Caribbean slaves, did not bypass the Dutch Cape entirely. Even before the arrival of British missionaries right at the end of the century, a profoundly conservative evangelicalism emanating from Holland reached the Cape in the persons of the Dutch-born Rev. H. R. van Lier and M. C. Vos, Cape-born and Dutch-educated. They and their converts were responsible for the establishment of the South African Missionary Society in 1799, and for mission work on the farms of the south-western Cape and in Cape Town. Such men did not question the hierarchical slave-based Cape society; but neither did they subscribe to notions of the racial exclusivity of Christian people. Certain burghers of Lutheran persuasion, the very wealthy wine farmer and slave-owner Martin Melck among them, expressed an interest in promoting, or at least not obstructing, the Christianisation of their slaves. They clearly had little fear that this would threaten their interests as slave-owners. Indeed, it might have been such burghers who initiated the 1792 query from the Stellenbosch church council. All the same, these initiatives had negligible impact on the religious sentiments of slaves and servants.[11]

Nevertheless, the fear that owners might not countenance Christian instruction for their slaves as a consequence of the 1770 regulations moved Sir John Cradock to repeal them in 1812, establishing officially for the first time that Christian faith had no bearing on the state of servitude. The intention was to promote Christianisation; but the effect was to confirm that Christians could be held in slavery, as had long been firmly established in law in the former British colonies in North America. The repeal had little effect in promoting Christian baptism among slaves. One concern of the British was the widespread incidence of Islam, brought by captives and political exiles from the Dutch East Indies, among the slaves of Cape Town. By 1820 there were three times as many Muslim as Christian slaves. Indeed it seems that slave-owners were remarkably tolerant of the spread of Islam among slaves, as it stressed discipline and forbade the use of alcohol.[12]

Contrary to the MacCrone–Fredrickson thesis that baptism meant access to burgher status, there was in fact remarkably little correlation between baptism and manumission in the colony throughout the seventeenth and eighteenth centuries. Whereas the vast majority of baptised slaves belonged to the company, most manumitted slaves belonged to private owners. Among the 1075 *requesten* from private parties to the Council of Policy to manumit slaves between 1715 and 1791, only 8.4 per cent argued in the slaves' favour that they had been baptised, and indeed some were Muslim.[13] In fact, by the standards of the Latin American colonies, slave manumission at the Cape was of limited extent. Only 0.165 per cent of the slave force could expect to be freed each year, against about 1 per cent in Brazil.[14] Indeed, the company imposed conditions on manumissions, starting in 1708 when Commissioner J. Simons ruled that manumissions would only be permitted if the owner guaranteed that the freed slaves would not impose a burden on the church's poor fund for a period of ten years. Later in the century this regulation was extended, including provision that money be paid into the poor fund for each manumission (which became a lucrative source of income for the Dutch Reformed Church).[15] The purpose was to discourage the practice among owners of manumitting slaves on account of old age or disability in order to avoid the expense of maintaining them; but such provisions very likely made owners more reluctant to consider freeing slaves in general.

Just as conversion to Christianity or Islam was largely confined to the urban milieu of Cape Town itself, so was manumission largely an urban phenomenon. The farm slaves of the arable districts of the southwestern Cape were too valued as labourers in the fields to be liberally granted their freedom, except in unusual circumstances. Stereotyping by origin was also evident in manumissions. Of foreign-born slaves manumitted, those of Asian origin greatly outnumbered those of African or Madagascan origin, although their respective proportions of the population were not dissimilar. It was regarded as natural for slaves of Madagascan or African origin to work in the fields, while the skilled artisan and service-worker slaves in Cape Town, who were more likely to win their freedom, were largely of Asian origin. Locally born (creole) slaves and particularly part-European (mulatto) slaves came to be specially favoured for manumission.[16]

Urban slavery was always a more volatile institution than rural slavery, as urban slaves were often hired out by their owners, and lived relatively independent lives as members of a larger urban working class. Seasonal fluctuations in economic activity and the flexibility of wage labour often made slave-ownership uneconomic in the urban context. Hence a steady trickle of manumissions did not materially affect class relations and class authority.[17] An analysis of reasons given in *requesten* for manumissions reveals that the largest category was testamentary manumissions and manumissions caused by owners' departure from the Cape (over 30 per cent), while humanitarian reasons were given in only 7.6 per cent of cases. Of private slave-owners manumitting their slaves 28 per cent were women, at least half of these being widows, who granted freedom to slaves to a disproportionate extent. In 12.2 per cent of cases, slaves bought their own freedom or that of their children, spouses or parents. It is notable that a quarter of all manumitting owners were themselves free blacks, who bought slaves, usually relatives, with a view to freeing them, thereby uniting families. Slave women were manumitted to a greater extent proportionally than were slave men, many because they were a source of wives for European men, but perhaps also for sentimental reasons, given the greater intimacy of the female slave within the slave-owning household.[18]

The 'free black' community, concentrated in Cape Town, consisted mainly of manumitted ex-slaves (with some free immigrants from the East Indies such as sailors and political deportees), and was never a major element in colonial society. In the 1807 census, the first to enumerate 'free blacks' separately from the rest of the free population, only 1204 were counted in Cape Town (as against 29 303 slaves and 25 614 whites). It is the relative rarity of manumissions and the absence of a substantial class of free persons of colour (again in sharp contrast to the Latin American pattern) that have led recent historians, contrary to earlier views, to characterise slave society at the Cape as closed and rigid.[19]

The free blacks formed a heterogeneous community, increasingly influenced by Islamic culture from the late eighteenth century, much less so by Christianity, and was of diverse, but primarily Asian, origin. They were occupied in servicing the transient population of the port, working in hostels or wine shops; they provided the artisanal skills of the town as tailors, coopers, shoemakers, saddlers, masons, carpenters and fishermen; and they were active in small-scale retail trade. In terms of economic function and cultural life there was little to distinguish many urban slaves from free blacks.[20]

The legal status of free blacks was ambiguous, but it is clear that through the eighteenth century the tendency to treat them as a separate status group from the free burghers grew. In the seventeenth century, when the agricultural colony was young, the company authorities gave some free blacks land in the new Stellenbosch district; they did not however last. Although in general there was little discrimination in law against free people of colour, at least until the late eighteenth century, the social order was never colour-blind. In 1722 free blacks were enrolled in an unpaid and compulsory fire brigade – responsible for putting out fires often started by slaves – perhaps so that free blacks would police the urban slaves. The free blacks were compelled to carry passes whenever they wished to leave town for more than a few days. In 1727 poorer European burghers in Cape Town saw to it that free blacks were excluded from a variety of occupations. Free persons of colour were excluded from burgher lists drawn up for militia purposes (although the indigenous Khoi in the employ of the company or the colonists did most of the colony's fighting in frontier regions), and in practice they were discriminated against in social and economic life.[21]

But in considering the different status groups in colonial society, we must remember that we are not dealing with watertight genetic compartments. White, Khoi, slave and free black were all categories that had a legal, political or social meaning (whatever terminology was employed), yet a fair amount of genetic mixing occurred from the start. According to Commissioner Goske in 1671, three-quarters of the children born to the company's slave women had European fathers. The large numbers of company servants (few of whom brought wives with them) and the transient population of sailors and soldiers made for a very skewed sex ratio among the free population of the port, and the company slave lodge apparently served throughout the company period as Cape Town's main brothel, much to the disapproval of official visitors. The offspring of casual liaisons did not, however, pose a problem of group definition, as they usually retained their mothers' slave status, despite the official policy laid down by Commissioners Goske in 1671 and Van Reede in 1685 that such mixed-race slaves had a right to baptism and manumission.[22]

It was when white men took baptised, freed slave women as their wives that preconceptions of racial identity were tested. In the seventeenth century there were some company officials and settlers who did take as wives baptised slave women, whose freedom they bought. These women were of Asian (often Bengali) origin rather than African, but in due course Dutch-speaking Cape-born women of mixed parentage became the preferred partners. Clearly, somatic as well as cultural preferences were at work here.[23] When the arable districts of Stellenbosch and Drakenstein beyond the Peninsula opened up for settlement, a few burghers took wives of Asian origin along with them. However, by the eighteenth century these arable districts had a fairly even ratio of white male to white female and a stable family structure in its European population. Marriage and concubinage outside that community seem to have become very unusual, although a degree of casual miscegenation no doubt continued to occur. So, in these wine- and wheat-farming areas, we can assume that a sense of bourgeois respectability came to set its face against race mixing. Group endogamy was fairly rigid throughout the eighteenth century; and the relative absence of a free black population of any consequence reinforced this rigidity.[24]

By contrast, on the pastoral frontier beyond the arable districts, the sex ratio within the European population tended to be highly skewed, more especially in newer areas of infiltration. This, as in Cape Town itself, led to much miscegenation but (unlike Cape Town) not much Christianisation and intermarriage. Here Khoi women usually provided the only sex partners. As we shall see, the result was the emergence of the Bastaard population.[25]

In Cape Town, unlike the rural areas of the immediate and further hinterland, intermarriage continued through the eighteenth and into the nineteenth century. No attempt was made to prohibit it. But after the early decades of settlement in the seventeenth century, intermarriage was confined mainly to the lowlier elements of the European population (often, no doubt, company employees, sailors and soldiers). Their wives were generally Cape-born and acculturated to some degree; and many of these women would have been of partial European descent themselves, as a result of the casual miscegenation out of which many Cape slaves and free blacks issued. Race mixing continued to be hypergamous; that is, men from the dominant group took partners from dominated groups. The incidence of European women taking slave or free-black partners was very rare. Black men were likely to be much more savagely punished by the courts for sexual crimes against white women than were white men. Slaves were put to death or banished for the merest suggestion of an unwanted sexual advance against settler women.[26] Thus slave and free-black men, despite having a great deal more economic independence in the urban context than slave women, were more restricted in their choice of partners. On the other hand, slave and free-black women could secure their freedom or improve their own and their children's status by marrying into groups that were accorded a higher status in society.

Earlier scholars following Theal and MacCrone emphasised the lack of race consciousness at the early Cape, and tended to regard group boundaries as being fluid and permeable. In the MacCrone interpretation, intermarriage would not initially have been remarkable, as religion and not racial origin was the decisive factor in defining group membership. Fredrickson, who tends to follow MacCrone in this interpretation of early Cape practice, places great stress on the legacy brought by the Dutch to the Cape from their Asian possessions. Since this was not an empire of settlement but of commerce, no attempt was made to replicate Dutch society in the Orient, and company servants in the East were permitted, even encouraged, to take Christianised native wives. The system sanctioned the incorporation of the children of Dutch fathers and native mothers into the colonising community, a pattern quite unlike that prevailing in the Americas. In the East Indies, Eurasians were in time to accede to the full status and rights of Dutch citizens. The initial impulse at the Cape, argues Fredrickson, was to follow this pattern.[27]

Fredrickson tends to the view that intermarriage was 'surprisingly frequent and socially acceptable' before the late eighteenth century – compared with British North America and even the Caribbean islands. He draws on the researches of Heese into the founding marriages of ('white') Afrikaner families still extant today. Of 2122 such marriages between 1688 and 1807, 500 involved a 'non-European' spouse (a proportion of 23.6 per cent). Of the 500 mixed marriages, only 69 involved full-blooded freed slave women, and the rest women of mixed parentage. A further large number probably occurred among those whose families died out, emigrated, or became classified later as 'coloured'. The incidence of 'mixed' marriages, in the Heese sample of founding unions, increased rather than declined through the eighteenth century. Heese concluded that there was 7.2 per cent of 'non-white blood' in the 'white' Afrikaner population today. Fredrickson further suggests that the offspring of such mixed marriages were commonly absorbed into the ranks of the dominant burgher community. Female offspring were more likely to be absorbed because of the shortage of marriageable women, and male offspring were likely to be so absorbed if they were light-skinned and possessed some education and property. But others of lower-status birth and greater somatic distance from a European ideal were likely to find themselves classified with the free blacks, who were increasingly denied full burgher status on grounds of racial difference, poverty and the preference of many of them for Islam and their imperviousness to Christianity.[28]

More recent historians have tended to downplay the significance of race mixture, contending that it did not modify to any great extent the closed and endogamous nature of colonial society and the rigidity of status lines. While the genetic make-up of the slave population was greatly affected by miscegenation, this was far less the case with the dominant European population. Elphick in particular criticises Fredrickson for being too 'idealist' in assuming that company policy as evolved in the trading empire of the East Indies shaped actual social development in the colony of agricultural settlement that the Cape became. He argues that the evidence Fredrickson uses for gauging the extent of race mixing is misleading. Heese only dealt with founding marriages of first-generation immigrants to the Cape, which took place mainly in Cape Town. Thus the extent of intermarriage was a reflection perhaps of demographic necessity, but it was not necessarily an indication of the social attitudes of the settled colonial population, among whom there is very little evidence of inter-racial marriages – certainly in the rural districts.

Elphick stresses what Fredrickson overlooks: that intermarriage was a large-ly urban phenomenon, confined by the eighteenth century to the poorer and propertyless class of colonists, and that the evidence cannot be generalised to colonial society at large. Casual miscegenation on its own does not of course imply any degree of racial tolerance, but can be seen as a further form of racial exploitation. In fact interracial marriages did not pose any threat at all to the racial hierarchy that was a feature of colonial society by the eighteenth centu-ry. Other historians have questioned the extent to which the offspring of mixed marriages could gain acceptance into dominant burgher society, some suggest-ing that the male offspring at least were almost certainly ostracised.[29]

Further, Guelke argues that the fact that the Cape was unlike other Dutch possessions, and contradicted VOC intentions, in developing a self-perpetuat-ing settler community is of crucial significance in understanding the pattern of race mixing at the Cape. For this community sought to replicate the exclusive and endogamous standards of the metropolitan society with its cultural and class consciousness. At the same time it rejected the more tolerant standards encouraged for purely pragmatic reasons in the male-dominated trading dias-pora – although Cape burghers differed from metropolitan ideals fundamen-tally by incorporating imported slaves in their household arrangements.[30] What seems to have been crucial in the transition from an outpost to a puta-tively European society, with a corresponding shift in attitudes and behaviour, was the presence of significant numbers of settler women.

Clearly, whatever happened lower down the social scale, race and status consciousness became increasingly developed through the eighteenth century within the burgher bourgeoisie of town and countryside in the arable south-western Cape. By 1765, the Council of Policy was seeking to dictate the dress of free-black women: they were forbidden to ape the European ladies of the town by appearing in public in hoopskirts, fine laces and adorned bonnets. This race and class consciousness was given institutional expression to an increasing degree towards the end of the century. Thus in 1787 a free corps of the militia was created to cater for people who, though not born in slavery, had not been born in wedlock, a definition soon expanded to include all those whose parents, even if married, had not been born in a state of freedom. The implication was that one had to be of putatively European ancestry to be fully accepted within the ranks of the dominant, respectable free burgher population. In 1788 a group of burghers in Stellenbosch petitioned that they were unwilling to serve under a certain burgher, Johannes Hartogh, with the rank of corporal (although they were prepared to serve with him as a common soldier) on the ground that he was 'of a black colour and of heathen descent'. In 1790 Jan Smook, who had manumitted and married a baptised slave, was summoned to enrol his son in the free corps. Smook indignantly refused as his son was a full burgher and eligible therefore to join an ordinary burgher company. But the burgher military council would not submit to Smook's entreaties. The son of a slave-born mother, no matter how outwardly respectable, was clearly ineligible for full burgher status. Whatever had been the practice earlier, by the late eighteenth century it was clearly very difficult for the male offspring of mixed marriages to aspire to such status (although it might have still been marginally easier for females to pass into the burgher community).[31]

The British, coming from a more dynamic bourgeois society, were, if anything, even more conscious of race and class hierarchies than were the older Dutch bourgeoisie at the Cape. On supplanting the VOC they took over and formalised the racial restrictions they found. In 1801 'all slaves or people of colour' were subjected to a curfew, and were liable to arrest if found in the streets after 9 o'clock 'without lighted lanthorns'. The first British census of 1807 enumerated 'free blacks' as a separate category for the first time. And it was the British who for the first time explicitly cut the Gordian knot by declaring unreservedly that the status of slavery was unaffected by religious affiliation. British law entrenched differential rights and obligations of various status groups, by extending legal disabilities to 'Hottentots' and 'free persons of colour', which included both Cape Town's 'free blacks' of part-slave descent, and indigenous Khoi and Bastaards in the rural areas.[32]

In the maturing bourgeois community of late-eighteenth- and early-nineteenth-century Cape Town, colour and descent were clearly defining marks of respectable society. To be of European descent was a necessary, but not a sufficient, precondition for membership of the colonial bourgeoisie. Quite apart from slaves, there were many others nominally free who were excluded from the ranks of the respectable. 'Heathen descent', which was implied by a non-European physical appearance, was a criterion for exclusion. Thus although some Muslims acquired wealth in slaves and other property, demonstrated advanced artisanal skills, and achieved standing in the Islamic community, they were always regarded as 'free blacks' and never respectable in the eyes of those who wielded power and authority. But equally, white servants and workers, who served others for wages, shared the subordinate and dependent status of the free blacks. The prejudice was deeply entrenched that labour in the service of others was not fitting for the dominant class in colonial society.[33]

A pervasive colour prejudice was thus clearly present at the Cape, but it did not constitute a racial ideology. Explicitly racial terminology was seldom used; aversion was directed at cultural rather than physiological traits; and people were not defined primarily in racial terms. Class distinctions were as germane as distinctions of race and ancestry in the making of bourgeois civil society. Certainly it is fair to assume that among the subordinate classes, skin colour or racial identity was not as significant as their shared subordination; hence the ongoing incidence of marriages between white men and free-black or slave women at the lower social levels. But at the same time, poorer colonists of European ancestry might well gain advantage and opportunity through racial solidarity, from which persons of non-European ancestry were excluded. In the self-definition of the dominant bourgeoisie, Dutch and British, colour prejudice cut across considerations of class, culture and religion. Class distinctions were more permeable than race and ancestry; and legal disabilities were increasingly laid on persons of non-European ancestry but were not imposed on persons who were perceptibly Europeans.[34]

By the beginning of the eighteenth century the company policy of maintaining a monopoly of the cattle trade with the Khoi chiefdoms was breaking down. Not only were the Khoi chiefdoms disintegrating under the pressures on them and the ravages of smallpox, but much illicit private trade between Khoi and colonist was taking place.[35] The company thus began entering into contracts with private colonists for supplying cattle; and colonists, initially envisaged as cultivators, were encouraged to apply themselves to the raising of sheep and cattle. From 1703 permission was granted to them to spread further afield than the established settlement in search of grazing. Thus was the trekboer frontier established.

In 1714 a system of loan farms of some 6000 acres each (distinct from the quitrent tenure applied in the arable districts) was introduced as a means of regulating the occupation of land (and water sources) in the grazing hinterland. By the 1740s, some 400 loan farms had been granted, about half of which were leased to individuals resident in the agricultural southwest, whose stock was sent to grazing lands under the supervision of managers or sons. The rest were permanently occupied by stock farmers, their families and dependants: these were the first of the so-called trekboers of the frontier. Loan tenure in practice became as secure as quitrent, and loan farms came to be freely bought and sold. Sale of land was common after the death of the landholder, given the partible inheritance system, which also facilitated the settling of new land by children of landholders, as all received some portion of the estate. What is more, from the start many colonists were without any claims to land and led a largely nomadic existence as herders on their own account or in the employ of others, typically taking a share of the increase in payment. The numbers of stock farmers grew from natural increase, Cape-born men moving further afield in search of new opportunities for independent existence. They were augmented by a steady trickle of new arrivals, many of them discharged company employees. Stock farmers represented some two-thirds of all colonial farmers at the Cape by the year 1770.[36]

Expansion was rapid in the eighteenth century as the Khoi, whose pastoral economy dictated small-scale polities and dispersed settlement, offered sporadic and ineffectual resistance. In addition, the lack of capital and markets offered no opportunity to colonists for diversification or more intensive production methods. What emerged was an undifferentiated and unspecialised economy, without urban centres of any consequence, and without any artisanal or commercial class to speak of. Formal slaves of alien origin were also far rarer in the pastoral regions than in the arable southwest: their cost made them unattainable for most frontier colonists.

This very extensive economy was serviced mainly by Khoi labour. The Khoi were incorporated as clients and servants much as they might have been in their own societies, but gradually lost any claim to economic self-sufficiency until their status subsided to an unmitigated condition of servility. While in theory a free people, Khoi were not granted any of the privileges of burgher status, most notably the right to lay claim to land. On the contrary, the interests of the colonists in securing labour was the predominant reality shaping the way in which Khoi were integrated into colonial society. Informal practices designed to keep Khoi bound to the farms and in employ evolved long before they were inscribed in law.[37]

MacCrone in the 1930s painted a picture of intense group self-consciousness and cohesion in trekboer society, representing it as a distinctive and idiosyncratic offshoot of the parent community of the southwestern Cape, with a heightened sense of racial hostility and fear. This view was effectively challenged in 1970 by Legassick, whose nuanced interpretation has been fleshed out, refined and contradicted in some respects by subsequent researchers. Legassick argued that given the thinly spread diaspora in which trekboers found themselves, there was far less consciousness of group identity than MacCrone had assumed. Instead, Legassick saw the frontier as a place where the absence of any single source of legitimate authority promoted mutual acculturation between colonists and indigenous Khoisan. Cooperation and interdependence were features as notable of frontier relations as were enmity and conflict. Enemies and friends were not rigidly defined along racial lines. Legassick also argued that trekboer adaptation to the pastoral environment must have been shaped in large part by their dependence on Khoi labour and skills; and the trekboer economy depended in some degree on the trade relations (shading often into outright raiding) that they were able to forge with indigenous communities.[38]

This line of thinking has it that, far from racial group consciousness and hostility towards others hardening in trekboer society, the trekboers in some degree were drawn into new social relationships and a new cultural melting pot, which did not invariably follow stark racial or ethnic divisions.[39] But clearly, as Legassick also stressed, this imagery conceals as much as it reveals. There were strong links with metropolitan society, which were rarely completely broken. Trade ties through the sale of livestock and other animal products, in return for manufactured items required for the trekboer lifestyle, tied them back to the original settlement on Table Bay. So did the need to register land title, to legitimise marriages, to baptise children, and to secure a supply of ministers and teachers for their children. The idea of the exclusiveness of Christian people was usually present among trekboers; and although historians no longer hold the notion that early colonists were inspired by a primitive Calvinism to see themselves as a 'chosen people', the term 'Christian' was widely seen as being coterminous with the community of European origin. This was not a theological principle so much as an aspect of their cultural chauvinism. At the same time, racism as an explicit doctrine of biological superiority was seldom enunciated, it seems; but race was implicit in the self-definition of the colonists. In practice, competition over land and the resources of water and grazing reinforced attitudes of inclusiveness and exclusiveness. The sheer brutality with which claims to land and water resources were sometimes enforced, stock theft was punished and servants were subjugated, was facilitated by a sense of racial or cultural otherness.

We need therefore to disaggregate the picture. Giliomee went some way towards allowing us to do this with his conception of 'open' and 'closing' frontiers. The open frontier was characterised by the absence of a single source of coercive authority, by a relatively low population density, by fluidity in group relations, by pragmatic resort to policies of cooperation and mutual accommodation, and by clientage rather than bondage as the basis of labour relations. There was also of course endemic violence, but it was inconclusive and could not yet form the basis of a new hierarchical social order founded on coercion, accumulation and dispossession. This nascent social order grew as the frontier closed, as the colonists, with the government at their back, imposed their hegemony over indigenous peoples and exerted a growing monopoly on productive resources, and as coercion increasingly became the basis of group relations and the organisation of labour. On the closing frontier, too, stratification within the ranks of the colonists sharpened, with a decreasing proportion being landholders, and growing numbers becoming propertyless and dependent.[40]

Clearly there was an implicit intention among at least some colonists, from the time the settlement first expanded beyond the arable southwest, to replicate in an entirely new environment the social and cultural norms of the original society, just as the emerging slaveholding gentry in the arable districts were doing by the early eighteenth century. In the context of the isolated stockfarming enterprise, this entailed building a patriarchal community of kin and dependants, permanently settled on land to which the patriarch had a legal claim registered in Cape Town, and aspiring to the accoutrements and outward signs of civilised Christian living (even though this was very difficult to achieve). With or without the presence of slaves of foreign origin or descent, such a community depended heavily on control over indigenous servants or clients in various conditions of servility.

But central to the self-image of respectability, which harkened back to met-ropolitan norms, was the presence of the European wife and the European family at the core of the community. As a general proposition we can assume that the more balanced the ratio between men and women of European origin in any particular region, the more its white inhabitants sought self-conscious-ly to reproduce metropolitan standards of respectability and class and cultural exclusiveness. In these circumstances, where the frontier was already closing, racial hierarchies were most marked, race mixing was most frowned upon, and racial discrimination in terms of economic opportunities most apparent. To refer to such colonists as 'trekboers' (with its assumption of mobility) is inap-propriate, as their self-image was wrapped up in their ownership of property and their sense of belonging (although of course exigencies of drought, over-grazing or warfare might force mobility on them). Indeed, loan farms com-monly remained under the same owners for entire lifetimes.[41]

To what degree were aspirations to gentry status attainable on the frontier? Neumark in the 1950s hypothesised that frontier expansion was closely syn-chronised with the expansion of the demand for meat and animal products, and that the trekboer economy was essentially entrepreneurial and commer-cial.[42] Guelke effectively discounted this thesis, arguing that the trekboer econ-omy, although not a purely subsistence economy, was marginally linked to the Cape Town market, and its expansion was driven by the absence of economic alternatives. But the nature of this economy was such that the viability of the stockfarming enterprise declined as the land became overused and less pro-ductive, and as the distance from Cape Town increased. Thus the average value of trekboer estates declined between 1731 and 1780, the years Guelke exam-ined.[43]

Newton-King has argued that Guelke greatly underestimated the range of necessary imported goods on which stock farmers depended not only for pro-ductive independence, but also for the maintenance of their self-image as respectable colonists. Every household required a host of items which could only be obtained by trade. Imported and locally purchased commodities formed a very significant proportion of moveable assets revealed in the liqui-dation records of deceased estates. But in contrast to the Neumark image of a dynamic market economy, this dependence on markets in reality made the stock farmers, especially those at greatest distance from Cape Town, exceed-ingly vulnerable. Apart from a tiny minority of really prosperous households in the Graaff-Reinet district in the final decades of the eighteenth century whose material position compared favourably with the well-to-do gentry of the arable southwest, stock farmers struggled to achieve the rough comfort to which they aspired. A full 40 per cent of Newton-King's sample in the Graaff-Reinet district were barely able to make ends meet. The monopsonistic organ-isation of the meat market ensured that prices paid to farmers were kept arti-ficially low; and the prices of goods imported to the Cape were not only greatly inflated but subject to wild fluctuations, given the restrictions on retail trade. In addition, dependence on butchers' *knechts* and neighbours or kin willing to endure the two or three months' trip with wagons to Cape Town and back, and reliance on credit, all made solvency a very fragile condition for stock farmers on distant frontiers.[44]

The further away from Cape Town they found themselves, the greater was the colonists' isolation, their distance from markets, and the insecurity of their lives. This meant they were less and less likely to escape debt or to accumulate capital on a sufficient scale to attain the kind of material culture to which they aspired. Seen in this view, the trekboers were not a separate and distinctive social entity, evolving in isolation, but were all too closely subservient to the metropolitan economy and culture, yet in ways which made it virtually impossible for them to fulfil their cultural aspirations.

In reality there was a wide spectrum of forms of adaptation to frontier conditions. Ties to the metropolitan culture could be very weak: formal education and institutional church membership often fell into abeyance. When settlement was new, insecure and contested, and when colonists had few institutional means of coercion to depend on, adaptations and compromises, in lifestyle and in relations with indigenous peoples, were inevitable. Descriptions of the living arrangements of colonists on further frontiers suggest that they often had much in common with the Khoi.[45] Circumstances, rather than ideology or aspirations, dictated responses to the social milieu. There were those who committed themselves more fully to the forging of new identities free of the social mores of metropolitan society (with its insistence on ethnic and racial exclusivity). These were MacCrone's 'border ruffians', who had reverted in his analysis to the level of the native inhabitants among whom they lived, cohabiting with Khoi women and turning their backs on 'civilisation'. For MacCrone, they were the deviant cases that proved the rule about the majority.[46] But in fact those who 'went native' were simply adapting rationally to a frontier environment of culture contact and competing sources of authority and legitimation. They were people without resources, who could not therefore find European wives. Theirs was the sort of pragmatic adaptation to inescapable circumstances that was to be found elsewhere on colonial frontiers, such as in the Americas or Australasia.

One important dynamic in the process of stratification was the relative difficulty of becoming an independent stock farmer – at least by the last third of the eighteenth century, when frontiers of colonial settlement were pressing against natural and human barriers. Loan farms were then not as easily acquired as they had been earlier in the century, and in desirable locations with water sources they fetched very large sums of money, sometimes saddling purchasers with crippling debts. (Nominally it was the *opstal* or fixed improvements that were sold, but in fact the land market reflected the actual value of the land.) Nor were livestock very easily acquired on a scale sufficient for independent farming, and accumulation from caring for stock on half-shares of the increase in the accustomed fashion was very slow.[47]

Giliomee says that in the 1770s it was still possible for a young colonist with little or no capital to acquire land and start raising cattle. But according to the 1798 *opgaaf* in Graaff-Reinet, 39 per cent of married men owned farms, and by 1812 this had shrunk to 25 per cent. Landownership itself was also unequal. In 1798, 174 inhabitants in Graaff-Reinet district held one farm each, 63 held two, 14 held three, and 2 owned four farms. Typical newcomers to the frontier during the eighteenth century that failed to become independent stock farmers were company employees (*knechts*) who took their discharge at the Cape, such as the many soldiers of German origin who became overseers for absentees (some of the latter being arable farmers from the southwest), or teachers in the employ of more substantial stock farmers – the notorious *meesters* of colonial legend. Such *eenlopende* men could also lead very mobile lives as hunters, traders and herders. By 1810 landdrost Anders Stockenström reported that in Graaff-Reinet district some 800–900 colonists without farms roamed about, staying for a while on one farm before moving off.[48] But ultimately the dominant mores of the pastoral frontier, as in the urban and rural settings of the arable southwestern corner of the colony, were those of the settled family units who aspired to the material and cultural adjuncts of a colonial elite, and not of those who had to build their social and sexual relationships on the margins of colonial and native societies.[49]

During the eighteenth century the commando became the single most important symbol of the cultural and social cohesion of the frontier burghers, and the chief instrument of their common interest in dispossessing and subjugating indigenous peoples. But the commandos also revealed how tenuous that cohesion and common interest could be, for they were typically riven with faction, and burghers were often very reluctant to take up arms at the behest of the military authorities. At first, commandos were officially organised under company officers. In 1715 the first purely colonial commando took the field with official approval, but under the command of a free burgher. After 1739 commando service became obligatory, and burgher officers with the rank of *veldkorporaal* were appointed to take charge of commandos when on service. Although the government was nominally in charge, commandos largely operated independently. With their ready access to horses and firearms, they were used to intimidate and punish recalcitrant Khoi groups, and in the process provided a supply of looted Khoi cattle for colonists. Later in the eighteenth century when 'Bushman' resistance beyond the escarpment posed for the first time a serious obstacle to colonial expansion, the burgher community became more militarised, violence became more systematic, and a supply of women and children captives became a by-product of commando campaigns. Leadership within the commando implied privileged access to important resources of land, labour and livestock. Thus the commando became both a reflection and an instrument of stratification among colonists.[50]

In fact most of the ordinary members of a commando were not burghers at all, but loyal Khoi servants, allowed the use of horses and firearms by burghers who did not care much for military service themselves. So the commando was a powerful means of acculturation. But equally it served the colonists' sense of their own superiority. For Khoi or part-Khoi soldiers were always quite explicitly subordinates, servants even, in the organisation of the commando. Over time the social stratification of the commando changed, and in particular came to reflect the declining status of the part-European on the frontier. Most offspring of colonist–Khoi relations would have been absorbed in the Khoi community of which their mothers were members. But a wholly new social stratum – the Bastaards – emerged, often we may assume the offspring of rather more lasting relationships in which European fathers remained heads of mixed-race households, so that the mixed offspring grew up in the Dutch language and with Dutch names and a modicum of European culture, including in some cases adherence to Christianity.

The Bastaards' position in frontier society was ambiguous, never being fully accepted, but enjoying some of the rights of burghers, provided they were baptised in the Dutch Reformed Church. In this they were not unlike the free blacks of mixed descent in Cape Town. Possibly some became fully absorbed in the community of the respectable – particularly females, given the shortage of suitable wives of European origin. In 1798 in Graaff-Reinet district, 5–6 per cent of married couples could be described as 'mixed', in that one of the partners had a grandparent who was not European (no doubt an underestimate). Most, we may assume, were poorer and marginal people in the burgher community, and some offspring may have become 'white', others not. At the same time some baptised Bastaards held registered loan farms; others owned considerable herds and flocks, without formally holding land. But there were few of them: in 1798 there were 136 baptised Bastaards counted in Graaff-Reinet, compared to 4262 Europeans, 8947 Khoisan and 964 slaves.[51]

But the lines of exclusion and inclusion, here too, tended to harden as economic pressures on the frontier intensified in the second half of the eighteenth century. Penn suggests that on the northern frontier it was the ecological crisis from 1770 onwards, arising from the natural and human barriers to further expansion combined with overgrazing in older settled areas, that led to the decline of Bastaard status, as competition for resources increased. The incessant wars against Bushmen from 1770 meant greater reliance on the military service of often reluctant and rebellious Khoi and Bastaards as crucial rank-and-file fighters, while at the same time their economic status was coming under attack. This in turn intensified racial hierarchy and racial dominance within the frontier community. Thus in the 1770s, for the first time, Bastaards were singled out as a specific category of subjects liable for military service, and simultaneously there were moves to define them as a separate and inferior group in terms of their access to burgher rights. 'Burgher trades' such as hunting, driving wagons and bartering were increasingly reserved in practice for burghers of undisputed European origin.[52] In consequence Bastaards, including landholders, increasingly moved beyond colonial borders. Economic opportunities beyond the colony on either side of the Orange River opened up as those within the colony closed. Taking advantage of these opportunities, independent political communities of Khoi–Bastaard origin flourished in the north for a while in the early nineteenth century, and the frontier remained open and fluid there long after it had closed within the proclaimed colonial borders.[53]

A further variable significant in shaping frontier relations was the nature of the indigenous peoples themselves. For indeed there was more heterogeneity about the native peoples than about the colonisers. The instrumentalism, pragmatism and variability of frontier relations cannot be understood without taking this into account. Thus Newton-King, puzzled by the contrast between initial symbiosis and interdependence on the colonist–Khoi frontier, and later evidence of frequent and savage violence inflicted on the native people of the Cape, particularly from about 1770 on, points to differences in origin and lifestyle between propertied and more tractable cattlekeepers with a tradition of clientage, on the one hand, and the cattleless 'hunter-robbers' living mostly beyond the mountain escarpments, which were infiltrated by the colonists from the 1760s, on the other. No accommodation was possible between European colonists and these Bushmen (or San), whose entire way of life was profoundly threatened by the spread of cattle farming.[54]

Thus beyond the rim of the mountain escarpments both in the north and in the east where the Bushmen were concentrated, colonial expansion was greeted with widespread and implacable resistance. In reaction Khoi cattlekeepers who had already become subordinated to the colonists sought to distance themselves from the mountain bands of hunter-robbers, which were subjected to merciless search-and-destroy tactics by burgher commandos. This sense of separate identity was exploited by colonists, who enlisted Khoi dependants and servants in commandos, rewarding them with captured livestock and, in some cases it seems, with the services of human captives.[55]

But the warfare that engulfed the frontier from 1770 precipitated a reign of fear and violence which infected relations on the farms as well, so that even loyal and long-serving Khoi servants and dependants came to suffer severe brutality. And it was under these circumstances, as we have seen, that those of part-European descent found themselves increasingly treated as a separate and inferior class. Indeed, the warfare against the hunter-robbers of the late eighteenth century seems to have been shockingly indifferent to human life. It was from this period that Boer references to natives as *schepsels*, as being subhuman, were reported in the observations of travellers and officials. They reveal Boer reactions to the threat of cultural annihilation at the hands of a people who were culturally thoroughly alien and resistant to assimilation (much more so than the pastoral Khoi).[56]

War captives became a major element in the labour force of the colonists. (Slaving was a by-product of commandos' activities, the primary goal being to incapacitate enemies.) By the last decade of the eighteenth century, captives may have outnumbered the officially acknowledged slave population of Graaff-Reinet district by two to one. The majority were women and children, who were 'apprenticed' (*ingeboek*) until the age of 18 or 25, although they seem generally to have had little opportunity to leave employment when the period of 'apprenticeship' nominally expired. Apprenticeship (more accurately, indenture) in the South African context was a euphemism for bound labour. The presence of large numbers of forcibly bound servants who had been alienated only very partially from their societies of origin explains why coercion on the farms tended often to take on extremely brutal forms. Within the realm of the colonists' pastoral enterprise, distinctions were lost between the *huisboorlingen* (those born on the farms of colonists) and captives. All were regarded as 'Hottentots', whose heathen status meant that they could lay claim to no rights, and who were increasingly perceived by their masters to be of *de facto* slave status.[57]

Incessant frontier violence, the failure to impose a moral hegemony on servants, and the pressures of land exhaustion and incipient land scarcity, combined to precipitate the crisis of the 1790s, when colonists rebelled against the landdrost in Graaff-Reinet, H. C. D. Maynier, as local representative of an autocratic and unsympathetic company government. Although the government nominally supported the colonists in the 'extirpation of the said rapacious tribes' and ensured a supply of arms and ammunition, it otherwise left the colonists to fend for themselves. Rather than providing military support, the government seemed to the colonists to be more inclined to blame them for their travails. Further, Maynier's concern for the rights (albeit very limited) of servants made his authority an affront to many of the colonists. It was widely regarded as an intolerable intrusion upon the authority of the master when local officials and local courts sought to mediate relations and subject masters to the rule of law, however loaded in their favour it might be. Hence also the outrage expressed when British missionaries, who arrived at the turn of the century, began to propagate notions of the oneness of humanity and the universality of the Christian message. Yet Maynier's unwelcome warnings of the consequences of unalloyed reliance on coercion were vindicated when in 1799 an unprecedented alliance of Khoisan and Xhosa, servants and independent peoples, erupted against the colonists.[58]

The supremacist impulse, though always present among colonists, was contingent rather than absolute, instrumental rather than immanent. Colonists could seek to ensure their survival in ways that do not conform to the picture of unmitigated enmity and violence which the 'Bushman wars' evoke. There were many examples of colonists, including respectable landholders, living in apparent harmony with Bushmen while elsewhere merciless war was being waged against them.[59] Indeed, the 'Bushman wars' provide one model of frontier relations, which grew out of a wide chasm of cultural, social and economic incompatibility, but it is one that cannot be generalised to other frontier situations elsewhere. The Khoisan frontier within the boundaries of the established colony had closed by the early nineteenth century, and the frontier of Bushman warfare had moved northward towards the Orange River, and across it into Transorangia by the 1820s. At the same time, a new and far more significant frontier had opened: that with the great phalanx of Bantu-speaking mixed farmers, with whom colonists had been in competition for land since the 1770s in the Zuurveld of the southeastern Cape.

As settled cultivators living in cohesive chiefdoms, and with a far more complex social structure than the Khoisan, the Africans were clearly not going to be subverted and dispossessed by colonists with the resources at their command. On the one hand the cattle trade between colonists and Xhosa (illegal because of official prohibition) flourished. But equally, conflict was present here too from the start over land and cattle. Yet the recurrent warfare, far from coinciding starkly with ethnic or racial lines, involved Europeans allying with the Rharhabe Xhosa against the smaller chiefdoms west of the Fish River (the colony's self-proclaimed boundary) and then allying with one branch of the Rharhabe against another. Conflict that arose from a failure to establish mutually recognised boundaries reached explosive proportions in the 1790s, but it was never simply a matter of colonists versus the Xhosa.[60]

There was never any doubt that for most colonists, the Xhosa, like the Khoi, were cultural outsiders, separated from people of European origin by an unbridgeable gulf, of which heathenism was an explicit and physiology an implicit element. Group endogamy and exclusiveness were cherished values for the majority of settled colonists, and miscegenation was probably far rarer with Africans than with Khoi. But it seems that attitudes towards Xhosa were significantly different from those expressed towards the Bushman hunter-robbers of the interior mountains. The Xhosa were rarely regarded as *schepsels*; eliminating or enslaving them was never considered appropriate or realistic. Practical realities dictated a very different adaptation to conditions on the mixed-farming frontier, one which recognised that Africans could be allies, patrons even, trading partners, competitors for resources, as well as enemies and servants.

The way of dealing with Xhosa chiefdoms, and all cohesive and stable political communities of African farmers subsequently encountered, was to seek agreements on boundaries and territorial rights. This was the goal not only of successive Cape governments, but of colonists themselves when acting independently of colonial authority. Of course, colonists always sought to maximise the land at their disposal, and took advantage of opportunities to seize cattle and secure labour whenever and wherever possible. But when acting individually or in small groups beyond the reach of the colonial authorities (such as on the early Sotho frontier) they could turn to African chiefs as the source of patronage and legitimate authority to secure their land rights. More often than not, there was a rough equality of military might between the burgher commandos and the more substantial African political communities, especially after Africans had armed themselves with European firearms. African societies had the self-assurance of numbers and social cohesion. What is more, population densities in the chiefdoms were greater than among the colonists. It was simply pragmatic and realistic to accept the inevitability of a policy of live-and-let-live wherever the power equation dictated it. Indeed, it was common for factions of colonists and, later, Boer emigrants north of the Orange River to seek out alliances with black chiefdoms in their own internecine conflicts. Across the Vaal, where, if anything, Boer communities had less access to coercive power than in the colony, they entered into agreements with chiefs for the supply of client labour, and even, in remoter fringes, were known to pay tribute to chiefs.[61]

The force ultimately responsible for closing the frontier, in the eastern Cape as elsewhere, was in fact not the mythical isolated and group-conscious 'frontier mentality', supposedly bred on an ideology of the chosen race and a rigid enmity towards the African 'other'. Rather, it was the force of British imperialism – always reluctant and penny-pinching until the final third of the nineteenth century – that established the hegemony of colonial society and enforced adherence to boundary lines. This entailed driving Xhosa out of the Zuurveld across the Fish River in a decisive campaign of 1811–12, in which 900 burgher militia and 700 men of the Cape Regiment (made up of Khoi) served under British command, with 500 British troops bringing up the rear.[62] At the same time, within the colony, the British were institutionalising the servile status of the colonial Khoisan, while extending the rule of law at the Cape.[63]

In all this, the British at first enjoyed the overwhelming support of respectable colonists (as evidenced in the support the authorities received when dealing with the Slagtersnek rebels in 1815). But as British rule became more intrusive and more influenced by anti-slavery and humanitarian thought in the 1820s, the Boers of the eastern Cape became increasingly antagonised by the dismantling of the coercive and hegemonic institutions which underpinned their patriarchal authority, and by the pressures on their land and on their trading patterns caused by the presence of large numbers of British settlers. Their attitudes towards British military power became more ambiguous. Throughout the subsequent decades, it was (very anti-humanitarian) British settlers, and not Boers, who developed a rhetoric of racial and cultural superiority to justify ongoing imperial subversion of the Xhosa. Boers increasingly resented this imperial militarisation of the frontier districts, proved unwilling military conscripts, and even on occasion showed some fellow feeling towards the African chiefdoms. Certainly, when new frontiers of imperial aggression were opened up north of the Orange during the brief period of British rule there at mid-century, Boer and Sotho were to throw in their lot together quite openly at crucial junctures against the British presence.

The Great Trek itself, beginning in the mid-1830s, was in part a rebellion against British policies of legal equality and the elimination of discriminatory treatment of the colony's servile classes, introduced during the humanitarian ascendancy of the 1820s. But the Trek cannot be said to have been motivated by a desire to conquer and subjugate. If anything, as that prominent Afrikaner frontiersman born and bred, Andries Stockenström, pointed out, Boers were indifferent, if not hostile, to the acquisitive machinations of British settlers and rogue governors bent on military expansion. As Stockenström wrote, 'The theory which makes the black irreclaimable savages, fit only to be exterminated, like the wolves, was not of Boer origin' – implying (correctly) that explicitly racist notions about the Xhosa and other African peoples were a British innovation.[64]

The predominant ideology of the colonial frontier was thus decidedly predicated on the ideal of racial or ethnic exclusiveness. But this did not imply that subjugation of the great mass of African farming peoples encountered beyond the Khoisan frontiers was either a practical possibility or even a desired ideal. This is where the earlier liberal interpretation breaks down. The power, the desire, the need to impose racial supremacy on a subcontinental scale at the level of the state and its institutions was an impulse that had other origins at other historical junctures. White supremacy as a total system of hegemony and subjugation grew from the centres of power – meaning (in the main) centres of imperial power – outwards, and not the other way round. It was not on isolated frontiers that such an ideal took root.

CHAPTER THREE

Imperial Renewal

Britain's uniquely fluid and dynamic social structure in the eighteenth century grew out of an economy transformed by the remaking of the countryside in the direction of capitalist relations and market production. Thriving and growing urban centres, spreading communications and transport networks, relative agricultural abundance, and a vibrant trading economy underlay the belief that the English (increasingly redefined through the eighteenth century as the British) were a uniquely privileged and free-born people, characterised first and foremost by their adherence to Protestantism, free of the superstitions, brutalities and oppressions of continental Catholicism. In this they were quite unlike the enemy, papist France, with which the English seemed to be incessantly at war, for in France the great mass of downtrodden peasant farmers remained tied to the land by the compulsions of ancient rights and obligations, and increasingly subjected to tax exactions to support a bloated absolutist state and its military adventurism.[1]

All the same the British ruling class right through the nineteenth century remained a landed ruling class. Wealth, status and power continued to be largely associated with landed property rather than trade or industry. The titled and territorial patriciate still controlled the high offices of state, the military, the church and the judiciary.[2] Nevertheless, there was general agreement that the cult of commerce was the foundation of Britain's identity and her pre-eminence in the contemporary world. In eighteenth-century England, there had been a remarkably close symbiosis between the exercise of power by the Whig oligarchy and the practice of commerce. It was the merchant community as well as the landed class which funded the imperial wars of the eighteenth century. It was trade that provided the tax base on which the state depended. Conversely, command of overseas trade depended on the government's investment in the navy and in imperial expansion. In peace time, 40–50 per cent of the government's expenditure went on servicing its debt, effectively redistributing wealth to its domestic creditors. In sum, British power and commercial profit went hand in hand. For the developing mercantile class, patriotism paid.[3]

The late eighteenth and early nineteenth centuries formed a bridge between the old British imperial system of largely self-governing colonies of settlement and the nineteenth-century polyglot empire of dependencies. Prior to 1763 (when Britain took over French North America at the end of the Seven Years War), colonial accretions (notably the North American colonies) resulted largely from the colonising efforts of private parties and companies, often operating under royal charter. They were Protestant, Nonconformist, anglophone, and relatively homogeneous.[4] In contrast, the possessions acquired in 1763 included Quebec with some 70 000 French Catholic inhabitants, as well as large stretches of Asian territory with manifestly non-European and non-Christian populations. This new empire posed new problems of military control and administration, and brought new challenges of redefining Britain's imperial mission. How were these recent imperial responsibilities to be reconciled with the self-imagery of a freedom-loving and commercial people, whose role in the world was different from the bloody and brutal imperialisms of the Catholic states?

The first casualties of the new imperial activism called into being by these recent encumbrances were the thirteen original North American colonies, which rebelled against the assertion of long-discarded powers of taxation by the British parliament. The American revolutionary wars further emphasised the changing nature of empire, and plunged Britain's ruling class into a crisis of confidence, evoking on a new scale doubts about its competence and its capacity and right to rule. These developments were followed by the French Revolution and the era of continental warfare. The Age of Revolution, thus inaugurated, challenged as never before the legitimacy of ruling elites, their status based on land and birth, and their hold on the instruments of power. Warfare taxed and disrupted the economies of European states on an unprecedented scale; it also undermined the loyalty of many, including those with mercantile interests, who had largely subscribed to the political *status quo* previously. In Britain, challenges to authority and the prerogatives of class entered the mainstream of popular culture in the 1780s and 1790s.

But more fundamental than imperial and continental developments in challenging the rule of the landed oligarchy were developments closer to home. In the last three decades of the eighteenth century, British society entered a period of rapid economic and social change, traditionally called the industrial revolution. In recent times, economic historians have tended to play down the significance of the industrial revolution, even to abjure use of the term. And indeed, in terms of macroeconomic indicators (such as productivity growth, national income and industrial output) the period now seems hardly to have been revolutionary. Factory production and capital-intensive methods were restricted to certain industries and processes before 1850. The typical worker of the industrial revolution was still the craft worker, the outworker, the casual labourer. But in the longer view, the late eighteenth and early nineteenth centuries were indeed years of dramatic and fundamental change, ushering in an era of sustained per capita income growth, an era in which the limits placed on production by pre-industrial technology and culture were decisively broken. In terms of social change, urbanisation, proletarianisation, popular politics and culture, government and law, these years were, and were experienced at the time as being, revolutionary.[5]

The fact that Britain was the world's first industrial nation may indeed have been a comparative disadvantage in the longer term, but that does not diminish the extent of the transformation when measured qualitatively rather than in terms of macrostatistics. Social protest and unrest on an unprecedented scale followed. Although much recent work, in reaction against the more radical scholarship of the 1960s and 1970s, has played down the extent of class consciousness, stressing fragmentation of experience and the ongoing manifestations of loyalism, royalism and patriotism, nevertheless it is still true to say that the world was a vastly different place for most British workers in the 1830s than it had been in the 1760s. For them the loss of independence and the decline of the household economy were particularly marked.[6]

It is testimony to the extent to which the British ruling class had adapted to and incorporated the dynamics of a capitalist society that it emerged not only intact, but stronger, wealthier, larger and more self-assured at the end of the Napoleonic period than before. By the end of George III's sixty-year reign in 1820, Britain's rulers had successfully reconstructed their authority and their image, imbued themselves with a new aura of patriotic virtue, and re-legitimated their exercise of power. The landed elites of the Celtic fringes had been drawn into the centre of political life more fully, and a pan-British ruling class was greatly consolidated, homogenised and strengthened as a result.

Members of this class consciously sought new forms of cultural expression that confirmed their inclusive British identity. And so the fiction was born that aristocratic property was the people's heritage. The Napoleonic wars also gave them the opportunity to reassert a cult of patrician heroism. In civil life too, the generation of William Pitt the Younger immersed themselves in the nation's work, and dedication to service and personal morality became the aspirations of the sons of the aristocracy. From the 1780s, an unprecedented number of men were raised to the peerage for service to the state. Without substantially diluting the ranks of the traditional aristocracy, sufficient recognition was paid to meritocratic principles so as to create the impression of an elite open to landless talent and dedicated to the national good. In a real sense, the British ruling class reinvented itself at this time.[7]

Similarly, the modern monarchy in large part dates from the same period. The eighteenth-century Hanoverians were unspectacular and disliked, foreigners imported by parliament to keep the Stuart pretenders at bay. But beginning from the time of the American wars to the death of mad George III in 1820, the king's apotheosis had been achieved. The monarchy became the focus of patriotic celebration, highly visible and splendid, and, in ostentatious contrast with the artificial pretensions of republican France, the symbol of popular mobilisation against threats from abroad.[8] Of course the transformation of the British state, its institutions and image, went hand in hand with a high degree of repression of popular dissent. And those who publicly revered the idea of monarchy and volunteered for service in defence of the realm against the French could also use their experiences of mass organisation and discipline in unforeseen ways, far more threatening to the established order. But threats from below were always dissonant and unsustained.

The resilience of the landed ruling class in Britain has been pointed to by scholars grappling with the evident economic decline of Britain by the 1960s, as the fatal flaw in the British body politic. Thus the archaic and uncompetitive nature of modern British capitalism has been ascribed to the original failure of Britain to undergo a thorough transition to bourgeois democracy, and its consequent lack of meritocratic, technological and acquisitive cultural values. An essentially pre-modern political culture, antipathetic to industrial innovation and technological advance, is the price Britain has had to pay for having been the first global power of the capitalist age. Later comers had to undergo far more disruptive and violent political metamorphoses, but in the process emerged far more adapted to global competition.[9]

From the vantage point of the 'post-industrial' 1990s, however, British backwardness looks far less distinctive. More recent writers have tended to play down the extent of British particularity.[10] But the prevailing wisdom continues to stress the continuities in British social structure throughout the period of the industrial revolution: the rising bourgeoisie never seized control of the levers of state power; industrial enterprise never became the dominant sector of British capitalism (as against commercial and financial services); non-industrial forms of wealth enjoyed a higher status than wealth derived from production.[11] A currently influential interpretation in British imperial history picks up these themes, and concludes that this 'gentlemanly capitalism' was the driving force behind British expansion. It also asserts that industrial growth, the desire for raw materials and markets for manufactures, had less weight than the interests of the City of London as bankers, insurers and carriers of the world's trade – sectors in which the landed elite had more direct interests – in driving forward imperial enterprise.[12]

But in reality there was a convergence of the commercially minded landed aristocracy and the capitalist manufacturers and merchants. They came to forge a united class through threats external and internal to property, through the merging of capitals and the interdependence of sectors, through intermarriage and middle-class enfranchisement from 1832. The old landed elite in some senses was transformed into a successful capitalist class by the early nineteenth century. Further, at local level and in civil society, the new middle class came to exercise real power. Assimilation was a two-way process, cultural and social as well as in terms of economic interest. Indeed, the economics and ideology of *laissez-faire* and free trade were as much a product of the landed interest as of the manufacturing districts, tempered only by specific considerations such as the post-war need to maintain agricultural incomes through the corn laws. And in terms of imperial commitments, it is in practice difficult to disentangle the interests of the City of London from those of the manufacturing north.[13]

❖

The new imperial system after 1815 cannot be understood without regard to the central role of overseas markets in fuelling Britain's industrial revolution. It is true that foreign markets were always dwarfed by soaring domestic consumption throughout the period: external trade accounted for some 18 per cent of GDP in 1800, falling back to perhaps 14 per cent by 1850. But foreign demand had a much larger impact in those sectors involved in the mass manufacture of homogeneous goods, in which technological innovation was most marked: notably textiles and iron and metalware.[14] Surges in external trade had widespread repercussions, and had a strong impact on transport and the financial and commercial infrastructure of industrialising regions. Indeed, the prospect of infinitely expanding demand for manufactures was a *sine qua non* of ongoing investment in revolutionising the productive forces of society. An economy increasingly based on factory production and proletarian labour could only be justified by the expectation that demand would always keep pace with galloping rates of increase in productivity. Hence, as industrial capitalism took off in the heartland, so merchant capital, surging out into the nether regions of the globe as never before, was bent to its service.

In essence, the significance of the Napoleonic wars was that they were the climactic stage in the century-long battle for global pre-eminence between Britain, increasingly dominated by an accumulating mercantile and landowning elite, and France, the most powerful and (until 1789) the most successful of the absolutist *anciens régimes*. By 1815, industrialising Britain had eliminated all rivals for command of the world's markets. Latin America, for example, had become virtually a British economic dependency, a position entrenched by the political independence of Latin American countries from Spain and Portugal, largely achieved by 1825. Indeed, throughout the nineteenth century, formal British possessions always paled in comparison with independent lands in the scale of Britain's non-European trade.[15]

If the North American colonies were at the centre of the old formal empire, India was at the centre of the new. It is certainly true that annexations of territory in the late eighteenth and early nineteenth centuries were not made with any explicit purpose of serving metropolitan industry. India was not conquered at the behest of the Lancashire textile manufacturers – Lancashire did not penetrate Indian markets before the nineteenth century. But it is true that Lancashire's exports to the Americas gave Britain bullion to finance wars in India at the same time as in continental Europe. Furthermore, the Indian military and civil administration was funded in large degree by local taxation and loans from locally based merchant houses. Their wealth in turn came from profits from the export trade to Europe (increasingly in raw materials such as indigo) and by the export of Indian opium to China to pay for the tea which was in increasing demand in the industrialising districts of Britain. And very considerable profits were repatriated to Britain, which must further have promoted economic activity and state revenues. Thus imperial expansion, if not driven by manufacturing interests, was closely linked to the changes taking place in the British economy as a result of the advance of British manufacturing.[16]

The East Indies had traditionally been a major producer of cotton goods. But cotton textiles were of course the major manufacture of Britain's early industrial age. And so in the nineteenth century, India's mercantile interests were subverted to the interest of Britain's new industrial economy, and India was systematically de-industrialised to serve as a market for Lancashire's dark Satanic mills. Indian village looms could not compete with Britain's factory production and cheap transport. In 1820 India consumed 11 million yards of British cotton textiles; by 1840, 145 million yards. What was being wrought was a historic turning point. Since earliest times Europe had always imported more from the East than it had exported there. Nothing much that Europeans produced was wanted by the advanced civilisations of Asia, in return for the spices, silks, calicoes and jewels that Europeans eagerly sought and acquired by exporting bullion or by outright theft. This relationship was, however, reversed by the industrial revolution. The pre-eminence of European industrial capitalism was nowhere more starkly proclaimed than in the Indian subcontinent. This was accompanied by the inexorable penetration of the largest remaining non-European bastion of economic self-sufficiency, China, whose vulnerability to the attractions of Indian opium kept pace with the demand for Chinese tea of Britain's working classes.[17]

Whatever the commercial advantages of India, the colonies acquired during the wars against Napoleon – including the Cape – were taken over mainly for reasons of war and strategy. Striking at continental enemies on the periphery (including Holland after 1793) was logical for a power which boasted naval supremacy over her adversaries. Much of this new dependent empire was of little practical interest to the British, and was given up when peace returned in 1815. Those colonies retained were not generally of intrinsic value, but were strategically important in promoting and protecting British trading interests and her command of the sea.[18] Mauritius, the Seychelles and Maldives were retained for their harbour facilities and to deny continental powers access to potential naval bases. Ceylon was retained for the port of Trincomalee, with its command of the Bay of Bengal. And the Cape was retained as the essential link in the chain of communication with the Orient. The Cape, thus, was of interest and value solely as a way-station on a major sea-route. There was nothing else at the Cape or in its hinterland that awakened the slightest interest.[19]

What these new colonies of occupation had in common (like other acquisitions such as Guiana taken from the Dutch, and Tobago and St Lucia from the French) was that they possessed their own established legal and administrative systems. Until 1815, they were under temporary military occupation with unclear constitutional status. Hence the British were reluctant to interfere with established institutions. What this meant was that the relative constitutional uniformity of the older British colonies of settlement, whose settler inhabitants enjoyed the full rights and legal status of 'free-born Englishmen', was destroyed. Instead, the new colonies came to be saddled in practice with autocratic governments, which made little effort to impose British law or British institutions. In this respect, the developing British dominion in India in the late eighteenth century had provided a model. In particular, the British conquerors, mindful of the consequences of weak imperial control and strong local assemblies in the erstwhile American colonies, were determined at first to deny any constitutional rights to newly acquired colonists, such as the Afrikaners at the Cape. Hence Admiral Pringle's warning in 1795 that the Cape, if allowed to, might develop into a second United States, and 'more likely in time to rob us of India than to secure it to us'.[20] Even in the older possession of Canada, the British were determined at this time to minimise the rights of colonists.

After 1815, temporary military government was replaced by the more permanent status of crown colony. But wartime administrative expedients were conveniently maintained intact and autocracy became entrenched in colonial government. At the same time, intense opposition to rights for newly acquired colonists was also being increasingly mounted in humanitarian circles, concerned to protect indigenous peoples in the Cape as elsewhere from the supposed slaveholding mentality of European settlers.[21] This tendency towards autocracy was reinforced by the fact that colonial governorships were regarded as fit offices for redundant members of aristocratic lineages, usually with military careers in the Napoleonic wars behind them. At the Cape, all governors before Cathcart in the 1850s were military men except Caledon (1807–11) and Pottinger (who was governor for less than a year in 1847); and all had served in the Peninsular War under the Duke of Wellington, except Lord Charles Somerset (1814–26), who had served at court and in parliament for much of the war period (his brother had been Wellington's military secretary). Somerset, second son of the Duke of Beaufort, and an undistinguished British general whose military commission had been bought, was typical of the early governors. The Beaufort family were heavily represented in the pre-Reform Act parliament because of their extensive landholdings, and they enjoyed great powers of patronage.[22] After Caledon had left the Cape in 1811, governors were appointed to both civil and military command, and many were closely aligned to the Horse Guards and the Duke of Wellington in London, and were sceptical of Colonial Office control. The Age of Reform was not immediately apparent in the new empire of the early nineteenth century.[23]

Colonial governors had enormous leeway to formulate local policy, partly because of a long history of imperial administrative decentralisation going back to the sixteenth and seventeenth centuries.[24] Such was the distance from Downing Street that the control that the Colonial Office was able to exercise over the governors was tenuous at best. Communications took several months to travel from London to Cape Town and back, especially before steamships appeared in the 1840s, and the time-consuming process of manual transcription of correspondence greatly slowed the process. Moreover, colonial secretaries and under-secretaries in London were political appointees, who might have a relatively short tenure of office. Their knowledge of the colonies over whose fate they exercised authority was likely to be sketchy, and their interest in matters of colonial policy was unlikely to be very considerable. If they were ambitious and talented men, the Colonial Office was a place they were likely to want to escape from. Parliament and the cabinet showed scant interest in colonial matters except when things went wrong.[25]

In the Colonial Office continuity was provided by the permanent officials, from the permanent under-secretary downwards. These legalistically minded men, of whom James Stephen was the leading exemplar in the first half of the nineteenth century,[26] were likely to regard as their prime responsibility the maintenance of stability and the minimisation of military and administrative costs. No great vision of imperial mission was likely to flourish in such an environment. Although for a time, as we shall see, evangelical humanitarians were heavily represented at the Colonial Office, considerations of economy and order always outweighed all others. Much time was spent in controlling damage caused by rogue governors who, plunged into the maelstrom of colonial politics, allowed themselves to be swept along by local currents, threatening to involve the exchequer in military and other expenditure that it did not feel inclined to meet. No current was stronger than that set in motion by accumulating settler elites, intent on initiating processes of dispossession and subjugation against indigenous peoples, and anxious to bring imperial muscle to bear on their own behalf. As we shall see, the Cape had its share of such settler elites and rogue governors.

Despite administrative autocracy, the new nineteenth-century empire was permeated by the ideology of free trade. Mercantilist restrictions were everywhere in retreat, as the theories underlying them had lost all credence. This philosophical conversion, well advanced in England by the early nineteenth century, grew out of the indisputable fact that Britain was the world's supreme naval power and easily dominated the world's long-distance trade. The country also needed ever-expanding markets to fuel its manufacturing sector, and could only benefit by the breakdown of all protectionist barriers behind which other powers still preferred to cower. It was for this reason that the British could abolish the very profitable slave trade in 1808: it was assumed that alternative avenues for mercantile profit would quickly compensate for the losses incurred in terminating the traffic in humans. Further, centralised control of colonial economies was less desirable than ever, once restrictive commercial regulations had become obsolete. Thus in 1813, the East India Company's monopoly of Indian Ocean trade was abolished (with the exception of the China tea trade). By 1830 Britain had opened her colonial trade to all foreign states which gave her reciprocal advantages. Finally, after the abolition in 1846 of the corn laws protecting British farmers from imports, all remnants of imperial preference were gradually done away with.[27]

The determination in Downing Street (seat of the Colonial Office) to minimise the costs of empire was reinforced by the doubts raised whether, in an era of free trade, any real compelling economic benefit accrued to the metropole from expenditure on colonial administration and defence. After all, Britain's trade with the politically independent republics of the Americas was considerable and growing. By comparison, colonial possessions such as the Cape were of marginal importance. Hence the colonies were ideally intended to be self-sufficient in the generation of their own revenues. There could be no economic justification for expending metropolitan revenues on maintaining such possessions.

Thus, one inevitable result of the triumph of free-trade ideology in Britain was a vigorous questioning of the appropriateness of holding overseas possessions at all, especially the autocratically ruled yet uncentralised empire of conquest of the nineteenth century. Many dissenting radicals, schooled in the doctrines of Adam Smith (which were increasingly taking on the force of a liberal orthodoxy), thought colonies were an archaism. This, and the fact that imperial expenditure and territorial expansionism were in disfavour generally in official circles, led historians for long to maintain that the mid-nineteenth century in Britain was an anti-imperial age. But this view was decisively challenged in the 1950s. Anti-imperialism never took on the trappings of an orthodoxy at any point in the nineteenth century. Preserving existing overseas possessions was a matter of strategy, commercial interest and, not least, prestige.[28]

Indeed, in unofficial circles, a whole new sense of imperial mission was developing in the first half of the nineteenth century – though governments were reluctant to embrace these ideas unless they coincided with their more mundane priorities. At one level, the new imperial ideology had a strong evangelical, civilising, humanitarian edge to it, manifested for example in the abolition of the slave trade in 1808 and the subsequent efforts to ameliorate and eventually abolish the institution of slavery. This aspect was also manifested in the rise of the new mission societies to social respectability and popular approbation.[29]

On another level, colonial emigration and settlement were incorporated into the tenets of classical political economy as it evolved in the first half of the century.[30] Although colonies suitable for free settlement were not actually sought by Britain in the transition to the new nineteenth-century empire, they fell into her hands for reasons of strategy or, in the case of New South Wales, for the transportation of convicts. In the age of mercantilism, emigration had been regarded as detrimental, for population was seen as an index of a nation's power and wealth. People were a national resource.[31] Ever since the days of the first Elizabeth and the early Stuarts, colonial settlement was undertaken by individual entrepreneurs, and was not encouraged by the state. Nevertheless, strong mercantilist arguments had developed for colonies as providers of food or raw materials for the metropole in a closed trading system.

Once these arguments had been superseded by free-trade ideas in the early nineteenth century, new rationales for retaining and developing colonies of settlement were formulated. In the projected free-market system of the nineteenth century, when finding ever-wider markets became a central preoccupation of imperial policy, colonies of settlement had the great advantage of being safer and more predictable markets than foreign states. The spectre, of course, was the United States, which in 1812 had supported revolutionary France in war against Britain. Colonial markets could be depended on and could not be closed at the whim of foreign governments. Further, contrary to older mercantilist thinking, colonies were seen in the free-trade era not simply as resource pools serving the interests of the metropole. Colonial economies had to thrive and grow if they were to generate an expanding demand for the products of British factories. And thriving, growing colonial economies could only be built by a constant accession of productive British settlers. 'Shovelling out paupers' was not enough; men of capital were indispensable to the colonial project.[32]

Emigration also came to be seen in certain influential circles as in fact beneficial, not only in terms of economic advantage, but also in draining Britain of its 'redundant' population. Malthusian spectres of an exponentially growing population, which outstripped food supplies and resulted in famine and anarchy, made emigration seem essential. Moreover, the post-Napoleonic years were marked by intense underclass unrest and radicalism, and unemployment and poverty began to threaten the social order. Tens of thousands of soldiers were discharged after the wars, and war industries shrank. Perhaps 15 per cent of the population was indigent at this time. Emigration as a means of draining the able-bodied poor to the colonies seemed an obvious palliative.[33] In this way economic, social and political arguments for state-aided emigration reinforced one other.

Although state-aided emigration became a subject of intense interest for the first time in the years after Waterloo, these ideas of the advantages of colonies of settlement did not easily or readily move the official mind to action. The government of Lord Liverpool, faced with its own burdensome post-war financial woes, was in practice reluctant to commit itself to funding emigration in anything but the most perfunctory way – notwithstanding the campaigning of enthusiasts such as R. J. Wilmot Horton, under-secretary at the Colonial Office from 1822 to 1828, and the positive proposals of various parliamentary select committees.[34]

The government's initial half-hearted moves in this direction grew out of alarm at the extent of population movement to the United States, now firmly ensconced as a rival and hostile power, despite the burgeoning trade between the two countries. Emigrants in search of better opportunities were inexorably drawn to the young republic rather than to British territories. In colonies held at the end of the Napoleonic wars, British settlement was very slight: Canada was colonised by French settlers and by American royalists fleeing the wrath of the republic. Scarcely 400 free settlers (as opposed to convicts) had arrived in New South Wales. Government schemes such as the Rideau settlement in Canada were designed to keep emigrants within the colonial sphere, where they could be relied on to serve Britain's economic interests, and to keep them away from the expanding republic to the south. But, as we shall see, the largest state-aided emigration scheme of the time (to the Cape in 1820) was motivated largely by a temporary crisis of domestic unrest in England.[35]

During the Liverpool years from 1815 to 1826 when six such experiments in state-aided emigration were promoted, only one in nineteen emigrants was state-funded – constituting no more than 11 000 people in all.[36] In the 1840s, owing to the agitations of the 'systematic colonisers' who followed E. G. Wakefield, the Colonial Land and Emigration Commission set about implementing a policy of paying for emigration from the proceeds of the sale of crown land in the colonies. Otherwise, emigration continued to be organised by private entrepreneurs, who were given grants of land for the purpose under prescribed conditions – such as the Byrne settlement of Natal in the late 1840s. But neither the efforts of the state nor those of the systematic colonisers stemmed the flow of emigrants to the United States.[37] Nevertheless, as colonies of settlement slowly grew and developed, autocracy was bound eventually to become inappropriate and counterproductive. Thus in the 1820s the practice of colonial administration and law began to be reformed, and by the 1840s thoughts had turned to the possibility of settler self-government.

The early British governors at the Cape ruled in some ways more autocratically than their Dutch predecessors. Proclamations and laws were issued in the governor's name only; no formally constituted body of officials or settlers advised him; his executive powers were effectively unlimited; and appellate jurisdiction in the judicial sphere rested in his hands alone. The great majority of government appointments (including the secretary to the government) were dispensed by the governor as his patronage. At the highest levels, the administration was manned by military men, from the governor down. For the most part, however, the Dutch administrative and judicial systems were taken over intact. Dutch officials continued to administer justice (in the Dutch language) and to collect revenue under the British, as before. There was nothing to stop them gaining private incomes from their public posts. Judicial training was not necessary for elevation to the bench, and judges were appointed from the offices of wharf-masters, collectors of revenue and land surveyors, and most held more than one office of state at the same time.[38]

At first the British were reluctant to interfere with existing privileges and perquisites. The ancient corruptions and monopolies persisted for a time. Public officials collected the greater part of their salaries from fees for services rendered to the public. Many ran private businesses, and often gave themselves public loans and contracts. At the same time, government control of licensing and of commercial credit through the system of *pachts*, or monopolies, created a tight oligarchy of businessmen closely linked to official patrons. The government's Lombard Bank, established in 1793, the Orphan Chamber, and the

Vendue Department, which conducted public auctions, reserved their favours for a select circle of people of power and influence.[39]

But British rule brought new economic forces which increasingly challenged and undermined old restrictions, eventually making them obsolete. Commerce had been firmly under VOC control, although this control was weakening towards the end of the eighteenth century.[40] Under British rule, the possibilities for private profit from trade increased greatly. Firstly, the Cape's international trade was decisively reoriented towards Britain and its empire – far and away the most dynamic mercantile network in the world. British ships, already dominant in trade between Europe and the East, came to dominate the imports and exports of the Cape. British merchants arrived at the Cape with commercial and financial connections in England, many becoming agents for English firms. They soon dominated the economic life of Cape Town, overshadowing the older Dutch merchants, such as the Van Reenens, who had for some years been struggling to rid themselves of the stifling stranglehold of the VOC and its officials on the economy of the port town.[41]

But at the start, the anachronistic mercantilist restrictions of the eighteenth century had to be contested. The English East India Company attempted by order-in-council to assert a monopoly on the Eastern trade, and to prevent Cape Town from becoming an entrepôt of trade instead of merely a way-station. It granted limited concessions to local merchants to import (for example) rice for sale locally from the East, but on the whole strove to retain tight control over the sea trade. After the Mascarene islands (Mauritius, Réunion, Rodrigues) had been taken from the French in 1809–10, a flourishing trade was pioneered from the Cape, with the firm of Ebden & Watts taking the lead, subject to prohibitions on the re-export of Asian goods from the islands to the Cape. Colonial produce for the British garrison on the islands was exchanged for coffee. In turn produce traded from the Mascarenes was sent to England to pay for imports to the Cape. From 1815, with the beginnings of Napoleon's six-year exile on St Helena, that island, with its large military presence, also became an outlet for colonial produce.[42]

In 1813 the East India Company Charter Act greatly curtailed the company's monopoly of the Eastern trade, although its continued monopoly of the China tea trade remained an obstacle to Cape merchants' access to the Asian markets. Then, in May 1820, an order-in-council effectively turned Cape Town into a free port. Foreign ships were accorded trading privileges on a basis of reciprocity. Imports into the Cape from friendly countries were permitted, except for cotton, wool, steel and iron; and Cape exports (and re-exports of goods imported to the Cape from the East, except tea) could be transported wherever markets could be found by any ship of any friendly country (although higher duties were to be paid by foreign merchants).[43]

The new mercantile elite of Cape Town were a small and relatively tight-knit community, closely associated with mercantile firms in England. These respectable and well-connected men sought to replicate in the colonial world the pursuits deemed appropriate to their class position, and tended to become part of the upper echelons of colonial society, together with the higher officials, military officers and the leading landowners. Those who were well established in Cape Town prior to the 1820s included J. B. Ebden, son of an army surgeon and nephew of an Anglican churchman in Hampshire; Hamilton Ross, a former officer in the Scots Guards; Antonio Chiappini, an Italian raised in England, whose sister was married to the Irish peer Lord Newborough, and who initially arrived at the Cape en route to India where he had been commissioned to decorate the ceilings at Government House in Calcutta; and Ewan Christian, brother-in-law of a rear-admiral.[44]

Many Cape Town merchants were birds of passage, temporary residents spending short spells in the colonies to acquire first-hand knowledge of commercial conditions. Some of the earlier arrivals such as Ross and Chiappini took Dutch wives, but many tended to maintain a sense of their own distinctiveness as expatriates. Some who stayed on at the Cape (such as Ebden) went back to England for long periods to find wives or have their children educated. Their names were to recur on the committees of charitable and voluntary organisations, and they were often associated with cultural and educational causes. Eventually the more prosperous of them (such as Ebden and Ross) carved out country seats for themselves in what are today the southern suburbs of Cape Town.[45]

In some cases, Cape Town merchants were sons or brothers of London merchants. London-connected Cape Town firms in the 1820s included Venning, Busk & Co., associated with Wm Venning & Co. of London; Phillips & King of London and Cape Town; and Borradaile, Thompson & Pillans of Cape Town, associated with Abraham Borradaile of London. The Collison brothers, John and Francis, who arrived in 1815 and 1822 respectively and established a leading export firm, were sons of a substantial London linen-draper and wine merchant. Thomson, Watson & Co. of Cape Town were associated with J. R. Thomson & Co. of London. J. R. Thomson himself had arrived in Cape Town in 1808 and eventually returned to London to take control of the business there, leaving the Cape Town business to his son. Ewan Christian represented his brother-in-law Henry Nourse in Cape Town, setting up Nourse, Christian & Co. in 1816.[46]

In the free-trade era, when international commerce paid no heed to the formal boundaries of empire or national sovereignty, a cosmopolitan mercantile diaspora developed, with agents and connections straddling the globe, operating under the informal protection of British naval supremacy of the oceans. This cosmopolitan bourgeoisie were to retreat towards the end of the century into a narrower nationalism more dependent on the imperial state. But in the early decades of the century they were sublimely confident of their global reach and the supine accessibility of global markets.[47]

The local mercantile elite, feeling the need to coordinate their efforts to promote commercial interests, both with the authorities in Cape Town and with

the commercial powers in England, founded in March 1817 a Commercial
Exchange in George's Coffee House in Berg Street. A joint-stock company, the
first in the colony, was set up to erect the Commercial Exchange building adja-
cent to the Grand Parade. This neo-classical structure, completed in 1822,
dominated public life in Cape Town for much of the nineteenth century. The
Commercial Exchange building was symbolically important in providing a
space in which the mercantile elite could assemble, formulate common ideas
and strategies, and establish a sense of class solidarity. Rituals of inclusion such
as the annual commercial dinners (males only) were among the functions of the
Exchange.[48]

The mercantile elite's connections with London merchant houses found
institutional expression in the London-based Cape of Good Hope Trade
Society, established in March 1825 to protest against the removal of preferential tariffs for Cape wines in Britain. Proclaiming itself as representing
'Merchants, Shipowners, Manufacturers and others interested in the trade of
the Colony of the Cape of Good Hope', the society was the conduit through
which the Cape merchants of the Commercial Exchange made their voices
heard in London. A founder member of the London society was J. B. Ebden,
who had returned to England in 1819 for a few years to see to the education
of his children, leaving his Cape Town business in the hands of his brother-in-
law R. W. Eaton, before returning to the Cape himself later in the year 1825.
The society's chairman was Abraham Borradaile, London connection of the
Cape Town firm Borradaile, Thompson & Pillans.[49]

This London connection was of paramount importance in the development
of Cape commerce, in the provision of credit, the supply of manufactures for
trade, and in financial advice and services. By the 1830s and 1840s there were
over fifty London mercantile houses with interests in the Cape trade. The
London merchant community, together with the banking, insurance and shipping interests of the City at their back, had considerable influence with officials
of the Colonial Office and maintained allies in parliament. Politicians, civil servants and leading figures in the City moved in the same circles and often over-
lapped. Although the Cape trade was never of much importance in global perspective, those with interests in the Cape trade – even when it was a subsidiary
item in their portfolio of overseas activities – were often able to secure a hearing where it mattered.[50]

The older Dutch elite at the Cape was from the start another crucial support
of the colonial order under British rule. A close functional relationship quickly grew between the local Dutch bourgeoisie and the British administration.
For many colonists, the British must have seemed like liberators from the deca-
dence and corruption of VOC rule in its dying days. There were also increased
possibilities for economic enterprise and for enjoying the patronage of all-
powerful governors, who in their turn had a vested interest in securing the
acquiescence of the older colonists, and no desire to subvert existing institutions. The Dutch elite of Cape Town quickly developed a sense of class soli-

darity with British officials. Intermarriage was not uncommon, due mainly to the dearth of marriageable expatriate British women at the Cape in the early years. The children of leading Dutch citizens were often educated in English.[51]

These relationships extended beyond Cape Town into the winelands of the arable southwest. Indeed, under British rule there was no great divide between the urban Dutch bourgeoisie and the leading wine farmers. Under VOC rule, on the other hand, company officials, who were commonly born in Europe, were not allowed to own farms or engage in private trade, though there were always some who did so by subterfuge. This was a major grievance among colonists. In the 1780s the Patriot movement at the Cape pitted the landed colonists against VOC officialdom. But by the late eighteenth century this situation was changing, partly because of the gradual collapse of VOC authority. Under the British, officials such as W. S. van Ryneveld, fiscal during the first British occupation, and J. A. Truter, chief justice from 1812, commonly owned farms and slaves themselves,[52] and there was a concentration of both farming resources and official patronage in the leading families. This urban–rural elite was heavily intermarried, and linked by an extensive credit network. The same names recur wherever landed wealth, power and patronage were to be found – Van der Bijl, De Villiers, Marais, Cloete, Myburgh are some. Rayner estimates that 21 families, mostly well connected and interrelated with high officials, produced over half the colony's wine, and also owned some two-thirds of the wine-farm slave population by the 1820s. Moreover, there had been a strong degree of continuity in the identity of this elite over generations.[53] The wine farmers were undoubtedly the 'gentry' of the Cape.

In the early nineteenth century, eight out of every ten slaves lived in Cape Town and the arable southwestern districts. Wine farmers owned an average of 16 slaves each (quite unevenly distributed) while the average slaveholding throughout the colony in 1834 was 5.6 slaves per owner.[54] Moreover, slave-ownership, constituting a major investment of capital, was an important cement of the dynastic alliances that held the gentry together. Slaveholdings were kept in the same families or on the same farms from generation to generation, so that a high proportion of the slave force enjoyed relative geographical stability. Slaves were commonly incorporated in inheritances, marriage portions and land purchases. *Inter vivos* transfers between generations were quite common.[55]

The British set about cementing their alliances with the older colonial population by promoting agricultural production, particularly in the wine industry. Wine was far and away the most important export commodity from the Cape in the 1810s and 1820s. Wheat, the other main arable crop of the southwestern districts, was a very unreliable export crop (mostly shipped to the islands of the southern oceans and to the East), and had to be imported as often as it was exported. Thus it was wine farming that the British sought to promote in order to reduce the trade deficit, so that the market for British commodities could be extended, and to increase colonial revenue. During the first

British occupation, wine production started growing, largely as a result of the presence at the Cape of the British garrison, which numbered up to 4000 soldiers until the early 1820s.[56]

Before 1810 the export of Cape wine had been sporadic.[57] In 1810 Ebden & Watts began to send Cape wine and brandy to the Mascarenes on their brig *Fancy* to slake the thirst of the British garrison there.[58] Export production was particularly promoted in 1813 by the reduction of duties payable on Cape wine imported into Britain to one-third of those levied on Iberian wines, the Cape's main competitors, and Britain became the Cape's major market.[59] At the time Sir John Cradock was governor at the Cape. Cradock was not only (like nearly all colonial governors) a military veteran but also, like so many of the landed classes, an agricultural enthusiast. He introduced a series of measures designed to increase wine production and improve quality, being determined to establish the 'success of Cape commerce in this her great and native superiority'. Thus in 1812 he set up the office of taster of wines, who had to certify the quality of wine before it could be exported.[60] In response, export merchants such as Ebden & Watts, John Collison & Co., and Daniel Dixon invested in the wine trade, building wine stores in Cape Town. For their part the maintenance of preferential tariffs on wine became the British merchants' main cause, in collaboration with their London contacts such as T. P. Courtenay, the colony's agent.[61]

In 1808–10 there were fewer than 15 million vines in the colony; in 1823–5 nearly 32 million. Between 1809 and 1825 the output of wine increased by 83 per cent. In the early 1820s, wine constituted 72 per cent of the value of exports, and was the only colonially produced export of substance until the take-off of wool farming in the 1830s.[62] Apart from Britain, St Helena was a large consumer during Napoleon's exile there until his death in 1821, when the large garrison on the island was withdrawn. Mauritius, New South Wales, Brazil and the East Indies provided subsidiary markets.[63] However, Cape wines always suffered from a reputation for inferior quality. The working capital available to most wine farmers was insubstantial and methods of production were basic. Furthermore, slaves and land were heavily mortgaged, especially to the government's Lombard Bank. Indebtedness was aggravated by the tendency for prices to fall over the years.[64]

The promotion of wine farming took place in a situation in which the slave population was growing very slowly, as a result of the abolition of the oceanic slave trade in 1808. At the time, Governor Caledon had expressed concern over the consequences of abolition for supplies of labour in the colony, even suggesting that the Hottentot Regiment be disbanded in order to divert Khoi labour to farms.[65] In the eighteenth century the average annual growth rate of 2.5 per cent in the slave population was due solely to slave importation, as mortality rates were greater than fertility rates among Cape slaves.[66] Although by the nineteenth century the slave population was reproducing itself (showing a growth rate of 0.8 per cent each year between 1808 and emancipation), the number of adult slaves fell increasingly below the demand for them. Thus between 1808 and 1823 slaves dropped from 40 per cent to 29 per cent of the total colonial population.[67] At the same time the price of slaves rose – fourfold for the most desirable male field-hands – as they became more valuable in the farming districts.[68] Cape Town slave-owners also began engaging in speculative selling and hiring out to rural districts.[69] Nevertheless, the slave population of the eastern districts grew more rapidly than in the arable southwest, owing in part to the migration eastwards of slave-owners.[70]

Indeed, the number of slaves per wine farm fell steadily after 1807 as many farms were subdivided; and the number of vines per slave shot up.[71] On arable farms slave labour was supplemented by indigenous Khoi, whose lot worsened as a result of increased demand for their services, and by the purchase and hiring of slaves and 'prize negroes' (indentured Africans 'rescued' from captured slave ships) belonging to urban owners.[72] Labour shortages were also eased somewhat by regular interchanges of slaves between wheat and wine farms, since peak labour seasons dovetailed.[73] But labour exploitation seems to have become more and more intense, and work-loads grew ever greater. Slave women and children (the latter a rapidly increasing proportion of the slave population by the nineteenth century) and older men were used more intensely in the fields.[74] But this exploitation would not go unchallenged. For if the regime was based on an alliance of interests with the landholding and slave-holding elite, it was also increasingly answerable to humanitarian sentiment at home. This was to lead to contradictions which became more intense over the years.[75]

Not only in the environs of Cape Town and Stellenbosch did the British rule through, and to the benefit of, the older colonial elite. Important district offices throughout the colony, in nether reaches where governors rarely travelled, were controlled by local Boer notables. While landdrosts were appointed from Cape Town, the elected boards of *heemraden* (six to eight for each district) continued to play important roles in constituting the local courts, in the assessment and collection of revenues, in processing applications for land, and in the disposition of labour. They were assisted in each *wyk* (ward) by field cornets, who were selected from the 'most respectable' of the property-owning inhabitants. Indeed, their powers were greatly extended by British legislative interventions, for example in the field of labour control. District secretaries, who performed most of the executive tasks of the boards, were 'constantly exposed to the influence of local partialities, of hereditary prejudices and of family connections', in the words of an imperial commission of enquiry in the 1820s. Some landdrosts were accused of being enmeshed in debt and hence malleable in the hands of local creditors. Boards freely loaned money to friends, and the power to assess taxes was allegedly abused frequently. In the allocation of lands and the assessment of quitrents, the commission of enquiry found the boards guilty of 'a sacrifice of the public revenue, either in subservience to their own views, or to the interests of their neighbours'.[76] These Boer notables benefited at first from British rule. Little wonder that at the time of the Slagtersnek rebellion of 1815, when a group of frontiersmen took up arms against the British rulers, the most prominent and propertied of the local colonists supported the reassertion of British authority. Those who resisted and resented British rule were people who resisted and resented the Boer notables – the marginal types, such as the Slagtersnek rebels.[77]

As one of the primary functions of government at the Cape, the British were concerned to impose their regulatory stamp on Khoi labour relations in the pastoral districts of the further interior, in order to stabilise and control the labour force, and to douse the violence that seemed inherent in such relations. In this pre-reform age, the attitudes of Britain's autocratic, military governors were still those of the eighteenth-century English countryside. Here paternalism and the natural prerogatives of class had produced a hierarchical order in which status groups enjoyed differential rights and duties, and the law was there to terrorise and coerce as well as to protect and placate the lower orders. The rule of law did not imply equality of all before the law: indeed, the definition of crime and the severity of sentencing depended on the social rank of the accused.[78] At the Cape, the anarchic state of violence and brutality that seemed to characterise relations between colonists and Khoi called out for legal intervention. Not only was this state of affairs brought insistently to official attention by the first generation of missionaries at Bethelsdorp in the eastern Cape, but it had erupted in a prolonged state of warfare that raged during the first British occupation. Colonel Richard Collins, sent to the frontier to investigate conditions, reported that colonists were up in arms over labour shortage and the disruptions allegedly caused by the Bethelsdorp missionaries and their agitations.[79]

Caledon's 1809 'Hottentot proclamation' provided for the registration of all Khoi and their 'fixed places of abode' so as to counteract Khoi 'vagrancy'. It also provided for the mandatory drawing up of contracts of service in the presence of officials. Any change of abode or employment had to be approved by either fiscal or landdrost, who would issue a certificate declaring that the previous contract had expired. The proclamation entrusted to landdrosts and field cornets the responsibility of granting passes to Khoi work-seekers or travellers. Any European might detain a Khoi who could not produce a pass. This power enabled officials, even the lowliest, to control the lives of Khoi, and forcibly to contract out those Khoi without formal employment or without passes to colonists with influence, thereby greatly extending official powers of patronage. The proclamation also provided for 'domestic' discipline – meaning that any local official (including field cornets) could inflict corporal punishment without the formality of a trial.[80]

At the same time protection for Khoi labourers was secured, in keeping with the spirit of eighteenth-century paternalism, by enforcing the payment of wages and outlawing debt bondage, and providing for the prosecution under the common law of masters who ill-treated their servants. The system was designed, though, to make it as difficult as possible for servants to lay complaints. It effectively codified existing labour practices without providing the wherewithal for the enforcement of employers' contractual obligations or restrictions on their treatment of servants. Likewise it greatly increased the powers of local officials, who themselves were widely seen as hopelessly compromised instruments of the master class.

At the same time, a more reliable judicial system in the interior districts than that provided by the courts of landdrost and *heemraden* came to be demanded by missionaries. With increasing support from humanitarian elements in Britain, they complained of the systematic abuse of the pass laws and labour legislation.[81] In 1801 a system of circuit courts had been suggested by the fiscal Van Ryneveld to Governor Dundas. They were instituted by Cradock shortly after his arrival in 1811, so that more serious allegations of ill-treatment could be heard by courts uncompromised by local loyalties and relationships. Under pressure from William Wilberforce, the leading humanitarian in parliament, who had in turn been lobbied by the Cape-connected London Missionary Society, the Colonial Office instructed Cradock to undertake a thorough investigation of abuses. The Boer population was, however, hardly likely to be sympathetic to a court whose purpose was to investigate their treatment of their servants, and in which the evidence of masters was called into question by their servants under missionary encouragement and protection. Indeed, in colonist historiography the circuit of August–December 1812 is remembered as the 'black circuit', and is regarded as a singularly perfidious episode by many Afrikaners, almost on a par with the crushing of the Slagtersnek rebellion in 1815 in the political mythology of Afrikaner nationalism. But neither episode had the significance at the time that they were subsequently to acquire.[82] On the whole, the alliance between the British administration and the notables in Afrikaner society was hardly undermined by the extension of the rule of British law.

The 'black circuit' in fact returned few verdicts favourable to Khoi plaintiffs. The court invoked the custom of granting legal weight to the evidence of Khoi witnesses on a selective and partial basis. The extent to which the testimony of non-Christians might be relied on had been an unresolved issue for the Dutch, as non-Christians could not swear an oath (although in practice slave and Khoi testimony had commonly been used in criminal cases). The fact that by 1812 many Khoi on the farms in the eastern Cape professed Christianity does not seem to have made an impression on the judges – Dutch colonists all. It was therefore difficult for any white to be convicted unless white witnesses were willing to testify against them.[83] Verdicts were thus by and large predetermined. The judges shared the fundamental assumptions of the colonists who were being tried, and published a report which was an implicit defence of the colonists and their labour system. This assumed that Khoi, as an inferior order of humanity, enjoyed an inferior order of natural rights, and in consequence had an obligation to render service to the colonists. The rule of law clearly did not imply that all enjoyed equal legal status. Little wonder that the judges condemned the mission institutions as incubators of laziness, dirt and moral degradation.[84]

In the larger view, the significance of the legislative interventions of the time was that they were ultimately designed to entrench and stabilise the authority of masters and the proletarian status of Khoi, whose rights of mobility and free contract were severely limited. These measures had precedents in British vagrancy and settlement laws, which were justified by reference to the need to restrict freedoms for the greater social good. At the Cape the British did not seek to deliver Khoi from exploitation and subservience, but from a kind of anarchic state of nature which was the inevitable result of the absence of legally sanctioned instruments of coercion. Cradock's apprenticeship regulations of 1812 further enabled landdrosts to coerce children and young adults between 8 and 18 by 'apprenticing' them to any farmer who had maintained them in their infancy, thereby also immobilising their families. This measure confirmed practices going back to the eighteenth century. As usual in the colony, the term 'apprenticeship' was used to disguise the fact that the law effectively sanctioned forced labour.[85]

As a result of measures like these, it seems that from the early 1810s there was a decline in reports of overt brutality and random violence practised against the subordinate classes within the settled parts of the colony. It seems that oppression became more institutionalised with the closing of frontiers and the abolition of the slave trade. The anarchic oppression of masters was replaced by the systemic oppression of the colonial order. Thus Khoi were more completely subjugated at the same time as they became increasingly indispensable as labourers in a developing frontier economy. Meanwhile the 'Bushman' frontier of random violence, raiding and slaving had moved northward towards and, by the 1820s, across the Orange River.

The 'Hottentot codes' and the judicial system of circuit courts laid the basis for the development of a common view, uniting British rulers and Afrikaner notables, of the power of the law as a means of social control.[86] The use of a seemingly even-handed law to protect servants as well as to promote the interests of masters was essential to the legitimacy of colonial government. A degree of nominally impartial legality, even if its impartiality was largely a fiction, was the key to the more efficient and profitable management of productive relations. Governor Cradock, who believed explicitly in the 'authority, power and property of the master', supported such a view of the role of the law. The problem for the authorities was to persuade the Khoi themselves of the legitimacy of the law and its usages, and for them to accept the paternalistic assumptions underlying it. It was probably those most exposed to the missionaries' message who were most amenable to the potential benefits of British law; but it was also they who were bound to be most severely disenchanted with its reality.

Cradock acted in other ways to modernise and develop the colonial economy, always with a view to improving its productive and its revenue-generating capacities. One important innovation was the introduction in 1813 of free-hold land tenure under a perpetual quitrent system in place of the old loan-farm system. No new loan farms were to be recognised, and henceforth loan farms were gradually to be converted to perpetual quitrent, which approximated freehold but involved annual rent payments to the government. A free market in loan farms (or, more exactly, in the fixed improvements or *opstal*) had developed over the preceding century, although individual landholders did not have title to the land. Farms were not surveyed, and were theoretically circular areas of at least 6000 acres defined as the area described by a certain radius from a fixed point (usually a water point). Loan farms could accommodate an extended family, kinsmen and *bywoners* (customary tenants) commonly residing on the land of the landholder, but could not be legally subdivided.

On coming to power the British regime, like the VOC before it, was reluctant to expand the colonial borders to accommodate applicants for new loan farms, and by 1813 two thousand applications for loan farms were still unanswered. The generally chaotic state of the colony's landholding system is indicated by the fact that in 1795 it was estimated that arrear *recognitie* payments on loan farms amounted to 376 360 rix-dollars – about seven times the annual amount due.[87]

The British authorities generally assumed that revenue would be greatly increased under a more efficient landholding system. It was further believed that private freehold in property would promote agricultural development and capital investment in what was still a very undercapitalised rural economy in the pastoral districts. Private property would likewise promote entrepreneurial attitudes, closer settlement and more progressive farming methods. With their extreme reluctance to expand the colonial borders northwards or to condone further settler expansion at the expense of the indigenous peoples, the British hoped that the trekboer and slaveholding economy would be replaced by a more intensive one in which landless whites would be converted into a useful and skilled class of artisans, workers and consumers who would fuel the economic development and commercialisation of the colony. The fiscal Van Ryneveld had expressed precisely such sentiments as early as 1797.[88]

But despite these innovations, no great change was immediately apparent. The conditions and costs involved in conversion to quitrent were such that the colonists resisted any interference with their less formal landholding arrangements. It was not until the 1820s that attempts were seriously made to implement the measures. In the meantime, no new loan-farm titles could be issued, and requests for land title continued to pile up in Cape Town. 'Request farms' became an informal system of registering claims, much like the old loan-farm system, and land was bought and sold on this basis. By 1824, a thousand of these 'request farms' were to be found in the Graaff-Reinet district, but not a single farm had been converted to quitrent.[89] Moreover, trekboers commonly pushed beyond colonial borders in search of new lands to use for their stock, despite official attempts to stop them.[90]

The linchpin of the colonial economy continued to be the wine industry, and British hegemony continued to a large degree to depend on the welfare of the industry through the governorship of Cradock's successor, Lord Charles Somerset (1814–26). As has been indicated, the substantial expansion of wine production in the 1810s and early 1820s contrasted with a relatively slow increase in the slave population of the wine districts. Under these circumstances, any attempt to improve the lot of colonial slaves, subject to ever greater work-loads, was bound to face obstacles. From the start, the British abolished torture (which had been liberally used by the Dutch authorities), and placed limits on the forms of punishment that slaves could be subjected to.[91] From their experiences of rebelliousness elsewhere they were well aware of the need to temper slave treatment. In parts of the Caribbean, the radical-democratic ideas of the revolutionary age were transforming slave consciousness, and the slave revolution in Haiti seemed to threaten the entire institution everywhere. At the Cape, as in the Caribbean colonies, the creolisation of the slave population – the growing predominance of locally born slaves – in the early nineteenth century brought with it the potential for a more assertive and perhaps a more rebellious slave culture than before (although individual creole slaves were more valued and often more trusted than imported slaves).[92] In this situation the alliance of interests between the colonial administration and the Afrikaner slaveholding elite was strained by the need to placate British humanitarians, while simultaneously maintaining control over the slave population. The British rulers sought to meet the challenge by extending and refining the exercise of legal paternalism, granting to slaves, as to the Khoi, legal rights to protection from arbitrary and excessively demanding treatment.[93] The difference was that, unlike the Khoi, slaves were private property, and hence legal intervention was more hesitantly and reluctantly undertaken.

Legal paternalism was in evidence when Willem Gebhard was sentenced to death for the murder in 1822 of his father's slave. The chief justice, the Cape-born J. A. Truter, passed the sentence, and Governor Somerset confirmed it.[94] The Gebhards were outsiders in Cape Town society, and convenient scapegoats for an administration under pressure from rising metropolitan and local pressures for the amelioration of slave conditions. Gebhard's execution came at a time when new forces were coming to the fore in Cape society, which as we shall see were to transform it in radically different ways. Gebhard, in a sense, was a sacrificial offering, intended to appease the new humanitarian forces. After all, in July 1822 the Commons in London had debated Cape slavery, and in consequence a commission of enquiry had been appointed to investigate the Cape's system of government, an alarming prospect for such as Somerset.[95]

As a further sop to the newly revived anti-slavery forces, Somerset issued a proclamation in 1823 seeking to place limits on what punishment masters could inflict upon slaves. For the first time, Christian slaves were allowed to contract legal marriages, and Christian married couples could not be sold separately. Christian slave women could not be separated from their children under the age of 10. Christian slaves could go to church, and could give evidence in court. Of course, the masters had made sure that few slaves were baptised Christians, and many slaves in Cape Town preferred Islam. By 1831 only three legal Christian marriages between slaves had been recorded. Furthermore, limits were placed on the number of hours slaves could be required to labour (twelve hours a day in summer, ten in winter – except during ploughing or harvesting or on 'extraordinary occasions').[96] Such measures did not in any way challenge the property rights of slave-owners, but were intended, it seems, to shore up and legitimise the slave economy. They may well have also been an effort to pre-empt the more thoroughgoing reforms being touted in the British parliament.[97] In broad terms, the 1823 proclamation proved acceptable to the Afrikaner slave-owning elite. It was less liked, though, by the Colonial Office, doing its best to cope with the rising tensions between slaves, masters and humanitarians in the West Indies. The Earl of Bathurst made it clear that the proclamation fell far short of the slave regulations being imposed in the Caribbean islands, and the missionary leader at the Cape, John Philip, rejected it as 'trickery'.[98]

But despite Somerset's attempts to legitimise the slave regime through paternalism and amelioration, the demise of his autocratic regime was clearly foreshadowed when, in 1825, William Huskisson, president of the Board of Trade and the scourge of all economic protectionists, persuaded his colleagues in government in London that imperial preferences were an obstruction to Britain's informal conquest of the world, and removed the advantages enjoyed by Cape wine.[99] At the same time, duties on wines imported from foreign countries were reduced by two-thirds. In 1824, 557 Cape wine farmers and merchants petitioned the British government against these forthcoming changes, which they said would 'annihilate' the export wine trade. With invested capital having doubled since 1811 to £1 500 000, and mortgages totalling 3 155 282 rix-dollars (£236 646), 'irretrievable ruin' faced them, they asserted. The Cape of Good Hope Trade Society, which as we have seen was formed in London by merchants directly involved in the wine trade to lobby the government, sent a deputation including the Cape merchants J. B. Ebden and Daniel Dixon, to see the chancellor of the exchequer on the issue. Huskisson did reduce the tariff on Cape wine from 2s 6d to 2s, but this did not placate the Cape lobby, given the great distance Cape wine had to be carried. The Colonial Office suggested unsympathetically that the quality of Cape wine should be improved in order to compete, or else capital should be invested elsewhere.[100]

In the same year of 1825, the slave-owning economy of the southwestern Cape was further shaken when a slave insurrection erupted in the Koue Bokkeveld, led by one Galant, resulting in a dramatic show trial.[101] The justices pronounced that the slaves had been misled by 'so-called Philanthropists and evil-minded persons' into believing that the powers-that-be were on their (the slaves') side. The prosecutor, Daniel Denyssen (an embodiment of the pro-

British Dutch elite), warned of external agitators insinuating ideas into the minds of slaves.[102] The truth is that slave rebelliousness was fuelled by the knowledge that their masters were fighting a rearguard battle for their slave-owning rights. Galant had overheard his master talk of plans to resist the British when they came to free the slaves. In succeeding years slave rebelliousness continued to haunt the slave-owners, conjuring up for them the subversive and dangerous consequences of state intervention in undermining the authority and property rights of owners. Governor Somerset and the chief justice, J. A. Truter, representing the Dutch gentry, were determined that liberalisation of the slave regime had gone far enough. In their eyes the ethos of paternalism, the essential cement of social relations, was under threat.[103] But they had been overtaken by events, and the regime that they represented was now thoroughly discredited.

After 1825, the wine industry was plunged into depression, as was the Dutch gentry. The amount of Cape wine exported to Britain dropped by three-quarters, and attempts by merchants such as Ebden and Ross to open new markets in South America and the West Indies did not take up the slack. Acting-Governor Bourke tried to set up a triangular trade in 1826 involving Cape wine, New South Wales wheat and Mauritian sugar and coffee, but without much success. Wine sales in London were soon showing heavy losses, further forcing down the prices paid to farmers. Wine prices, the value of land in the wine districts, and the value of slaves, all declined substantially. Insolvencies became frequent, as the huge burden of debt closed in.[104] Slave-ownership became an incubus, so much dead capital. George Thompson, a Cape Town merchant, observed in 1827: 'the colonists are suffering more or less in proportion as they are possessed of slaves; or, in other words, are receiving a smaller return from their capital, than if it were otherwise invested; and there are few slaveowners, beyond the lines which surround Cape Town, who, after estimating the cost of their agricultural property, can say that they receive an adequate return from their capital.' By contrast, wrote Thompson, stock farmers of the interior pastoral districts, who owned few slaves, were flourishing.[105]

Economic depression was aggravated by the depreciation of the rix-dollar. At the time of the second British occupation in 1806 the rix-dollar equalled four shillings. In 1825 the value was fixed at 1s 6d, owing to the accumulation of debt to Britain for imports which had for years exceeded exports. This meant that the purchasing power of the old colonial currency was slashed, greatly impoverishing many colonists.[106] But out of the ruin of the slave economy and of the Cape gentry there was to arise a new colonial order, very different from the old autocracy, and built on fundamentally new foundations. But before we consider that, we must turn our attention to the new forces developing on the eastern fringes of colonial society in the 1820s.

❖

In the early years of British rule at the Cape, much thought was given to the possibility of introducing a white working class into the colony from among the unemployed masses of post-Napoleonic Britain. Extending non-European slavery was unthinkable in the climate of the day; at the same time the established rural working class of Khoi origin was not regarded as suitable material on which to build a colony of settlement. Africans had not yet been incorporated into the colony – indeed the thrust of imperial policy was to keep them beyond the colonial boundaries, by military force if necessary, and to enforce a policy of non-intercourse. In the years after 1815 a number of private emigration schemes were mooted in Britain. Central to all of them was the prospect of making a profit out of transforming unemployed Britons into a productive colonial working class. They were given official approval, especially since they did not entail public expenditure, and also in light of the flood of emigrants to the United States and the extent of unemployment and discontent at home. Indeed, Somerset disingenuously suggested in 1817 to the secretary of state for the colonies that imported British labour would lessen the value of slaves and thus gradually lead to the abolition of the institution.[107]

The most ambitious scheme was that of Captain Benjamin Moodie, impoverished laird of Melsetter in the Orkneys, who shipped out to the Cape some two hundred unemployed Scottish 'mechanics' and workmen and their families. The bulk were settled in the vicinity of Swellendam, to the east of Cape Town, where their indentures were sold to local employers, and they were rapidly absorbed into the colonial population. Although Moodie and his brothers became successful colonial farmers, the emigration scheme left them with debts, as many settlers absconded.[108] The eminent merchant Henry Nourse was another who submitted a plan in January 1818 to the government for sending unemployed workmen to the Cape, where their indentures could be sold to local employers. But this scheme did not get off the ground.[109]

Much more significantly in the longer term, the Cape was the beneficiary of the most ambitious state-aided scheme of emigration of the time, which led to the arrival in 1820 in the southeastern corner of the colony of some 4000 British settlers. A small sideshow in the flood of emigration (one million between 1815 and 1840) leaving Great Britain and Ireland, it nonetheless had a disproportionately large impact on South African history. The arrival of the 1820 settlers is as much a landmark in the colonial mythology of South Africa as the Afrikaners' Great Trek was to be a decade and a half later. But stripped of its perceived and celebrated significance as the foundation stone of a peculiarly 'South African English' people and culture,[110] the settlement of 1820 is of great importance from our perspective, for it set in motion new social forces that were to play a fundamentally shaping role in nineteenth-century South Africa.

Thus for us it was not that the settlers planted British culture and British institutions on South African shores that is of significance. Rather, their significance lies in the fact that they carried with them an ideology conducive to the development of productive capitalism. They also brought with them the full support of British merchant capital in pursuit of their own enterprises, largely denied to non-Britons. And they enjoyed access, on the margins and at certain times, to the forces of (an admittedly largely reluctant) British imperialism to enable them to proceed with their expansionist cause. They developed an ideology of accumulation and dispossession that was a new force in colonial society. But none of this was immediately apparent. The intention behind the settlement, and the actual composition of the settler parties, did not prefigure the social dynamics that would in due course be unleashed.

The idea of promoting emigration to the remote eastern Cape was certain of a lukewarm response from official quarters if it meant much in the way of state expenditure. The notion of barricading the eastern border against the Xhosa by promoting immigration from Britain was first broached by Colonel Collins after his official tour in 1809. In 1813 a settlement of Scottish Highlanders there was canvassed by Colonel John Graham, who in 1811–12 was responsible for the expulsion of the Xhosa beyond the Fish River (an expulsion which, as always, proved temporary and ineffective).[111] Governor Somerset took up the idea particularly in 1817 when he set about attempting to seal the frontier by recognising the Rharhabe Xhosa chief, Ngqika, as the paramount African authority in the region, and entering agreements with him for the recovery of stolen livestock by a system of patrols. At first Somerset hoped to persuade Boers to resettle the Zuurveld, which many had abandoned owing to friction with the Xhosa.[112] These efforts coincided with news that a substantial reduction of military forces on the frontier had been ordered as a result of severe financial constraints prevailing in the wake of the Napoleonic wars. Somerset then suggested that men of capital be sent out, accompanied by parties of 20–50 labourers and artificers each, to be settled on 4000-acre farms, as a matter of urgency to secure and stabilise the frontier and keep the Xhosa at bay. He wrote to the colonial secretary, Bathurst, describing the area as 'the most beautiful and fertile part of the Settlement. I know not how to give an idea of it, unless by saying that it resembles a succession of Parks from the Bosjeman's to the Great Fish River.'[113]

The idea of a state-aided settlement scheme, which had been in circulation for some years, seems to have been taken up simultaneously in Cape Town and in London in 1817. The Colonial Office then advertised for applications from prospective emigrants, and 90 000 letters of application flooded in. But without adequate funding from the Treasury, the scheme did not immediately get off the ground. However, in July 1819 quite unexpectedly a grant of £50 000 was made by the chancellor of the exchequer, Vansittart, for the emigration of settlers to South Africa. At the time, the Cape was being widely promoted in Britain by propagandists and pamphleteers as an ideal destination for settlers. In the same month as Vansittart's announcement, the traveller William Burchell testified in London before the select committee on poor laws that South Africa was in every way preferable to North America. In particular he spoke glowingly of the eastern Cape frontier zone. John Barrow, the noted authority on the Cape, wrote in the *Quarterly Review* of July 1819 that the Cape was 'a land which may literally be said to flow with milk and honey'.[114]

The immediate purpose of this apparently spur-of-the-moment allocation of £50 000 was to relieve alarming, potentially destabilising tensions then stirring in post-war Britain. The social dislocation that the industrial revolution was bringing in its train was increasingly reflected in movements of civil disobedience. The year 1819 was the year of Peterloo and the Six Acts, restricting rights of free assembly. The Prince Regent warned of the 'traitorous designs' of those who wanted to 'subvert the constitution' under the 'pretence of Reform'.[115] Hence the emigration to South Africa of some 4000 people in 1819–20 originated as a domestic political gesture, designed to pull the teeth from the forces of radicalism. It was the most ambitious state-aided emigration scheme yet, and nothing on the same scale was to be repeated. Like other smaller-scale emigration schemes of the decade or so following 1815, it was a deviation from the general rule that the promotion and financing of emigration were the domain of private entrepreneurs; and it grew out of specific circumstances of domestic upheaval. Interest in government-sponsored emigration faded as soon as the immediate crisis was over.[116]

Despite the publicly propagated view that the settlement was a form of pauper relief, pauper emigration was never in reality a practical consideration. Humanitarianism in this case was largely symbolic, and stretched only so far as financial considerations permitted. What the Colonial Office envisaged was the recruitment of parties of emigrants, under the leadership of men with sufficient capital to recruit their own labour force of at least ten men each, and to pay a deposit of £10 per head. A grant of 100 acres per man was then to be made to the head of the party, with title to be granted after three years and quitrent payable only after the first ten years. Thus the clear and quite unrealistic object was a close settlement of gentlemen arable farmers, each with his own community of labouring dependants. Within a couple of years it was to become apparent that the soil and rainfall could not sustain such a settlement.[117]

In fact the vast majority of the applications came from individuals or single families, rather than from leaders of parties of dependent servants. Typically they were people from the respectable lower-to-middle ranks of society – including artisans, mechanics, tradesmen, clerical workers, merchants and 'petty gentlemen' – who in the depression of the times were faced with reduction of status, and who certainly did not have the wherewithal to take with them large numbers of dependants as a labour force. Many 'broken tradesmen' and 'distressed artisans'[118] had lost their property and independence, or possessed skills that were under threat from technological innovation. Indeed, contrary to expectations of a settlement of farmers, the great bulk seem to have been townsfolk, although at the time many would have been first-generation town dwellers, suffering the consequences of large-scale underemployment in burgeoning towns after the demobilisation of 1815–16. A good proportion were relatively well educated by the standards of the day, and a number were army officers on half pay.[119]

Since only parties under a leader could be accepted as participants in the scheme, groups of individuals banded together under a nominal figurehead, and pooled their resources. In practice, the Colonial Office did not inquire too deeply into the composition of the parties. These 'joint-stock' parties constituted the bulk of the emigrants, some numbering over a hundred individuals plus families. Only about a dozen parties out of some sixty in all that embarked were 'proprietary' parties – that is, groups of indentured labourers led by men of substance and social standing.[120]

These proprietary parties, whose leaders were the closest thing to a prospective farming gentry among the settlers, were plagued from the start by absconding indentured labourers, who demanded the same wages as were paid in the colonial towns. Their employers had to pay wages as well as rations during the first few wretched years when they were attempting to raise crops on the unpromising soil of the Zuurveld (or Albany district, as it was now renamed). Rations were granted to the employers by the authorities against the deposits they had paid, and then on credit when the deposit money was exhausted. Unable to mortgage the land (title to which had not yet been granted), they rapidly used up their capital and became impoverished.[121]

This aspirant gentry – Thomas Philipps, Duncan Campbell, George Pigot and Donald Moodie being pre-eminent examples – led a furious agitation against Somerset's regime. Such men styled themselves the 'Albany radicals', and demanded larger land grants, tighter labour controls, appointment to local public office, and other perquisites of access to official patronage (such as grants of urban plots). Acting-Governor Rufane Donkin (1820–1) was prepared to oblige; he hoped 'to raise a sort of aristocracy or gentry who might lead and encourage the labouring classes'. When Somerset returned to Cape Town from leave at the end of 1821, he quickly turned on the 'Albany radicals'. Ironically (given his own social background), he had no time for place-seeking settler factions trying to replicate the privileges and patronage of English rural society. He did not think it wise 'to make Dukes of Bedford of Heads of Parties'.[122]

In the early 1820s, these potential 'Dukes of Bedford' were indeed suffering from the failure of the agricultural settlement to prosper. Having invested their capital in the land and unable to pay their labourers, they looked at a bleak future. By way of contrast, many of the middling and lowlier people were beginning to do well for themselves in trade, services or wage employment in town. A society for the relief of distressed settlers was established in Cape Town, which distributed the great bulk of its funds to those who had expended capital in pursuit of agricultural improvement – namely, the heads of the proprietary parties, those who were perceived to be of the highest social standing and who had brought out most capital from Britain. But its impact was limited. These, the 'Albany radicals', tended to end up as servants of the colonial state, or otherwise faded from the scene.[123]

The failure of the 1820 settlement as an experiment in the transplanting to Africa of English rural society also brought to an end any notion that there was a future in South Africa for a white working class.[124] In 1823 the Colonial Office entered an agreement with one John Ingram to transport 341 indentured servants from southern Ireland to the Cape. But like Benjamin Moodie's earlier experiment in 1817, this enterprise ended in conflict and financial loss, and the Colonial Office henceforth steered clear of private, speculative schemes for the emigration of indentured labourers. The colonists were clearly not in a position to pay the wages and indemnities required. Somerset's suggestions in 1825 for a further supply of 600 boys and 250 girls at government expense to shore up the Albany settlement fell on deaf ears.[125] When Governor Lowry Cole in the early 1830s sought views at the Cape on possible labour immigration schemes under government auspices, he received only eleven responses, and those suggested that white labour was too expensive, and not as easily controlled (or exploited) as black labour.[126] In view of the existence of coerced black labour systems in the colony, white immigrants were singularly reluctant to embrace wage labour as a viable or acceptable avocation, certainly under the conditions which local employers had grown used to.

The true social significance of the British settlement of 1820 is to be found elsewhere than among the early aspirant, yet frustrated, landed gentry. Despite their heterogeneity of class and social origin, the great bulk of the settlers, those in the joint-stock companies, were neither potential gentry nor a likely labouring class. In fact they were typical of the sort of enterprising men who would grab any opportunity (generally closed to them in Britain) to profit and to prosper. Colonial emigration presented them with virtually limitless prospects of social mobility. In the colonies, resources were seemingly abundant and waiting to be exploited. The potential expansion of mercantile enterprise (conducted especially with indigenous peoples previously peripheral to the colonial trading economy) was apparently enormous.

Soon after their arrival the joint-stock companies, comprising individuals determined to make their own way in the new environment, began to break up as members moved off to take to trade, or to sell their services, according to whatever skills or experiences they brought with them. Even in the under-developed economy of the Cape, wages and demand for skills and services were high. The cooperative communities some hoped to see established in Albany district were not to be. The official response was to try to keep the settlers on the land, but with little success. In due course, a distinctive settler bourgeoisie began to take shape, with its base in Graham's Town.[127]

A crucial element in the corporate identity of the bulk of the settlers was their adherence to Wesleyan Methodism. In some degree this shaped their perceptions, and helped form a settler identity in an age and place in which religious affiliation played a significant political role. In England, Methodism was essentially a lower-middle-class, artisanal and working-class movement, reflecting the changes occurring in the transition to a more urban and industrial society. John Wesley himself was a Tory churchman with no time for political agitations, who split from the lethargic and materialistic established church very reluctantly, in order to take the evangelical cause to the poor and dispossessed. Methodism spoke to the needs of lowly people, in ways that the hierarchical established church could not, in the new and alienating environment of the industrial town and factory. Emergent working-class organisations in England copied the Methodist cell-like structure, with its lay class meetings; and Methodism gave many ordinary congregants their first experience of participating in organisational networks beyond the reach of authority or officialdom.

On the other hand, many have seen in Methodism not only the breeding ground of working-class political organisation, but the dead hand of middle-class control, preaching the virtues of subservience, submission and work discipline. This was certainly the message of Wesley's nominated ministers and the annual conferences. Élie Halévy's celebrated thesis was that Methodism prevented a revolution akin to that in France from taking place in England. Semmel has argued that Methodism did this because it was itself a quasi-democratic revolution, a progressive, modernising movement, but one which steered away from the antinomian excesses of earlier dissent, and channelled enthusiasm in non-political, non-confrontational and spiritual directions. Whereas anti-clerical sentiment pervaded the more radical elements in revolutionary France, Methodism played an important role in consolidating working-class Britain behind the authority of church organisation.[128]

In the Methodist movement there was always a tension between the democratic and authoritarian tendencies inherent in it. On the one hand, church government at the centre was sacerdotal and hierarchical. On the other, centrifugal and democratic tendencies operated, reaching their height immediately after Wesley's death in 1791, in the heat of Jacobin agitation and before reaction set in. But from the mid-1790s onwards, as Methodism spread through working-class communities, it became more of a stabilising, socially repressive force, shedding secessionist sects such as the Primitive Methodists, who rebelled against church organisation. A new bureaucracy of professional ministers arose, determined to assert order and bring dissidents to heel. Jabez Bunting – ironically, great-grandfather of the founder of the Communist Party of South Africa – was pre-eminent among those in England who from the 1790s set about removing the taint of Jacobinism from the Methodist movement, and asserting a loyalist, monarchical ideology. Local self-government by laymen and women within the church was undermined. The morally redeeming quality of regular and disciplined labour was at the heart of the Methodist message, and gave it its utility to employers. While it provided a social network for the displaced and newly urbanised, it also channelled psychic tumult and insecurity into the quest for personal salvation, and directed its earnest followers away from political and social activism.

If Methodism gave cheer to the hopeless, it also spoke to the hopeful. It was above all things the religion of the artisanate rather than the displaced masses. It incorporated an ethic of individual redemption, discipline, self-improvement, austerity and frugality. It sanctified the moral economy of acquisitiveness through diligence, hard work and sacrifice. If it offered consolation in the afterworld, it also provided a vision of worldly reward. It thus resonated well with many of the 1820 settlers in South Africa, who were keen to grasp any opportunity to climb into the ranks of the new colonial bourgeoisie of the early nineteenth century. The colonial economy provided expanded opportunities for small men with some education and initiative to profit and accumulate in modest ways. Methodism's hierarchical and participatory organisational structure, and its reliance on lay leaders in local communities, suited well a new frontier society splintered from the metropolis, seeking to establish institutions of authority and control where they existed very weakly, and intent on colonising an untamed landscape, physical and human. Jabez Bunting and his kind were the spiritual forebears of the settlers of 1820.

One of the largest joint-stock parties of settlers was Hezekiah Sephton's Methodist party from London. They settled initially at Salem, south of Graham's Town, and, in Thomas Pringle's words, associated themselves 'like the early American colonists on principles of religious as well as civil communion'. Many of the subsequent settler elite came from Sephton's party, and from other parties of similar composition.[129] From Sephton's party came the leading Methodist minister, William Shaw, who was to play a major political role in the Cape for many years as spokesman for settler causes and opponent of the humanitarians.[130] By 1823 he had established the Methodist mission station at Wesleyville, the first of a string of stations that spread up through Nguni territory towards Port Natal. Most of the early Methodist ministers and missionaries were 1820 settlers or their offspring. Leading settlers gave strong financial support to the church and mission. By the 1830s Graham's Town was largely a Methodist town, and eminent citizens like Robert Godlonton played prominent lay roles in the church.[131]

The initial route to accumulation lay, as always, not in farming but in trade. Accumulation from productive enterprise alone was limited, given the relative lack of capital and of local markets, and the absence of any obviously desirable raw material or crop which might be produced locally by settlers as an export commodity. Investment in rural productive enterprise was more likely to be a function of entrepreneurial success in speculation and trade than the other way round. Thus men of generally lower-middling and working-class social origin from the joint-stock settler parties, without the means initially to invest in land and labour, but with the ambition and energy to transform themselves into a colonial bourgeoisie, saw in mercantile enterprise their road to fortune.

Once established by the 1830s, this emergent settler elite were to become more directly predatory, and put their full weight behind the processes of dispossession and military expansionism whereby indigenous land and labour were shaken free for settler speculation and settler use. To this end they were periodically able to exploit imperial military muscle to their own profit and enrichment. Speculation and investment in land and, from the 1830s on, in woolled sheep gradually gave rise to a fully fledged settler capitalism that was to spread well beyond the original settler nucleus in Albany district. In the 1820s these developments lay in the future.

The epicentre of the emergent settler economy was the district capital of Graham's Town. Before 1820 it was purely a military post. Ten years later it was a thriving trading entrepôt, linking the port in Algoa Bay, Port Elizabeth, with not only the immediate eastern Cape hinterland, but also with the far north beyond the frontiers of colonial settlement. By 1828 there were 400 settler dwellings in the town. Other towns further inland, Graaff-Reinet for example, were infiltrated by mercantile enterprise in the 1820s, and themselves became the bases of much interior trade.[132] In Graham's Town, men such as P. Heugh, C. and H. Maynard, W. R. Thompson, Benjamin and Joshua Norden, William Wright, James Howse and W. Ogilvie became prominent as merchants, making large profits. Not all were themselves 1820 settlers, but all became part of the eastern Cape British elite that grew out of the arrival of the settlers. Behind these Graham's Town merchants were the credit and capital of Cape Town. Cape Town merchants with direct access to principals in London (Henry Nourse, Frederik Korsten and George Thompson were prominent in this regard) established branches, set up agencies, and entered partnerships with the men of Graham's Town.[133]

J. W. D. Moodie described the ease with which settlers without capital could enter the mercantile networks: 'Anyone of the class of mechanics or artisans who possesses industry and steadiness, may easily raise himself to a higher situation in society; for, as soon as he has acquired a little capital he may readily obtain credit with the merchants of Cape Town, who will give him goods to sell for them on commission; and he soon acquires the means of carrying on business on his own account.'[134] Profit margins could be very large. William Southey asserted that they ranged from 20 to 100 per cent profit on goods sold. One merchant store in Graham's Town boasted a 'clear profit' of 50 000–60 000 rix-dollars in two years in the early 1820s. Benjamin Norden later claimed that he had accumulated something between £40 000 and £60 000 in the frontier trade in under two decades.[135] But inevitably amongst men so inexperienced in business, there was a degree of attrition: 'their ambition generally leads them to live expensively and to speculate beyond their means, and after going on for a few years in apparent prosperity, they become bankrupt and are obliged to return to their original employments,' wrote Moodie.[136]

At the most vulnerable end of the mercantile chain was the small trader interacting directly with indigenous African consumers and middlemen. As we have seen, the VOC tried to restrict the right to trade to company representatives – licensed butchers or official trading expeditions. In this way the company sought to secure a monopoly on the supply of meat to Cape Town. But private trading expeditions continued throughout the eighteenth century, bringing back cattle and ivory. Although little documented, they elicited a string of proclamations from the authorities prohibiting all such trading contacts. The British took over the Dutch prohibitions, and they were reiterated after the Xhosa were expelled across the Fish River in 1811–12.[137] In the years before the arrival of the 1820 settlers, such trading contacts seem to have greatly intensified, stimulated by the advent of coastal shipping. Much trade was carried on by the missionaries.[138] In 1817, as part of his attempt to shore up Ngqika's authority as a colonial collaborator, and in an attempt to check illegal barter and cattle raiding, Governor Somerset allowed the chief's representatives to bring their produce to Graham's Town to trade. But private colonial traders were excluded from the barter, which was restricted to officials.[139]

Early attempts to limit trade to official channels were unsuccessful. In 1824, for the first time, Somerset, under intense settler pressure, permitted private traders to participate in the trade fairs established at Fort Willshire near the Keiskamma River. He hoped thereby to curtail the burgeoning illegal traffic to which the British settlers of Albany district were increasingly turning. Trade was still prohibited other than at Fort Willshire, where fairs were to be held for three days a week throughout the year. Sales of arms and ammunition and liquor were disallowed, as was at first the purchase of cattle, for it was feared that this would encourage stock theft. Typically the Africans who came to the fairs (some from far distances) brought with them ivory, horns, hides and skins, gum arabic, maize, sorghum, pumpkins, honey, and small manufactures such as baskets, mats or whips. Settler traders had to apply for licences from the magistrate at Graham's Town; and 196 such licences were issued in the first year of the fairs – overwhelmingly to British settlers. These traders were financed by, and acted as agents for, the merchants of Graham's Town. In general they were based in that town and travelled weekly to Fort Willshire in wagon trains.[140]

A breakdown of licences issued reveals that hardly any applicants identified their occupation as merchants or traders. Farmers, carpenters, shoemakers, gardeners, bakers, painters, bricklayers, tailors, wheelwrights, masons, smiths and fishermen all featured, a cross-section of the lowlier of the British settlers.[141] Some went on to become established merchants and landowners in their own right. For example George Wood, who was still a teenager when he started trading at the fairs, went on to own a number of stores in Graham's Town, made a fortune as a wool broker, and by 1849 owned four farms. James Howse followed a similar course.[142] Wood and Howse were exceptional, and many settler traders ended up bankrupt, but there is no doubt that enormous profits could be made, both by the Fort Willshire traders and by the Graham's Town merchants. The Xhosa trade was a launching pad for much settler accumulation.

Many of the Xhosa were themselves middlemen, building on a long history of inter-regional trade between African communities, a history going back long before colonial penetration made much of an impact on their economies. The Rharhabe Xhosa chief, Ngqika, sought to control the trade from the African end, levying a toll on all produce sold, particularly ivory. The main trade items exchanged for African produce were buttons and beads: these functioned as a form of currency among Africans, who used them to buy cattle from other African peoples, and had for long been in circulation throughout southern Africa.[143] Between the establishment of the Fort Willshire fairs in August 1824 and the end of 1825, an estimated £19 317 worth of produce was obtained from the Africans. In the first year, 82 672 lb of ivory, 10 864 hides and 58 602 lb of gum were bought.[144]

The Fort Willshire fairs were only the most visible manifestation of the exploding cross-border trade in these years. The northward trade which operated through Griqua and other middlemen, and in which Boers were much more important than in the eastern frontier zone, was also considerable, as we shall see. There is no knowing how much illicit trade was being conducted. The colony's trade deficit declined substantially in the years after 1824, despite the decline of the wine industry. The fact is that frontier trade was now the most important support of the colony's mercantile bourgeoisie. Cory was not far from the mark when he wrote that ivory 'came to the rescue' of the British settlers after the initial failure of the envisaged Albany agricultural community.[145]

The Fort Willshire fairs (and other less prominent fairs established subsequently on similar lines in the eastern and northern frontier zones) were no more than a temporary expedient. Illegal trading, particularly in firearms and cattle, could not be stamped out, and indeed spread as the profits to be made at Fort Willshire fell. The terms of trade soon turned against the colonial traders. Firstly, the demand for beads pushed the price up for the colonial merchants; and simultaneously the great boost given to trade meant that the price demanded by Africans for trade goods, especially ivory, rocketed. The only way to maintain the initial extraordinary rates of profit was by decentralising trade and permitting traders free access to independent African communities beyond colonial borders.[146]

Acting-Governor Bourke in 1826 sought to liberalise trading regulations, but the restrictions were such that few licences were issued until, in 1830, the pressures of surging merchant capital caused the final lifting of all restrictions and the final closing down of the official trade fairs.[147] By the mid-1830s, the estimated annual turnover of trade beyond the eastern border of the colony amounted to £34 000. Between 150 and 200 traders were active beyond the Keiskamma River, deep in Nguni territory, at any one time.[148] By the 1830s, however, beads and buttons had so saturated Xhosaland that they ceased to be the main item of exchange, and were replaced by manufactures such as blankets, ironware, and arms and ammunition. Increasingly, arms and ammunition became central, if illegal, trade items on the eastern frontier, as was the case in the trade across the northern frontier, where Boers and Griquas were the main mercantile agents. Furthermore, as elephant herds were shot out, ivory had to be brought from longer distances to the Graham's Town market. More and more, the Xhosa and neighbouring peoples were becoming dependent on the colonial exchange nexus, and relied on the export of their crops and cattle for increasingly non-discretionary manufactured imports. As a result of competition from trade goods, indigenous manufacturing declined.[149]

It is not surprising, given the surge of mercantile activity spreading out from Graham's Town, that among the earliest speculative enterprises by leading settler entrepreneurs like John Bailie and William Cock was the effort to raise funds for harbour developments at the mouths of the Fish and Kowie rivers. In 1825 the Albany Shipping Company was formed, with a view to profiting from the inevitable urban and commercial development that landing facilities would bring. For a time, there was even a customs house at the Kowie River mouth (present-day Port Alfred).[150] But despite many efforts over the years, Port Elizabeth in Algoa Bay, site of a military fort since 1799 and a regular port since the arrival of the settlers in 1820, remained the only viable and safe anchorage on the east coast.

Both Dutch and British regimes at the Cape had insisted that all external trade be channelled solely through Cape Town, under the eyes of the customs authorities. In the second decade of the century, before the arrival of the settlers, regular coastal trading traffic began to develop, reaching the Breede River mouth near Swellendam, then Mossel Bay, Knysna by 1817, and as far as Port Elizabeth with the arrival of the 1820 settlers. This was of course a dramatic development in the means of transport available to producers and consumers in the eastern part of the colony. But until 1826 the rule remained in force that external trade could only take place through Table Bay. In 1826, bowing to mercantile pressure, the authorities allowed direct exports and imports to be loaded and landed at Port Elizabeth, and established a customs house there. The export–import trade through Port Elizabeth increased from £18 500 in 1828 to £122 661 in 1834.[151] Previously, coastal freight of sugar, for example, from Cape Town to Port Elizabeth was some 35 shillings per ton, compared with 40 shillings per ton from London to Cape Town. So direct contact with foreign ports was a considerable boon to the eastern districts. Port Elizabeth and Graham's Town began to capture the trade of the interior districts, such as Graaff-Reinet, from Cape Town. One result of the freeing of foreign trade was the opening up of an export trade in, for example, salted meat from Port Elizabeth to Mauritius in the Indian Ocean and St Helena in the Atlantic.[152]

Typically, the more successful settler entrepreneurs channelled profits into landownership in Albany district and further afield in Somerset, Cradock and Graaff-Reinet districts, and began to import merino sheep. In this, they also enjoyed substantial backing from the mercantile community in Cape Town, which, after the decline of the wine export trade, was very receptive to new possibilities for profitable investment further afield. The take-off of the wool industry was perhaps the single most important economic development initiated by the British settlers. In the long run, it was the merino sheep and export trade in wool that would transform the economy of the colony. Right up to the mineral revolution in the last third of the century, wool was to be the basis on which a settler capitalism would evolve.[153]

The 1820s saw a greatly increased demand for wool in Britain, and much of the dry interior of the Cape beyond the southwestern corner was ideal for woolled sheep farming. Although the traditional Cape fat-tailed sheep was a dependable source of meat, and tallow for candles and soap was made from its body fat, it had little commercial value. Initially, some of the aspirant gentry who headed the proprietary parties – Campbell, Pigot, Bowker and others – began to experiment with new sheep breeds. In the 1820s Richard Daniell of Sidbury Park was the leading light, acquiring thoroughbred merinos from Australia in 1827. Lt. T. C. White of Table Farm near Graham's Town imported fine wool Saxons, and had one of the finest studs in the colony.[154]

But the wool industry only really started its take-off in the 1830s. Those who propelled it and profited from it were not the decaying settler gentry of the early settlement, but the new men emerging as an elite on the base of mercantile and speculative activity. In 1833 a joint-stock company was formed to import sheep from overseas. Thirty of the fifty shareholders were Graham's Town businessmen, including White, Thomas Philipps, Robert Godlonton and Charles Griffiths. They imported merino stock from Germany and British breeders such as Lord Western. Sheep were bred and sold throughout the eastern districts. By 1834 there were an estimated 12 000 woolled sheep in Albany district alone – an indication of the extent of the development in the rural economy that had already taken place before the mass emigration of Boer farmers known as the Great Trek. Land was already being bought or hired further into the interior by the leading settlers for speculative and sheep-farming purposes. Tariffs discriminating against colonial wool were lifted in the early 1830s.[155]

Thus by the 1830s the fundamental group dynamics set in motion in Cape colonial society were clearly defined. In the process, the settler elite of the eastern Cape, already spreading out from its base in Albany district, was developing a corporate identity and a corporate sense of self-interest which would become a shaping influence in the processes of accumulation and dispossession during the crucial middle decades of the century. This elite was moving into a more advanced phase of economic consolidation from the stage of individual enterprise characteristic of the 1820s. In the course of things, they acquired their mouthpiece and their major spokesman. The *Graham's Town Journal* was launched in 1831 by L. H. Meurant. But the man who was most energetically to represent settler interests through the columns of the *Journal* and in print generally was Robert Godlonton. He contributed substantially to the tone of Meurant's newspaper from the beginning, and took over the editorship in 1834, also becoming a partner in Meurant's trading business – a necessary source of income given the uncertainties of journalism as a profession.

Meurant's capital continued to sustain the paper, until Godlonton eventually took over ownership.[156]

The *Graham's Town Journal* represented typical entrepreneurial interests vigorously and persistently over a number of decades. Attracting immigration and capital investment was at the top of the agenda for the settlers. The *Journal* sought to propagate the attractions of the eastern Cape generally, in the hope that a flow of population and capital would follow. Larger settler population densities would increase trade and the prices of land and produce, and would spur capital investment in both production and infrastructure such as roads, bridges and port facilities. Vagrancy laws and other legislation controlling the indigenous peoples were propagated ceaselessly. In these ways Godlonton and his colleagues sought to promote a booming settler economy, in which fortunes could be made by commerce, speculation and productive investment.[157] The *Journal* provided a public sphere for the common articulation of bourgeois values and aspirations in the context of a threatening physical and social landscape. It was the *Journal* more than anything else which defined this settler elite as a historical reality, subjectively and collectively, and differentiated it from those who were excluded from membership by reason of social class, culture or racial characteristics. The menacing proximity of strong and cohesive African chiefdoms loomed large in the perceptions of this emergent elite, both as a threat and as an opportunity.[158]

Godlonton was himself a typical self-made settler of humble origins. He had been an apprentice printer at the King's Printing Office in Shacklewell in London; a wooden printing press, given him by the manager of the printing office, had been confiscated in Cape Town en route. He emigrated to South Africa as a member of John Bailie's joint-stock party, and through a combination of commercial and official employment (in 1828 he became chief clerk to the civil commissioner of Albany and Somerset districts) was able to attain a degree of respectability. He took with alacrity and energy to the business of business and of political agitation. He branched out into various fields of speculative enterprise. As early as 1825 he was elected treasurer of the Albany Shipping Company; in 1832 he was agent to the Graham's Town Orphan Chamber; and in 1833 he became a major shareholder in, and secretary to, the Eastern Province Joint-Stock Sheep Farm Association.[159]

By the mid-1830s, Godlonton had acquired rural land and urban plots in different parts of the eastern Cape, and had become a substantial sheep farmer. He had also established himself, in his role as editor of the *Graham's Town Journal*, as the chief propagandist of the settler bourgeoisie, a role he fulfilled in subsequent decades by issuing a number of books designed to serve the cause of the accumulating class which he represented. In this he was joined by other articulate and enthusiastic settler propagandists, men such as J. C. Chase and Donald Moodie. The *Journal* was to be followed by other small-town newspapers whose perceptions were similar and which took their lead from Godlonton.

In due course it became clear to men such as Godlonton that nothing much could be achieved without a degree of political separatism. The colonial state was penurious and dominated by western Cape interests, and unable to expend much on public works for the promotion of trade and transport in the eastern districts. Strong local government, free from the political domination of Cape Town, was essential for development. Thus the *Graham's Town Journal* pushed for the establishment in Graham's Town of those essential supports of a capitalist economy: a local commercial discount bank and a deeds registry office, to promote the flow of loan capital and credit, and to facilitate the operation of the property market. All these functions were based in Cape Town six hundred miles away, and under the control of men whose interests diverged from those of the settler elite in the eastern districts. Moreover, in the early 1830s postal communication with Cape Town took place only once a fortnight.[160]

A petition from Graham's Town businessmen in August 1833 called for a 'resident authority' in the east, 'who shall have the entire controul [*sic*] of all local matters, civil and military'.[161] At a meeting in the town at the end of the following year called to protest against their impotence, William Cock said that easterners 'were not represented in a way they had a right to expect. Look at the neglect of their commerce, the indifference with which their just demands had been treated for a pier at Algoa Bay, for a lighthouse on Cape Recife, and for other important improvements, and then it would be seen how necessary it was that they should have a voice in the legislature of the country.'[162] This demand extended to municipal government for the more efficient regulation of markets, slaughterhouses, auctions, and other manifestations of a growing commercial economy.[163]

However, the fundamental compulsion which came in the 1830s and 1840s to dominate all others was the need to shake resources free for settler accumulation from the neighbouring African peoples. This project required more than just a degree of local self-government; it required military intervention. Bellicosity, repeated war panics, exaggerated reports of Xhosa depredations and spoliation, became the stock in trade of settler propaganda. An imperial commitment to the militarisation of the frontier would mean expanded markets, potentially massive war profits, and the ultimate promise of accumulation through subjugation and dispossession of the indigenous African farmers. It was to settlers such as these that the historian Merivale was referring when he wrote (implying a rather permissive definition of 'crime') that in the colonies it was 'an admitted principle that all means short of crime are legitimate for obtaining money'.[164] The extreme reluctance of the imperial authorities to underwrite the settlers' agenda with public funds was regarded as a major obstacle to settler accumulation. But every so often a rogue governor would arrive at the Cape willing to use his relative independence of action to indulge in military adventures to the profit of the settler elite – until roped in by Downing Street.

CHAPTER FOUR

Liberal Reform and the Humanitarian Movement

The Age of Revolution brought another force to bear on the economic relationships in which the colonial world was enmeshed: evangelical humanitarianism. This was as much a product of the new industrial era as the ideology of free trade. At one level, the evangelical revival was a movement of spiritual renewal, starting in the mid-eighteenth century in Britain and New England, as well as other parts of Protestant Europe. In Britain, it brought new life to the old churches, leading to the establishment of new denominations such as Methodism, and finally infiltrating the established Church of England from the last decades of the eighteenth century. According to the evangelicals, external observance of religious rites was of no consequence without inner conviction and personal conversion. Salvation only occurred through personal contact with God; and the process of conversion, of rebirth, was spontaneous rather than intellectually premeditated. At the same time evangelicals believed that church discipline was no substitute for the active workings of God's spirit. The complacency of the established church, riddled as it was with ruling-class patronage, was thus rejected in favour of the religious enthusiasm of the spiritually committed. Evangelical revivalists also rejected the Calvinist notion of predestination, actively seeking out sinners in the villages and in the slums. Evangelism through lay preaching and itinerancy came to be regarded as a primary religious duty. In sum, the evangelical revival stressed spiritual experience over doctrinal knowledge, and played down denominational distinctions.[1]

The evangelical revival most affected the mobile ranks of the upper working classes. It was the industrial transformation of large parts of British society that created the material conditions under which revivalism thrived. Young artisans with a degree of independence and control over their own destiny, but faced with the insecurity of a rapidly changing social and economic environment, were the typical adherents of the new religious culture, with its emphasis on individual redemption, self-realisation and the resolution of anxiety.[2]

Indeed, evangelicalism in eighteenth-century Britain was by no means a dominant religious current. Itinerant preachers met fierce resistance from Anglican clergy, who feared that their local authority would be subverted. Those inflicted with enthusiasm were widely regarded in the established church as threatening the entire social order. This was particularly the case at the height of the revolutionary onslaught in continental Europe in the 1790s, when many dissenters in England took up the Jacobin cause. Something of a ruling-class moral panic set in, and a Bill was introduced in parliament that was designed to prohibit itinerant preaching.[3]

Nevertheless, the Age of Revolution spurred evangelical revival within the ranks of the established church too, which had so unceremoniously exorcised the earlier manifestations of religious fervour in the persons of John Wesley and his colleagues. Although Anglican evangelicals did not challenge the ecclesiastical framework of the established church, they sought to infuse it with new purpose. As a result of the upheavals of the 1790s Anglican evangelicals were pushed in more conservative directions, and became concerned to profess their loyalty to church and state. They asserted the value of hierarchy and conceded that access to spiritual enlightenment could be gained through a gradual process of doctrinal education and adherence to the disciplines of the church.[4] In Britain in general, as the wars against Napoleon drew to a close, a much more bourgeois evangelicalism came to permeate the respectable middling ranks of society. Increasingly in subsequent years evangelicalism took on the trappings of an ideology of social control in the established church, as it had done in the Methodist movement when the Bunting reaction took hold.[5]

Many evangelicals believed that political and social issues were central to the concerns of Christians. They extended, in other words, the notion of Christian redemption to include redemption from temporal bondage and deprivation. To the religious enthusiasm of the seventeenth-century dissenters they brought the concerns of the eighteenth-century Enlightenment. The ascendancy within the Anglican Church of Arminianism, the belief in free will and personal responsibility, was combined with a belief in man's capacity to transform the world. It was in this nexus that evangelicalism took on the trappings of humanitarianism.

Thus evangelicalism was also a great crusade in pursuit of secular causes. In the early nineteenth century it became the moral arm of bourgeois reformism – political, economic and social.[6] It embraced the cause of liberalisation, most obviously in the fields of productive and commercial relations, both in Britain and in the wider international sphere. Indeed, in practice it is impossible to divorce evangelical humanitarianism from the pervasive ideology of free trade. The one was inextricably associated with the other. To the humanitarians, free markets were a precondition for the triumph of 'Christian civilisation'. In their understanding of Christian civilisation, they did not recognise any dichotomy between spiritual and secular realms. Material culture, attitudes towards work, patterns of consumption: all these were intimately germane to the Christian life. People driven to labour by moral compulsion and the laws of supply and demand were bound to be more productive than those who were coerced or bound. Moreover, free labour freely entered into (even if the alternative was starvation or the workhouse) was the only path to personal redemption and salvation. So humanitarian evangelicalism also served the interests of the new accumulating elites of industrialising Britain, concerned as they were with extending production and markets at every turn.

Humanitarianism was a central element in the broad movement managing the adaptation to an industrial economy and society. Its involvement in reform movements encompassed the fields of education for the masses, poor relief, judicial and penal institutions, treatment of the insane, leisure activities, and family reconstruction.[7] People associated broadly with evangelicalism were thus at the forefront of charting new social values and social institutions apposite for an urban, industrial age. While these values and institutions were grounded on the belief that individual self-interest was the optimal spur to productive labour, they also involved new regimes of social control, surveillance and regimentation. They assumed too that individuals and societies were malleable, and that social behaviour and institutions, being formed by the environment, could be transformed. Their goal was to inculcate a discipline of virtue to replace the old coercions. This required a thorough cultural reconstruction of the lower classes, a process that was not without resort to new forms of compulsion. The poor house or penitentiary was always there to accommodate those who failed to respond appropriately.

Embedded in this broad movement of liberal reformism was an underlying tension between humanitarian sentiment and the more utilitarian liberalism associated with Jeremy Bentham. For the former, the freedom of the individual from artificial restraint or overt coercion was essential for the reconstitution of the self. Only through the exercise of free choice and personal responsibility could redemption through labour be achieved. For the utilitarians, on the other hand, results were more important than the state of people's souls. Efficiency and discipline were essential to progress, and, if necessary, authoritarian means should be employed to impose them. These tensions were not immediately apparent in the optimistic years of humanitarian advance up to the 1830s. But when optimism faded, in Britain as well as in her colonies, humanitarian idealism was to give way to tougher-minded utilitarian prescriptions.

At one level, humanitarianism was an ideology that served to shore up and legitimise the rule, at home and abroad, of the ruling classes, under pressure at this juncture from the seething masses of the impoverished and underemployed. With memories of the French Revolution still haunting people's minds, it was apparent that the moral base of class rule had to be reinvigorated. Not surprisingly, therefore, humanitarianism infiltrated the self-consciousness of sections of the British elite, not only the new bourgeoisie, but some of the old landed oligarchy as well. Thus among the ardent patrons of the humanitarian cause were members of the landed gentry and the aristocracy. Men like William Wilberforce and the Clapham sect were effective in carrying evangelical humanitarian views into the upper reaches of British society, where many of them were well connected.[8]

Bourgeois humanitarians often reflected all the class prejudices and anxieties of a rising middle class. For they were threatened from below by a mass of discontent, and were often scandalised by the forces of popular radicalism. The humanitarian reformers were by no means Jacobins. On the whole they clung to a rigid conception of the rights of property (although property in human beings posed a different set of problems, as it conflicted with a superior right to freedom). Like all paternalisms, the paternalism of the humanitarians in industrialising Britain was only partially effective, and radical leaders routinely criticised them for being blind to the conditions under which the marginalised underclasses lived and laboured. They were more interested with slaves in the colonies, it was charged, than with the plight of the Irish in England. The archetypal humanitarian, William Wilberforce, supported legislation in parliament designed to crush political dissent after the Napoleonic wars – such as the combination laws and the suspension of habeas corpus. In Wilberforce's opinion, working-class grievances were born of an over-anxiety with 'the concerns of this world'.[9]

Abroad, there developed out of the humanitarian movement a passionate commitment to extending rights and freedoms to all peoples subjected to coerced labour systems, notably the considerable slave populations over whom the British held sway, but also those not formally enslaved yet held in servile relations, such as the South African Khoi. Indeed, it was the campaign against the great wall of slavery and the whole political system built around the institution in the colonial world that gave the humanitarian moment its special historical significance. To the reformers, human bondage was a mountainous obstacle to both moral upliftment and economic progress. Slavery impeded not only the extension of Christian civilisation, but also the extension of markets and mercantile enterprise. Again, the two imperatives, moral and material, were inseparably linked.

As a movement of reform in the colonial world, humanitarianism was often far more confrontational and explicitly political than in the metropole. In close alliance with elements of merchant capital, humanitarians (who were often merchants themselves) pushed for the restructuring of colonial government and colonial labour relations, and indeed of Britain's relations with the outside world generally, in more liberal directions. As we have seen, the nineteenth-century empire of free trade, in strong contrast to the mercantilist era, was predicated on maximum expansion of demand in colonial markets rather than on the rigid subordination of colonial economies to the needs of the metropole. And coerced labour was widely perceived as an inadequate base on which to build dynamic and prosperous colonial economies. For the humanitarians, free markets and free contracts freely entered into by free people were preconditions for the attainment of Christian civilisation in both its secular and spiritual dimensions.

The popular perception of empire was closely bound up with the anti-slavery cause. In the 1790s Britain was responsible for the transportation of 45 000 Africans annually to the Americas, representing perhaps 60 per cent of the total slave trade.[10] This trade was a major component of British overseas commerce. But after the loss of the thirteen American colonies, the slave trade became the focus of a considerable popular ferment, in which middle-class evangelicals took a lead. In 1787 they were instrumental in establishing the colony of Sierra Leone as a private settlement for freed and runaway slaves on the west coast of Africa.

The anti-slavery movement, which became the broadest-based mass petitioning campaign of the nineteenth century, was in one sense a quest for national atonement and redemption, a way of asserting the supremacy of British values and British liberties against the pretensions of both American republicans and French revolutionaries. When Napoleon reimposed slavery in the French Caribbean colonies and attempted to reimpose it in revolutionary Haiti in 1802, anti-slavery increasingly became part of the British ruling class's reassertion of its own superior qualities as a class. (In the 1790s, in contrast, when French revolutionary fervour was at its height, Britain in its reactionary phase had been intent on crushing Haiti's slave revolution.) In 1808 Britain abolished the slave trade, not because the trade had become uneconomic – far from it – but because abolitionism was a cause that more than any other legitimated Britain's evolving ruling order, and provided the new empire of conquest with a sense of moral idealism and mission.

After the Reform Act of 1832 had brought middle-class influence to bear at Westminster as never before, the final Act of emancipation in 1833 was to be the culmination of this great crusade, a crusade that ultimately served the cause of Britain's rulers without greatly threatening any fundamental national interest. Like parliamentary reform itself, emancipation became a potent symbol of legitimacy, calculated to evoke the consent of non-slaveholding classes. Everywhere, the rise of emancipationism coincided with political crises, metropolitan and colonial, and it became an instrument in shoring up established authority. Everywhere, it coincided with the growth of radical social movements from below (whose own role in the anti-slavery movement was considerable). In Britain, the older ruling oligarchy (still over-represented in state office) skilfully embraced the issue too, and thereby deflected more far-reaching domestic reformism, not to mention more radical pressures. In general, dominant classes sought to legitimate and validate a new capitalist domestic order by contrasting an idealised vision of it with the horrors of exploitation abroad. In this way the problematical concept of freedom in the age of free trade and free labour was defined in contradistinction to the institution of slavery. Finally, emancipation was facilitated by the fact that, although still profitable, the economic significance of slave regimes was no longer great in the metropolitan perspective, once the possibility of free trade in sugar had been accepted, as it was by many in the reformed parliament of 1833.[11]

Apart from reform of labour systems in the colonial world, humanitarianism also played an important role in developing a new sense of moral commitment towards indigenous peoples in the colonial world over whom the British now exercised their rule. This notion that the colonisers had a special moral obligation to the spiritual and material upliftment of the colonised would have been meaningless to the denizens of the older mercantilist empire of self-governing settler communities. But with the establishment of the new nineteenth-century empire a concept of imperial trusteeship matured.[12] The fact that these same indigenous people were actual or potential consumers of British manufactures added the essential material foundation to the expression of evangelical concern manifested in the newly rampant missionary movement.

Specifically, a zeal for proselytising non-European peoples, something largely lacking in Protestantism hitherto, grew out of the evangelical fervour of the time. Converting aliens was a natural extension of the conversion of Britain's new working classes. This expansion of evangelical horizons was assisted by a number of contemporary developments: the development of literacy and the information networks created by the spread of evangelical culture and itinerant preaching through Britain, the burgeoning market for cheap publications, and the growing mobility and self-confidence of the Nonconforming religious leadership from the lower ranks of society. More broadly, Britain's expanding empire of commerce, the voyages of Captain Cook, the rise of popular geography, and the increasing dissemination of propaganda about the slave trade, all provided the popular imagination with new possibilities for mission work abroad.[13]

Thus in the years after 1790 a number of missionary societies came into being, arising not so much from the mainstream Christian establishment, but out of the lower and more marginal elements of eighteenth-century evangelicalism. The first was the Baptist Missionary Society in 1792, founded by William Carey, a pioneer of missionary activity in India. The London Missionary Society was established in 1795, the Glasgow Missionary Society in 1796, the Church Missionary Society in 1799, the British and Foreign Bible Society in 1804, the American Board of Commissioners for Foreign Missions in 1810, and the Wesleyan Methodist Missionary Society in 1813. In keeping with the general tendency of the evangelical movement, these missionary societies were mostly non-denominational. Confessional divides and conflicts were unappealing to people who stressed personal religious commitment. While the Church Missionary Society was nominally an Anglican organisation, the London society (LMS) was more typical of the early missionary movement, drawing into its ranks representatives of a wide range of Nonconformist backgrounds.[14]

Indeed, missionary culture, like evangelical revivalism as a whole, initially had a strong supra-national focus, drawing on volunteers from continental Europe. The redemptive action of God, it was believed, did not recognise national boundaries. But although the mission enterprise was conceived of as being supra-national, British evangelicals regarded Britain as playing a special role, having been spared from the ravages of war and civil breakdown for God's purposes. Gradually, as the mission movement took on the trappings of an established element in dominant British culture from the second decade of the nineteenth century, it became more nationalist in its rhetoric and its appeal, and more intertwined with notions of the imperial civilising mission and the beneficence of British commercial enterprise. But these were not preoccupations of the first generation of missionaries or the bodies they represented.[15]

The early missionary movement was driven largely by people of the skilled working class – the 'pious mechanicks' of the LMS. It was, moreover, largely secular in its leadership.[16] Like the anti-slavery movement, the missionary movement was regarded with deep suspicion in certain establishment circles in the revolutionary age, including leading Tory churchmen, particularly in years of heightened Jacobin agitation. Within the colonies in which missionaries operated, there was usually a wide social gulf between the military class who filled gubernatorial posts and the humble missionaries, who were typically men of artisanal background. For most colonial governors, missionaries represented the presumptuous new classes seeking to push their way to influence and position. To many of the older ruling class in the colonies, the missionary movement did seem to be part of a new democratic order that was threatening to subvert their system of privileges and patronage.[17]

The mission movement was domesticated within the dominant culture of Britain as it came to be accepted by the ecclesiastical establishment of the Anglican Church. Distrust of the early mission movement – exemplified by the LMS with its suspect class base, theology and social assumptions – was displaced by the growth of mission activity under the authority and discipline of the church. The focus of this activity was the Church Missionary Society (CMS), established in 1799 by a small group of evangelical clergy in London. From the start, patrons of the CMS included prominent middle-class Claphamites, associated with domestic reform and the anti-slavery campaign, among them men with extensive imperial experience. Zachary Macaulay, Charles Grant, James Stephen and Henry Thornton had experience in Africa and India, through the East India Company, and were involved in founding the evangelical colony of Sierra Leone (of which Macaulay had at one time been governor).[18]

It was in relation to India that the missionary cause was to enter mainstream debate about the purposes of empire, once the receding threat of revolution and the prospect of victory against Napoleon permitted a thawing of attitudes towards mission enterprise. The East India Company had been very reluctant to encourage or support mission activities in territories under its authority – although evangelicals who were politically cautious were tacitly allowed to operate. The official fear was that Indian collaborators, notably the sepoy troops on whom the British relied, would strenuously object to any attempt to undermine their faith. Then in 1812 the CMS organised a campaign in Britain pleading the needs of the Indian people for access to Christianity. In 1813 a breakthrough was achieved when the company's charter bound it to the religious and moral 'improvement' of the natives. Succeeding years saw an unprecedented surge in support for missions across Britain and across denominational lines. The newly won approval of church and state made the missionary cause respectable. At the same time it became more nationalist and more closely tied to ideas of imperial mission and commercial enterprise. The empire of conquest and free trade thus also took on an aura of evangelical self-justification.[19]

In the post-Napoleonic period, the newly respectable mission movement generally tended to become more institutionalised, more conservative, and better-off financially. By the 1820s the mission cause was disseminated widely in Britain through recruitment drives, fund-raising, and the widespread promotion of humanitarian causes. Popular culture became permeated with images of benighted and deprived indigenes being redeemed by contact with Christian civilisation.[20] Through the 'Saints' in parliament (dominated by Wilberforce and T. F. Buxton) and through the patronage of leading lights in Britain's aristocratic families, the missionary cause found itself not short of influence or access to the highest forums in the land. Exeter Hall (the generic name given to the missionary movement as a whole, after the venue off the Strand where the various societies held their annual meetings) became a force to be reckoned with in public affairs and in the formulation of imperial policy.

In the 1820s and 1830s, when the moral bases of Britain's relations with the colonial world were being reformulated, humanitarian influence was deeply rooted in the Colonial Office in Downing Street. Here the Clapham sect was represented by the most influential of the Colonial Office bureaucrats, James Stephen, son of the ardent abolitionist and CMS patron, and nephew by marriage of William Wilberforce. He became legal adviser to the Colonial Office in 1813, rising to the position of permanent under-secretary from 1836 to 1847, although he had long before that date been an important formulator of policy. Charles Grant, Baron Glenelg, who was secretary of state at the Colonial Office from 1835 to 1839, was also the son of a founder of the CMS and of the British and Foreign Bible Society. Both Stephen and Glenelg, like their fathers, were on the committee of the CMS.[21]

But just as advocates of colonial settlement schemes were confronted by official reluctance to commit public resources to their cause, so the missionary movement was seldom a decisive factor in the making of imperial policy, despite the intimate access of humanitarian advocates to the corridors of power. It was when humanitarian concerns coincided with those of fiscal prudence that humanitarian influence became most persuasive. In general the missionary cause was an imperial and not an anti-imperial force, concerned with the extension of British influence and control. But, as we have seen, the informal imperialism of free trade was grounded on the principle that an accumulation of territorial encumbrances was to be avoided as far as possible, given the assumed efficacy of informal means of control in the colonial world. In the final analysis humanitarian influence in the corridors of power was limited.

The first missionary endeavour among the dispossessed Khoi in South Africa was undertaken in 1737 by the Moravians at Baviaanskloof (later known as

Genadendal), beyond the Hottentots Holland mountains east of Cape Town. The missionaries left in 1744, not to return until 1792. The Moravians, whose stations in the nineteenth century were all situated close to the arable south-western heartland of the Cape Colony, were always relatively uncontroversial and amenable to the authorities. Their theology too was more congenial to the High Church Anglicanism of the colony's rulers than that of the Noncon-formists of the London Missionary Society, with whom they were often favourably compared. They enjoyed a higher social standing and more politi-cal influence in early-nineteenth-century Britain than the bulk of the dissenting evangelicals. At the Cape they did not challenge the colonial hierarchy, nor did they question the paternalistic prerogatives of the master class. Even more def-erential was the Cape-based South African Missionary Society, an outgrowth of the Dutch Reformed Church; its members included slave-owners.[22]

But the history of the missionary factor as a force to be reckoned with in Cape society and politics began with the arrival in 1799 of the Hollanders Dr T. J. van der Kemp and J. J. Kicherer of the London Missionary Society. They were shortly thereafter followed by James Read and by William Anderson, mis-sionary pioneer of Griqualand, in 1800. Van der Kemp's first plan was to establish a mission among the Xhosa, as a gateway to other African peoples of the subcontinent. But the authorities frowned on the idea and, confronted with the Khoi rebellion of 1799–1803, encouraged the missionaries to set up instead an institution in the eastern Cape under government patronage as a means of reconciling the Khoi to the authorities. Here at Bethelsdorp, the LMS's flagship mission near Algoa Bay, the missionaries were expected to act as a go-between with Klaas Stuurman, the rebel leader. The authorities in Cape Town also envisaged that the mission Khoi, most of whom had participated in the rebel-lion, would serve as a workforce for white colonists and would be a source of recruits for the Hottentot Corps.[23]

Van der Kemp, senior missionary at Bethelsdorp, was the leading figure among the early evangelists and gave the early mission presence at the Cape its distinctive character. He was an unlikely and atypical missionary. A Dutch medical doctor from a well-off family, he spoke a brace of languages and was the author of books of philosophy and theology. As a young man he had turned his back on his social background and rejected the trappings of respectability. After leading a profligate life, he devoted himself to expiating his sense of guilt through Christian service. This is what took him to South Africa in the service of the LMS.[24] In his rejection of conventional norms of social hierarchy, Van der Kemp was very different from subsequent generations of missionaries, who were to conflate the experience of Christian conversion with the process of acculturation. Van der Kemp had little time for such 'civilisation' and self-consciously 'went native', living in very humble circumstances, and tolerating a lifestyle among converts which differed little from that of other Khoi. He married a 14-year-old slave girl whose freedom he had purchased. Other early missionaries also took indigenous partners, and distanced themselves from the colonial social order.[25] For them, as for Van der Kemp, the Christian community thrived best when least infected by contact with the false Christianity of metropolitan civilisation.[26]

The Bethelsdorp model of Christian society, in its egalitarian and separatist aspects, was profoundly subversive of the colonial order. This was especially so for the Boers, for whom Christianity was a status marker which dictated differential access to the legal system and to the protections and patronage of government. Khoi testimony, for instance, was regarded as inadmissible as evidence in courts of law since Khoi could not swear on the Bible, even if they were baptised converts (a customary assumption invoked by the 'black circuit' of 1812). It had also long been regarded as improper to teach Khoi to read and write, skills which were central to missionary instruction. Bethelsdorp was thus an affront to the moral universe of the master class. The very act of proselytisation was a challenge to Boer claims to exclusive access to God's word, and also to the productive relations which underpinned their economy and society.[27] Little wonder that the colonists, both burghers and local officials, did all they could to obstruct Khoi from settling at the station.

For the Khoi, the mission was a haven for those escaping the shackles of service, or a place where family members could be sheltered from exploitation and children from 'apprenticeship', while the menfolk went out in search of work. But although a modest accumulation of property was possible at Bethelsdorp and her sister stations subsequently established, life there nevertheless was by and large wretched. All the same, Bethelsdorp became a focus for the reintegration of Khoi society and the reassertion of indigenous political leadership.[28]

Rates of conversion among Khoi were high compared with those in the more resilient and self-contained African chiefdoms that subsequently received missionaries. For mission Christianity enabled Khoi to make sense of their experiences in terms of concepts of evil and original sin, and provided an explanation and expiation of suffering. The power of the Christian message, mediated by their own historical and cultural understandings, spread among Khoi on farms far and wide, as Khoi converts themselves spread out as preachers along wagon routes or as seasonal workers, with the encouragement of the missionaries.[29] In keeping with the early missionaries' emphasis on spiritual commitment rather than civilisation or acculturation, and in view of the general lack of social distance between missionaries and their charges, there was little to prevent converts from being used as evangelists themselves. It was, after all, early LMS policy to establish independent, self-governing churches without European supervision, according to the model of lay evangelism pioneered in Britain.[30]

Prominent early Bethelsdorp evangelists, or 'native agents', included Cupido Kakkerlak, Hendrik Boezak, Jan Goeyman and Gerrit Sampson. Boezak, for example, was an elephant hunter who preached on farms he visited while on hunting expeditions. Such Khoi evangelists established an outpost at Algoa

Bay, itinerated in Xhosaland, and eventually played a major role among Tswana, Griqua and Khoisan peoples north of the Orange, where Goeyman and Kakkerlak were prominent for several years. The idea of a 'native agency' was first introduced among the Griqua at Griquatown north of the Orange by the LMS director John Campbell on his visit in 1812–13. In consequence Jan Hendricks, Barend Barends, Pieter Davids and Andries Waterboer were appointed missionary agents at 100 rix-dollars a year. The literacy of Khoi or Griqua evangelists, imperfect though it may have been, meant that they had access to God's word in a very direct sense, in the form of the Bible, and thus enjoyed a status and authority that many white colonists could not match.[31]

The mission diaspora, spreading out from Bethelsdorp or Griquatown, carried trading frontiers and the zone of colonial influence and acculturation further north, even when the evangelists detached themselves from the direct control of the LMS. They played an important and controversial role politically and economically. For they were men who had been thrown up by and had rebelled against colonial society, and who fully shared the jaundiced view of established authority and the forces of colonial expansion held by their mentors Van der Kemp, Read and Anderson. They were forebears of an important class of men of colour, products and representatives of, but also rejects of, colonial society, establishing pockets of economic accumulation and independence in and around mission stations on and beyond the frontiers of colonial society, until eventually they were swallowed up as the forces of settler expansion gradually expropriated them.[32] Waterboer, who became an eminent Griqua captain, personified these processes.[33] Such men were to be of fundamental significance in formulating a sense of 'Hottentot', 'Griqua' or 'coloured' identity, and in mobilising resistance in decades to come.[34]

It is against this backdrop that the early history of the LMS at the Cape played itself out in the early years of the nineteenth century. Relations between missionaries at Bethelsdorp and the administration in Cape Town quickly soured. Van der Kemp and Read began to report to the authorities acts of ill-usage by Boer colonists against Khoi servants, and obstructed colonists' attempts to recruit labour at the station. The authorities soon realised that Bethelsdorp was becoming a major grievance among the local colonists. The latter complained of Khoi living in idleness and being taught to read and write; worse, they were imbibing notions of equality as Christians. Van der Kemp was accused of inculcating a belief in the Khoi that they were an oppressed race, and of fomenting rather than dousing Khoi rebelliousness. Further, Bethelsdorp recruits in the Cape Regiment (the former Hottentot Corps) proved refractory and insubordinate. Deserters reportedly responded to demands that they return by asserting that they now belonged to the army of Jesus, and Van der Kemp was their general.[35]

Such was the irritation caused that the Batavian governor, General Janssens, proclaimed it illegal to teach 'Hottentots' to write, and recalled Van der Kemp and Read to Cape Town in 1805, threatening to expel them from the Cape. He charged that they were British sympathisers, and situated dangerously close to the Algoa Bay anchorage.[36] After the British re-took the Cape in 1806, they allowed the missionaries to return to Bethelsdorp. Thereafter, J. G. Cuyler, landdrost at Uitenhage, clashed repeatedly with the Bethelsdorp missionaries over access to Khoi labour and military service, and he dismissed Khoi complaints of ill-treatment. He demanded the right to screen admissions to the station, and used his authority to harass all wishing to settle there.[37]

With their re-taking of the Cape the British were now committed to longer-term occupation than in 1795; and the issue of labour relations was at the forefront of their concerns. The history of violence and warfare between colonists and Khoi, and the ongoing ferment of missionary agitations and colonists' anger, forced the state of the further interior on to the reluctant attentions of the British authorities in Cape Town. When Colonel Richard Collins was sent on a grand tour to investigate conditions, he returned echoing colonists' complaints against the Khoi of rebelliousness, indolence and labour shortage.[38] In an attempt to bring order to the troubled frontier regions, Caledon issued the so-called Hottentot proclamation of 1809 and established circuit courts in 1811.[39] But matters were not so easily resolved. By the 1810s, with the growing acceptability of the mission voice in mainstream political and religious discourse in Britain, the LMS was emboldened to take its case to the Colonial Office, where evidence by South African missionaries of gross malpractices towards the Khoi was soon being heard. Moreover, in view of the hostile state of relations between the missionaries and the Cape authorities, the LMS directors sent John Campbell to the Cape in 1812 to investigate matters. He clashed with Governor Cradock over the purposes of the mission.[40]

Beyond the borders of the colony, William Anderson, the most notable missionary to the independent Griqua up to 1820, was expected by the authorities to act as an agent of the colonial government. In return for providing information on and exercising influence over indigenous rulers, he sought to gain privileges for baptised Griqua and negotiated for supplies of gunpowder. But in this region too, relations between administration and mission deteriorated to a state of crisis. The mission proved a magnet for runaway slaves, deserting Khoi workers and absconding criminals. In 1814 Governor Cradock sought to bring Anderson's mission under colonial control. The authorities tried to assert colonial law over Griqua territory, demanding that all deserters be forcibly returned, and that twenty youths be furnished to serve in the Cape Regiment.[41] But Anderson had no power to assert colonial authority over the Griqua even had he wished to. He refused to act as official government agent and declined to supply a levy of soldiers.[42]

Cradock's successor, Somerset, was particularly hostile to the missions and determined to bring the conflict with them to a head. Somerset expressed an aversion to missionaries operating independently beyond the borders as rival sources of influence to the colonial authorities. Nevertheless, by 1816 he was confronted with the inevitability of a curtailment of imperial expenditure and a reduction of the Cape garrison. He thus determined to use loyal missionaries as agents in maintaining peace and stability. On this account Joseph Williams was allowed to settle at the Kat River as a colonial representative with the Rharhabe Xhosa chief, Ngqika, to ensure the return of stolen cattle and runaway servants. Somerset's quite unrealistic plan was to set up Ngqika as collaborator-in-chief, through whom lesser chiefs could be controlled. But Williams, who received no remuneration from government, proved a less than devoted agent, and did not meet Somerset's expectations.[43] In 1817, thus disappointed, Somerset refused permission for four newly arrived LMS missionaries, including Robert Moffat, to leave for stations beyond the northern border. In 1818 he ordered the Bushman missions at Tooverberg (later Colesberg) and Hephzibah just south of the Orange to be closed, and the missionaries William Corner and Erasmus Smit were summoned back to the colony – at a time when Boer colonisation of the region was intensifying.[44]

At the same time as the government was attacking from without, the LMS was riven within by conflict. This had been growing since the elderly Van der Kemp's death in 1811. The mission movement as a whole was also becoming more respectable and more concerned to placate the established authorities. Elements within the LMS reflected this trend. At the Cape, a pro-government faction of the LMS, under the leadership of George Thom, was determined to mend relations with the administration, and in the process to get rid of Read and the 'radicals'. They were allied with the loyalist South African Missionary Society. Thom, who was based in Cape Town and was very close to the administration, called a quite irregular 'synod' in 1817, but only those based near to Cape Town were invited. This amounted to an attempt to purge the society of missionaries of the Van der Kemp–Read persuasion, whose scandalous lifestyles and lack of deference to secular and ecclesiastical authority were an embarrassment to a new generation of evangelists. A number of charges were laid against those missionaries who had aroused the ire of the colonists and the administration. In particular, Read, who had upset these circles by his marriage to a Khoi woman, was charged with adultery with the daughter of a convert (he had already confessed and been forgiven by the Bethelsdorp congregation), and was expelled from the society. The proceedings of the synod provided a vindication for the colonists and their subsequent historians.[45]

Thom and three others left the LMS themselves and joined the Dutch Reformed Church to serve predominantly the Dutch–Afrikaner colonists, whose anti-humanitarian world-view they shared. The Rev. John Brownlee, who had arrived in 1817, also resigned from the LMS and was seized upon by Somerset as government agent with Ngqika in place of the ineffectual Williams, who had died in August 1818. Brownlee was to be a paid government employee, and his letter of appointment was very comprehensive and specific, leaving no doubt where his primary loyalties were to lie. Henceforth, the government in Cape Town tried to ensure that all missionaries beyond the eastern frontier were under government control, by imposing conditions on them to report regularly to the chief government missionary at Ngqika's. From 1821 to 1830 this was William Ritchie Thomson, a Scot recruited by Thom; he resigned from the Glasgow Missionary Society to take up government employment. Thomson never swayed from his loyalty to government, and ended up a Dutch Reformed minister himself. But as Thomson was to realise, missionaries who bent over backwards to serve colonial authorities found themselves in an invidious and compromised position, unable to establish their bona fides among the independent people they were trying to serve.[46]

With the LMS at the Cape in a state of collapse, the directors in London decided to send out a resident director to be permanently based in Cape Town, whose task it was to put the society's affairs in order and to sort out its relations with the Somerset regime. John Philip's arrival at the Cape in 1819 signalled the coming of age of the humanitarian factor as a political force in colonial society. Philip was to become for many of the dominant classes in colonial society, then and subsequently, the personification of villainy. Yet Philip was a typical figure of his times and social origins, representing what by the 1820s was a mainstream current of thought in Britain. Whereas his predecessors at the Cape had mostly positioned themselves on the margins of colonial society and, certainly since Van der Kemp's death in 1811, had been unable to carry forward their cause in the face of the hostility of the administration, Philip himself was to champion the cause of the colony's dispossessed and exploited on a larger stage than anyone before. The cause he espoused was now a cause which touched the sensibilities of the respectable middle ranks of British society. In sharp contrast to his predecessors, Philip had the polemical skills, the social standing, the political connections, and the indefatigable zeal to make his voice heard where it counted. Philip's significance derived from the fact that he represented an increasingly broad social and moral consensus at the heart of the British body politic about the responsibilities of empire.[47]

But after the crisis of 1817 the LMS at the Cape was still rent by schism. Philip's main antagonist for years to come was Robert Moffat, who had arrived in 1817, and had at first been inclined to ally himself with the LMS conservatives. As a good Congregationalist who opposed church government, he regarded Philip as having papal aspirations, and became increasingly vociferous in his condemnation of Philip as the latter grew closer to Read as his confidant and informant, and became more involved in the struggle for Khoi rights. Both Philip and Moffat were dogmatic and combative men with a zeal for the causes they espoused, and with a talent for exaggerated polemic. In this they were not out of step with the general tone of colonial politics at the time.[48]

In particular, Moffat, who devoted his life to serving the Tswana-speaking Tlhaping beyond colonial borders, deeply resented the native agents based at Griquatown. He saw them as agents of the humanitarians' evil designs to establish a political dominion over African peoples and their missions. He also condemned the practice of baptism by profession which was associated with the Van der Kemp–Read tradition within the LMS, and which spawned (as he saw it) an army of coloured apostates who caused trouble wherever opportunities for trade and land grabbing presented themselves.[49] In all this, Moffat espied the stirring connivance of Dr Philip. For Moffat, Philip was the embodiment of the political missionary, as he was for many other critics, then and subsequently. The truth, though, was that the missionary enterprise was always profoundly political, even when it was disinclined to admit it (and men like Philip asserted that they were guided solely by the imperatives of their spiritual calling). For Philip, based in Cape Town, came to see more clearly that the whole colonial system of subordination and thraldom had to be challenged if the indigenous people were to develop fully as redeemed individuals.[50]

In fact, Philip's and Moffat's differences were differences of means rather than ends, and derived in part from their different geographical locations. Both were men of the second generation of missionaries, more attuned to middle-class prejudices and perceptions than the likes of Van der Kemp and Read. For them, conversion ultimately implied acculturation to bourgeois norms. In their view Christians were defined not only in terms of their spiritual commitment, but in terms of the cultural traits and values of the missionaries' brand of civilisation. At the same time neither Philip nor Moffat was inclined to compromise with indigenous cultures. But both knew that the evangelical project was gravely threatened by the land and labour hunger of the colonists. For this reason integration of the Khoi and other African peoples into the larger colonial economy and society was beneficial and necessary, but on their own terms, ideally through independent production and commercial enterprise, rather than as dispossessed and subjugated labourers.

The social origins of the missionaries explain something of their ideology. Scotland was the breeding ground of many of the most influential early-nineteenth-century missionaries and colonial humanitarians – including those who played so important a role in South African history, such as Philip, Campbell, Moffat and Livingstone.[51] Scottish society and culture were far more radically captured by the evangelical movement than was England, with its less malleable class structure and its weight of established interests. In contrast, the class system of the Highlands had been dismembered after Jacobite resistance was crushed at Culloden in 1746, and the Highlanders had been integrated into a very new society. Then again, the Scottish agricultural revolution from about 1760 had produced one of the most advanced agricultures in Europe. The old peasant economy disappeared before the onslaught of enclosures, innovations and capital investment. Simultaneously the industrial revolution produced a new urban life centred on the textile industry. At this time, too, Scotland's uniquely democratic university system, fostered under the auspices of the Presbyterian kirk, engendered an intellectual golden age, the Scottish Enlightenment. The educational opportunities that opened up were exploited by the rapidly growing and prosperous new middle class and artisanate (such as the weavers, whose skills were not taken over by factory technology for several decades into the nineteenth century). Men of humble background became men of letters, innovators, and political and social reformers. Evangelical revivalism found a fecund breeding ground among such people, many of whom turned their gaze overseas as an outlet for their talents and their zeal. The new British empire of direct rule over alien peoples was forged in large part by Scottish administrators, soldiers, merchants and missionaries, for whom colonies offered opportunities for fulfilling their aspirations.[52]

It was inevitable that these new men would challenge the authority of the old eighteenth-century Presbyterian ruling elite – the lairds in the countryside, and the oligarchic councils in the burghs, who controlled the local communities in part through their control of appointments and patronage in the kirk. The new classes rebelled against this archaic elite, a rebellion which, as in England, led to a reform movement within, and also secession from, the established church. New Congregationalist and Baptist congregations, which were so important in the missionary movement, emerged in the 1790s. In Scotland at this time, as in England, the proximity of the French Revolution and the proto-democratic spirit of the times aroused the ire of the old ruling classes. And inevitably the new evangelical currents and their humanitarian after-tow, notably the anti-slavery and missionary movements, were roundly condemned in reactionary circles as subversive and even treasonous, particularly in the volatile years of the early 1790s following the French Revolution. Again, however, that which might initially have seemed fairly radical, eventually became (like English Methodism) itself a defender of new established interests, once captured by dominant forces in society for their own purposes.[53]

John Philip, who was born in 1785, was a handloom weaver's son from the fishing town of Kirkcaldy on the Firth of Forth. He was thus one of that prosperous Scots artisanal class with unprecedented opportunities for education and upward mobility. His formal schooling ended at the age of 11, when he started to learn his father's trade. He was reared in a bookish atmosphere, in which reading and writing were valued as leisure-time activities. He grew up to be a self-educated man, attending evening classes at an academy while in employment, and attained at a young age the position of manager of a spinning mill in Dundee. Caught up in the evangelical revival of the 1790s, Philip became a committed Congregationalist. After study in England he made a name for himself as a prominent minister in Aberdeen, in great demand as a preacher, and a leading spokesman for the missionary cause in the northeast of Scotland. When the directors of the LMS sought a dynamic representative to rebuild its activities at the Cape, they fixed their eyes on Philip, and set about seducing him with honorary doctorates from those evangelical schools across the ocean, Columbia and Princeton, according to the evangelical custom. Eventually he succumbed, and took leave of his Aberdeen congregation.[54]

Philip shared the belief of others of his class background that indigenous peoples in southern Africa were in no way naturally inferior to Europeans (in fact he claimed that many were morally superior to white colonists); and insisted that if they imbibed evangelical Christianity and its associated literate culture and values, they were as capable of achieving solid prosperity as were the artisans and yeomen of his native Scotland. They were embryonic small farmers and craftsmen, teachers and evangelists. After all, in Scotland did not an essentially tribal, warlike culture (or so it seemed to peace-loving Lowlanders) survive until the middle years of the eighteenth century, when it was ruthlessly cut down at Culloden and dismembered? And were not the sons of Culloden (at any rate, some of them) making their way in the new Scotland of the universities and the professions?[55] The mission station in the colonies was thus intended to become the seedbed of a new society, designed to replicate the metropolitan social order which the missionaries themselves represented.[56] Discipline, sobriety, literacy, 'respectability' (not least with regard to codes of dress, gender roles and family life) and, above all, material progress through hard work in the nexus of market relations: these were the means of getting ahead. Productive labour and consumption of European manufactures: these were the outward signs of inward virtue.

The missionaries were unquestioning of the absolute superiority of 'Christian civilisation' in both its spiritual and material dimensions. But they also believed implicitly in the capacity of indigenous peoples in the colonised world to adapt to their conception of both Christianity and civilisation. For individuals and societies were seen as infinitely malleable. It was a constant theme in missionary literature that the 'backward' races were the victims of their environment. This belief arose out of the Enlightenment view of humanity as being part of the natural world, instead of standing above it. Missionary ideology was specifically shaped by Scottish Enlightenment thinking on the organic, unilinear evolution of societies according to uniform laws of cultural development towards a common goal, of which European civilisation was the ultimate expression.[57] Although scientific racism was also a product of Enlightenment thought, mission ideology (contrary to scientific racism) held that all people belonged to the same order of humanity, and shared a natural propensity to embrace civilisation once they were brought to a state of divine revelation and self-realisation.

But if their potential was to be realised, indigenous people such as the Khoi had to enjoy the full rights of citizenship, on an equal footing with white colonists. This meant that barriers to knowledge, to mobility and freedom of contract, to landownership, the pursuit of trade, and the raising of capital, all had to be removed. In particular, the Khoi had to be protected from exploitation and coercion. Philip was a disciple of fellow-Kirkcaldian Adam Smith, and he believed in the efficacy of free trade and the abolition of all restraints on enterprise and personal advancement.[58] Such beliefs coloured Philip's attitudes towards colonial government. Hence he was to embrace a range of reformist causes at the Cape, and suffered the opprobrium that is the invariable lot of the crusader.

But Philip was no friend of radicalism, and was as staunch an upholder of the hegemony of class and property as any of his contemporaries. He was much concerned with maintaining proper relations between the 'respectable' and the common mass. When British settlers were being selected under the official scheme of assisted emigration in 1819, Philip warned that 'if they are the refuse of our manufacturing towns, dissipated Mechanics whose political principles have been acquired in the Schools of Sedition, those connected with their settlement will have little pleasure in the undertaking'. He urged that preference be given to the unspoilt rural classes, especially from the Scottish Highlands.[59]

These culture-bound attitudes also came in time to temper the initial enthusiasm of missionaries about the readiness of indigenous peoples for the Christian life. Moffat, based among the independent Tlhaping, became cynical about his charges when they proved highly resistant to his message; and even Philip was inclined to believe that the full transformation of the indigenous peoples might take generations. The 'unspoilt rural classes' of Africa turned out to be less malleable than missionary propaganda had assumed. Missionary optimism was eventually to wane, and the humanitarian moment in metropolitan life was in due course to be surpassed by other preoccupations.

On his arrival at the Cape, Philip was much occupied in turning the mission stations into model communities, in order to prove the fitness of the mission Khoi for absorption into the ranks of the colonial community as full citizens with full rights. In October 1821 he presented an improvement plan to the Khoi of Theopolis and Bethelsdorp. This required the destruction of the old reed-and-daub houses, and their replacement by stone houses built in rectangular pattern along straight streets surrounding a village square. As part of the plan, trading stores were to be established and 'artificial wants' inculcated. Inasmuch as physical reconstruction implied moral regeneration, Philip believed the external appearance of Christian Khoi communities was all-important in persuading observers, and public opinion in Britain, that the converts were economically and socially progressive, and thus worthy recipients of the full rights and privileges of citizens.[60]

Philip's first task on his arrival at the Cape was to restore good relations with the colonial authorities. Somerset initially tried to secure Philip's support for his policies across the frontiers.[61] Then Acting-Governor Donkin lifted the ban on new LMS missionaries working beyond colonial borders in 1820, after being persuaded by Philip of the utility of LMS missionaries in securing stability and peace. Indeed, for a couple of years, Philip was inclined to criticise his predecessors, Van der Kemp and Read.[62]

But the honeymoon with the Tory establishment that ruled the colony was not to last. In 1821, after a confrontation with Acting-Governor Donkin over a series of charges, originating from James Read at Bethelsdorp, that local officials were coercing Khoi labour, Philip took up the cause of the colony's Khoi working class. Although Donkin absolved landdrost Cuyler of Read's charges, Philip subsequently found documentary evidence of their veracity, convincing him that Read and others had in fact been justified in their charges against the colonists and the administration all along. 'The Hottentots are acknowledged to be a free people', wrote Philip in October 1822, 'but labour is every day becoming scarcer, and the colonists are resolved to indemnify themselves for the loss of the slave trade by reducing the Hottentots to a condition of slavery the most shocking and oppressive.'[63] After this episode Read and, later, his sons became close confidants and informants of Philip in all his campaigns.[64]

At the centre of the oppression and exploitation of the Khoi, Philip contended, was the system of passes. This severely restricted their rights of movement and rendered them liable to prosecution for vagrancy if caught passless; thereupon they could be contracted out to anyone at the whim of the local official. Further, the system of 'apprenticeship' of children was nothing other than a means of immobilising Khoi families. In general, Khoi were subjected to a system of forced labour. Philip realised that it was no longer enough to take up individual cases of mistreatment of Khoi workers by masters: the entire colonial system at the Cape had to be transformed.[65] In the process he was to antagonise the ruling elite at the Cape. Governor Somerset soon developed an extreme hostility towards Philip – a representative, after all, of the stirring classes, who took up causes for which Somerset had no sympathy at all.[66]

But Philip learned early on to exploit skilfully the increasingly powerful humanitarian network in London. Through the LMS and other friends in high places, not least at the Colonial Office and the Saints in parliament itself, he made sure he was heard on behalf of the colonial labouring classes. Already in 1822 Philip was telling the LMS in London that the question of native rights in South Africa would have to be thrust before the British parliament in order to get action taken. By June of the following year he reported: 'You will perceive that everything possible has been done by me to bring the Government to reason in order to avert this struggle. Nothing can now be of avail to save Africa but British statutes. I should be guilty of dereliction of duty if I quitted the subject till everything was done in my power to obtain emancipation for the wretched aborigines of South Africa.'[67]

Philip's sources of information were many and diverse. He became acquainted with the situation in the further reaches of the Cape Colony and beyond its borders better than just about any official in Cape Town. Not only was he an indefatigable traveller who personally came to know most political leaders of consequence in the colony and over its borders, but he received a steady stream of communications from mission stations scattered throughout the subcontinent.[68] Using this mass of evidence Philip appealed to the metropolitan humanitarian network to expose the plight of the Khoi. It was a particularly fruitful appeal, for it coincided with a new and more intense phase of abolitionist fervour in Britain, which took off from 1823.

The agitation on behalf of the colony's labouring poor greatly debased the image of the Boer colonist. The humanitarians sought to convince the Colonial Office that frontier Boers were cruel savages whose atrocities were responsible for the ills of colonial society. After all, were they not slave-owners? (British settlers were specifically disallowed from owning slaves.) Since labour relations and living conditions on Boer farms, even where formal slavery did not exist, fell far short of the idealised conditions of freedom regarded as essential for upliftment, Boers came to be portrayed as monstrous tyrants. British observers and travellers – Barrow (in 1799), Bruce, Bannister, Thompson and Pringle, for example – tended to exaggerate and generalise what they saw or heard, and painted a dark picture of Afrikanerdom as a whole. Philip's own *Researches in South Africa* of 1828 was a damning indictment of the Christian morality of the colonists.[69]

It needs to be said that Philip and the humanitarians were not dogmatically opposed to settlers. Indeed, Philip aligned himself strongly with the leading British settlers in the early 1820s in the battle against the 'old corruption' of Somerset's regime. He was, for example, active as chairman of the society for the relief of distressed settlers, established to help the immigrant gentry of 1820 who had been impoverished by the agricultural failures of their settlement in Albany. The society was vehemently opposed to Somerset, and the governor tried to undermine it at every turn. Many of the early settler gentry – Campbell, Moodie, Philipps – corresponded voluminously with Philip and his colleagues.[70] But by the late 1820s, relations between humanitarians and settlers had soured.

Philip considered that the interests of settlers should not be raised above those of other elements of colonial society. The colonisers, he asserted, had a special duty to protect and uplift the indigenous peoples. Anything which interfered with this sacred obligation, whether it be exploitative labour conditions or military predations, had to be vigorously opposed. So once the dynamics of their emergent society became apparent, the British settlers, too, came to be seen as obstacles to the humanitarian cause, to be opposed from every platform. Humanitarianism sought to blight at every point, not settler capitalism *per se*, but settler capitalism of an exploitative, coercive variety and settler accumulation that was predicated on subjugation and dispossession.

At the same time Philip and the humanitarians were forging alliances with Cape Town's expatriate mercantile bourgeoisie in the 1820s. Humanitarian and mercantile interests became closely intertwined in a broad-ranging campaign for the reform of colonial society. Humanitarianism held out a vision of material as well as moral advance through the substitution of free labour for the labour of the servile. In this view people encouraged to produce and consume as free individuals, motivated by moral imperatives and by the prospect of personal betterment, were in the long run not only better Christians but also more productive and hence more profitable for employers and for the commercial classes than those whose labour was owned or coerced by others.

Of course there is nothing homogeneous or static about merchant capital.

Mercantile enterprise was endlessly adaptable, being essentially parasitic on whatever productive system or dispensation offered opportunities for exchange and profit. In the 1810s and early 1820s a number of prominent Cape Town merchants such as J. B. Ebden invested heavily in the wine industry, in mortgage loans to wine farmers and in constructing wine-storage facilities. But the wine industry had limited long-term prospects and, as we have seen, wine declined from the mid-1820s as a viable export commodity, as did the slave economy on which it was based. Merchants who had invested in the wine industry found themselves caught in a vice between their indebtedness to London merchants and that of their farming clients. As Ebden said: 'unlike the general merchant who can go to his bales and dispose of them at the market price of the day, we are unfortunately tied up to property inconvertible to other purposes.'[71]

For the merchant class there were few attractions in the narrowly restrictive colonial economy of the mid-1820s. Somerset's alliance with the Dutch–Afrikaner notables was far too limited a base on which to develop a dynamic mercantile economy. It was with a degree of equanimity that many of the Cape Town bourgeoisie witnessed the decline of the slave-based agricultural economy of the southwestern Cape in the later 1820s, as the shallow and limited prosperity of the wine-export boom faded. Some, like Ebden, with substantial capital invested in the wine industry, suffered greatly; but their long-term interests had to lie elsewhere, as they no doubt knew.

At the same time as the wine industry was declining, the entrepreneurial instincts of the British settlers in the eastern Cape were opening up the Xhosa frontier and the hinterland of Port Natal as major fields of investment and profit. Out of this new enterprise – which spread into the further interior through both Boer and Griqua middlemen – a new accumulating British settler elite in the eastern Cape was born. Merchants in Cape Town must have seen a new Eden beyond the arable southwest.

For a time in the 1820s, a particular mercantile vision predominated – of free indigenous communities, generating ever-expanding markets for British produce. It moved beyond any narrow reliance on the colonial economy or exclusive alliance with colonial interests. For the colonial economy was fragile, underdeveloped and unpromising. But beyond settlerdom lay a great hinterland of potentially free producers and consumers, innocent of the archaic inhibitions of imported slavery and Khoi servitude. At this point mercantile interests and humanitarianism joined forces in agitating for the reform of colonial society – away from slavery and other forms of servility in labour relations, away from restrictions on trade and enterprise, away from autocracy and patronage in politics. Their ultimate goal was the overthrow of the old corruption of Somerset's regime as well as the alliance with Afrikaner notables on which it was built. Humanitarian struggles on behalf of the Khoi working class thus became, from the mid-1820s on, one element in a broad-based reform programme that was to shift the basis of legitimacy of the colonial regime.[72]

Imperial intervention on behalf of reform was made in the form of a commission of enquiry into the civil and judicial affairs of the Cape, Mauritius and Ceylon. This was approved by the British parliament in July 1822, at the same time as Philip and his friends were greatly intensifying the agitation for Khoi rights at the Cape.[73] In London leading free-trade colonial reformers were conscious of the need to liberalise internal economic relations and to 'anglicise' judicial and administrative systems in colonies of military conquest such as the Cape. To men of this persuasion autocratic government, superimposed on pre-existing and alien institutions, seemed inappropriate once these crown colonies had been confirmed as permanent possessions. Acquired for strategic reasons, they had to be turned into paying propositions by the stimulation of industry and enterprise. Central among the colonial reformers was R. Wilmot Horton, permanent under-secretary at the Colonial Office from December 1821 to January 1828. Horton was more of an architect of the new empire than was his political boss, Bathurst.[74] Another pivotal figure was William Huskisson, president of the Board of Trade and, later, in 1827–8, secretary for the colonies. He was the scourge of all protectionist restrictions and impediments to free trade.

The crown commissioners appointed in 1822 to undertake the enquiry were to investigate not only the civil and legal affairs of the Cape, but also the conditions of the slave and Khoi populations. These groups were included in the enquiry as a result of the intervention of William Wilberforce, who argued that one part of the population (the colonists) could not be liberated from archaic restrictions while others remained enslaved. The commissioners, J. T. Bigge (chief justice of Trinidad) and Major W. M. G. Colebrooke (an Indian army officer, later to serve as governor of various West Indian islands), arrived in Cape Town in mid-1823, but did not submit their initial report until 1826, and their final report until 1831.[75] They were thus in Cape Town at the same time as the local battle was joined against the Somerset regime. External and internal pressures for reform were converging. At the centre of the reformist alliance in Cape Town in the 1820s was of course the commanding figure of John Philip, who busied himself marshalling facts and opinions, drawing up 'memorials' for the commissioners, and courting their favour. He organised visits for them to mission stations in order to propagate these communities as models of what could be achieved by liberal and humane policies, stepping up his plans for reconstructing mission villages along rational planning lines for the commissioners' benefit. He even persuaded a visiting judge from Ceylon, Sir Richard Ottley, to draw up a plan for a revamped judicial system for the Cape.[76]

A focal point of the local struggle against gubernatorial autocracy was the campaign for press freedom and freedom of expression and dissent generally. An important early figure in this struggle was Thomas Pringle, leader of a party of Scottish Presbyterians who came out with the 1820 settlers and were settled on the Baviaans River east of the Fish (modern-day Bedford district), north of the main body of immigrants. But Pringle was very atypical of the bulk of the settlers, not only in terms of religious affiliation. For he threw in his lot with the humanitarian cause, becoming by the late 1820s distinctly anti-settler, like all the humanitarians. A man of letters, he had practised as a journalist in Edinburgh's golden age of intellectual flowering – he had been co-editor of the literary *Blackwood's Magazine* – and wrote poetry of a romantic and epic kind. He also brought with him a letter of commendation from his friend Sir Walter Scott. He was undoubtedly a child of the Scottish Enlightenment. In September 1822, Pringle moved to Cape Town where he hoped to follow a career in journalism and education. There he got a job in the public library, and launched a small school. He then invited his friend John Fairbairn (they had been students at Edinburgh together) to join him in his undertakings at the Cape – not least in the launching of a local newspaper.[77]

Fairbairn was of a typical Scottish Presbyterian background, coming from a Berwickshire weaving family. He had started studying medicine in Edinburgh before being diverted by his literary preoccupations, and then took up a post in Newcastle where he taught classics. He contributed translations to *Blackwood's* and gave lectures on literary topics to the Newcastle Literary and Philosophical Society. He sailed for Cape Town in June 1823, persuaded that the colonial environment provided virgin territory for the practice of literary journalism and educational enterprise.[78]

Pringle and Fairbairn are honoured in the pantheon of liberal heroes as the fathers of the free press in South Africa. Indeed, they faced severe obstacles from the proconsular despotism of Somerset's regime in their enterprises. When Pringle first approached the government to start a newspaper in Cape Town, Somerset refused permission on the grounds that it would become 'an active and uncontradicted Engine directed against our Civil and political Establishments and most probably particularly against the Established Church'. Pringle, charged Somerset, was an 'arrant Dissenter'.[79] The only thing approaching a newspaper in the colony was the *Cape Town Gazette*, an official publication containing chiefly government notices and official advertisements.

In December 1823 Pringle and Fairbairn managed eventually to gain the governor's permission to publish a quarterly journal, provided it contained no references to matters of political or personal controversy. But by mid-1824, after two issues, it had ceased publication, after the fiscal had warned the editors that any more articles on the condition of the 1820 settlement in the eastern Cape would not be tolerated. Pringle and Fairbairn also accepted the joint editorship of the *South African Commercial Advertiser*, a paper started by George Greig, a printer, under the same restrictive conditions. But that enterprise also ended precipitately when in May 1824 Somerset ordered the press to be sealed and Greig to be banished from the colony, following publication of court proceedings which embarrassed the governor. Even Pringle's humble academy was denounced by Somerset as a 'seminary of sedition', where the 'most disgusting principles of Republicanism' were espoused. The governor even went so far as to refuse permission to the two intrepids to found a scientific and literary society. He wrote to Bathurst in London that Philip himself was 'the real writer for that seditious Press', and demanded that he be removed, denouncing 'Scotch Independents' who dabbled in politics.[80]

But Somerset's increasingly anachronistic autocracy was now seen in London as counterproductive and inappropriate, and his days were numbered. He was informed in no uncertain fashion that he had overstepped his authority. The *Commercial Advertiser* recommenced publication in 1825, but lived a precarious existence, again closing down for a few months from April 1827, until in 1829 an ordinance was enacted which finally secured the freedom of the press. In general, the rise of a colonial press ushered in a new era of public discourse in colonial society, unknown in the closed society that had prevailed before. Not only did newspapers begin in Cape Town and then further afield such as in Graham's Town, Port Elizabeth and Graaff-Reinet from this time on, but public life was increasingly characterised by the regular publication of polemical pamphlets on the major issues of the day, and not a small degree of litigiousness.[81]

Pringle remained in South Africa only until 1826, but on his return to Britain he continued to exercise an influence on South African affairs (on the commendation of John Philip) as secretary of the Anti-Slavery Society – so much so that settlers of the eastern Cape in the mid-1830s were still angrily accusing him (after his early death in 1834) of being responsible for fuelling Xhosa aggressions against them by his philanthropic agitations.[82] In the meantime Scottish teachers and ministers continued to arrive, many of them kindling the humanitarian impulse. As children of Scotland's intellectual golden age, these men saw education as fundamental to the spread of Christian civilisation. As early as 1821 Philip envisaged the establishment of a college in Cape Town for the local training of teachers and preachers, and Pringle started his school a couple of years later. In 1829 the South African College, forerunner of the University of Cape Town, was established, although at first it was little more than a high school. It was a monument to the humanitarian–mercantile alliance that dominated Cape Town politics at the time – although it is indicative of the fundamentally conservative nature of that alliance that people of colour were not regarded as yet ready for admission.[83]

Fairbairn, now sole editor of the *Commercial Advertiser*, became firmly entrenched as the chief propagandist for the humanitarian–mercantile lobby. He crystallised their cause when he wrote: 'To stimulate Industry, to encourage Civilisation, and convert the hostile Natives into friendly Customers, is ... a more profitable speculation than to exterminate or reduce them to Slavery.'[84] Indeed, the *Advertiser* continued to be the chief organ of Cape Town mercantile interests until Fairbairn's death in 1859, altering its stance as the interests of the mercantile lobby shifted. The big merchants enthusiastically backed the struggle to secure a free press, and men like Ewan Christian, C. S. Pillans and

A. Chiappini featured in a petition of 1824 protesting against the closure of the *Advertiser*. In 1827 Fairbairn was made an honorary member of the Commercial Exchange.[85]

From the start the *Advertiser* reflected the limitations and contradictions of the humanitarian liberalism of the 1820s, particularly the uneasy coexistence of philanthropic and more overtly utilitarian thinking. Fairbairn was an enthusiastic proponent of the unity of colonists, Afrikaner and British, and of the granting to them of representative institutions (although ideas of building solidarity between British and Afrikaner colonists and the granting of such institutions must have seemed very unrealistic in the 1820s and early 1830s, when reformist initiatives profoundly alienated the old Dutch–Afrikaner elite).[86] While he remained through the 1820s and 1830s a firm adherent of the humanitarian position on the legal rights of the colony's underclasses and the rights of independent African chiefdoms beyond colonial borders (even when these causes were deeply unpopular among colonists), Fairbairn was also a firm proponent of colonial economic development, a process which was predicated on securing a disciplined and orderly labour force. At the same time as preaching the humanitarian gospel of the assimilability and malleability of indigenous peoples, Fairbairn was also very concerned in his columns to depict a civilised colonial realm separate from the barbarism surrounding it. Although the prospect of incorporating the underclasses into the ranks of civilised Christian society was always held out as fundamental to the imperial mission, simultaneously there was also an exclusivity (not least racial) about the way in which colonial bourgeois identity was constructed.[87]

This colonial society included the older Dutch–Afrikaner colonists, provided they embraced bourgeois values of free enterprise, free trade and free labour. But the underclasses, the potential recipients of Christian civilisation and candidates for eventual inclusion in the ranks of the respectable, were also a source of threat and defilement, against which bourgeois society defined itself. This tension in fact pervaded the entire post-1815 humanitarian enterprise, riddled as it was with assumptions about respectability and cultural superiority. The contradictions were resolved only when in the 1840s Fairbairn finally broke his rhetorical allegiance to the humanitarianism of the 1820s and accepted the colonial wisdom that the underclasses were largely irredeemable and that a level of coercion was necessary in dealing with them, either as labourers or as neighbouring societies. By then it had become abundantly clear that mercantile profit and development were to be powered by a colonial capitalism that required an ongoing measure of racial subjugation and control. As pessimism about the indigenous and servile people set in, so the purely utilitarian strand in the liberal reformist thinking of the 1820s took over.

However, in the 1820s, humanitarian and mercantile concerns seemed perfectly compatible, as both were preoccupied with the dismantling of the old order, based on monopoly and patronage, coercion and unfreedom. The reformist alliance between mercantile and humanitarian forces was apparent, for example, in the struggle against remaining restrictions on freedom of trade, not least of which was the East India Company's monopoly on the China trade in tea. In 1825 the prominent Cape Town firm of Borradaile, Thompson & Pillans, with advice from the Cape of Good Hope Trade Society (whose chairman was the London partner of the firm), ordered a cargo of tea, bought at the East India Company's London auctions. Borradaile's opinion was that the reshipment was not a transgression of provisions of the company's charter. But when the tea arrived in Table Bay in January 1827 aboard the *Kerswell*, the customs department impounded it in defence of the company's trade privileges. There followed a sustained campaign, led by the Commercial Exchange and Fairbairn's *Advertiser* in Cape Town and the Trade Society in London, and Acting-Governor Bourke eventually intervened to allow the tea to be sold.[88] The *Kerswell* test case went some way towards undermining the company's prerogatives. This episode and the larger struggle against company monopoly were marked by the mobilisation of liberal opinion at the Cape. Fairbairn's paper played a central role as the local conduit of liberal agitation. Further mass meetings and petitions on the issue of the company's outmoded privileges were organised by the Commercial Exchange and fully reported in the *Advertiser*.[89] The noises coming from Cape Town were hardly likely alone to move government in London; but the company's charter was nonetheless eventually abrogated in 1834, as an anachronism in an era of growing free trade.[90]

Somerset's deportation in 1824 of George Greig, printer of the *Commercial Advertiser*, scandalised reformers in Britain. In consequence, in May 1825 the Council of Advice was established at the Cape, a toothless body of officials, but nonetheless the first attempt to temper autocracy with some degree of corporate responsibility.[91] The discredited Somerset's recall was delayed by the overbearing influence of the 'Beaufort interest' in the unreformed British parliament. However, he left the Cape in March 1826 on leave, not to return. Yet it was only in 1827, once the Liverpool government had been replaced by Canning's Whig administration after twelve years in office, that his tenure was finally ended, concluding what Fairbairn called that 'consummation of earthly ills – the Government of Lord Charles Somerset in South Africa'.[92] Somerset's very different successor was General Sir Richard Bourke, a Whig reformer, whose role at the Cape has been much underestimated, in part because he remained acting governor from 1826 until his departure for New South Wales late in 1828. Bourke oversaw many of the fundamental reforms of the time, deriving in part from directives of the Colonial Office based on the recommendations of the crown commissioners, in part from his own initiatives in the Council of Advice. In all his endeavours, Bourke was zealously supported by the liberal government secretary in Cape Town, Sir Richard Plasket.[93]

It was in 1827–8 that these various initiatives really bore fruit. There was no corner of Cape society that did not feel the waves of reform. First, the commissioners were concerned to stimulate productivity and enterprise, and hence to promote trade and increase the size of the Cape market. All restraints on free economic activity had to be stripped away. In 1826 Bourke opened Port Elizabeth and other ports to import–export traffic, dismantling Cape Town's monopoly of commercial contact with the outside world. Then all remaining monopolies (those of the butchers, bakers, wine traders and vendue masters), *pachts* (licences) and special concessions, dating back to VOC days, were done away with in 1827 and 1828. The Vendue Department was replaced by private auctioneers. Local *opgaaf* taxes and tithes on produce were abolished, and better communications and postal services were planned. What these measures aimed at was dismantling all restrictions that inhibited economic demand, prevented the growth of the internal market and drove up prices of provisions in country areas.[94] Further, in 1828 the Cape Land Board was established, and the first qualified land surveyors were appointed. These attempts at improving the land tenure system were the first since Governor Cradock's reforms of 1813.[95]

Judicial reform was the most important measure to flow from the labours of the crown commissioners. The Charter of Justice that came into force on 1 January 1828 established an independent bench with a chief justice, free from the domineering control of the governor. The reforms, which followed the lines of Ottley's report in 1823, included the introduction of a jury system (although Ottley's recommendation that juries should not preside over cases in which black and white confronted one other was ignored). Judges in future were to be appointed from the British bar, and the governor lost his role as final court of appeal. The fiscal was replaced by an attorney-general appointed in London. English was for the first time introduced as the language of the courts – inevitably so, given the fact that the old Dutch–Afrikaner ruling class was being displaced by properly qualified professional jurists. This also meant that proficiency in English was a prerequisite of jury service. The English common law was introduced, to operate side by side with the older Roman–Dutch law. The more important senior civil appointments now became the prerogative of the crown rather than the governor. Civil servants could no longer hold other posts simultaneously, and could not profit from their offices, for example by demanding fees for their official services or for the granting of licences or concessions.[96]

The deeper significance of these reforms was that the class of Afrikaner notables was being ejected as the essential pillar of support of the colonial regime. Initially the British administration had been constructed on the foundations of pre-existing institutions, administrative and judicial. Now in 1828 the fiscal and the old colonial judges were being ousted by British-appointed and legally trained officers, and at a local level landdrosts and *heemraden* were being replaced with resident magistrates and civil commissioners.[97] (In practice, though, the splitting of judicial and administrative functions was not implemented because of expense, and the posts of magistrate and civil commissioner were usually filled by one and the same man.) What this all meant was that Boer notables, prominent farmers and community leaders lost their pivotal and often arbitrary role in local judicial administration, the raising of revenue, the disposal of land, and the disposition of labour. On the whole, Boers were not regarded in a flattering light by the commissioners, who referred to them as indolent and unenterprising. They suggested that a tax be levied on servants and slaves in order to counteract what they saw as Boer sloth, and force them to become more industrious and less dependent on servile labour. These radical tax proposals (10 shillings per head) evoked a storm of protest and were not implemented.[98]

In pursuit of a more productive and enterprising economy, the commissioners also supported calls for the removal of all legal disabilities and restraints on the Khoi, although here other forces at work at the Cape and in England were more important than the labours of the commissioners. (In any event they were divided on the issue and did not produce a report until 1830.) The very lack of urgency in the commissioners' deliberations on the matter caused Philip and his colleagues to chafe. For the condition of the colony's Khoi working class was the cause closest to their hearts. In the view of the Cape humanitarians, the question of slavery could safely be left to the now rampant abolitionist movement in Britain, and needed no extra agitations from the Cape. But in Britain the fate of the Khoi might easily be ignored in the larger picture of the anti-slavery movement. So by 1825, while the crown commissioners were still involved in their investigations at the Cape, Philip was ready to make good his promise to carry the cause to Britain. In May he set out on another extended tour of the mission stations to gather information and evidence with which he would persuade the British government to put 'the aborigines ... upon the same footing as Europeans with respect to law and privilege'. On his arrival in England in early 1826, he intended to 'lay before Lord Bathurst numerous and large documents, and, if that fails, shall instantly and on my own responsibility lay the whole before the British public'.[99]

Clearly, Philip's presence in London was an important catalyst in bringing the issue of Khoi rights to a head. He campaigned ceaselessly, with the aid of anti-slavery forces in parliament (notably T. F. Buxton, Wilberforce's political heir), to ensure that the condition of the Khoi should not be overlooked. In the Colonial Office, Philip had the strategically important support of James Stephen.[100] Apart from a busy schedule of meetings, Philip also set about writing an extended polemic, *Researches in South Africa*, which was eventually published in April 1828. This book asserted the beneficial effects civil equality and liberty would have on good order and mercantile profit in the British empire. In it Philip traced the historical origins of the dispossession and degradation of the Khoi to the seventeenth century. Like Barrow and others before him, Philip challenged the traditional derogatory stereotypes of Khoi society held by the colonists and earlier writers. But at the same time he tended to fall back on the conventional imagery of barbarism when comparing the precolonial Khoi with the converts of the mission stations. This ambivalence, common in humanitarian ethnography, grew out of the perceived need to protect the Khoi from the oppressive and corrupt dominion of the colonists on the one hand, while promoting the urgent task of redemption and reclamation confronting the missions, on the other.[101] Although Philip's book has become a symbol to colonial apologists of virulent anti-Boer propaganda, the ultimate target of his invective was the colonial legal system. But, despite his fierce opposition to the autocratic and archaic system he had encountered at the Cape, Philip revealed himself in the *Researches* as unashamedly pro-imperialist in his conviction of the ultimate beneficence of British rule.[102]

Action had been delayed by the political changes taking place in 1827 with the fall of the Liverpool administration. But after meeting with Philip in late 1827, the reformer William Huskisson, now colonial secretary, issued orders to Acting-Governor Bourke in Cape Town to take the matter of native rights in hand. At a time when the abolitionist movement held the commanding heights of public opinion, the legal status of 'free' coloured persons in the empire was a potentially embarrassing issue. In July 1828, therefore, the Wellington cabinet, aware of the publicity evoked by Philip and his book, supported a motion in parliament, drawn up by Philip and Buxton, requesting that the Cape government be sent instructions to secure the same 'freedom and protection' to the natives as those enjoyed by the white colonists. But this proved redundant, as two days after the parliamentary motion was passed, Bourke at the Cape introduced Ordinance 50.[103]

In response to Huskisson's directive, Bourke had asked Andries Stockenström, erstwhile landdrost at Graaff-Reinet and now commissioner-general for the eastern districts, to draw up a 'report on Hottentot conditions' in early 1828. This outlined the basic principles of what became Ordinance 50 of 1828. John Philip had kept in contact with Stockenström from his earliest foray into the interior in 1819 (when Stockenström was landdrost in Graaff-Reinet) and had clearly found (after much initial suspicion) that they shared common ground on the question of Khoi rights. The foundations for such a law as Ordinance 50 had perhaps already been laid in these communications between the two men before Philip's departure for England. Bourke was himself very receptive to suggestions on the issue, having been primed by the LMS before taking up his post in Cape Town in 1826. And the commissioners Bigge and Colebrooke had expressed themselves forcefully on the subject of legal constraints on free labour. Thus it was at the Cape that Ordinance 50 of 1828 was drawn up and promulgated.[104] Philip's purpose in London reached its ultimate fruition with the ratification of Ordinance 50 by the British parliament in January 1829. This contained the additional clause, fundamentally important to Philip, that the Cape government could not repeal or amend the ordinance without the express sanction of the King-in-Council.

The ordinance disposed of all pass laws and statutory criminalisation of 'vagrancy', prohibited summary punishment without benefit of trial, and abolished all forms of compulsory service (such as labour demanded by magistrates of mission residents). It affirmed the right of Khoi to buy or own land in the colony. All contracts of service were to be freely entered into by mutual consent. Oral contracts could only hold from month to month; and written contracts (very much the exception) could not last for more than twelve months, and had to be registered before an appropriate authority. Children could not be indentured without parental consent. The duties of the children of a labourer were to be separately specified in any contract, and spouses had to enter separate contracts. Ordinance 50 was thus a wide-ranging measure, whose only defect in the eyes of Philip was that it applied to 'Hottentots and other free persons of colour', instead of being colour-blind.[105]

The ordinance has generally been seen by historians as one of those defining moments in South African history: to some the culmination of missionary meddling in the natural relations between black and white; to others the foundation stone of a proud tradition of liberalism which was to last into the twentieth century, until it was finally overwhelmed by the alternative tradition of the frontier. In general, in both colonial and liberal traditions, the significance of the ordinance has been exaggerated.[106] Particularly in colonial contexts where the colonial state on the local level was weak, there must be severe doubts about the practical efficacy of such statutory interventions in rural social and economic relations. Nevertheless, the ordinance did represent, on paper at least, a kind of charter of rights for the colony's Khoi working class.

The effort on the part of metropolitan and missionary forces to liberalise the legal status of the Khoi working class did not derive in the first instance from any consideration of labour supply in any direct, functional sense – contrary to one influential analysis.[107] Those in charge of the colonial state in 1828, in London and in Cape Town, and those most influential in formulating colonial policy, had their own humanitarian–mercantile visions of reconstructing the colonial economy: they did not place the labour requirements of unprofitable settler farmers at the centre of their concerns. For in the commissioners' words, the whole colonial system of tied and coerced labour gave rise to 'indolence and indifference', and the entire edifice had to be replaced if industry, enterprise and productivity were to take off. Certainly Governor Somerset, tied by links of patronage to the Afrikaner elite, had been closely concerned with questions of labour supply and control, more specifically as they touched the slave economy of the arable southwest. But such considerations faded somewhat under the reformist impulses that arose out of the demise of his regime.[108]

Nevertheless, Stockenström, who played an important role in formulating the ordinance, was not unaware of the labour needs of colonists, nor was he unsympathetic. Ordinance 50 did in fact coincide with a growing awareness by some colonial officials in the interior districts that the old coercions tended to be counterproductive and likely to intensify resistance and conflict. Stockenström was very aware of the history of resistance among Khoi and the need to remove the potential for class antagonism implicit in relations between Khoi and colonists – particularly in light of the history of, and potential for, Khoi–Xhosa alliance against the colony. The rebellion of 1799–1803 was still a formative memory. Stockenström was also influenced by the utilitarian arguments of the wider anti-slavery movement, and saw eye to eye with the reformist view of the need for incentive and reward in increasing the productivity of labour. So, in the eyes of a colonial official close to the ground such as Stockenström, Ordinance 50 was not unrelated to issues of labour needs.

Labour needs were more directly addressed in Ordinance 49, introduced by Bourke at the same time as Ordinance 50.[109] Ordinance 49 provided for the entry of Bantu-speaking African people into the colony to seek labour, provided they took out passes for the purpose. Ordinance 49 in a sense was an acknowledgement of a *fait accompli*: refugees from the warfare of the further interior to the north (the 'Mantatees') had been entering the colony since about 1825, and had been permitted by Somerset to enter the service of colonial farmers. It was Somerset who in 1826 had suggested to the Colonial Office that the policy of non-intercourse with Africans beyond the colony be abandoned. Clearly, on inland pastoral farms African herders, with or without families, content to be paid in livestock (or guns), were a boon to many farmers.[110]

When asked originally for his opinion on allowing Africans to enter the colony to seek work, Stockenström had advised that they should be obliged to find employment 'on pain of being taken up and severely punished as vagabonds if they go about or collect in gangs'.[111] In consequence, while Ordinance 49 (like Ordinance 50) stipulated that verbal contracts were only valid from month to month, indenture of children was disallowed, and wages could not be withheld, it also laid down (unlike Ordinance 50) that Africans from across colonial borders seeking work were not allowed to move about without passes.[112] Similarly, in formulating the provisions of Ordinance 50, Stockenström had intended that a vagrancy ordinance should accompany it, providing for the carrying of passes by Khoi. All in all, Stockenström envisaged the two ordinances, 49 and 50, as being of a kind in seeking to secure a market in labour which avoided the outward appearance of coercion, while minimising disruption for employers by providing statutory controls over the mobility of workers. Stockenström was a utilitarian liberal who saw anti-vagrancy legislation as in the best interests of the Khoi as well as their masters. For humanitarians like Philip, however, any form of legislative coercion or constraint robbed labour of its morally uplifting qualities.[113]

Most colonists considered Ordinance 50 to be the work of the devil. When Philip returned to the Cape in September 1829 he discovered that his agitations in Britain had turned him into an ogre in the eyes of the colonists generally.[114] To the Afrikaners in particular he had become a symbol of the whole humanitarian movement, which had systematically stripped them of access to the patronage of public office, threatened to undermine their authority as a master class, and held them up to the calumny of the world. Disaffection over Ordinance 50 was intense. These sentiments were broadly represented in *De Zuid-Afrikaan*. This Dutch-language newspaper, launched in Cape Town in 1830, sought to counteract what it saw as the pernicious influence of the humanitarian-oriented *Commercial Advertiser* of John Fairbairn. *De Zuid-Afrikaan* represented in part a Dutch–Afrikaner bourgeoisie, many with commercial and business interests, but with few direct ties to Britain. They were attuned to the feelings of the mass of older colonists, sympathetic to their sentiments on race and class relations, resentful of the more established British mercantile elite, and increasingly antagonistic to its humanitarian inclinations.

Having cheerfully collaborated with the sympathetic Tory regime of Somerset, Afrikaner colonists were now embittered at having been jettisoned by the reform movement, under the auspices of the mercantile–humanitarian lobby. The role of Afrikaner notables as the agents and allies of the Somerset autocracy was being removed. The only people in South Africa who regretted Somerset's departure were the Afrikaners, specifically the more substantial among them. The seeds had been sown for the great movement of mass emigration of the mid-1830s known as the Great Trek.

The British settlers of the eastern Cape, in the process of throwing up their own bourgeoisie on the basis of trade and speculation, were also deeply alienated by humanitarian agitations and by Ordinance 50. When Philip and Fairbairn, his future son-in-law, travelled through the eastern districts from January to June 1830, they were inundated by complaints (a 'panic' Philip called it) of desertion, vagrancy, insolence and disobedience, theft and banditry, on the part of Khoi servants, as a direct result of Ordinance 50. Fairbairn took it upon himself to summon Graham's Town employers to answer charges of non-payment of wages, and 'by a curious coincidence', reported Philip, 'among those who were condemned for injustice to the Hottentots were some of the inhabitants of Grahamstown who had taken the most active part in promoting the panic that has been described'.[115] For many years the issue of Khoi rights continued to demand attention, as colonists pushed for a vagrancy law which would to some extent counteract the evils they perceived as flowing from Ordinance 50. But by the mid-1830s, when war on the eastern frontier had erupted, the question of relations with the Xhosa chiefdoms, whose land and labour the British settlers increasingly coveted, was what came to distinguish the latter most sharply from the humanitarians.

As the settler economy developed from the 1830s, and as Cape Town capital became more and more bound up with it, the mercantile–humanitarian comity was broken. Fairbairn's commitments continued to be riddled with ambiguity. Then in the 1840s he was finally to follow the general mercantile stampede in favour of aggressive and expansionist policies towards the Xhosa, and broke with the policies and ideals of his father-in-law. In general, mercantile interests, Janus-faced as ever, were increasingly to throw in their lot with white colonists in pursuit of a racially repressive order. In the process, the ambiguities at the heart of the humanitarian movement itself were also revealed. For Fairbairn's later commitments were not inconsistent with his earlier adherence to humanitarian prescriptions. After all, acculturation and incorporation of the native peoples as a dependent class was always the humanitarian vision, and if that could not be achieved by moral suasion, then conquest and dismemberment of African societies might be presented as logical alternative means to the same end.[116] But in the 1820s all that lay in the future.

There remained one last issue of the greatest concern to humanitarians that had not yet been resolved: the question of slavery. Uncharacteristically, John Philip and his colleagues at the Cape were relatively silent on the issue. It was an issue that was not greatly influenced by forces specific to the Cape Colony itself, and did not require agitations from the Cape to keep it on the boil in British political life. Indeed, the issue of slavery at the Cape in these years was decided by struggles focused on Caribbean sugar-plantation regimes and the battle against slave-owning legislatures there. These West Indian colonies of settlement dated back to the older eighteenth-century British empire, and had their own legislative assemblies, not to mention a strong West Indian party in the British parliament. The Cape was a newer colony of conquest, without any institutional means of defence against gubernatorial decree or imperial orders-in-council, which did not require any approval or sanction by the British parliament. Especially after Somerset's obstructionism had been removed, the Cape had imposed on it regulations and laws relating to slavery designed primarily for West Indian slave systems.[117]

Abolition of the slave trade in 1808 had had a twofold purpose: to end British complicity in the capture and transport of human beings, and to force slave-owners, now reliant on natural increase, to improve the conditions of their slaves' lives. But by the early 1820s when the anti-slavery agitation revived, it had become clear that the lives of slaves had by no means improved. In January 1823 the Anti-Slavery Society was established in London, represented by powerful voices in parliament. In the same year a slave rebellion in Demerara (Guiana) jolted public opinion in Britain. Thus in May 1823 it was decided by parliamentary resolution that slavery must be brought to an end, but that this could not happen quickly. Slaves had to be made fit for freedom through a gradual process of amelioration imposed by metropolitan edict as far as possible. Already several months before the parliamentary resolution in London, Somerset's toothless and placatory proclamation had been issued in Cape Town. Somerset had been spurred by the Commons debate on Cape affairs the previous July and the subsequent appointment of the commission of enquiry, to pre-empt the kind of Colonial Office intervention that was already being proposed for Trinidad. Bathurst at the Colonial Office regretted Somerset's proclamation, and Philip concluded that it would in no significant way benefit the slaves.[118]

From 1825 on, the Colonial Office became unashamedly interventionist, demanding of Somerset that he adopt an ordinance along the lines of the

Trinidad one. His successor, Bourke, who was more sympathetic to the anti-slavery cause, complied by enacting Ordinance 19 of 1826. It caused uproar.[119] The previous year a slave insurrection had taken place, and Somerset had just left the Cape with a flood of warm valedictory petitions following in his wake from Afrikaner beneficiaries of his rule. Landdrosts, often slave-owners themselves and disturbed by the waves of reform that were washing around them, refused to implement the ordinance. But the outrage of Cape slave-owners was hardly a significant constraint on Colonial Office meddling in their domestic relationships. At this time the moving forces at the Colonial Office were men like James Stephen whose immediate concern was to prepare slaves for a role as a free, albeit subservient, labour force. Promoting a work ethic and a stable, Christian family life among the slaves was their purpose: the intention never was to upset the hierarchical order of things. They were committed to maintaining a proper sense of authority and to securing the long-term acquiescence and productivity of colonial labour. Thus the British were caught between the dictates of their free-labour ideology and the need to subordinate and control workers. Little wonder that ameliorative measures had unintended consequences.[120]

Colonial Office interventions sought to regulate work routines and to limit physical punishment, encourage religious instruction, facilitate Christian marriage and prohibit the separation of children under 10 from their mothers, extend the legal rights of slaves, allow slaves to own property, and mandate manumissions if slaves could come up with a fair purchase price. Intervention took the most visible form in the person of the slave guardian or slave protector (his name changed over time) and his assistants in district towns. They were given increasingly extensive powers, including (from 1830) overseeing a system of punishment record books, which had to be presented twice a year for inspection. In February 1830 and November 1831, by which time the emancipation movement was becoming more radicalised, the Colonial Office simply bypassed the colonial authorities with orders-in-council enforcing and extending the rights of slaves. At the Cape Governor Cole, who was no abolitionist, responded that such interventions made 'that species of property [slaves] worse than useless'.[121] He was not entirely wrong. The absolute authority of masters, the only basis on which a slave regime could be maintained, was being undermined by the existence of countervailing and inherently antagonistic authority, which undercut masters' pretensions that they were the sole source of protection, indulgence and discipline for their slaves. Such edicts directly challenged the patriarchal ideology which was the mainstay of their entire social edifice.[122]

The slave guardians or protectors were hardly the friends of the slaves. But the regulations they had to implement – and the people in London they were answerable to – ensured that they would have a very unsettling influence, as far as the slave-owners were concerned. The slaves were increasingly aware that they had legal rights, and that there were channels available to secure them. They were encouraged to take their complaints to the guardian, and were entitled to provide witnesses if that person felt it proper to take the case before the magistrate. Although slaves were not slow to use the presence of the guardians to threaten their owners, only a small proportion of complaints reached the courts. The significance of the system lay in fact elsewhere. The masters of the time complained bitterly of their slaves' growing insolence and disobedience. Historians have also noted a decline in 'slavishness' and deference. Slaves used the law to improve their physical conditions of life and to protect themselves from physical abuse, as well as to keep their families together and to win their freedom by demanding the right of self-purchase.[123] These challenges to the moral hegemony of masters coincided with the depression in the slave economy of the Cape's southwestern districts from the mid-1820s.

Amelioration measures also had a direct effect on the viability of urban slavery in Cape Town itself. In fact urban slavery was disintegrating, a process that had begun long before the amelioration policy was instituted.[124] As the urban economy became more diverse and complex, requiring a more flexible and skilled labour force, there was a considerable shift away from reliance on slave labour to wage labour. Slaves were replaced by free blacks and European apprentices, and increasingly began working alongside free labourers as hirelings, earning similar wages. In terms of economic function, they became indistinguishable from the rest of the working class. Many slaves, particularly skilled artisans, were free to find employment for themselves upon payment of a proportion of their income to their owners. It was common for them as well to rent property and establish their own independent living arrangements.[125]

Under such conditions, owner surveillance was impossible and it became more and more difficult to maintain control over the urban slave population, now increasingly creolised (Cape-born) after the abolition of importation, and immersed in the working-class sub-culture of the city. In work and in leisure, slaves and free rubbed shoulders and shared space. A cosmopolitan urban society was emerging in which the slaves were only one strand in a diverse working class. In this subaltern community, which grew increasingly autonomous and assertive, socially and culturally, Islam was an important force, uniting free blacks, urban slaves and other elements.[126]

Slave amelioration measures were a decisive solvent of the institution of urban slavery. From the later 1820s the guardians processed one or two hundred manumissions annually (90 per cent of which were in Cape Town): perhaps most of these would not have occurred had it not been for the provisions of the law of 1826. Freedom had to be bought. Skilled tradespeople often could pay their owners off by instalment; others (more commonly) had free friends or relations who could give or loan the necessary money. Free men thus bought freedom for their slave wives and children.[127] Moreover, some slave-owners were only too willing to sell their slaves their freedom, as slavery for many owners seemed no longer economic. Some slaves were sold or hired out to the arable farmers, increasingly hungry for labour. In the urban context, therefore, the legal status of slavery was increasingly anachronistic.[128]

As slavery in both rural and urban areas became less and less profitable, relations between colonial reformers and the Afrikaner slave-owning elite continued to deteriorate. By the 1830s, throughout the empire, earlier optimistic projections of a peaceful and evolutionary path to emancipation were being undermined by slave-owner resistance, slave rebelliousness, and the failure of amelioration measures to improve the lot of slaves. As a result anti-slavery rhetoric hardened in Britain, and immediate emancipation came to the fore as the goal of the humanitarian lobby.[129] Then, as imperial intervention became more intrusive in 1830 and 1831, slave-owner resistance intensified. At the Cape, slave-owners refused to comply with the system of punishment record books. This led to brief outbreaks of violence in Stellenbosch in April 1831, with the local magistrate tacitly siding with the rebels.[130] In 1832 Cole introduced an ordinance imposing sentences of four months' imprisonment on anybody participating in meetings which excited agitation against the law of the land. In early 1833 at least half the slaveholders in the colony signed a petition calling for the repeal of the latest order-in-council.[131] The close social relationships established in earlier years between Afrikaner and British elites in and around Cape Town had broken up into mutual hostility.

Such disaffection was represented in the pages of *De Zuid-Afrikaan*. This Dutch-language paper, committed to furthering colonists' interests, first appeared in 1830, having been founded by a syndicate of some eighty prominent Afrikaner citizens. Many of the Dutch–Afrikaner intelligentsia of the Cape – attorneys, ministers, doctors – had been trained at Dutch universities, where a conservative, anti-revolutionary Protestantism prevailed, in reaction against French domination, and where anti-slavery had the aura of a suspect foreign ideology.[132] One prominent member of this group was Christoffel Brand, a Cape Town lawyer, who played a particularly important role in shaping *De Zuid-Afrikaan*'s political character, being responsible for many of its editorials. Brand was the son of J. H. Brand, a member of the early Court of Justice and a deeply pro-British loyalist. Christoffel was educated in law at Leiden in Holland, and became an advocate in Cape Town in 1821.[133] Much influenced by ideas picked up in Europe, he threw himself into the struggle for more representative institutions and for press freedom, representing the *Commercial Advertiser* in its legal battles with Somerset's regime. But by the 1830s, he and his Afrikaner colleagues had broken ranks with the humanitarians and reformers on the issue of liberal reform in general and, particularly, on the issue of official intervention in relations between masters and their slaves and servants. In 1831 Brand defended seven burghers of Stellenbosch accused of rioting against the punishment record-book system. These slave regulations he considered a contravention of rights and an inquisition.[134]

The launching of *De Zuid-Afrikaan* amounted to an organised challenge to the humanitarian–mercantile solidarity in favour of liberal reform among the Cape Town bourgeoisie which had marked the 1820s. Letters to the paper dripped with venom towards Philip and the missionaries, the commissioners of enquiry, and the *Commercial Advertiser*, which was dubbed the 'Hottentot Advertiser', representing supposedly the interests of 'vagrant Hottentots and heathens' over those of 'whites, Christians and property owners'. References to 'colonists' or 'South Africans', as opposed to the 'philanthropists' or the 'English', in the public agitations of the day suggest a mobilisation of local sentiment against meddling outsiders. In *De Zuid-Afrikaan* as well as in *De Zuid-Afrikaansche Tijdschrift*, of which Abraham Faure was editor, an Afrikaner world-view was developed in the 1830s. This raised Jan van Riebeeck, founder of the Dutch settlement, to the position of founding father, and justified colonial land rights and dispossession of the Khoi against the claims of the humanitarians. In this periodical literature a colonial historiographical tradition was established, parallel to the far more influential tradition established by British settler propagandists.[135]

But despite the enormous heat that was generated in the early 1830s, the Afrikaner elite was not unconditionally in favour of slavery as an institution.[136] *De Zuid-Afrikaan* was unremittingly committed to the sanctity of property, including slave property, and deeply resented ameliorative measures which interfered with owners' rights and moral authority. Yet it also supported initiatives which promised gradual and piecemeal abolition, provided all interference by the state in relationships between masters and slaves was ended. Emancipation was not rejected out of hand. Indeed, letters to the newspaper suggested that slave-owners were often sympathetic to plans for gradual emancipation under certain conditions – mainly monetary compensation and the assurance that labour supplies would not be disrupted. As an editorial concluded in late 1830, 'a general desire to emancipate their Slaves is becoming apparent among the Colonists'. Although a few correspondents defended slavery in principle as a natural order of things, in general slave-ownership was no longer widely regarded as being profitable or a necessary underpinning of the colonial economy.[137]

The common formula put forward by colonists, including many slave-owners, to avoid parliamentary abolition, entailed the emancipation of new-born offspring of slaves. This would stretch out the process over a generation or more – the justification often being that adult slaves would not be able to look after themselves if granted their freedom hastily. Proposals like this came from unexpected quarters, such as meetings of slave-owners in the interior town of Graaff-Reinet held at landdrost Stockenström's instigation in August and October 1826 in response to Bourke's ameliorative Ordinance 19. At one meeting, Stockenström and the district *heemraden* proposed fixing a date after which every female child of slave mothers would be freed – with the clear demand that if such a scheme were implemented, there would be no need for Ordinance 19 and other ameliorative regulations.[138] Similar trade-offs between gradual emancipation and repeal of the ordinance were suggested at other meetings called at the time in different parts of the colony.

This approach to the issue of slavery had the broad support of Afrikaner slave-owners such as the ex-chief justice, J. A. Truter, and J. W. Stoll, former colonial treasurer, men who had been firm allies of Governor Somerset's regime. What they angrily opposed was intrusion in their private affairs and property rights by the liberal bureaucrats of the Colonial Office and the busy-body humanitarians at the Cape.[139] For them, self-government, for which *De-Zuid-Afrikaan* campaigned vociferously, embodied a greater ideal than the maintenance of the increasingly unprofitable slave regime. In 1831, for instance, prominent Afrikaners in Cape Town petitioned the British parliament that should a representative assembly be granted to the colony, they would be agreeable to the freeing of all slave girls born after that date.[140] In all, the fierce antagonisms of the early 1830s were not so much about slavery *per se*, but about the impotence felt by Afrikaner colonists at their loss of influence and authority, and the threat they perceived to the hierarchies on which their social order was based.

On the other side of this divide in colonial society, it is equally notable that the humanitarians were relatively reticent on the issue of emancipation, in contrast to their strident condemnation of the exploitation of Khoi labour prior to Ordinance 50 of 1828. Men like Philip and Fairbairn did not doubt that slavery was morally wrong and an impediment to productive expansion and diversification. But despite their intense dislike of the concept of property in human beings, they also believed in the absolute and inalienable right to the privileges of property. For the rights of property were the foundations of the entire capitalist edifice, and were clung to the more vehemently by the British middle classes as new populist, even socialist, ideas began to question them. In consequence, humanitarians had tended initially to look to gradual emancipation, based on preparing slaves for the responsibilities of freedom.[141]

Philip often asserted that the condition of the Khoi (prior to Ordinance 50) was much worse than that of the colony's slaves, as colonists had had no proprietary interest in the welfare of their Khoi dependants. The truth is that the lack of proprietary interest in Khoi labour made their cause unproblematical for one whose commitment to the inviolability of property was so strong. Philip became much hotter under the collar about the colonists' determination, as emancipation came closer, to secure a vagrancy law (a measure he saw as a particular threat to Khoi) than about the cause of slave emancipation itself. Vagrancy laws, he declaimed in 1834, were 'the most demoralizing, the most degrading, and the most cruel and pitiless of all systems of slavery ... on the face of the globe'. On the whole, Philip wanted a system of 'prudent and gradual emancipation': precipitate emancipation would be 'too glaring' to consider. He also counselled colonists to undertake a programme of emancipation themselves by freeing all slave children, without waiting for parliamentary decree.[142]

This surprising degree of common ground on the question of slavery between the Afrikaner slave-owning elite and the local humanitarian lobby, whose interests and visions otherwise diverged so heatedly, was reflected in editorials in Fairbairn's *Advertiser*. Initially in the 1820s, Fairbairn had been careful not to alienate the colony's slave-owners, characterising Cape slavery as mild, and using the West Indies for the projection of anxieties and moral qualms over slavery. He refrained from moral judgement, but concentrated on utilitarian arguments about the greater productivity and profitability of free labour. At one stage, too, Fairbairn cooperated with Brand in calling for greater self-government for colonists. But by the 1830s, Fairbairn's attitude, in keeping with shifting abolitionist currents generally, had shifted to one of more rapid abolition on the basis of monetary compensation. At the same time he began to distance himself from the cause of colonists' rights as long as the issue of the rights of people of colour had not been resolved.[143] In June 1832 Fairbairn wrote that under current circumstances petitioning for a legislative assembly would be 'a ridiculous insult to the common sense of mankind'. An assembly of colonists, he foresaw, would be inclined to put down 'all Societies formed for the Improvement of the Colony, to expel the Missionaries – to revoke the Ordinance conferring Civil Rights on the Natives – to strip the Slave of all legal protection, and leave him, like other "goods and property" entirely to the magnanimity of the owner.'[144]

By the early 1830s colonial opinion had become sharply polarised between liberals and their opponents. Nevertheless, while the two parties spat venom at each other through their newspapers, they both in reality continued to agree on the fundamental importance of property rights. Labour discipline and social order had to be maintained, argued Fairbairn, and emancipation should occur with 'least shock to property and vested rights'. What this meant in practice was that there was 'but one way, consistent with justice, of making slaves freemen – by redeeming them with money'.[145]

This idea of monetary compensation became the central issue in the entire slavery debate, and one on which there was essential agreement across the spectrum from John Philip to the Afrikaner slave-owners themselves. In the public debates which reached their climax in the early 1830s, the common thread was that slavery had become uneconomic and unprofitable, and abolition was thus inevitable, even beneficial. Governor Cole summed up the prevailing mood when he reported to London in 1832 that the farmers' 'ruin seems to be actually sealed by the necessity of their keeping up large establishments of slave labour for which no profitable employment can be found'.[146] But if the liquidation of this redundant and costly asset was to respect slave-owners' property rights and make reparation for the loss of capital resources, an influx of metropolitan funds in the form of compensation payments would be essential.

The idea of compensation was embodied in the activities of a philanthropic society 'for aiding deserving slaves to purchase their freedom', established in June 1828. Dominated by merchants, clergymen and civil servants, this conservative and unthreatening society was the one institution in the colony which embraced the divergent and hostile forces in Cape Town. Philip raised funds for the society in London, and both he and Fairbairn served on the executive committee of the society in the early 1830s. P. A. Brand, one of the leading lights in *De Zuid-Afrikaan*, joined the society in 1832–3. Many Afrikaner slave-owners were also members, such as the ex-chief justice, Truter. As Governor Cole, who, though no anti-slavery advocate, was yet patron of the society, wrote to London, it had the 'zealous support' of many slave-owners.[147]

The purpose of the society was to purchase the freedom of 'deserving' (Christian) female slaves, mainly young girls, at the proposed rate of fifty a year. This would lead eventually to the demise of the institution altogether, with the full consent of the owners. In July 1833 the society reported that it had been responsible for freeing 126 slave children.[148] Their owners were well compensated, with money largely collected in Britain. Many of those who sold slaves to the society were themselves members, and slaves thus freed were usually apprenticed back to their former owners until the age of 18. One of the society's chief concerns was that freed girls be trained as proper servants. Behind the enterprise lay a conception of women's roles as mothers and wives in the moral construction of a free, subservient and industrious working class. They had to be taught to play their proper social function in the household.

The society was in fact a preliminary, unofficial experiment in metropolitan-funded compensation of the sort the reformed British parliament was to provide for in the Abolition Act of 1833. What precipitated the Act was the bloody Trinidad slave rebellion of 1831 and its vicious suppression. These events brought home clearly that amelioration, acculturation and Christianisation, meant to make slaves fit for freedom, had instead made them, in the words of Viscount Goderich, 'unfit for slavery'. The passing of the Act led to the emancipation of slaves throughout the empire, including some 38 000 at the Cape, on 1 December 1834. After emancipation, the ex-slaves were to be tied as 'apprentices' (a euphemism for bound labour) without wage payment to their masters for a further period of years, a plan devised to ease the transition to a free-labour regime.[149] At the Cape, the period was fixed at four years. The Act also provided for £20 million to be paid in compensation to slave-owners in the nineteen British colonies where slavery existed. Eventually the Cape Colony was allocated £1 247 401, or £34 per slave – far short of the more than £3 million (or £73 per slave) computed by the committee appointed to evaluate the colony's slave assets.[150]

An editorial in Fairbairn's *Commercial Advertiser* in November 1833 summed up the significance of compensation: 'it is perhaps not too much to say that this sudden influx of capital will raise the Colony as much in five years, in point of wealth, as we could have hoped to see it rise in Fifty under the present System of stinted Labour, and deficient Capital.'[151] The editor returned to the theme in the same month:

> Unfortunately for this colony a great portion of its agricultural capital was locked up in vineyards from which it could not be withdrawn, even when

the wine trade became unprofitable. And still more unfortunately, a very large portion of it was swallowed up, and in danger of being utterly lost in the person of the labourer ... What no man could have hoped for, time has brought about of its own accord. The vineyards can attract ... no more capital, and the money sunk in the labourer is about to be recovered by the colonist, through the justice and generosity of the mother country.[152]

Purely humanitarian considerations evaporated altogether from Fairbairn's mind at such a prospect. His father-in-law, John Philip, also supported compensation, but preferred to put a humanitarian gloss on it. The slaves were heavily mortgaged, Philip argued, and without compensation the farmers would become bankrupt. Bankruptcy would throw ex-slaves out of employment and leave them without the means of subsistence. Thus, to Philip, compensation was 'an act of humanity to the slaves themselves'. He preferred 'an excess of generosity' to the opposite.[153] But in reality, compensation was more of an act of philanthropy to the bourgeoisie of Cape Town than to the slaves.

Compensation had a wider significance than simply making reparations to slave-owners who were being deprived of their property. For one thing, by 1834 mortgages on slave property stood at some £400 000; and so the interests of creditors were involved as well. Further, the secretary of state insisted that all claims be settled in London. While this was convenient for West Indian slave-owners, many of whom were absentees living in England, it allowed middlemen to intervene as agents on behalf of the three thousand slave-owners at the Cape. Cape Town merchants, who were themselves often major creditors of the slave-owners, eagerly vied for such business. Merchants bought claims from the slave-owners at a discount, exploiting their often desperate need for cash to pay debts. They also often charged high commission fees for their services as agents. Commission of 5 per cent was common, and claims were commonly sold at a discount of 10–20 per cent. Cape Town merchants with London connections were at the forefront of those who acted as compensation agents under power of attorney: Venning, Busk & Co., Borradaile, Thompson & Pillans, Thomson & Watson, and Ewan Christian, among others. Commonly, the influx of compensation money also provided the opportunity for Cape Town creditors to call in their loans to farmers. All in all, the beneficiaries of slave compensation were not only (or mainly) the struggling and undercapitalised wine farmers who had been deprived of their slaves, but the Cape Town mercantile bourgeoisie as well.[154]

The compensation money which entered the colony in 1836–8 had a considerable impact, coinciding as it did with a considerable expansion of the colonial economy, and a new and unprecedented period of prosperity. Never in the history of the colony, wrote Macmillan, had there been such a liquidation of assets.[155] During the years following the formal Act of emancipation, bankruptcies in the colony declined. At the same time, the level of private specie imports soared, and money in circulation doubled during 1837. Interest rates throughout the colony dropped sharply as a result. Imports also jumped in value: in 1834 customs revenue stood at £15 778, and in 1839 at £51 395. In 1837 the first private commercial bank in the colony was established. But in this new period of prosperity the productive economy was to have its epi-centre, not in the vicinity of Cape Town, but in the far-flung drier districts to the east, where the woolled sheep ushered in a wholly new phase in the Cape's economic history. While wine exports fell from 41 to 8 per cent between 1838 and 1850 as a percentage of the total export trade in agricultural produce, wool exports rose from 11 to 62 per cent. There was indeed a flood of Cape Town-based merchant capital eastward into the sheep-farming areas.[156]

This shift to wool farming after the decline in wine farming was personified by the prominent Cape Town merchant J. B. Ebden, pioneer of wine export-ation in earlier years. In the early 1830s he began experimenting in the impor-tation of merino sheep from New South Wales. In November 1831 he was involved with the formation of an association 'for the improvement of Cape wool' to encourage sheep breeding and the export of wool, together with fel-low Cape Town merchants A. Chiappini, E. Christian and H. Ross. In the same year Ebden's son settled in New South Wales as a general agent; through the 1830s that state provided a market for Cape wine exports, initiated by the Ebdens, which paid for the supply of Australian merinos to the Cape. When in 1835 shiploads of sheep arrived in Cape Town for auction on the Grand Parade, Ebden advertised that 'Claims to the Compensation Money will be taken in payment' – revealing the close relationship between slave emancipa-tion and the release of productive capital for the take-off of a new phase in colonial development. In fact the promised compensation money was used to promote wool farming before the money actually reached Cape Town. A cor-respondent to the *Commercial Advertiser* advised slave-owners to invest the capital due in the colony in 'wool speculation': this he predicted was about to become the colony's staple export. Ebden's lead was followed by other mer-chants, who supplied goods in exchange for the transfer of compensation claims into their hands.[157]

But the question arises: what was the shape of the society and the productive system that emerged from the liberalisation of labour relations represented by Ordinance 50 of 1828, and from the abolition of slavery? Macmillan's view, repeated by subsequent generations of like-minded historians, was that a sig-nificantly 'liberal' tradition was established at the Cape at this time, meaning a colour-blind order in which merit and attainment were paramount.[158] If one leaves aside the fact (to which Macmillan was impervious) that even colour-blind societies can be built on the basis of class domination and exploitation, his characterisation is dubious, notwithstanding the non-discriminatory forms that Cape legislation tended to adopt. For the Cape continued to be built on a basis of racial hierarchy and racial subjugation. It is revealing that the Khoi themselves, according to their missionary spokesman Read, were not greatly excited by Ordinance 50, for by itself it did not hold out any promise of economic independence or an end to *de facto* discrimination. Without land, their newly won legal equality did not seem of great consequence. Land continued to be their greatest need and most urgent demand, poverty the most essential fact of life.[159] Those on the mission stations, far from being a model peasantry, remained in fact a depressed and propertyless underclass for the most part. Very few conformed to the idyllic vision of the noble agriculturist which metropolitan humanitarians and missionary propagandists fondly imagined.[160]

The inability or unwillingness of the authorities to turn humanitarian rhetoric into reality was the ongoing source of anger and frustration for Khoi, torn between their missionary-inspired conviction of the benevolence of the British crown, and the hard truths presented by the malevolence of the British settlers. By the time of Ordinance 50, indeed, evidence suggests high rates of alcoholism and social despair among mission communities. Indebtedness was a common condition.[161] Philip's improvement plans of the early 1820s, and his attempts to persuade the commissioners of enquiry and the Saints back home of the successful metamorphosis of Khoi converts, could not hide a shabbier reality.[162]

In 1829 a settlement was established for Khoi people on the Kat River, on land from which Xhosa had been expelled, bringing hope for many. Its ultimately forlorn history reveals much about the kind of social order being forged despite the liberalism of the law. Though he disliked humanitarians and had no fondness for the Khoi, Governor Cole had nevertheless supported Stockenström's suggestions of planting Khoi settlers in the Kat River territory as a barrier against Xhosa seeking to return to lost lands.[163] Cole anticipated that such a community would fall under government patronage and hence be free of pernicious LMS control, unlike stations such as Bethelsdorp and Theopolis. To this end he appointed W. R. Thomson, previously government missionary to the Xhosa, as Dutch Reformed minister to the Kat River Khoi. But Cole was to be disappointed. For most of those who moved to the Kat River came from LMS stations within the colony, or were people who had been in close contact with the LMS sphere of influence, and they wanted their own LMS missionary rather than a government-appointed one. The majority of the new inhabitants of the Kat River Settlement decided therefore to petition Philip in Cape Town for the appointment of James Read as their minister. To this Philip agreed. By 1834, some three-quarters of the five thousand inhabitants of the settlement claimed allegiance to the LMS. It seems that many who attached themselves to Thomson were in fact 'Bastaards' (people of European–Khoi parentage) who claimed social superiority and sought to distance themselves from the Khoi majority.[164]

Read, a carpenter by trade, was typical of many members of the evangelical missionary corps, being ill educated and unordained on his arrival in South

Africa in 1800. In 1816 he founded the first mission to the Tswana at Lattakoo (Kuruman), which was taken over a few years later by Robert Moffat. Read was widely regarded by the colonists (and many of the more socially self-conscious missionaries of the post-1815 generation) as an object of contempt and, as we have seen, was expelled in 1817 from the LMS by conservatives for adultery. He married a Khoi woman, and his sons followed in his footsteps as powerful leaders of the coloured population. In 1821 his rehabilitation began when Philip called him back to Bethelsdorp to take charge of his improvement scheme there, as an artisanal mission assistant. Read's rehabilitation was sealed with his call in 1830 to Kat River, where Philip ordained him. While most missionaries had come to accept that the Khoi were far from imbibing the moral values and material attributes of civilised society, and kept a distinct social distance from their charges, Read associated himself indistinguishably with the people whom he served.[165]

Read's importance lay in the fact that he, as much as anyone else, oversaw the forging of a whole petit-bourgeois class of coloured people, originating at Bethelsdorp or Theopolis. Many of them moved with him to Kat River, and from there spread out in a diaspora that took in mission stations further north across the Orange River. As traders and transport riders, artisans and teachers, they spread the Christian message and humanitarian ideology to other coloured peoples, and did much to forge a coloured, or (in the language of the day) 'Hottentot', sense of national identity. Widely seen by the white colonists as a blight on the landscape, for a period they were men of stature and influence, who beyond colonial boundaries could rival white colonists as accumulators of land and resources, enjoying the patronage not only of missionaries but also of Griqua and Kora captains and African chiefs. However, this flowering of a coloured class, growing out of the mission nexus, was not to survive the rise of centres of colonial state formation, in the Cape and north of the Orange, which were more inclined to promote racially exclusive accumulation. The Kat River Settlement under the stewardship of the Reads was an important seedbed of this mission-shaped class, as Bethelsdorp had been in earlier years.

The commitment to national regeneration evident among the LMS-oriented Khoi leadership at Kat River was manifested in their investment in education and literacy. By 1834, seventeen schools served the LMS community, all staffed by local people under the supervision of the Reads, and attended by 700 pupils.[166] It was this aspect of the settlement that humanitarians presented to the world as evidence of what native peoples could aspire to, if freed from the shackles of subjugation and coercion. In his correspondence with Buxton in London, Philip provided much sanguine material for use in humanitarian propaganda in the early 1830s. These were years when the conditions under which slave emancipation would take place were very much the subject of debate; and the humanitarians had, in the case of the Khoi of Kat River, a community of the imagination which could be evoked against those who were inclined to a pessimistic view of life after slavery. In this discourse Ordinance 50, the seminal code of native rights, was held up as an act of economic and spiritual redemption which had saved the Khoi from a state of degradation, and transformed them into the noble yeomanry of missionary legend.[167]

But the Khoi themselves were keenly aware of the insecurity and marginality of their position in colonial society, especially in the year of slave emancipation, 1834. For in that year came the first abortive colonist-led effort to roll back the humanitarian tide, in the form of a vagrancy law. In September the unofficial members of the newly constituted Legislative Council, spurred by a barrage of petitions from nervous employers anticipating disruption as a result of the implementation of emancipation, pushed through a draft vagrancy law for the control not only of Khoi servants but also of ex-slaves. It reintroduced passes, and provided for the arrest of any person as a vagrant if he could not account for how he had subsisted over the previous three days.[168]

Stockenström and other utilitarian liberals considered vagrancy legislation a civilising measure, intended to counteract an alleged Khoi tendency to idleness and indolence. For the majority of colonists, however, its purpose was to make it as difficult as possible for Khoi and ex-slaves to escape a life of servility. And indeed, the law made no distinction between the 'idle' and the economically independent, such as Khoi stock-owners or transport riders. Although Godlonton at the *Graham's Town Journal* was still inclined in 1834 to echo liberal sentiments in support of the law, arguing that Khoi and ex-slaves needed to be 'taught to understand the value of the social compact', this reasoning was unlikely to find much resonance with settlerdom in general. In fact the notion of the 'social compact' was to give way very quickly in Godlonton's writing to a language of racial hostility and domination.[169] More typical of colonial sentiment was the developing stereotype of the Khoi or ex-slave as potentially criminal. For most colonists in the 1830s and after, vagrancy legislation was increasingly seen, in the western as in the eastern Cape, as necessary for the control of the criminal underclasses, which tended to be defined in implicitly and explicitly racial ways.[170]

In opposition to the vagrancy law of 1834, all the humanitarian propaganda of the previous years was invoked. Philip, the missionaries and the Khoi themselves launched a furious petition campaign with the full support of the humanitarian lobby in England. Philip wrote in a letter to the *Commercial Advertiser* in May 1834: 'Will the English nation, which has engaged to pay £20 million for the redemption of the slaves of our colonies, suffer itself to be cheated out of that money by allowing the iron chains of the Hottentot to be substituted for the leathern thongs of the slaves?'[171] The humanitarian position was that the Khoi had advanced sufficiently in civilisation to be trusted with freedom. More to the point, humanitarians saw the exercise of free choice, responsibility and self-discipline as essential to moral upliftment. Human dignity and human coercion could not coexist; and redemption as members of civilised society was impossible, in the view of the humanitarians, without the dignity and self-worth that came from self-motivation.[172]

The agitations against the vagrancy law of 1834 were especially significant in that the Khoi themselves played a major role, much to the appreciation of their missionary mentors who were keen to demonstrate their charges' political maturity. Scores of 'Hottentots' (including 401 LMS congregants from Kat River) signed petitions to the governor condemning the law as an instrument of oppression, declaring that Khoi 'vagrancy' was caused solely by cruel treatment and fraudulent dealings. The columns of the *Commercial Advertiser* overflowed with agitation against the draft law, including many letters from people describing themselves as 'Hottentots'.[173] In August 1834, well-publicised meetings were held at Philipton on the Kat River to discuss the vagrancy legislation, at which Khoi spokesmen identified themselves as representing the 'Hottentot' nation, robbed of its heritage, discriminated against and oppressed, but seeking equality of opportunity and status with white colonists and, above all, land. They used the language of missionary humanitarianism, as if they had a clear understanding of the role they had been assigned in the campaigns of the day. If Khoi had not been greatly excited by Ordinance 50 in 1828, in 1834 it was the touchstone of their agitation. For by presenting the vagrancy law as a return to the state of enslavement from which they had allegedly been liberated in 1828, they hoped to touch a nerve of anti-slavery sentiment in Britain.[174]

By the 1830s the armed resistance of the past had been displaced by the integration of the mission Khoi into a new social and cultural order, whose fruits, hitherto reserved for white colonists alone, they wished to share. But memories of the Khoi servants' rebellion of 1799–1803 were still strong. For years after the rebellion, Khoi believed that they had been persuaded to lay down arms in return for promises of independence and equality which never materialised, a belief that would form a powerful element in what became 'Hottentot nationalism', and the basis of continuing appeals to British justice.[175] Long after the Khoi had been subsumed into the colonial economy as a working class, the Khoi captaincy remained of enduring importance, and Khoi captains continued to serve as potential focuses of resistance well into the nineteenth century – which is why colonial authorities sought to manipulate the captaincy to recruit Khoi for military service, handing out staffs of office to their appointees in the early 1800s. There was thus a degree of ambiguity in Khoi political and cultural struggles, both backward- and forward-looking, both nationalist and incorporationist.[176] On the one hand the deep-seated belief in British benevolence and justice was revealed when, in the frontier war of 1834–5, the Khoi of Kat River disappointed their Xhosa neighbours by throwing their weight (with a few exceptions) behind the colonial forces as auxiliaries and in the Kat River legion. At the same time, the Kat River adherents of the LMS revealed the Janus-faced nature of their position: for they were strongly suspected of serving as a conduit in the provision of armaments to the Xhosa, and of providing a gateway into the colony for passless Africans.[177]

And in due course, as we shall see, the option of armed rebellion was again to suggest itself.

The 'Hottentot nation' as defined in the agitation against the vagrancy law in 1834 was a heterogeneous one. Afrikaans/Dutch was apparently more common than Khoi languages at Kat River, and the 'Hottentots' were by no means all aboriginal Khoi, but included people with heavy admixtures of European, Xhosa and Bushman ancestry. Even those of slave parentage reportedly called themselves Hottentots. In 1835, Captain A. B. Armstrong, the magistrate at Kat River, complained that Read had 'taught the Hottentots to consider themselves a distinct Tribe, to consider their interests as apart from others of His Majesty's subjects in the Colony'; and that Read 'encouraged all classes of coloured people whether Bastards, Gonahs or Fingoes to assume the appellation of *Hottentots*'. Moreover, reported Armstrong, Read had sought to persuade the 'Hottentots' that they should be governed by their own magistrates, elected by themselves.[178] This was by no means the only time missionaries in southern Africa were to busy themselves with the task of brokering identities.

A case in point was Andries Stoffels. According to Donald Moodie, he was a 'Gonah' captain who had become 'the voluntary champion of the Hottentot races', although he could 'claim no other affinity than that the first tribe of Caffres encountered by the Colonists were by them called Gonah Hottentots'. An early Bethelsdorp resident, Stoffels had been a long-time companion of Read, accompanying him to set up the first mission to the Tswana in 1816, and for many years was a mainstay of the Bethelsdorp and Kat River communities. His continuing faith in British intentions and British power for good was strong enough for Stoffels to lead Khoi as a field cornet under Captain Henry Somerset against the Xhosa in the frontier war of 1835. In 1836 Stoffels accompanied Philip, the Reads (father and son) and a petty Xhosa chief, Jan Tshatshu (another scion of Bethelsdorp), to England to appear before Buxton's select committee on aborigines. He spoke to religious groups throughout England, including thousands at Exeter Hall, on the past sufferings and future aspirations of his people. Here was a shining exemplar of the transforming power of the mission. The empire of free trade and of free men was on display. Stoffels, however, was likely to be aware of the dissonance between imperial promise as represented by Exeter Hall, and colonial reality as represented by the frontier settlers, whose land-grabbing proclivities were becoming ever more evident. He returned to Cape Town a very sick man, and died within months.[179]

The draft vagrancy law of 1834 which sparked the mobilisation of the 'Hottentots' was not, however, implemented. As we have seen, all legislation bearing on Ordinance 50 was reserved for the sanction of the British government. Governor D'Urban warned the Legislative Council that the draft law would never be accepted under prevailing circumstances in London, where the Colonial Office was having to deal with a flood of obstructionist legislation, coming from West Indian planter assemblies, designed to mitigate the effects of emancipation. And indeed, the Cape vagrancy law was promptly disallowed, to the anger of the eastern Cape settlers and Afrikaner interests represented by *De Zuid-Afrikaan*, who used the issue to intensify the campaign for representative institutions.[180] But this was a Pyrrhic victory for the humanitarian lobby, and would not obstruct for long the realisation of dominant colonial interests.

Indeed, the contradictions at the heart of the humanitarian cause itself were soon revealed once slavery had been formally abolished. The period of 'apprenticeship', which delayed the achievement of freedom for ex-slaves, divided humanitarian sentiment in Britain. While the purists continued to insist that there was no justification for delaying unfettered freedom, more pragmatic humanitarians (such as Buxton), wary of the ex-slaves' readiness to exercise the responsibilities of freedom, were more inclined to support the temporary need for disciplinary constraint and control. Faith in the benefits of freedom began to waver when confronted with the realities of emancipation. As the earlier abolitionist optimism wore off, the utilitarian concern for surveillance and policing came to the fore.[181] At the Cape, those who fought passionately against vagrancy legislation (such as Philip and Fairbairn) seem to have been unperturbed by the apprenticeship provisions, perhaps in part for the same reasons that they found the cause of slave emancipation less problematical and less urgent than the rights of the Khoi.

The Cape ordinance enacted in January 1835 for administering the apprenticeship system (in reality, indenture rather than apprenticeship) introduced stringent measures to discipline the ex-slaves and to appease employers' demands that their interests be secured. It represented also an attempt to extend an apparently impartial rule of law to replace the arbitrary authority of the slave-owners. Masters could not inflict physical punishment as before; but special magistrates, retired army and navy officers sent out from Britain, were given powers of summary jurisdiction in cases of default, misdemeanour, idleness and desertion, with wide powers to impose punishment. Refusal to work could earn the recalcitrant 'apprentice' thirty lashes or a month's hard labour. The rationale was that slaves had been inadequately prepared for freedom inasmuch as the amelioration measures had been resisted and undermined by the slave-owners. In reality, the apprenticeship regulations and the machinery set up to implement them merely increased the dead weight of oppression on ex-slaves. They revealed too the advancing bureaucratisation of government and law, and the increasingly authoritarian, utilitarian reformism of the imperial state.[182]

The apprenticeship laws were more strongly weighted on the side of the masters than the amelioration regulations had been. They emphasised the duties of ex-slaves rather than their rights. Henceforth masters appeared in courts less often as defendants and more often as plaintiffs. At the Cape the apprenticeship system was weakly supervised, for there were only eight special magistrates appointed, all quite unfamiliar with the colony and its languages. In effect the law meant that ex-slaves were maintained in a situation of legal servitude after emancipation. Indeed, they could still be bought and sold, although they could not be displayed at auctions. They received no cash wages and no training such as would fit them for any occupation other than servile labour. Moreover, it seems that masters commonly removed rights and privileges enjoyed previously, and refused to accept responsibility for unproductive ex-slaves who were too old to work, or to support ex-slaves' children unless they were indentured. But provision was made for apprentices to buy their freedom, as under slavery, and this continued to occur.

The issue of labour control came to the forefront of masters' consciousness more sharply and pertinently when the four-year period of apprenticeship of ex-slaves came to an end, freeing them from further servile obligations. The real moment of emancipation was 1 December 1838, a rain-drenched day recalled in folk memories right up to the mid-twentieth century. Reports immediately began to surface of labourers leaving the farms of the southwestern Cape. *De Zuid-Afrikaan* was filled with complaints of the disappearance of thousands of ex-slaves. Many simply squatted on vacant land or moved away to settle on mission lands or with the independent Griqua. Many more moved to town. It was at this time that the problems of urban indigency and overcrowding in Cape Town and elsewhere became a matter of middle-class concern. One result was a boom in working-class housing in Cape Town, boosting slumlordism as a source of income for the newly rising bourgeoisie.[183] As for the rural districts, statistics of cereal crop production showed a sharp decline from 1838 to 1841, although this was as much the result of drought and disease as labour shortage.[184] All in all, these were years of incessant complaint by white farmers of adverse labour supply and lack of control over workers. When they complained of idleness and fecklessness, they in effect were describing a determination by ex-slaves to define the conditions under which they worked.[185]

The desire to establish independent households, to gain access to church communities and educational institutions, and to earn higher wages, drew the ex-slaves away from their places of servitude. Emancipation meant escape from the patriarchal embrace of the slaveholding unit, and meant too the reconstruction of families and communities of the freed. Broken and divided families were united, and ex-slave men began to assume the role of heads of their own patriarchal households. Immediately after emancipation day, mass registrations of baptisms and marriages among the newly freed were reported. In this way legal protection was assured, children were legitimised and property could be passed on.[186]

Married women and children withdrew from the labour market as far as possible, although this was in practice difficult to sustain. There was a widespread shortage of domestic labour reported in both rural and urban white households. The ex-slaves' determination to maintain the integrity and independence of their domestic units was one reason for the proliferation in the arable districts of labour tenancy of a sort that had long prevailed among Khoi on livestock farms, by which tenants could work their own land and accumulate modest stockholdings in return for their labour services. Labour tenancy arrangements became a new focus of conflict over the labour of dependants within subordinate labouring households. The ex-slave families fought to ensure physical and psychological distance from employers, and the labour of married women and children was kept as far as possible out of the employers' clutches. For many, this was the essence of the struggle over the meaning of freedom.[187]

Labour tenancy was only possible on larger landholdings in the wine and wheat districts, and the poorer white farmers bitterly resented it.[188] On the other hand, the emancipation of 1838 resulted in a more even distribution of casual labour to those who had found it difficult to afford slaves. Long-term contracts were anathema for most ex-slaves, as being reminiscent of slavery. The most obvious change in productive relations on the land therefore was the shift to short-term, task or daily work arrangements – although the limited availability of land for independent existence hardly provided much scope for discretion in entering such arrangements.

The alarms of the time hid a deeper reality: so advanced was the extent of proletarianisation and economic dependence among the labouring classes that their chances of real freedom from servility were severely limited in the longer term. Skills and resources were few. Squatting on public land was precarious at best; private land available for independent living, such as that attached to mission stations, was very restricted. Mission stations in fact became valued sources of labour supply to farmers rather than a drain on the supply of labour.[189] Humanitarians, Khoi and ex-slaves continued to argue that without the provision of land for independent farming, emancipation was an empty promise. For their part, however, the authorities were strongly inclined to do all in their power to reinforce the *status quo* and to secure the subordination of workers, rather than promote alternatives such as peasant production. Thus in rejecting the provision of land for Khoi, Glenelg wrote in 1837: 'The most desirable result would be that they would be induced to work for wages as free labourers. Whatever tends to counteract that object seems to me unadvisable, with a view to the interest of all classes.'[190]

Freedom became a terrain of struggle over mobility, family and labour. Most ex-slaves stayed on the farms, or eventually returned there. What emerged on the arable farms of the southwest was a very insecure and impoverished workforce consisting of hired seasonal labour (from mission stations and towns) working at day or task rates, and permanent farm residents, who did not necessarily receive cash wages,[191] but whose dependence on employers' land, food, housing, clothing and alcoholic sustenance secured their submission. This pattern was facilitated by the very seasonal nature of farm work. Labour tenancy thus provided little scope for challenging the chains of dependency. For white employers, this was a more flexible, albeit less easily subordinated, workforce than slavery had been. Indeed, despite the disruptions of emancipation, the

1840s and 1850s would see a long boom in agricultural production.[192]

External sources of labour continued to arrive at the Cape, not least from Britain. The Children's Friend Society was responsible for importing some 700 juvenile delinquents between 1833 and 1839, mostly boys of 14 and younger, as apprenticed labour mostly on farms in the southwestern Cape, thus perpetuating pauper apprenticeship, which had long been abolished in Britain.[193] Although the idea of adult indentured labour from Britain met with much resistance among farmers, who regarded white labour as too expensive and insufficiently subservient, the idea of voluntary, subsidised immigration from Britain remained attractive for those like Fairbairn, Ebden and Brand who looked to an influx of people and capital to propel development in the colony. It was one cause which united the Cape Town bourgeoisie. After 1845 there commenced the systematic importation of adult male volunteers from Britain, when a committee of the Legislative Council approved a scheme of the imperial Land and Emigration Commission. A sum of £10 000 was voted to finance this scheme to provide a thousand immigrants with free passage. Harry Smith, governor from 1847, took up the cause of immigration; and during 1848–59, the colonial government subsidised immigration to the tune of £36 000. On some well-established and profitable arable farms, British labourers formed a component of the workforce for several years. But the great majority of immigrants joined the urban underclasses, and white labour never became a significant part of the rural labouring population.[194]

By the 1840s, clear shifts were taking place away from Colonial Office interventionism in advancing and protecting the rights of coloured working people in the colonies. When ex-slaves did not respond to freedom in a way that abolitionists regarded as appropriate, coercive measures were increasingly resorted to. As sugar production began to fall in the West Indian islands, strict anti-vagrancy and masters and servants measures were introduced, and increasingly restrictive franchise provisions were applied, with the approval of the Colonial Office.[195] At the Cape the question of legislative intervention in the labour market was again much under discussion in the late 1830s. In July 1839 the Legislative Council adopted an ordinance regulating the rights and duties of masters and servants. This ordinance was explicit in discriminating racially, referring to 'persons of colour' but excluding Bantu-speaking Africans, 'Bushmen' and any woman of colour 'lawfully married to any European'. Governor Napier argued that racial distinction was necessary in order to attract European immigrants to the colony. But Lord John Russell, the Whig colonial secretary, insisted that the ordinance be redrafted without racial references. The amended ordinance was passed in March 1841.[196]

The law as passed was designed to stabilise the new labour system that had emerged since 1838. Effectively it repealed Ordinance 50 of 1828. Unlike the latter, which applied to 'Hottentots and free people of colour', the ostensibly colour-blind 1841 ordinance could be held up as an advance on the 'class legislation' of 1828. Thus Macmillan argued that though Ordinance 50 was repealed, 'its work was done; and its principles established'. 'The effect of repealing the Ordinance was actually to place the coloured population of the Colony on a footing of complete legal equality with Europeans, and to give them at last the full legal protection of the ordinary law of the land. The Cape Colony ceased to know any legal distinction between "white" and "coloured."'[197] Here the whole mythology of the Cape liberal tradition can be seen encapsulated.

The reality was that the masters and servants ordinance was aimed at the coloured working class, and was universally so interpreted. It bound workers with severe criminal sanctions for breach of contract, including such subjectively determined 'crimes' as disobedience, defiance and resistance. While providing workers (and their families) with protection from abuse, the crucial effect was to strip workers of their means of defence against the will of employers, by throwing the weight of the law behind the latter. Field cornets were given power to enforce provisions of the law and to authorise written contracts of service. Special magistrates appointed to oversee the apprenticeship system were kept on to enforce labour relations provisions. The ordinance sought to buttress the racial hierarchy and to reinforce the subordination of coloured workers, as well as the subordination of women to men in labouring families. The legal underpinnings of a racial order did not require that the law be couched in overtly racial terms.[198]

After emancipation there was little official commitment to the promotion of the welfare of the coloured population, and no real attempt by the colony's dominant classes to provide greater educational opportunities for the liberated slaves or Khoi, although there continued to be a few mixed Dutch schools for poor children in Cape Town as there had been under Dutch rule. The schools founded to teach in English from the early 1820s were almost exclusively white. Education for coloureds was left to the mission schools (attended by many poorer whites as well); these began to receive nominal state aid only in 1863. In Cape Town, polarisation along race lines sharpened in the 1830s and 1840s, although *laissez-faire* attitudes and practices continued to prevail at the lower social levels, accompanied by a paternalist tendency among the 'respectable' elite, which was axiomatically confined to people of European origin. If anything, the insecurities introduced by emancipation heightened race consciousness in the perceptions of the dominant classes.[199]

The overthrow of Cape slavery also meant the final overthrow of the old regime. It clearly represented a climactic point, a culmination of the transforming, liberalising forces which had taken hold of colonial government in the 1820s. The consequent freeing of the colonial economy for the forces of accumulation was in large part driven by humanitarian forces, closely associated with mercantile enterprise. At its height, therefore, humanitarianism had served a profoundly important material purpose. In the 1820s and early 1830s the ascendancy of humanitarian influence coincided with the structural reform of colonial society along lines more apposite to an imperial economy of free trade dependent on expanding markets. Most obviously, of course, there were nominal and ultimately evanescent advances in the human rights of many people, if not a corresponding improvement in their quality of life. In other areas too, the structural reform of colonial society was evident, such as administration and the law. Although humanitarian influence did not necessarily dictate imperial or colonial policy, it could reinforce or legitimise it profoundly when the official and the humanitarian mind coincided, as they did quite often in the 1820s and 1830s. So the humanitarians played a major role in opening up the Cape for enterprise and accumulation, by their exertions in propagating the destruction of the corruption, despotism and mercantilist tyrannies of the older colonial regime.

The end of the slave economy cleared the decks and opened the way for the emergence of a settler capitalism. This colonial capitalism was to be the fundamental force driving imperial expansion and black dispossession for decades to come, as subsequent chapters will attempt to document. By the 1840s, moreover, humanitarianism was on the retreat. The humanitarian movement thrived only so long as the settler economy was weak and underdeveloped. While philanthropic impulses served a purpose in the transition to a bourgeois colonial society, once settler capitalism had been launched as a vital force these impulses faded. The irony was that the capitalist economy which emerged from the transformations of the 1820s and 1830s was to be based on the ever more rigid assertion of racial hegemony. Because the colony's underclasses, rural and urban, failed to conform to the optimistic humanitarian ideal of a sober, subservient and tractable workforce, new forms of social control and subjugation had to be forged to replace the older, counterproductive coercions of unfree legal status.

The forces of dispossession and marginalisation grew more intense in subsequent years for Khoi everywhere. For the Kat River people, overcrowding in the locations eroded any opportunity for economic advance or independence, and was compounded by increasing hostility from neighbouring settlers. The fate of ex-slaves and indigenous people faded from the public conscience in Britain after the 1830s, as evangelicals became more narrowly concerned with religious matters, as missionaries withdrew from social and political activism and, at the Cape, the settler economy became more profitable and more insistent on a docile labour force. In 1851, with local representative government (dominated by the white colonists) in the offing, the Khoi of Kat River would once again throw in their lot with the military resistance of Xhosa farmers seeking to preserve their independence from conquest. The result, for Khoi as for Xhosa, was to be disaster.[200]

In the end, liberal humanitarianism turned out to be a shallow, tawdry, deceptive thing. The LMS, the very seedbed of humanitarian thought in the

1820s and 1830s, was by the 1840s and 1850s becoming infected with racial sentiment. LMS congregations in the towns of the eastern Cape became segregated. New missionaries like Henry Calderwood, who arrived in the eastern Cape in the late 1830s, were deeply hostile to the Reads, whom they regarded as unsuitable because of the elder Read's marriage to a Khoi woman and his sons' coloured status. Philip found himself fighting a rearguard action in defence of the mission institutions as LMS property. One of his Cape Town congregants started a storm when he wrote to an evangelical journal in England in 1848 declaring that the institutions had become an evil, and were not needed any more as the coloured people had won full civil rights. Eminent missionaries such as Moffat and Livingstone argued that the colonial stations should be sold to the inhabitants as freehold proprietors, and mission resources be concentrated on the vast masses of uncolonised African peoples in the further interior. Indeed, from the mid-1850s, financial aid was withdrawn from the colonial and Griqua stations.[201] With the decline of the LMS, the only real legacy of the humanitarian moment at the Cape was that the law retained a formally non-racial character.

CHAPTER FIVE

Colonial Initiatives and the Dynamics of Accumulation

The humanitarian cause reached a high point in 1834, with slave emancipation and the rejection of the colonists' vagrancy law. But the issue which was to represent most clearly the violent clash between the humanitarians and their colonial enemies once emancipation had been accomplished was not so much labour relations as policies towards independent African peoples beyond the colony's borders, notably in the first instance the Xhosa. It was on this issue that the eastern Cape settlers were to develop an intense hostility towards the humanitarians, at the same time as racial enmity hardened towards the Xhosa. It was also on this issue that mercantile interests in Cape Town most obviously broke from their former humanitarian allies. For in military advance and dispossession to the benefit of settlers lay the prospect of far greater and quicker profit than that to be won from the expanding frontiers of trade. This became clear when, at the end of 1834, the eastern frontier was plunged into war. The settlers were on the march.

Trekboer and Xhosa routes of expansion had initially met in the Zuurveld between the Gamtoos and the Fish rivers in the 1770s. Their meeting initiated a long period of interaction, interdependence and conflict. From the start, frontier warfare over resources of land and cattle erupted as colonists were sucked into – or took advantage of – rivalries and fissions between chiefdoms (and vice versa), rather than as the result of irreconcilable racial enmity, as the traditional colonial historiography assumed. From the time of the VOC onwards governments sought, in vain, to regulate relations between trekboer and Xhosa by prohibiting all trading contacts and the employment of Xhosa in the colony. Given the impotence of the authorities, raiding continued to destabilise the frontier, and African herders competed for access to the grazing resources of the Zuurveld.[1]

The salient elements of the colonial government's frontier policy were spelled out by Colonel Collins, who in 1809 travelled east as emissary of Governor Caledon to interview the Xhosa chiefs. His report issued on his return insisted on firm adherence to the policy of non-intercourse and segregation, except for the establishment of official trade fairs to discourage irregular commercial contact. He recommended the expulsion of all Xhosa beyond the Fish River, and the settlement of British settlers in the Zuurveld in order to stabilise the border. With the French expelled from the Mascarenes, the British garrison at the Cape could be turned to local use by 1810.

On the basis of Collins's recommendations, Colonel John Graham was

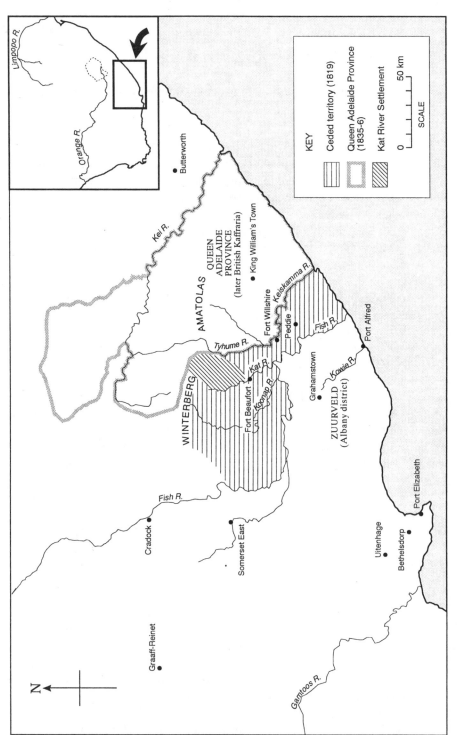

The Cape eastern frontier

Within the map:

Limpopo R.

Orange R.

Butterworth

KEY
Ceded territory (1819)
Queen Adelaide Province (1835–6)
Kat River Settlement

50 km

0

SCALE

Kei R.

QUEEN ADELAIDE PROVINCE (later British Kaffraria)

King William's Town

AMATOLAS

Keiskamma R.

Fort Willshire

Peddie

Fish R.

Port Alfred

Tyhume R.

Kat R.

WINTERBERG

Fort Beaufort

Koonap R.

Grahamstown

ZUURVELD (Albany district)

Kowie R.

Fish R.

Cradock

Somerset East

Uitenhage

Bethelsdorp

Port Elizabeth

Graaff-Reinet

Gamtoos R.

N

deputed to expel the Xhosa from the Zuurveld, which he did with great brutality in 1811–12. An estimated 20 000 Xhosa were expelled, and 27 military posts, manned in the main by Khoi troops, were set up near the Fish River, from Cradock in the north to Graham's Town in the south. At the same time the colonial authorities exploited divisions within the Rharhabe branch of the Xhosa who predominated west of the Kei, and formed an alliance with Ngqika. Ngqika recognised the utility of the imperial presence in shoring up his authority against Ndlambe, his uncle and regent before his accession, and thus was willing to accept the Fish River as the boundary, as well as the withdrawal of all Xhosa behind it. As was so often to be the case in the subcontinent, African factionalism facilitated their subjugation.[2]

Governor Somerset set about implementing Collins's prescriptions. Being denied the military force he required owing to the retrenchments of 1816–17,[3] he turned to other expedients, including the use of government missionaries among the Xhosa people as agents and informants, and the deployment of burgher militias to counter stock theft through a policy of reprisals. He recognised the authority of Ngqika, the senior Rharhabe chief, over the other chiefs, and entrusted him with responsibility for keeping the peace and ensuring the compliance of all in preventing theft and punishing thieves. But Somerset completely misunderstood the segmentary nature of chiefdom politics.[4] Other chiefs refused to accept that Ngqika had such authority over them, and combined under Ndlambe to defeat him at Amalinde in October 1818. Somerset sought to settle the issue in a campaign of 1818–19 against Ndlambe. After the war, in which the prophet Nxele carved a place for himself in the history of resistance, and Graham's Town was attacked in mass formation, Somerset declared the land between the Fish and Keiskamma rivers northwards to the Winterberg range as a neutral territory, thus removing Ngqika from his own country, and proving to Xhosa allies the limitless capacity for perfidy of the British. But despite public avowals to the chiefs that this would remain an empty corridor, Somerset's intention in private was eventually to people the land with settlers. Far from being neutral land, it soon became known as the 'ceded territory'. The conflicts of succeeding years grew out of this act of dispossession, and the intermittent efforts of the colonial military to remove Xhosa from the territory.[5]

All the while, Xhosa society was being fundamentally changed by the encroaching forces of colonialism. In an earlier chapter, in the context of the history of the British settlers of the eastern Cape, we traced the development of the trading economy in the 1820s, which undermined Xhosa self-sufficiency, eroded chiefly prerogatives, and reoriented economic activity to new patterns of production and consumption.[6] Another aspect of colonial penetration came in the form of the mission station. Van der Kemp first made contact with Ngqika in 1799, and in 1817 Joseph Williams became the first missionary at Ngqika's great place on the Kat River, where he was expected by Somerset to act as government agent, a role he was very reluctant to fulfil. Subsequently it was mainly the Methodists who took up the task of setting up stations among the Xhosa beyond the Cape frontier, with Somerset's blessing.[7]

The Methodist Missionary Society, which initially had been denied permission to work at the Cape when Somerset was fighting with the LMS, really took off after the arrival of the 1820 settlers. These British immigrants, as we have seen, were largely of the Methodist persuasion, and provided the society with a number of prominent missionaries, such as William Shaw, William Boyce, John Ayliff and John Shepstone.[8] Unlike the LMS's initial strategy of concentrating on the Khoi and Griqua – people captured or forged in the colonial nexus – the Methodists concentrated on the Nguni and Tswana beyond colonial borders, establishing a chain of stations eastwards through modern-day Ciskei and Transkei from 1823, and among the Rolong and other groups in what became known as the Transvaal and Free State. They acceded to the government's terms. In the Nguni region this meant undertaking to work under the supervision of the government missionary agent William Thomson (Williams's successor), and to report regularly to him on all matters relating to the political affairs of the chiefdoms.[9] In contrast to the dominant strand in the LMS and other non-denominational, Scottish-influenced societies such as the Glasgow society, the Methodist missionaries were politically cautious and were careful not to antagonise the settlers or the administration by taking up the cause of the colony's working class, or by promoting the political and economic rights of indigenous people. While the Methodists were conscientious proselytisers among the indigenous Africans, they never forgot that their first political allegiance was to the British settlers, from whom they drew personnel and monetary support.[10] They never regarded these two priorities as being contradictory, as did the humanitarians of the London and Glasgow societies.

Missionaries played a crucial role in representing independent African societies to the outside world and shaping imperial policy towards these societies. Although they sought to establish islands of acolytes free from the constraints of chiefly rule and the redistributive economy of chiefdom, clan and lineage, in reality most missionaries active among independent peoples beyond colonial borders were obliged to attach themselves to indigenous authorities as clients, agents and advisers if they were to establish themselves. Such were the resources at their disposal – intimate knowledge of the British imperial forces at work, skills in literate communication, their role as forward agents of merchant capital – it was inevitable that missionaries would play a crucial political role among indigenous peoples during a period of great instability and political flux. In situating themselves at the interface between mercantile expansionism and indigenous societies, they helped shape in important ways the outcome of the interaction between these forces. It was of profound significance to which political patrons the missionaries chose to (or were allowed to) attach themselves, and under the auspices of which focuses of chiefly power they operated.

Chiefs saw the missionaries as crucial adjuncts and supports of their rule, and often suspected that they had mystical powers and privileged access to spiritual as well as material resources. But, as they also suspected, the inherent consequence of missionary enterprise, if not restricted and controlled, was the subversion of the entire edifice of African society and culture. Rather disingenuously the missionaries insisted on the separation of church and state, and thus declared their intent not to interfere with the secular power of the constituted chiefly authorities to rule over their peoples, while reserving the right for themselves to transform the spiritual realm of African societies. But in reality no such separation of spheres of authority was possible. To attack the powers of diviners or rainmakers, for example, was to attack the whole indivisible fabric of authority that regulated social and economic life, as embodied in the person of the chief. For every aspect of African life was influenced by nonmaterial forces. The dualisms of post-Enlightenment European culture found no resonance among Africans.[11]

Relations between missionaries and chiefs were fraught with ambiguity and misunderstanding, and conflict always lay close to the surface. Conflict not only concerned the allegiance of followers, acolytes and converts, or the powers and privileges of chiefs. It also concerned more deeply and less explicitly (in the Comaroffs' words) 'a long battle for the possession of salient signs and symbols, a bitter, drawn-out contest of conscience and consciousness' – about 'linguistic forms, spatial forms, the forms of rational argument and positive knowledge'.[12] This was a battle over the very shape of everyday life. The missionaries saw their task as the capture of souls, but in the process they proved a powerful solvent of indigenous political, social and economic systems. Whatever their intentions, they served wittingly or unwittingly as agents of a pervasive economic and cultural imperialism.

In important respects, the Methodists and the more humanitarian-oriented LMS had much in common, believing implicitly in the capacity of indigenous peoples to imbibe Christian civilisation and its related individualistic material values. But despite similarities in ideology, the mission societies followed different political strategies in establishing space for themselves in independent African societies beyond colonial borders. Hence rivalries between mission societies could take on the dimensions of, and to an extent helped shape, political struggles between and within African societies in the 1820s and 1830s. For instance, the Methodist alignment with the settler cause was reflected in the emphasis of their mission work. Both in the eastern Cape and in the area north of the Orange River, the Methodist society attached itself politically to weaker and more fissiparous centres of chiefly power,[13] and set its face firmly against those (such as Ngqika and his sons in Xhosaland, and Moshoeshoe and his sons in Transorangia) whose claims to authority implied a centralisation and consolidation of black state power and black means of resistance.[14] In both areas they came into conflict with the LMS and its allies (the Paris Evangelical Missionary Society in Transorangia), who favoured the stronger chiefs and their claims to regional hegemony, as bulwarks against settler expansionism and settler power, and who actively promoted the arming of their patrons. The competing mission societies fought for dominion like rival imperial states, and conflicts over rights to land of the societies or their chiefly patrons featured prominently in disputes between missionary organisations.

Apart from their political role, missionaries were particularly important as forward agents of the trade frontier.[15] Missionary trade began with the very first missionaries of the LMS.[16] Van der Kemp traded with Ngqika's people as early as 1799, acquiring milk cows for thirty metal buttons each, an ox for forty. The universal currency of the chiefdoms at first was buttons, beads and brass wire. It is little wonder that Van der Kemp and Read wanted to establish a button factory near Algoa Bay in 1802. Beads and buttons were used not only for trade, but for wages, tribute and gifts to chiefs. As far as the societies were concerned, trading activities were entirely legitimate, indeed necessary for the survival and development of mission stations, but officially they frowned on trade conducted by missionaries solely for profit. However, the missionaries themselves often did not share such moral qualms.[17]

Both the LMS and the Methodist missionaries constantly demanded supplies of beads and buttons from their home societies, specifying styles and colours required according to the fashion of the time or the requirements of a particular market. The subject took up much space in the correspondence of men like William Shaw, the Methodist missionary leader. Shaw wanted these trade items shipped directly from England, as Cape Town merchants apparently made profits of up to 500 per cent on them. In August 1824 he asked for half a ton of beads and three hundred pounds of brass wire. In July 1825 the Rev. Stephen Kay wrote to the Methodist society in London stating that each station would require four to five hundred pounds of beads per annum for the next few years. It is thus clear that the settler trade that played so important a role in the rise of a new settler elite in the eastern Cape in the 1820s was pioneered in part by missionaries.[18]

Trade at mission stations was formalised by the setting up in the 1820s of trading stores under missionary control, supplied by principals at Port Elizabeth or Graham's Town.[19] The store at Wesleyville, the first permanent establishment set up beyond the eastern frontier (in 1827), conducted its business in the name of Messrs Cock & Co. of Graham's Town – William Cock being one of the most successful of the settler entrepreneurs.[20] The missionaries' intention was to promote African enterprise and handicrafts, by purchasing corn, aloes, gum arabic, baskets and mats, in exchange for European clothes and other 'useful articles', and to avoid the trade in hides and ivory which would compete with the secular trade. Such produce would then be resold at Graham's Town, where the inhabitants, wrote Shaw, were 'enriching themselves by the rapidly extending trade in ivory, hides, gums, aloes, etc.'.[21]

By the end of the 1820s, new demands were displacing buttons and beads as desired commodities among Xhosa. Apart from the acquisition of textiles and metalware, they were becoming gradually armed with European weapons.

Surprisingly, missionaries of a humanitarian persuasion were often willing collaborators in the arms trade in the interior. In their view, if Africans were to defend themselves against the aggressions of settlers, British or Boer, they should be provided with the means to do so. Humanitarians thus vehemently opposed the official prohibition on trade in guns and ammunition.[22] One justification of their position was the presumed threat posed by the militaristic Zulu. The imperial commissioners of enquiry in the 1820s concluded that 'the gradual introduction of fire-arms among the Caffers, when the relations of Trade have connected their interests more firmly with those of the Colony, would in the same manner enable them to resist the threatened attack of a warlike tribe of savages on their eastern confines.'[23] A further concern lay behind this. Fairbairn warned in January 1831 that American and other foreign interests would secure a foothold on the subcontinent by providing Africans with guns if British traders were not allowed to supply them. Fairbairn held out the dire prospect of the Nguni people looking towards Port Natal as the 'emporium of their growing trade', to the huge detriment of British interests.[24]

Indeed, by the 1830s arms and ammunition were becoming a central, albeit still illegal, trade item on the eastern frontier. A similar situation prevailed in the trade across the northern frontiers, where Boers and Griqua were the main agents of commerce. Despite government restrictions, a profitable smuggling trade flourished, and certain officials were known to make substantial profits out of the government monopoly of the supply of gunpowder. But a royal order-in-council in February 1832 allowed merchants to import and sell ammunition to their private account. Although the prohibition on selling arms and ammunition to African peoples was maintained, it was brazenly ignored, on the Xhosa frontier to the east as much as to the north. This resulted in an enormous increase in officially recorded imports of gunpowder. In 1833, 30 000 lb were shipped into Cape Town alone in a period of six months. A considerable proportion of this ended in the hands of indigenous peoples. In response Acting-Governor Wade in November 1833 raised the licence fees and import duties to stem the flood, but the ordinance was disallowed after the Cape of Good Hope Trade Society petitioned the Colonial Office against it, on the grounds that it would merely lead to increased smuggling and the taking over of the trade by American suppliers. In 1834 the Cape government secretary complained that Cape Town merchants were using the colony as a 'convenient road for supplying its neighbours and future enemies with ammunition merely because it would give them an advantage over their rivals'.[25]

It was widely contended that Graham's Town was an important entrepôt in this trade. Names of eminent members of the settler bourgeoisie, such as W. R. Thompson and James Howse, were mentioned in this connection. But in the three years up to the end of 1833 this trade reportedly resulted in only two prosecutions and one conviction in Graham's Town. The Khoi of the Kat River Settlement were one conduit in the gun-running business originating in Graham's Town. Klaas Platje in 1835 testified to having often seen Andries

Stoffels, whom we have met as a close confidant of the missionaries, selling muskets to Xhosa intermediaries for an ox each at a house belonging to James Read. 'All the people ... knew of Andries Stoffel selling guns to the Gonahs for the Caffres, and ... it was generally said you can buy guns of Andries Stoffel at Mr Read's.'[26] Boers (such as Louis Tregardt) and Griqua from the northern frontier were also accused of selling weapons to the Xhosa; and the schooner *James,* which anchored beyond colonial jurisdiction in July 1835, was reported to be offloading guns for the Xhosa, then at war with the British.[27]

The settler merchants of Graham's Town continued through the 1840s to be a major source of armaments for the Xhosa. It may seem paradoxical that the settler bourgeoisie, who dedicated their public lives to urging the dispossession and subjugation of the African chiefdoms, should simultaneously be involved in providing them with the means of armed resistance. But profits spoke volumes to these men, and guns and powder fetched incomparable profits after the collapse of the buttons and beads market. The guns, moreover, were of a very inferior description, being usually obsolete, and were no match for the armoury of the British and colonial forces. The Xhosa were also wholly untrained in using them, typically firing indiscriminately from the hip.[28] As far as the merchants were concerned, supplying Africans with guns must have seemed perfectly compatible with the larger purpose of crushing them militarily, and in the process enticing high levels of British military expenditure to the colony. The missionary David Livingstone, who was himself to be implicated in the arms trade among the Tswana, some years later described the role long played by the local bourgeoisie: 'The Graham's Town merchants who are the principal getters up of the war sell their goods to the troops at enormous profits, and then when the war is concluded they supply the Caffres with guns and gunpowder and call for a war again, and that great idiot John Bull has to pay the piper. This system has gone on for years.'[29]

By the 1830s the ivory frontier had receded, and increasingly Africans were becoming dependent on the sale of livestock, animal products and agricultural produce for access to British manufactures. In the process colonial traders began to raise the ire of the chiefs. Not only did they undermine self-sufficiency, and drain cattle resources, but the chiefs were unable to regulate and profit from their activities. Traders were closely allied with the Graham's Town elite and the Methodist missionaries, and flaunted their influence with the colonial military. They also flagrantly disregarded the laws and usages of the chiefdoms. The result was that when war broke out in 1834–5, a number of traders were killed, despite the fact that white civilians were seldom attacked by the Xhosa in time of war.[30]

❖

The Xhosa had every reason for wishing to arm themselves. In terms of the reprisals system, instituted officially by Governor Somerset in 1817, military patrols, accompanied by aggrieved farmers – sometimes verging on full-scale commandos – could invade Xhosaland to recover allegedly stolen cattle by following its spoor. If found, the cattle could be seized, or else compensation could be demanded and seized. In practice, the system shaded into utter lawlessness, it seems, and certainly there was a constant stream of complaints from missionaries and others of quite indiscriminate and arbitrary depredations. Acting-Governor Bourke in 1826 issued instructions that colonists were not to enter Xhosaland in search of lost cattle, but to no avail. Sir Lowry Cole's governorship (1829–33) was particularly characterised by policies of military coercion against the chiefdoms. Colonel Henry Somerset, military commandant on the frontier (and Lord Charles's son), was determined to drive the Xhosa across the Keiskamma and out of the 'ceded territory'.[31]

By 1829 frontier tensions were building up to breaking point. A severe drought raised the levels of conflict over grazing land, both between the chiefdoms, and between Xhosa and colonists.[32] Adding to the chronic instability on the frontier, the colonial military under Colonel Somerset had in 1828 joined with Thembu and Xhosa in attacking the Ngwane refugee chiefdom at Mbholompo deep beyond the Kei, and refugees had begun creating additional pressures on the frontier.[33] Then in 1829, the ailing chief Ngqika's most powerful son, Maqoma, and his people were driven from the Kat River region of the ceded territory to make way for a settlement of Khoi smallholders in the Kat River valley. The pretext was the raiding of Thembu villages by Maqoma's people.[34] The idea of such a settlement of Khoi on the eastern boundary had first been mooted in 1823 by Thomas Pringle as a system for stabilising the frontier and, in the process, further extending the humanitarian preoccupation with establishing prosperous and independent communities of the dispossessed Khoi working class. Despite the humanitarian origins of the idea, the fact that the settlement was situated on land from which Maqoma's Xhosa had been expelled would appal people like Pringle.[35]

As commissioner-general in the eastern districts from 1828 to 1833, Andries Stockenström opposed the policies of commando raids and reprisals. To Stockenström, the arbitrary and provocative nature of Somerset's aggressive policies would lead inevitably to war. Stockenström's alternative proposal was a treaty system, built on mutual cooperative agreements with the chiefs (who, after all, held sway beyond the borders of British rule) for the stabilisation of frontier relations. In his autobiography, Stockenström criticised the military, with settler interests at their back, for desiring 'a chain of sanguinary wars which were to cost the mother country some millions of money ... but would popularise themselves by bringing enormous fortunes to some dozens of speculators, and overwhelm head-quarters with patronage'. He described 'the eternal din of those who were already on tiptoe of excitement at the prospect of millions which the military chest was to pour forth, and the promotions, patronage, and popularity, which that only inexhaustible source was to spread over our thirsty land'.[36] In evidence before the select committee on aborigines in London in 1836 he was to advocate his point of view fiercely, as we shall see. Colonel Somerset refused to submit to Stockenström's authority, whom he regarded as an upstart colonial. Stockenström for his part regarded Somerset's appointment as military commander in the east as evidence of nepotism.[37] Constantly frustrated in his attempts to impose his authority on the military and to prohibit the arbitrary seizure of Xhosa cattle, Stockenström eventually decided that his job as commissioner-general for the eastern districts was a 'fraud upon the public'. 'As long as one single soldier could be moved with hostile intent, without my requisition or sanction, my political responsibility was a sham and a hoax,' he later wrote. He recommended that the post be abolished, which it was in 1833.[38]

In Cape Town Fairbairn at the *Commercial Advertiser* began to publicise the alternative policies espoused by Stockenström. In 1832 he was already pushing for the adoption of a treaty system as opposed to the policy of military coercion and depredation. He urged the recognition of an executive authority among the Xhosa with which the colonial government could treat as equals on diplomatic terms. 'In every respect they should be treated as a nation having a regular Government, and a regular Executive, responsible to us, and we to them in every case.'[39]

At this time Philip appeared again at the forefront of the humanitarian cause. After his return from England in 1829, having obtained the liberalisation of labour relations within the colony which had been his primary preoccupation through the 1820s, he turned his attention more fully to the cause of the independent African societies beyond colonial borders. With Fairbairn, he visited the eastern districts early in 1830. There they expressed their indignation at the plight of the Xhosa, at the atrocities of the military, and the predatory and provocative intentions of the settlers. To them, the instability of the frontier region was attributable to the settlers' determination to dispossess and subjugate the indigenous people.[40] Summarising his impressions on this tour of 1830, Philip wrote:

> Slander and defamation, and the injuries done them [the Xhosa] by the colonists, have already done their work, and their slanderers are now waiting an opportunity to excite a quarrel that will furnish a pretext to the Government to drive them from their lands, when they hope to share their cattle and their land. In such a colony there are numbers of toadeaters, civil servants who want estates. These men are on the very borders, from them the Government secures all its information respecting the Caffres, and they are incessant in their exertions to accomplish their objects. Frontier Boers, Field Cornets, magistrates, friends of magistrates want new grants of land, and these grants must be taken from the Caffres.[41]

Thus as early as 1830 Philip identified the forces of frontier destabilisation that were already well advanced. However, we need to be wary of Philip's evidence, which rings with polemical intent and anti-Boer prejudice. He knew what notes to play to appeal to an ignorant home audience. The term 'Boer' was used typically as a useful shorthand for settlerdom in general and, in the context of the time, one intended to have maximum impact on humanitarian sensibilities. As we shall see, the really predatory enemies of the Xhosa were not Boers at all, but British settlers.

Philip was back in Xhosaland in 1832, ready to take up the African cause with a vengeance. While at Kat River he met Maqoma, Tyhali and Sandile, the major sons of the late chief Ngqika, to whom the LMS had long been attached.[42] Philip was kept closely informed on frontier affairs by Stockenström and by James Read at the Kat River, who, together with his coloured and especially Gonaqua Khoi friends that travelled extensively and dealt with the main Xhosa chiefs, was in a good position to keep a finger on the pulse of frontier politics.[43] A crucial agent in this communication network was Jan Tshatshu. Son of a minor Xhosa chief, he had served the LMS for many years, from the time of Van der Kemp's days at Bethelsdorp, and was to accompany Philip and Read to England in 1836.[44] Other informants who emerged at this time were John Ross of the Glasgow society and Frederick Kayser of the LMS. Ross was attached to Maqoma's people, who had been expelled from the Kat River to make way for the Khoi.[45] (By this time the colonial authorities no longer vetted the establishment of missionaries among African peoples, as Somerset had done.) There can be no doubt that these missionaries in the Philip camp were up to a point trusted by the chiefs, whereas government agents such as the missionary Thomson and the Methodists were certainly not, as Thomson's biographer concedes.[46]

Meanwhile, repeated efforts were being made during Cole's governorship to clear remaining Xhosa beyond the Keiskamma. At the same time land beyond the Fish River in the ceded territory was increasingly taken up by white settlers and speculators – though the secretary of state for the colonies, whose opinion of the allegedly slaveholding Boers was formed by humanitarian propaganda, explicitly prohibited Boers from settling there.[47] In 1831 and 1833 troops drove people and cattle indiscriminately over the Keiskamma, burning huts and crops, during a period of severe drought.[48] Militarists on the frontier thought a salutary war would put the Xhosa in their place. It was only a matter of time, it seemed, before full-scale war erupted. Cole, confronted with the paucity of regular troops at his disposal, and the reluctance of Boers to turn out on commando, attempted to bolster the old commando system by imposing penalties on colonists failing to heed a call-up. Particularly alarming was the provision in Ordinance 99 of 1833 that any junior official down to acting field cornet could call out colonists on commando, a provision (in the eyes of the critics) virtually licensing anarchy. But Lord Stanley at the Colonial Office (under intense humanitarian pressure) disallowed the ordinance.[49] The opening shots had been fired in a war between settler accumulators and their military allies on the one hand, and the humanitarians at the Cape and their metropolitan allies in England on the other.

In 1833 Philip began in earnest feeding Fowell Buxton, leader of the Saints in the House of Commons, with information on frontier affairs for use in his campaigning in parliament. 'Furnish me with facts,' Buxton asked Philip, and the latter obliged. In 1834 Buxton pushed in parliament for a select committee on aboriginal affairs in the colonies, but he had to wait a year before it was appointed. The initial success of the humanitarians was reflected not only in Lord Stanley's rejection of Governor Cole's commando ordinance of 1833, but in Stanley's instructions to the new governor, Sir Benjamin D'Urban, who arrived at the Cape in January 1834.[50]

D'Urban brought with him a plan hammered out at the Colonial Office, much influenced by William Ellis, secretary of the LMS. Closely similar to Stockenström's proposed treaty system, this was based on a proposed system of alliances with independent chiefs. In terms of the plan the chiefs undertook to accept responsibility for the peaceful conduct of their followers, in return for annual gifts in recognition of their independent authority.[51] At the Cape, Philip used his considerable influence to win D'Urban's ear, and for a time exercised great influence over the new governor.[52] Although Philip (in contrast to some of his closest colleagues) would have preferred a massive extension of British sovereignty and British expenditure to the benefit and protection of Africans against the depredations of the settlers, he gave the proposed treaty system his blessing as the next best option.[53] It was a great improvement on the essentially militarist policies followed by Governor Cole and Colonel Somerset previously. Late in 1834, Philip went east to the frontier to sound out the chiefs pending D'Urban's arrival to implement a treaty system. He used the opportunity to gather further information and evidence for Buxton in London, and in the process aroused dark suspicions among the settlers about his motives. As the avalanche of negative publicity emanating from Cape Town grew towards them, so the more enraged became the settler elite of the eastern Cape.[54]

After a long history of expulsions and cattle-lifting expeditions against the Xhosa, which reached a climax in a series of incidents in 1834, war broke out a couple of days before the Christmas of that year.[55] The Ngqika Xhosa, under the late chief Ngqika's sons Maqoma and Tyhali, took the initiative in bringing tensions to a culmination, in the hope of regaining the steadily diminishing lands in the ceded territory from which they were being systematically ejected. Some 12 000 Xhosa poured over the frontier in small raiding parties, easily evading Colonel Somerset's concentrated frontier troops and sending the white farmers of the district fleeing to Graham's Town.[56]

The war of 1834–5 brought factional tensions within colonial society to a boil too. It constituted one of those key moments when accumulative dynamics were sharply revealed. The war and its consequences were certainly seen by people at the time as a crossroads. Was settler militarism to prevail in securing state support, or were countervailing priorities to stabilise the colonial society as a low-cost outpost of merchant capital? Was imperial power to be mobilised in pursuit of settler speculative profit and accumulation of resources, or were African peoples to be incorporated as free producers and consumers into the colonial embrace?

Fairbairn at the *Commercial Advertiser* charged that the settlers had provoked the Xhosa invasion. 'Indeed,' he declared, 'it required no supernatural powers to predict that violence would beget violence, and that unjust inroads into their country on our part, would, some time or other, be followed by destructive retaliation on the part of the Caffers.'[57] In his turn Godlonton at the *Graham's Town Journal* accused Philip, Fairbairn and their colleagues of sowing the seeds of war in the minds of the chiefs by their agitations on their visits to the frontier and through their published propaganda. A Xhosa informant was brought forward in Graham's Town to testify that it was 'common knowledge' among the Xhosa that on his visit in 1834 Philip had promised the chiefs that their lost lands would be restored. A storekeeper from Kat River alleged too that Philip had been heard boasting to the chiefs of his role in liberating the Khoi from oppression.[58] Indeed, when war broke out in December 1834, an organised boycott of the *Commercial Advertiser* was launched in Graham's Town, accompanied by a petition signed by 479 people specifically blaming Fairbairn for complicity in the Xhosa aggression. Fairbairn had 'endeavoured to advocate the proceedings of the ruthless barbarians who are now ravaging the colony,' wrote the editor of the *Graham's Town Journal*. The result was a 'deep and universal feeling of indignation and disgust' in Graham's Town.[59]

For the settlers, the sympathy of the home public and of the politicians in London was of crucial importance at this juncture. On their approbation hung many things: the stationing of a large and profitable military force on the frontier (with the vastly augmented local market that would thus be created), the establishment of a more substantial and responsive local government in the eastern districts with an autonomous governor or lieutenant-governor stationed at Graham's Town, and settler claims for financial compensation for war losses (real or imagined). All of this depended on general acceptance of the settlers' view of the causes and significance of the war. It was of the greatest importance to them that the Xhosa be seen as bloody savages who had to be subjugated and displaced before civilisation could triumph. Yet the humanitarians in Cape Town and London threatened to subvert them at the very moment when they seemed on the verge of success.

So Godlonton set about putting forward the case of the settlers against their critics by publishing within a few months of the war's commencement the first instalment of his work *Introductory Remarks to a Narrative of the Irruption of the Kafir Hordes*, based on material originally published in his *Journal*. In this, he sought to show that Xhosa depredations and savagery were a continual and intolerable threat to peace, and stressed the forbearance and peaceful intentions of the colonists. Godlonton was particularly concerned to show that the Xhosa were recent usurpers of the land west of the Kei (as recently as the

1780s), land which had belonged to the Khoi and the Boers. An unambiguously anti-liberal and anti-Xhosa rhetoric now pervaded settler propaganda.[60]

At one level, the contending forces predictably confronted each other in religious guise. Accusation and counter-accusation of culpability for the war led to a veritable war of words between the Methodists, represented particularly by William Shaw and William Boyce, and the humanitarians, represented by John Philip of the LMS. The Methodists were concerned to defend the British settlers; some at least repeated the charge that Philip and his allies had instigated the chiefs to invade the colony. To the Methodists, this invasion was an 'unprovoked aggression' by the Xhosa, who had 'most wantonly, cruelly, and ungratefully commenced this war with a people who sought and desired their welfare and prosperity'. To the London and Glasgow societies, on the other hand, the Xhosa were the victims of settler-inspired military aggression.[61]

Certainly, as far as the settlers were concerned, whether they consciously sought to instigate war or not, the war brought with it great opportunities. Firstly, it brought Governor D'Urban to Graham's Town, where he was based for an unprecedented eleven months. War had broken out before D'Urban could turn his attention fully to frontier matters (he had had first to oversee the emancipation of the slaves). But once confronted with the war on the frontier face to face, he swiftly turned his back on the instructions that he had brought out with him from London to implement a system of treaties. For D'Urban was first and foremost a military man with a firm belief in the efficacy of military solutions.[62] He was not the last governor to turn rogue once plunged into the maelstrom of settler politics.

In Graham's Town, D'Urban soon fell under the influence of the settler bourgeoisie, and he became convinced that Philip had misled him about the situation in the eastern districts. He was enraged by evidence of Xhosa devastation of settler farms, and soon believed that there was a conspiracy of chiefs at work. The settlers, he claimed, had been grievously misrepresented.[63] He wrote to Graham's Town settler leaders in July 1835 that he had observed 'not without painful astonishment, the dangerous efforts of some (I would fain hope but a very few) persons within the colony to sacrifice the cause and to degrade the character of their fellow-countrymen, in defence of those of a savage and treacherous enemy.'[64]

Prominent settlers attached themselves to D'Urban as advisers on the grounds of their special knowledge of Xhosaland as traders: the Bowkers, Southeys, Theophilus Shepstone, Walter Currie, John Bisset, Abel Hoole. In the military government set up in Graham's Town, prominent townsmen like Robert Godlonton, W. R. Thompson, J. D. Norden, William Wright and James Black were appointed wardmasters.[65] The Methodist missionaries in particular made an impression on D'Urban, who reported to London (quite inaccurately) that 'all the Missionaries upon the borders ... concur in one opinion, of the wanton atrocity of their [the Xhosa] invasion, and of the impossibility of any other remedy than the Sword'. In fact, of course, only the Methodists held such opinions. The Methodist missionaries also performed a valuable function in acting as D'Urban's emissaries to the chiefs.[66]

D'Urban soon agreed with the settlers that the solution to problems of frontier instability lay not in treaties with independent chiefs, but in extending imperial sovereignty and pushing the boundary further east to the Kei, and in crushing and expelling the Xhosa – incidentally, also thereby throwing open Xhosa lands to settler land-grabbing. Subjugation and dispossession was the settler creed, and D'Urban set about implementing a policy of military expansionism, relying largely on commandeered burgher forces.[67] Having been 'most pacifically inclined' towards the Xhosa the previous year (according to the settler Thomas Philipps after an interview), D'Urban was now describing them in official pronouncements as 'treacherous and irreclaimable savages'.[68]

The Xhosa paramount, Hintsa, chief of the Gcaleka Xhosa across the Kei well to the east of the border, was seen by D'Urban as the evil genius lurking behind the treachery. The governor ascribed to Hintsa an authority which in practice he did not possess. While Hintsa undoubtedly sympathised with the invaders of the colony and sheltered colonial cattle lifted by them, he did not control the more westerly Xhosa in the way D'Urban assumed. Nevertheless, D'Urban determined that Hintsa and his people must be made to pay for the aggressions against the settlers. In all this D'Urban was egged on by his second-in-command, Lieutenant-Colonel Harry Smith, who was himself to become another, even more expansionist rogue governor at a later date. D'Urban and Smith were seeking to invest the 'Xhosa nation' with a spurious political cohesiveness, and to undermine it by attacking it at its centre. Thus the aggressions of some of the chiefdoms in the cisKei provided the pretext for launching a strike at the Xhosa heartland – a strategy that was to become characteristic of wars of dispossession in the subcontinent generally. And behind the governor were the agitations of British settlers and Methodist missionaries who saw that their own interests would best be served by striking at the heart of Xhosa legitimate authority. By the end of April, D'Urban's force had crossed the Kei into Gcaleka territory.[69]

Hintsa (who made no effort to resist the British invading force) was made responsible for proclaiming and implementing the cessation of all hostilities, and he was obliged to pay a huge and quite unrealistic number of livestock as indemnity to the colonial authorities. He was held hostage in the governor's camp pending the implementation of the settlement. On trying to escape, he was shot dead and his body mutilated. D'Urban gloated in a dispatch that Hintsa deserved his fate. But the episode became a *cause célèbre* for humanitarian propagandists, and they made much use of the commission of enquiry appointed to investigate it. Buxton's and Philip's standing as informants on frontier affairs was much enhanced at the Colonial Office as a result.[70] For the Xhosa, this act of unmitigated barbarism was to remain the central event of the war; hence it became known to them as the War of Hintsa.[71]

But D'Urban's most dramatic step was yet to come. In May 1835 he proclaimed the annexation of what was to be called Queen Adelaide Province right up to the Kei River, more than 7000 square miles in extent, and announced his intention to expel the cisKeian Xhosa chiefdoms beyond the river.[72] Militarily, pushing the boundary further east to the Kei made sense, as it lay in open country and was thus much more easily patrolled than the thick bush of the river valleys further west. But the settlers had more pressing preoccupations than military considerations, faced as they were with the prospect of several thousand square miles of attractive farming land being opened up and cleared of its human population. Philip explained the war to Buxton in January 1835 thus: 'The frontier colonists have long set their hearts upon Caffreland – they already calculate upon having it given them as sheep-farms and the general cry is "blood! blood!"'[73] One of their number, Holden Bowker, scion of a prominent settler family, recorded in his war journal that the 'fine land' of the Xhosa through which he campaigned beyond the Keiskamma would 'make excellent sheep farms'. It was 'far too good for such a race of runaways as the Kaffirs'. The *Graham's Town Journal*, representing such acquisitive elements, enthusiastically sought to justify this impending massive forfeiture of territory by many thousand Xhosa as just punishment, and essential to security and progress; 'if any Governor of this Colony had a debt of gratitude due to him from its inhabitants, it is Sir Benjamin D'Urban'.[74]

The prospects for land speculation were unprecedented and intoxicating. Settlers scrambled to secure the patronage of the governor for the land grab that was to come. The frontier land surveyor Frederick Rex assured his father in a letter that the governor was so favourably disposed to his land claims that he 'could get almost anything done'.[75] Among the four hundred or so who submitted claims to land grants in the new province the Southeys and the Bowkers were prominent, as were Theophilus Shepstone, Charles Maynard (with three requests), W. R. Thompson, George Wood, Henry Nourse, James Howse, the four Cawood brothers, James Collett, George Jarvis, William Ogilvie, P. W. Lucas and Abel Hoole – a veritable 'who's who' of British settlerdom, merchants, speculators, accumulators all. D'Urban himself was not above exercising patronage towards the specially favoured. He assured J. M. Bowker in writing that the applications of himself and his family, as well as the Southeys and Shepstones, would receive precedence over all others, should his measures be approved by London.[76]

These sanguine expectations were to collapse, as we shall see. But in the meantime, another welcome and predictable side-effect of war provided further unprecedented opportunities for the settler elite. Imperial war-chest disbursements on the war amounted to £154 000, and that was only a part of the increased expenditure that can be ascribed directly or indirectly to the war – amounting perhaps to £500 000. Commissariat contracts enriched many a Graham's Town merchant: the supply of forage and wagon transport was a prolific source of profit. Prices generally soared for marketable commodities.

William Cock, the 'army butcher', for example, was a 'made man' after the war as a result of his meat contracts, and was to play a leading role in the affairs of the eastern Cape as an eminent public figure for years to come. William Southey and Godlonton himself were apparently successful contractors too.[77]

In the circumstances of war, public funds were available to be plundered, and those who held the military purse-strings were no less averse than the governor himself to extending patronage towards loyal settlerdom. Shady, not to say fraudulent, dealings seem to have been the result. George Wood, another Graham's Town merchant of modest origins, who began as an itinerant at the Fort Willshire fairs and who was well on his way to becoming a man of great wealth (he was not yet 30), was involved in a scandal that arose from his highly inflated contract for the supply of cloth for the uniforms of the Khoi troops, for which he apparently raked in £6000 or £7000.[78] The Quaker traveller Backhouse, visiting Graham's Town in 1839, was appalled at the 'nature of the things they [the merchants] persuaded those commissioned to make purchases for the army, to take', and the 'charges for supplies'.[79] War thus was not a calamity but an opportunity for these accumulating men. They acquired a reputation as warmongers, a reputation that was to spread and increase as the years went by. The critical observer Lennox Stretch noted in his diary the militant posture of the 'Graham's Town worthies', who were determined that the 'war *should proceed*, the Caffres were not *sufficiently punished*'.[80]

Apart from the prospect of sharing in the great land alienation that seemed imminent, and the opportunity to share in the profits to be gained from military expenditure during the war, there was also the prospect of benefiting from the compensation for war losses that settlers felt sure a beneficent government would not deny them. As early as February 1835, a 'committee of merchants and others connected with the trade of Grahamstown' petitioned the government for 'aid by loans upon real property and by advances upon the compensation which may be eventually made for losses sustained through the invasion of the colony by the Caffers' (a request turned down by the Executive Council in Cape Town).[81] The statistics of losses sustained which were collected by the civil commissioner were without doubt greatly exaggerated.[82]

The whole settler agenda seemed set fair to materialise in mid-1835. The massive 'freeing' of Xhosa land (and, presumably as a consequence, labour too), the presence in the east of a sympathetic and resolute governor backed by a substantial military force, the expectation that at last a commitment to strong government and economic development had been accepted by the imperial authorities – all this indicated that a turning point had arrived, and that humanitarianism was a beaten force. But these assumptions were premature.

Not all Africans were to be expelled beyond the Kei in the proposed settlement after the war. The Mfengu, for one, were to be 'liberated' and resettled within the colony. Although the identity of the Mfengu (or 'Fingoes') has become a topic of considerable scholarly dispute, most agree they were an amalgam of immigrant groups of various northern Nguni origins who arrived in Xhosa territory from different directions over a period of time. Such newcomers would typically have attached themselves at first to the Xhosa as clients and dependants, either as individuals or as larger clan groups or lineages, exchanging both cattle and women. The paramount Hintsa himself married a Bhele (northern Nguni) woman to cement the 'friendship'. Some may have achieved positions of authority, and would have begun to accumulate wealth. Like the 'Mantatees' of colonial literature, 'Fingo' came to be loosely used as a blanket term for refugee labourers entering colonial employment from Xhosaland in the 1820s and 1830s.[83]

By the 1830s a centre of Mfengu settlement had been established at the Methodist mission station at Butterworth, where John Ayliff was stationed. It is not clear whether Mfengu were singularly attracted, as relative outsiders, to the apparent advantages of mission affiliation, or to what extent mission-attracted people found it appropriate to embrace Mfengu identity (which after all was, like all identities, an infinitely flexible thing). But what is clear is that by 1835 relations between Ayliff and the Xhosa paramount, Hintsa, had soured, as Ayliff's station became an alternative and antagonistic centre of temporal authority to the paramountcy. And it seems that relations between the Mfengu and their Xhosa hosts were also becoming tenser, with Xhosa accusations of Mfengu witchcraft and the 'eating up' by Xhosa of Mfengu cattle on the increase. The role of missionary activity in fomenting these social cleavages is clouded by the nature of the evidence. But there can be little doubt that Ayliff was concerned to spread the notion both to Mfengu and to colonial authorities in 1835, when British invasion across the Kei seemed imminent, that the Mfengu were an enslaved and oppressed people, whose emancipation from Xhosa thraldom was an imperial duty. In consequence, many Mfengu saw potential advantage in looking to Ayliff as their source of political patronage. At one level this is an example of the way missionaries commonly sought to manipulate and engineer ethnic identities. (The Mfengu were not very distinct culturally or linguistically from the Xhosa, and passing from one identity to another was presumably quite easy.) Nonetheless, the political intention of Ayliff quite clearly was to sabotage the relative cohesion of an independent African chiefdom, by promoting ethnic conflict and separatism.[84]

In March 1835 Ayliff wrote to the *Graham's Town Journal* warning that, according to his Mfengu spies, Hintsa was planning to destroy his station at Butterworth and personally do the missionary to death. Ayliff then told D'Urban that the Mfengu earnestly requested deliverance from their enslavement at the hands of the Xhosa. When D'Urban arrived across the Kei, Mfengu representatives came to his camp pleading to be accepted as British subjects under British protection. D'Urban and Smith immediately saw the advantages of turning the Mfengu into colonial allies, settled as a buffer on the colonial borders, between the Fish and Keiskamma rivers, and also of supplementing colonial labour supplies. In their migration to their new home, the 16 000 or 17 000 Mfengu reportedly took with them some 20 000 head of cattle that in large part apparently belonged to Xhosa patrons.[85]

D'Urban bought Ayliff's special pleading unreservedly, and justified the 'emancipation' of the Mfengu in his dispatch to London not only in terms of their usefulness as a 'buffer state' or as labourers, but as consistent with the anti-slavery convictions of British governments. Indeed, the 'emancipation' of the Mfengu was even more justified than the freeing of slaves in the empire in the previous year, he wrote, 'since in no instance did that extensive Emancipation rescue any race from a life of misery bearing any comparison to the wretched state of slavery and oppression under which this nation groaned'.[86] Here we see the potent impact of Methodist missionary propaganda, which, whatever other considerations might have prevailed, had the deliberate effect of disrupting cohesion and solidarity within an independent African society faced with an external imperialist threat. Independent focuses of legitimate black authority were anathema and had to be undermined. In this, as in so much else, the Methodists fully represented the interests of settler accumulators. The rhetoric of anti-slavery was both flexible and useful.

The incorporation of the Mfengu into the colony, as well as the reformulation of Mfengu identity, was the single most important consequence of the war, and the one which was to serve the settler elite best in the expansion of labour supplies. The Mfengu for their part were to experience various fortunes, some becoming an archetypal colonial peasantry, others becoming part of the colonial working class.[87] In the locations at Peddie and Tyhume, chiefs were placed over them, often it seems with scant regard to historical antecedents.[88] They also settled at mission stations such as Kat River (1500 of them) and Theopolis (where Mfengu and Sotho 'Mantatees' made up the bulk of the population in the 1840s), on farms and in towns such as Graham's Town, Port Elizabeth and Uitenhage. This influx of the Mfengu precipitated, as much as anything else, the decline in the status and opportunities of the mission coloureds, sending many eventually to seek alternative havens elsewhere, such as north of the Orange.[89] Numbers of the Mfengu were to prove loyal and dependable military allies of the colony in subsequent conflict with the Xhosa.

The settler-inspired forward march of imperial force on the eastern frontier was, however, to falter and then collapse. Firstly, D'Urban began backing away from his policy of total expulsion of the Xhosa from his new Queen Adelaide Province. In the well-wooded, mountainous country beyond the Keiskamma, the Xhosa warriors could not be decisively subdued; nor could the thousands of Xhosa be removed (and kept across the Kei) without military resources of an altogether different order from those available. Thus by September 1835

D'Urban fell back on a policy of providing defined locations for the chiefdoms. The Xhosa in the Queen Adelaide Province were to become British subjects, and British magistrates were to ensure that British justice should prevail. For the first time, intact indigenous societies were to be incorporated with their own institutions under British rule – a proposed increase of some 70 000 souls in the colony's population. The settlers were aghast at this reversal of policy, and D'Urban's reassurance that large tracts would still be left vacant between the locations for the 'occupation and speculations of Europeans' did not placate them.[90]

Within the new province D'Urban's policy was to erode the power of the chiefs, and reduce them 'to the most wholesome position of subordinate magistrates (or field cornets) acting under prescribed rules and limits'.[91] Colonel Harry Smith, the new ruler of Queen Adelaide Province, developed grand ideas of himself as supreme chief over the African chiefdoms, dispensing the magical benefits of civilisation to his grateful subjects.[92] Although this rhetoric of civilisation was not dissimilar to the humanitarians', the utilitarian means were radically different. Innovative ideas like these were to be implemented two decades later by another governor, Sir George Grey, but by then Xhosa independence had collapsed. In 1835, such notions were premature – notions of incorporating Xhosa people within colonial society as subservient subjects waiting for 'civilisation' to transform them into a dutiful working class.

All the same, the agenda of the authorities in London was not that of the settler bourgeoisie of the eastern Cape. The officials at the Colonial Office were not averse to imperial commitments; but they were averse to financing grand imperial projects whose benefits did not seem to justify the expenditure required, and which bore risks of ever-greater commitments with little prospect of profit except for a self-aggrandising settler elite. But while it was the commitment to economy – the essential principle of the informal imperialism of free trade – that dictated policy, it was the rage of the humanitarians at Governor D'Urban's annexations and dispossessions that provided the public rhetoric.

Humanitarian pressures had been at work in London since news of the outbreak of war arrived. Buxton and William Ellis of the LMS brought pressure to bear on the new colonial secretary, Lord Glenelg, himself very much a scion of an evangelical family, and hence susceptible to influence from such circles. They were fed a constant stream of information on the causes and conduct of the war by John Philip at the Cape. Philip indeed became the major source of official information on Cape affairs at this crucial moment, especially after the circumstances of Hintsa's death became known, and in consequence Governor D'Urban's sparse correspondence was overwhelmed. In mid-1835, Buxton gained parliamentary consent for his select committee on aborigines, which he had unsuccessfully sought the previous year. This committee was intended to examine the state and treatment of indigenous peoples throughout Britain's overseas possessions, but in practice became an inquisition into the iniquities of border policy towards African people on and beyond the eastern frontier of the Cape Colony. The committee held 54 public meetings in 1835 and 1836, and interviewed 46 people, most of whom were of a humanitarian persuasion. Philip, accompanied by the Reads, Stoffels and Tshatshu, arrived in London, where they were lionised and paraded. In the process, the settlers (both Boer and British) and the colonial military were painted as the villains of the piece in no uncertain terms. The committee's report, demanding atonement for past wrongs committed against the native races, represented something of an apogee of parliamentary humanitarian activism in Cape affairs.[93]

The most damaging evidence before the committee came from none other than Andries Stockenström, until 1833 commissioner-general for the eastern districts, who had been called to London from a visit to his ancestral home in Sweden to give evidence. The fact that he was a born colonist, for years land-drost of the frontier district of Graaff-Reinet (as his father Anders had been before him), and of an Afrikanerised parental family, gave his evidence extra weight. He agreed strongly with the humanitarian condemnation of the militarist policies towards the Africans. He thus neatly complemented the flood of evidence coming from Philip in the Cape that much of the lifting of cattle from African villages as reprisals and compensation for theft, which had been going on for years, was in fact based on fraudulent claims by settlers, and that the settlers were activated by a desire to get possession of Xhosa territory.[94]

Philip himself declared before the committee that he supported the annexation of territory, provided that no land be given to settlers, but argued that it be secured for the Xhosa under their own independent authorities. In this Philip revealed himself as an arch-imperialist in support of the humanitarian cause. 'Annexation up to the tropics' was his prescription.[95] But so discredited was the very idea of territorial expansionism among the humanitarians in England, bearing as it did the taint of settler greed about it, that Philip's vision was drowned in the clamour to see D'Urban's measures exposed, discredited and overturned. In any event, humanitarian impulses at the end of the day did not drive imperial policy. What determined the fate of D'Urban's policies was primarily considerations of costs and benefits rather than the well-being of African peoples.

Hence the new secretary of state and those around him at the Colonial Office (such as James Stephen) had little compunction in overturning all D'Urban's proposals for the annexation of territory and the subjugation of the Xhosa. In his famous dispatch dated 26 December 1835, Glenelg enraged the settlers and delighted the humanitarians by declaring that the Xhosa had had 'ample justification' for invading the colony, and rebuked D'Urban for referring to the Xhosa as 'irreclaimable savages'. The Xhosa, wrote Glenelg, had been goaded beyond endurance 'by a long series of acts of injustice and spoliation' conducted under 'the express sanction and guidance of the authorities, civil and military, of the frontier districts'. He upheld the causes for the war alleged by Philip and the witnesses before the select committee. Glenelg further rejected any parallel between the 'liberation' of the Mfengu and slave emancipation.[96]

Queen Adelaide Province was to be abandoned, and any further extension of territory was to be avoided at all costs. In particular, any long-term, large-scale military commitment to the frontier (which was what the local settler bourgeoisie desired as the necessary basis for economic development and profit) was anathema to Glenelg and his officials. Instead he fell back on the prescription of a suitably disciplined local militia under imperial command – such as the 1820 settlers had originally been intended to constitute. In these ways the settlers would themselves have to pay for their own defence rather than relying on the British taxpayer. This would also have the desirable effect of dampening their expectations of benefiting from the militarisation of the frontier. As far as administration of frontier relations was concerned, Glenelg, influenced by Stockenström, wanted to see a return to the proposed treaty system which D'Urban had originally been sent to the Cape to implement, and which had the great advantage of being cheap. 'In other words,' wrote Glenelg, 'we must look to the Chiefs, and to them alone, and must no longer take upon ourselves to make reprisals upon the people.'[97]

In his dispatch, Glenelg thunderously gave his and the humanitarians' judgement on the whole project of settler accumulation in the colonies:

> Of all the Chapters in the History of Mankind, this is perhaps the most degrading; nor is there any one great course of events, on which every humane mind dwells with such settled aversion and shame, as on that which records the intercourse between the Christian States of Europe and the Heathen nations of America and Africa. I know not that a greater real calamity could befal Great Britain, than that of adding Southern Africa to the list of the Regions which have seen their aboriginal Inhabitants disappear under the withering influence of European neighbourhood.[98]

In this declamation Glenelg was passing the judgement of the Age of Capital on the whole centuries-old imperial enterprise which had made that age possible. The truth, though, was that the real motive forces behind imperial restraint in the region were far more prosaic than those implied in the rhetoric of philanthropy.

It was not surprising after Stockenström's condemnation of military solutions to frontier conflict, and his espousal of treaty relations with independent chiefs,[99] that he should be appointed to implement the border policy in the new post of lieutenant-governor of the eastern Cape. In his instructions to Stockenström, Glenelg wrote that his main task was to put in place a system 'as may ensure the maintenance of peace, good order and strict justice in the intercourse and relations between the inhabitants of European and African origin and descent on either side of the eastern frontier'. Glenelg clearly saw Stockenström's appointment as returning frontier administration to civil government, after it had fallen under permanent martial law with the 'administration of justice being left to the Commandant and his soldiers'.[100]

When they heard of Stockenström's appointment, the British settlers centred on Graham's Town were furious. That their sworn enemy and arch-critic, who represented all that stood in their way as an accumulating bourgeoisie (and was a 'Boer' to boot), should be appointed to rule over them was the ultimate humiliation. The settlers' ire at Stockenström's testimony against them before the aborigines committee was great, and seven hundred people in Graham's Town signed a petition demanding a formal inquiry to investigate his charges. 'It is lamentable', wrote the editor of the *Graham's Town Journal* on hearing of the appointment, 'to reflect how often the cup of prosperity has been dashed from our lips at the very moment of anticipated enjoyment.'[101]

In general the commercial bourgeoisie of Cape Town were as strongly opposed to Glenelg's disannexation as to Stockenström's policies. Indeed it was on the issue of policy towards the Xhosa that the humanitarian–mercantile alliance of the 1820s came undone. In June 1835 a public meeting in Cape Town addressed by a number of prominent citizens right across the political spectrum had expressed the colonists' satisfaction with D'Urban's measures to extend and stabilise the eastern frontier through a process of dispossession. But when Glenelg's dispatch became widely known and the nature of Stockenström's brief became clear, another public meeting in November 1836 demanded from the British government a commission of enquiry to investigate on the spot the causes of the war and the accusations levelled by the secretary of state and his humanitarian informants against the colonists. J. B. Ebden chaired this meeting, and also compiled a petition to the British parliament to counter humanitarian propaganda. Ebden and C. J. Brand in 1837 were among a group of sixteen eminent Capetonians who promised financial assistance for the publication of a collection of official documents designed to justify aggressive policies towards the Xhosa, and prove that the frontier settlers were victims of the chiefdoms' malevolence. In mid-1836 the discredited D'Urban, for whom such an exercise would be a vindication, had asked Donald Moodie, a former Royal Navy officer who had settled in the eastern Cape in 1819, and who had served as protector of slaves, to undertake such a compilation. Moodie's task, which proceeded in fits and starts, culminated in 1843 with the publication of *The Record*.[102]

It is noteworthy that this anti-humanitarian movement coalescing around frontier policy encompassed the spectrum of the local bourgeoisie in Cape Town – from the British merchant elite through to the rising and increasingly assertive Afrikaner professional and business class. For this bourgeoisie, humanitarian sentiments would not be allowed to get in the way of new sources of accumulation from which mercantile profit could be expected to flow. Barely any merchant of consequence openly supported the humanitarian position in the war of 1834–5. Nevertheless, Fairbairn at the *Commercial Advertiser* was still firmly in the humanitarian camp and was unwaveringly loyal to his father-in-law, Philip. In his columns, Fairbairn poured scorn on Moodie's labours, and accused Ebden and others of stirring up public opinion against the imperial government.[103] Clearly, when settler accumulation on frontiers was at issue, the humanitarians did not represent any substantial element of colonial opinion. In due course, though, Fairbairn was also to embrace the cause of frontier expansion and the subjugation of the Xhosa.

From the outset the thwarted local expansionist forces in the eastern Cape were vehemently hostile to Stockenström and his administration. (This rage is understandable when one considers that men like A. G. Bain, William Southey and Duncan Campbell all lost farms in the abandoned territory which they claimed to have already begun to develop.)[104] The discredited Governor D'Urban was vindictive towards the new lieutenant-governor; the local military under Colonel Somerset were contemptuous of him; his officials (with one or two exceptions) undermined his authority; and the British settler bourgeoisie campaigned tirelessly against him. He was blamed for the fact that the settlers were not awarded war compensation, and was resented for his refusal to extend any patronage or tolerate any corruption or laxity in administration (particularly with regard to land transactions, the basis of settler wealth). Stockenström even had to put up with a charge of murder dating back to a frontier clash in 1813. In this the chief rumour-mongers were the leading settlers Godlonton, Chase, Donald Moodie and Duncan Campbell (who as civil commissioner was directly implicated in corruption in respect of land administration). As a result a libel suit was brought against Campbell but was dismissed. At the same time Fairbairn, who had described the campaign against Stockenström as a 'criminal conspiracy ... organised by a pack of gun-runners and war-profiteers on the eastern frontier', was successfully sued by Moodie. Clearly, litigiousness had become an integral element of political life, arising from the ascendancy of the printing press as an instrument of political agitation.[105]

In his treaties with the chiefs, signed in December 1836, Stockenström recognised their sovereign authority beyond the Fish River (including Somerset's ceded territory) and extended to them responsibility for maintaining peace and good order among their subjects in their relations with the colonists. Specific provisions were included relating to the recovery through diplomatic channels of stolen livestock. The obligation was placed on colonists to ensure the proper herding of their stock by armed guards.[106] Opponents of the system argued that frontier security would be severely threatened by a system that accorded independent African chiefs coequal responsibility in maintaining law and order, and left settler farmers defenceless in the face of Xhosa cattle theft. A great deal of ink was expended in seeking to prove that the incidence of Xhosa depredations against the colonists was much greater under the treaty system than under D'Urban's rule. The Godlontonians painted a sombre picture of the state of affairs in the region in order to undermine Stockenström and his treaties, and subsequent historians, such as Theal and Cory, came to rely heavily on their evidence and judgements.[107] D'Urban himself, fed ammunition by partisan frontier officials such as J. D. Warden and J. M. Bowker, resident agents to the Xhosa, continued the campaign of vilification against Stockenström in dispatches to London, warning darkly of the consequences of his policies. The governor's sense of grievance did not dim, and after his retirement to Wynberg in 1838, he spent much time amassing evidence to defend his frontier settlement.[108]

Nevertheless, many contemporary observers commented on how peaceful things were on the frontier in the late 1830s and early 1840s.[109] Thus C. L. Stretch, diplomatic agent to the Ngqika, in a letter of August 1842, ascribed the passivity of the Xhosa at a time of conflict between British troops and Boer emigrants in Natal, to the treaties: 'If in the present defenceless state of our borders the Caffer chiefs and nation had been groaning under compulsory British domination, or the horrors of the old system, they would upon the first report of the check of the troops in Natal have done with Albany, Somerset and Cradock ... In short, "*those villainous treaties*" are our only anchor which keeps us from destitution.'[110]

However, it was eventually realised in London that Stockenström was so disliked by the colonists that he had to be replaced in order to cool tensions in the eastern Cape. He was eased out of office with a baronetcy and replaced by Colonel John Hare in 1839.[111] With Stockenström's dismissal, the trust of the chiefs – the foundation of his treaty system – evaporated, and conflict again began to build up, especially when new restrictions and conditions were unilaterally imposed on the chiefdoms in 1844, leading eventually to the renewal of war.[112] Years later, when war was again ravaging the frontier, Stockenström was again to be found expounding the virtues of a treaty system against what he called the 'D'Urban system', which he considered the cause of war. He warned in 1851 in a letter to the chairman of a select committee in London that under the policy of military domination 'South Africa will be to England what Algiers is to France'. If the 'Glenelg system' of treaties had been adhered to, it would have saved 'a few millions of money and prevented all the bloodshed and crimes which have befallen the Cape frontier for the last five years'.[113]

There was nothing overtly philanthropic or delusory about Stockenström's conception of frontier policy. Rather it was rooted in mundane considerations of the limits of state power and the destabilising effects of militarism on insecure frontiers. 'Civilisation', he thought, could not be forcibly imposed, but must grow out of the indigenous people's own experiences of superior institutions and influences. The end result, the incorporation of Africans as a subordinate element in colonial society, was to be the same, but the means of attaining it were to be pacific and gradual. As his attitudes had revealed in the agitation over the rights of the Khoi in the 1820s, Stockenström was always first and foremost persuaded of the futility of coercion. A Dutch-speaking colonist himself, he abjured solutions predicated on greater British military intervention in the region.[114] But by the 1850s the foundations of Xhosa society were already disintegrating, and the problem of 'frontier policy' was resolving itself by the incorporation of the cisKeian Xhosa as a dependent, but differentiated, underclass. That, however, lay in the future.

In the 1830s and 1840s the settler elite pushed for a strong, local executive government in the east. The fact that colonial government had been effectively centred on Graham's Town for most of 1835 served to strengthen the resolve of easterners in their drive for local government. They had seen how the local state could function as an engine of patronage on their behalf. They had had direct access to an administration with the authority to take decisions concerning state expenditure and the allocation of public resources. They had been able to stake a claim to the considerable patronage which D'Urban and the military could dispense. Settlers came closer in 1835 to realising their dream of an interventionist and expansive imperial power serving to promote their own acquisitive interests than ever before. But Glenelg, Stockenström and the humanitarians had killed all that. What these settlers certainly knew was that Stockenström's lieutenant-governorship, and the pacific and penurious policies he sought to implement on behalf of a misanthropic and unsympathetic imperial power, were not at all what they had in mind.

Fully *representative* government was not on the agenda of the British settlers of the eastern Cape. Indeed, it would be quite counterproductive, especially as the settlers feared Afrikaner domination. Also, representative government without separate eastern government would mean continued domination by Cape Town, which was believed to be strongly neglectful of the east. One suggestion (initially put forward by Governor D'Urban himself) that gained much support in the east was the removal of the colonial capital lock, stock and barrel from Cape Town to Graham's Town. But either way, a local state with imperial funds and resources to dispense, and amenable to the pressures of local settler interests, was indispensable to the British settler elite's long-term prospects.[115]

In response to the argument put forward by Glenelg in defence of his policies (that military withdrawal and reliance on local militias and treaties with independent chiefs were the way to secure peace), the settler propagandists argued that this was 'false economy'. In his book published during the war, Godlonton had already formulated the reasoning that was to be habitually repeated: the war would never have occurred had a sufficient military presence, backed by a strong local state committed to the advance of 'civilisation', been set in place. 'The expense of repelling and chastising the late irruption, will amount to a sum equal to the cost of a separate government for the eastern province for a period probably of fifty years.'[116] And, by extension, such a 'separate government' with a complementary military force would be the only insurance against further and more devastating warfare on the frontier in future. The *sine qua non* of the kind of 'separate government' that Godlonton had in mind was of course a more spendthrift government in London than seemed remotely likely.

In the event Godlonton and his settler colleagues had to be content with the granting of municipal government in 1837, in accordance with Ordinance 9 of 1836. Governor D'Urban had been instructed to institute such local government in 1834, but the ordinance had been delayed by the war of 1834–5.[117] Municipal institutions in the Cape were introduced simultaneously with their introduction in England, and arose out of the same impulses that saw the Reform Act of 1832 widen the British parliamentary franchise to include the great middle class. The Municipal Corporations Act of 1835 in England replaced the old oligarchic corporations with municipal governments elected by ratepaying householders.[118] But in the Cape, the institution of municipal government was also part of an economy drive. The posts of magistrate and civil commissioner in the districts had already been amalgamated. In 1831 Governor Cole, rejecting the idea that boards of *heemraden* be resurrected to take up some of the strain of district government, suggested that townsfolk be allowed to manage their own affairs and levy rates for this purpose. Thus municipal government was set up as a *quid pro quo* for the amalgamation of magisterial and civil offices in each district.[119] The newly elected municipal commissioners of towns like Graham's Town and Uitenhage quickly used their newly won powers to establish greater control over the settlements of impoverished work-seekers, many of them refugee Mfengu and Xhosa after the war, who had located themselves in the vicinity.[120] But municipal government was a poor substitute for the strong local state that the local bourgeoisie desired.

One way of galvanising greater imperial commitment to the promotion of settler accumulation was, of course, by inducing an influx of settlers and capital into the eastern districts. This was a central preoccupation of the settler propagandists in the years following the war. Promoting emigration was widely regarded in England in the 1830s as an important function of formal empire, owing in large part to the popular theories of E. G. Wakefield and the systematic colonisers. In South Africa, immigration of men of enterprise was seen as essential in advancing production and trade and the value of property. Papers like the *Graham's Town Journal* and the *Eastern Province Herald* of Port Elizabeth lent themselves enthusiastically to the cause of promoting every speculative proposal, realistic or not.[121]

Men like Godlonton and J. C. Chase issued a flood of literature in their efforts to lure immigrants to the eastern Cape. Prominent were Godlonton's *Sketches of the Eastern Districts of the Cape of Good Hope*, published in 1842, and Chase's *Cape of Good Hope and Eastern Province*, published in 1843.[122] Chase in particular was an avid purveyor of statistics, often highly coloured in order to inflate the potential of the eastern districts.[123] In 1844 the twenty-fifth anniversary celebrations of the launching of the settlement of 1820 were used to trumpet the scheme as a great success story whose prospects were limitless. A new civilisation and a new 'African Empire' had been planted in the fertile soil of the eastern Cape.[124]

At one level, men like Godlonton and Chase were concerned to counter the negative image created by their antagonists such as Philip and Stockenström. As Chase wrote to the *Graham's Town Journal*, his purpose was to 'cleanse the colonial character from those *dark stains* with which zealots and philanthropists ... [had] for their own purposes blackened the history of their [the settlers'] intercourse with the native tribes'.[125] Electoral considerations under a possible future representative form of government also lay behind the British settler agitations for the promotion of British immigration. 'Were it not for the superior energy of the English, we should long since have been swamped,' wrote Richard Southey. 'We should therefore encourage by every possible means the increase of the English population – vote as much as possible to bring out English labour, and in every way encourage capitalists to come.'[126]

But settler propagandists constantly undermined their own efforts to sell the eastern Cape as a destination of emigration. In their bid to spur the authorities to commit more resources and finances – especially military – to the eastern Cape, a sustained chorus of warmongering and scare tactics marked settler rhetoric in the 1830s and 1840s. The projected image of a paradise for the aspiring settler was constantly contradicted by the warnings coming from the same quarters that disaster could only be diverted by a large and permanent investment of imperial military muscle on the frontiers of settlement. These divergent chords were struck presumably for different audiences, but they were intended to secure the same end – namely, a state-sustained process of accumulation and development in the eastern districts.

A strong military presence meant the power to coerce and control the African peoples and to eat away at their economic independence. It meant a large market for all kinds of produce and services, a climate of confidence and security for investors, and upward pressure on land values. It meant state investment in infrastructure and public works. And there was the larger prospect, briefly raised by Governor D'Urban in 1835, of Xhosaland being thrown open to white landownership, settlement and exploitation. Moreover, there were still memories of the private fortunes made in 1834–5. As Thomas Stubbs recalled in later years: 'the people on this frontier liked a Caffer War better than peace ... I could if I wished enumerate a great many who owe their present positions [to] the Caffer Wars.'[127] Hence the war scares, the rumours of African chiefs' intrigue, the warnings of imminent invasion. The *Graham's Town Journal* in particular seems to have indulged in deliberate misrepresentation in order to create a war psychosis (at the same time as it advertised the attractions of the eastern Cape as a destination for settlers).[128]

Invariably the reports of imminent Xhosa invasions and war plans and sightings of black armies gathering were found to be groundless. This did not stop the settler leaders in the eastern Cape sending off a series of highly charged petitions, referring to the 'atrocity of the outrages of our Kaffir neighbours', their 'almost continuous aggressions', their 'continued and increasing outrages'. Settlers like J. M. Bowker gave themselves over fully to fanning this racial hysteria. In a famous speech of August 1844 he urged that like the tens of thousands of springbok that had once roamed the plains, the Africans too must give way: 'Is it just that a few thousands of ruthless, worthless savages are to sit like a nightmare upon a land that would support millions of civilised men happily?' Their land should be 'taken, sold and settled', Bowker declaimed.[129]

Those who were unsympathetic to the preoccupations of the settler elite were cynical about what the latter were seeking to achieve. Lennox Stretch, diplomatic agent to the Ngqika Xhosa under the treaty system, and one of the few frontier officials to support Stockenström's policies against the settlers, was particularly unimpressed in his assessment of settler propaganda. He dismissed as fabrication 'the clamour of Graham's Town' about the extent of Xhosa depredations: 'The sense of all the Noise is to prevent the Military Expenditure being withdrawn from the Colony which the Graham's Town contractors dreaded. The robbery of the Caffers is nothing – "a flea bite" – if we can keep the troops and rob the tax payer in the United Kingdom.'[130]

Dispatches by Lieutenant-Governor Stockenström and his successor, John Hare, were full of descriptions of rumours and alarms – 'scandalous falsehoods' – that were assiduously spread by the settlers. Stockenström was convinced that 'a "Cabal" and "War Party" *want* a blow up – that they may share in the scramble'. Hare complained repeatedly of fabrications and misrepresentations in the *Graham's Town Journal*, referring to the 'machinations by which it has been attempted to keep this Frontier in a permanent state of ferment'.[131] Hare also noted the ironic, but not inconsistent, involvement of these self-same settler forces in the arming of their enemies, which was continuing in the early 1840s as it had in the run-up to the war of 1834–5. He was certain that the Graham's Town merchants were 'deeply implicated' in the arms trade with the Xhosa, mentioning Wright, the Nordens and Howse, whose names had come up in court cases then in progress. 'I have not the slightest doubt that every merchant of the town is deeply concerned in this unlawful traffic,' Hare wrote to Governor Napier, 'and that all are equally culpable.' These were, as Napier wrote, 'the very persons most clamorous against the Kafir nation'.[132]

Governor Napier, who succeeded D'Urban in 1838, quickly perceived the settler purpose. He had a much clearer idea than his predecessor of what the proper role of a Cape governor should be, and of the limits of his function. In 1839 he wrote to his brother:

All looks peaceful again, and will remain so, I feel convinced, in spite of the rascals who work hard in Graham's Town, aided by the *Graham's Town Journal*, whose editor is a rascal, to bring on a war! But they *shall not*; by God I know them! I know their machinations! and they can't do a thing I shall not have timely notice of! I hate listening to *secret* intelligence or having anything to say to *espionage*, but I *am forced* to have recourse to it now and then, in order to counteract the evil designs of villains as *regards the Caffers*.[133]

A few years later, Napier was still expressing to the authorities in London his exasperation at 'the alarms and panics to which they [the British settlers] are continually abandoning themselves, upon the slightest, and generally speaking, the most unfounded reports'.[134] And in 1845, the attorney-general, William Porter, as progressive an official as the Cape produced, saw fit to warn Governor Maitland before the Legislative Council:

> While saying and doing everything apparently calculated to bring on a war, they [the settler elite of the eastern districts] represent at the same time the powers of the Kafirs as most formidable, and tell Your Excellency that you have not troops to meet them. If I could suppose these gentlemen to be playing a game, I could understand them. By exaggerating the depredations of the Kafirs, and the designs of the Kafirs, and the powers of the Kafirs, a state of excitement is produced which must keep continually upon the Eastern Frontier a large military expenditure.[135]

However, despite the rhetoric of impending doom, the eastern districts in the years after the 1834–5 war entered a period of economic boom, stretching through the 1840s into the 1850s. The one central feature of this sustained period of productive development was the woolled sheep. From 1840 onwards, the British wool clip declined while the demand for wool by British manufacturing industry continued to expand with increased mechanisation, rising from 171.1 million lb annually in 1830–4 to 262.6 million lb annually in 1855–9. The demand for wool imports thus entered a phase of rapid growth. Whereas in 1820 Britain imported 31 per cent of its raw wool, by 1850 the proportion was 49 per cent, and by 1900, 80 per cent. Cape wool production, although never as large as that of Australia, was considerably boosted as a result, especially as it enjoyed an advantage in freight costs. The Cape's annual wool exports, according to customs reports, increased from 117 634 lb in 1835, to 3 194 602 lb in 1845, and 5 447 000 lb in 1851, by which time wool comprised 59 per cent of all Cape exports. By 1855 the figure stood at 12 million lb. In 1859, 15 465 632 lb were exported through Port Elizabeth alone. Further, prices increased gradually each year to 1860. In 1840–4 the annual average wool exports were valued at £73 000, and in 1855–9 at £984 000.[136]

Inevitably, labour demand increased proportionately with the development of the farming economy. As a result of the war and the removal of the Mfengu into the colony in 1835, African labour became more readily available than ever before.[137] But labour shortage was a constant complaint of settlers. Despite the ongoing pleas of Godlonton and others for greater immigration from Britain as an answer to the problem, there was no real alternative to local sources as far as farmers were concerned. Agitations for anti-vagrancy and masters and servants laws mounted in the late 1830s and 1840s. Ordinance 2 of 1837 prohibited unauthorised 'native locations' and authorised the arrest of 'native foreigners' without passes; and the masters and servants ordinance of 1841 increased the powers of control available to employers of labour, as we have seen. Polemical attacks on mission stations mounted likewise, especially as by the 1840s it was clear that these communities fell far short of being the progressive bastions of the civilising mission that men like Philip had envisaged. Even within the mission movement the stations were beginning to be seen as an insupportable burden. More and more choice grazing land was being given over to woolled sheep, and independent coloured and African communities were increasingly hemmed in and on the retreat as a consequence. The mid-1840s were years of drought and famine in Xhosaland, and large numbers of impoverished people streamed into the colony in search of sustenance – in contravention of ordinances which sought to regulate such influx through the issuing of passes. While labour was thus becoming available, the problems of labour control, vagrancy and petty depredations heightened the demands for statutory intervention.[138]

The spread of wool farming in the Cape was facilitated by the exodus of some 15 000 Boer emigrants into the Transorangian interior, in the large population movement known as the Great Trek. Although the mass emigration had started prior to the war of 1834–5, the bulk of the emigrants left after the war had ended. They often sold out for very low prices. Frequently it was reported that they had sold farms in return for trading goods, guns and ammunition, or wagons for the trek. Farms were sold, according to F. P. van Gass, *voor een appel en een ei*, or as J. H. Hatting remembered, rather less proverbially, for anything from £7 10s up to £300 or £400.[139] An Australian visitor testified before an 1844 New South Wales select committee that

> some excellent farms were given away for a waggon and team of bullocks to carry farmers on to Natal. I have seen excellent land that had been sold by these parties at the rate of 1s 6d per 'morgen' ... There were a number of farms sold about the time I was there, and they varied from 9d to 5s an acre, according to the improvements that had been made upon them; great advantages are given there by the landowners to the settlers. I have heard of land sold in the Cradock district at about 2s 6d an acre, with twenty years credit, the purchaser paying interest, or rent, at ... 6 per cent.[140]

Those who invested most heavily in grazing farms throughout the eastern districts and in woolled sheep were the British settler elite, as well as some Cape Town entrepreneurs who bought land in the sheep districts at the time, such as F. S. Watermeyer and Fred Liesching.

British landownership spread dramatically into the interior north and north-west of Graham's Town, into what became known as the Cape Midlands – Somerset, Cradock and Graaff-Reinet districts – which was much more suited to wool farming than the sour veld of Albany. The Southey and Rubidge families pioneered an exodus from Albany into Graaff-Reinet district (where only two farmers had invested in merino rams by 1838), and bought up large sheep runs of some 85 000 acres in that drier Great Karoo region. George Southey reported that he had bought two farms near Graaff-Reinet town for his father-in-law Rubidge, comprising 15 000 acres, for £375. He boasted that a short time previously (prior to the Boer emigration) these farms would have fetched £1500. The Southey family apparently owned at least 27 farms in 1849. The Graham's Town merchant James Howse became a large landowner as a result of his trade connections with emigrant Boers from whom he bought farms, using no doubt money he had made as a contractor to the commissariat during the 1834–5 war. The high road from Graham's Town to Fort Beaufort on the Kat River reportedly passed through Howse's land for a distance of 25 miles. By the end of the 1840s, he owned some 30 000 acres in the Fort Beaufort district, where he pastured some 23 000 woolled sheep. The Bowker family also bought up much land at the time, as did James Collett, who became a major sheep farmer on the Koonap River north of Graham's Town.[141]

The truth was that just as the Boer emigration made cheap land widely available, so war profiteering combined with a surge of loan capital enabled many British settlers to exploit the opportunities for further profit and accumulation thus opened up. Once the land left behind by emigrating Boers had been bought up and wool farming had taken off, land prices boomed, doubling in a few years in the late 1830s and early 1840s, and leading to substantial speculative profits.[142] Subsequently the woolled sheep gradually spread into the drier Karoo regions of Beaufort West district and beyond, westward and northward. Those responsible here tended as well to be merchants and speculators of British origin, rather than members of the older Boer population. Thus G. W. Prince, J. R. Thomson and H. Watson, all partners in big Cape Town merchant houses, bought considerable property in Beaufort West district in 1841 in what was described as the biggest single land sale ever in the colony.[143]

At the time many noted the contradiction between settler propaganda of impending ruin due to the indifference of government to the alleged Xhosa threat, and the evident extent of settler investment in land and sheep in these years. The ceaseless demand for land suitable for sheep grazing, and the consequent inflation of land values, right on the borders of Xhosa territory, could hardly be squared with the constant war scares that emanated from exactly the same quarter. Lieutenant-Governor Stockenström, in a letter to John Fairbairn in April 1838, noted the irony: 'The fellow who pretends to believe that the Hottentots and Caffres are preparing to *eat us up*, gives £200 for a sheep farm *bordering on the Fish River bush*.' In 1841, Governor Napier wrote to the secretary of state, Lord Stanley: 'No merchant of any importance in Graham's Town has not within the last few years invested considerable sums of money in the purchase of farms along the immediate border, and in stocking these farms with sheep.'[144] In August of the following year Stockenström, now retired on his farm not far from the Xhosa borderlands, wrote to Philip:

> Is it not a fact that hitherto there has been no new war, no fire, no slaughter, though the [treaty] system has been in operation for six years; that instead of being ruined, the clamorous themselves boast that what they bought for a rix-dollar before, during and soon after the war, is now worth a pound? ... I have been on or about my estate for the last two years. So much is the country improved ... that I have often been absent, leaving my family (women and children) entirely in charge of blacks; and in spite of alarms, rumours of wars, we have never felt ourselves more at ease anywhere. Property for which no one would have given three thousand pounds in 1836, I would not now take ten for, and my nearest neighbour has lately refused £3375 for land which in 1834 cost him six hundred.[145]

Economic boom also brought about regional rivalries within the eastern Cape. During the 1840s Port Elizabeth, the eastern Cape's major port, was beginning to rival Graham's Town as an entrepôt of trade. By the end of the 1840s the Zuurberg pass north of Port Elizabeth had greatly strengthened the port's direct access to large stretches of territory to the north – Somerset, Cradock, Graaff-Reinet, Colesberg and the regions to the north of the Orange River. The mails from Cape Town to Graham's Town, sent three times a week instead of once as previously, now came by sea via Port Elizabeth rather than overland via Uitenhage; and the long-awaited lighthouse on Cape Recife had been erected. Port Elizabeth began to develop its own political identity, with John Paterson's *Eastern Province Herald*, founded in 1845, as its major mouthpiece. Paterson, a Scottish schoolmaster from Aberdeen, pushed the port's claims to regional primacy as the capital of the eastern Cape.[146] To counter Port Elizabeth, the Graham's Town bourgeoisie's pet scheme was the proposed harbour at the Kowie River mouth, which for long had been promoted by the 1820 settler William Cock as the natural port for Graham's Town. In 1839 he had drawn up a private Bill for opening up the Kowie mouth to be presented to the Legislative Council, and when he became the first easterner on the council in 1847, he pushed his schemes insistently, albeit largely unsuccessfully.[147] In the event, however, Graham's Town's commercial as well as financial pre-eminence in the east was not yet shaken by the end of the 1850s.[148]

Notwithstanding developments in the east, the colonial economy was still dominated by the merchant and financial bourgeoisie of Cape Town. That Albany district was, in William Porter's words, 'the most energetic, enterprising, American and "go-ahead" part of the entire colony' did not alter the fact that in the 1830s and 1840s money was still concentrated in Cape Town.[149] Cape Town continued to be the link in the chain of dependence between the metropolitan and peripheral economies. For a time in the late 1830s the major element in this exchange was the inflow of capital in the form of slave compensation payments, which spread out through the colony as mortgage capital and credit to fuel the wool economy. The importance of Cape Town capital was referred to by John Fairbairn in the *Advertiser* in September 1847: 'With respect to mortgages, it will probably be found that a considerable portion of the fixed property in the eastern province is thus pawned to capitalists in the western province, with nothing reciprocal from the east.'[150] Again, he told a parliamentary select committee in London in 1851: 'A large proportion of the money in Cape Town is derived from mortgages on frontier farms and frontier estates; a large portion of the trade of Table Bay is connected with the frontier, and a great many people in Cape Town have an interest in estates in the eastern province.'[151] As there was little demand for mortgage capital in the west at the time wool farming took off in the east, capital thus flowed eastward. Western Cape merchants became the chief financiers of the first eastern Cape wool boom, a dependence the easterners resented.[152]

Leading Cape Town merchants (including Hamilton Ross, J. B. Ebden, C. S. Pillans, A. Chiappini, Dickson, Burnie & Co., and Borradaile, Thompson & Hall) financed the interior trade based largely in Graham's Town and its port, Port Elizabeth. For their part, eastern Cape merchants acted as agents of Cape Town firms. Further, Cape Town investors commonly supplied the mortgage loans and credit for the purchase of farms, fuelling the land price inflation, and many bought land directly themselves as speculative investments. Cape Town merchants commonly advertised imported woolled sheep, wool bags and shearing equipment for sale in the newspapers. They supplied credit to farmers through local agents for the purchase of sheep or for investment in fixed assets, against future consignments of wool, and their notes became common currency. This access to mercantile credit was especially crucial given the long time-gap between shearing and the realisation of wool sales in London.[153]

Important regional merchants in the wool districts with close Cape Town links included the Mosenthals. German Jews with strong financial connections in London, they established their headquarters in Port Elizabeth in 1842. Through the 1840s they set up a chain of stores and agencies in small towns throughout the Cape interior, manning them with fellow German Jewish immigrants from Hesse–Cassel. They pioneered the close commercial relationship between Graaff-Reinet and Port Elizabeth, and dominated trade in new towns such as Burghersdorp and Aliwal North, founded in the late 1840s in the northeastern reaches of the colony near the Orange River.[154] J. Barry & Nephews, founded in 1834, played a similar role in the southern Cape with their base at Swellendam. They too had strong Cape Town links as shareholders and agents of several Cape Town companies. When wool farming took off in the Overberg in the 1840s, the Barrys established a large degree of commercial dominance throughout the region. Joseph Barry's wife was related to the wealthy Van Reenen family and had considerable farming connections. The Barrys built up an entrepôt at the mouth of the Breede River, and their ship the *Kadie* was the first steamship to sail up the river. Between 1847 and 1850 they purchased over a million pounds weight of wool.[155] Both the Mosenthals and Barrys issued banknotes, handled farmers' estates, and took shares in sheep farms. They laid great store on the improvement of wool quality, for example by giving awards for good quality wool.[156]

The era of steamships had arrived by the 1840s, and Cape Town immediately secured control of the coastal steamship business. Ebden and other Cape merchants set up the Cape of Good Hope Steamship Company with a capital of £20 000 in £10 shares as early as 1836, when Cape Town was flush with expectations of slave compensation money. This was a pet project of Fairbairn, who propagated it in his editorials. The Graham's Town merchant William Cock was the first easterner to acquire a steamship in 1843. Growth in shipping was rapid. The number of vessels calling at Port Elizabeth increased from 159 ships in 1840 to 274 in 1850. In the 1840s, over half of the ships through Port Elizabeth were trading directly with overseas markets, but the rest plied between Port Elizabeth and Cape Town, and Cape Town maintained its position as the colony's primary import–export terminal into the 1850s. By 1854, however, exports through Port Elizabeth overtook those through Cape Town, although Cape Town with its larger population and greater concentration of wealth remained the premier port of import. It also remained the port of call and revictualling for the substantial number of ships rounding the Cape between the western and eastern oceans.[157]

Other sectors of the economy also experienced a take-off in the 1830s, among them financial institutions such as banks and insurance and trust companies. Again, slave compensation was the major impetus. The first private commercial bank was the Cape of Good Hope Bank, founded in Cape Town in 1837. Until then, banking had been a government monopoly which had been firmly protected as a source of government revenue, despite attempts by merchants connected with the Cape trade in 1815 and 1825 to set up a joint-stock bank. The bank established in 1837 was initiated by the Cape of Good Hope Trade Society in London in order to obstruct an attempt by persons not connected with the Cape trade to obtain a charter for banking in Australia and South Africa. The society approached the Commercial Exchange in Cape Town, which welcomed the proposal, in the conviction that sufficient capital existed in the Cape for launching such an institution. J. B. Ebden, H. W. Watson and G. W. Prince were appointed to draft a prospectus. The bank was incorporated by local ordinance, and capital of £75 000 was to be subscribed in £50 shares. Ebden was appointed chairman, a post he retained until his death in 1873. Although Fairbairn had campaigned for such an institution for years, it only became viable in the economic conditions following the emancipation of slaves and the economic stimulus given by the 1834–5 war. The bank established a branch in Graham's Town in 1838, charging higher rates for credit in the east, where demand for capital was higher, than it did in Cape Town.[158]

In 1838, after slave compensation money had begun to arrive, company formation spurted. In that year six joint-stock companies were formed in Cape Town, as many as had existed previously. The joint-stock company enabled a number of individuals with limited personal wealth to share their resources in more profitable enterprises than could be achieved severally. Shares in new banks and insurance and trust companies were widely advertised in Cape Town newspapers in 1838. In Graham's Town too, the Eastern Province Bank was established in 1838 by local merchants, but it always lived under the shadow of Cape Town capital, as did all such institutions subsequently founded in the east.[159]

The capital behind these new institutions in Cape Town in the late 1830s was often different in provenance from that of the big mercantile establishments, which, with their close ties to the City of London, had dominated the economic life of Cape Town previously. Several of these companies were controlled by Dutch–Afrikaans-speaking directors and shareholders. Representing a rising local middle class of colonially oriented businessmen, retailers, merchants and professionals, they were increasingly to challenge the economic dominance of the more established merchant elite. Indeed, an Afrikaner-dominated South African Bank was set up in direct competition with Ebden's Cape of Good Hope Bank, with which this elite was associated. These new joint-stock financial institutions joined the eastward flow of capital to fuel and feed off the wool economy. The South African Mutual Insurance Company, for example, was estimated by Fairbairn to have three-quarters of its funds invested in the eastern districts on first mortgage. This spurt of company formation was superseded by a slump, which set in in 1840; but a fresh spurt commenced with the establishment of the Colonial Bank in 1844 and the Union Bank and Western Province Bank in 1847, as the burgeoning wool economy began to pump increasing life into the Cape's commercial economy.[160]

Thus a new layer of the colonial bourgeoisie was emerging, created in large part by emancipation and the payment of slave compensation money. For one thing, many such men had been themselves slave-owners or had held mortgages against the security of slave property, and some had acted as agents for other slave-owners in securing compensation.[161] In fact, all those involved in the commercial business of the colony would have benefited from the great surge in liquidity as well as demand in the colonial economy. This rising Dutch–Afrikaner bourgeoisie comprised men who had come to terms with the entrepreneurial spirit of the age, no longer harboured any regrets for the dismantling of the slaveholding economy, and no longer relied on the patronage of the old regime represented by Somerset's displaced autocracy. Many of them had strong agricultural connections. Prominent for example was F. W. Reitz, a wealthy sheep farmer with extensive landed interests in the Overberg. Others were lawyers such as J. H. Hofmeyr and C. J. Brand, founder of *De Zuid-Afrikaan*, committee member of the agricultural society and, later, Speaker of the Cape parliament. Among Afrikaner businessmen who were very much part of this rising bourgeoisie were J. H. and J. A. H. Wicht, P. M. Brink, J. A. Bam, F. S. Watermeyer, O. J. Truter, J. J. L. Smuts, A. F. Carstens, J. S. Leibbrandt, J. M. Wentzel and F. H. Kunhardt, all of whom were prominent figures in trade and professional life.[162]

This new bourgeoisie established a political identity and secured a political power base by gaining control over the elected Cape Town municipality which was established in 1840 (some three years after municipal government was introduced elsewhere in the colony).[163] Among the commissioners of the Cape Town municipality, Afrikaners predominated from the start. But there was very little sense of ethnic exclusivity apparent. The English-speakers associated with this rising bourgeoisie were generally of humbler origins than the old British mercantile establishment, and had no pretensions to being members of the colonial social elite. They tended to belong to dissenting or Nonconformist congregations, rather than to the strongly pro-establishment local Anglican Church.[164] This increasingly powerful 'municipal party', Afrikaans- and English-speaking, sought in the 1840s to use the municipality as a counter-weight against the ineffectual Legislative Council set up in 1834. In this council, dominated as it was by officials and controlled by the governor, the merchant elite was well represented in the persons of Hamilton Ross, J. B. Ebden and C. S. Pillans.

The rising commercial class which controlled the municipality was particularly marked by its speculative accumulation of residential housing. The leading municipal commissioners were generally large-scale proprietors of urban and peri-urban property. Commissioners like H. Jarvis, A. F. Carstens, J. J. L. Smuts and J. A. H. Wicht (originally a linen-draper and ironsmith) owned 'hundreds of houses' in Cape Town – rows of cheap and usually unhygienic dwellings in the courts and alleys of the more densely populated and racially mixed parts of town, such as the Waterfront, Constitution Hill (later, District Six) and Lion's Rump. Wicht's property in and around Cape Town came to be worth some £55 000 (out of an estate worth £122 000 overall in 1867). By the 1860s he owned no fewer than 374 dwellings in Cape Town, mostly without any sewage disposal, housing some 4000 tenants. Commissioners like him – including O. M. Bergh and J. S. Leibbrandt, both affluent wine merchants – also commonly held considerable mortgages on household property. They were joined on the municipal board in 1848 by J. M. Maynard and in 1852 by R. Arderne (originally a cabinet-maker), owners of large stretches of land in the southern suburbs. By the 1870s Maynard owned property in Cape Town and the Cape district worth £60 000. These landlords unashamedly used their positions to push for municipal expenditure in areas in which they owned property.[165]

The subdivision, sale and accumulation of property in Cape Town and suburbs seem to have greatly accelerated in 1838–9, at a time when economic
activity in general was greatly boosted in the immediate aftermath of slave
compensation payments. The loss of slaves may have resulted in the ownership
of larger slave-worked *erven* becoming an unviable proposition. A great deal
of new building activity occurred at the same time, as evidenced in the increase
in the number of brickfields in Cape Town, from four in 1834–7 to ten in
1838. What this indicates is a considerable growth in the urban population:
emancipated slaves moved to town (especially after their four-year apprenticeship terms had ended in 1838), and those who had previously lived on owners'
premises moved into new rented dwellings. The Cape Town housing market
would have been boosted by the expansion of a market in artisanal and craft
skills as a result of emancipation, and by the monetisation of the urban economy which accompanied the replacement of slave labour with wage relations.[166]

The Cape Town municipality was made up in the first place of a board of
commissioners, representing the propertied. Such were the property qualifications for candidates for the board that membership was restricted to the
wealthiest proprietors, only 326 men out of an overall urban population of
22 000 being so qualified. The subsidiary board of wardmasters was a more
broadly based body consisting of representatives of householders in each ward
of the city. The wardmasters were usually men of the lower-middle class –
tradesmen, shopkeepers, artisans and craftsmen. Over the years there was a
slow seepage of wardmasters into the ranks of the commissioners. Men of
colour were not excluded, though few met the property qualifications as householders. Only one coloured man is known to have been elected a wardmaster
in 1844; he resigned shortly afterwards.[167]

Much municipal politics revolved around the issue of public finance. For
their part the municipal commissioners were determined to minimise the tax
burden on the proprietors of fixed property, and to pass as much of the tax
burden as possible on to such sources as the buyers and sellers at the municipal market and tenants of property. They also sought to shift expenditure on
to the colonial state, by trying to force the government to pay rates for water
supplies and on state-owned property, and to pay for the municipal police. At
the same time the commissioners were concerned to minimise expenditure that
was not of immediate benefit to their own propertied interests, being very
reluctant to appoint streetkeepers to maintain the cleanliness of the town. They
also used their status to pursue their own business interests. When gas lamps
for the streets of the town were erected in 1848, the Cape of Good Hope Gas
Light Company, of which several commissioners were shareholders, was contracted to do the job.[168]

Apart from their municipal power base, this rising business and professional class sought to establish their own institutional platform by attempting to
launch a Cape of Good Hope Chamber of Commerce in opposition to the

Commercial Exchange, which was in practice controlled by a small group of shareholders in the Exchange building. The first attempt in 1841 had the enthusiastic backing of leading municipal commissioners. But opposition to the scheme came from the elite merchants G. W. Prince, R. W. Eaton and J. B. Ebden, who denied the need for a rival institution to the Exchange. In the event the attempt was still-born, as were later attempts, but it did indicate that those less firmly established in the commercial firmament were seeking their own voice.[169]

It would be wrong to be too mechanistic about the economic interests represented by factions within the commercial bourgeoisie of Cape Town.[170] Differences of emphasis or perspective in economic matters derived as much from the fact that the bigger merchant houses of the Commercial Exchange had, on the whole, a longer history of engagement with the imperial economic system, and closer and more personal links with metropolitan capital. They were longer established, better connected and more financially stable. They also tended to identify with the Commercial Exchange and the Cape of Good Hope Bank and its affiliated institutions. These elite merchants' religious and cultural affiliations made them more acceptably part of the social coterie that centred on Government House, with its strong military and politically conservative ambience. A large part of their wealth derived from their businesses, mainly import–export, rather than from residential property (although many elite merchants had suburban estates and interests in wool-farming property).[171]

In terms of economic activities, there certainly was no deep incompatibility of interests between the older, more outward-looking merchant capital, and the newer, more colonially oriented wealth and speculative enterprise. Wherever profits were to be made, whether in copper mining in Namaqualand, docks or railway schemes, or the commercial exploitation of wool or wine farming, entrepreneurs of every political shade were likely to be involved.[172] In the years from 1849 to 1853, leading up to the granting of representative government, there was a bitter conflict over the desirable extent of the democratisation of the colonial state, as we shall see. But the Cape Town bourgeoisie was united on the broad principles of constitutional and economic development.

As new vistas for profit from colonial enterprise opened up in the 1840s, the humanitarian impulses of the 1820s and 1830s were receding fast. The bitterness that had accompanied emancipation and the Boer emigration was dissipating in the 1840s, and a new sense of common purpose across the language divide became apparent.[173] Fairbairn and his *Commercial Advertiser* had lost much of their humanitarian fervour by the 1840s, and were largely reconciled with the rest of the commercial bourgeoisie. The forces of colonial capitalism were clearly ascendant. At the same time extraneous considerations, such as the fate of the Xhosa or the rights of the colony's coloured working class, were pushed into the background. Newspaper editors like Fairbairn, Brand at *De Zuid-Afrikaan* and William Buchanan at the *Cape Town Mail* strongly supported the 'municipal party', and became proponents of unity as a necessary precondition of economic and constitutional progress. In the early 1830s Fairbairn had opposed an elected assembly for the colony as long as the legal rights of coloured people were in doubt.[174] But by the 1840s he was ready to put his weight and that of his paper behind the drive for representative government – at the same time as the rights of coloured people were coming under more intense attack. As the colonial bourgeoisie grew in size and self-confidence, so concerns for the place of coloured people in colonial society receded as an obstacle to constitutional development, both in Cape Town and in London.

In the 1820s and early 1830s Afrikaner politics had been defensive and embattled, focusing on the status of the colony's coloured and slave working class and on the colonists' prerogatives as a master class against humanitarian interference. By the 1840s a language of enterprise and the rights of citizenship had taken over, uniting colonists both English- and Afrikaans-speaking. This was based on a common understanding of the efficacy of new means of social control over the colony's subordinate peoples, different from those provided by older institutional forms of coercion and unfreedom, and encompassed a vision firmly fixed on future possibilities rather than past prerogatives.[175] Within this increasingly assertive colonial bourgeoisie, there was little sense that the culture of rights and opportunities to which they laid claim as British citizens extended to the colony's people of colour.

Cape Town's rising bourgeoisie, quite substantial by the late 1840s, began to chafe at their lack of leverage over the governor and his administration. The colonists had scarcely any role in the higher branches of the administration, which were peopled by metropolitan or gubernatorial appointees. The imperial authorities had long resisted all supplications from the colony for greater representation, on the grounds that colonists could not safely be entrusted with managing relations with indigenous people within and without colonial borders.[176] In 1841 the agitation for representative institutions moved up a ratchet when the newly constituted municipality took the initiative in petitioning the Queen. C. J. Brand told a special meeting of the municipal commissioners that the obstacles to representative institutions had been removed: slavery had been abolished, and 'party feeling' had died away. While 'millions of taxes' had been paid by the colonists over the years, there was not 'a single penny to lay out on any colonial improvement'. A committee was thereafter deputed to draw up the petition, which was endorsed at a public meeting. But Lord Stanley at the Colonial Office was still not to be moved, repeating the objections made by his predecessors that representative institutions might be 'perverted into a means of gratifying the antipathies of a dominant caste, or of promoting their own interests or prejudices, at the expense of other and less powerful classes'.[177] This was, however, soon to be an anachronistic viewpoint.

The colony's Legislative Council became a particular object of popular opprobrium. It was regarded as an illegitimate institution whose nominated unofficial members were wholly unrepresentative. Although the prominent merchant Hamilton Ross managed for a time to combine membership of both the Legislative Council and the municipal board, the unofficial members of the council, who were outnumbered by officials, were regularly criticised for their ineffectuality and impotence. Elite merchants like Ebden sought to use the council to promote the cause of wider representation, but at the end of the day their vision of colonial democracy was of a far more conservative and restrictive kind than that demanded by the municipality.[178]

There were definite material benefits to be gained by the rising bourgeoisie from representative institutions. Safe and profitable investment opportunities were eagerly sought in the 1840s. This was a period of excessive speculative frenzy in Britain, especially in the floating of companies to build railways. At the Cape, speculative undertakings included the launching of a company to build a railway to Swellendam and beyond in 1845, and the launching of a syndicate to investigate the potential of copper deposits in Namaqualand in the same year. Joint-stock companies were set up to cultivate cotton in Natal and to provide urban amenities and coach transport services.[179] But whereas in Britain there was at the time a relative excess of investment capital, in the Cape capital was limited. The transfer of capital from the northern hemisphere to the Cape continued to be very insubstantial after the arrival of slave compensation money, being largely confined to mercantile credit and individual shareholdings in Cape companies by London merchants with Cape connections. Attempts to float companies in London for business in the colony all failed to materialise prior to the 1850s.[180]

Access to metropolitan capital was necessary for the successful implementation of speculative company ventures. Municipal guarantees were not, however, sufficiently secure to raise the kind of capital required for railway construction, mining, telegraphs, waterworks or gasworks. The Colonial Office made it clear that it was not prepared to provide imperial guarantees for colonial investments such as harbour improvement projects. Under these circumstances, local businessmen became determined to gain access to a new, popular colonial legislature free of Colonial Office control, and answerable to local and not metropolitan interests. Only in this way would loans for speculative ventures be guaranteed.[181]

CHAPTER SIX

Expanding Frontiers:
The Great Leap Forward

The Griqua had their origin in groups of 'Bastaards' who moved northwards from the region of the Khamiesberg towards the Orange River from about 1780. Their migration indicated a hardening of racial attitudes and antagonisms in the areas of trekboer expansion northwards and northeastwards from Cape Town towards Namaqualand and the Roggeveld.[1] For by the 1770s the ecological and military constraints on trekboer expansion were becoming intense. The consequence was intensifying pressures on labour, land and livestock within the limits of trekboer settlement. Penn notes that the word 'Bastaard' rarely appears in official records before the 1770s and indicates the redefining of people of mixed descent or illegitimate birth who had previously enjoyed some burgher rights. In the military crisis of the 1770s their services were increasingly needed for commando duty against the Khoisan within and on the borders of the colony; yet at the same time their civil rights were being eroded. As Khoi deserted from service and as the Bastaards removed northwards rather than serve on commando, the authorities threatened to impose passes indiscriminately on all who were not of putatively full European descent.[2]

The northward movement of Bastaards, who were often substantial stockowners and claimants to colonial land, was to lead to the establishment of new statelets beyond the boundaries of the colony. More immediately, the migration of Bastaard groups with their associated families and retainers expanded the reach of the colonial economy. The area to the north of the colony had long attracted hunters, traders and cattle raiders. It was also already settled by independent Khoi bands (the Nama and Kora) involved in economic relationships with peoples further north, such as the southernmost Tswana. While trading and raiding across colonial borders were formally illegal, nevertheless such activities had long been carried on with impunity, with even local officials participating. As they became increasingly concentrated on the Orange River, the Bastaards (or Griqua, as they were subsequently known) emerged as middlemen between white colonists to the south and the independent Khoi communities beyond the Orange, in the 1780s and 1790s onwards. For the Bastaards trade was essential if they were to maintain access to necessary items of colonial material culture, notably firearms, powder and horses, without which they would have lost their status as colonial frontiersmen. To their north the Nama and Kora were very willing to exchange cattle for colonial beads, but raiding and hunting were often more profitable and effective when European trade goods for barter were unavailable. Raiding activities extended as far as the southern Tswana chiefdoms.[3]

In particular, the colonial government sought to maintain strict control over the trade in armaments: powder could only be bought from government stores and re-sale was prohibited. Such prohibition did not prevent Bastaard middlemen from becoming effectively armed with the help of their white trading partners in the colony. (Trade in arms with Khoi or African groups to the north remained, however, strictly proscribed, being considered against the interests of both white and Bastaard frontiersmen.)[4] This collaboration in illegal trade to mutual advantage was to be a central feature of the economics and politics of the northern frontier zone right up to the 1840s, until white infiltration of Transorangia once again plunged the Griqua and whites into competition for land and political hegemony.[5]

From the early years of the nineteenth century the Bastaard/Griqua frontiersmen began a process of state building in mid-Transorangia under the patronage of LMS missionaries.[6] These new political communities were offshoots of colonial society, and were made up of people who were the forward representatives of that society. It was their racial identity that had pushed them to the further margins, where new political and economic opportunities were available to be exploited. In Transorangia they wished to lay claim to the status denied them within the borders of an increasingly hostile colonial order. Their eager embrace of mission Christianity, at least its outward trappings, was crucial in this respect. Christian baptism, with the rights that went with it, was fundamental to burgher status within the colony. Even though racial criteria rather than church status had become the central prerequisites for acceptance in the world of the white colonists, it was exclusion from the church that most dramatically symbolised outcaste status in the burgher community.[7] But equally, the Griqua sought to secure their political independence, not least from the colony itself, in order to recreate the society from which they had removed themselves. There was great diversity of opinion about what such a society should be. Was it to resemble the extensive patriarchal pastoral society of the trekboer, in which trading, raiding and hunting were crucial elements; or, more ideally, the settled agricultural community which the missionaries envisaged? Either way, political communities were built around the central institution of the mission. However, contrary to contemporary missionary propaganda,[8] the Griqua states were by no means solely the creation of the LMS.

The wealthiest and most influential Griqua families that had moved up from the colony were the Koks and the Barends. In Transorangia, through their dominance of long-distance trade, they amassed great wealth. In 1801 it was reported that the Koks possessed 45 000 head of cattle. They collected around themselves large followings of associated families, retainers and clients in loose alliances without territorial definition. Under the auspices of the LMS missionaries – initially William Anderson, who arrived in 1801 – these communities, which incorporated a diversity of elements under the authority of the

Griqua elite, forged a larger political community centred on Klaarwater, which was to become known as Griquatown. Adam Kok II and Barend Barends were appointed nominal chiefs over the community.[9] From 1805 magistrates, all members or close adherents of the Kok and Barends families, were appointed at various outstations. But it was the missionaries who formed the crucial link with the outside world, representing the colonial authorities and the Griqua elite to each other, and giving the community its historical voice.

The missionaries at first were accepted informally by the authorities in Cape Town as agents among the Griqua. They gave the Griqua access to essential supplies of gunpowder, previously acquired through illicit trade, which were necessary for the maintenance of the Griqua economy and Griqua hegemony over subject or neighbouring peoples. Under missionary patronage, the extent of trade controlled by the Griqua elite boomed. For their part the authorities in Cape Town and the missionaries did all in their power to encourage legitimate commerce as opposed to illicit trade by the Griqua with frontier Boers. Thus the traveller Burchell found Barend Barends with twenty followers in Cape Town in 1811 selling a ton of ivory and cattle for 'gunpowder, muskets, lead, flint, porcelain beads, knives, tinder boxes and steels, tobacco, woollen jackets and trowsers, horses and wagons'. The Griqua demand for gunpowder, essential to hunting, was insistent.[10]

As the southernmost Tswana as well as the Khoi bands of the region were decisively drawn into the colonial trading system, the Griqua elite were provided with new opportunities for profit from the large discrepancies in values between the Tswana and the colonial markets. The catchment area of the colonial frontier zone was thus greatly expanded. Cattle and ivory, 'hides and horns', flowed southward from Tswana country, while beads flowed northward, supplemented by colonial tobacco and, increasingly, sheep. The Griqua established *maats*, or trading partners, amongst the Tswana. Tswana chiefs jealously guarded access to the further interior, so that by 1820 the Griqua were still familiar only with the area south of the Molopo and west of the Vaal–Harts river system.[11]

Not only was the trading frontier expanding as a result of Griqua enterprise, but acculturation was also spreading under the auspices of the Griqua church. The idea of a 'native agency', first applied by Van der Kemp and Read at Bethelsdorp, was transferred to Griquatown by John Campbell, director of the LMS, and Read during their 1813 visit. Men like Cupido Kakkerlak and Jan Goeyman from Bethelsdorp, who settled among the Griqua, were to play a considerable role in forging a pan-'coloured' identity, which would be of some significance in subsequent decades. And men from the Griquatown church were in years to come to play an important role in spreading Griqua and missionary influence into the lands of the Tswana. It was Campbell who suggested the adoption of the name 'Griqua' (a corruption of the name of a Khoi group originally living near the southwestern Cape). This facilitated the integration of the Griqua community by giving it a new identity. Campbell also

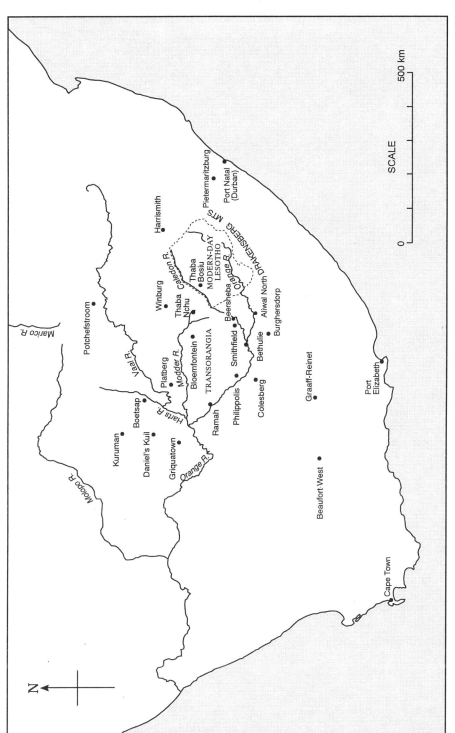

The Cape northern frontier and Transorangia

provided a new constitution for the Griqua state.[12] These various measures implied the rise of a new class of humble origin at Griquatown – people who were not dependent on the 'old captains' (the Kok and Barends families), but were products of the mission, and had come closest to fulfilling the missionary ideal of a progressive agricultural yeomanry. The most important exemplar of this class was Andries Waterboer. Allegedly of Bushman extraction, he was appointed a lay preacher after Campbell's and Read's visit in 1813.[13]

It was Waterboer who came to the fore as the chief accommodator when relations between the mission, the colonial authorities and the 'old chiefs' began to crumble from 1814 on. Governor Somerset (as we have seen) turned on the LMS with the charge that the Griqua state was serving as a haven for a stream of absconding labourers. The situation was aggravated when his demand for military conscripts from Griquatown was refused by the missionary Anderson.[14] When the governor put an end to Griqua trading privileges, the Griqua elite were simply driven back to illicit trade with frontier whites (which had never ceased). At the same time the missionaries suffered a general collapse of influence and prestige as they ceased to have any usefulness as intermediaries with the colonial authorities.[15] In addition, the peripatetic 'frontier ruffian' Coenraad de Buys proved a complicating factor in the politics of the region. Allied from 1815 with Griqua rebels, he greatly facilitated the illicit southward trade in cattle and (possibly) captured Bushmen in exchange for the crucial commodity of gunpowder.[16]

In an effort to deal with the problem of widespread illegal trade between the old Griqua elite and the frontier whites, Somerset instituted an annual fair in 1819 at the new landdrostdy of Beaufort (West) on the same principle as the fairs in the eastern Cape. This marked a resumption of legitimate commerce. The old captains, Kok and Barends, whose influence and wealth had so heavily depended on their role as middlemen, responded with alacrity by bringing in August 1819 a party of 120, with 25 wagons and 50 spans of oxen, bearing 200 tusks, 700 head of cattle, as well as skins, soap, wheat, honey, salt, and sundry 'curiosities'. Significantly, a party of Tlhaping came as well. But the white traders who had taken out licences to trade at the fair did not have the goods to sell which were in demand by the Griqua – imported manufactures, notably arms and powder. Thereafter the Beaufort fairs, like those in the eastern Cape, went into sharp decline. Official consideration was even given to the idea of forcibly bringing the Griqua back within colonial borders – a scheme dismissed by Stockenström, the frontier landdrost at Graaff-Reinet.[17]

Meanwhile, in order to restore order at Griquatown, the missionaries secured the election of their chief acolyte, Waterboer, as Griqua chief in 1820. His election brought about the rehabilitation of the agricultural community of Griquatown, to which end he introduced much-needed regulation of its affairs. To the pastoralist captains, Waterboer was a colonial upstart. Waterboer's election, however, presented the colonial authorities with the opportunity to establish a collaborative relationship with a submissive Christian chief, but this time with a salaried government agent in attendance representing colonial interests, rather than relying on the LMS missionaries as in the early days of Griquatown. John Melvill, appointed in 1822 as government agent with Waterboer, was empowered to issue passes to 'orderly' Griqua to enter the colony to trade. But he too was to confront the problem that evading official trade regulations was easier and more lucrative for the Griqua, in the absence of any effective policing of the frontier. The 'loyal' were penalised by restrictions on what might be traded, while the 'rebellious' had access to ready supplies of ammunition (and, increasingly, brandy) from frontier whites.[18]

Indeed, the dissidents among the Griqua, those who regarded Waterboer and Melvill as representatives of a discredited colonial regime, assumed a distinctive identity from 1822 as the so-called Bergenaars. The Bergenaars' raiding activities across Transorangia intersected with and were stimulated by the waves of destabilisation originating in the conflicts east of the Drakensberg, that are conventionally known to historians as the Mfecane. These began to disrupt life seriously among the Sotho–Tswana on the highveld and beyond with the invasion of Matiwane's Ngwane in 1822.[19] The old Griqua chiefs, displaced from Griquatown, meanwhile formed their own autonomous settlements, Barends at Daniel's Kuil and later at Boetsap, and Adam Kok at Campbell and later at Philippolis. Here the missionaries set about trying to re-win their loyalty and wean them away from the rebellious Bergenaar raiders, with whom they were inclined to throw in their lot for a time.

The violence and instability in the entire region were to be fuelled by new forces. The land frontier south of the Orange was closing, and the relatively privileged status of the Bastaards in that region was again eroding. Whereas the initial northward thrust of the Bastaards in the late eighteenth century originated in the area north of Cape Town towards Namaqualand, now the more easterly swath of colonial expansion up through the northern reaches of the Graaff-Reinet district was closing off access to land, as the boundary of white settlement began to impinge on the Orange River region. Fresh Bastaard emigrants from the colony, who had been radicalised by the experience of dispossession, began to augment the Bergenaars. They were to exert a strongly anti-colonial influence and play a prominent part in the raiding in the region.[20]

Such new emigrants into Transorangia brought with them new trade routes and illicit sources of ammunition. The earlier areas of illicit trading with Boers stretched north from Khamiesberg in the west, Little Namaqualand and Graaff-Reinet district in the east, where cattle could be exchanged for arms, ammunition and horses. Increasingly, the LMS 'native agents' – men mainly from Bethelsdorp sent to man outstations to the Bushmen and other refugee groups along the Orange – were involved in channelling illicit merchandise northwards from the eastern Cape, where the 1820 settlers were becoming a new engine of mercantile enterprise. Thus Melvill in March 1824 reported that on their trips south into the colony such native agents 'very frequently take with them disaffected Griquas without passes who by that means have an opportunity of gathering ammunition. The Gunpowder procured on a visit to Bethelsdorp in company with one in the service of the [London Missionary] Society is now employed by the Party of Griquas who have become a Banditti.'21

Philippolis, established as a mission station to the Bushmen in 1823, soon became a major distribution point for trade of this kind, and in this the Bethelsdorp native agents Andries Pretorius and Jan Goeyman – who were reportedly related to Bergenaar leaders – played a leading role. According to Peter Wright, LMS missionary at Griquatown, Pretorius was in 1827 indebted to an amount of 1600 rix-dollars to white farmers for trade in horses and 'contraband articles' for the Bergenaars.22

In another respect too, the volatility of the Transorangian region was being greatly aggravated, with more important long-term consequences. For in the 1820s white frontiersmen started for the first time crossing the Orange in search of pasture. The region south of the Orange known as Bushmanland was being parcelled out to Boer land claimants. By 1825 landdrost Stockenström at Graaff-Reinet was issuing temporary permits enabling white farmers to graze their livestock north of the Orange, on condition that they did not trade, put up buildings or cultivate the soil. As far as the authorities were concerned, this was a one-off concession arising from the severe drought in the northern reaches of the colony. It was impressed on the trekboers that this concession was not to be regarded as a precedent and that no further extension of colonial boundaries would be contemplated. But although the authorities were opposed in principle to trekboers moving beyond colonial borders (indeed it was formally illegal without permission), they had no power to stop them. By 1828 trekboers were no longer asking for permission, but merely informing the magistrate in Graaff-Reinet that they were moving over the Orange. From 1830 onwards the movement north of the Orange became a regular seasonal migration rather than simply an *ad hoc* reaction to temporary climatic conditions. Landless families tended to stay behind in Transorangia permanently; and by the later 1830s colonial landholders started disposing of their own land permanently and remaining north of the Orange too.23

But the trekboers were careful to ensure that their ties with the colony were not broken, and eagerly sought colonial recognition of their land claims north of the Orange – with no satisfaction. They even returned in large numbers to the colony for the annual *opgaaf* (tax census) well into the late 1830s and beyond. When Colesberg was established as a frontier magistracy just south of the Orange in 1837, farmers from far north of the Orange attended quarterly *nagmaal* services there, and brought their children to be baptised. Nevertheless, the trekboers early on sought to place their access to land in Transorangia on a permanent footing by entering into agreements through their field cornets with local communities, initially Bushmen. In the late 1820s they paid over large numbers of livestock for the 'purchase' of vast stretches of land from Bushmen, indicating that they regarded the river valleys of Transorangia as permanent *trekvelden* for their stock.[24]

The intrusive trekboers were a destabilising influence in Transorangia, adding to the conflict caused by the rebel Griqua–Bergenaar raiders and the groups sent flying across the highveld by the rise of Zulu power to the east. As white trekboers infiltrated, the long-established and illicit trading relationships between Griqua and white frontiersmen shifted their centre of gravity northwards across the Orange. Indeed, the 1820s seems to have seen an intensification of such trading relations. Further, again repeating earlier patterns, individual whites were widely involved with Bergenaar raiders right across the length and breadth of Transorangia. ('Bergenaar', like 'Bastaard' or 'Griqua', was, after all, a social or cultural category as much as – or more than – a racial one.) As firearms and ammunition flooded across the Orange, the jealously guarded restrictions on access to firearms north of the Orange broke down. For decades the Bastaard/Griqua frontiersmen had ensured that whatever arms and powder were available in the northern frontier zone did not reach the non-Christian Khoi, Bushmen or Sotho–Tswana. Now European weaponry began to be diffused more generally through the region.

With all this intrusion and intermingling of peoples in Transorangia, the dynamics of the region became intricate and complex. Thus the Bergenaar raiders, originally rebellious Griqua, became more heterogeneous, as newly arrived Bastaards from the colony, Kora (Khoi) bands and even whites were involved. Eventually the Kora emerged as the predominant raiding force in the region. In the process they were transformed from loose bands into larger communities under a new military leadership – such as, for example, Jan Bloem and Abraham Kruger, the half-Khoi sons of earlier white frontiersmen.[25]

The victims of cattle raiding were Sotho–Tswana communities, already disrupted by the incoming groups from east of the Drakensberg. Captured cattle were channelled south in payment for arms, powder, horses and (in increasing demand) Cape brandy, brought north in Boer and Bastaard wagons. But it is also clear that a very important commodity being sold southwards in the 1820s was human captives. This trade was not new, but was taking on wider dimensions in that turbulent decade. Particularly vulnerable to capture were the Bushmen, who had little to offer raiders other than their labour power, and rarely had the means of armed resistance. The Bushmen were finding it more and more difficult to evade the sights of white and coloured frontiersmen's guns as their hunting grounds and springs north and south of the Orange were gradually taken over – just as they had been further south in the eighteenth century. [26]

It was also commonly reported that destitute people were offering children for sale. In 1824 Robert Moffat and, a few years later, Samuel Broadbent were offered children by Rolong in exchange for an ox or sheep and some beads. Andrew Smith reported that Bushmen were selling their children for goats or sheep to Boers, although they claimed that the children had been instructed to abscond from their new masters. Moffat wrote that the practice was prompted by pressures from the Griqua (whom he disliked); but Broadbent declared that selling children was 'a general practice' among the Rolong, and was accused by Chief Sefunelo of interfering with their rights when he opposed the practice. The extent of this trade in captives is difficult to gauge, given the episodic nature of the evidence. No doubt it was a significant spur to violence in the region; but there is no evidence to suggest that it was in any way a systematically organised traffic dependent on the deployment of large quantities of capital, such as characterised slave-trading elsewhere.[27]

Some of the victims of raiding were not without resources of their own, and were quick to seek access to firearms for themselves. Indeed, the 1820s witnessed not only disruption among the Sotho–Tswana, but also the consolidation of new centres of state power in reaction to the insecurities of the time. Thus the Tlhaping west of the Vaal–Harts soon regrouped, having found themselves in the eye of the storm arising both from other African peoples dislodged by the invaders from below the Drakensberg and from Bergenaars and Kora raiders.[28] Their missionary, Moffat, complained in December 1827: 'They frequently interrogated us as to where the Corannas [Kora] procured their guns, horses, and ammunition. We, of course, could not deny a fact so notorious, that they purchased these articles from the farmers on the northern limits of the Colony.'[29]

Commodities like these facilitated the emergence of new centres of authority under Tlhaping rule out of the ruins of the old Tlhaping state. Bent on restoring depleted cattle herds and rebuilding their economy, the southern Tswana were now more closely tied to, and dependent upon, access to colonial markets, where ivory, stock, produce and labour were in demand. This closer involvement in the colonial economy made missionaries all the more attractive to Sotho–Tswana communities, for although conservative evangelists like Moffat were strongly opposed to arms sales, missionaries did tend to attract traders and open up channels of communication with the colony.[30] By the 1840s new technology, most obviously the plough and irrigation, had begun to transform Tswana society. The presence of firearms and the consequent shooting out of wild game hastened this transformation.[31]

British traders, hunters and explorers from the eastern Cape were also infiltrating the land of the Tswana by the late 1820s, increasingly drawing the Tswana more directly into long-distance trade relations. Now that all attempts at controlling commercial intercourse across the northern boundaries of the colony had failed, in January 1825 Governor Somerset for the first time allowed colonial traders to venture over the northern borders with licences issued by the landdrost, and under the authority of the government agent at Griquatown, who would supposedly enjoy a monopoly over the supply of gunpowder. This did not in any way alter the fact that the great bulk of the trading continued to be conducted illicitly, on a minor, *ad hoc* scale by small parties of Boers or Bastaards with wagons and little capital. The restrictions on officially sanctioned trade in fact placed the law-abiding at a positive disadvantage. By contrast, men like A. G. Bain, Thomas Biddulph and J. C. Chase, all prominent 1820 settlers, saw themselves as pioneer adventurers, concerned to chart unknown territory and open up commercial opportunities to the British commercial class, and to communicate widely their findings. They were not interested in the petty commodity trading of the Boer diaspora. Instead they headed straight for the sources of ivory in Tswana territory way to the north. It was they who established the route from Graham's Town via Philippolis to the land north and west of the Vaal, as the main road to the north.[32]

In 1826 Bain and Biddulph reached Molepolole at a latitude of 24 degrees. In 1827 Robert Scoon and William McLuckie reached the headwaters of the Marico River and, two years later, Mzilikazi's Ndebele in the vicinity of modern-day Pretoria. They made a profit of £1800 on this journey. As a direct result of these journeys the missionaries Archbell and Moffat visited Mzilikazi, following in the footsteps of the men of commerce. David Hume was perhaps the most important of these British traders, establishing himself at Kuruman in the 1830s, and travelling in search of gold north of the Limpopo. The larger merchants of Graham's Town provided the capital for such ventures. From 1830 permanent stores were established at mission stations among the Tswana, such as at Kuruman and Platberg. In 1835, Scoon reported that when he had begun trading, the Tswana had only wanted beads, but would now provide only milk or firewood for beads. Their main desire was for European clothes, and they had begun to pay with money earned through the sale of ivory or in service. What Scoon did not mention was that he was suspected also of carrying supplies of arms and ammunition northwards for sale.[33]

Much more important, though, than any Tswana chiefdom in the longer-term development of colonial and imperial policy was Moshoeshoe's emergent Sotho state in the Caledon valley. This valley, previously peopled by small Koena chiefdoms, had been devastated by the troubles of the 1820s. By the early 1830s Moshoeshoe, heir to a Koena chieftaincy, had emerged as the ruler of a state of increasing size and wealth. He extended his sway up and down the Caledon valley between the open plains to the west and the mountains to the east, by incorporating a diversity of Sotho and Nguni refugees. By means of his control of cattle wealth (gained in part through raiding, and protected against Kora and Griqua by the inaccessibility of his pasture lands), Moshoeshoe built up a considerable authority through the *mafisa* system of cattle loans, especially for bridewealth purposes, which bound young men and their lineages to him in the idiom of kinship relations.[34]

Moshoeshoe's state was, more than any other African chiefdom, constructed in direct symbiotic relationship with the expanding colonial economy. For one thing, some of those who fell under his authority had sought temporary refuge in colonial employment, bringing back European goods and technologies such as firearms. Further, the Caledon valley was, in sharp contrast to territory occupied by Griqua, Tswana or trekboers, fertile grain country; and the

Sotho were increasingly able from the 1830s to acquire guns and horses from trekboers and Griqua by providing them with cattle and grain. Indeed, Lesotho would become the focal point of a thriving regional trade network in which the Boers of the northern Cape and the Transorangian plains featured prominently. (Long-distance British traders avoided Lesotho because it did not contain the much-prized ivory.) Moshoeshoe's state was always a loose confederation, very different from the centralised military states spawned by the rise of Zulu power. But the chieftaincy always retained authority over the economic and commercial life of the chiefdom. By the 1840s Moshoeshoe was widely believed to have more firearms and horses than any other chief in southern Africa.

Moshoeshoe's importance in the politics of the region was enhanced by the sought-after presence from 1833 of French Protestant missionaries among his people. Close allies of Philip and the humanitarian lobby, they acted as advisers and interlocutors between the paramount and the outside world. For some years, owing to the circumstances of the kingdom's creation on the cusp of an expanding colonial order, the missionaries had considerable success in converting not only the marginalised, but also senior figures in the royal lineage itself. In the end, however, this success did not outlive the appearance of the ugly face of British imperialism in the late 1840s.[35]

The humanitarian lobby in South Africa saw the Christian Griqua – recognisable offshoots of the colonial society from which they had separated themselves – as ideal vectors of their vision of a non-racial Christian civilisation in the subcontinent. It was altogether in keeping with John Philip's humanitarian imperialism that, increasingly in the 1820s and 1830s, he sought to promote the Christian Griqua state as a political bulwark against the forces of chaos and subjugation, represented by Bergenaar and Kora raiders on the one hand, and white trekboers on the other.

For Philip, the Griqua, like the products of colonial missions such as Bethelsdorp, were pre-eminently the creatures of the LMS. When Anderson and his colleagues first came into contact with them in 1800, Philip wrote, they had been a 'herd of naked and wandering savages ... without knowledge, without morals, or any trace of civilisation, they were wholly abandoned to witchcraft, drunkenness, licentiousness, and all the consequences which arise from the unchecked growth of such vices'.[36] From this fate the missionaries had saved them, and had led them along the path of civilisation. Philip believed that the LMS stood in the position of trustee or guardian to the Griqua state under Waterboer's captaincy. In what was a gross historical distortion, Philip claimed in 1832 that the Griqua chiefs 'did not find a country for the Missionaries, but the Missionaries found an unoccupied country for them. This new country they did not take possession of in their own name, or in the name of any men among them, but in the name of the LMS, and the Colonial Government sanctioned the deed.'[37]

In this way Philip was promoting the LMS as the ultimate authority not only over the Griqua political community, but over vast and infinitely expandable stretches of territory as well. It was in relation to the Griqua beyond colonial borders that the political dimension of the humanitarian vision was most fully developed. For here the humanitarian lobby (represented by the LMS) was acting not only as a powerful pressure group, but quite explicitly (or so it thought) as an autonomous territorial power in its own right, using Griqua institutions and Griqua military capacity as organs of LMS policy.

During the turmoil of the 1820s, Philip held up the Griqua as natural allies of the colony in maintaining law and order beyond the reach of colonial authority, in the same way that the mission Khoi of the eastern Cape could be trusted to act as loyal servants. In 1825 he argued that the Griqua had saved the colony from having to station a military force of a thousand men on the northern border. But on a visit to Transorangia in that year, Philip came face to face with the extent of illicit trade across the northern frontier, and the degree of dislocation that pervaded the region. To strengthen the 'loyal' Griqua against Bergenaar and Kora raiders, he authorised the settlement of Adam Kok II and his followers at Philippolis mission. He also transferred his protégé, Peter Wright, from Theopolis to Griquatown, where he was to play an important role as Philip's right-hand man north of the Orange, consistently representing Waterboer and his state in the most favourable light as the bastion of civilisation and imperial defence on the northern frontier.[38]

In 1829 Philip returned from his lengthy stay in London. There he had agitated for the passing of Ordinance 50 of 1828 and had written his *Researches*, in which he stressed the destructive effects of the trade in firearms and slaves. On his return to the Cape he was alarmed at the spread of white settlement north of the Orange. This he considered to pose a threat to his Griqua protégés and his ambitions for them. Having won, as he saw it, the battle for civil rights for the Khoi inside the colony, he launched a campaign to persuade the colonial authorities to recognise the Griqua state as the only legitimate authority north of the colony. He suggested that the Griqua be formed into a 'kind of Frontier Militia to prevent aggressions committed by the farmers, and the reaction that might arise from these aggressions'.[39] Being incapable of seeing white colonists in anything but the darkest light, Philip could not conceive that a good many Griqua, with their access to colonial markets, might not be as alarmed at their presence as he. He was also blind to the fact that many Griqua were just as much a predatory force against the hapless Bushmen as were the Boers.

After a visit to the north in 1832, Philip came up with concrete proposals. Either the Griqua territory should be incorporated within the colony on the same terms as the Kat River Settlement – that is, a distinct and self-governing territory under LMS guardianship (an option Philip very much preferred) – or else Waterboer should be made commandant over the whole Transorangia and allowed to acquire sufficient arms and powder to bring order to the region. If given the authority by the colonial government, the Griqua could assist in 'confining the boors within their present limits' as well as preventing direct contact 'between white colonists and the raiding groups or "banditti."' Philip held out the Ndebele of Mzilikazi, based on the northern edges of the highveld, as a major new threat to the stability of the region, even though Mzilikazi at the time was seeking a missionary presence at his capital.[40]

In 1834 Philip's prescriptions to the colonial government bore fruit. When Governor D'Urban brought with him from Downing Street instructions to enter treaty relations with the Xhosa, war erupted on the eastern frontier before they could be implemented. But Philip ensured that treaty relations were extended to Waterboer's Griqua without delay. In December 1834, Waterboer and the missionary Wright arrived in Cape Town, where the captain was wined and dined by the local elite, attended banquets at Government House, and was carried around town in the governor's carriage. He took back with him to Griquatown a treaty declaring that he was the 'friend and ally' of the colony, bound to protect the colonial frontier by sending back fugitives and assisting colonial forces against external dangers. He was to receive a salary of £100 and a supply of arms and ammunition. At the same time the missionary Wright accepted the post of government agent. Significantly, the Griqua territory was not geographically defined in the treaty. As far as Philip was concerned, the spread of 'Christian civilisation' to neighbouring African peoples beyond the northern frontier would go hand in hand with the spread of Griqua political authority. This formal recognition of Griqua statehood thus reflected Philip's and Waterboer's efforts to expand the scope of Griqua (and hence LMS) power in Transorangia.[41]

For some years before 1834 Philip and his missionaries had been actively asserting the hegemony of Waterboer and Griquatown over other centres of Griqua settlement and political authority. After Waterboer's rise to power the 'old chiefs', the Koks and Barends, had established themselves elsewhere in the 1820s. But the LMS missionaries claimed that Cornelis Kok at Campbell was an appointee of Waterboer, a claim that had no truth to it; Barends at Boetsap, they argued, had no status as a chief. Barends was a particular thorn, as he had fallen under the influence of rival Methodist missionaries based amongst the Seleka Rolong (a Tswana chiefdom) at Platberg. This was to lead to a clash between the LMS missionaries and the Methodists over itineration rights among Barends's people.[42]

But it was Philippolis, where Adam Kok II had settled under LMS auspices in 1826, that would be a particular focus of conflict – not least because Kok's claimed territory lay in the path of trekboer expansion north of the Orange. Philip had approved Kok's settlement there in an effort to bring the rebellious Griqua raiding groups under control. He had also been concerned to ensure that Kok recognised Waterboer at Griquatown as the hegemonic authority in the whole region. But by the mid-1830s he was forced to take Kok and his captaincy more seriously as an independent entity, since it was the Philippolis Griqua who were the main bulwark, as Philip saw it, against the intrusive white settlers.[43]

At first there was no particular friction between Griqua and white trekboers: after all they were trade partners historically. But Kok's relationship with the LMS and hence with the colony gave him alternative and potentially more lucrative sources of patronage to those provided by the trekboers. Thus not surprisingly, an ambivalence developed among Kok's people. Some sought settled respectability in close contact with the mission, while the Bergenaar–Kora element continued raiding activities from the river valleys further north (such as the large-scale expeditions against Moshoeshoe in 1830 and against Mzilikazi in 1831). The raiders were closely allied with trekboers through the illicit trading linkages of the frontier. Publicly, Kok and his council at Philippolis, seeing the advantages of responding to missionary pressures, tried to secure the cooperation of the colony in upholding their own authority. In 1829 they sent memorials to the governor (apparently drafted by the missionaries) requesting that trekboers be confined to those parts of the country that they (the Griqua) designated. They were also concerned to check the indiscriminate trading of firearms with the rebellious, and to regulate relations between white employers and Griqua labourers. Yet Kok himself was also implicated in raiding activities.[44]

Inevitably, conflicts over legitimate authority sometimes flared, with Kok determined to exploit the advantages of his relationship with the LMS to the full in order to extend his claims to territorial hegemony. The trekboers' main grievance, as articulated by their field cornets, was that the Griqua (with their missionary spokesmen) were recognised as having sovereign rights and autonomy beyond colonial borders, whereas the trekboers north of the Orange were officially regarded as outside the law and therefore without any legal recourse or protection, despite their determination to remain loyal colonial subjects.[45] Yet on the whole, despite occasional alarms, relations between the Griqua and the trekboers were not antagonistic. The trekboers were willing to pay for grazing rights, and the Griqua elite, who parcelled out land rights between themselves, profited from the trekboers' presence. In practice, the trekboers recognised Griqua rights over the land. A pattern began developing in the 1830s whereby the Griqua, despite strong opposition from the missionaries, sacrificed the long-term integrity of their territory for short-term financial gain, by leasing out their land to trekboers.[46]

Thus Kok's people on the whole were not the close ally of the mission and the colonial government that Waterboer was. Historically, Kok's followers had been a pastoral rather than an agricultural people, less susceptible to mission influence than those at Griquatown. Stockenström was always more sceptical of Kok's Griqua, whom he regarded as interlopers, than were Philip and his missionaries, who saw the white trekboers as the perpetrators of villainy and the Griqua as the fount of civilising influences north of the Orange. In the end Philip's vision for the Griqua proved as illusory as the vision Stockenström had once held of Transorangia as a Bushman reserve. But in the 1830s the humanitarian lobby was still at the peak of its influence and optimism.

Persuaded of the importance of shoring up Kok's power base, in view of his strategic location at Philippolis, Philip was already by 1834 entertaining the idea that Kok should enjoy a similar and equal status to that extended to Waterboer. Kok, again at missionary prodding, thus visited the colony in 1835 in search of colonial recognition of his sovereignty. But war on the Xhosa frontier precluded any consideration by the governor of the Griqua situation. Kok died while in the colony, and it was to be some years before a formal treaty was signed with his son Adam Kok III. In February 1837, though, a treaty was signed between Kok and Waterboer formalising the division of the Griqua into two separate states, with separate governments and separate laws, but providing for joint council meetings and cooperation in warfare and defence. Ramah on the Orange was established as the border line between the Griquatown and Philippolis captaincies. But for the rest, boundaries were not defined, in keeping with the missionary assumption that Griqua expansion was beneficial and inevitable.[47]

Between 1834 and 1840 some 15 000 Boer colonists left the colony in a series of trek parties in a determined effort to remove themselves from direct British rule. This exodus is known today as the Great Trek, although that term was not used before the 1870s.[48] From early 1834, a year of intense drought, reports began to reach Cape Town of Boers from the districts of the eastern Cape – Albany, Somerset, Uitenhage – moving beyond the borders of the colony with no intention of returning. The pretext given was that they refused to allow their slaves to be emancipated under the legislation passed the previous year by the British parliament. Although many slaves taken out of the colony by the emigrants absconded and returned to the colony, it is remarkable, and often overlooked, that many Khoi or coloured servants showed little inclination to desert service rather than accompany their masters on trek. At least as many coloured servants as 'white' Boers left the colony during the exodus, and large numbers of the servants seem to have willingly participated (although little is known of their role or perspectives).[49]

What made this movement so novel was that the trekkers seemed determined to throw off the yoke of British rule and British law. There was a new note of rebellion about it. Significantly, the emigration had its origins in the eastern districts close to the epicentre of the British settler economy, where British imperial adventurism had impinged most destructively on African societies, and pressures on economic resources were most intensely felt. This was in sharp contrast to those loyalists in the remoter northern parts who since the

1820s had moved beyond the Orange River boundary, and who petitioned for an extension of colonial boundaries to incorporate them, and continued to pay taxes and sustain relationships with the colonial church.[50]

The trek is a major theme in traditional South African historiography, and has taken on different symbolic meanings in different traditions.[51] It has generally been seen as a political or ideological movement of rebellion against British authority – as an expression of proto-nationalist sentiment, and hence as an essentially unified movement, imbued with a sense of cohesion and common purpose. The search for 'causes' of the trek has been one of the great themes of Afrikaner historiography – so much so that the history of the years prior to 1834 is often seen solely in terms of the trek's origins. Slagtersnek – the incident in 1815 when five frontier Boers were hanged for fomenting rebellion against the authorities – was the most evocative precipitating event in earlier interpretations, although it has been demonstrated that at the time of the trek, Slagtersnek was hardly a memory. In fact it was resurrected much later.[52]

Usually the search for 'causes' is pushed back to a quest for the Afrikaner's Calvinist-inspired 'calling' or 'mission', sometimes invoking biblical imagery of the exodus of a chosen people.[53] In the nationalist literature, moreover, there is often a sense of primordial Afrikaner identity, growing out of shared historical and cultural experience, just waiting to be realised in a movement of national liberation. As far as many of the nationalist historians are concerned, the trek was a movement of unique significance, not reducible to the comparative history of colonial settlement or colonial expansion. It was very specifically a nation-forming event of almost mystical dimensions.[54]

In this tradition, apartheid ideology can often be explicitly traced back to the trek. The trek preserved and fostered an independent Afrikaner nation free of alien cultural influences and alien political domination. It established the policy of territorial segregation and racial differentiation as the ascendant ideal. In some versions, it even liberated oppressed African groups from the yoke of Ndebele and Zulu domination, and hence served as a vehicle for the liberation of other oppressed 'nations' as well. If it had not taken place, racial equality and integration would have been imposed by the British, and white South Africa would have been swallowed up by black Africa and would have lost its racial identity, unable to defend itself in the absence of an autonomous state power.[55] But the ideals embodied and preserved in the trekker republics, which were established in the interior as a result of the trek, were strong enough to triumph in the modern unified state which emerged in the twentieth century. In this tradition – in some ways very similar to the liberal formulation described earlier – the trek becomes a titanic struggle for survival, a struggle which was to culminate in the victory of republicanism and apartheid by the 1960s. This highly teleological and self-justifying interpretation ascribes fixed and static ideological positions to imposed ethnic and national categories, and effectively closes off any real consideration of the actual historical processes involved.

In fact, little essence of Afrikaner political consciousness is to be discovered in the expressions and intentions of the trekkers themselves. For all the later emphasis on their republicanism and striving for independent nationhood, these sentiments find only the most transient reflection in the evidence of the time. Because any self-conscious sense of national mission is absent, generalisations about the causes of the exodus are difficult to make – although, clearly, material factors can be identified. These material factors are normally described as the intolerable conditions under which the Boers lived in the British-ruled colony. But much more positive motives relating to the extension of frontiers of trade and opportunity were in play as well, as we shall see.

In the frontier districts of the Cape the old alliance between the British and the Boer elite had begun to break down by the 1830s. With the abolition of the boards of *heemraden,* and the subordination of the commando system (with its hierarchies of privilege) to British military authority, the old lines of patronage and authority in the districts were being dismantled. Anglicisation of administration and the courts was symbolic of a larger process of disempowerment. In consequence the field cornets often found themselves ignorant of law and administrative procedure, and out of touch with the larger governmental framework within which they were supposed to operate. From about 1828, when the old administrative system was replaced, Stockenström, for one, discerned a growing resentment towards the British and a growing sense of powerlessness. '"Everything is becoming so English, that we, with our old Dutch habits, feel as if we are no longer in our own country," was everywhere heard, and many of the Boers openly declared their desire to know a little more of the interior of Africa.' Stockenström also revealed the sense of bewilderment and alienation among Boers, no longer able to rely on the advice and mediation of the 'voorstanders van 't volk' in their dealings with government, 'for our oldest and wisest men know as little of the Government as we do'.[56]

At the same time the economy drive of the Cape government had pared away the administrative resources of the colony. Low-paid and overburdened personnel were left to man the districts, and very thinly at that. It was common for very considerable field-cornetcies never to see any magistrate or civil commissioner. An older system of authority had been dismantled and replaced by something alien and wholly inadequate. In general it was the ineffectiveness of the administration as much as its intrusiveness that evoked grievance and resentment. The colonists considered themselves to be 'totally neglected', wrote Stockenström; and they were left feeling 'helpless and ignorant'. The ineffectuality and unresponsiveness of the local administration were particularly serious in an area where British military adventurism had for a couple of decades been destabilising indigenous societies, and access to land was at a premium. The result was bound to be a heightened degree of tension over encroachment, cattle theft and labour relations. Finally, the pressing reality of drought in the early 1830s may have been a further precipitating factor in causing disgruntled people to start thinking of leaving the colony.[57]

Underlying heightened tensions throughout the eastern Cape and Midland regions lay the question of declining access to land. The Boer economy was land-extensive and, especially in times of drought, dependent on seasonal trekking in search of alternative grazing. By the 1830s a majority of Boers were non-landowners, and those many who did not personally own land were increasingly finding it difficult to gain access to land for their stock.[58] Because of the problems surrounding the system of quitrent tenure introduced in 1813, a new informal system of 'request places' came instead into being. This was land to which claims had been lodged, and to which no title had yet been issued, although they had often been surveyed years before, at great expense to claimants. Without title, there was little real security, and the transfer or testamentary disposition of land was of dubious legality. There were hundreds of 'request places' in Graaff-Reinet by 1824, but no quitrent farms. The first Land Board served by qualified surveyors was set up in 1828 following recommendations by the commissioners of enquiry, but their core suggestions were neglected, and the survey department became even more mired and underfunded. The colonial land registry, too, operated in a state of advanced disarray, and despite the costs involved to claimants in registering claims and securing surveys and inspection reports from overstretched officials, the issuance of title-deeds remained years behind schedule.[59]

Added to all this, the corruption and incompetence of surveyors were aggravating factors. In 1834 it was discovered that literally hundreds of farms in Albany, Somerset and Graaff-Reinet districts had been wrongly surveyed and had to be re-surveyed before title could be issued. The surveyor W. F. Hertzog, who was assigned in 1837 to rectify matters, found that in many cases no records of claims, surveys or inspection reports could be found; receipts of survey fees in farmers' hands were the only evidence of such activity. In effect, concluded Hertzog, the activities of certain surveyors had amounted to large-scale fraud committed on the farming population.[60]

The insecurity of land tenure in frontier districts was heightened by the increasingly aggressive speculation of British settlers, whose access to official patronage was greater than that of most Boers – not least because so many settler accumulators themselves held official appointments. The surveyor Hertzog recorded that it was a cause of great bitterness that so many Boers who had submitted land claims, had had the land surveyed, and worked it for years, were forced to make way for English-speaking claimants, who might already own far more land than they could use. Hertzog noted that he could itemise twenty such cases which he had come across in Graham's Town alone.[61] The closing of land frontiers simply meant that by the 1830s thousands of Boers had moved or contemplated moving beyond colonial frontiers. Those further from the northern frontiers and under the greatest pressure were more likely to make the bold leap into a conscious breaking of ties. All in all, the importance of land and grievances about its administration cannot be underestimated in explaining the exodus.

Accounts of the trek have laid stress on no single factor more than the perceived revolution in labour relations caused by the liberal reforms of the 1820s, and the amelioration and eventual abolition of slavery. The effects of these measures on labour supplies and labour relations in the frontier districts are difficult to assess. But there were enough prosecutions under the new laws to serve as a threat, and farmers must have been very aware that there was no legal sanction for coercive practices any longer. For farmers, labour supply was never sufficient or, in other words, sufficiently exploitable and obedient at the remuneration and under the conditions employers could afford. For years, white farmers hungry for labour had bemoaned the extent to which blacks were able to evade servile status, and regretted their own failure to impose a moral hegemony over the servant class. There was nothing new about this. But in the early 1830s a growing dissatisfaction among Boers about labour and class relations seems to have fed into a general sense of crisis, for which an inept and unsympathetic government was held responsible. In particular their grievances focused on the *gelykstelling*, or equalisation, implicit in the new politico-legal order, which threatened the established patriarchal authority of the Boer household. Within the household, consisting of the core Boer family plus dependants and servants (including slaves), the hierarchy of authority was built on the patriarch's control over relationships in the domestic sphere. In the new legal order the emasculation of this authority, perhaps more threatened than real, must have seemed like an attack on the very foundations of Boer society.[62]

Although only a small minority of Boers in the frontier districts owned slaves, the questions of amelioration, emancipation and slave compensation were repeatedly cited as major grievances by trekker leaders and observers at the time. We should remember that those who owned slaves were also those most likely to be leaders of the exodus. Gert Maritz, for example, owned twelve slaves valued at £1540, and Louis Tregardt had ten. Some had been investing in slaves from the western districts at a time when prices were rising as a result of the abolition of the slave trade in 1808. Then again, many western slave-owners had been moving to eastern districts in search of new opportunities.[63] Others accounted as slaves in the eastern districts may have been child captives from the north.[64] Slaves in the pastoral eastern districts, unlike workers of Khoisan origin, were culturally alien to the indigenous peoples, and therefore were particularly valued. They were trusted often to travel alone and carry guns, and often supervised Khoisan servants. And like many nominally 'free' servants, they commonly had livestock and gardens of their own.[65]

In 1832 Stockenström commented on the hostility evoked in the eastern Cape by the restrictions and conditions placed on the use of slave labour by regulation, at a time when Khoi or coloured labour had been freed from legal restrictions.[66] After emancipation in 1834, slave-owners became particularly vulnerable to fraud, because of their dependence on agents and middlemen – often their creditors – for the collection of compensation moneys. Many had little choice but to sell their claims in return for trade goods. Others had to pay commission of 20 per cent to agents. Typically, frontier slave-owners received about one-fifth of the assessed value of their slaves. Many received no compensation at all, and some refused to accept payment of what they regarded as derisory sums. Although the issue of slave emancipation directly affected relatively few, no doubt great propaganda advantage was made of the perfidy involved.[67]

In all the agitation about labour and class relations, it is very difficult to discern the trekker voice, although there were many historical voices seeking to represent it. What is certain is that grievances were deliberately propagated by people with particular motives. And these trekker spokesmen and observers who reported on the exodus were often people who had the clearest and strongest political agendas. It is not unlikely that for many trekkers the political battle over rights for coloured people, or humanitarian influence, or the question of the Stockenström treaties was quite remote. Nevertheless, on a more subliminal level these issues must have fed into a general psychosis, the sense of a society under siege and in danger of expropriation – not least because of the stridency and arrogance of much British humanitarian rhetoric concerning the evils of Boer society.

The exodus should also be seen in terms of the squeezing of the Boer economy by the surge of British commercial enterprise, dating from the 1820s, when the British settlers of the eastern Cape began to turn to trade in a big way. Many settler traders moved around the Boer farms in search of custom. One consequence of the coming of the trader's wagon was the commercialisation of the Boer economy on an unprecedented scale. Although some Boers further away in the northern Cape and beyond benefited as middlemen, in the eastern Cape itself – closer to the areas of most intense British commercial activity – increasing indebtedness may have been a result. The fact is that few export commodities of value came from white farms before the widespread adoption of woolled sheep, and those without the wherewithal to trade or hunt (options which in any event were increasingly closed off) found themselves economically in a squeeze. This was particularly the lot of the more substantial Boer landowners and officials who had themselves had experience of the commercial nexus and the world the British settlers represented – men who, because of their ethnic background, may well have been excluded from credit or commercial favour.[68] It was such men who became leaders of trek parties. Several of those leaving on trek left unpaid debts behind them. Indeed, indebtedness for some may have been a prime motive for trekking.[69]

This levelling down of the Boer elite – their land rights and their privileged hold over tied labour under threat, and their access to official patronage choked off by government reform and the rise of the British settler elite – can be seen in the lives of individual trek leaders. The first important trek leader was Louis Tregardt, member of a prominent family of officeholders in the central eastern frontier who had participated in the rebellions of the 1790s. In

1833 Tregardt resigned from the post of provisional field cornet, disposed of his farms in the Tarka region of Somerset district, and arranged for the settlement of his affairs in the colony. Then he and a group of some thirty Boer families (relations and *bywoners* among them), together with a total of fourteen slaves, moved away and settled beyond the Kei in territory under the control of the Xhosa paramount, Hintsa, who allegedly gave Tregardt a substantial farm of 12 000 morgen. They lived in apparent harmony with Hintsa and his people, with whom they at first planned to stay permanently, before moving off northwards across the Orange in the course of 1835. Seeking temporary grazing beyond the borders was very common at the time. What was unusual, however, was that Tregardt apparently had no intention of returning. Tregardt's grievances had been long in gestating. For the authorities had declared in 1826 that no land title would be issued east of the Fish River to Boer slave-owners, as they were too close to the frontier and might be encouraged to enslave Africans. Tregardt, a substantial stock farmer, had ten slaves. And although he had paid fees and quitrent for land, he could not gain title. To the Boers, the British policy seemed designed to ensure that land would become available to British speculators, whose sole concern, complained Tregardt and 120 others in 1827, was not to maintain their families but to make money.[70]

Removing his slaves across the border in the year of emancipation was an act of rebellion in the eyes of the authorities. Captain A. B. Armstrong was consequently dispatched in November 1834 with a detachment of Cape Mounted Rifles by the magistrate in Albany to secure Tregardt's slaves' release. Tregardt was informed that emancipation legislation provided that removal of slaves beyond colonial borders involved a punishment of transportation beyond the seas for up to fourteen years, quite apart from fines of £100 per slave.[71] It was possibly this aggressive posture by the authorities that persuaded Tregardt to move well beyond the reach of colonial law and seek succour in the far northern interior in communication with the Portuguese authorities at Delagoa Bay. Towards the end of 1835 he and a small party made their way to the Limpopo valley, from where they reached the Portuguese port, only to succumb to the ravages of malaria. In all, Tregardt's trek was an idiosyncratic and failed experiment.[72]

More important was A. H. Potgieter's departure with a much larger party, also from the central frontier zone (the Tarka region north of the Winterberg). Potgieter (of whose origins little is known) avoided the dangers of the Portuguese hinterland and established himself across the Vaal, where he remained a considerable influence in the politics of the region until 1854. He founded the western settlement of Potchefstroom and the eastern settlement of Ohrigstad, and pioneered colonisation of the far northern Zoutpansberg. Like Tregardt, Potgieter fully intended that he would have nothing further to do with the British, and always followed a policy of avoidance by moving further away from their influence, even as others were taking on or accommodating the advancing forces of British imperialism. It is perhaps significant that Potgieter's communities were far less predatory and more compatible with the political geography of the Transvaal interior (after the Ndebele had departed) than the bulk of the trekkers who followed. Unlike Potgieter, these were more intent on carving out racially exclusive states.[73]

Indeed, the exodus had two distinct waves, each with its own distinctive characteristics. While Tregardt and Potgieter were inclined to break all ties with Britain, the great majority of the trekkers who left later – from early 1836, after the war on the eastern frontier was over – were far more ambivalent in their attitudes, and in fact continued to cling to British colonial trade links as their umbilical cord to markets. There is every indication that subsequent trek leaders saw themselves as establishing satellite communities within the informal sphere of British colonial hegemony rather than seeking to break ties altogether. These leaders were members of a frustrated colonial accumulating elite, who wished to create new economic spaces for themselves away from the suffocating pressures of British settler dominance and administrative inertia. But they still considered themselves members of that colonial elite after they had left.

The trekkers were not an undifferentiated mass. The leaders tended to be men of substance in the colony – men who had enjoyed above-average access to economic resources, who had held office and had a knowledge of the wider world. Men like Piet Retief, Gert Maritz and Piet Uys had strong links with the market towns of the eastern Cape and Midlands, and were very much in touch with British settler opinion and the British settler economy. They were certainly not unaware of the possibilities of accumulating resources, notably land, through establishing state structures (republican or not) in which they, as men with greater education and administrative and legal experience, would play leading roles. It is most likely that such men envisaged becoming a landowning and business elite wherever they settled. They were not fleeing from the colonial nexus, but carrying it into the interior of Africa. Nevertheless, their capacity to fulfil their dreams without the active succour of the imperial power proved to be limited.[74]

The satellite states that men like these envisaged represented in one sense a leap forward of the colonial trading frontier. There had long been close relations between British merchants and Boer itinerant traders in the northern reaches of the colony and well beyond the Orange. By the 1830s, the sources of the most sought-after export commodities, ivory especially, had receded far to the north, and the trekkers were to pursue the receding ivory frontier to the richest areas of supply beyond the southern Nguni. The most developed trading frontier outside the colonial borders was that radiating from the settlement of Port Natal (present-day Durban) on the southeast African coast, way beyond the Cape's eastern frontier, on the fringes of the region of northern Nguni settlement.

British traders were established at Port Natal from as early as 1824. Here they involved themselves in the politics and trade of local black peoples such as the Zulu, took black women as wives or concubines, founded their own communities of African followers, and laid claim to extensive tracts of land. They fed to the outside world a picture of fierce Zulu militarism, and of devastation over a wide area of Natal. This 'devastation stereotype' took on a useful propaganda role among those of the Cape mercantile bourgeoisie, in Cape Town and the eastern Cape, who saw in Natal rich potential pickings. The threat of foreign intervention to subvert British hegemony was also widely touted.[75]

The Port Natal trading community was in some degree an offshoot of the Graham's Town community. James Collis, an 1820 settler, arrived at Port Natal in 1828, where he became a leading merchant in collaboration with C. and H. Maynard and B. Norden of Graham's Town. In 1834, shortly before his death, he was reported to be on his way from Graham's Town to Port Natal with twelve wagons full of merchandise. Dick King, who had arrived with the settlers in Albany at the age of 8, moved to Port Natal in 1830, where he became a prominent figure. Other Albany settlers who by the early 1830s had begun to exploit the rich potential of the Natal hinterland included the four Cawood brothers; in 1832 they returned from a hunting and trading trip to Port Natal with produce, mainly ivory, valued at £2000. Robert, son of Alexander Biggar, who had led his own party of 1820 settlers to Albany, settled at Port Natal in May 1834, to be followed the next year by his father and brother. As a result of the enterprise of men like these, a rough transport road from Graham's Town through southern Nguni territory had been opened up by the mid-1830s, linking as well the chain of Methodist mission stations stretching up to the land of the Mpondo.[76]

The mercantile agitation surrounding Natal reached a peak on the eve of the Boer emigration. Both Saxe Bannister, a former attorney-general of New South Wales, and Nathaniel Isaacs, who had been one of the earliest residents at Port Natal, launched separate campaigns in Cape Town in the early 1830s to gain sanction for joint-stock companies to develop and settle Natal. In 1832 the director of the South African Museum in Cape Town, Dr Andrew Smith, eminent explorer and naturalist, spent several months visiting Natal, when deputed by Governor Cole to establish contact with the Zulu king after Dingane had sent gifts to Graham's Town through Port Natal traders. Arriving back in Graham's Town in August, Smith wasted no time in publicising his findings in the local press on the eminent suitability of the territory as a colony of settlement. Together with the settler propagandist J. C. Chase, who had himself done much to open up the land of the Tswana to the north in the 1820s, Smith was instrumental in establishing the Cape of Good Hope Association for Exploring Central Africa, officially sanctioned by Ordinance 81 of 1833.[77]

Smith and Chase persuaded the committee of the Commercial Exchange in Cape Town to take up the cause of the military occupation and colonisation of Natal with renewed vigour. As a result J. B. Ebden, Chase and R. W. Eaton were delegated to draft a petition to the secretary of state in London, which was to be discussed at a public meeting in Cape Town in January 1834. At the meeting visions were presented of foreign powers arming the warlike Zulu against the colony, and the praises of Natal's commercial and agricultural potential were sung. A petition with 190 signatures was forwarded to the Colonial Office urging the setting up of a 'Government establishment at Port Natal, with an adequate military force for the protection of the trade with that place'. Governor D'Urban supported the petitioners' pleas, pointing to the strategic significance of the Natal coast, and stressing the commercial possibilities of the hinterland. However, the secretary of state's response was that the colony's finances made it impossible to sanction any new settlement. In the following year the arrival of American missionaries served to alarm D'Urban further into warning that American annexation might be imminent – again to no effect in moving the British government.[78]

Prominent Boers were receptive to reports of new lands awaiting settlement and commercial exploitation, and were active in their own investigations. One colonist who accompanied Smith was Hermanus Barry from Swellendam, son of the merchant Joseph Barry whose wife came from an Afrikaner family. On his return, Hermanus reported enthusiastically to frontier Boers on what he had seen, asserting that he would move to Natal as soon as it was declared a colonial district.[79] Among those who would have heard such reports was Petrus Lafras Uys from the Lower Bushmans River ward of the Uitenhage district, not far southwest of Graham's Town. He soon set about organising his own reconnaissance trip to Natal. This party of 21 Boers and a number of coloured servants left on 8 September 1834 and travelled through Xhosaland to Port Natal. Uys's father, J. J. Uys, was known in the 1820s as a pioneering merino sheep farmer, and 36-year-old Piet himself was a successful horse-breeder who was on good terms with British officers and officials in the Uitenhage and Albany districts. According to his son, he participated in the very English sport of horse-racing in the district towns, and once spoke of emigrating to the United States.[80]

The Uys party were warmly welcomed at Port Natal by old acquaintances such as Alexander Biggar, who was well known to the Boers of Uitenhage and Albany districts, where he had served as a transport rider. Uys came away with the clear impression that the British traders of Port Natal would welcome any white settlement of the hinterland; and some members of the party made clear their determination to settle there. Their three months in Natal were largely spent hunting for ivory, horns and hides in the area between Port Natal and the Tugela River – a territory they found to be teeming with elephant and buffalo. The commercial aspect of the trip was very apparent. Furthermore, Uys confirmed the widely reported perception that Natal south of Zululand proper was an empty country available for white settlers – a highly dubious yet influential assumption.[81]

Although Uys presented the grievances of his fellow Boers to the authorities, he was not inclined to promote anti-British rebelliousness. On his return in June 1835 he declared that his party had 'never expressed an unfriendly feeling towards the Government' and repeated what he claimed to have often said: 'if the British Government would take possession of that Country [Natal], I would have no objection to go and reside there provided I could form a large party.' As late as January 1838 Uys, then in Transorangia, was assuring Governor D'Urban of his loyalty towards the government.[82] But on his return from the expedition of 1834 the findings of the Uys commission were widely disseminated, and were very influential in promoting the idea of emigration as a solution to widely felt problems.[83]

The propaganda campaign in favour of Natal as a destination for the land-hungry seems to have reached new heights during and after the frontier war of 1834–5. Dr W. Robertson of the Dutch Reformed Church, who like his colleagues disapproved of this wanderlust, reported in March 1836 that 'The most extravagant notions have been given them [the Boers] by means of journals and Letters of the fertility of the Soil and the Beauty of the Climate – "They may have three crops in a year" – "It is always summer there" – "Every sort of manufacture may be purchased for *one fourth* of the price for which it can be obtained in this Colony ..."' Land could be picked out for nothing in the new territory, it was trumpeted. This rising agitation promoting Natal as a paradise for settlers was communicated through the press, such as the *Graham's Town Journal* and *De Zuid-Afrikaan*, and indeed through the informal channels of the market town and the itinerant trader. Boers in frontier districts, feeling alienated from British rule to an increasing degree and eager for new economic opportunities, would have responded positively.[84]

At the time many strongly suspected that British settler interests were deliberately encouraging the emigration fever. Those who were cynical about the machinations of the Godlontonians generally were inclined to impute base motives to the British settlers. The Quaker traveller James Backhouse, for instance, suspected that the *Graham's Town Journal* was being used by those wishing to buy up cheap land thrown precipitately on the colonial market by prospective emigrants.[85] Blatant scare tactics were apparently resorted to. It was rumoured that Stockenström, newly appointed lieutenant-governor, intended turning the burghers into soldiers by militia laws, and planned to hand all government land and 'request farms' over to emancipated slaves and Khoi. Stockenström himself later recalled that settler propaganda about the enforced introduction of Roman Catholicism was 'poured into their [the Boers'] ears by fraudulent speculators who hoped to frighten them out of the Colony and buy their lands for a song'.[86]

Philip, admittedly no impartial observer himself, considered that 'The agitation caused by the newspapers contributed largely to the emigration of the Boers'. In the panic thus created,

they sold their farms much under their value to English settlers, while those who had created the panic became purchasers, and are now selling the farms again at three or four times the prices at which they bought them. They expatriated themselves originally under a delusion created in the first instance by the supineness of the Government, later under the influence of disaffection created by those who wanted their farms at low price.[87]

The realisation was dawning on British settlers that conditions of speculative boom were in the offing. Not only did D'Urban's campaigns against the Xhosa hold out the prospects of long-term military commitment and war profit on the frontier, but many set great store by the anticipated arrival of slave compensation money, and the potential of woolled sheep in transforming the farm economy of the frontier districts. In fact war expenditure and (a few years later) compensation payments were to provide the capital for buying out Boer assets through the eastern Cape and Midland districts.

Whatever the combination of factors involved, the major wave of emigration took place after the war was over, from early 1836, although, as we have seen, the first parties had left earlier. Harry Smith reported to D'Urban in March 1836 that 'For some time past, the Boers have refused in payment everything but specie ... they had given 23 shillings for a sovereign, and literally have drained Graham's Town of all its metallic currency'. In August the *Commercial Advertiser* reported that some trekkers had taken as much as 40 000 rix-dollars with them in specie.[88] In the process, though, emigrants often lost a great deal. Maritz, leader of the Graaff-Reinet trekkers who left in September 1836, computed his personal loss at £908. But those who left in 1838 benefited by the arrival of slave compensation money. Large sums of specie brought into the colony for that purpose, and then channelled into commerce and land purchase in the east, were reported to have been removed by the trekkers. The Pretorius trek from Graaff-Reinet (they left early in 1838) was thus a more financially liquid affair. It greatly expanded for a time the trading opportunities at Port Natal and its hinterland once the party had arrived there.[89]

But the removal of specie from the colony did not constitute a net loss to the colonial economy. For the emigrants who headed northwards over the Orange River from early 1836, in the expectation of finding alternative and easier access to the coast beyond the southern Nguni lands compared with the route Smith and Uys had followed, were not breaking ties with the colonial market. Rather they were greatly extending its geographical range. Their crucial supplies of lead and powder, the basic means of survival as well as their means of production for the market, were provided by colonial traders, whose lines of communication and supply led back to the colonial market towns, and eventually to Graham's Town and Port Elizabeth. The ox-drawn wagon was not only the trekkers' vehicle of removal but also their lifeline.[90]

Parties of English-speaking traders followed the trekkers with wagons of merchandise (ammunition included no doubt), trading with black peoples on the way (including perhaps grain for re-sale to the Boers).[91] But trekking was inevitably an impoverishing experience, as flocks and herds were bound to suffer attrition, and consumption requirements tended to drain liquid assets. In the event, political conflicts, both with indigenous powers and imperial forces, were to aggravate the impoverishing effects of the trek, and it was to be years before satellite centres of accumulation under stable government were established in the diaspora.

In short, it is a myth that the trekkers were hardy pioneers headed for the unknown wilderness in order to establish their own republican nationhood, removed as far as possible from the hated British. They certainly harboured deep and bitter grievances against the British rulers of the Cape. But it is also true that by the 1830s the interior of the subcontinent, not least the hinterland of Port Natal, had been well explored and was ripe for more intense commercial exploitation and colonisation. Long-distance hunters, traders and explorers had already spread a great deal of knowledge about the subcontinent. Other colonists, even less secure in their status in colonial society – the Bastaards, or Griqua – had long preceded them north of the Orange, and had pioneered commercial contact with African peoples there. In fact the great era of opening up was the 1820s, rather than the 1830s. Wherever they went, north of the Orange and Vaal and down into Natal, the trekkers were moving into *terra cognita*.[92]

After the 1834–5 frontier war, the way the Boer exodus was seen became inextricably bound up with conflicts in colonial society that had little to do with the emigrant Boers themselves. The propaganda purposes for which it was used at the time also deeply influenced the way in which the Great Trek was later interpreted by historians. In particular, Godlonton at the *Graham's Town Journal* began increasingly in the post-war period to use the emigration as a weapon in his struggle against the appeasement and false economy that he associated with the policies of Glenelg and Stockenström. It was in the interests, after all, of the British settler elite to pin the blame for the Boer exodus on those policies which they so ardently opposed and wanted to see subverted. Thus the exodus, in the propaganda of the day, was blamed firmly on the reversal of D'Urban's policy and the abandonment of Queen Adelaide Province. By mid-1836, when the true extent and nature of the exodus had become apparent, and it had become clear that D'Urban's policies had been decisively rejected in London, Godlonton was asserting that the two were causally linked. In his view the emigrants were escaping from the insecurity, odium and suffering arising from an inadequate frontier policy 'and the mischievous misrepresentations of designing men'. Britain's lack of military commitment and the humanitarian-inspired refusal to allow burghers to mobilise their commandos against the Xhosa threat had only brought ruin and degradation to farmers in the frontier districts.[93]

The persistence and shrillness of the settler propaganda about the consequences of Stockenström's policies and about the threat of 'Kaffir depredations' may have had the intention of promoting an urge to trek. Not only was the settler rhetoric presumably aimed at an audience in Cape Town and Britain where policy was formulated, but men like Godlonton must have been aware of the effect being wrought on the public mood in the eastern Cape, not least among the Boers themselves. Those interests which Godlonton represented stood to profit from the conscious promotion of trek fever. In this way the emigration was provided with its public and historical voice, not only by the emigrants themselves, but also by others with their own sectional interests to serve.

The Godlontonian line of argument had been used by D'Urban in justifying to the secretary of state his annexation of Xhosa territory up to the Kei and their expulsion in 1835. This policy was necessary, he wrote in June, because otherwise the frontier districts of Albany and Somerset would be altogether deserted owing to the 'frightful perils' of the close proximity of the Xhosa. When Glenelg ordered the retrocession of the new province, D'Urban immediately predicted that 'abandonment and ruin' of the frontier districts were now certain. In his dispatch of June 1836 he drew more clearly the links with the Boer exodus from the colony, which was then picking up steam. The Boers, he wrote, had relinquished their earlier plans for emigration when he had announced the annexation of Queen Adelaide Province in May of the previous year, 'seeing in that measure a promise of more efficient protection'; 'but now, when they will know that the new Province is actually to be renounced by the end of the year, and despair ... of any compensation for their losses, they will assuredly again prepare to go away; and the order for evacuating Adelaide will be the signal for their departure to seek their fortunes in the interior of the country.'[94]

Quite apart from the fact that those who had been regarded as suitable applicants for land in the new province were invariably British settlers and office-holders, D'Urban failed to acknowledge that the main trek parties were already being organised before any intimation of the reversal of policy could have reached them. Nevertheless, this official argument endured among D'Urban's lieutenants. Thus when Harry Smith returned to the Cape nearly a dozen years later as governor, he based his policies in part on the assumption that the treaty system had been responsible for the emigration, and that a return to the 'D'Urban system' (which he had been responsible for implementing as military commander) would reconcile the Boers to British rule, facilitating their reincorporation. This was a foolhardy assumption, as he was to find out.[95]

For the Godlontonians, the humanitarians remained the arch-villains of the piece. The hostility of their rhetoric was reflected in an 'open letter' to Glenelg published in the *Graham's Town Journal* in May 1836. 'AB' ascribed the exodus to the machinations and calumnies of 'an irresponsible faction in the colony stronger than the government' (meaning the Philip camp), by whom the emigrants had been 'held up to the execration of the world'. Glenelg was warned that he would go down in history as one who 'allowed the tyranny of a one-sided philanthropy, and the misrepresentations of a worthless faction, to depopulate a virtuous and industrious colony'. The implication always was that Boers were emigrating from the colony because of British failure to crush the black chiefdoms (or their refusal to permit Boer commandos to do so). The only way the emigration could be halted was by jettisoning Stockenström's 'false, vicious but fine-sounding theory', and reverting to the 'common sense and practical view' of the experienced men on the spot – namely, the policy of dispossession and military expansion.[96]

These perceptions found a receptive ear among those commercial interests in Cape Town which had adopted the militarist cause during the war. The bulk of the Cape Town bourgeoisie, old and new, were also opposed to the Glenelg policies and Stockenström's treaties, and shared Godlonton's views on the causes of the Boer exodus. At a meeting on 19 November 1836 to protest against the retrocession of Queen Adelaide, Ebden asserted baldly that the exodus would not have occurred if D'Urban's policy had been sanctioned by the British government.[97]

In keeping with the image of the emigrants as victims of execrable policies, the *Graham's Town Journal* opened its columns to trek leaders as their official organ, publishing their proclamations and statements. Piet Retief, the most famous and articulate of the trek leaders, was painted in the most favourable light in the paper's editorial columns as the victim of the administration's perfidy and double-dealing, and championed as the major representative and spokesman of the emigrants. Retief used the *Journal* to publicise at length his disagreements with Stockenström and his grievances with the colonial government, and later channelled reports to the paper during his trek north and east over the Drakensberg. In particular, upon his departure early in 1837 he published his famous manifesto, widely regarded as the official declaration of Boer principles.[98]

But despite his later status in Afrikanerdom as a national hero of near-legendary proportions, Retief was no typical frontier Boer. He was himself a colonial businessman with a long history of official contracting, speculation and dealing with the colony's small-town commercial class. He was born in the western Cape to a wealthy wine-farming family, but moved to the east in 1812 to escape creditors. After the frontier war of 1811–12 he became a contractor for government supplies in the new frontier military village of Graham's Town, but failed to meet his obligations, leaving his creditors holding debts of up to 30 000 rix-dollars. Nevertheless, he was well established within local military circles, and was able to obtain in subsequent years grants of up to seven farms totalling more than 120 000 morgen; he also acquired more than thirty *erven* in Graham's Town as well as several in Uitenhage and Port Elizabeth, with huge livestock holdings to match.[99]

When the 1820 settlers arrived, Retief used his contacts to monopolise the supply of corn and flour to them, making a good profit. In 1822 he was award-ed the contract to build a new barracks and drostdy in Graham's Town, but again failed to meet his commitments. From there on his career was a down-ward spiral, marked by attempts to stave off bankruptcy, and play one debtor off against another. A variety of dubious occupations such as selling liquor and timber failed to keep him out of debtors' prison, and he was eventually declared officially bankrupt in June 1836. Shortly thereafter he was stripped of his title as commandant. His was a long history of exploiting access to the patronage of the colonial state for personal financial gain – except that Retief proved not very successful at it. Significantly, too, his real travails began as the settlers started to acclimatise to their new circumstances and discovered that they, too, in large numbers, could tap official patronage and commercial opportunities to their own benefit. Retief was of the type, but an Afrikaner, and one with a reputation for fraudulent dealing. By the mid-1820s he was expendable to the British officials, and by the 1830s no doubt an embittered man.

In Graham's Town, where he lived much of the time and carried on any number of business ventures, Retief was on good terms with many of the British elite. He stayed there with his friend Meurant, Godlonton's printing and publishing partner, while preparing for departure from the colony in early 1837. It is perhaps significant in assessing his motives for emigrating, that on the day of his departure from Graham's Town in February 1837, he was being pestered by creditors, and was subsequently declared to be in default when he failed to appear in the local court. His manifesto, which purported to explain the reasons for the emigration, was initially published in Godlonton's *Journal*. Far from expressing some essence of Afrikaner national sentiment, it likely rep-resented in part the grievances of the settler-dominated Graham's Town bour-geoisie, of which he was a frustrated but long-standing member. Quite possi-bly, Meurant and perhaps Godlonton himself played some material role in drawing it up.[100]

But the *Journal*, for all its self-righteous lamentation at the plight of the Boers, nevertheless had its eyes firmly fixed on its own agenda: provoking the imperial power to a policy of annexation and military advance, which was a far cry from any striving for independence from the British yoke which the emi-grants might have felt. It is ironic that Retief, the only self-conscious polemi-cist among the emigrants, was also the trek leader most closely involved in the battles for the heart and soul of the imperial power being waged by the settler imperialists centred on Graham's Town, although he himself had increasingly been marginalised by the rise of settler influence from the 1820s on. It is uncer-tain whether such struggles were of any great significance for most Boers of the frontier districts.

However, there were other voices at work representing very different points of view – even in Graham's Town, which by 1840 was clearly big enough to contain quite separate factions. For a few brief months in 1840 an opposition voice arose there, the *Colonial Times*, published by a fierce foe of Godlonton, Dr A. G. Campbell. During the war Campbell had supplied Philip and Buxton with much information, particularly on the circumstances of Hintsa's murder. The tone of the *Colonial Times* was exemplified by one Robert Baxter, who in the correspondence columns in February 1840 accused Godlonton's *Journal* of having been

> a leading instrument in encouraging the *Trekking Mania*. It constantly held forth to the world that these 'bold peasantry' (the Boers) *trekked* in consequence of Captain Stockenström's policy; whereas it is well known ... that the mass of the *trekkers* had no connection with the frontier ... It [the *Journal*] justified trekking and aggression on the lands of the natives, and infected with ridiculous conceit about their capacity for self-government, such men as Maritz, the Graaff-Reinet blacksmith, Retief, and others of a similar cast ... It encouraged these deluded men – gave an undue importance to their complaints – published many documents in their names, but which it is doubtful if they proceeded from them.[101]

The most vociferous proponent of this point of view – that the Godlontonians were using the exodus for their own ends – was none other than Stockenström, who as lieutenant-governor in the eastern districts at the time was a harsh critic of the emigrants. In retrospect he had little doubt that the settler imperialists represented in and by the *Journal* were culpable. In a letter written to a select committee in London in 1851, Stockenström asserted that in their determination to portray the frontier in a state of chaos as a result of the Glenelg retrocession, the Godlontonians had 'scraped together' addresses 'from factions and ignorant men to give some likelihood' to the assertion that the Boers were emigrating because of Glenelg's policies. The trekkers in fact, wrote Stockenström, were 'perfectly indifferent about the Adelaide Province'; they 'had openly declared that they would not live in it'; and they had been moving off 'long before the Glenelg Treaties had been heard of'.[102]

Colonially oriented and conservative historians have usually assumed that Stockenström was wildly unpopular among Boers because of his liberal views and his advocacy and implementation of the treaty system as lieutenant-governor from 1836. But some years later, when the first popular elections were held at the Cape, Stockenström clearly emerged as the major representative of Afrikaner opinion in the eastern Cape and Midlands; and in the war of 1846–7, he served the Boers as their popular commandant. It was to Stockenström (his 'best friend and father') that the trekker leader A. W. J. Pretorius turned in 1847 and 1848 in his determination to resist Smith's annexation of Transorangia, trusting to Stockenström's advice and support, and even asking him for supplies of powder and lead. In the 1830s, too, there is much evidence of his popularity. Reportedly, great affection was evinced by the mass of Boers on his return to the eastern Cape as lieutenant-governor in 1836, in the face of massive propaganda from British settler sources opposed to his appointment.[103]

The truth seems to be that Stockenström, an Afrikaner himself, was far closer to the Boers and their sentiments than Godlonton or D'Urban, despite stark differences of view on the question of labour relations and the rights of black people. He certainly caused outrage among British settlers by his evidence before the aborigines committee in London in 1835–6, and by his role in having D'Urban's annexations overturned, but Stockenström himself scorned the suggestion that the feelings of the English-speaking settlers permeated Boer society. There is no reason to suppose that his well-publicised and acrimonious exchanges with Retief, when the trek leader was dislodged as commandant in the Winterberg in 1836, prior to his decision to emigrate, characterised in any way his relations with the frontier Boers in general. Rather we should question whether Retief was in fact a popular hero among the frontier Boers. (Despite the prominent role he played during the exodus, his own party of followers was relatively small.)[104]

Even though historians have tended to discount them, Stockenström's views merit a good deal of respect. His own position was that the destabilisation and dislocation of the frontier were a result not of the *lack* of British military commitment, as Godlonton and D'Urban so vigorously argued, but of the very expansionist military adventurism that the settler imperialists sought to promote, and the 'real, direct and positive evils' that arose from it. The disruption caused by the war of 1834–5, which no doubt did accelerate the exodus, was, for Stockenström, the direct consequence of D'Urban's policies. Insecurity and general failure of law and order in rural areas, as well as the decision not to compensate farmers for losses, were real grievances. But the notion, so general in the propaganda of the time, that the Boers' sense of grievance arose from the failure of British military resolve and refusal to crush the Xhosa and drive them beyond the Kei is unconvincing. It was the British settlers and expansionists, with their own political and ideological agendas, who propagated most vociferously notions like these, in their determination to draw imperial power irrevocably into the subcontinent. They, not the Boers, agitated for greater imperial military involvement on the frontier.[105] What the Boers for their part wanted was peace and security, which Stockenström's treaty system was designed to ensure.

The fact that Boers in general were very reluctant to take up arms or to be incorporated into D'Urban's militia system seems to show that most Boers did not share the British settlers' commitment to policies of subjugation.[106] In 1836 and 1837, when the exodus was at its height, there was no direct indication of general Boer disaffection with Stockenström's more pacific policies towards the Xhosa. Indeed, there is little evidence that the majority of Boers harboured dreams of conquest and dispossession against African peoples during the mobile phase of the exodus. Throughout their travels, the emigrants showed a preference for negotiation and treaty-making with African chiefs. Certainly, they wanted security, land and servile labour, and were prepared to take up arms to secure them (as they did against the Ndebele and Zulu while on trek). But in general their attitudes towards the chiefdoms were quite accommodating and respectful, despite their sense of themselves as the bearers of a greatly superior Christian civilisation. Indeed, it was not uncommon for Boers to throw in their lot with black chiefs, militarily or otherwise, against stronger African rulers or against threatening imperial exercises of power north of the Orange in subsequent years. As on the early Xhosa frontier, when Boers took up arms they usually did so in alliance with one or other African chiefdom.

For example, we have seen how the first conscious rebel against British government, Louis Tregardt, settled for a time in 1834–5 beyond the White Kei with the Xhosa paramount, Hintsa. There is evidence that Tregardt supplied Hintsa with firearms, and undoubtedly endeavoured to turn Hintsa strongly against the British. Ayliff, the Methodist missionary at Butterworth, who was no friend of the Xhosa paramount and who was in contact with the trek party, suspected that Tregardt was inciting Hintsa to go to war against the colony. The paramount's mother, Sutu, told the missionary Ross that some Boers had encouraged the Xhosa to attack the colony in 1834. And indeed one Christiaan Muller attempted to enter into a peace agreement on behalf of the Boers with Hintsa early in the war. To this, Hintsa reportedly responded that the Boers should 'remain on one side, and allow the [Xhosa] to drive the English from the frontiers'.[107] When Tregardt finally moved northward towards the Orange River, he trekked in the company of the old Chief Mnyaluza, an uncle of Maqoma. A Xhosa spy explained this relationship to the colonial authorities thus: 'These Boers abused the English very much, [and] said "We have no powder yet, but we shall have; tell your chiefs to come to us; the English will seize them as they have done others before and will make servants of the whole of you. Do not trust the English."' The Xhosa are also said to have asserted: 'Louis Trichard and Umjaloosie [Mnyaluza] are our chiefs.'[108]

During the early months of 1835, when D'Urban and the settlers were planning their campaign against Hintsa and his people beyond the Kei, the trek leader Piet Uys was also enjoying the paramount's considerable hospitality. Uys and his party were on their way back from their reconnaissance trip to Port Natal. They stayed at Hintsa's great place for two days (although invited to stay longer), and were presented with several slaughter oxen and horses, and guides to conduct them back to the colony in safety. On their return to the Cape in March, Uys and one of his companions, Pieter Moolman, reported that Hintsa was entirely innocent of any aggressive intention against the colony, that he undertook to hand over any of his people guilty of taking up arms against the colonists, and harboured no cattle belonging to the colonists. The *Graham's Town Journal* reacted with scorn to this report, insisting that Hintsa was engaged in a campaign of subterfuge and disinformation in order to escape the retribution he knew was coming. Here again, the forces of expansion and dispossession on the frontiers of settlement were represented by the British settler elite and not by Boer farmers.[109]

North of the Orange, the Boer emigrants accepted the Rolong chief Moroka at Thaba Nchu and his Methodist missionaries as their patrons and hosts. Winburg, their first 'capital' (in reality a couple of huts), was planted on land 'ceded' by a Taung chief 'in exchange for a troop of cattle and the promise of protection' against the Ndebele. The trekkers were very dependent on African peoples for supplies of grain and vegetables to supplement their own meat and milk. Sheep and goats (the indigenous variety) were among the items given in exchange. But when confronted with resistance or hostility, the trekkers could use their firearms, horses and military know-how (which was considerable when concentrated) to great effect, as Mzilikazi and Dingane found out.[110]

Unlike the British settlers, the Boers had not acquired the kind of corporate ideology or sense of identity that arose with the development of intersecting institutions of civil society. They were not motivated by the same sense of corporate mission to establish a racial hegemony, as were the settlers. All the same, the Boers were just as likely to take up accumulative, subjugatory attitudes as and when opportunities arose. They could very easily become violent accumulators at the expense of African communities, especially when settled communities began to throw up elites who controlled the resources of land and labour and the means of warfare. As more advanced centres of state formation evolved in the diaspora, locked into the larger commercial networks radiating out from colonial ports, attitudes and practices could rapidly adapt. There was nothing static or fixed about the attitudes and practices that characterised the mobile phase of the exodus. Nevertheless, in large areas of the Transvaal, nominally incorporated in the South African Republic, Boer political institutions remained embryonic, and Boer tenure remained insecure and contingent on maintaining good relations – even tributary relations at times – with African chiefdoms.[111]

The trekkers were disunited on questions of tactics and policies. Their initial attempts at state formation were not very successful, and revealed a high tendency to factionalism. Although basic regulations were promulgated while they were gathered at Thaba Nchu, and an embryonic republic was established in Natal, there were clearly divisions between those who sought to create strong institutions, and those who resisted the pretensions of others to an elite status. These tendencies, which reasserted themselves repeatedly in subsequent decades, were disclosed in Natal in divisions between commandant-general Andries Pretorius and the Volksraad, an essentially occasional and informal body. This body objected to Pretorius's military forays against small chiefdoms, such as the Bhaca to the south.[112] The Natal Republic (which claimed to incorporate those trekkers still on the highveld) did not last. After British military intervention at Port Natal in 1842, a mobile – and levelling – phase began again, and the Boers returned slowly to the highveld, only in 1848 to meet with British interference there again.

Pretorius – who already in Natal had demonstrated the tendency for accumulating and military elites to arise once opportunities presented themselves, and who led the fierce resistance against the British in Transorangia in 1848 – made his peace with the British when they finally recognised Boer independence north of the Vaal in 1852. From the Potchefstroom settlement on the Mooi River, he was to launch a new round of violent state formation and dispossession against the neighbouring Tswana. In contrast, Potgieter (whose concern was to get as far away from the British as comfortably possible rather than set up satellite statelets in a colonial trading system) had a far less intrusive or disruptive influence on the African social environment (at least once the Ndebele had been expelled). He resembled more an African chief in his assemblage of diverse followers and dependants and in the complexity and fluidity of the relations he established with indigenous chiefs. Well into the late nineteenth century the highveld republics continued to be racked by conflict between accumulating elites dependent on trade linkages and state power, and those who resisted state authority and remained less inclined to regard African chiefs as potential enemies.[113]

Besides opening up large tracts of land within the colony for speculation and investment, the Boer emigration opened up the long-coveted opportunities of the Natal hinterland for land speculation, settlement and commercial exploitation by British commercial interests, provided the British government could be prevailed upon to extend its rule over the emigrants. Natal was seen as a new frontier for British settler enterprise in ways which replicated the earlier development of the eastern Cape. Such considerations had long lain at the back of merchants' minds in Graham's Town and Cape Town.[114] While the trekkers, as in the northern Cape, might serve as a vanguard of British commercial penetration, acting as forward agents and middlemen, only British settlers under British government could exploit the potential of the region.

Agitation for the extension of British rule over Port Natal and its hinterland concentrated on the destabilising effects of Boer military activity and slave raiding,[115] as well as on the enormous potential for British settlement and commercial enterprise. In London, the Cape of Good Hope Trade Society urged annexation, and Saxe Bannister published a pamphlet to drum up support. In 1839 a Natal Association was established, and merchants from Liverpool and elsewhere presented petitions to parliament. Rumours circulated of the presence of tin, copper, lead and coal deposits in Natal, and the richness of the soil for producing cotton, silk, sugar and wool.[116] Merchant interests widely assumed that the Boers were 'deficient in energy' for exploiting these resources. As their specie drained away, the emigrants' impoverishment threatened to undermine the trade potential of Natal which British merchants had begun to exploit.[117]

The British authorities, very reluctant to extend British rule and doubtful of any real economic benefits, were nevertheless drawn into authorising the annexation of Natal by 1842. Once Governor Napier had been persuaded that a military force was necessary at Port Natal, annexation seemed to Lord Stanley at the Colonial Office to be the path of least resistance.[118] Under the circumstances, direct British rule was probably the safest way of minimising the dangers of unmanageable conflict, and of dissuading mischievous foreign adventurers, like J. A. Smellenkamp, the Dutch supercargo on the ship *Brazilia*, from inciting the Boers by pretending to represent European powers.[119] Stanley may well have been confident that Natal at the very least would pay for its own administration. However, the annexation of Natal ultimately had little to do with considerations of commercial profit, as far as the powers-that-be in London were concerned. Formal imperial advance in the era of informal empire did not necessarily obey direct economic motives. Moreover, Natal was at the time not widely regarded as an economically attractive proposition despite mercantile propaganda.

Nevertheless, particular local mercantile and speculative interests, loudly supported by a section of the mercantile community in Britain, must have had some bearing on developments on the colonial frontiers. We shall see how important a force settler imperialism was to be later in the 1840s in the expansion of British sovereignty north of the Orange, when a more settler-oriented governor, Harry Smith, exercised a free hand locally. Although the extension of sovereignty over Natal was not as clear cut, we should not underestimate the extent to which local governors and military forces, with considerable autonomy of action, might be influenced by local economic forces whose interests were mostly parochial and self-serving. The failure of the Republiek Natalia to provide, in fact as well as in theory, a reliable and effective government for the region was fundamental in persuading these interests of the need for imperial rule. Such were the considerations that moved empires in the first half of the nineteenth century, when economic penetration did not necessarily require acquisition of territory, but when acquisition of territory was not wholly excluded as a matter of policy. And there is little doubt that specific economic interests, in South Africa and in Britain, not in themselves capable of moving the imperial government, created the climate and provided the local pressures which made imperial advance possible and ultimately inevitable. In short, the annexation of Natal emphasised once again the importance of local impulses rather than grand imperial forces in extending the British empire.

The prospect that most excited speculative imaginations, among eastern Cape British settlers and Cape Town merchants, was land accumulation and land settlement. Land speculation by merchant interests on a massive scale followed the annexation of Natal. When the speculators arrived on the scene, prices of 1d or 2d per acre were common. F. Collison of the firm Prince & Collison of Cape Town bought fourteen farms (84 000 acres) in 1843 at a low price, and opened an office in London where emigration was promoted once annexation had been confirmed. In 1847 J. B. Ebden, Edward Chiappini, Jonas Bergtheil and the Sufferts established the Natal Cotton Company. The company intended settling 500 immigrants, and requested 50 000 acres for their operation, which was sanctioned by the secretary of state. By 1849, however, the directors had decided that indigenous labour was preferable to immigrants, and conceded that most of the land was unsuited to cotton cultivation. The company's land was thus reclaimed for the crown, and assigned to J. C. Byrne for his scheme of emigration to Natal.[120]

Boer grievances over land, which had been apparent in the eastern Cape, re-emerged in Natal. For the British administration from the start proclaimed a policy of recognising only Boer land claims which had been occupied and productively exploited; yet in sharp contrast, English-speaking absentee speculators were soon able to get hold of large stretches of land in the territory.[121] Thus although many of the Boers initially accepted the British annexation in light of the financial collapse of their own republic, most moved back on to the highveld by the end of 1848.

Annexation of Natal produced a number of colonisation schemes, official and unofficial, by entrepreneurs, speculators or religious bodies. Byrne's Emigration and Colonisation Company was the most important. Between 1849 and 1852, some 5000 immigrants arrived in Natal, but (like the 1820 eastern Cape settlers) few of them actually settled productively on the land.[122] The land market remained deflated and the operations of the settlement companies ground to a halt. The early colony of Natal vindicated the opinion of the Colonial Office that economically it was a dubious acquisition. But, like the early colonists in the eastern Cape, many of the early settlers in Natal flourished as traders and transport riders, opening up the hinterland in the process. Pietermaritzburg, the old trekker headquarters, came to play the role of Graham's Town to Port Natal's Port Elizabeth. Trade slowly took off, particularly in animal products, including products of the hunt from both white and African sources. As an example, the Cawood family, 1820 settlers based in Graham's Town, were heavily involved in Natal in the 1840s. From this source they fulfilled their contracts for the supply of meat to the commissariat and the governments of Mauritius and St Helena, in return for sugar and other tropical products. In general, the transport road between Graham's Town and Port Natal through Xhosaland was much in use, and trade overland and by sea between the Cape and Natal increased rapidly in the 1840s. Ivory continued to be a major export, supplied by individual African hunters using guns that were provided by whites in return for half the haul. The European colony, slowly augmented by new arrivals, many from the eastern Cape, soon became dependent on the purchase of supplies of maize, vegetables, milk and wood from African farmers.[123]

As in the eastern Cape, the Methodists developed a special relationship with many of the Natal settlers who arrived in the 1840s, and enunciated a settler ideology of accumulation, enterprise and development.[124] With it went, as in the eastern Cape, a commitment to the conversion and civilising of the local Africans – in a way that complemented rather than challenged the interests of the settler economy. In this the Methodists embodied the ideological continuity between the 1820 settlers in Albany and the early settlers in Natal.

An important figure was James Archbell, who had come to the Cape in 1818, and had been a pioneer Methodist missionary in Namaqualand and Tswana territory north of the Vaal and in the Caledon River region. Then, as a minister in Graham's Town, he had fallen easily in with local merchants such as W. R. Thompson, who owned land in Natal and showed an early interest in cotton cultivation there. In 1841 Archbell rode to Port Natal, where he built a small church to minister to the settlers. In 1845 he moved to Pietermaritzburg, becoming a large landowner in the vicinity (with three extensive farms) and a newspaper editor serving settler and mercantile interests. Another prominent Methodist, the Rev. W. C. Holden, arrived in Port Natal in 1847, and came to serve a similar role, as settler scribe, to that of J. C. Chase in the Cape. He published his pioneer *History of the Colony of Natal* in 1855.[125] In England too, the Nonconformist network (which by the 1840s was distinctly losing its humanitarian zeal once slave emancipation was a *fait accompli*) actively promoted emigration to Natal.[126]

It was in Natal, for the first time, that white rule was deliberately imposed on a large population of Africans living in a homestead economy. Here the essential instruments of coercion and control, which would later be elaborated elsewhere in southern Africa, were first developed. And it was here too, earlier than elsewhere, that there first developed that parasitic relationship between a colonial society and its black suppliers of peasant produce, and between white absentee landowners and rent-paying African homesteads. Thus was established the essential source of conflict that characterised Natal politics, and that later in the century pervaded struggles throughout areas of historical African settlement into which whites had moved and established their own rights of ownership over land. These involved efforts by whites to minimise the alternatives available to African cultivators, to restrict their freedoms and bargaining power, and to extract maximum surpluses from them. Struggles within settler society involved control over the colonial state: between those speculative, mercantile and official interests which profited from exploiting the surpluses from black farming (either as traders in black produce or as landlords), and those employers of labour who wished to see black economic independence subverted in order to increase the supply of labour and cheapen its cost.[127]

In Natal, the system of 'locations' proved a flashpoint early on. Theophilus Shepstone, member of an 1820 settler family and the son of a transKeian Methodist missionary, was appointed as 'diplomatic agent to the native tribes' in Governor Martin West's first administration in 1846, responsible for overseeing the African population. Despite the widespread belief that he single-handedly persuaded Africans to segregate themselves within 'locations' in

1846–7, the locations system was probably little more than a recognition of existing realities in a rough and ready way. At the same time large numbers of Africans continued to live on white-owned and crown lands. Rather than an indication of Shepstone's personal wizardry, his system was an index of the colony's administrative weakness.[128] However, the small settler farmers and other employers, Boer and newly arrived British, saw the locations, mission stations, absentee-owned farms and crown land as threats to their labour supplies as well as sources of competition in supplying markets. In particular they used the Natal Native Affairs Commission of 1852–3 to demand action to dislodge African labour from the independent homestead economy, not least by reducing the amount of land available in locations drastically.[129] Underpinning policy debates was the erroneous assumption that Natal's Africans had entered the territory after its colonisation by whites, and that therefore they were a rightless people whose access to land was permanently on sufferance. In this early history of conflict over land and labour in Natal lay a foretaste of later developments. It is ironic that these struggles between colonial forces and African farming communities being brought under colonial rule should first be manifested well beyond the eastern Cape frontier. For white and black societies had first met in the eastern Cape as early as the 1770s, and in the 1840s the eastern Cape frontier was still characterised by relations between nominally independent political communities, despite the enormous degree of interpenetration, physical, cultural and economic, that had already occurred.

CHAPTER SEVEN

Colonial Crises, Imperial Resolutions

In June 1846 Robert Peel's Conservative ministry fell. This was a dramatic moment in the history of Britain's nineteenth-century empire: by throwing in his lot with the free-trade lobby, Peel split his party and let the Whigs back into power. The immediate circumstance was the controversial repeal of the corn laws, which had protected Britain's agricultural interest by keeping out foreign grain. At the same time sugar preferences, which were a mainstay of the West Indian colonial interest, were repealed. With enactments like these the ideology of free trade, already largely a conventional wisdom in most areas of commercial activity, was battering against the last bulwarks of protectionism, and winning. On coming to power Lord John Russell's Whig administration, with Peelite support, proceeded with the final repeal of the navigation laws in 1849. This elaborate body of law, which dated from the seventeenth century, discriminated against foreign shipping, but had been chipped away at since 1815. With its repeal in 1849 went all vestiges of colonial preference protecting select colonial products imported into Britain.

Both Russell and his colonial secretary, Earl Grey, were partial converts to the colonial reform programme with which E. G. Wakefield, the advocate of colonial settlement, was closely associated. Colonial reform incorporated the idea of responsible local government in the colonies; for if colonies were to consist of free settler communities pursuing mutual advantage with the mother country, free of constraint or regulation, then autocratic rule had to be replaced by representative and responsible local institutions. The grant of self-government to colonies in the nineteenth century was thus the product of deliberate British disengagement, and not just a series of concessions to the forces of colonial particularism. However, except for a radical fringe represented by Richard Cobden, self-rule was certainly not envisaged as leading to the dissolution of imperial bonds. On the contrary it was regarded as perfectly compatible with the maintenance, even the strengthening, of colonial ties through economic interdependence and mutual goodwill.[1]

The nineteenth-century colonies of conquest were for these reasons deliberately launched on a process of constitutional development leading to self-rule, although the speed of the process depended ultimately on the resources and stability of the settler society in question. The idea had been first formulated in the days of Melbourne's Whig ministry (1835–41) in relation to Canada. That colony's governor, Lord Durham, in a famous report of 1839 recommended that gubernatorial jurisdiction over all internal affairs be surrendered to an elected government of colonists. In 1840 the Union Act was passed, though it did not go as far as Durham had suggested. After coming to power in 1846 Russell and Grey realised that British interests in North America would be safeguarded most effectively by fostering a sense of Canadian nationhood, and by granting institutions the colonists would be prepared to defend against the pretensions of the powerful republic to the south. At the same time Russell and Grey insisted that the British government retain residual powers, to ensure that colonial legislatures did not depart from the fundamental principles of the imperial relationship, most particularly in the area of free trade and open markets. After all, colonists would be sorely tempted to use tariffs to boost revenue.[2]

Financial self-sufficiency was the goal for the colonies, which also entailed responsibility for defence. It was on this issue that Wakefield and his followers, who feared that dependence on imperially funded military garrisons would allow colonists to become parasites on the commissariat, came into conflict with humanitarian sentiment. Exeter Hall, now much reduced in influence, deplored the proposed abdication of imperial control over settlers wherever they lived cheek by jowl with indigenous populations, and indeed where the indigenes had been integrated into colonial societies. This clash of view was particularly manifested in the 1840s in relation to New Zealand, where systematic colonisation of the sort Wakefield advocated inevitably involved expropriating Maori land.[3] In situations like this, humanitarian interests still looked to the imperial government to act as the guardian of native peoples. But the Colonial Office had no intention of playing this role if it involved taking on greater responsibility for policing the colonies. What the politicians and officials in London wanted was stability and economy, peace and quiet – secured, ideally, on the settlers' terms under settler government with settler resources.

In the shorter term, though, in a colony such as the Cape with its problems of frontier security, the Colonial Office believed that garrisons had to be retained under imperial control. Thus the reason why the Cape (unlike Canada) was not yet regarded as fit for full self-government was not that the Colonial Office feared for the fate of the Xhosa, but that the local financial and military resources were not yet sufficiently developed to manage relations with them. At the same time Russell's ministry contemplated a fully elected legislature for the Cape – albeit without parliamentary control over the executive for the time being – as a first step towards a fully fledged settler state. As for Grey, he was confident that no 'society of British birth or origin' would oppress the natives.[4] The fact that most colonists, and probably most of those who would get the vote, were not of British origin reveals the vacuousness of the sentiment; but Grey was prepared on the basis of this premise to overlook the misgivings of Exeter Hall.

❖

In the 1840s, the colonial state at the Cape itself was expanding its functions and improving its efficiency. And so the scope for competition and conflict between the state and its unenfranchised subjects grew, and with it demands for greater participation by colonists in the colonial government. This was especially so after the arrival of John Montagu as government secretary in Cape Town in 1843 as successor to John Bell. Montagu was a hard-nosed arch-conservative and an instinctive autocrat who surrounded himself with men who owed him favours. But he was also an exceptionally able and energetic administrator, and left a permanent mark on the colony's infrastructure. He greatly extended the functions and responsibilities of his post and his department, and established functional primacy over all other state departments. Soon he was second only to the governor in power and influence. During Maitland's governorship (1844–7) James Stephen in London regarded Montagu as the real ruler at the Cape.[5] He laid the foundation of a modern civil service by introducing an examination system for civil servants, antedating such a system in Britain. He also quickly put an end to the long-standing practice of government officials using their positions for private gain.[6] Montagu determined to undertake the urgent task of improving colonial communications. Means of reaching markets were still rudimentary, slow and expensive, in the absence of navigable rivers and given the mountainous terrain. Clearly the potential of the Cape's wool economy was severely constrained by the problems of transportation.[7]

Montagu had cut his teeth in Van Diemen's Land (Tasmania), where his wife's uncle George Arthur had been lieutenant-governor. He had first gone to Hobart as Arthur's private secretary, and from 1834 to 1842 had served as government secretary. In this capacity he had been responsible for managing the colony's large transported convict population, assigned as labourers to free settlers and on public works. Though the Cape was not a penal settlement, it did have its own local convict population, sentenced by the colonial courts. Up to this time men under sentence of hard labour were generally sent to Robben Island, and employed in quarrying stone and making lime. After a week on the island in December 1843, Montagu concluded that labour was woefully misdirected and conditions were quite inadequate for the reformation of the convicts.[8] He introduced many features of convict management from Van Diemen's Land, using convict labour systematically in gangs under close supervision on improvements to the colony's transport system, building main roads, mountain passes and bridges.[9]

To this end Montagu set up a central road board with official and unofficial members, supplemented by elected road boards in the districts. With the use of convict labour and the skills of engineers such as the 1820 settler A. G. Bain, the mountainous barriers between the interior and the coast were breached by passes such as Bain's Kloof and Mitchell's Pass in the southwestern Cape, and the Montagu Pass between Oudtshoorn and George, which greatly facilitated communication between the western and eastern districts. This went hand in hand with considerably improved postal services, when carriages replaced horses.[10] Another pet scheme of Montagu's, in collaboration with the big merchants of Cape Town, was the improvement of harbour facilities, especially the construction of a new breakwater in Cape Town to assist oceanic trade.[11]

In his use of convict labour on public works, Montagu introduced the system of rewards and punishments developed in Van Diemen's Land, including evening literacy classes, the prospect of remittance of sentence for good behaviour, and compulsory church attendance. Ordained ministers were appointed to some of the road stations. Montagu claimed great success for his convict system. Under the regime that had prevailed till then, Montagu wrote, 'what we call the prevention of crime, becomes the promotion of crime, and the prison, instead of being an abode of correction, is turned into a school of vice'. On the contrary, prison discipline, in his view, was primarily concerned to promote habits of industry and to combat indolence. In 1848 a board was established to oversee the reform of the prison system, a project carried through by the Cape's representative government from 1854. Montagu was clearly steeped in early industrial society's utilitarian prescriptions for the exercise of disciplinary and corrective surveillance over the criminal.[12]

How were public works such as road construction to be paid for? Montagu was confronted on his arrival with a large colonial public debt – standing at £180 000 in 1842 – and payments of taxes and quitrents were seriously in arrears. The government's promissory notes circulated like cash. In view of the commitment of Sir Robert Peel's ministry in Britain to financial efficiency, the colonial secretary, Lord Stanley, in his instructions to Montagu at the end of 1842 stressed the need for reorganising the Cape's finances. Within two and a half years of Montagu's arrival the debt was paid off. He gained control over fiscal affairs, confining the treasurer-general's duties to the disbursement of public money. He raided colonial funds, such as the guardian fund, the storm fund and the 'prize negro' fund, which were reserved for specific purposes. He tackled the large-scale circulation of promissory notes. He amended the rules of revenue collection and enforced them ruthlessly. Most important, the windfall discovery of guano deposits on the Ichaboe islands off the west coast brought in £80 000 in licence fees. On the expenditure side, Montagu cut deeply into the discretion of officials, requiring that no expense be incurred without written authorisation.[13]

For the first time the Cape government, expected to be self-financing by the Colonial Office with respect to internal administration and development, had some leeway to improve the economic infrastructure of the colony.[14] For a few years in the 1840s, Montagu's public works absorbed about a sixth of the colony's total revenue. But to some extent Montagu's financial success was illusory. Based on temporary expedients, creative accountancy and windfalls, it was reminiscent of the methods of company promoters in Britain during the 'railway mania'. It could not be sustained, and the income generated by the frontier war of 1850–3 probably saved the colony from bankruptcy.[15]

Nevertheless, Montagu's public works greatly improved the commercial potential of the colony as a whole.

Montagu's determination to improve the state of the colony's finances brought about conflict between the colonial bourgeoisie associated with the Cape Town municipality and the colonial authorities. At one level, this was reflected in squabbles over the extent of the colonial government's responsibilities for funding the Cape Town police, and the rights of the municipality to levy rates on state-owned property.[16] Then in 1843, the attorney-general, Porter, was obliged in the face of criticism to withdraw a Bill which provided for the funding of the construction of a hard road over the Cape Flats by taxing the owners of fixed property in the Cape and Stellenbosch districts.[17] To meet these objections Montagu wisely provided for his public works programmes to be funded by grants of the Legislative Council from the colonial revenue.

A major clash arose from Montagu's introduction of a Stamp Bill in December 1844, designed to raise revenue by imposing a stamp tariff on all legal documents – bills and promissory notes, insurance policies, deeds of partnership, marriage licences and land rent receipts. In January 1845, in response to publication of the Bill, a meeting was held in the town hall at which the 'tyranny' of government was condemned in no uncertain terms. Wardmaster David Buchanan, whose brother edited the municipal mouthpiece, the *Cape Town Mail*, raised the spectre of Somerset's despised regime and launched an attack on Montagu and his henchmen – 'the placemen who luxuriate on handsome incomes'. He argued that the only grounds on which the government could tax the people were 'the defence of the country, the maintenance of order … and the promotion of the people's happiness'. The meeting resolved that the proposed tax would 'obstruct and injure the interests of the Banking Establishments, Merchants and Traders' of the colony, as well as insurers and mortgagees. At the same time the elite merchants of the Commercial Exchange were derided as demonstrating 'the most solemn and ludicrous obsequiousness': their spokesman in the Legislative Council, Ebden, supported the principle of revising stamp duties, though not to the extent proposed. His main concern, however, was that the Bill had been drawn up without reference to the unofficial members.[18]

A full-scale campaign against the Bill ensued throughout the colony, not least in the newspapers. At a second public meeting in Cape Town, Captain J. H. Vanreenen of the municipality (an English immigrant who had served in the Bengal army) reminded the audience that it was the Stamp Act of 1765 'which lost England the United States'. Numerous petitions in protest against the measure were presented in the Legislative Council. The Stamp Bill was withdrawn by Governor Maitland when he realised that a serious confrontation was looming. But the municipal commissioners of Cape Town, in particular, had flexed their muscles. There was no issue more likely to gain them credibility among the colonists than taxation without representation. Henceforth the municipality of Cape Town considered itself the standard-bearer in the struggle against the governmental oligarchy, and laid claim to represent the colonists in their struggle against unrepresentative government. 'After this,' declaimed *De Zuid-Afrikaan*, 'it will be in vain for any future Government of the Cape to attempt to force any unpopular tax down the throats of the people.'[19]

Montagu, who quickly became in the eyes of the colonists the embodiment of unrepresentative and irresponsible rule and a lightning rod for their frustrations, hit back in April 1846 by introducing legislation designed to limit the municipal market tariffs, which were a mainstay of the municipal income. As far as the municipal commissioners were concerned, any interference with their prerogatives on the matter of taxation was 'unconstitutional'. A petition to the governor requested him 'to prevent any encroachment upon the chartered rights and privileges granted by Her Majesty to this Municipality'. But municipal government had been introduced by an ordinance of the Legislative Council, which could amend it at will, and Montagu proceeded to push through the first of his market bills, removing the obligation of sellers of produce to sell at the municipal market.[20]

At this, the municipality cut off all communications with Montagu. In a letter to the governor they condemned the government secretary as a 'fearful enemy' who sought to destroy their 'acquired liberties'.[21] A petition was sent to the Queen asserting that the nominated Legislative Council neither represented public opinion nor afforded 'a sufficient check against any undue influence being exercised, to the detriment of every corporate institution, and the Colony at large'. The prominent municipal commissioner J. M. Maynard told a crowded meeting in the town hall on 29 November 1847 that the members of the Legislative Council were 'a mere set of automatons' who 'nod, or sit still, just as the Governor chooses to pull the string'. Clearly, the issue at stake was the unrepresentative nature of the colonial state.[22]

The increasingly self-confident and assertive bourgeoisie looked forward to the formal extension of the public sphere in which they operated and exercised their influence. The mercantile–humanitarian alliance of the 1820s that had set out to free the colonial economy and society from archaic restrictions had been overwhelmingly metropolitan in its perceptions and orientation. By the 1840s, however, public discourse in Cape Town was dominated by local colonial forces, Afrikaans- and English-speaking, with precious little time for humanitarian concerns. They enjoyed support among colonists far and wide beyond the confines of Cape Town. The Cape's Afrikaner elite, so seriously alienated by the reform of the status of the labouring classes in the 1820s and early 1830s, had been reconciled to the essentially bourgeois world-view of the British middle classes; at the same time the liberal reformers of the 1820s (such as Fairbairn) had lost their humanitarian optimism and their enthusiasm for the moral redemption of the colony's underclasses. This rising colonial bourgeoisie defined themselves in terms of who was excluded as much as who was included in their ranks. The colony's people of colour were not considered as candidates for membership, or as potential beneficiaries of their growing influence. Indeed, coloured people were more likely to condemn the granting of greater constitutional authority to the colonists than to welcome it, even though any future constitution for the colony was bound to be formally non-racial. At the same time, the settler elite of the eastern Cape centred on Graham's Town were determined to resist any development likely to entrench authority in Cape Town and diminish their access to British military power, the only source of coercion and subjugation suitable for their purposes. More imperial intervention, not less, was their goal.

Conflict over municipal prerogatives and taxation was only the prelude to a developing crisis of legitimacy and control for the colonial government during the period leading up to the eventual granting of representative institutions in 1853. By 1846, renewed war with the Xhosa, long inevitable, was furiously brewing. Two years earlier, under settler pressures the governor, Sir Peregrine Maitland, abrogated Stockenström's treaties with the chiefdoms, heralding a partial return to the old system of military reprisals.[23] Settler propagandists insisted from every forum that war was imminent. At meetings held throughout the eastern Cape in the early months of 1846, the characteristic war hysteria reached new heights. The Colonial Office in London was deluged with warnings that the settlers were in dire danger from the Xhosa owing to the lack of imperial military commitment.[24] In a letter to Governor Maitland of February 1846, Lieutenant-Governor Hare warned of 'mischievous rumours … circulated by men of desperate fortunes, who desire War for the sake of plunder'. In March he wrote that 'instead of meditating aggressions upon the Colony, [the Xhosa] were themselves thrown into a state of great alarm from the state of excitement into which the colonists had thrown themselves'.[25]

War broke out in April 1846 when Colonel Hare, no longer able to contain the tide of bellicosity rising around him, invaded Xhosaland with a mixed force of regulars, Cape Mounted Rifles and colonial volunteers. But the Xhosa were much better armed than in 1835, the arms trade from Graham's Town having paradoxically continued apace, and their resistance was fiercer and more determined than before. With the British lacking the military muscle to root out the Xhosa warriors from the thickly vegetated valleys and mountains of Xhosaland, the outcome was again inconclusive.[26] The military stalemate angered the settler imperialists. Having failed to win the war in 1835 because of (in their view) a lily-livered, humanitarian-inspired failure of nerve, they were determined it would be won this time round.[27] And winning the war meant confiscating African land, expelling the Africans from it, and making it available for settler speculation and settler use. Such an imperial commitment was a precondition of the sort of profiteering that these settlers felt was their due. It was also a precondition for the further sustained development of the economy of the region.

The contrast between these sentiments among British settlers and those of their Boer compatriots was stark. Such was the extent of Boer indifference, even resentment, towards British military imperialism that they refused to come out on commando under British command. It was only when Maitland persuaded Stockenström, then in retirement on his farm, to take command of colonial forces as a colonel on the staff that the burghers agreed to take up arms in defence of the colony. The Boers' enthusiastic response to news of his emergence from retirement contrasted sharply with the bitter dislike of the British settler faction, who had long regarded him as a negrophile and friend of the humanitarians. It was ironic that the British military had to turn to him, of all people, as the only man under whom the Boer population would serve in a war against the Xhosa.[28]

Stockenström's view of the purposes of the war was very different from the official British view. Stockenström still believed in preserving and protecting African independence, and in regulating relations with them by treaty. Although he envisaged a rapid campaign aimed at punishing the chiefdoms for their infringements and re-stabilising the frontier, he did not wish to proceed any further. After marching across the Kei and eliciting a treaty of submission from the Gcaleka Xhosa paramount, Sarhili, he withdrew his troops. But Maitland, who had initially granted Stockenström full powers to use his own discretion, repudiated the treaty, precipitating a damaging row. The burgher troops began to drift off home, even more embittered against the British authorities. As a consequence Stockenström emerged more clearly than ever before as a popular leader of the eastern Cape Boer population.[29]

In Cape Town there was no anti-war party to speak of in 1846–7, in sharp contrast to 1834–5. The increasingly self-conscious Cape Town business community was more and more inclined to throw in its lot with an expanding settler capitalism. Philip was old and disillusioned, and the missionary lobby under the influence of such men as Moffat and Livingstone had tired of colonial causes and shifted their focus northwards. Nothing revealed the collapse of humanitarianism as a political force more than John Fairbairn's desertion of the cause. The editor of the *Commercial Advertiser* was by the time of the War of the Axe in 1846–7 an ardent militarist. As his example reveals, the interests of the mercantile community and the ideals of humanitarianism were becoming increasingly antagonistic. When in 1845 the South African Mutual Insurance Society was established in Cape Town with Fairbairn as chairman, three-quarters of its initial assets were invested in mortgages in the eastern districts: this might explain in part Fairbairn's new interest in the clearing of Xhosaland. Fairbairn wrote in October 1846 that the Xhosa had to be 'put down or expelled, though it should require 10 000 regular troops to accomplish it ... not victory but conquest is to be the end of this outbreak.' Fairbairn's volte-face stunned his erstwhile enemies. Chase, writing to Sir

Benjamin D'Urban, asked, 'Are you not astounded at the extraordinary change in Fairbairn's tone? ... I suppose he found the influence of his party was gone. He is very generally despised for this ratting, for which he has not been honest enough to offer an excuse.'[30]

Given the military stalemate on the frontier, the new colonial secretary in London, Earl Grey, began to rethink the bases of frontier policy. Stabilising the Xhosa frontier once and for all appeared to him the necessary prelude to the eventual granting of representative government. By late 1846 Grey was persuaded that Maitland had to be replaced by someone younger and more resolute. He chose Sir Henry Pottinger, who had proved implacable in his dealings with the Chinese, obliging them to open their ports by the Treaty of Nanking in 1842. In his instructions to Pottinger, Grey signalled a return to the D'Urban ideals of 1835–6. The Xhosa were to be pacified and subjugated, and British sovereignty was to be re-proclaimed over Xhosaland up to the Kei. Grey wrote that 'the welfare of our uncivilised neighbours, and not least the welfare of the colonists, require that the Kaffir tribes should no longer be left in possession of the independence they have so long enjoyed and abused'. The chiefs were to be won over by material rewards and used as agents of British suzerainty, but no tribal rights were to be defined or recognised. 'Religious knowledge, Moral Instruction and an Acquaintance with the Arts of a Civilised Life' were to be inculcated by encouraging missionaries and artisans to settle among them. The conquered were also to be taxed as a 'stimulus to Industry'. Furthermore, in order to cope with the wide scope of his responsibilities, Pottinger was the first Cape governor to be given the title of high commissioner for South Africa, with legal authority to act across colonial borders. He was also that rare governor, a civilian, and Sir George Berkeley was appointed commander of the troops, a function usually fulfilled by the governor himself. Finally, Pottinger was instructed to report on the readiness of the colony for constitutional advance. All this amounted to a decisive shift in imperial policies and perspectives.[31]

Once he had arrived at the Cape in January 1847, Pottinger, like D'Urban before him, fell heavily under the influence of those in colonial society most committed to military solutions to frontier problems. Like D'Urban before him too, he decided that the Xhosa had to be driven across the Kei. Pottinger's resolve to accomplish what his predecessors had so conspicuously failed to do filled the British settlers with enthusiasm.[32] But one problem that had stymied Maitland the year before – the reluctance of the burghers to take up arms – still remained a major stumbling block to the realisation of Pottinger's military plans. He thus issued a proclamation offering the burghers all the booty they could capture as an inducement to joining up. This attempt to turn the burgher forces into plundering parties disgusted Stockenström, and he simply refused to cooperate. But British loyalists such as Richard Southey set about assiduously trying to raise men for raiding expeditions into Xhosaland. Efforts like these to raise colonists for military duty nevertheless failed, and, like D'Urban in 1835, Pottinger had to admit that policies of mass removal were impractical. Once again, imperial and colonial resources had proved unequal to the task of subjugation and expulsion that the Cape governor had decided upon.[33]

As 1847 wore on, the expenses of the war on the eastern Cape frontier began to embarrass Grey. When he had revolutionised Colonial Office thinking on frontier management by deciding that the Xhosa were to be pacified and incorporated, instead of being kept at a distance across boundaries regulated by treaty relations, he had assumed that this was the shortest route to stabilising the frontier. But the British settler elite saw things differently. Sensing new opportunities for sucking as much out of the imperial treasury as possible, the settlers formed numerous citizen forces, which in fact had little military value, operating more as a home guard than as an offensive military force, at large expense to the military chest. Pottinger reported that C. H. Maynard, a leading Graham's Town merchant, had drawn pay for himself and his 'levy' comprising his coloured farm-hands, though they in fact continued to work on his farm. And the Fort Beaufort settlers spent £10 000 of military funds on equipping, from their own stores and farms, a 'volunteer force' of 4000 men also comprising in large part their own labourers and tenants. The monthly outlay in Graham's Town was estimated at £3000, although most of the 'volunteers' were 'following their usual occupations and only did duty by drawing their pay'. 'The consequence was that merchants, shop-keepers, editors of newspapers, hotel-keepers, etc., etc., were living at home and enjoying equal pay with the officers of Her Majesty's regular service, whilst thirty or forty men could not be found to take two outposts ... within a few miles of Graham's Town.' Those implicated in such profiteering included a number of leading settler entrepreneurs – H. Blaine, William Cock, T. H. Bowker, the former military commander Colonel H. Somerset, and Godlonton's early partner, L. H. Meurant. As Governor Smith was to report in 1848, 'those who have amassed large sums of money by the late war are anxiously looking out for the means of employing their capital', and forecast a period of unusual speculation.[34]

As in years past, the settlers also had at the forefront of their minds the possibilities that forward imperial policies held for land grabbing. Thus for Godlonton at the *Graham's Town Journal*, Providence had assigned to the Albany settlers 'the task of colonizing Kaffirland'. A Graham's Town petition submitted that in 'Kaffirland ... there is a wide and most fertile tract of country which must, to preserve the advantages the British forces have gained over the Kaffir tribes, be occupied by British subjects'. The time was ripe, the petitioners wrote, to connect the eastern Cape with the new colony of Natal. Moreover, now that British settlers had begun to establish themselves north of the Orange, 'British sway must ere long be extended in that direction'.[35]

As the war effort lost momentum, Pottinger began to express the same frustration towards the settler elite as that of his predecessors. He wrote to Grey in October 1847 of the obstruction he had experienced in his efforts to account for military expenditure. Nowhere was this worse than in Graham's Town: 'In none were greater opposition and undue influence and misrepresentation, used to bias or change my decision, and in none were the jobs, abuses and irregularities demonstrated to be more extensive, more expensive to the public, or more barefacedly carried on.'[36]

Pottinger's frustrations were aggravated by the fact that he was a civilian, and the army officers who authorised expenditure did not feel obliged to answer to him. At the same time, the editorial columns of the *Graham's Town Journal*, so full of praise for him on his arrival, became decidedly less flattering. But by this time even more sanguine hopes had been aroused by the news that Pottinger was due shortly to be shuffled off to Madras after less than a year at the Cape, and to be replaced as governor and high commissioner by Sir Harry Smith.

Smith was appointed towards the end of 1847 because he persuaded Earl Grey that he could achieve what his predecessors had failed to accomplish, the pacification and subjugation of the Xhosa, while simultaneously reducing Britain's military commitment. Smith had been closely associated with formulating and implementing the policy of conquest and overrule as military commander under D'Urban's governorship in 1835–6. Now in 1847 he had just returned in adulation to England, the popular hero of the Indian army after his triumphs in the Sikh War, with a considerable reputation as a soldier. When Grey approached him for his advice on the situation at the Cape, Smith seized the opportunity to vindicate the discredited frontier policies in South Africa with which he had been associated. Annexation of territory, military rule and the dismantling of chiefly rule were Smith's prescriptions for the cisKeian Africans, prescriptions which fitted well with Grey's own views as expressed in his instructions to Pottinger.[37]

Smith suggested that as soon as the war was over, the British garrison could be reduced by a third. Once peace had been restored in the eastern Cape, a force of 1500 or less would suffice to guard the frontier (as against Pottinger's estimate that 5000 British regulars were required). 'The Kaffir, like every other barbarian, is a desponding creature; and, when once subdued, easily kept subordinate.' As the Xhosa lapsed into 'quietude and docility', so could the military force be substantially reduced. Thus were the chiefdoms to be permanently pacified, at minimal long-term expense to the exchequer.[38]

Smith's massive ego and blinkered vision led him to believe that he could bend black chiefdoms and white colonists alike to his will, and even use colonists (Boer and coloured) to enforce British hegemony in the region in the absence of an adequate imperial military force. Among his major misconceptions was his belief that the emigrant Boers could easily be persuaded to resume their allegiance to British authority. Ascribing all that had gone wrong in South Africa since the mid-1830s to the policy of drift and concession, Smith believed that British power and authority had to be brutally asserted if peace and security were to prevail and the disaffected Boers were to regain their confidence in British rule. He was convinced that his prestige and his will would do the job. In the event Smith promised far more than he could deliver, and succeeded in plunging the colonial government to its lowest ebb in public legitimacy. Far from stabilising southern Africa, he was to militarise it.

Many of Smith's perceptions had been formed in association with the settler bourgeoisie of the eastern Cape. He had been intimate with them in the 1830s, and had shared their ignominy at the hands of the humanitarians before the aborigines committee in London in 1835–6. Like Smith, the British settlers had never forgotten or forgiven those who had painted them and their policies towards the Xhosa in the blackest light. Not surprisingly, they greeted the news of Smith's appointment with unbridled enthusiasm. Their cause was, it seemed, vindicated.[39] But Smith's arrival at the Cape was more than a vindication for the settler elite; it was also an opportunity. Eminent British settlers were soon appointed to official positions. Particularly significant was the appointment of that archetypal settler figure, Richard Southey, close associate of Godlonton, as the new secretary to the high commissioner. Southey had been Smith's close friend and aide during the 1834–5 frontier war, and had served as resident agent with some of the Xhosa chiefdoms under Smith's brief governance of the short-lived Queen Adelaide Province in 1835–6, before the annexed territory was abandoned at Glenelg's behest. Smith and Southey had continued to correspond in the intervening years. Now Southey was to become the *éminence grise* in the formulation and implementation of policy on and beyond colonial frontiers.[40]

Smith's first initiative as governor in December 1847 was to travel to the eastern Cape, where the War of the Axe had left the chiefdoms in a state of exhaustion. In a remarkable display of boorish self-assertion, he went out of his way to belittle and humiliate the Xhosa chiefs, in the belief that once cowed, they would stay cowed. He threatened to crush them once and for all should they take up arms again. Smith proceeded to extend colonial boundaries over a wide area to the northeast, encircling the southern Nguni; he incorporated Somerset's old 'ceded territory' between the Fish and Keiskamma as the district of Victoria East; and he established the land between the Keiskamma and the Kei rivers (D'Urban's Queen Adelaide Province) as the dependency of British Kaffraria, over which he would rule as high commissioner and great chief. 'I make no treaty,' asserted Smith, tearing up a sheet of paper before the assembled chiefs; 'I say this land is mine.' By mid-January 1848 Smith was on his way towards the Orange River with his entourage, convinced that he had established permanent peace amongst the cisKeian Xhosa, and set them on the road to becoming a loyal and useful subject people, Christian and subservient, ruled over by military officers and missionaries, under the despotic overlordship of Smith himself.[41]

Smith took seriously Grey's prescriptions about the moral and material upliftment of the Xhosa. He obliged the bemused chiefs to reject witchcraft and polygamy – 'the sin of buying wives', as Smith would have it. He also set about undermining chiefly authority, establishing military courts under army officers to try serious cases such as would otherwise have fallen under chiefly jurisdiction, and insisted that the chiefs recognise no other paramount than the Queen of England.[42]

The missionary lobby was by now so reduced that it could safely be co-opted as a tool of economic and cultural subjugation. In pursuit of his 'civilising mission', Smith sought out the aid of the Aborigines Protection Society in London (which he secretly despised). 'My object is to induce [the tribesmen] to clothe themselves and, by habits of industry, to teach them the use of money,' he wrote. The society provided him with agricultural implements for the Xhosa. In Cape Town, Smith consulted Philip and other unlikely collaborators on how to teach Africans to plough and follow 'habits of industry', and on the setting up of schools. An elaborate schedule of fines was devised to suppress traditional customs, and another of rewards for promoting 'European attitudes'.[43] This utilitarian liberalism, very different from earlier humanitarian views, was authoritarian, coercive and without any illusions about the role of Africans in colonial society.

The truth was that in the aftermath of the War of the Axe, Xhosa society was in a state of severe shock. It would reach its nadir in the great cattle-killing episode of a few years later. By the time of Smith's governorship, the consequences of colonial penetration and aggression among the cisKeian Xhosa were glaring. Whereas a census of 1835 had recorded 56 500 Ngqika Xhosa between the Fish and Kei rivers, by 1848 the total had fallen to 27 000, with an equal number said to be seeking food in Thembuland, Gcalekaland beyond the Kei, and in the colony. Smith was quick to see the benefits to be gained from exploiting Xhosa vulnerability and imposed a tax of £1 on African plot-holders in the locations that were provided for them in the newly annexed territories in accordance with Grey's instructions. He threatened that he would 'turn those who do not pay off the land or seize cattle to the value required'. He also allocated money to meet the expenses of recruiting youths for indentured service in the colony, thereby reclaiming them 'from a life of idleness, ignorance and lawlessness', and planned the introduction of a vagrancy law.[44]

Smith ushered in an era of massive land alienation and speculation for those close to his administration, both in newly annexed territory in the eastern Cape and in the new Orange River Sovereignty north of the Orange. With the annexation of Victoria East and Albert districts there was an influx of settlers from Albany in search of sheep runs – almost all of British origin. (Stockenström told the Legislative Council in 1850 that there were not fifty Boers in Victoria East district.) The Graham's Town merchants Blaine, Black, Wood and Howse all acquired land by public auction; Henry Nourse of Graham's Town bought three farms in the Peddie area; and William Southey boasted of speculative profits he had made on land deals. In addition Smith was persuaded in July 1848 to extend the borders of Albert district further eastward in order to incorporate part of Thembuland within the colony.[45]

But there were limits to the extent to which Smith could meet the aspirations of the settlers. After all, his appointment had been predicated on his undertaking to reduce military expenditure. The withdrawal of troops which he had promised, coinciding as it did with a commercial depression in 1847–8, ran directly counter to the interests of the eastern Cape settler bourgeoisie. Godlonton reported that business in the town of Fort Beaufort on the Kat River had 'gone to the dogs' since the departure of the 7th Dragoons. Smith's popularity with the business community had suffered in consequence of his failure to keep up military expenditure of half a million pounds a year. However, the settler businessmen of Graham's Town and Fort Beaufort were too closely tied to Smith's regime for these grievances to cause an estrangement.[46]

But a much more serious source of disenchantment with this newly aggressive imperialism was brewing. Old battles with the British settler imperialists over relations with the Xhosa had left their scars, and Stockenström once again took up the cudgels. He started a correspondence with Earl Grey in London denouncing Smith's plans ('so sneeringly and contemptuously' proclaimed) as a 'delusion', and pointed out the impossibility of permanently cowing the Xhosa. But his warnings to London fell on deaf ears: Smith was still implicitly trusted at the Colonial Office. Stockenström simultaneously appealed to colonial opinion through the press, as well as through the occasional pamphlet denouncing imperial policies on the frontiers. The *Cape Frontier Times*, to which Stockenström gained access through the agency of Henry Hutton, his aide-de-camp in 1846 and later his son-in-law, became a vehicle for his polemics.[47] Godlonton in his *Journal* responded in kind, with a renewed campaign against Stockenström and the evils of the old treaty system. In all this rhetoric, the war of 1835 and its aftermath formed again and again the reference point. 'I read Stockenström's letters with attention', Godlonton wrote to Southey (now the high commissioner's principal aide),

> and can think of no word but *infamous* which can be appropriately applied to them. In my own opinion his object is to stir up the Colony to rebellion ... He richly deserves prosecution, and would be prosecuted were he not in a position which enables him to defy the government with impunity. He knows he is backed by a good many disaffected Boers and by two thousand Kat River vagabonds.[48]

Smith soon discovered that the Boer population as a whole, like Stockenström, were not as pliant as he had thought. They were alienated by the summary execution of one of their number after the Battle of Boomplaats against emigrant Boer rebels who resisted Smith's designs on the territory north of the Orange.[49] Then, unwilling to accept the lessons of the past, Smith published in mid-1848 a draft ordinance amending the law relating to burgher military service. The colonists were enraged, and petitions poured in from almost every district. Smith was forced to withdraw his proposal. The truth was that the bulk of the Boer colonists saw no reason to take up arms in the service of an aggressive imperialism. As this episode demonstrated, Smith's unrealistic undertaking to transfer the responsibility for military service on to the colonists themselves was unravelling. Increasingly alarmed at the spectre of another rogue governor in the colony, Grey could only warn again that the British army would not protect the colonists in the event of another war.[50]

The resistance against Smith's oligarchic regime also became intense in Cape Town. The rising Cape Town business and professional class were certainly not averse to the subjugation of the Xhosa or the extension of colonial territory. But these were now secondary to their demand for representative institutions answerable to colonists rather than to London. Although John Fairbairn, for one, at first welcomed Smith (one of his arch-enemies in the 1830s) back to the colony, even becoming secretary of a committee to collect funds for an equestrian statue of the governor on the Grand Parade, he soon changed his attitude. To the business class, with which Fairbairn was now closely associated, the ruling oligarchy had to be displaced by a more malleable and sympathetic regime if their own interests were to prosper. In the event, the equestrian statue was never erected; subscriptions soon dried up.[51]

Control over public financing remained at the centre of disaffection in Cape Town. In 1848 Montagu's plans to extend the income base of the central roads board, by targeting the proprietors of urban property, evoked renewed outrage from the municipal commissioners. While supporting the upgrading of the road system, they decried what they considered an unfair tax burden on their shoulders, especially when none of the money was expended on the town's roads. A meeting in May 1848 denounced the Legislative Council as Montagu's 'pet council', whose members, 'like drilled men, must bow to whatever he proposes'. 'We have nothing to hope from the Council as it now exists,' concluded J. H. Wicht, slumlord supreme. Another futile petition was dispatched to the Queen praying that the Road Amendment Bill be disallowed, and accusing Montagu of seeking 'to apply his utmost ingenuity to misrepresent the facts, arguments, and proceedings' of the petitioners.[52]

Despite the fact that Stockenström and Fairbairn had parted company on the question of policy towards the Xhosa, the pages of the *Commercial Advertiser* were made available to Stockenström for the propagation of his views. This was indeed a marriage of convenience by people who shared an antipathy to the regime. A new and more insistent mouthpiece for such 'popular' sentiments was established in January 1849 when F. S. Watermeyer began publishing the *Cape of Good Hope Observer* in Cape Town. This he used to attack mercilessly the corruption and nepotism of oligarchic government. Watermeyer was related to Fairbairn and F. W. Reitz – both prominent spokesmen for the 'popular' party – and a close associate of Stockenström, who used the pages of the *Observer* as another outlet for his views. Stockenström joined the clamour for representative institutions for the colony as a whole, as necessary to re-stabilise frontier relations.[53]

This degree of collaboration between English- and Afrikaans-speaking colonists across the colony in opposition to the regime was something new, and formed the basis for what became a loose 'popular' party. For Afrikaners, theirs was no longer the rearguard struggle of the 1820s and 1830s against liberal interference in their privileges and prerogatives, but a common struggle for civil and political rights which were the due of British citizens. By the 1840s the issue of class and race relations was no longer divisive within white ranks. In fact the issue of relations with independent peoples beyond the eastern frontier was more likely to be a source of conflict. For while the western Cape business and professional class was now supportive of the use of military force to shake free resources for colonial exploitation, the Boers of the eastern districts were more likely to take up pacific attitudes. However, in the intensifying crisis of the Smith years, the Cape Town business class was inclined to put the cause of colonial unity and constitutional advance first, and this meant opposition to the warmongers of the frontier whose interests were antagonistic to these goals.

As disaffection against the Smith regime and its policies in the subcontinent grew, so the 'conservatives' – those opposed to the 'popular' party – dug in their heels. The conservative party, too, would increasingly unite previously distinct groups across the length of the colony. Prominent among the conservatives were the leading British settlers based in the eastern Cape. To men like Godlonton, Southey, Cock and Chase, the idea of the British government abdicating its internal responsibilities at the Cape to a representative government, dominated presumably by Afrikaans-speakers, was abhorrent. They demanded a separate government for the eastern districts; self-government for the colonists they did not want.[54] The conservative party was also strong in Cape Town. Here John Montagu took the lead in resisting the pressures of the local business community with their power base in the municipality. He was supported by the longer-established and larger merchants with their close imperial ties. Although most senior officials like Montagu accepted the need for representative institutions, they insisted on stiff property qualifications for the franchise and even stiffer for membership of such institutions, and sought a strong and independent executive authority answerable to the colonial secretary in London rather than to a local parliament.[55]

An important accession to the conservative cause was Bishop Robert Gray, who arrived at the Cape in 1848 as the first Anglican bishop of Cape Town.[56] The Anglican Church, shorn of its evangelical schismatics, was still a bulwark of *ancien régime* Toryism, profoundly suspicious of humanitarians and missionaries. Gray was no exception. An extreme conservative with a profound dislike of political reform of all kinds, he blocked attempts to grant assistance to other denominations. He formed a close alliance with Montagu, and was allocated extensive grants of land in Caledon, George and Port Elizabeth –

arousing fears of 'an insidious and intruding Puseyism' among other denominations. Under Gray the Anglican Church at the Cape took on the trappings of an established church with a hierarchy of authority.[57] The conservative cause had won a powerful ally.

❖

As yet by early 1849 disaffection with the colonial regime was uncoordinated and *ad hoc*. Petitions focused on local or factional grievances. Elective politics was confined to the level of municipalities and district road boards. What was required was a mobilising issue before disaffection could reach the proportions of a broad popular movement. The issue that brought the crisis of legitimacy to a head and out on to the streets was convict transportation. This was an issue which in 1843 had already aroused the unalloyed wrath of the Cape colonists, when a proposal to send fifty juvenile convicts to the colony was withdrawn after a flood of petitions had arrived in London.[58] In 1846 Montagu's successful road-building projects using local convict labour again alerted the Colonial Office to the possibility of sending convicts to the Cape for labour on public works. But the scheme again elicited strong disapprobation from colonists, and never materialised.[59]

Transportation of convicted felons, and in previous years parish paupers as well, went back to the very earliest settlement of the eastern seaboard of North America. After American independence, Botany Bay in New South Wales became the receptacle for transported convicts. The first arrived there in 1787, and were assigned as tied labourers to free settlers. Assignment as labourers in the service of free settlers was ended in 1840, and was replaced by a 'ticket of leave' system, meaning that convicts were transported on parole. But as convicts began to compete with existing settlers in the market for skilled employment, resistance to transportation grew. Continued transportation was also seen as an obstacle to the granting of self-government.[60]

In the late 1840s the immediate problem for the British authorities was where to settle two thousand Irishmen convicted of minor agrarian crimes during the potato famine. Because of opposition from settlers in other colonies, Grey looked to the Cape to receive a proportion of these petty offenders, and decided that 282 Irish convicts should be transferred on board the *Neptune* to Cape Town.[61] When Grey sought Harry Smith's opinions on the matter in 1848, the latter foolishly advised the colonial secretary 'to take measures for conferring this boon ... with as little delay as possible'. Although Grey asked Smith in August to canvass the feelings of the colonists on the issue, at the same time he issued an order-in-council establishing the Cape as a penal settlement. This made the transportation a *fait accompli*. Grey's idea was that the convicts would labour on public works for a period, and then be dispersed through the colony with tickets of leave to make their own way.[62]

Grey considered that the colonists had an obligation to Britain arising from imperial expenditure in the recent frontier war, amounting to £1 200 000, an argument Smith repeated in the Legislative Council. Nevertheless, a public meeting in Cape Town on 18 November unanimously objected to the reception in the colony of convicts. Reasons given in the resolutions of the meeting were the vast extent and thinly populated nature of the colony that made efficient policing difficult, the effect the transportees would have on the morale of both colonists and indigenous people, and the probability that free immigrants would be deterred from settling at the Cape if it were a penal colony.[63]

Despite clear colonial resistance to the idea, news reached Cape Town in March 1849 that the convict ship *Neptune* had been ordered to the Cape. A formal pledge was posted at the Commercial Exchange and the Cape of Good Hope Bank for signature, declaring that no convict would be offered employment or shelter. On 19 May a meeting of some five or six thousand people on the Grand Parade, allegedly the largest public meeting to have been held in Cape Town, deputed J. B. Ebden and H. E. Rutherfoord, elite merchants, and H. C. Jarvis, president of the municipal board of commissioners, to present petitions of protest to the government. On 31 May a meeting of some five thousand people at the Commercial Exchange, including some from other parts of the colony, elected a committee (later called the Anti-Convict Association) with the merchant Ebden as its chairman, to resist the landing. The association was pledged to 'discountenance and drop connection with any person who may assist in landing, supporting, or employing such convicted felons'. The leading banks and trust and insurance companies all publicised their support for the pledge in newspaper notices. All divisions within the colonial community were apparently papered over in a common cause – although there were already those who resented Ebden's leading role in the movement. He was, after all, a member of the hated Legislative Council.[64]

Behind the single issue of convict transportation lay the wider fact that gubernatorial oligarchy was unacceptable to the emerging local bourgeoisie, seeking every opportunity to invest and prosper. The convict question, wrote Fairbairn, 'has convinced all men here that the colony needs the protecting shield of a local parliament'.[65] It was for this reason that the Legislative Council with its official majority and its nominated unofficial minority of approved merchants and landed notables became the special butt of popular calumny in the anti-convict campaign. The council was the symbol of the powerlessness of the colonists. Its bitter rival for political influence was the municipality, the power base of the newer colonial business class. When it came to the question of transforming the Cape into a penal settlement, even the metropolitan-oriented elite merchants, such as Ebden and Rutherfoord, Hamilton Ross, George Thompson and A. Chiappini, were inclined to lend their weight to the popular campaign against officialdom, though they were likely to resist any attempts to supersede legal measures or to whip up mob emotions.[66] On the other hand, in the view of the municipal commissioners and newspapermen like Fairbairn at the *Advertiser*, Watermeyer at the *Observer*, Brand at *De*

Zuid-Afrikaan, and Buchanan at the *Mail*, the Legislative Council had to be rendered incapable of continuing its routine business. The disruption of the council would enable the elected municipality to pose as the real voice of the people in challenging the authorities on the issue of transportation.

Matters came to a head in July 1849. At a mass meeting on the 4th, the pledge was extended to the social and economic ostracism of all who aided the government's policies. When an unofficial member of the Legislative Council, Pieter van der Bijl, died, and Ebden and Ross resigned, the Anti-Convict Association announced that anyone accepting appointment to the body would be subjected to the pledge. By now, the issue had brought crowds, including 'respectable' citizens, out into the streets of Cape Town. When the Swedish consul, Jacob Letterstedt, and two others accepted nomination to the council and were sworn in, they were manhandled by a large crowd, and pelted with mud. They soon resigned. Letterstedt's flour mill was attacked, and boatmen refused to unload goods belonging to him in Table Bay harbour. His business was closed down by boycotts.[67]

The effect of the agitation was dramatic: the Legislative Council effectively collapsed, local officials in the districts began to submit their resignations, and government was paralysed. Only William Cock, a Godlontonian from the eastern Cape, refused to resign from the council – not surprisingly as Smith's patronage was indispensable to his pet project, the development of a harbour at the Kowie River mouth near Graham's Town. In consequence of his obduracy, Cock was refused accommodation at all the hotels and lodging houses in Cape Town, and had to be put up at Government House; no washerwoman in town could be found to wash his clothes. Supporters of Smith were threatened with foreclosure of mortgages and expulsion from rented premises. Several civil suits against the Anti-Convict Association followed from people who claimed to have been libelled or even ruined by the application of the pledge.[68]

When the *Neptune* arrived in Simon's Bay on 19 September, a stalemate ensued. The 282 convicts were to remain on board, denied supplies, while the crisis ashore developed. Until further instructions were received, Smith could not take any action. Meanwhile, the Anti-Convict Association moved steadily in a more extreme direction, and its leadership passed from the merchant Ebden to a more radical faction led by Fairbairn and H. C. Jarvis of the municipality. The association instituted a boycott of everyone providing supplies to the government and its personnel, including the military. Merchants declined to tender, even for the supply of policemen's clothing. But the more conservative mercantile elite were not prepared to support the boycott of the executive government, the military and the police. They had entrenched interests at stake, and thought Smith was doing enough by ordering that the convicts should not come ashore.

From 10 October the *Commercial Advertiser* and the *Cape Town Mail* published names of all who continued to have dealings with any department of government. Spies were stationed to watch the business premises of suspected renegades, including former leaders of the Anti-Convict Association such as Ebden, who was accused of supplying wheat to the government, and who was now treated in the newspapers with open contempt. The situation was virtually out of hand. 'Nothing can exceed the disorganisation of the government, of commerce, of agricultural interests, of every branch of trade,' reported Smith. In the British parliament, the colonial reformer Charles Adderley took up the colonists' cause.[69]

Elsewhere in the colony, local Anti-Convict Association committees had been set up. In Graaff-Reinet, for example, J. J. Meintjes, a relative by marriage of Stockenström, was elected chairman. J. F. Ziervogel, a close associate of Stockenström who was to represent the district in the first elected Cape parliament, was among those who resigned their commissions as justices of the peace in protest against the government. When news of the *Neptune*'s arrival in Simon's Bay was received in Graaff-Reinet, the bells tolled, the shops were closed, and door handles covered with crêpe. A black flag was raised at the municipal offices. A story ran through the district that a thousand men were assembled, awaiting the arrival of the trekker leader Andries Pretorius, who had taken on Smith's forces at Boomplaats north of the Orange the previous year; they were to march on Cape Town and unseat the government.[70]

Eventually, in November, Russell's cabinet forced Grey to back down and order the *Neptune* on to Van Diemen's Land.[71] On 21 February 1850 the ship sailed out of Simon's Bay, more than five months after its arrival. Meanwhile, leading conservatives in Cape Town, alarmed at the rebelliousness of the popular party, began to demand that Smith ruthlessly assert the government's authority. Montagu was the leading spokesman for this group of hardliners, who preferred to throw in their lot with the metropolitan power rather than suffer an excess of colonial democracy. Although on the whole opposed to permanent convict settlement at the Cape, they were more alarmed at what they saw as the radicalism of the agitators, and were suspicious of their motives. Some feared that the convict issue was being used as the pretext for whipping up anti-British emotions among Afrikaners. One T. B. Bayley of Caledon wrote to Southey:

> The real object of Wicht, Truter and Co. is to promote Dutch ascendancy and accustom the Afrikander to public meetings, agitation, and political feuds. I should like to know what Sir Harry thinks now of a *Representative Assembly*, and what kind of a thing it would be if established now. The same machinery which rules the Anti-Convict Association (so called) would ensure the return of nineteen Afrikanders and one Englishman, *and what would be the result*?[72]

Smith and the leading conservatives used the agitation to frighten Grey in London into agreeing to the delay of representative government. Smith reported to the secretary of state in January 1851:

It would be difficult for me to convey to your Lordship any idea of the change which has taken place in the character of the community during the last two years and the hostility which has during that period been roused against the English government. This feeling it will take a long time to remove and I can entertain no doubt that, if the new legislature be entirely popular, the legislation at first will be entirely anti-English.[73]

The anti-convict agitation thus saw the crystallisation of distinct factions, with all those opposed to a broad representation in the government of the colony gathering around the figures of Montagu and the conservative Bishop Gray (in Cape Town) and Godlonton and Southey (representing the British settler elite of the eastern Cape). And increasingly, wealthy merchants such as Ebden, Rutherfoord and Norden, who had at first identified with the Anti-Convict Association, were inclined to throw in their lot with the conservative cause.[74]

In turn, the Godlontonians in the eastern and Midland districts found themselves more bitterly disliked than ever before by the Boer majority and by many English-speaking settlers too, particularly in the growing coastal town of Port Elizabeth. For one thing the loyalty shown to the rejected Smith regime by the British settler elite during the convict crisis had discredited the cause of eastern Cape separatism. For another, Graham's Town's primacy was being challenged, and its dominant elite in disfavour, as never before. The completion of the Zuurberg pass north of Port Elizabeth in 1849 greatly strengthened Port Elizabeth's access to the large stretches of territory to the north. A correspondent in the *Graaff-Reinet Herald* declared in August 1849 that the majority of farmers in the district would no longer have dealings with such as Godlonton and Cock, and were seeking an alternative market for their produce to that provided by Graham's Town. The *Eastern Province Herald* of Port Elizabeth also increasingly cultivated a Port Elizabeth–Graaff-Reinet axis. John Paterson, the editor, began in 1848 to push the claims of Uitenhage against Graham's Town as the potential capital of the eastern Cape. The failure of the Kowie River harbour scheme to get off the ground compounded Graham's Town's commercial misfortunes.[75]

The fierceness of the reaction to the imminent arrival of nearly 300 petty Irish felons, more victims than victimisers, might at first seem strange. We need to remember, though, that in 1849 there was widespread unemployment in Cape Town, due in part to a serious trade depression following the 1848 uprisings in Europe; and the more violent element in the Cape Town mob during the crisis months were people, mainly of the coloured working class, who had been reduced to penury as a result. But the middle-class leadership of the agitation had other fears. The emergent colonial bourgeoisie were very aware that their status as respectable men of property was based on their own exertions in a new society. In the colonial context, there was relatively open entry into the avenues of speculative and commercial accumulation. These self-made men were conscious of the slightly disdainful image of the 'colonial' in middle-class Britain, especially since so many of that kind elsewhere in the colonial world were tainted with the suspicion of convict ancestry. It is in this light that we should understand the emotive symbolism of convict transportation to the Cape. The self-conscious desire for respectability was threatened by the proposal to turn the Cape into a penal settlement. Furthermore, leaders of opinion expressed the concern that if the convicts were allowed to land, the colony's coloured underclasses would be 'polluted' by 'sinful white men', in Governor Smith's words.[76] The hierarchies of race and class were under threat. Contrary to the assertions of Smith, Montagu and Godlonton, the bourgeois agitations of the day were by no means inspired by radical-democratic ideals.

But beyond these considerations, the convict issue was clearly exploited for more immediate political purposes. It was a very convenient pretext for the propaganda battle against gubernatorial oligarchy and the arbitrary rule of Colonial Office appointees. Hence the Legislative Council was singled out as the singular object of mass anger and boycott. It was also feared that convict settlement would delay the granting of representative institutions and even imperil the freedom of the press, won after a long battle with the Somerset regime in the 1820s. For autocratic government was perceived as being an integral aspect of penal colonies. F. S. Watermeyer, editor of the *Observer*, explicitly set out the connection: 'The people chose no longer to have others rule them; ... they insist that the Representative Legislature which had been so long promised them, shall be withheld no longer ... If we wanted to be roused, surely the convict question is sufficient for our purposes.'[77]

Watermeyer likened developments at the Cape to upheavals then sweeping Europe: the 'revolutionary genius of the age' had reached Cape Town. On the other hand, Fairbairn drew parallels with events leading up to the American War of Independence. To use another analogy, the anti-convict agitation was a rite of passage for the Cape colonists, British as well as Afrikaner. Untrammelled gubernatorial rule was now untenable. A veil of mistrust and suspicion hung over relations between the colony and the imperial authorities in London while the threat of disruption and boycott continued to haunt the colonial administration. And the Cape Town municipality, having tasted victory, was not going to give up the initiative.

Although his confidence was shaken in the readiness of the Cape colonists for representative institutions, Earl Grey submitted to the colonial government in the early months of 1850 his constitutional proposals. Already in 1848 William Porter, the Cape attorney-general, had put forward a draft in response to Grey's request, but matters had been delayed both by the crisis in the colony, and by a lengthy process of consultation within Whitehall.[78] Grey now required Smith to call on the Legislative Council to fill in the details in the proposed constitution. But the council had been rendered inoperative during the agitations of the previous year. Moreover the 'popular party' demanded a central influence over the process of constitution-making: they demanded 'the substance as well as the form of self-government'. Fairbairn at the *Advertiser* suggested that the colonists draft their own constitution, and make it clear to the imperial authorities that 'no other form of government can be carried on here'. A meeting in the town hall in April 1850 resolved that a 'committee of delegates' be elected by the whole colony to frame a constitution.[79]

Faced with a quandary by Grey's instructions to reconvene the Legislative Council, Smith hit upon the expedient of asking municipalities and district road boards – the only elected institutions in the colony – to submit names for nomination. In this way he hoped to deflect the objections of the 'extreme' party, as he called them. While the conservatives saw this concession as a dangerous precedent, the leaders of the opposition saw it as an opportunity. The Cape Town municipality headed the campaign to get opponents of gubernatorial rule nominated, sending voting tickets throughout the colony. In the event, the five candidates they put forward at the head of their list – Brand, Stockenström, Reitz, Fairbairn and Wicht, all leaders of the anti-convict agitation – headed the overall returns in that order. Stockenström, who enjoyed overwhelming support in both eastern and western parts of the colony, was hands-down winner in the eastern districts.

All in all, this first colonial 'election' was a pretty hit-and-miss affair. But it was a rough indication of popular feeling among white colonists. It revealed starkly the unpopularity of the conservative supporters of the administration. Godlonton, spokesman for the eastern Cape British settlers, came eleventh overall. But Smith was determined to include Godlonton as a counterweight to the 'radicals', and appointed him ahead of Wicht to the council. With five official representatives on the council, Smith hoped that the 'extreme' voice would be drowned.[80]

The four 'popular' members challenged Godlonton's appointment, unsuccessfully. But what sank the Legislative Council yet again in September 1850 after a two-week session was the governor's determination that it should not confine itself to constitution-making, but pursue general business as well, as was its legitimate function. For their part the popular members were determined that the council should sit only as a constitutional assembly, and no more. Then, when they were outvoted by eight to four they resigned, issuing a document entitled 'Reasons for Dissent'. Without a quorum, Smith converted the rump of the council into a commission to complete the details of the constitution. In a dispatch, the governor referred to the four seceders as representing 'a violent party, generally Dutch ... who, while they cry out for Liberal and Free Government, had rather be without any government whatever'. Godlonton wrote four days later to Southey that 'Fairbairn and his clique' stood 'in full relief as a dangerous factor, destructive to British interests and ruinous to the prosperity of the country'.[81]

The Cape Town municipal commissioners once again turned to popular agitation. Those who had resigned from the council were called upon to draw up a 'popular draft' constitution. In keeping with Porter's 1848 draft, they proposed a £25 property franchise for voters to both chambers of the elected parliament, broad enough to stymie the obstructionism of pro-imperial elites, but sufficiently restrictive to ensure that the propertyless working classes, white and coloured, were effectively disfranchised.[82] For their part, the conservatives were concerned to ensure the highest qualifications for membership in such an institution, even proposing a fully nominated second chamber; and they were adamant that the minimum of powers be vested in it. A strong, autonomous executive responsible in the first instance to the imperial government was their prescription for progress and prosperity. In particular they were determined to keep power out of the hands of the Afrikaans-speaking majority. Committed as they were to the imperial connection, they warned incessantly of the supposedly backward-looking and unprogressive attitudes of the majority. As Southey wrote to Godlonton, they would be 'swamped' by 'Dutch and *coloureds*' if an excess of democracy were permitted. Godlonton himself warned in his *Journal* against a constitution which would give the franchise to 'the untutored aborigines of the Kat River'. He wrote to Southey in January 1851: 'One thing is quite clear, that the people are not fit for those liberal institutions proposed for them, and I believe they will not be ripe for many years to come.' A few months later, Southey was writing to Godlonton that every effort should be made to delay the constitution for at least five years. If representative institutions along 'popular' lines were introduced, 'the first Parliament will be Dutch ... and the next will be elected by the Coloured population'. Their 'only safety', he wrote, lay in a 'higher franchise and higher qualifications for members of both houses'; otherwise they should rather opt to be 'governed from Downing Street'.[83]

Fairbairn and Stockenström, those old campaigners with all their experience of lobbying imperial opinion, were deputed to carry the popular constitutional demands to Britain. Their mission was made all the more urgent for Cape Town businessmen by the fact that at this time negotiations were under way for the construction of a railway from Cape Town to Wellington and Stellenbosch for half a million pounds, to be raised in debentures. As we have seen, the value of representative government for local business interests lay in the ability of a colonial legislature to provide satisfactory guarantees for loans. Fairbairn left Cape Town in October 1850 while Stockenström waited until the northern spring on doctor's orders. He used the delay to travel through the colony collecting evidence of popular support for their cause to present before the British authorities, and met with an overwhelmingly positive response.[84]

Fairbairn and Stockenström's mission produced a flood of invective from the pen of Godlonton. Their object was 'to secure for Cape Town the government of the rest of the colony, to augment the political power of the servile classes, so as that they may stand in successful antagonism to those who possess property'. The conservatives sent James Adamson of the South African College to London to ensure that their voice was also heard. Their major concern now was to delay the introduction of representative institutions as long as possible. In London Russell and Grey were still committed to the abandonment of gubernatorial oligarchy and the introduction of more liberal institutions, but they were haunted by the spectre of anti-British agitation at the Cape. This was played up by the leading local officials. And when warfare on the eastern frontier again erupted in December 1850, Smith and Montagu urged that popular demands be resisted.[85]

Since his arrival in 1847 Smith's policies of reducing the cisKeian Xhosa to a state of subordination, ruled over by magistrates, military officers and missionaries, had been proceeding. Colonial rule was a harsh imposition for the Xhosa. British law assumed that Xhosa had lost all title to their land since they had fallen under British rule, and Smith asserted his assumed rights in this respect with impunity. Within British Kaffraria, people were shifted from grazing land to grazing land to suit administrative convenience. In Victoria district between the Fish and Keiskamma, Xhosa land was sold off wholesale to English-speaking speculators at public auctions in order to fill colonial coffers. In the preceding several years thousands of Xhosa had entered the colony for the first time in search of work. Starvation was regularly reported by 1850, as landlessness was aggravated by severe drought. The missionaries, with few exceptions, were now unsympathetic towards the humanitarian concerns of their predecessors, and generally took the side of the authorities. The officials, civilian and military, who ruled Kaffraria usually spoke little Xhosa, and often shared the settlers' almost total misunderstanding of Xhosa society. Smith, preoccupied with conflicts in Cape Town, was himself impervious to any warning that the policies being followed towards the Xhosa were leading to an explosion.[86]

In October 1850 Smith visited the frontier to calm settler alarm. He summoned the chiefs to King William's Town, capital of Kaffraria, to answer charges that they were behind the prevailing unrest among the Xhosa. The Ngqika paramount, Sandile, refused to come, terrified of again being imprisoned as he had been in 1847. He was proclaimed deposed, and replaced by magistrate Brownlee. It was at this point that the killing of cattle was ordered by the prophet Mlanjeni in preparation for a millenarian struggle against the British. When a colonial force was sent as a show of force against Ngqika strongholds, it was ambushed and twelve men were killed. By the end of December the Xhosa had overrun the frontier, and many workers and squatters on farms and members of mission communities throughout the eastern Cape deserted and turned against authority in a widespread outbreak of rebelliousness.[87]

The war which began in December 1850 at first followed a familiar pattern. There were no battles to speak of, but much small-scale skirmishing in the dense bush of the river valleys and mountain fastnesses of the Amatolas, where the Xhosa concentrated. British tactics as always involved burning huts, destroying crops, capturing cattle. But more than this, there were widespread atrocities committed. Women and children were not immune from this kind of treatment. Indeed, Peires calls this the 'longest, hardest and ugliest war ever fought over one hundred years of bloodshed on the Cape Colony's eastern frontier'. It was, writes Mostert, the single biggest conflict between black and white south of the Sahara in the nineteenth century. It would reach its peak of ruthlessness in the early months of 1852 when Lieutenant-Colonel William Eyre unleashed methods of terror and destruction in a desperate effort to end the war. Some 16 000 Xhosa died in the War of Mlanjeni, more than were to die in the Zulu war of 1879–80, and the consequence was the terminal disruption of cisKeian Xhosa society. Within a few years the great cattle-killing movement was to achieve more in reducing the Xhosa to penury than any number of imperial guns could have hoped to achieve.[88]

For British settlers on the frontier the war also brought the usual welcome opportunities for profiteering. Commissariat prices doubled and trebled during the war, as they always did in wartime, and British traders and contractors again exploited the possibilities for enrichment. The old missionary James Read on the Kat River told Fairbairn that there was a dread of war everywhere except at Graham's Town and Fort Beaufort – the centres of British business activity. The larger and longer-term goal, pursued since the 1830s, was expressed to Godlonton by William Southey, brother of the secretary to the high commissioner, in mid-1851: 'It would be easy to subjugate all Kaffirland and take it for ourselves for ever if men would generally turn out for the work ... All Kaffirs, even to Natal, must be subdued, their lands conquered *from them* and they themselves made *servants*. This will, however, not all be effected *at once*, but I shall live to see it.'[89] As the war seemed in danger of petering out because of mutual exhaustion, Southey wrote: 'I am seriously afraid the Kaffirs won't continue the war now they find us too strong for them. Six months more will ruin them completely.'[90]

The Boers again were reluctant to have anything to do with the 'governor's war'. Smith wrote to Grey of the burghers' 'apathy and indifference'. The burghers' spokesman was once again Stockenström: this time he declined to support the call to arms. The government alone had provoked the war, he wrote in a polemical pamphlet penned while in London in 1851, pointing out that the burghers had had nothing to do with British designs in Xhosaland 'except as instruments in systems they could neither institute nor control'. In fact, in the absence of a burgher law such as Smith had failed to carry in 1848 in the face of massive opposition, there was nothing the governor could do to coerce compliance with his call to arms. In Graaff-Reinet, burghers at a meeting told magistrate W. C. van Ryneveld that they would only go if the government first provided them with horses – remembering how their loss of horses in the previous war had gone uncompensated. In the event, only small groups from Graaff-Reinet, mainly British settlers, served in Smith's war. William

Southey, one of the British settlers of the district, wrote to his brother that the local Boers were '*very anti*-English in their *hearts, far more so* than I had supposed'. And Smith himself noted that while he did not suspect that Stockenström had 'tampered with the Kaffirs',

> I have no doubt that they have been encouraged to revolt, by the disunion within the Colony with which he has been so mixed up; and though I do not charge him with inciting the Kat River Hottentots to rebellion I have no doubt they believed they were promoting the views of their patron by taking up arms against a Government which he has constantly vituperated; and though I do not allege that he has counselled the Boers to refuse to serve against the enemy in the present war, his organs of the press have openly done so.[91]

Just as he had done in 1835, Godlonton spared no time in compiling a book on the war, consisting of material originally published in the *Journal*, designed to paint the Xhosa as treacherous and cunning savages, egged on by unscrupulous philanthropists. He also designated Stockenström as the 'leader of the discontented oppositionists to British rule in South Africa'. Dark suspicions were fostered by the fact that Stockenström's farm near Bedford was the only farm in the area not ransacked. (Stockenström was subsequently told that Sandile had in fact posted a guard to protect the property.) Unknown settler elements took their revenge on Stockenström by burning his house to the ground while he was away in London, an event that confirmed in him a deep sense of bitterness which he carried to his grave.[92]

Predictably, much of the conservative rhetoric about the causes of the war sought to prove that it was an extension of the anti-British rebelliousness manifested in the anti-convict campaign; that it had been instigated deliberately by traitorous Afrikaners and their coloured allies to end British rule and drive out the British settlers. Thus a connection was made, in conservative propaganda, between the war and the dangers of granting a liberal constitution to the colonists. Indeed there is no coincidence in the fact that the British settler imperialists who surrounded Smith and egged him on in his expansionist enterprises (as they had D'Urban in the 1830s) also firmly resisted the granting of representative institutions to the colonists. More representative government ran directly counter to the kind of imperial military expansionism on which their interests relied.

With his allies in the Cape Town business community opposed to Smith's administration, Stockenström took the opportunity presented by the war to embarrass the governor, by launching a frontal assault on his policies through the pages of opposition papers such as the *Advertiser*, the *Observer* and the *Mail*.[93] When in London in 1851, Stockenström also took advantage of the select committee appointed to look into the causes of the war, which sat between June and July. He called the Kaffrarian government a 'regular speculation', and used the occasion to vindicate his treaty system at length, blaming the state of warfare that had been endemic since 1846 on the colonial government's betrayal of treaty obligations. Having absolved the ordinary colonists of any responsibility for war, he placed the blame squarely on the shoulders of an aggressive regime and its local hangers-on. He assured the committee that a more representative colonial government would restore stability and accept full responsibility for maintaining peace without imperial involvement. As long as government by force and coercion persisted, Stockenström asserted, 'South Africa will be to England what Algiers is to France'. He denounced that 'insignificant fraction' which

> rejoiced in war as long as it was profitable to themselves ... Where ten make their fortunes by war, ten thousand suffer in some shape or other, and I have long felt convinced that if the ... colonists had had the control over public affairs by means of free institutions, the mere publicity of truth and exposure of falsehood would have prevented the deplorable condition of South Africa, which we are now so deeply lamenting.[94]

Before the same committee John Fairbairn, whose interest in the frontier was largely opportunistic, hit at the elite Cape Town merchants who had thrown in their lot with the conservative faction, asserting that 'British merchants and their agents' in Cape Town were trying to prolong the war for private gain.[95] But by the early 1850s the situation on the frontier had irretrievably changed, in ways which would have met with Fairbairn's approval. The cisKeian Xhosa had already been conquered by a process of attrition, and their independence irrevocably lost. No return to the treaty system was possible. The only question to be answered was how the colony would rule over large numbers of African subjects incorporated under colonial rule.

Whereas in the mid-1830s criticism of policies of dispossession against the Xhosa had come from the humanitarian lobby with a particular vision of an expanding empire of free trade in the subcontinent, by the 1850s the same criticisms against the same imperial forces were coming from an emergent colonial bourgeoisie chafing at the bit of imperial hegemony and challenging restraints on local enterprise and investment. For most colonial polemicists in Cape Town (such as Fairbairn), criticism of Smith's frontier policies provided a convenient peg on which to hang their campaign against gubernatorial rule, rather than a reflection of philanthropic sentiment. They had already shown in the 1840s that they were enthusiastic at the prospect of the Xhosa being swept aside in the interests of development and profit. But by the early 1850s they were no longer prepared to support military adventurism to the benefit of a small group of elite settlers who subsisted on the fruits of imperial patronage and favour. The cause of constitutional advance now came first.

❖

The War of Mlanjeni had much wider, long-term significance. In previous frontier conflicts much of the actual fighting on the colonial side had been done by coloured auxiliaries. But in the War of Mlanjeni, Smith was confronted with more than a war against the Xhosa. Large numbers of the colony's coloured population rose in rebellion too. The epicentre of coloured rebelliousness was the Kat River Settlement. As the wool industry developed and property values climbed during the 1840s, so the Kat River Settlement came to be seen by colonists as a community of idlers and wastrels, whose unproductive hold on the land had to be removed. The settlement, which was becoming increasingly overcrowded, lay in the midst of highly valued and well-watered sweet grass veld of the kind on which woolled sheep flourished. Fort Beaufort on the edge of the settlement was growing rapidly as a market town by the 1840s. And as a result of the wholesale exodus of local Boers on the trek north in the 1830s, farms in the vicinity had fallen into the hands of British settlers, speculators and farmers. Mission stations everywhere were under attack, even from within the ranks of mission societies themselves. 'The voice of every colonist', wrote the editor of the *Graham's Town Journal*, 'must be loud in demanding, that every Institution, where a number of the coloured races are, or can be drawn together, shall be broken up, and restricted from re-assembling.' This was an increasingly uncontested view in employer circles.[96]

During the war of 1846–7, Kat River people had participated fully on the colonial side, as they had in 1834–5. For their pains their settlements were devastated by invading Xhosa. In 1847 Pottinger appointed an archetypal settler figure, T. J. Biddulph, as magistrate in the Kat River. Biddulph saw no good at all in the continued existence of the embattled settlement. He described the inhabitants as 'incorrigibly idle' and 'thoroughly corrupted', and demanded that they be forced into service. The original foundation of the settlement he condemned as 'nothing but the most transparent piece of humbug ever practised on the public, to serve the purposes of unscrupulous, intriguing people'. Biddulph's report was approvingly published by Godlonton in his *Journal*. In response to the report, Pottinger described the settlement to Grey in London as a 'concourse of rebellious, idle paupers', which was 'worse than useless'. Pottinger imposed a debilitating tax on timber, the sale of which was the only means the Kat River people had of surviving the calamitous losses of the war. Inevitably, the perennial call for a vagrancy law was sounded again.[97]

For the various factions within white colonial society at the time contesting the extent of constitutional change, the rights and freedoms of coloured people were not at issue. Their claims evoked little sympathy. The people of Kat River had few friends anywhere among the white colonists, British or Boer. Notwithstanding conservative warnings that the popular constitution would lead to a swamping by coloured voters, it was never disputed by the 'popular party' that racial hegemony was the essential base of the colonial social and economic order. If the British settler elite posed the most immediate threat to the Kat River people, that was because they had the acquisitive drive and the access to capital and to state patronage to carry through their designs on Kat River land. The imperial government, still bound by its obligations under Ordinance 50, disallowed Smith's renewed attempt to get vagrancy legislation enacted in 1848. But this was clearly an issue on which white colonists across the spectrum agreed, and it remained on the colonial agenda pending the granting of self-government.[98]

With the reincorporation of the remnants of the old 'ceded territory' (between the Fish and the Keiskamma) into the colony as the district of Victoria East, the Kat River Settlement no longer straddled the colonial border with Xhosaland. That it no longer served a military function as a buffer against the Xhosa robbed it of its original usefulness. In 1848 T. H. Bowker, the new magistrate and member of a leading settler family, set about recalling government weapons from the inhabitants, which they had held since 1830. White landowners took up farms in the new district, displacing many Mfengu communities. When these were removed to the Kat River, they placed extra strain on the resources there. Smith whittled away at Kat River land by granting land to those, such as Godlonton, who had claims on his patronage. Meanwhile, the campaign of vilification against the coloured inhabitants of the settlement continued in the pages of the *Graham's Town Journal*, increasing the sense of insecurity and deprivation among the people. While the editor of the *Journal* was orchestrating this campaign, he was writing to his old colleague Richard Southey, secretary to the high commissioner, thanking him for promises concerning lands beyond the Kat, and requesting prior information on impending land sales in newly acquired territory.[99]

In 1849 eight Kat River people petitioned the Aborigines Protection Society in London for deliverance from 'the insatiable thirst of colonial oppression'. At the forefront of the resistance of Kat River people to the encircling forces of colonial oppression was James Read, Junior, himself regarded as 'coloured' as a result of his mother's Khoi ancestry. His father was now an old man and had handed over his life's work to his son. Stockenström, the founder of the settlement in 1829, and still an enemy of settler greed, took up the cudgels too, warning the government secretary in July 1850 that the 'malicious calumny' and 'denial of justice' suffered by the Kat River people, who had saved the colony in two frontier wars, might yet have serious consequences. As always, Stockenström was willing to take a longer view than his Boer followers. And he was to be vindicated. When the War of Mlanjeni erupted in December 1850, the Kat River people (like the Boers) refused to turn out in support of the government forces, mindful of the severe losses they had suffered in previous wars when they had dutifully obeyed official summonses.[100]

Such was the level of disaffection and insecurity that many of the inhabitants under the leadership of Hermanus Matroos, a former ally of the government and son of an absconded slave and a Xhosa woman, joined the Xhosa and rebelled against the colonial authorities in 1851. The spirit of rebellion spread, drawing in landless coloureds from the farms and the mission stations, as well as deserters from the Cape Mounted Rifles. Mfengu levies also refused to re-enlist. In July 1851 Smith was forced to discharge his remaining Khoi conscripts for fear of further mutinies. A pensioner from the corps, Willem Uithaalder, became the leader after Matroos's death. The rebellion took on nationalist overtones. Uithaalder tried to elicit the active support of the Griqua captains Kok and Waterboer in a campaign on behalf of the coloured 'nation' (*geslacht*), warning that the colonists planned to pass 'irregular and oppressive laws, such as vagrant laws, which tend to oppression and complete ruin of the coloured and poor of this land, a land which we, as natives, may justly claim as our mother land'.[101]

Undoubtedly, the imminent prospect of representative institutions which were bound to be dominated by white colonists was a potent threat and pushed men like Matroos and Uithaalder to extreme measures – although the leaders asserted that their quarrel was not with the Boers but with the British. They saw through the rhetoric of non-racialism to realise that even the most liberal of colonial constitutions would remove the protections they enjoyed against the avarice of the employing classes. For when it came to the demand for labour coercion and control, there was little to differentiate British settler from Boer. The colony's working people could no longer rely upon humanitarianism, so powerful a force twenty years before, to plead for or protect their interests. The forces of colonial oppression seemed inexorable by the time of Smith's governorship, and men such as Uithaalder, who had served the colony in previous military conflicts, must have felt they had nothing to lose by taking up arms against the colonial authorities. That they represented themselves as a coloured 'nation', determined to assert its national independence against colonial rule, was itself a significant form of racial self-identification. Reminiscent of the 'Hottentot' nationalism of earlier years, it had grown out of an increasing sense of alienation and isolation from the racially defined dominant classes of the colony.

At the same time, there was clearly a strong sense of Xhosa–coloured solidarity. In the 1834–5 war, the Xhosa had strenuously tried to win the support of Khoi, but the latter were still firmly committed to proving their loyalty to the crown (despite their missionaries' condemnation of the war). By 1851, all this had changed, and Khoi were prepared in large numbers to desert the colonial cause, even as they continued to plead loyalty to the crown. In this alliance of the oppressed, an element of class solidarity coexisted with the rhetoric of national liberation.[102]

The fate of the Kat River Settlement was sealed. The land of all those considered to be disloyal was confiscated, and the settlement was opened up to white land-grabbing, despite the protests of Stockenström. Plots fetching less than £20 before 1851 were changing hands at £1000 and more within four years. In the process the Kat River Settlement was decimated, and many of its inhabitants dispersed through the colony and beyond. Andries Botha, local field cornet and a leader of the Kat River forces in the war of 1846–7 – as loyal a subject as could be found in the settlement – was tried for treason in Cape Town. The *Graham's Town Journal* triumphantly summed up the significance of his trial thus: 'The case of "the Queen versus Andries Botha" is in reality the case of "The Colonists versus the Kat River Settlement."' Botha was sentenced to death, although the sentence was subsequently commuted.[103]

Thus it was that when Fairbairn and Stockenström in 1851 set about appealing to the British government to grant representative institutions immediately to the colony along the liberal lines demanded by the popular party, constitutional issues had again been clouded by the renewed outbreak of conflict on the eastern Cape frontier. In the colonial secretary, Earl Grey, they found a man who had become jaundiced against their cause. Grey regarded the defeat of his convict order-in-council as a personal humiliation and (so he was persuaded by his senior officials in Cape Town) the work of a revolutionary, anti-British faction. He was thus little inclined to welcome the two delegates of the popular party. All Stockenström's and Fairbairn's attempts to persuade the colonial secretary of the consequences of continued autocratic rule at the Cape were met with a lukewarm response. In the event, all that the delegates could obtain from the Whig ministry was a commitment to introduce representative institutions when the time was ripe.[104]

In May the Colonial Office sent 'additional instructions' to Smith allowing him to continue to rule through a Legislative Council consisting solely of official members, as most of the unofficial members had resigned in protest the previous year. This alarmed the delegates in London, for it suggested that representative institutions were not going to be introduced soon. In the colony, the *Cape Town Mail* declared that the government had now become 'a naked and undisguised despotism', while a Graaff-Reinet meeting declared that 'political corruption and bureaucratic power' would now be entrenched. The threat of mass resistance in Cape Town was resurrected.[105]

But despite Earl Grey's distaste for what he termed the 'Cape Town mob', and his newly awakened fears of Boer and coloured disaffection, he was forced to proceed with the constitution as it stood. The law officers ruled that the draft could not be withdrawn.[106] Once again the Legislative Council, now without any pretence of being representative of 'popular' opinion, was called upon to deliberate on the constitution. This was broadly in line with the proposals of the popular party. Grey and the officials of the Colonial Office knew that anything less would defeat their purpose by vesting power in the hands of a small elite, thereby aggravating rather than stabilising tensions in the colony.

But the conservatives who controlled the council in Cape Town were still determined to delay the introduction of representative institutions for as long as possible. Apart from the absence of any provision for the separation of the east, the £25 franchise for both houses and the property qualifications for membership were far too low for the conservatives as a whole; and they also found unacceptable the fact that the second house was to be elected and not nominated. The *Graham's Town Journal* rejected it with more than a touch of hyperbole as 'a universal franchise in all but name'. In the western Cape the conservatives assiduously fanned fears of coloured rebelliousness, alleging a conspiracy of the colony's coloured underclasses. Montagu reported to Godlonton in alarm that coloureds returning from frontier service were expressing the seditious opinion 'that the Hottentots and Caffres are fighting for *land* formerly theirs and are right in so doing'. The result was something of a panic in the western districts at the prospect of an armed rising by servants. A government commission concluded that the panic had been deliberately fanned in order to arouse fears of the consequences of extending the franchise on a low-franchise, non-racial basis.[107]

By the end of 1851 Grey was coming to the end of his tether with Smith. Although thoroughly antagonised by Smith's enemies in the colony since the anti-convict agitation of 1849, Grey was beginning to suspect that the unremitting bluster of the governor had blinded him to some colonial realities. He now believed that Smith was ultimately to blame for the destabilisation of the subcontinent. Grey had long been deeply suspicious of Smith's annexation of Transorangia in February 1848. But it was the state of war on the eastern Cape frontier which increasingly alarmed Grey, for it represented the failure of everything Smith had been sent to the Cape to accomplish. Had not Smith been sent to South Africa on the understanding that imperial military expenditure would be reduced and peace secured by imposing British rule over the cisKeian Xhosa? Yet the Xhosa, far from being pacified and reconciled to British rule as Smith had promised, had proved more intractable and desperate than ever before. And the colonists had refused to take up arms – had even been mutinous. Smith's dispatches on the frontier situation had proved hopelessly misleading and self-congratulatory, full of imagined victories when the reality was grinding stalemate. In fact, Smith had revealed himself, like D'Urban before him, as another rogue governor, captured by local settler interests to further their own agenda of military aggression and dispossession.[108]

Grey decided to send out two 'assistant commissioners', Major W. S. Hogge and C. M. Owen, to investigate the situation and restore peace. Both had commanded levies in the 1846 war, and neither was a friend of the Xhosa. Nevertheless, Hogge reported that Smith was misrepresenting the military situation, and was incapable of securing a lasting peace. So, early in 1852, Smith was recalled (not without opposition from within the cabinet, the prime minister and Wellington objecting). He left the colony in April. Montagu followed in May on sick leave, never to return. Thus fell the bastion of Tory reaction in Cape Town.[109]

The final enactment of the Cape constitution was delayed further by the return of a Tory ministry from February 1852 to January 1853. But the new administration at the Cape under Sir George Cathcart had a very different approach to colonial government from Smith's and Montagu's regime. Cathcart, who had been aide-de-camp to Wellington at Waterloo, had seen military service in several parts of the empire, notably Canada, but had no experience of colonial administration. He was primarily appointed to end the war and achieve the lasting peace that Smith had been unable to secure. Because Cathcart was to be stationed at the frontier until the war was ended, Charles Darling was appointed as his lieutenant-governor in Cape Town. Darling had served under Lord Elgin in Jamaica and then as lieutenant-governor in St Lucia. He was far better disposed towards the rising middle class centred on the Cape Town municipality than Smith or Montagu had been. Thus the colonial bourgeoisie, who had so bitterly opposed Smith's oligarchic regime and pressed for representative institutions, found themselves at last close to the centre of influence.[110]

Darling set about dismantling the private empire Montagu had built, reclaiming for Government House the powers which the government secretary had usurped. By the time Smith and Montagu were recalled, the latter was clearly in charge of the government in Cape Town, as Smith had become embroiled in the frontier military conflict. The conservative newspaper, the *Monitor*, was to all intents and purposes issued from Montagu's office. The treasury was under his control. After his departure many of Montagu's more obviously political appointees were retrenched. Richard Southey, secretary to the high commissioner in Smith's time, was removed from office after it was discovered that copies of government papers were being sent to Montagu in London in an effort to discredit Darling and to get the constitution obstructed.[111]

Despite conservative resistance in Cape Town to Darling's measures, he soon became a popular figure among the colonists as a whole, in sharp contrast to the officials who had preceded him. Petitions, memorials and addresses praising him arrived from throughout the colony. In November 1853, Darling wrote to the colonial secretary that those who supported his measures were the

> native or permanently settled colonists … who feel that true social prosperity depends upon something more than the rapid accumulation of wealth (not even perhaps to be reinvested in the country where it has been acquired) as contradistinguished from those who merely regard the colony as a convenient and profitable trading station, to be deserted when their purpose of achieving independence is attained, and who, viewing this object as the 'greatest good' not unnaturally conceive that Public Policy ought to be exclusively directed to its promotion and to the maintenance of the paramount influence of those engaged in its pursuit.[112]

On the eastern frontier, Governor Cathcart was equally determined to distance the administration from its former conservative allies. He brought the

War of Mlanjeni, festering since December 1850, to an end. No real military victory had been won, but the Xhosa had been so reduced in circumstance and so brutalised that no further resistance was possible. In his settlement of the frontier Cathcart sought to placate the chiefs and to restore their dignity. His emphasis on ruling through the chiefs was not, however, a return to the treaty system associated with Stockenström, as the chiefs were now unquestionably subordinate officials of government, and not independent authorities. Unlike the Glenelg settlement of 1836, there was to be no withdrawal from Smith's British Kaffraria to the *status quo ante*. Cathcart's rule over Kaffraria was in fact a fairly naked military occupation, enforced under martial law.[113] In practice, no matter how strong was the official British desire to withdraw from responsibility for directly ruling the Xhosa, the internal cohesion of the Xhosa chiefdoms was so disrupted that it was impossible to restabilise them as units of local administration.

Nevertheless, for the Godlontonians on the frontier, Cathcart's summary termination of the hostilities smacked of a failure of imperial will comparable with the withdrawal of 1836. But Cathcart saw through the 'Graham's Town faction', and warned against profiteers who tried to obstruct the restoration of peace in the frontier region by spreading 'false rumours' – rumours which Godlonton was assiduously publishing in his *Journal*.[114] In a private letter of February 1853, Cathcart wrote that 'a set of covetous, profligate, unscrupulous, land-jobbers of colonists expected that I was to use the Queen's troops, not in support of justice, but to aid and abet, and support them in injustice and rapacity, at the expense of commencing another war'. The following month he wrote that 'peace is ruin to them, and the expenditure of public money during the war has been the making of their fortunes, in war prices for their goods, contracts for provisions and waggons etc. ... I am heartily disgusted and sick of these mean, dishonest people; the Kafir is much the finer race of the two.'[115]

In 1853 the new colonial secretary, the Duke of Newcastle, brought an end to the back-and-forth shuttling of constitutional drafts that had been going on since 1848. The constitution was promulgated on 1 July. It retained the £25 property qualification for the franchise – a more liberal franchise, indeed, than that enjoyed in Britain at the time. It also finally rejected the principle of nomination rather than election to the second chamber (which had been used to secure British interests in Canada). All this mortified Cape conservatives, who raised the spectre yet again in their Cape Town organ, the *Monitor*, of coloured and Afrikaner domination and the swamping of the British. In the eastern Cape, the British settlers condemned the failure to provide for separate government, and the grant to the western districts of a slightly larger proportion of seats than the eastern (24 to 22 in the House of Assembly and 8 to 7 in the upper Legislative Council). Nevertheless, there were safeguards built into the new constitution which ensured imperial interests would be maintained – such as the civil list, which reserved a proportion of the colonial revenue for prescribed purposes. And of course representative government fell short of fully responsible government, in which the executive was drawn from and answerable to the parliament. Twenty years would pass before fully responsible government was to be granted.[116]

From the time of the anti-convict crisis of 1849 on, a crisis of state legitimacy, a breakdown of consent, gripped the subcontinent, not only in the Cape but also in Smith's Orange River Sovereignty. In 1848 Smith and his senior officials had been content to allow the liberal attorney-general, Porter, leeway to draw up a draft constitution designed to provide for a broad electoral base, in his own disingenuous words, 'not dependent on class or caste'.[117] But within a couple of years reaction had set in. Underlying cleavages had been brutally exposed. The rising colonial business class, including Afrikaner farmers and professionals, and the bulk of the Boer pastoralists in the interior had all revealed a disdain for and rejection of oligarchic rule from Downing Street and Government House. If the convict crisis had not brought this home to those in Britain who feared for imperial interests in southern Africa, the overwhelming disaffection with the re-opening of war against the Xhosa must have done so. On the other hand, further democratisation of colonial political life was resisted by senior officials such as Montagu, the elite merchants with their close metropolitan ties, the Anglican hierarchy and the British settler elite of the eastern Cape. Behind their expressed fears of Afrikaner and coloured domination lay fear of the withdrawal of the civil and military patronage on which their economic interests rested.

Earl Grey, who came to the Colonial Office in 1846 imbued with reformist ideas, allowed his best intentions to be partly subverted by conservative bluster from Smith and Montagu. However, warfare in the eastern Cape frontier region as well as north of the Orange in 1851 gave Grey pause. The reports of special commissioners Hogge and Owen persuaded him that Smith had lost control of the situation, that he had deliberately misled his superiors, and had to be recalled. Not only could the wholesale disaffection of the colonial population not be gainsaid, but the narrow base and self-serving nature of the oligarchy in Cape Town and on the frontier were now apparent. Cathcart and his lieutenant, Darling, were dispatched to salvage the British position in South Africa. Both men quickly realised that re-stabilising the region meant dismantling oligarchic rule, extending more liberal institutions, shifting the bases of state support to a broader mass of colonists, making peace with the Xhosa, and withdrawing formal sovereignty from Transorangia. After a brief Tory interregnum in London, in January 1853 a new regime was installed in Downing Street totally at one with the new forces at work in the colony. Clearly, there was not enough at stake for Britain in its South African possessions to justify the kind of expenditure required to support the self-enriching projects of the settler militarists and expansionists. Co-option was preferable to coercion.

The 'popular party' at the Cape represented in part a rising local bourgeoisie, combining commercial and agricultural interests, English- and Afrikaans-speaking, but without close links to the metropolis. Their political assertiveness and self-confidence by the late 1840s grew out of the economic development that had already taken place since slave emancipation, and out of frustration at the considerable obstacles to raising capital for infrastructural development and company formation. They shared a growing aversion to the military coercion that was part and parcel of the Smith approach to frontier relations, although they had little sympathy for Xhosa independence or the rule of chiefs. Thus Watermeyer at the *Observer* saw Smith's frontier policies as an extension of the patronage that was an integral feature of autocratic government: militarisation of the frontier meant war profits for a small band of merchants, contractors and speculators. In a similar vein, the bilingual pro-Stockenström *Graaff-Reinet Courant* accused the Graham's Town people of seeking to provoke the Xhosa to war, because they 'could willingly see the welfare of the colony ... succumb to their own sordid ends'.[118]

However, the opposition of the popular party to the war effort against the Xhosa in the early 1850s should not be overstated. The marginal nature of humanitarian concerns had been revealed when war broke out in 1846, before political factions had coalesced around the convict issue. There was virtually no anti-war propaganda within colonial society then, and Fairbairn had eagerly supported the war effort. It was only when the real issues at stake began to crystallise out over the nature of the colonial state and the interests it was to serve during Smith's governorship that an anti-war stance hardened within the alliance that opposed the regime. Policies towards the chiefdoms, both on the eastern frontier and in Transorangia, were part of the terrain of conflict; but the fate of the chiefdoms was not really the issue at stake. The cattle-killing disaster of the 1850s, the culmination of decades of warfare directed against the chiefdoms, was widely regarded by whites within the colony as a salutary development, advancing the cause of civilisation and progress.[119]

Similarly, the adherence of most white leaders in the colony to the principle of constitutional non-racialism did not imply any real intention to dilute racial hegemony in political or economic spheres. The constitution of 1853 was not a triumph of democracy. Despite its non-discriminatory form, it was the culmination of a process of economic development which brought in its wake gradually narrowing opportunities for coloured people and, indeed, a gradually encroaching wave of dispossession and subjugation. In 1830 the secretary for the colonies, Sir George Murray, had dismissed representative government as incompatible with the interests of the colony's coloured population, who, he considered, were not yet in a position to defend their rights against white domination. It is doubtful whether the Cape was any fitter for representative institutions by this criterion in 1853 than twenty or thirty years before. But by the mid-century humanitarian principles had become severely diluted and, in sharp contrast to earlier policy, the Colonial Office was turning a blind eye to fiscal measures in Jamaica and elsewhere which were designed to limit the enfranchisement of blacks in these British colonies.[120]

Certainly, the disaffection of the coloured population was as intense as it had ever been. In the early 1850s the Kat River Settlement was being dismembered by white land-grabbers at the very time the new constitution was introduced; and the old mission stations within the colonial borders, such as Bethelsdorp, were in a chronic state of decline – a process deplored by Stockenström, who remained something of a champion of the independent coloured artisan class, but who was powerless to halt it. At the same time, segregation was being introduced where it had never been practised before, such as in the Dutch Reformed Church. Whereas in 1834 Fairbairn was reported to have said that 'he will not advocate the measure [a legislative assembly for the colony] any more till the Hottentots and people of colour are fit to take their places in it along with the white population',[121] by the 1840s his attitude had shifted. This change of mind had little to do with any change in his assessment of the 'fitness' of coloured people for the vote, but much to do with the development and increasing profitability of a racially defined colonial capitalism.

Fairbairn continued in his newspaper to espouse the benefits of a non-racial franchise, and there is no reason to doubt his sincerity. But it was also evident that the reconciliation and unity that he so passionately advocated was restricted to colonists of European descent, English- and Afrikaans-speaking. He stressed their comity of interests as the 'ruling class' in sharp contrast to the indigenous people. Under a representative government, he reassured his readers in 1848, it was perfectly clear that 'both the electors and the elected would be of their [the whites'] body'. Many spokesmen for the colonists' cause regarded the non-racial franchise as a necessary and not very significant concession to the sentimentality of British public opinion. The old ethnic divisions within white ranks over the issue of rights for the colony's coloured working classes, and the historical prerogatives of Afrikaner colonists, had given way to a struggle for ascendancy by a self-confident colonial bourgeoisie which crossed ethnic, if not racial, lines. They had discovered that non-racial legal formalism did not in any way threaten the hegemony of class and race. It was autocratic government that stood in the way of their further advance.[122]

Electoral returns in the first elections under the new constitution demonstrated the fading away of older ethnic divisions within white society. Stockenström and his colleagues proved overwhelmingly popular, not only among the Afrikaans-speaking population, but also among many British colonists in the eastern districts and Midlands who did not identify with the Godlontonians. As for the rising business class of Cape Town, they saw in Stockenström and the considerable mass of Boer colonists who looked to him for leadership, an essential accessory in their drive to wrest power away from those who obstructed their economic advance. Moreover, in the western Cape Fairbairn, who in the 1820s and 1830s had been seen by the burghers as the embodiment of an interfering humanitarianism, was now in the embrace of

Afrikaner farmers. In 1854, this most urban of commercial polemicists was elected to the new Legislative Assembly as representative of the rural and largely Afrikaans-speaking constituency of Swellendam.[123]

Far from greeting the non-racial franchise as securing their liberty, coloured colonists on the whole seem to have anticipated representative government with trepidation. The direct rule of propertied colonists, the employing class, and the removal of the protective embrace of the Queen, seemed to them a retrograde step. Indeed, coloureds were to be a marginal factor in the electoral politics of the colony. In the elections of 1854, coloured voters at the Kat River and at mission stations such as Bethelsdorp were virtually unanimous in their support of Stockenström.[124] But the humanitarian impulses that had produced Ordinance 50 of 1828 and had blocked vagrancy legislation in the 1830s were essentially something of the past, despite Stockenström's lingering adherence to them. The white colonists as a whole, many of whom also regarded Stockenström as their champion, saw no reason why they should not use their newly acquired voting powers to secure the sort of repressive legislation that they had been seeking for years for the better control of the colony's working classes. The popular party of the 1850s was by no means a standard-bearer for democracy.

The coming of representative government coincided with a boom in colonial trade, spurred in part by the development of gold mining in Australia. A period of wild speculation began at the Cape, reaching its height in 1854. Companies mushroomed in Cape Town, started up by businessmen associated with the municipality.[125] The coming of an elected colonial legislature seemed to promise the necessary guarantees for gaining access to international capital markets. Further to the north, British sovereignty in Transorangia, proclaimed by Smith in February 1848, was withdrawn in 1854, and Britain handed government over to collaborating whites. In this way the re-stabilisation of South Africa for the purpose of consolidating imperial hegemony was achieved by the empowering of local elites.

CHAPTER EIGHT

Colonial Advances, Imperial Retreats

Philip's grand design for Transorangia extended well beyond securing recognition for the sovereignty of the Griqua states at Griquatown and Philippolis. From the early 1830s he envisaged that the Christian Griqua would act as agents of LMS missionary expansionism, by spreading Christianity, education and civilisation to the surrounding Sotho–Tswana, who were busily rebuilding community life after the ravages of the 1820s. In further pursuit of this goal, Philip undertook a grand tour of Transorangia in 1841–2, ten years after his previous visit, and was accompanied by his old lieutenant, James Read.[1]

By 1842 new and seemingly menacing forces were stirring north of the Orange. It was some years since the main body of Boer emigrants had passed northwards from the colony on to the highveld and down the escarpment into Natal. When in 1842 the British occupied Port Natal and extended control there, the trekkers began to extend territorial claims more determinedly in Transorangia. In the area between the Orange, Vaal and Caledon rivers, many of the growing numbers of white farmers were decidedly more hostile to the imperial factor in southern Africa than the longer-established trekboers concentrated in the south of the region. Their presence there had to be reckoned with.

Philip had the ear of Governor Napier in Cape Town, whose interest in, and anxiety over, the northern frontier region was aroused, just as his alarm had been awakened by the trekker presence in Natal. Philip warned too of the extent of slave trading in Bushman children by Boers. As many of the Philippolis Griqua, whose country was being eaten away by Boer land settlement, were taking to Bergenaar-style raiding again, Philip warned that 'If their property and land are not secured to the Griquas, and the protection of the Colonial laws, before ten years there will not be a single Griqua in the country'. Philip realised now that treaties were no longer enough: only direct imperial intervention could prevent the trekkers from overwhelming the Griqua and seizing their land.[2]

But there was another power to be reckoned with to the east of the region: Moshoeshoe's now very substantial state centred on the Caledon valley. Unlike the Griqua states, Moshoeshoe was consolidating and even expanding his authority over people and territory in the 1840s. The real significance of Philip's and Read's tour of 1842 lay in the fact that it marked the first formal colonial recognition of Moshoeshoe's importance as a centre of power north of the Orange. Through his contact with the French Protestant missionaries, with whom Moshoeshoe had developed a close relationship, Philip had already been aware of Moshoeshoe's position as a strongly accommodationist chief with growing power over both territory and people, firmly within the LMS sphere of influence. Now in 1842 Philip realised that Moshoeshoe held the key to the future of Transorangia, and was not slow to seize the initiative.

Philip contended that Lesotho was attractive to the Boers because horse-sickness was unknown there. 'The Boers know that without their horses, which they cannot keep without the possession of this Country [Lesotho], they never can carry their ambitious designs into execution,' he wrote to Lieutenant-Governor Hare. As for Lesotho's strategic significance, it lay between two sections of disaffected Boers. In Boer hands it would link a united republic from the Orange River to the Indian Ocean. A commitment by the British to protect Moshoeshoe's chiefdom, Philip asserted, would be a lot cheaper 'than it will be to fight the Boers and expel them from the country when they shall have exterminated these tribes and got possession of the country and horses of Moshesh'.[3]

Moshoeshoe was very receptive to the idea of an alliance with the colony, for he had learnt enough of the outside world to stand in awe of British power and civilisation; and he was easily persuaded at this time of the humanitarian and disinterested nature of British imperial motivations in southern Africa. In May, the Rev. Eugène Casalis, on the chief's behalf, wrote to Hare expressing Moshoeshoe's desire to 'make his relations with the colonial government more regular and intimate than has been the case hitherto … He is increasingly convinced that the existence and independence of his people are possible only under the protective aegis of the Sovereign whom you represent.'[4]

For Philip, outright annexation of territory was the 'only possible expedient of safety'.[5] But Governor Napier, who considered Philip's anxieties exaggerated, could recommend only that treaty relations be extended to Moshoeshoe and Kok. These two chiefs he was prepared to accept on Philip's advice as the major established indigenous authorities north of the Orange (apart from Waterboer to the west, with whom a treaty had been signed in 1834), and thus useful collaborators in maintaining stability in Transorangia. In August 1842 Napier issued a proclamation in which he warned the Boers not to 'molest, invade or injure any of the native tribes, or to take or maintain unlawful possession of any of the lands to those tribes belonging'.[6] For Napier, any greater responsibility or financial obligation north of the Orange than that entailed in signing treaties and issuing salutary proclamations was unthinkable. He and other makers of policy did not share Philip's humanitarian imperialism: crusades to protect the natives had no place in imperial or colonial policy.

As a result of developments in Natal the political temperature in Transorangia intensified in late 1842. Jan Mocke, a teacher from Koup in Beaufort district, who had accompanied the trekkers to Natal, led a large party of Boers from north of the Vaal to Natal in mid-1842 in order to evict the small British garrison at Port Natal. Failing that, he had returned to the highveld with dyed-in-the-wool rebels determined to give the British and their allies a bloody nose. In October a party of 300 armed Boers arrived at Alleman's Drift on the Orange to proclaim that river the southwestern border of the Republic of Natalia. Hearing of Mocke's intention, the redoubtable Judge Menzies, on circuit in Colesberg, arrived at the drift two days before and proclaimed the sovereignty of the Queen up to 25 degrees South. When Mocke's men arrived, Menzies delivered them a lecture on the evils of rebellion and sedition. Needless to say, Menzies's proclamation was hastily disavowed in Cape Town. At the same time, complaints of Boer harassment were made by missionaries in the LMS fold and their adherents in Transorangia, who all shared the assumption that imperial advance would support their enterprise as evangelical empire-builders. They thus had their own motives for raising the alarm. Casalis at Thaba Bosiu reported a rumour that missionaries would be expelled unless they acknowledged the authority of the Natal Volksraad. Fearing an organised revolt, Lieutenant-Governor Hare in Graham's Town sent to Colesberg in December a force of 850 men. This obliged the Boer rebels to disperse northwards again.[7]

Once approval from Downing Street had arrived, treaties with Moshoeshoe and Kok were drawn up in Cape Town in close collaboration with John Philip, the only man in Cape Town with first-hand knowledge of the situation north of the Orange. The treaties obliged the chiefs to cooperate with the colonial government in the preservation of peace and security, and promised them an annual present (£100 plus arms and ammunition for Kok, at least £75 in money or armaments for Moshoeshoe). In this way Kok was granted a nominal paper importance for a brief time, but to no avail in stopping the fatal process of land alienation. Whereas mechanisms for dealing with land disputes were not included in Kok's treaty (a recognition perhaps of the hopelessness of the case), rough boundaries were described for Lesotho.[8] These boundaries were to be the cause of much conflict with the Methodist missionaries. For the small Methodist communities on the west bank of the Caledon, such as Moroka's Rolong settlement at Thaba Nchu, objected to the recognition of Moshoeshoe's overlordship in the treaty provisions.[9] As in the eastern Cape, the Methodists in Transorangia were concerned to undermine focuses of black power and independence such as presented by Moshoeshoe.

But by 1843 Philip himself was a spent force. In June he offered his resignation as superintendent of the LMS. Though he was persuaded to withdraw it, his public career was all but over, as was his public influence.[10] Philip's espousal of the native cause after his grand tour of 1841–2 was his last hurrah. Indeed, by this time treaties were an anachronism, as Philip himself realised. This was the last time that treaties were to be used as the medium of ordering relationships with indigenous authorities. For they and the humanitarian impulses that gave them birth were soon to be overwhelmed by more powerful and insidious imperial forces – the very antithesis of everything Philip stood for – which would surge north of the Orange in a few years' time, jettisoning treaties and humanitarian concerns as an irrelevance.

At the time, the treaties seemed to the Boer radicals further evidence of British perfidy and of the machinations of the missionary lobby, provocative and thoroughly inimical to Boer interests. They had every reason to suspect that it was their own subjugation the missionaries were after. What they particularly resented was the recognition granted in Kok's treaty to the authority of the Griqua chief and his council over the territory they claimed, which was nowhere defined, but in which many Boers lived, while the Boers themselves were regarded as British subjects enjoying no independent rights to order their legal or political affairs. Kok himself read the treaty as recognising his full judicial authority over whites as well as Griqua. Conflict was thus inevitable. For the treaty with the colonial government had imposed on Kok's shoulders the duty of maintaining the law over people who did not recognise his authority, and without supplying his fragile captaincy with the means to establish any kind of authority at all.[11]

The Boers also resented the alliance between the British and Moshoeshoe's kingdom, so assiduously pursued by Philip and the French missionaries in Lesotho. Just as Moshoeshoe was pinning his colours to the mast of British imperialism, the more activist Boer rebels increasingly saw him as an arm of British power in southern Africa, and their attitude towards him and his people soured. 'In general the audacity of the Boers has very much increased of late,' reported Moshoeshoe to Governor Maitland in May 1845, 'and they make it no longer a secret that it is their intention to carry on their plans without any reference to the native chiefs.'[12] Imagining that his British allies would readily respond to appeals to their humanitarian instincts, Moshoeshoe tended to exaggerate the danger posed by Boer encroachment on his land and the bellicose intentions of the Boers. It seemed to him too that greater imperial involvement in the affairs of the Transorangian interior would shore up his own authority and increase his own security and prestige. Moshoeshoe was an unusually perceptive and far-sighted leader with considerable diplomatic skills; but his perceptions of the world of Europeans were formed almost exclusively at first by his missionary advisers, especially Eugène Casalis, himself a keen propagandist in the cause of evangelical imperialism.[13] Yet although Moshoeshoe's unquestioning faith in the ultimate goodness of British intentions was sincere, he was to learn that the reality of imperial power was less rosy than its promise.

The Boers who took up assertive attitudes towards Moshoeshoe, Kok and other mission communities in the 1840s were acting on behalf of the *maatschappy*, the corporate body of the emigrants. But the *maatschappy* was a tenuous and elusive entity, which waxed and waned in visibility and influence. In fact, the extent of state formation envisaged or set in train by the trekkers was very limited. The *maatschappy* was the union of the impoverished and the mobile, particularly after the Natal Volksraad had bowed to British pressure and dissolved in 1843. While the *maatschappy* Boers were just as inclined as others with guns and horses in the region to raid for cattle and captives, and while they had no particular regard for the rights and liberties of indigenous peoples, it is not true to suggest that they were bent on wholesale dispossession or subjugation. They never evinced any particular desire to make war on the chiefdoms unless deemed necessary (as with Mzilikazi and Dingane), and their relations with African chiefdoms were generally based on mutual accommodation.

In contrast to the *maatschappy*, most Boers in the south had no sense of themselves as representing a separate political community.[14] Boer and African settlements were becoming most intermingled in the lower Caledon valley, in the southwestern reaches of Moshoeshoe's territory where trekboers had been settling for longer or shorter periods since the 1830s. These Boers were mostly content to validate their individual claims to land by reference to Moshoeshoe or his subordinates. They had generally sought Moshoeshoe's permission to settle there and had never directly challenged the Sotho chief's overall authority. However, they had their own conception of the nature of the land tenure they had been granted. In contrast, Moshoeshoe's missionaries, who had their own axe to grind, insisted that while the chief was content to allow the farmers to stay on the land they occupied as an act of sufferance, he had refused to accept any remuneration or to grant them any documents which would assure them of indefinite possession of the land in the future. Casalis even insisted that the Boers had asked only for temporary rights but had later denied this when they 'thought themselves strong enough to throw off the mask'.[15] On the other hand, the trekboer J. de Winnaar was to claim many years later that Moshoeshoe, on a visit to the south of his territory in 1840, had expressed delight that whites were settling in the country, for this would 'contribute to his safety against the attacks of his enemies. He told me that I must plant trees and a vineyard, and build houses, as a proof that I would continue to inhabit the farm.'[16]

Whatever the truth, Moshoeshoe was clearly alarmed by the implications of the informal market in land that was bound to arise, a market he regarded as incompatible with his authority over the land and the personal nature of the patronage he had extended. No doubt the activities of local *maatschappy* men also alarmed him. In October 1844 he visited the south again and discovered that not only were long-term investments being made on the land by Boers, but some Boers were selling their land to newcomers from the Cape Colony. He thereupon issued a notice to the farmers warning them that all sales of farms, springs, houses, cattle kraals or any improvements were contrary to Sotho law, and therefore illegal and invalid. But the market in land continued to grow despite Moshoeshoe's determination to stamp it out.[17]

❖

In this fluid state of group dynamics and political allegiances north of the Orange, imperial involvement, once begun, could only increase. In 1845, when Kok sent a commando to arrest a Boer who had flogged his servant, the *maatschappy* commandants called out their followers to confront the Griqua. They were not inclined to tolerate Kok's attempts to exercise judicial authority over the Boers in Griqualand. To protect Kok against the *maatschappy* forces, Governor Maitland immediately dispatched troops under Captain Henry Warden, and at Swartkoppies in April 1845 the Boers were dispersed. Having been put to flight by Warden's force, the *maatschappy* leaders and their more committed followers moved northwards beyond the reach of British power.

Determined to impose order on Transorangia, Maitland himself crossed the Orange, the first governor to venture so far into the interior, and called the chiefs of Transorangia to meet him at his camp at Touwfontein in June. What he sought was a strengthening of the British alliance with Moshoeshoe and Kok, and a bolstering of their authority vis-à-vis the Boers living within their territories. Maitland was no friend of treaties, which he had emasculated on the eastern frontier the previous year; but faced by the deteriorating situation in the eastern Cape (where war was to erupt within a few months), he could do little more than reinforce existing makeshifts north of the Orange. Provision was made in new treaties with Moshoeshoe and Kok for the appointment of a British Resident permanently stationed in Transorangia. His duties included enforcing 'order and obedience among all British subjects' (that is, Boers), with judicial authority to 'prevent or punish all crimes or injustices meditated or committed by any such subjects' against the chiefs. To this end he was empowered by the Cape of Good Hope Punishment Act of 1836. (The Act remained, however, unenforceable, despite the provision of a small military force for the Resident's use.) On the assumption that conflict could be managed by an unscrambling of the egg, the Maitland treaties also arranged for the demarcation of 'alienable' portions of both Kok's and Moshoeshoe's territories, where Boers were to be permitted to lease land (without reducing either chief's paramount authority within his own territory). Boers living within the 'inalienable' remainder of their territories were, however, to be removed. Inevitably, these provisions were quite unworkable, and no effort was made to enforce them.[18]

Most of the Boers in the lower Caledon were not particularly concerned to elicit British intervention in 'closing' the frontier and placing geographical limits on Moshoeshoe's authority. The drawing of boundaries and the enforcement of racial segregation were not preoccupations of either Moshoeshoe or the Boers who enjoyed his patronage.[19] Some of these Boers in the lower Caledon had become Moshoeshoe's friends and supporters in a more direct way. Prominent among them was Jacobus Theodorus Snyman. Until 1843 Snyman had been a *maatschappy* commandant and companion-in-arms of the radical Mocke, whom he had accompanied on an abortive commando over the Drakensberg in July 1843 to challenge the British annexation of Natal. After this final attempt to turn back the tide of British advance on that front, Snyman relinquished all ties with the *maatschappy*, became reconciled with the British, and accepted Moshoeshoe as the ultimate source of political patronage in the region on either side of the lower Caledon River, and the final authority over the land. In 1845 Snyman accompanied the chief to his meeting with Maitland at Touwfontein, conveying him in his own wagon. By this time, clearly, the hold of the French missionaries on Moshoeshoe was being tempered by other influences. Henceforth, Snyman's voice was to sound loudly on the chief's behalf.[20]

This empathy for Moshoeshoe and his people in the lower Caledon valley was undoubtedly related to the trading relations between the Boers of the district and the Sotho chiefs. For most Boers, trading was no more than a periodic, small-scale activity, supplying items of consumption and the means of war, and carrying wagon loads of grain southwards for local use or sale in the trading towns of the colony. But there were some who enjoyed more regular and profitable intercourse with Thaba Bosiu, and nobody more so than the Hoffmans. Josias P. Hoffman, later to become the first president of the Orange Free State Republic, was another confidant and adviser to Moshoeshoe in the later 1840s. He visited the chief frequently, and provided him with large supplies of ammunition in exchange for grain and cattle. On their visits to Thaba Bosiu, Hoffman and his brother Jacobus often gave Moshoeshoe gifts of percussion caps, which the chief valued greatly.[21] Other traders followed the Hoffmans' example. (The longer-distance and more capitalised British traders in search of greater profit concentrated on the Tswana areas beyond the Vaal, where the ivory came from.) Little wonder that Moshoeshoe's store of ammunition was regarded as the most impressive of any chief in southern Africa.

These bonds of interdependence with the Sotho were to issue eventually in a strong and self-conscious pro-Moshoeshoe Boer faction by the early 1850s, once British imperialism began to threaten them. Moshoeshoe himself was to realise that an imperial power at a distance and under philanthropic guise was a very different animal from an imperial power encamped on the very threshold of Lesotho. On the other side of the equation, an expansive, independent, powerful Lesotho suited British purposes up to a point. But once British purposes had been bent to the service of British settler interests, as was the case from 1848, Moshoeshoe was quickly to become a *bête noire* of imperial policy. However, in the mid-1840s Moshoeshoe and the British still regarded each other as firm allies.

Imperial encroachment was soon to take on a dramatic new form – the outright annexation of the entire territory between the Orange and Vaal rivers. Annexation was unlikely to be fuelled by the humanitarian concerns of a John Philip, or by the pleas of loyalist Boers: such considerations did not move empires. But a rogue governor with expansionist visions forged on the anvil of settler politics might commit the empire without its consent. The first indication of things to come was the arrival in the lower Caledon district in 1847 of

British speculative interests, represented most obviously by the Halse brothers, 1820 settlers from the eastern Cape. These men were a relatively new phenomenon here: land accumulators whose primary purpose was to provoke a price inflation in land by drawing the colonial government northwards after them to legitimise land title and to sponsor immigration, settlement and investment. They were also involved in money lending and commercial enterprise. The Halses quickly fell foul of the French Protestant missionary Samuel Rolland at Beersheba on the lower Caledon, a loyal and fierce upholder of Moshoeshoe's authority in the district, whom they clearly perceived to be an obstacle to their plans. In correspondence with the British Resident, they condemned the French missionaries as a cancer in the land, accusing Rolland of inciting Africans to occupy land they had bought.[22] To Moshoeshoe the Halses posed a wholly new and unexpected threat. For they represented the settler elite of the eastern Cape, and could potentially, given the right set of circumstances, enlist the full weight of imperial power in the pursuit of their purposes, as they had on the Xhosa frontier.

It is impossible to say when Sir Harry Smith decided to bring the troubled territory north of the Orange River directly under British rule. His course of action may have been conceived before he arrived at the Cape in late 1847; or it may have been implanted in his mind once he had consulted his friends in the eastern districts. But there can be no doubt that it was a course of action which was likely to meet with the unqualified approval of Smith's natural allies in Cape settler society. Men like Godlonton and Southey, Chase, Biddulph and Bowker considered the imperial government's distaste for colonial responsibilities and expenditure inexplicable. To them expansion of territorial commitments in the interests of settler accumulation and prosperity was self-evidently the business of empire. As for the Halse brothers and their friends, they had not hesitated to exploit the networks of influence to make known to the authorities in Cape Town the desirability of extending colonial boundaries to incorporate them. After all, land purchases had little legitimacy without state authority to enforce them against counter-claims, and the credit that was part and parcel of the commercial system could only be secured by such authority. The new high commissioner would have been apprised of all this soon after his arrival in Cape Town.

By mid-January 1848 Smith was on his way towards the Orange River with his entourage, convinced that he had established permanent peace amongst the cisKeian Xhosa, and had set them on the road to becoming a loyal and useful subject people. Smith's journey to the interior had been preceded by an invitation from loyalists of southern Transorangia to visit them and hear their pleas for an extension of colonial rule. He was also aware of the desperate pleas of the loyalist Boers at Winburg to the north for military protection against the *maatschappy* party. On his arrival at the headquarters of H. D. Warden, the British Resident at Bloemfontein, Smith received deputations begging that colonial boundaries be extended to incorporate the loyalists, so that they could again enjoy the benefits of settled government, churches and schools, and title to their land. These requests Smith took to indicate a general sentiment among Boers north of the Orange.[23]

The high commissioner was not alone in grossly underestimating the intensity of the emigrants' political sentiments and their sense of deprivation at the hands of the British. Their spirit of rebellion had hardened as a result of British attempts to constrain and obstruct their independence, most notably by the invasion and annexation of Natal in 1842. Moreover, by 1848 the bulk of the emigrants were straitened in circumstances and thoroughly impoverished after years of uncertainty and impermanence. They were thus likely to greet Smith's projects with an angry show of resistance. Nevertheless, Smith believed that a display of imperial resolve would bring the emigrants to his feet. He quite simply assumed that he knew their minds better than they, and any lingering disaffection would be dispelled once his paternal beneficence had been manifested.

While at Bloemfontein, Smith peremptorily changed the treaty that the Griqua captain Adam Kok had entered into with Governor Maitland in 1845. Kok's leasable territory north of the Riet River was now to be permanently transferred to the possession of its Boer inhabitants, who had hitherto held it on lease from the Griqua. In lieu of his income from the quitrents collected by Warden from the Boers, Kok had to submit to accepting £300 per annum. Kok's land was now confined to the area south of the Riet. Treating Kok with impatience and intolerance, Smith had clearly decided that the Griqua were no longer of much use to the British. Kok's ramshackle, fissiparous captaincy no longer provided collaborative support for British hegemony north of the Orange; and with the demise of humanitarian influence, there was little advantage to be gained from shoring up his position in relation to the Boers in his country. Smith wrote to Grey that 'Kok and his followers are mere squatters, and have no more hereditary right to the country in question than the Boers themselves'.[24] After this, Kok's position was to deteriorate steadily, and by the early 1860s the Philippolis Griqua had moved off in search of pastures new, leaving their extensive tracts of country to Boer farmers.

But Moshoeshoe was still a power to be reckoned with, and was still regarded as a major pillar of British designs – for the time being. Smith met the Sotho paramount at Winburg. Together they subscribed their names to a vague document in which Moshoeshoe welcomed the proposed annexation of Transorangia, including Lesotho, to the crown. (After all, he had suggested such a step as early as 1842 shortly after meeting Philip.) The Sotho were to be left to rule themselves in their traditional way, under the protection of the British government as the paramount authority in the region as a whole.[25]

But there was a sting in the tail – representing a decisive break from past imperial policy – which must have indicated to Moshoeshoe that the forces behind imperial expansion in 1848 had very different motives from those animating Philip in 1842. Already in his reply to the loyalist white inhabitants of the lower Caledon who had waited on him at Bloemfontein, Smith had revealed the tenor of his thinking: 'you shall hold your lands from the Queen of England and from no native whatever,' he had told them.[26] With that one sentence Smith swept away all the assumptions underlying the policies of his predecessors. At Winburg Smith told Moshoeshoe that he intended to confirm the Boers in the permanent possession of all the land to which they laid claim, that this land would henceforth be under the Queen's authority and not Moshoeshoe's, that he would permit no further encroachments on Sotho territory, and that a commission would establish the boundaries between Lesotho and the white settlers. Though he undertook to pay the chief monetary compensation for all the land his people would thereby lose, Moshoeshoe declined the offer.

According to the missionary Casalis, who acted as interpreter, the chief told the governor that 'his desire was that all should live together, that no limits should be made, and thus that no one should say to him "this land is no longer yours."'[27] But characteristically Smith was deaf to indications of dissent. Perhaps, too, Moshoeshoe's trust in British intentions overrode any qualms he may have felt. But Smith was quite clear in his own mind that the Sotho were to lose all claims to land on which whites had settled. In this way all previous treaties were to be disposed of.

By the beginning of February 1848 Smith was in Natal, no more than a few weeks after crossing the Orange. Near the banks of the Tugela River he met the emigrant leader Andries Pretorius at the head of his followers undertaking their final exodus from the British colony rather than submit to the required oath of allegiance. Pretorius hoped to persuade Smith to withdraw British sovereignty over Natal and leave the Boers to enjoy their independence in peace. But nothing was further from Smith's mind, and on 3 February he issued his proclamation annexing Transorangia to the crown as the Orange River Sovereignty while still encamped close by the Tugela. The most he was prepared to concede in the face of the Boer leader's protestations was that British sovereignty would extend no further than the Vaal River. Smith proceeded to Pietermaritzburg and thence by sea to the Cape, satisfied that he had turned the tide of South African history.[28]

In a dispatch to Earl Grey in London, Smith justified his radical extension of British rule with an undertaking similar to that which had won him his appointment in the first place. Just as he had held out the prospect of permanently pacifying the eastern Cape frontier while at the same time reducing military expenditure, he assured Grey that the 'entire expense' of the new Transorangian administration would be borne by the colonists themselves, and the surplus would be devoted to the erection of churches and schools and the employment of ministers and teachers.[29] Not only did the high commissioner have a very optimistic view of his capacity to carry the mass of Boers with him (to the point of relying on burgher commandos to compensate for the shortage of regular troops). But he also clearly envisaged that an influx of settlers and capital would rapidly create the base for a more sophisticated state structure. This certainly was the sanguine expectation as well of many prominent British settlers, ready to take advantage of any speculative or commercial opportunity presented by the extension of British government northwards.

Fundamental in the formation of a state system was the formalisation of landownership. For land in the pre-industrial age was the primary productive resource, and control over it dictated class status and ultimately control over human labour. Moreover, formal registration of landownership was the primary source of state revenue, through registration fees, quitrents and transfer dues. By these means Smith expected the state to be strengthened as speculative capital entered the territory and as productive development took place. Although Smith's optimistic projections of development and prosperity were not in the event to be realised, the processes set in motion had long-term significance for the eventual creation of a larger white-controlled dominion in Transorangia.

Initially, three magistrates cum civil commissioners were to be appointed – at Winburg, Bloemfontein and on the lower Caledon. Each was to be assisted by a clerk and two constables, and a small Cape Corps force was to be stationed with Warden as Resident in Bloemfontein. The crucial first duty of these officials was to inspect land claims, issue certificates and impose quitrents. Smith estimated that initially income from quitrents and licences would amount to £5000–£10 000 a year, leaving a handsome surplus. Each district was to have its own elected, part-time commandant and a number of field cornets, who would serve as military officers of the burgher forces should they be called out. Those appointed to the magisterial posts were, predictably, men with very close ties to the British settler elite of the eastern Cape.[30]

However, these very basic arrangements were barely being implemented when it became clear that Smith's expectations of Boer compliance in the new Sovereignty were based on fallacious assumptions. News of a rebellion brewing under Pretorius's leadership reached Smith soon after his arrival back in Cape Town. Pretorius was busy seeking the support of Moshoeshoe to his cause. In April Pretorius wrote a letter to the chief reminding him that the emigrants had always endeavoured to live in peace and friendship with the Sotho.

> Is it not since we came to reside with you that you and your people have become secure against all the enemies ... who ten years ago surrounded you? and notwithstanding all this we perceive an arrangement which you made with the Governor Sir Harry Smith, in which you have ceded to him all the land which we occupy, and which is the cause that British jurisdiction is now extended over us. We therefore, as your old friends, know not what to say of you, whether you are our friend or enemy.[31]

But Moshoeshoe's reply was hardly likely to mollify Pretorius. He assured the Boer leader that the emigrants' best interests would be served by once again submitting to the benevolent protection of the colonial government, which had their welfare at heart. 'If it be your meaning that my friendship for the Boers should be shown by withdrawing myself from the Government, then you are mistaken.'[32] Moshoeshoe was soon, however, to revise his opinions of the nature of British imperialism, and to discover that he had much in common with the Boer emigrants in their determination to escape the rule of an expansionist imperial power.

By mid-July 1848 news reached Bloemfontein that Winburg had been occupied by 500 men under Pretorius. Rebel patrols were commandeering wagons and oxen, and a march on Bloemfontein by a force of over a thousand men was being planned. Warden, who had only some seventy men under arms at his disposal, set off for the Orange River, surrendering the Sovereignty to Pretorius. Smith immediately dispatched a large military force from the eastern Cape to Colesberg, and he himself arrived on the Orange on 9 August. The high commissioner was undoubtedly embarrassed at this turn of events. His assurances to London now seemed to be dangerously ill-informed. In order to meet Pretorius's challenge he was obliged to leave the eastern Cape vulnerably denuded of troops. The rebels, many of them unsure whether they wished to face British guns, were swept aside at the Battle of Boomplaats, and the Queen's sovereignty was reproclaimed.[33]

Pretorius fled back across the Vaal and settled in the Magaliesberg. He was declared an outlaw and a price was placed on his head. But in due course Pretorius was to make his peace with the British, once he had re-established an economic base in the Transvaal that he and his followers had been deprived of in Natal. In the absence of a communal political ideology, the emigrant Boers were never able to sustain concerted, organised action for long.

For his part, Smith had learnt enough of a lesson and sanctioned the building of a fort in Bloemfontein where a small garrison was to be stationed. But much more he could not do without incurring an expansion of imperial military commitments that he had promised would not be necessary. On his way back to the Cape, Smith addressed a large meeting of loyalists on the Caledon River, much dominated by the Halses and their friends; here he was assured of their imperial resolve and patriotism.[34] The one regret that these British settler interests may have felt was that the high commissioner had failed to commit a much larger and permanent military presence to the Sovereignty.

Now that British rule had been re-established, the registration of land title could commence in earnest. Land commissions began work in the various districts.[35] Apart from Boers who had settled north of the Orange prior to British annexation, many land claimants were in fact British. Speculation in land was particularly rife among the British establishment – the civil and military officials in the Sovereignty – and prominent among them were persons with close ties to the settler elite of the eastern Cape. It was in the nature of government in this pre-democratic age that there was a close relation between office and profit. High-placed officials who owned six or twelve farms were not uncommon.[36]

Those in the know were able to buy up land north of the Orange from Boers before Smith proclaimed annexation on 3 February 1848, although there was as yet no administration to sustain the pieces of paper which were the only evidence of title. Immediately after the proclamation, sought-after farms in the rich lower Caledon, which had cost £100–200, were fetching £1000 as the demand by speculators for land soared. Thereafter land prices sagged when Boer rebelliousness threatened the collapse of the flimsy new administration. But as many of those implicated in Pretorius's insurrection moved northwards across the Vaal River, disposing of their farms north of the Modder River as best they could, new opportunities opened up for British officials and speculators to acquire land for very low prices.[37]

While little land remained unclaimed by whites in the southern and central parts of the Sovereignty, large stretches of territory in the northern Vaal River district were vacant. Magistrate Paul Bester at the newly established village of Harrismith reported that there was 'abundant room' for some 500 or 600 farms to be carved out there, particularly in the northeast, where by the late 1840s only small isolated villages remained of the dense Sotho-speaking population that had lived there prior to the upheavals of the 1820s. This part of the Sovereignty, above the Drakensberg escarpment and north of the thickly populated Caledon valley, was quickly seen to be a speculators' paradise. As part of its drive to increase its revenue, the administration began in mid-1850 to dispose of farms here by the dozen at the upset price of £20 each, plus an annual quitrent of 30s.[38]

Proponents of colonial immigration generally assumed that development of landed resources depended on allowing settlers access to 'waste' land on the easiest terms possible, and on condition that the land be settled and developed. In line with this, Smith approved the sale of unoccupied land in the Vaal River district with the proviso that 'particular care must be taken to prevent the land falling into the hands of speculators. It must be ascertained that the purchasers of farms at this low rate intend *bona fide* to occupy them.'[39] But in practice settlers and capital were slow to arrive; and speculation in land inevitably prevailed. Smith's injunction was brazenly ignored.

Magistrate Bester visited Bloemfontein to sell farms to the townsfolk, many of them British officials and army officers, and in no time had disposed of fifty. Also prominent among those who grabbed farms in the district were members of the Cape settler elite, for example Robert Godlonton. Henry Southey, who was brother of the secretary to the high commissioner, and who owned much land in the Graaff-Reinet district, visited Vaal River district to buy up land for himself and for his friends. Much speculative money from Natal was also tied up in the district: the Nourse family owned large tracts of land in the vicinity of modern Memel, and Adolph Coqui, a Portuguese Jew who traded in the interior from Port Natal and set up a store in Harrismith, owned eleven farms.[40]

After the local land commission had laid out farms in the district, critics alleged that the commission had distributed land 'indiscriminately amongst its favourites and friends'. An observer remarked: 'Instead of contributing to the progress of the district, these holders of land reside in other districts, even in the old colony, and merely wait the time when these munificent grants of land can be turned into a handsome sum of money, and further do not trouble their heads about a district where no outlay of their capital interests them.'[41] Such was the level of absentee ownership in the district that in 1854 the newly independent government of the Orange Free State Republic withdrew the local landdrost, declaring that the town of Harrismith, on the trade route down into Natal, was 'like an oasis of occupation in a wilderness of hundreds of square miles of speculators' unoccupied farms'.[42]

The free grant of land was a form of patronage reserved for those specially favoured at Smith's court. Commonly, land grants were used as payment for services rendered. For example, A. H. Bain, member of a prominent 1820 settler family, was granted 16 000 acres for his services in the Pretorius rebellion of 1848, in 'assisting the Commissariat in obtaining Griqua wagons for transport in a country unknown to the officers and in conveying intelligence'. The high commissioner similarly authorised that Charles Halse and his brother-in-law J. A. Poultney be granted farms in Vaal River district as compensation for losses sustained and services performed during the rebellion. Old soldiers who had served under Sir Harry were given farms by their commander too.[43]

While no flood of new settlers into the interior of southern Africa materialised, land prices hardly stagnated. In September 1850, it was claimed that landed property had risen in value by 400 per cent since the Pretorius rebellion of two years earlier. Unimproved farms in Vaal River district which had been sold to speculators at £20 each were selling for £75–£300 by mid-1851. But in the more progressive and densely settled southern reaches of the territory, the profits to be made were far greater. In September 1849 H. Joubert bought a farm for £1500; eighteen months previously it had fetched £60. John Norval was offered £4000 for Batfontein on the banks of the Caledon in 1851; the farm had been sold in 1848 for £75.[44] Unquestionably, farming – above all, sheep farming – in the Caledon River district in the south was becoming more capitalised than elsewhere during the Sovereignty period. In the district town of Smithfield in April 1853, the first agricultural show north of the Orange was held. Many of the prize-winners were men who were also involved closely in trade, money lending and speculation (including the Halse brothers, James Poultney, Thomas Spiller and Robert Finlay).[45]

Such men had their own decided political agenda. They were enthusiastic imperialists whose perceptions and interests were identical to those of the eastern Cape British settler elite. They had their own mouthpiece, the newspaper

The Friend of the Sovereignty, established in Bloemfontein in 1850 by Robert Godlonton, proprietor and editor of the *Graham's Town Journal*. Under the editorship of Godlonton's nephew, Thomas White, it faithfully echoed its older relative in pushing for a more militant, aggressive, aggrandising commitment of imperial power on the frontiers of settlement. To *The Friend*, land settlement and capital investment were the twin pillars of development and progress in the temperate colonies.[46] These, however, were to remain unfulfilled expectations in the short term. For the political uncertainties and lack of confidence in imperial intentions were severe obstacles to investment in productive resources.[47] In fact the authority of the British administration was always tenuous and would collapse entirely in due course.

Despite the relative weakness of productive capitalism in the Sovereignty, the territory became more and more closely tied to the mercantile network of the larger colonial economy. The merchants and storekeepers of the Sovereignty towns were dependent on the credit and capital of bigger merchant houses in Graham's Town, Port Elizabeth and Cape Town. Bloemfontein, the capital of the Sovereignty, quickly became the centre of trade in Transorangia, and the forward base of trade with the Transvaal and Lesotho. As Warden's successor, Henry Green, wrote, Bloemfontein was supported 'by the Port Elizabeth and Cape Town merchants to whom the houses of many of the inhabitants, most of whom were engaged in trade, were mortgaged as security for the capital advanced them'. Port Natal was also a source of merchant capital, but the Natal trade with the highveld beyond the Drakensberg escarpment remained small compared with the linkages with the Cape.[48]

The merchandise passing through Harrismith from Natal inevitably included quantities of firearms and ammunition, bound not only for the Boers of the Transvaal but also for African chiefs. This illicit trade from Natal with African chiefdoms, reported magistrate Biddulph in Winburg in March 1851, was 'carried on to an extent almost incredible'. He had found large quantities of gunpowder and lead in traders' wagons loaded in Pietermaritzburg for the 'kaffir trade'. Likewise the trading ties described earlier between Moshoeshoe and many of the Boers of the lower Caledon region strengthened; indeed, they were to become politically significant as British policy towards the chiefdoms became more militant and bellicose.[49]

At mid-century Moshoeshoe's state, centred on the Caledon River valley, remained pivotal in the regional trading economy, as it had been for years past. Much of the trade of Bloemfontein was with the Sotho, whose grain fed the increasing population, urban and rural, of the Sovereignty, and now also the men and horses of the British military garrison. From Bloemfontein the road eastwards to the rich arable lands of the Caledon valley was well travelled by the wagons of Boer, Rolong and Bastaard middlemen and hired transport riders. Many Boers bartered grain for their own consumption or for sale to friends and neighbours. Lesotho was regarded as the 'principal granary' of the Sovereignty. During periods of disruption chiefs and missionaries were particularly concerned to keep the wagon routes open and safe for travellers.[50]

Once British sovereignty had been established, Moshoeshoe's role as the pillar of British hegemony, a role defined by treaty relations with Smith's predecessors, began to erode very quickly. Representatives of British settler interests were from the start concerned to knock the Sotho paramount off his pedestal. Typical was T. J. Biddulph, the 1820 settler who had done much to malign and destabilise the Kat River Settlement during his period as magistrate there. Now magistrate in Winburg, he warned his friend and associate Richard Southey, secretary to the high commissioner, that if the weaker communities under Methodist tutelage were not supported against Moshoeshoe's power, 'the upshot will be the annihilation of the smaller tribes, who will for ever be blotted from the Map of Africa, to gratify the ambitious views of Moshesh and his sons, every one of whom expect in their turn to become Great Chiefs, and they seem to rely upon Government to support them in this'. Biddulph wrote that the 'favour and distinction' accorded to Moshoeshoe had aroused a feeling of jealousy in the rival chiefs, and induced in Moshoeshoe's sons an unquenchable ambition to dominate the entire Caledon basin. 'Now is the time to assert and maintain the Sovereignty over the chiefs … by showing a physical force,' wrote Biddulph.[51]

William Shaw, superintendent of Methodist missions and himself an 1820 settler, took the opportunity while visiting Thaba Nchu in May 1848 to promote his clients' cause. 'The Government having resolved to pet Moshesh, have hitherto treated Moroko [the Rolong chief based at Thaba Nchu] with *worse than neglect*. In the matter of his lands he has been dealt with most *unjustly* to gratify the unbounded ambition of Moshesh.' Shaw pointed out that while Adam Kok and Moshoeshoe had been permitted to obtain supplies of gunpowder under their treaties with the British, Moroka's every application had been refused for several years past.[52]

What the smaller chiefdoms objected to was a natural process of expansion into land to which Moshoeshoe had always laid claim. As the Sotho continued to expand the limits of their settlements and establish new villages further away from Thaba Bosiu, they were resisted by the smaller chiefdoms (who had immigrated from elsewhere). In this the latter were aided by their Methodist missionaries, who sought diligently to elicit the intervention of the administration – with which the Methodists had from the start strong links – in drawing boundaries and rebuffing Sotho claims. Tensions began to boil up periodically between the Sotho and the Tlokoa of Sekonyela, by now heavily outnumbered and outarmed by Moshoeshoe's people. Sekonyela's people had occupied the upper Caledon – including Moshoeshoe's ancestral home – since arriving from the plains further north around Harrismith during the dispersals of the 1820s, but their power had now dwindled. Moshoeshoe had no intention of bending his knee to Sekonyela. At the same time he was cautious not to give the British any reason to regard his people as aggressors; but he could not restrain his subordinates. A new round of raiding began, led by his son Molapo, who controlled the northern reaches of Sotho settlement.[53]

Warden called a meeting to define a boundary line between the Sotho and the Tlokoa, a line which, if strictly enforced, could only favour Sekonyela's declining position against the inexorable infiltration of the expanding Sotho.[54] But such attempts to undermine Sotho power by drawing boundaries and recognising the sovereign authority of lesser chiefs – now almost clients of the administration and the Methodist missionaries – within their own defined territories, were almost a necessary consequence of expanding colonial power, and represented a stark reversal of policies followed under Philip's influence a few years earlier.

The most intense challenge to Sotho power came from the south in the lower Caledon region. There land speculators, with the Halses and the magistrate Thomas Vowe in the lead, had a strong financial stake in pursuing policies of belligerence and dispossession against the Sotho, and were pushing for a radical diminution of the territory over which Moshoeshoe and his subordinates laid claim. They impressed on Governor Smith at a meeting in September 1848 the need for a line of separation between white and black, who, they insisted, 'could not live mixed up with each other'. Smith entrusted Richard Southey with the task of defining the boundaries of Lesotho in the lower Caledon. Undeterred by Moshoeshoe's objections, Southey, after a cursory investigation, sent the chief details of his decision. The proposed new boundary line entailed a massive annexation of Sotho territory. What was more, Southey made it clear that all the Sotho living on the wrong side of the line would be expected to move beyond the boundary.[55]

Moshoeshoe had no intention of meekly accepting the annexation of so much territory and the radical diminution of his authority. He commented in a letter to Warden that the line would 'cut off the *half* of the habitable country, and some thousands of Basutos would be driven from their homes, it is said to give place to a very small proportion in number of British subjects. Mr Southey could not have been aware of this, but his proposition has filled me with grief and astonishment, and caused a sensation throughout this and surrounding tribes.' The chief added that he was sure the high commissioner would never accede to such an unjust proposal.[56]

Moshoeshoe's ally and agent, Josias Hoffman at Beersheba, warned against the drawing of lines between black and white. In a letter to his family in the Cape he wrote, 'This plan was clearly brooded at Smithfield', the district town where Vowe and the Halses were based, thus accurately identifying the forces behind the policy of dispossession that were coming to the fore. 'The natives will not consent to remove and will revenge such unjust treatment.' Hoffman estimated that three thousand Africans would be forced out by Southey's proposed line. 'If Southey thinks that he can bind the Boers to the British Government by giving them all the land,' wrote Hoffman, 'he is mistaken and knows neither the Boers nor the natives.' This letter, like others of Hoffman's, was intercepted by Vowe at Smithfield.[57]

The French missionary Casalis, Moshoeshoe's trusted adviser, heard of Southey's boundary line while on his way to Cape Town where he was to embark for France. He immediately wrote to Smith from Bethulie in protest. Much of the territory 'that would thus be taken from its legitimate owners is entirely unoccupied by Boers,' he wrote – missing the point that speculation in land was a more important motive force at this moment than occupation and development. Casalis pointed out that

> the Basutos and their Chief have never contemplated till now that the arrangements ... would necessitate the removal of any of them from their possessions ... The Chief did not object to the Sovereignty of the Queen being proclaimed, because, as he expressed it, he considered it as a cloak stretched over the Black and the White to cover and protect them all equally and maintain them all in what they actually possessed. He did not object to each Boer retaining his place, because he considered it as a warrant that no further encroachments on the part of the Colonists would be allowed.[58]

But he had not agreed to a boundary line beyond which his people would have to retreat. Casalis warned that given 'the attachment of the natives to their land ... nothing less than the employment of force can induce them to abandon that important part' of their territory.

Casalis's warning that only the use of force would oblige the Sotho to sacrifice their land in the lower Caledon proved accurate. Magistrate Vowe discovered that the work of the local land commission could not proceed because of armed Sotho resistance.[59] A British-appointed field cornet, H. J. Wessels, reported a conversation with a petty chief who told him that 'Moshesh would not make a line, and that when the Governor comes to make the line Moshesh would assemble his forces, and that where his skull lay there the first beacon should be planted, and that a stream of blood should that day run as large as the Caledon River.'[60] In fact, Moshoeshoe was too cautious and placatory a diplomat to have issued such threats, and despite his growing disillusionment he clung stubbornly to his belief in the fundamentally philanthropic character of British imperialism. But his subordinates, including leading members of his own family, by now had a far more pessimistic, indeed realistic, view of the nature of the imperial impulse.

The high commissioner, whose fingers had been burnt once by the spirit of resistance north of the Orange, knew full well, however, that the colonial secretary in London would not tolerate another military conflagration in his new Sovereignty. Smith realised how short his leash was. He thus trod uncharacteristically warily. He realised that no boundary line could be enforced without Moshoeshoe's assent. Warden was thus instructed to revise the boundary line, making sure this time that Moshoeshoe was consulted and his approval secured, by whatever means. The border line submitted by Warden to Cape Town in June 1849 was marginally less disadvantageous to the Sotho than

Southey's proposals had been, but still represented a massive diminution of Moshoeshoe's territory compared with the boundaries recognised by earlier governors in the treaties of 1843 and 1845.[61]

Meanwhile, in a campaign remarkably reminiscent of settler agitations in the eastern Cape against the Xhosa in preceding years, the advocates of dispossession in the lower Caledon took every opportunity to paint Sotho motivations in the blackest light, and to press for more militant forward policies against Moshoeshoe's people. Their ultimate goal was to secure imperial military intervention to drive the Sotho beyond the new borders and to subjugate them once and for all, with a view to opening up the district's resources for speculation, investment and settlement. Rumours of war plans being hatched at Thaba Bosiu were spread through the district, and reported to the authorities by Henry Halse and Vowe. With their extensive speculative claims to land in the district, it was in their interests to fan the flames of conflict and to pressurise the imperial authorities to intervene so as to break the power and independence of the Sotho.[62]

Warden relayed all these warnings, much of them exaggerated and highly polemical, to Smith in Cape Town. Then in August he requested that Smith dispatch a military force from the eastern Cape to the lower Caledon so as to compel Moshoeshoe to agree to the boundary line and to pacify the Sotho chiefs. 'The people of the Caledon expect Government protection; and I have sent out a notice to say that it shall be afforded to them when required.'[63] Apart from urging Smith to assert his military strength against the Sotho, Warden's stratagem now was to forge an alliance of the smaller Methodist communities west of the Caledon River against the expanding power and wealth of Moshoeshoe's state.[64] He was determined to overawe Moshoeshoe and his subordinate chiefs, and to confine them to the much-truncated Lesotho which he had defined.

Of course, intimidation could not bring about the physical eviction of the thousands of Sotho living on the colonial side of Warden's boundary without a large and permanent military presence, and this was not available. So complaints and demands continued to come from the white land claimants of the war party, alarms continued to be sounded, and the essentially impotent administration continued to blow hot and cold on the issue. As in other countries where settler capitalism confronted independent indigenous societies, the battle for dominance was a protracted one, only decided eventually when the development of a local state system and their own productive economy enabled the white colonists to assert control over the resources of land, labour and capital.

Nonetheless, despite these limits to the exercise of state power, the larger truth behind the developments described here is that a strong, independent Lesotho had ceased to be a useful instrument of imperial policy in the southern African interior. It was now increasingly an obstacle to British hegemony and to the further development of colonial capitalism. The drive to break

Sotho power and expropriate Sotho resources, most obviously the fertile arable lands of the Caledon valley, had become a dynamic force shaping imperial policy at the mid-century.

Many of the Boers on the frontier of white settlement in the lower Caledon were less enamoured of the intrusion of imperial power, and of the efforts to establish a fixed and closed frontier between black and white, than the settler war party. At a meeting of some sixty Boers in December 1849, speakers urged that they should now 'decline with thanks having anything to do with Government and the same with its functionaries, as they could do without them as they did before' – in the words of an observer, Hans Smit, who estimated that half of those present supported a decision to refuse to pay any taxes or quitrents to the Sovereignty administration.[65] Indeed, in September of that year Moshoeshoe claimed that in the previous three or four months he had issued papers to many of the Boers in the lower Caledon region securing them in possession of their farms.[66] It seems that whatever was happening on a diplomatic level between British and Sotho authorities, many Boers were continuing to look to Moshoeshoe as the source of security and patronage in the region.

In truth, a more complex reality was obscured by the widely disseminated image of the burghers clamouring for territorial segregation and denouncing Moshoeshoe's claims to authority over white-settled land. For every imperialist demanding policies of aggression and dispossession, there were several Boers who were not at all sure that imperial power, and the speculative interests it represented, were preferable to the ill-defined, *laissez-faire* patronage that Moshoeshoe had exercised over them. The majority of Boers in southern Transorangia had no history of specifically anti-imperial sentiment – few had been 'Voortrekkers' of later terminology. But they did not necessarily see their interests best served by the policies of the Smith regime.

These divisions among the white colonists were vividly reflected in the controversies surrounding the siting of the Caledon River district headquarters – what became known as the town of Smithfield, in honour of Sir Harry. The leading local representatives of British settler interests, the Halses, used their influence with officialdom to secure the right to set up a district town on their farm Waterfall in 1848. They were to sell *erven* at the proposed site to their own profit, over and above £500 due to the government for the building of a church.[67] In other ways too, they took steps to ensure that they benefited from the establishment of the town. All this was typical of the kinds of speculative advantage available to such men, and of the close relation between official patronage and profit.

But warnings were soon sounded about the suitability of the site. Frederick Rex reported that he had been told in Colesberg that 'Waterfall is so badly watered, that it could not have been chosen had not some deception been used'. The auction of plots by the Halses was a failure. When William Robertson, Dutch Reformed minister from Swellendam, passed through the district, he soon realised the reason for this: 'The money-making spirit of the proprietors of the farm where it was proposed to establish Smithfield was so evident that it seemed to us to have entirely defeated its object. Some of the leading men expressed to us their anxious desire to purchase another farm [for the site of a town].' Robertson added that the Halses seemed 'much disliked'. In the end the Halses' farm was reluctantly abandoned by the magistrate.[68]

This circumstance of disputed authority over the land revealed clearly the ambiguities of political identity and allegiance in the district. For it soon emerged that the British-appointed commandant for the district, J. T. Snyman, representing the informally elected church wardens, had approached Moshoeshoe through J. P. Hoffman with a request to grant Snyman and his colleagues the farm Rietpoort further up the Caledon as a 'church place', thereby recognising the chief's rights to the land as primary. The chief gladly granted the land for this purpose 'in peace and affection', gratified that his authority over the land was still recognised, despite the pretensions of the British. When the government surveyor Rex surveyed the site without consulting the church wardens, Snyman complained, and was further outraged when the British magistrate set about selling the *erven* to the government's account. On the day of the sale in November 1849, field cornet Van der Walt, one of the church wardens, rode to Rietpoort and declared before the assembled crowd that the farm had been granted by Moshoeshoe to the wardens as a church place, and the British Resident had no right to interfere. He called on the Boers not to buy *erven*. Although in the event forty *erven* were sold, most buyers were speculators rather than local burghers.[69]

The actions of Snyman and his colleagues were regarded as highly irregular by the British authorities. At that very time Warden was putting pressure on Moshoeshoe to accept his border delimitation. There was no doubt that according to that massive annexation of territory, Moshoeshoe had no authority whatever over the farm Rietpoort. Commandant Snyman was 'severely reprimanded' for his actions and, according to Vowe, took 'grievous offence' in consequence. In June 1851 he was replaced as district commandant.[70] Having broken his earlier ties with the emigrant *maatschappy* some years before, Snyman had subsequently acted as the local agent of the British Resident in the lower Caledon region; but when confronted with the reality of imperial expansionism he discovered that Moshoeshoe's patronage was more attractive than that of the British. Like many Boer notables in the eastern Cape before him, he soon became disillusioned with the realities of British power. And he was to become even more disillusioned as imperial power on the frontier became increasingly intrusive and aggressive towards the Sotho.

❖

Exasperated by the pressures on him, Warden began to plan a military campaign against Moshoeshoe during 1850. After conflict had broken out between the Sotho and the Rolong of Thaba Nchu, he wrote to the paramount in October with a hint of false bravado: 'Depend upon it, Chief Moshesh, that however strong you may imagine yourself to be, there is a stronger hand ready and able to punish the wicked doings of a people ten times more powerful than the Basutos.' Warden estimated in a letter to the governor that the allied chiefs, including Griqua and Kora living at a distance, could provide a force of some two thousand, and a burgher commando of perhaps three hundred could be raised. But, he added, 'the Natives unless supported by a Military force somewhat larger than the one we have at Bloemfontein would not act with that confidence of success against the Great Chief they otherwise would do.'[71]

However, the high commissioner had even less leeway to consider requests for military assistance than the previous year. For by the time Warden's request was made in November 1850, yet another frontier war had erupted in the eastern Cape, a war that would finally discredit Smith's regime and all it stood for. Nonetheless, Warden continued to press his ultimatums against Moshoeshoe. These were made with the full support of Smith, who had determined on a dramatic show of force using the league of allied chiefs, but in the knowledge that if it came to open war in the broken country of the Caledon River valley, Warden's force was inadequate to deliver a decisive blow against the Sotho, and indeed ran the risk of being humiliated.[72]

All the same, Smith and Warden hoped that a show of force would be sufficient to make Moshoeshoe and his subordinate chiefs and allies appreciate the seriousness of imperial intentions, and in this way avoid a protracted campaign. It was an overly sanguine expectation. But Warden had little choice: the most vociferous supporters and beneficiaries of British imperialism were clamouring for war.[73] Economic confidence, on which immigration, investment, the value of property and speculative prospects were all founded, was at a low ebb and unlikely to revive and flourish in prevailing conditions. The whole future of the Sovereignty was at stake, for there was little enthusiasm in London for this new territorial encumbrance; and no one could be in any doubt that should it threaten to impose endless demands on imperial military resources, the tolerance of the politicians would be quickly exhausted.

The shaky platform on which the entire expansionist policy of Smith and the settler elite was built quickly revealed its structural faults. In the Sovereignty as in the Cape, the mass of the colonists again proved reluctant to provide military support for the exercise of imperial power. On 9 June 1851 Warden reported that the field cornets had been unable to induce more than thirty ordinary burghers to report for military service. Moreover, Adam Kok's Griqua were slow in joining his force, unsure whether their antagonism towards Moshoeshoe was greater than their antagonism towards the British administration.[74]

In attempting to flex its muscles, Warden's force suffered a bloody nose at the Battle of Viervoet in early July. He retreated to Thaba Nchu, conceding that it was impossible to take on the combined forces at Moshoeshoe's disposal (estimated at 10 000 men) without the aid of a strong burgher commando.[75] He then fell back on a combination of threats and inducements to get the Boers to obey the call to arms. In circular letters reminiscent of Pottinger's inducements in the eastern Cape in 1847, he promised the Boers one-third of all captured livestock; and he warned them that they would forfeit their farms (which they held on condition of military service) if they disobeyed his summons again.[76]

Significantly, Warden fell back on racial rhetoric. He urged the necessity of 'putting down the common enemy of the white man'. He declared that 'the year 1851 must decide the mastery between the white and coloured race, both here and in the colony'. But this revealing appeal to racial sentiment and racial fears, stripped of the philanthropic rhetoric which had until recently characterised official relations with Moshoeshoe, fell on deaf ears. It did not have the same resonance for the Boers as it might have had at a later date. To the Boers of the 1850s, the world did not present itself in stark racial terms. In the ensuing weeks, even those who had accompanied Warden to Viervoet deserted his cause.[77]

For his part, Smith, with his attention focused on pacifying the Xhosa and the coloured rebels in the Cape, was content for the time being to warn Warden to 'risk nothing that is not founded on every prospect of success', for partial success would be inadequate, and 'failure would be attended with disastrous results'. In the meantime, Warden was to stockpile provisions in Bloemfontein for 1500 men and 500 horses which Smith hoped to be able to dispatch once the reinforcements he was expecting had arrived from Britain.[78] The Resident could do little but await developments, his authority and that of his administration effectively destroyed. In the event, the high commissioner's resolve to march an army across the Orange came to nothing by the time he was replaced in ignominy the following year. For what he did not yet realise was that the destabilisation of frontiers of settlement – the necessary consequence of his policies – had now drained the patience of his superiors in London. To those who made policy in London, the interests of those forces in colonial society which he represented and served were interests of very marginal importance.

Once aroused by British aggression, disaffection among the Boers grew to crisis proportions. Magistrate Vowe in Smithfield reported in mid-July 1851 that the Sotho were in constant communication with the disaffected Boers of the district, who his Mfengu informants had told him were more numerous than previously realised. Some were acting as spies for the Sotho, keeping Moshoeshoe and his allies informed of which burghers were expressing their loyalty to the British. In August Vowe reported that many Boers in his district had expressed their conviction that Moshoeshoe was still their friend, 'and why should they not visit and trade with him, instead of being compelled to go to war with him?' The underlying economic relations between African chiefdoms and Boer pastoralists continued in this way to assert themselves. Indeed, wagons were still plying the road from Lesotho to Burghersdorp across the Orange River, bearing merchandise northwards and bringing grain southwards to feed the markets of the Cape Colony, notwithstanding the state of war that officially existed. A trader in Moshoeshoe's territory was surprised to discover that 'while Moshoeshoe is proclaimed an enemy and war declared against him, a number of Boers are living in peace and security in the heart of the enemy's country'. When Vowe heard that the renegade ex-commandant J. T. Snyman was on his way to pay a courtesy visit to the Sotho paramount at Thaba Bosiu, the magistrate wrote in a fit of rage to Warden demanding that 'this indiscriminate communication between British subjects and these enemies … be put a stop to without delay'.[79]

Warden conceded that many Boers made no secret of the fact that 'they prefer the rule of the Chief Moshesh to that of the British Government'. The Resident was so used to the agitations and exhortations of British loyalists and imperialists that it came as something of a surprise to him to discover how apathetic, even hostile, the bulk of the burgher population was to the policy of forceful subjugation of the Sotho. He naively assumed that there had been a 'sudden change of feeling' towards the Sotho, which could only be accounted for by the correspondence disseminated by Moshoeshoe and his agents among the Boers. Warden charged that 'designing men' – among them the Hoffmans, Hans Smit and J. T. Snyman – were responsible for subverting the loyalty of the burghers in this way. Charles Halse wrote to Warden demanding that Josias Hoffman be charged with conspiring with enemies of the crown, 'from the fact of his receiving for circulation or publication amongst British subjects certain communications having a tendency … to induce them to refuse obedience to the orders of the proper authorities'.[80]

But the pro-Moshoeshoe faction in Caledon River district was not to be cowed. Gustavus Voesee, Jurie Gouws and Piet Labuschagne, delegates of the burghers of the district, made their way to Thaba Bosiu in September. There they signed a declaration in Moshoeshoe's presence 'that we have this day concluded a peace with the Great Chief Moshesh', and pledged 'that we shall not take up our weapons against him'. Magistrate Vowe conceded in October that in the field cornetcy of Koesberg particularly, closest to the heart of Moshoeshoe's power, most of the Boers were favourable to Moshoeshoe and hostile to British rule.[81]

What was particularly galling to the authorities was the considerable extent of trade in arms and ammunition being plied with the Sotho. Vowe issued instructions to the district commandant and field cornets to prevent wagons from entering Sotho territory. He declared that without a larger police force the flow of arms into Lesotho could not be checked.[82] A correspondent from Caledon River district wrote to the Bloemfontein newspaper *The Friend* in August about the scale of this trade:

as is well known, we have many disaffected farmers in the Sovereignty, many residing near the Colonial boundary (the Orange River) some of these men are (even during the present disturbed state of the country) constantly among the Bassoutas, and are carrying on a most lucrative trade in Kaffir corn, which they dispose of in Burghers Dorp – and which some of the shopkeepers of that place have no hesitation in paying for in gunpowder and lead.[83]

This correspondent quoted from a letter which he had just received from Burghersdorp, south of the Orange: 'A great number of Boers from your district have visited this place during this and the past weeks with loads of Kaffir corn, which they dispose of well, taking the chief part of their payment in powder and lead. It has been remarked that they all speak in the most friendly way of the Chief Moshesh and the Bassoutas.' Another correspondent pointed out that 'depots are actually formed at these Villages [such as Burghersdorp], from which the enemy is (perhaps indirectly) continually supplied with a sufficiency of ammunition to enable him to protract the war to an indefinite period – if not directly sold to the Kaffir, it is to the white man and by him to the Bassouta.'[84]

Hoffman, who traded on a larger scale with the Sotho paramount than perhaps anyone else, called meetings near Koesberg right on the borders of Lesotho, at which his supporters cheered his denunciation of British policy towards the Sotho. A meeting of some 120 Boers on 24 September 1851 chaired by Hoffman passed resolutions ascribing the 'pitiable state' of the Sovereignty to British policies of aggression towards the chiefdoms, including the enforcement of Warden's boundary line on Moshoeshoe in 1849 'against the wishes and interests of his people' – a very significant resolution in view of the fact that most of the burghers present at the meeting lived on land which had been regarded by all parties as under Moshoeshoe's authority prior to the paper annexations of 1849. Another resolution warned that if the burghers were to be forced to perform military service against Moshoeshoe, 'the greatest part of the white population will abandon the Sovereignty'. Hoffman and Snyman were deputed to draw up a memorial to the high commissioner incorporating the resolutions passed at the meeting.[85]

But the crisis of legitimacy into which the British administration was plunged took on more ominous forms than the rhetoric of public meetings. In the Winburg district to the north of Bloemfontein, loyalist burghers were subjected to a systematic campaign of plunder by a commando of Moshoeshoe's and Moletsane's men. The discrimination with which these thefts took place suggests a carefully plotted war of nerves aimed at political allies of the British administration among the Boers of the district. 'The frontier is now in the hands of Kaffirs and disaffected Boers,' wrote magistrate Biddulph from Winburg at the end of July. 'Only those who went on commando [against Moshoeshoe] are singled out for plunder – not one of the disaffected has lost a horse. The loyal inhabitants will soon have to seek refuge under the strongest party – there is not a night they are not robbed.'[86] Biddulph conceded that prior to the Viervoet battle of 30 June, depredations by Africans on the border farmers were unknown. 'We have frequently heard some of the most respectable Dutch farmers assert', wrote the editor of *The Friend*, 'that they have lived in this country for fourteen years, and had never met with any losses from robberies by the Natives previously to our late interference.'[87]

By October, according to a petition of 64 loyalists, all the British officeholders in the district had been 'obliged to fly from their homes, and are now wandering about with their families, and the remnant of their flocks'. The 'few loyal and faithful subjects' were surrounded by enemies, wrote G. H. Meyer, and all they had left were their lives. 'The great bulk of the people are against government, and with the Kaffirs,' wrote field cornet J. Fick; 'I am despised, reproached, and defied continually.' A correspondent wrote to *The Friend* that

> The bitterest part of all to the feelings of the sufferers, is the knowledge that the natives have been incited to these acts of plunder … by those Boers who are disaffected to the British Government, and who have adopted this step to embarrass the Government, and ruin those of their countrymen who have evinced their loyalty by obeying orders … With the exception of these few, all the farmers of the district are now opposed to the British Government.[88]

'The passive resistance of the majority has succeeded,' wrote Biddulph; 'they hold constant traitorous discourse with the Kaffir chiefs' and 'have headed marauding bands of Kaffir thieves into the immediate neighbourhood of Winburg'.[89]

Those now determined to expel the British from Transorangia directed appeals to the burghers of the Transvaal to come to their aid. At a meeting on 25 August, 139 Boers signed a memorial to Andries Pretorius, urging him to intervene with a force from north of the Vaal River. However, Pretorius had other priorities in mind. He saw the possibilities of exploiting the crisis in the Sovereignty in order to win formal imperial recognition of Transvaal independence. Hostility against the British was always difficult to sustain beyond the reach of British authority. The Potchefstroom *krygsraad*, or council of war, refused to sanction any military adventurism south of the Vaal – especially as the Boer economy in the Potchefstroom hinterland was now increasingly being built around linkages with the colonial economy further south and with the credit and mercantile networks reaching out from colonial ports.[90]

Meanwhile, the supporters of imperial advance kept up their agitations for a greater military commitment by the British government. 'Little wars have been the curse of the country,' propounded an editorial in *The Friend*, 'and will continue so long as turbulent natives and disaffected settlers [i.e. Boers] remain of the opinion that they will continue to be met with the same *little* military force and stinted resources.' The conventional wisdom in London that settlers should provide for their own defence was met on the frontiers of British settlement in southern Africa with the cry of 'penny wise, pound foolish'. A *permanent* reduction of expenditure in the colonies, it was asserted by such settler interests, depended on indelibly impressing the natives with a sense of imperial power and strength, and once and for all depriving them of the means of resistance. Unless imperial troops were committed to the Sovereignty in considerably larger numbers, the Sovereignty would slide further and further into crisis, and fail to attract the settlers, capital and entrepreneurial skills required for economic progress. Once such economic progress had been set in train, it was argued, the need for imperial expenditure would wither away.[91] But by the end of 1851 such arguments, as well as the Smith governorship, were thoroughly discredited.

The crisis of 1851 sealed the fate of the Orange River Sovereignty, for it finally confirmed the suspicions in London that Sir Harry Smith's expansionist policies were foolhardy and dangerous. The colonial secretary, Earl Grey, upon hearing news of the débâcle at Viervoet and the humiliation of Warden's force, presaged on 15 September the dissolution of the Sovereignty. In a dispatch that must have come as a devastating blow to Smith's pride, he reminded the high commissioner that the annexation had been sanctioned in 1848 on the understanding that the inhabitants overwhelmingly supported the extension of British dominion, and on condition that the whole cost of administration of the new territory (including military expenses) was to be met by those for whose benefit the annexation had supposedly been undertaken – the burghers. 'If the inhabitants will not support that authority, but on the contrary desire to be relieved from it, there is no British interest to be served by endeavouring to maintain it, and the sooner the force now there can be withdrawn the better.' British authority was to be withdrawn as soon as this could be accomplished 'with safety and honour' – meaning that the 'superiority of British arms' had first to be demonstrated in order to dispel any appearance of weakness in retreat, and that the interests of British allies north of the Orange had first to be secured.[92]

The first step in the process of withdrawal was the recognition of the independence of the Transvaal Boers, and the formal renunciation by the British authorities of their claims to the emigrants' allegiance as subjects. This was achieved at a meeting between representatives of the high commissioner and those of the Potchefstroom Raad on the Sand River in January 1852. Thus did the mass emigration of disaffected Boers from the 1830s receive, for the first time, the official blessing of the British as a *fait accompli*. But the Sand River Convention went further: all British alliances with black chiefs were forsworn, and the Boers were granted a monopoly of the supply of arms and ammunition bound for the Transvaal from colonial ports. In all this, the Convention provided a model for the terms under which independence was to be granted to the Sovereignty burghers two years later.[93]

North of the Vaal a new ruling class was emerging as Boers re-established their productive and trading enterprises after the long years of trekking. In the 1840s the emigrant town of Potchefstroom hardly existed as a centre of permanent settlement. By the mid-1850s, however, it was a modest commercial entrepôt, firmly linked to the trading networks spreading out from the British ports, and through it passed much ivory from further north.[94] The rising Boer elite of the southwestern Transvaal, many of whom had resisted imperial advance under arms a few years earlier, were by the early 1850s ready to take their place as forward representatives of colonial capitalism, eager to establish their own stable institutions of government, to regularise their relations with the imperial power, and to convince the British of their friendship.[95] In bilateral recognition of these realities, the Sand River Convention was signed in 1852. By the 1850s the emigrant Boers were being reintegrated into the colonial economy – on their own terms.[96]

But withdrawing British sovereignty from the territory between the Orange and Vaal rivers with due regard for Grey's strictures about 'safety and honour' proved much more difficult and complicated than the initial annexation had been. It was delayed in part by changes of government in Britain. But once Smith's regime at the Cape had been replaced, abandonment was only a matter of time. The new high commissioner, Cathcart, decided that first of all a short military display against Moshoeshoe was essential to restore British prestige in the quagmire north of the Orange River. The military adventure into the interior by 2400 regular troops late in 1852 was undertaken in the knowledge that continued British rule in Transorangia was counterproductive and profitless, but that first a final assertion of British will and power was necessary. The purpose was not to wage war against the chiefdoms, but merely to salvage some honour from the mess created by the discredited policy of aggression and dispossession which the previous British administration had pursued.[97]

Having elicited from Moshoeshoe a face-saving avowal of subservience to the paramount power, Cathcart's force withdrew. *The Friend* declared the campaign an impotent failure; the supremacy of British arms had manifestly not been asserted. The enemy should have been 'thrashed', the newspaper declared, and their cattle wealth confiscated.[98] The loyalists of Smithfield and the Caledon River district to the south, with the Halses in the lead, were predictably enraged at this conclusive evidence of the failure of imperial will to establish British hegemony in the subcontinent. Land prices had tumbled as a result, they wrote in a petition, and the morale of the British settlers had slumped dramatically, more particularly in view of the imminent departure of Cathcart's troops so soon after they had arrived.[99]

The high commissioner's unrepentant response was that he had not entered Sotho country with the intention of making war on them. He pointedly observed that some persons were apparently 'disappointed that I did not ... "eat up" and destroy the Chief Moshesh, in order that his rich lands might fall into other hands'. Some appeared 'to have anticipated, with no disinclination, a protracted Basuto War, requiring probably the expenditure of a large amount of British money for its maintenance'. Cathcart dismissed the imperialists in the Sovereignty as 'almost all land jobbers, possessed of title to numerous farms which they hold unoccupied with a view to profitable speculation', whose 'covetous and rapacious spirit' had been largely responsible for the destabilisation of the region.[100]

Sir George Clerk was dispatched as special commissioner to effect the disannexation. He eventually arrived in Bloemfontein in August 1853. His task, quite crucially, was to forge an independent successor state that could be relied upon to carry on the imperial task without threatening a continual drain on the imperial exchequer. He was met with a furious, sustained barrage of propaganda from the empire loyalists, determined to obstruct this act of betrayal. Like the Ulstermen of a later date, they threatened rebellion against the British authorities in order to secure continued British rule over them. Petitions and letters to the colonial press predicted the direst consequences should British sovereignty be withdrawn.[101]

But Clerk was not to be diverted from his task, which was in his own words 'to withdraw, if possible in a friendly manner, if not, to withdraw anyhow'.[102] He called a meeting of delegates from each field cornetcy with a view to drawing up a constitution for the independent state. But the loyalists succeeded in ensuring that their views predominated when the 95 delegates (who were not directly elected but indirectly nominated by the British-appointed local officials) met in Bloemfontein in September 1853. Confronted with their uncooperative attitude, Clerk simply set about finding other more amenable collaborators, undeterred by the furious objections of the loyalist delegates. This did not prove to be easy. In fact there was no great rush by burghers to take advantage of the special commissioner's determination to hand over the reins of government to anyone who would deal with him.[103]

But gradually an independence movement coalesced around a few men of diverse origin and political persuasion, some of them (like A. H. Stander) old *maatschappy* rebels, others (like J. P. Hoffman and J. T. Snyman) members of the old pro-Moshoeshoe alliance, and even some British officials like P. M. Bester, who had served as magistrate in the far-northern Vaal River district. Prominent in the movement were aliens such as A. Coqui, the Jewish trader from Harrismith, J. Groenendaal, an immigrant Dutch teacher, and J. Schnehage, a German storekeeper in Winburg. Stander in particular assiduously presented a memorial at public meetings through the country, offering to take over the government on easy terms. What is clear is that the strong anti-imperial instincts of the great bulk of the burgher population, who had plunged the Sovereignty into crisis and persuaded the British to withdraw their rule, did not translate readily into a self-conscious republicanism or sense of national identity. Nevertheless, at a meeting in February 1854 attended by 27 representatives of the independence movement, the Bloemfontein Convention was drawn up and signed, despite the efforts of the townsfolk to disrupt the proceedings. The Orange Free State Republic was now ready to be born, with an elaborate, racially exclusive constitution based very loosely on that of the United States of America.[104]

Meanwhile, Henry Halse and a group of his colleagues in Caledon River district announced to the world in January, amid much publicity in the colonial newspapers, that a fabulous gold reef had been discovered not far from the town of Smithfield and that a mining company was being floated – hoping no doubt to abort the abandonment by provoking a surge of speculative fever north of the Orange River. Clerk coolly responded that 'the inhabitants of Smithfield would find it more advantageous to their interests' to accept the inevitable, than 'to cling to hopes which cannot be realised'. As a desperate last resort, the Smithfield imperialists set up a 'committee of safety' in March, committed to defying the authority of the new republican regime.[105]

But men like Henry Halse were too aware of where their interests lay to resist the inevitable for ever. By April, Halse had been elected to the new Volksraad as member for the town of Smithfield. There he and other representatives of urban bourgeois and large landowning interests (Boer and British) played an influential role from the start. At a local level, British settlers accepted magisterial posts – such as J. Orpen in Winburg.[106] Indeed, independence did not imply the overturning of the existing social and economic order. The state continued to be dominated at local level by the elite interests that had arisen with the intensification and spread of settler capitalism particularly in the years of British rule. The difference was that the state now enjoyed a legitimacy that the imperial administration had never had; and it promoted and represented a far larger range of rising local Boer elites than the rather narrow clique of imperialists, concentrated in the south, and government employees whom the Sovereignty had primarily served.

The *maatschappy* radicals such as Stander soon understood these realities. The rise of a colonial state as an extension of imperial hegemony (albeit, from 1854, republican in form) was not what they had in mind. By September 1854 a flood of petitions had reached the Volksraad demanding the dismantling of the state and unification with the Transvaal Boers. Many of the petitions demanded that only members of the Dutch Reformed Church could be members of the Raad or hold public office, so as to subvert the continued influence of British settler interests. Some questioned the need for a state president and a professional civil service. Stander himself held meetings north of Winburg in October, campaigning for the replacement of the president by an unpaid commandant-general in the minimalist political tradition of the *maatschappy*.[107] The Orange Free State Republic was in large degree the vehicle of an informal, if often insecure, imperial hegemony in southern Africa, which outlasted the phase of formal imperial expansionism. And the mass of poorer emigrant Boers of the highveld continued to resist the rise of local ruling elites from among their ranks, and the elaboration of local state structures.

Settler imperialism had failed in its immediate objectives, not least because imperial expansion evoked massive resistance from both Boers and black peoples. Policies of aggression and dispossession aimed at independent chiefdoms evoked in fact, not support, but rebelliousness and sedition from the Boers on the frontiers of settlement, and contributed to a crippling crisis of legitimacy for the colonial government. Most of the Boers saw no reason to throw in their lot with British imperialism against black chiefdoms, and many of them, including those who lived closest to the centre of Sotho power, openly chose the patronage of Moshoeshoe rather than that of the British. For their part, the Sotho learned that an apparently benign imperial power, located at a distance and clothed in philanthropic garb, was very different from a predatory imperial power encamped at the very threshold of Lesotho. The imperial factor, as represented by the humanitarian lobby, proved in the event to be an illusion, behind which lurked a far more sinister force.

It was the misfortune of the settler imperialists that their influence in the making of policy at the Cape was at its height at precisely the time that the purse-strings in London were being tightened, and politicians were becoming determined to displace financial and military responsibilities on to local colonists. Tolerance for imperial aggrandisers and military adventurers on distant frontiers was at a low ebb. Despite the implicit promise of Smith's rogue regime at the Cape, the truth was that the British were no longer prepared to pay for the processes of accumulation and dispossession that were enriching the rising settler elite on the frontiers of settlement. Smith's successors at the Cape as well as the officials and politicians in London could differentiate more clearly between Britain's essential and her peripheral interests. Her essential interests could be maintained much more effectively through free trade and local self-rule than through the militarisation of colonial society that had been the necessary consequence of policies pursued since the late 1840s. Only peripheral interests were served by Smith's policies of territorial advance and subjugation. In fact, British withdrawal made little practical difference to the value of land, the profitability of the interior trading networks, and the well-being of the sheep farms and towns of the former Sovereignty – dire predictions of chaos and ruin notwithstanding. Further commercial and productive development did not require the maintenance of British authority.

Although in terms of its own programme Smith's governorship was an abject failure, in other respects he did leave a lasting legacy in shifting the essential supports of British power in the subcontinent. Indeed, Smith's governorship represented a watershed of lasting significance. This decisive moment was not marked by British abandonment of humanitarian responsibilities, as the earlier orthodoxy suggested, for the purposes of imperial policy did not change radically. Rather, it lay in the nature of the means by which the British exerted their influence. Ironically, the annexation of Transorangia had created the conditions for securing British interests without an ongoing accumulation of military commitments and territorial encumbrances. In this perspective, the temporary extension of formal sovereignty was a necessary step in the creation of a state system through which British interests in the region could be secured. A new, white, collaborating class with the requisite institutional muscle and economic resources emerged out of the Boer diaspora, much more suited to imperial purposes in the subcontinent than the indigenous authorities (such as Moshoeshoe and the Griqua captains) on whom the British had previously pinned their trust as allies. Contrary to conventional wisdom, the creation of the Boer republic was manifestly not a return to the *status quo* before imperial intrusion. Rather, it was made possible by the settler capitalism that was spreading most rapidly into the further interior from the late 1840s on the back of an advancing imperialism.

In the 1850s and 1860s republican policy towards the Sotho became increasingly militaristic. The policies of dispossession and subjugation against Moshoeshoe's people which the republican state pursued had first been initiated by the British under the Sovereignty administration. Indeed, in earlier years they had been much more characteristic of British settler imperialists than of the Boer emigrants. These continuities between British and Boer administrations and the interests they represented are striking. In Caledon River district, for example, the local notables of the 1850s and 1860s (such as H. Joubert and J. Klopper) – large landowners and speculators, wealthy sheep farmers, office-holders, and leaders of the war party – tended to be the same men who had most strongly allied themselves with the British administration's imperialist policies in the period of British rule.[108]

The Boer republicanism that emerged in the 1850s was also different from the *maatschappy* tradition of the earlier 'Great Trek' period. Then, the minimalist, part-time, *ad hoc* political institutions of the *maatschappy* were a product of relative classlessness, of the egalitarian democracy of the mobile and the impoverished. When emigrant communities were still unstable, unsettled and unstratified in the aftermath of the levelling experience of the emigration from the Cape, there was little need or inclination to submit to the rule of government. Government only emerged as and when the process of accumulation from economic and military enterprise threw up a stratum of local notables, who in turn required the protection and the patronage of stable, permanent political institutions. Until then, emigrant political life remained atomised and fissiparous. These factors explain the lethargy that confronted George Clerk when he tried to set up an independent republican government in the Sovereignty. As far as the mass of poorer Boers were concerned, political leadership served an essentially part-time military function. They had no time for rulers, and even declined to sanction the appointment of a permanent commandant-general in the territory.

In part, the struggle within Boer society was between different economic systems, and in part between different classes in an emergent rural society. The more radical of the Boer emigrants, who resisted the entrenchment of bureaucratic government, sought a more egalitarian, atomised and self-sufficient economic system, and one incidentally that posed far less of a threat to the security of black peoples. But theirs was a forlorn cause. For as long as there were opportunities for individuals to profit by closer integration into the larger colonial economy, the processes of state formation and the emergence of local elites were unavoidable developments in the long term.

The earlier anti-statist tradition continued to be manifested in a sort of rural populism among the mass of poorer Boers, always well represented in the Volksraad but always well insulated from the levers of power at a local level in the republican state. This populism of the propertyless revealed itself in a number of ways. Illicit ties with the Sotho and other African peoples (including large-scale gun-running) continued throughout the republican period. There was continual resistance to the accumulative drive of the notables in the districts. And finally, widespread resistance was offered to military service at the behest of the state, which would be evident even in the Anglo-Boer War at the end of the century.[109]

CHAPTER NINE

Conclusion:
The Stabilisation of Contradictions

In a European-dominated world in which race came to permeate the social orders established by colonial regimes, it is superfluous to argue about the origins of the South African racial order. Racial hierarchies were present from the beginnings of settlement at the Cape. European colonisers brought with them stereotypes and prejudices which did not amount to a racial ideology so much as an inherent ethnocentrism. These were activated into a social system of racial hierarchy by the struggle for control of resources against native peoples, and by the labour systems, based on coercion, on which the colonisers came to depend.[1] In the Dutch period, a hierarchy of legal status groups – free burghers, slaves and Khoi – laid the basis for a racial order which in its fundamentals was unaffected by the jettisoning of the legal foundations of inequality in the 1820s and 1830s.

However, structures of domination and subordination passed through different phases, and the essential forces propelling them changed over time. As for the early colonisers' struggle for the land and control over the destinies of the Khoisan who lived on it, this was propelled by the dictates of cultural survival as much as by any prospect of profit, which was remote indeed on pastoral frontiers. With the integration of the Cape into the British empire of free trade, new economic opportunities arose and new settler classes arrived with different entrepreneurial expectations and different resources at their disposal. New possibilities thus emerged for extending the reach of the colonial domain and, ultimately, the exercise of racial domination, beyond the Khoisan frontier into the very different realm of the mixed-farming African peoples of the colonial hinterland.

In the 1820s the British authorities began the liberal reform of the colonial economy and society at the Cape, seeking to remove obstacles to free enterprise and free trade, and to dismantle archaic legal and economic structures based on monopoly and patronage. A mercantile–humanitarian alliance coalesced for a brief period, agreed on the need to open labour markets and abolish the unprofitable slave economy which seemed to have become an incubus. In the process Afrikaner slave-owners and beneficiaries of previous authority structures were greatly alienated, in Cape Town as well as in the eastern districts of the colony. But the alliance between mercantile and humanitarian interests, based on visions of a society built on free contract rather than on hierarchies of legal status, rights and privileges, proved short-lived and partial. Merchants quickly perceived new possibilities for prosperity growing out of a developing colonial capitalism, which from the start was built on racial exploitation, albeit without the explicit legal foundations of older bound-labour systems.[2] Indeed the humanitarian vision of a society in which indigenous peoples were free of oppression was always a pipedream in a colony in which a substantial white population had already established itself as a dominant class, with control over resources of land and dispossessed labour. A new configuration of forces came into being, inimical to the humanitarian ideal of a thriving and independent peasant–artisan economy.

Partly as a result of the arrival of compensation money for the ex-slave-owners and their creditors and agents after emancipation, a new class of urban business people developed in Cape Town, typically involved in commerce, the professions, in company formation and in urban property ownership. Both Afrikaans- and English-speaking, they soon established a power base in the new municipality. Cape Town capital flowed eastwards to fund wool farming in districts being depopulated in some degree by the mass emigration of dis-gruntled Boers. The dominant landed classes in the pastoral districts were now in large measure British settlers who had been arriving in the eastern Cape from 1820 onwards, infused with acquisitive and entrepreneurial values seek-ing an outlet. As economic opportunities blossomed, hostilities between Afrikaans- and English-speaking colonists faded, and the newly emergent class-es set about challenging the narrow oligarchy that ruled the colony. The battles of mid-century between the 'popular' party and the conservatives were not about the rights and privileges of coloured or African peoples. If men like Fairbairn or Stockenström took issue with military adventures on distant fron-tiers, it was because they were conducted at the behest and to the benefit of a settler elite which had chosen the side of gubernatorial autocracy at the expense of the larger project of sustainable economic development. For though more immediate sources of speculative profit beckoned, in railways or mining for instance, these required access to capital markets, access that was being obstructed by the archaic nature of the political system. The fact is that the rights of coloureds and Africans within and without colonial borders had ceased to be an issue. These realities were reflected in the Cape constitution of 1853, for its major purpose was to maximise the political incorporation of white men. That some men of colour were incorporated at the same time was secondary.

The story told here is replete with irony. It is ironic that the triumph of lib-eral economic and social values in the nineteenth-century European world should have coincided with the intensification and spread of race consciousness and theories of racial supremacy. The humanitarians' propaganda and assump-tions were so unrealistic – indeed, so fraught with cultural absolutism and coercive impulses – that their project was bound to fail, and the failure of free-labour regimes to fulfil humanitarian prescriptions was in turn bound to pro-voke a post-emancipation backlash among dominant classes. The result was the spread of racist assumptions, not only in surviving slave societies such as the American South, but also in the British metropole.[3] At the Cape, slave emancipation brought in its wake not liberty and opportunity, but different means of control and subjugation, means less reliant on paternalism and family incorporation, and more reliant on the impersonal authority of the state. As for the Khoi, their freeing from legal thraldom went hand in hand with their further impoverishment and the closing off of any alternatives for them to servility.[4]

The contradictions of the humanitarian cause were implicit from the beginning. The missionary ideal propagated by John Philip was a radical one in the context of the time, and in terms of its logical consequence of a colour-blind society in which there was potentially no limit to the aspirations of civilised natives. But Philip was hardly a radical, much less so than Van der Kemp or Read. He, and others like him, represented the domestication of missionary humanitarianism in respectable metropolitan society, and this severely restricted their vision. For mainstream humanitarians, like all of their class at the time, were explicitly class conscious: even though they expressed little overt racial antipathy, the strong sense of class hierarchy which infused their thinking tended to have similar consequences. For seldom could respectable Europeans of the age envisage non-Europeans aspiring to their class status. The great age of European racism and conquest in the late nineteenth-century was in some degree made possible by the failings and the limitations of early-nineteenth-century liberalism.

The missionary cause, originally so convinced of the malleability of the human material at its disposal, and of Africans' receptivity to the cultural norms of the mission, became quite quickly suffused with notions of the innate inferiority of Africans once the initial flush of humanitarian enthusiasm had worn off. The initial belief that environment determined the 'backwardness' of natives gave way to a belief in innate racial difference. Whereas the principle of egalitarianism in mission communities, derived from the Congregationalist principles of Scottish evangelicalism, was implicit in the first generation of missionaries, by the 1840s it had faded when men like Moffat rose to influence, and was never translated into a commitment to democracy. When Christian converts at the stations were small and unsettled communities, egalitarian ideals were easy to maintain, but they lost their attraction as Christianity spread among the colonial working class. Subjected to paternalism, which shaded into explicit racial stereotyping, those Khoi and ex-slaves who had most eagerly embraced mission Christianity were steadily compromised and marginalised. At the same time the attractions of 'Hottentot' or 'coloured' nationalism, even armed resistance, increased, culminating in rebellion in the original heartland of mission enterprise, the eastern Cape, by mid-century.

The obverse of the ideal of Christian egalitarianism was the exclusion of outsiders from the embrace of civilised rights. This might mean exclusion of those who were not church members at Kat River or in the Griqua communities, but most clearly it meant the exclusion of the great mass of the African peoples, Nguni and Sotho–Tswana, who were still largely on the margins of or outside colonial society in the first half of the nineteenth century. It was far easier for men like Philip to envisage a colonial Christian society embracing white and Khoi or Griqua. But African peoples were culturally and economically more cohesive and thus more alien, and would not easily fit into the mould of 'Christian civilisation' on the terms of the missionaries. The humanitarian vision simply did not anticipate either the incorporation of such numbers of people as might displace their European missionary mentors, or the incorporation of people with cultures and political allegiances other than those of the colonisers, or indeed the incorporation of anyone on any other basis (initially at least) than as part of a dependent class.

Although humanitarians had to work under the auspices of indigenous political authorities beyond the borders of the Cape Colony, they never fully accepted their legitimacy, for that would have challenged their preconceptions. Thus the Griqua were presented, falsely, as the creatures of the mission, which in Philip's formulation took on the trappings almost of a territorial power operating through its Griqua surrogates. Upon conversion Africans beyond the frontier were required to submit entirely to the authority of the mission and its Griqua and coloured agents. Only once they had been transformed in the cultural image of the mission itself, and delivered from all trace of the political and social order from which they had come, could they aspire to equality. In this, ironically, humanitarianism merely rendered these independent peoples more vulnerable to conquest by other colonial forces and, in the case of the Griqua, to dispossession and dispersal.[5] In the end, mission imperialism was not so very different in its effects from the imperialism of the settlers. Indeed, Philip agitated for the extension of British rule further and further into the subcontinent, although his notion of British rule as a protective blanket under which the evangelical task could proceed unhindered was based on a misconception of what in reality was likely to drive imperial expansion in these years.

The decline of humanitarian idealism after the victory of the anti-slavery cause did not mean that the language of evangelical Christianity was subverted, but it was turned to more utilitarian purposes. Repressive laws were justified in terms of the need to inculcate responsibility, obedience and a work ethic.[6] Moreover, the conquest and subjugation of Africans was undertaken in the cause of Christian civilisation. In terms of his civilising policy, Governor Sir George Grey can be regarded as a champion of liberal values. The assimilationist ideals which he espoused in the 1850s, based on dismantling the rule of chiefs and expanding mission schooling, have been regarded as a high point of liberal administration at the Cape.[7] And yet to the Xhosa these were years of despair, when their independence was lost, their culture was subverted, and they were reduced in the main to a state of dependence on colonial labour markets. Here we confront the limitations of the liberal cause, whether in its earlier humanitarian guise or in its later official guise. It required that native peoples abandon not only their independence and their political systems, but all aspects of their social and cultural lives that did not accord with the liberals' definition of civilised standards and values, and that they submit to the tolerant paternalism of white patrons. The promise implicitly held out that they would eventually reach a state of equality with whites was remote and contingent, and was ultimately overwhelmed.

From the early 1830s colonial forces antagonistic to humanitarianism were promoting an agenda which in the final analysis tended towards the same goal of assimilating Africans at the bottom levels of colonial society. On the frontiers of settlement an English-speaking settler elite arose, with its base initially in the Albany district and centred on Graham's Town. For them, territorial acquisition and conquest were directly concerned with speculative profit and capital accumulation. This elite revolutionised commercial enterprise on the frontiers of settlement, accumulated land and stocked it with merino sheep, and called vociferously for military advance requiring generous outlays of imperial funds. They had access to political influence within the colony, and were on occasion able to enlist in their cause rogue governors susceptible to dreams of military glory despite Colonial Office strictures on the need for economy. In their view, neighbouring African societies had to be subjugated and dismantled, and Africans reduced to a state of subservience in the interests of economic progress.

Men with Albany roots were to be found on new frontiers of settlement in the subcontinent – in Natal in the 1830s and 1840s, and north of the Orange from the late 1840s – where the commercial, speculative and productive forces they represented proved to be powerful magnets, drawing imperial power after them. In particular, during the half-dozen years of Smith's governorship at mid-century, more spectacularly than at any other time before the mineral age, British imperial rule and British arms advanced hand in hand with settler land-grabbing, speculation and profit. The result was an unprecedented degree of destabilisation and disaffection over a wide front, involving war with African chiefdoms, coloured subjects and Boer rebels.

However, the forward march of the forces of racial subjugation and dispossession was unsustained, because the benefits were not such as to persuade the British authorities in London to underwrite the cost and provide the manpower. The settlers failed to harness the imperial state to their purposes over the longer term: their ambitions for self-aggrandisement outstripped the economic potential that could be realised. Thus the middle years of the century also saw a partial withdrawal of imperial responsibility from the subcontinent, with Britain recognising the independence of white colonists north of the Orange River, and granting representative institutions within the original colony itself.

The retreat of the early 1850s was a recognition of the fact that direct rule founded on a narrow base of settler support was costly, dangerous and unnecessary. It was also liable to manipulation by unrepresentative and opportunistic local elites that were keen on committing the imperial power to policies of military adventurism. The problem with the settler imperialists was that their interests were too narrowly based, too exclusive, too reliant on the politics of patronage and favour. That is why their goals could not be attained, no matter how much support and succour they might temporarily gain from rogue governors like D'Urban and Smith. The interests at stake were simply of insufficient weight for the British government to wish to be continually sucked into unnecessary conflict. Essential imperial interests could be upheld much more satisfactorily by broadening the base of white rule and making the colonists bear greater responsibility for maintaining the political order. Britain's intention therefore was to re-stabilise the subcontinent, and to establish a greater degree of legitimacy and consent without undermining imperial hegemony.

North of the Orange, there arose new collaborating white elites that had in essential ways been created by the prior exercise of imperial power. It now became British policy to rely on the ruling classes and political institutions emerging in the new republics to sustain the larger colonial economy. The Orange Free State Republic in particular proved to be an essential support of imperial interests for decades to come, more accountable and democratic (for whites only), and therefore more legitimate and stable, than formal imperial rule itself. British policy thus came to be firmly pinned to the mast of Boer republicanism, which in fact grew out of the social and economic forces unleashed by British territorial expansion and commercial enterprise. With the rise of new rulers more appropriate to British purposes, the Griqua, colonial pioneers in Transorangia, could be jettisoned.

When Waterboer died in 1852, his precious treaty of alliance with the colonial government died with him. Griqua statehood, so forcefully championed by Philip, became more and more an empty shell, although individual Griqua continued to pioneer trade routes far to the north in subsequent years. Griquatown, to the west of the main northward thrust of white settlement, lay in an area of little interest to white farmers. (With the opening up of the Griqualand West diamond fields in the late 1860s, however, they were quickly swallowed up in the land grab that followed.)[8] By 1861 the Philippolis Griqua under Kok, encircled and without champions any longer in colonial society, had surrendered their land to the Free State. In an epic and ultimately tragic trek across the southern Drakensberg, they moved down to the buffer zone between the southern Nguni and Natal, carving out what became known as the territory of Griqualand East, where they were to survive a while longer as a semi-independent entity. Many mission communities north of the Orange shared the same fate, finding themselves in the way of white land hunger, as had once been the case of mission communities all over the eastern Cape.[9]

From the late 1850s on, the new frontier of conquest was to be the Sotho frontier. Here Boer commandos, taking up where Warden's British-led forces had left off, eyed with greed the rich grain lands of the Caledon valley. After a series of invasions which followed much the same pattern as those against the Xhosa at an earlier date, the ageing Moshoeshoe had to admit defeat, the grain supplies which constituted the lifeblood and chief trade commodity of his kingdom having been repeatedly destroyed. He signed away vast stretches of his territory on both sides of the Caledon. But no one could doubt that this was a strategic and temporary retreat. In 1868, the high commissioner in Cape Town stepped in and annexed Lesotho, once it had been stripped of all lands to the west of the river. Compared with Smith's day, the Cape government no longer had any special interest in securing the rich resources of Moshoeshoe's territory – and certainly there was little philanthropy involved. But in its guise as keeper of the peace, Britain could not allow local conflicts to get out of hand and threaten larger conflagrations. However, at that very time, the first news was surfacing of the extent of diamond deposits to the west in the former lands of the Griqua. This would bring Britain back into the interior of southern Africa with a vengeance.[10]

In Natal the importation of immigrants and the development of cotton farming had largely fizzled out by the 1850s, and an economy based in the main on absentee landownership and native trade had developed. The British presence here was skeletal, and offered little immediate prospect for settler imperialists to profit from provoking military intervention. Having patched up a workable *modus vivendi* with the myriad small African groups living within the borders of the territory, the British were content to hang on to a possession which included a port controlling potentially important trade routes into the interior.

Unquestionably, the colonial societies emerging in the subcontinent were being built on the exercise of racial domination and exclusiveness. The Cape's commitment to non-racial legal forms was an indication that liberal ideology had become embedded in British public discourse, long after that ideology had largely lost its earlier humanitarian idealism. The exercise of racial domination within Cape colonial society took on a *laissez-faire* rather than a dogmatic character, allowing for some political participation and a degree of socio-economic interaction and race mixing among the lower orders, without threatening racial hegemony. The Cape's new political order was designed to mediate between different classes and communities, and to prevent local forces from again precipitating crises of the kind that Governor Smith's regime had presided over. At the same time, labour relations were as exploitative, and the condition of the colony's coloured labouring classes as impoverished and servile, as ever before.

Despite the modest take-off of an incipient productive capitalism after slave emancipation, the colonial economy was still weak, based on the export of a few primary products. Nor should we overestimate the capacity of the colonial state as an instrument of control and coercion. After 1853 the Legislative Assembly, representing a coalition of mercantile and farming interests, did not control the executive, which was still answerable primarily to London, and it was not always an adequate instrument in the hands of the 'popular' party, which had agitated so vociferously against gubernatorial autocracy. Although legislation to facilitate the importation and investment of capital and the establishment of businesses was passed, infrastructural improvements were slow in coming. The rural economy continued to suffer from a shortage of capital, and to rely on the service of labour tenants, 'squatters' and piece workers. Moreover, unattached communities of black people continued to cause anxiety to rural whites, who demanded, and obtained, legislation to further limit the rights of working people, such as the masters and servants law of 1856. But the modest prosperity of the 1850s, based in the main on wool farming and resurgent wine production, should not blind us to the severe limitations of colonial wealth and power.[11]

On the eastern Cape frontier, the partial disempowerment of the military and their settler hangers-on did not, however, mean peace for the Xhosa. The great millenarian cattle-killing movement among the Xhosa in 1856–7, an act of consummate despair, was the culmination not so much of decisive military defeats, but of cumulative colonial pressures which had undermined Xhosa society to the point of collapse. The disaster was then used by the Cape government to subordinate even further the cisKeian Xhosa already under colonial rule, by tightening the grip of magisterial rule over them and reducing their land reserves. Chiefs and their law were anathema to Governor Grey, the 'great civiliser', whose experience had been gained in warfare against the Maoris in New Zealand. The first governor at the Cape to have had previous experience of 'native government', he was committed to a coercive and brutal policy of assimilation based on the assumption that the optimistic and gradualist humanitarianism of an earlier age had dismally failed. He was, in short, the archetypal utilitarian liberal of his age. The incorporation of the Xhosa, conducted under Grey, involved, as under his predecessors, the dismantling of the chiefdoms and the subjugation of the people. The cattle killing provided Grey in fact with the opportunity to carry that project through more thoroughly than his predecessors could, and without resort to large military expenditures.[12]

Determined to exploit the pitiful condition of the bulk of the Xhosa population, Grey and his agents in British Kaffraria set about rooting out chiefs on the specious grounds that they had instigated the entire movement as an act of rebellion against colonial authority. Many landed up in colonial prisons, mainly Robben Island. A system of special courts was instituted, whose effect was to transport Xhosa in large numbers to work in colonial employ, often on the most arbitrary of grounds. When a 'Kaffir relief committee' was set up in King William's Town to cope with the flood of hungry refugees, a cry of rage went up that 'indiscriminate benevolence' would simply encourage indolence. Grey used his influence to destroy private relief efforts of this kind. His larger plan was to extend white rule and white land settlement right through the lands of the southern Nguni peoples to the borders of Natal – but such schemes were not, however, to be tolerated in London.[13]

The influx of Xhosa from across the Kei in search of work and succour, after the cattle killing had brought them to the point of starvation, alarmed the politicians. In 1857 the Cape parliament introduced the Kaffir Employment Bill to prevent the 'disgorging of Kaffirland', and enforce long-term (five-year) compulsory contracts of indenture on African work-seekers. As contracts were to be drawn up by the magistrates, the destitute, desperate for relief, had no say over where they were to be employed or what the terms of their contracts might be. By the end of 1857, nearly 30 000 Xhosa had registered as labourers in the colony, with perhaps an equal number entering the colony unregistered. For the first time, Xhosa in large numbers travelled as far as the western Cape to work. John Fairbairn, son-in-law and former ally of the humanitarian Philip, protested that the introduction of a large mass of Africans would 'form a savage element in the population', and that 'the armed savage was even less to be dreaded than the domestic savage'. *De Zuid-Afrikaan*, mouthpiece for progressive Afrikaans opinion, warned that 'every mountain and kloof would be infested with prowling savages'. 'If you allow such people to become proprietors, you cannot withhold from them that measure of political power which belongs to the elective franchise.'[14]

This anxiety was real, for in the eastern Cape an African commercial farming and trading class was emerging as an important economic and political factor out of the disintegration of Xhosa society. The independent Khoi communities of an earlier date had largely disappeared by the 1850s, especially with the demise of the humanitarian lobby that had championed them. But Africans, whose incorporation into the colony had only recently begun in large numbers, had the great advantage that they were mixed farmers with resources of skills and local knowledge, as well as a collective work ethic which would make them highly competitive farmers in the context of the colonial economy. For most, their experience of participation in the colonial economy by the 1850s was almost universally as labourers on farms and in towns. But the waves of dispossession which had begun to subjugate and incorporate African peoples could never reduce them uniformly to an underclass. Accommodations were always necessary. The devastation caused by decades of conflict and the undermining of their societies gave birth to a class of people who were sufficiently accommodationist and acculturated to take their place as full participants and independent producers in the colonial economy.

Some were prosperous and independent landowners; many others were still embedded in the redistributive networks of the homestead, but were nonetheless inextricably integrated into the commercial economy. It is not surprising that prominent among the most successful were Christian Mfengu and other products of the mission nexus, people most alienated from the tenets and values of native culture, the 'unbelievers' who had enraged the traditionalists by refusing to join in the cattle killing. From the perspective of the 1850s the high point of the black-controlled commercial economy of the region still lay in the future. Africans would be well positioned to take advantage of the spaces and opportunities created by the great surge of economic activity of the mineral era in the 1870s.[15]

In political terms, Africans who fulfilled the property qualifications for the vote for the Cape legislature were to become active participants in electoral politics in the eastern Cape. Indeed, Trapido has written of an alliance of white merchants and black 'peasants' playing a pivotal role in certain eastern Cape electoral constituencies. This 'small tradition' of liberalism in the eastern Cape was remarkably resilient, and rested on real economic benefits. A mission class of teachers, ministers and journalists forged a politics of accommodation, which survived long after accommodation was no longer feasible. There were prominent white liberals who were committed to the rights of this African elite, and many profited from their enterprise. The black elite could legitimately be held up as a buffer against the increasingly dispossessed majority, and against the still quite menacing authority of the chiefs, who could not be eradicated with the finality that the administrators might have wished.[16]

Nevertheless, the participation of Africans in economic and political life did not so much reflect the liberal convictions of the colonial rulers, as embody in a sense a compromise with social and economic realities. After the imperial retreat of 1853, the function of government became inevitably the maintenance of stability through co-option, in the absence of military force. 'Cape liberalism' was a form of partial incorporation at the margins, arising as much out of colonial weakness as out of ideological commitment. Few white colonists could conceive of such rights ever being enjoyed by more than a small minority of Africans.

The structures of racial domination have taken on different forms in South Africa. In the Cape, incorporation of the Khoisan was accompanied by the crumbling of their institutions, and their acculturation as an underclass in colonial society. The first African mixed farmers to be incorporated in the nineteenth century were not numerically overwhelming; and owing to the concentration of mission activity and the long history of culture contact, trade and warfare, many (notably the Mfengu initially) were already loosened from the hold of chiefly authority and traditional culture, and thus more susceptible to acculturation. Under these circumstances, an assimilative, *laissez-faire* form of race domination was possible. However, as circumstances changed, the Cape model became less and less tenable. After the discovery of diamonds in the late 1860s, a new imperial activism arose of a qualitatively different kind than before, this time fully endorsed in London. New economic opportunities and capital investment on an unprecedented scale provided the economic momentum to sustain policies of conquest and expansionism in southern Africa. The beneficiaries of the new surge of productive and commercial development were much wider spread and more influential at the centres of power, both locally and internationally, than the narrow settler elite which had sought to benefit from earlier bouts of expansionist fervour.[17]

The extension of colonial rule over African peoples in the last third of the century, from the transKeian Nguni and Zulu in the east to the Tswana in the west, and including the diverse African peoples of the Transvaal, required new adaptations to new realities.[18] A full-scale scientific racism was taking root in the European world, and in South Africa too there was a growing tendency to stress the unassimilability of Africans, and the dangers of loss of tribal identi-fication and allegiance. This was more pronounced in Natal, where assimila-tionist ideas could not be afforded, even of the most marginal variety as in the Cape, given the weight of African numbers within the colony from the start of white settlement and the relative cohesiveness of the local African communi-ties. But in the Cape too, the realisation developed that there were limits beyond which the political accommodation of the black elite was no longer feasible. In the final third of the century, the mineral discoveries eroded the util-ity of African production and made possible the construction of a more devel-oped racial order, just as the numbers of Africans incorporated under Cape rule increased rapidly, with the annexation of more and more transKeian territory. In consequence, the curtailment of such rights as the African elite enjoyed, and of the economic base on which they rested, became settled points in the poli-cies of colonial governments. The imperial authorities, now at a distance since the granting of fully responsible government to the Cape in 1872, fully con-curred.[19]

The newly incorporated African societies were culturally and socially cohe-sive, and chiefly rule continued to have real purchase in the lives of the people. At first, white administrators had to work through the authority structures they found, while employers of labour in new economic sectors had to make do with what labour could be cajoled or forced out of African societies. But by the twentieth century it had become clear that the use of pre-existing socio-economic systems and a co-opted chieftaincy, operating within radically cir-cumscribed land reserves and brought firmly under the control of the central state, provided ideal conditions for the mobilisation and direction of labour through the ubiquitous institutions of labour migrancy, pass laws and the urban compound. In these ways the labour costs of the industrial economy and the welfare costs of the industrial state would be subsidised by still-functioning rural societies. The policy of segregation was a clear case of turning immutable reality to advantage: African societies could not be dismantled or dispersed, but they could be used to impose a pervasive system of coercion and control, and for this the Natal system, which had been developed under very different conditions of colonial weakness and insecurity, was to provide the model.[20]

A co-opted chieftaincy was increasingly seen as a potent counterweight to the educated black elite, which in the nineteenth-century Cape had been incor-porated into the political system. In the twentieth century, however, this elite had become too numerous and too assertive, even nationalist, to be useful agents or collaborators for the much larger and more pervasive colonial state. African traditionalism, codified native law, chiefly rule, all served by a new science of anthropology, became the instruments of racial supremacy from the 1920s.[21] Culture came to be seen as something static, innate and inherent in defined racial or ethnic categories; while 'detribalisation' was now regarded as unnatural and socially dangerous. The wheel had turned. The intensely culture-bound assimilationism of the early mission movement, which saw nothing of value at all in African society, had given way to an exaggerated reverence for a perverted and prostituted 'traditional' way of life. A one-dimensional notion of culture, which tolerated no deviance from a prescribed ideal type, had been replaced by a notion of cultures as being impermeable and mutually exclusive entities. Both in their different ways were instruments of domination.

However, while South African society was built on the basis of racial supremacy from the very beginnings of Dutch settlement, it is clear that the immediate genesis of the racial order in its specifically twentieth-century form lay in the growing integration of South Africa into the world economy of nineteenth-century European capitalism. This integration had its roots in the early nineteenth century in the developments examined in this book, but really took off after the mineral discoveries of the last third of the century. The origins of the white-supremacist state of the twentieth century, in other words, did not lie particularly in the attitudes spawned on isolated, backward frontiers, where Boers struggled for survival against harsh conditions and hostile indigenes. Nor did those origins lie directly in the patterns of thought and behaviour engendered by the institution of slavery. These were certainly manifestations of the racial nature of the colonial society of the day, and left deep marks on the collective psyches of masters and servants alike.

However, there was a world of difference between, on the one hand, the individual master–servant relationships, brutal and harsh though they might have been, that characterised life on the wine farms in the days of slavery or on the Boer frontier, and, on the other hand, the systematic, institutionalised domination increasingly exercised by the state as the colonial economy intensified and developed. The Boers' domination of their servants was very localised and limited in scope, and very different from the large-scale, pervasive, state-initiated and state-sustained domination of the industrial age, a domination that encompassed not only black servants on white farms and in white homes, but blacks wherever they were to be found, in mines, factories, farms or reserves. The radically new idea that African societies outside the immediate realm of the colonial household or enterprise should be subjugated and ruled in the interests of the colonial economy did not derive from the era of slavery, nor did it derive from the Boer diaspora. In this, South Africa was fully in step with the new imperialism which was sweeping through Africa, and which saw African peoples everywhere subjugated to European domination.

It is true that Afrikaans-speaking elites were just as likely to take up acquisitive and predatory attitudes against African peoples as were British settlers, given the right conditions (as on the Sotho frontier in the 1860s). But in the nineteenth century, the Boers of the pastoral interior were as likely to see themselves as victims of imperial expansion, as they were to see themselves invariably as enemies of the African people with whom they shared the soil. Their political and religious communities were racially exclusive, and the only Africans they incorporated in their society became a rightless labouring class. But they also shared the land with independent African communities with whom they fought and allied, whom they sometimes dominated or by whom they were on occasion dominated, but over whom they could never have ruled, even had they wished to do so.

In all this, it would be true to say that British influence tended to harden the hierarchies of race rather than dissolve them, and to strengthen the hegemony of white colonists rather than weaken it. The permanent conquest of African societies was usually dependent on the exercise of imperial power. Throughout the nineteenth century, the dominance of colonists over cohesive African societies, whether in colonies or republics, could not be long sustained without the support of the imperial power. Indeed, it was direct British intervention north of the Orange in Smith's time at mid-century and (arguably) in the 1870s north of the Vaal (where white settlement had been on the retreat in the 1860s) that facilitated the establishment of viable Boer republican states.

While humanitarianism at times provided a useful rhetorical accompaniment, in reality imperial policy was dictated by the hard-nosed pursuit of British interests at minimal cost. This involved seeking out local collaborative agents and, where possible, solutions built on indirect rather than direct forms of imperial hegemony. The ideal allies and agents of British hegemony at the end of the day were white colonists rather than indigenous peoples, despite brief and transient recourse in the 1830s and 1840s to treaties with African chiefs and Griqua captains in areas where the colonists' presence was as yet weak and unreliable. By the 1870s, when imperial aggression against independent African peoples was at its height, the imperial authorities were simultaneously increasing their reliance on local white elites by granting responsible government to the Cape and toying with ideas of creating a larger white confederation under imperial auspices, combining all the white-ruled states of the subcontinent, including the Boer republics. And in the early twentieth century, immediately after the most costly war of conquest yet undertaken in South Africa, these visions were realised with the unification of British possessions as a self-governing white-ruled dominion.

References

Place of publication is London unless otherwise stated.
Abbreviations used:
AYB   Archives Year Book for South African History (Cape Town, 1938–)
BPP   British Parliamentary Papers, Irish University Press edition (Dublin)
BR   Basutoland Records, 4 vols. (1883, repr. Cape Town, 1964)
CCQ   W.M. Macmillan, The Cape Colour Question (1927, repr. Cape Town, 1968)
DSAB   Dictionary of South African Biography, 6 vols. (Pretoria, 1968–)
IJAHS   International Journal of African Historical Studies
JAH ·   Journal of African History
JSAS   Journal of Southern African Studies
OHSA   M. Wilson and L. Thompson, Oxford History of South Africa (Oxford, 1969–71)
SAHJ   South African Historical Journal
SSAS   R. Elphick and H. Giliomee, The Shaping of South African Society, 1652–1840, 2nd ed.
        (Cape Town, 1989)

Chapter One: Introduction

1. The concept 'frontier' is of course problematical, as it is itself a historical construct. Its significance and meaning will emerge in the discussion below.

2. Martin Legassick, 'The Frontier Tradition in South African Historiography' in Shula Marks and Anthony Atmore (eds.), Economy and Society in Pre-Industrial South Africa (1980), 44–79, is a seminal discussion of these historiographical issues. On the historiography in general, see C.C. Saunders, The Making of the South African Past: Major Historians on Race and Class (Cape Town, 1988); Ken Smith, The Changing Past: Trends in South African Historical Writing (Johannesburg, 1988). The discussion of the early liberal historiography here is not meant as a judgement on liberal historians in general, a category which at its broadest would include most of those who write about the past in the Western tradition of scholarship, but is an examination of a particular tradition of historical interpretation concerning South Africa that was influential between the 1920s and 1960s. It might seem unnecessary to some that this terrain should be revisited here; but in view of its lingering echoes in some still-influential writing, and since it forms an essential backdrop to the approach taken here, a brief review is necessary.

3. W.M. Macmillan, Bantu, Boer and Briton: The Making of the South African Native Problem, 1st ed. (1929), 166; cf. 2nd ed. (1963), 195. The 1963 edition was a more urgent and polemical work, but Macmillan's approach and ideas had not changed. In many places he spells out more explicitly in the second edition that which is implicit in the first. See also Macmillan, The Cape Colour Question (1927, repr. Cape Town, 1968), 142–3, 247–8, for further statements of this kind. See the essays in Hugh Macmillan and Shula Marks (eds.), Africa and Empire. W.M. Macmillan: Historian and Social Critic (1989) on Macmillan's place in South African history and historiography.

4. Macmillan, Bantu, Boer and Briton, 192–3.

5. Eric Walker, The Frontier Tradition in South Africa (1930); quotes from Walker, The Great Trek, 5th ed. (1965), 1, 376–7; Walker, 'The Formation of New States, 1835–1854' in The Cambridge History of the British Empire, VIII (Cambridge, 1936), 318. J.S. Marais also subscribed to this notion of the frontier tradition taking 'deeper root' in the post-trek republics; see The Cape Coloured People, 1652–1937 (1939, repr. Johannesburg, 1957), 160–1.

6. C.W. de Kiewiet, A History of South Africa, Social and Economic (Oxford, 1942), 56–9.

7. De Kiewiet, The Imperial Factor in South Africa (Cambridge, 1937), 13–14.

8. De Kiewiet, History, 212, 150–1; also Saunders, Making of the South African Past, 88–9.

9. I.D. MacCrone, Race Attitudes in South Africa: Historical, Experimental and Psychological Studies (Johannesburg, 1937).

10. André du Toit, 'No Chosen People: The Myth of the Calvinist Origins of Afrikaner

Nationalism and Racial Ideology', *American Historical Review*, 88, 4 (1983), 920–52; Du Toit, 'Puritans in Africa? Afrikaner "Calvinism" and Kuyperian Neo-Calvinism in Late Nineteenth-Century South Africa', *Comparative Studies in Society and History*, 27 (1985), 209–40; also Robert Ross with D. van Arkel and G.C. Quispel, 'Going Beyond the Pale: On the Roots of White Supremacy in South Africa', 74–81, and Ross, 'The Rise of Afrikaner Calvinism', 183–91, both in Ross, *Beyond the Pale: Essays on the History of Colonial South Africa* (Hanover, N.H., 1993). Further criticism of this literature is found in Irving Hexham, 'Dutch Calvinism and the Development of Afrikaner Nationalism', *African Affairs*, 79 (1980), 195–208. The 'Calvinist paradigm' is to be found in, e.g., MacCrone, *Race Attitudes*, 87–8, 129–30; Walker, *Great Trek*, 55–9; Sheila Patterson, *The Last Trek* (1957), 177–8; Maurice Boucher, 'The Frontier and Religion: A Comparative Study of the USA and South Africa in the First Half of the Nineteenth Century', *AYB* (1968, II); Gerhard Beckers, *Religiose Factoren in der Entwicklung der Südafrikanischen Rassenfrage* (Munich, 1969); Jan J. Loubser, 'Calvinism, Equality and Inclusion: The Case of Afrikaner Calvinism' in S.N. Eisenstadt (ed.), *The Protestant Ethic and Modernisation: A Comparative View* (1968); W.A. de Klerk, *Puritans in Africa* (1975); J. Alton Templin, 'God and the Covenant in the South African Wilderness', *Church History*, 37 (1968), 281–97; Templin, *Ideology on a Frontier: The Theological Foundation of Afrikaner Nationalism, 1652–1910* (Westport, Conn., 1984). J.N. Gerstner, *The Thousand Generation Covenant: Dutch Reformed Covenant Theology and Group Identity in Colonial South Africa, 1652–1814* (New York, 1991) has restated the thesis with more empirical sophistication, but still manages to reach conclusions that his empirical evidence does not really bear out. Donald Akenson, *God's People: Covenant and Land in South Africa, Israel and Ulster* (Ithaca, 1992) follows Templin in criticising Du Toit for concentrating on 'elite' or 'political' thinking rather than looking at private writings or 'folk theology'. But Carli Coetzee, in 'Individual and Collective Notions of the "Promised Land": The "Private" Writings of the Boer Emigrants', *SAHJ*, 32 (1995), 48–65, shows that those 'private' writings on which Templin and Akenson rely for their vision of the 'chosen race' paradigm, as represented notably in the Dutch-born missionary Erasmus Smit, were by no means a representative reflection of Boer thinking.

11. G.M. Theal, *History of South Africa*, 11 vols. (1892–1919, repr. Cape Town, 1964); George Cory, *The Rise of South Africa*, 5 vols. (1910–1930, repr. Cape Town, 1965); Saunders, *South African Past*, 9–44; Smith, *Changing Past*, 18–52; D.M. Schreuder, 'The Imperial Historian as "Colonial Nationalist": George McCall Theal and the Making of South African History' in G. Martel (ed.), *Studies in British Imperial History; Essays in Honour of A.P. Thornton* (1986), 95–158; F.A. van Jaarsveld, *The Afrikaner's Interpretation of South African History* (Cape Town, 1964); L.M. Thompson, 'Afrikaner Nationalist Historiography and the Policy of Apartheid', *JAH*, 3 (1962).

12. E.g. Alexander Wilmot and J.C. Chase, *History of the Colony of the Cape of Good Hope* (Cape Town, 1869).

13. Macmillan, 'The Frontier and the Kaffir Wars, 1792–1836' in *Cambridge History*, VIII, 316; Macmillan, *Bantu, Boer and Briton*, 1st ed., 124–5.

14. Macmillan, *Bantu, Boer and Briton*, 2nd ed., 232–3.

15. De Kiewiet, *History*, 51–2, 64.

16. De Kiewiet, *British Colonial Policy and the South African Republics* (1929), 21–2, 5.

17. Ibid, 7, 62–6.

18. De Kiewiet, *History*, 64–6. Also see De Kiewiet, 'The Period of Transition in South African Policy, 1854–1870' in *Cambridge History*, VIII, 391–428; C.J. Uys, *In the Era of Shepstone* (Lovedale, 1933), 34–5; Patterson, *The Last Trek*, 23–4. The persistence of this interpretation was revealed when the historian Arthur Keppel-Jones in 1959, asking whether the apartheid order could have been avoided, concluded that the original 'wrong turning' had been the failure to maintain British rule north of the Orange in 1854. A.M. Keppel-Jones, 'When Did We Take the Wrong Turn?', *Race Relations Journal* (Johannesburg), 26, 1 (1959); also Keppel-Jones, *South Africa, A Short History*, 5th ed. (1975), 71–3.

19. Walker, 'Formation of New States', 341, 355–6.

20. *Bantu, Boer and Briton*, 1st ed., 222–3, also 190, 203. By the second edition in 1963, this passage (256–7) was much toned down (reserves had a different connotation by then, and African urbanisation and rural degradation were much more advanced); and it was coupled with strictures against '*laissez-faire*' principles which had provided a pretext for benign neglect of African agriculture and economic development. From the start, Macmillan was preoccupied with the historical roots of contemporary African poverty. These concerns were fully present in *Complex South Africa: An Economic Footnote to History* (1930), which was gestating at the same time as his historical perspectives were being formed, according to Saunders, *South African Past*, 47–55,

62–4. Also see De Kiewiet, 'Social and Economic Developments in Native Tribal Life' in *Cambridge History*, VIII, 808–28, for another early investigation of the historical roots of the problems caused by land loss.

Although Macmillan was persuaded, following his protagonist John Philip, that territorial segregation under benevolent British rule would have been the ideal answer to the expansion of colonial settlement, he always clung firmly to the ideal of the common society, and firmly rejected the rigid and restrictive segregationism of early Union governments, in sharp contrast, e.g., to Edgar Brookes, whose *The History of Native Policy in South Africa from 1830 to the Present Day* (Cape Town, 1924) stressed cultural unassimilability. Prior to his departure for England in 1933, Macmillan was involved in conflict at Wits University with more conservative liberals, such as Winifred Hoernlé and J.D. Rheinallt Jones, whose interests lay in the field of 'Bantu Studies', which Macmillan interpreted as being an antiquarian pursuit of 'decaying cultures' aimed at accentuating racial differences and in danger of playing into the hands of segregationists. For similar reasons he disliked the South African Institute of Race Relations, established in 1929, with which Edgar Brookes was involved (although by then Brookes had moved in a more liberal direction). Saunders, *South African Past*, 56; Macmillan, *My South African Years* (Cape Town, 1977), 214–17; Paul Rich, *White Power and the Liberal Conscience* (Manchester, 1984), 57; Hugh Macmillan, '"Paralysed Conservatives": W.M. Macmillan, the Social Scientists and the "Common Society," 1928–48' in Macmillan and Marks, *Africa and Empire*. Thus, while Macmillan accepted the full implications of the fact that South Africa was a common society earlier than most, he also was impatient of any effort to understand the dynamics of African culture, regarding it as dangerous and backward-looking.

21. Macmillan, *Bantu, Boer and Briton*, 2nd ed., 339–41; 1st ed., 292–3; also *Complex South Africa*, 138–9, for Macmillan's criticism of Harry Smith's land policies along similar lines; and J.S. Marais, 'The Imposition and Nature of European Control' in Isaac Schapera (ed.), *The Bantu-Speaking Tribes of South Africa* (1937), 335–42.

22. Saunders, *South African Past*, 72–3.

23. Monica Wilson and Leonard Thompson (eds.), *The Oxford History of South Africa*, 2 vols. (Oxford, 1969, 1971); see, e.g., Francis Wilson, 'Farming, 1866–1966', 104–5; David Welsh, 'The Growth of Towns', 173, 242, both in vol. 2. The 'economy' is treated in a separate chapter by Hobart Houghton. Even the South African War (1899–1902) is treated as a conflict between imperialism and nationalism, not directly related to the changes wrought by the gold-mining revolution (II, 324, 289). The political forces embodied in Afrikaner nationalism are seen in René de Villiers's chapter ('Afrikaner Nationalism') explicitly in terms of the frontier tradition. The Afrikaners are seen as having already in the eighteenth century evolved a separate identity in isolation from the 'main stream of western thought and action', and the preservation of this separate identity necessitated domination of other groups which posed a threat to group survival (II, 364–5). Early critiques are contained in Anthony Atmore and Nancy Westlake, 'A Liberal Dilemma: A Critique of the *Oxford History of South Africa*', *Race*, 14, 2 (1972), 107–36; Shula Marks, 'African and Afrikaner History', *JAH*, 11 (1970); Marks, 'Liberalism, Social Realities and South African History', *Journal of Commonwealth Political Studies*, 8 (1972), 243–9; Martin Legassick, 'The Dynamics of Modernisation in South Africa', *JAH*, 13, 1 (1972), 145–50.

The 'capitalist system' is of course an abstraction, and in real historical situations capitalist economies are inevitably embedded in relations of conflict, over access to resources and privileges, over inclusion and exclusion, over the instruments of power and control. It makes no historical sense to separate these off as external to the economic system, as if economic systems can ever operate in a kind of end-of-history ideal state, as fixed determinants. Liberal democracies tend to work because they maximise opportunity, access and inclusion; but liberal democracies are political constructs, and are no more the 'natural' form of capitalist social organisation than any other form of government. It is absurd to assume that in undemocratic or divided societies, 'politics' or 'ideology' has intervened in order to obstruct the natural order of things.

24. A subsequent, more radical generation of Africanists was more inclined to see penetration by agents of European imperialism – traders, missionaries, soldiers, administrators – as disruptive and ultimately destructive, wittingly or unwittingly serving capitalist interests, which were intent on gaining control of resources and subjugating indigenous peoples to their own ends. J.B. Peires, *The House of Phalo: The Xhosa People in the Days of their Independence* (Johannesburg, 1981); Peires, *The Dead Will Arise: Nongqawuse and the Great Xhosa Cattle-Killing Movement of 1856–7* (1989).

25. J.S. Galbraith, *Reluctant Empire: British Policy on the South African Frontier, 1834–1854* (Berkeley, 1963).

26. George Fredrickson, *White Supremacy: A Comparative Study in American and South*

African History (New York, 1981), 49–53. Richard Ford, 'The Frontier in South Africa' (Ph.D., University of Denver, 1966), provides a similar comparative argument.

27. Fredrickson, *White Supremacy*, 52–3.

28. Ibid, 170–5, 52–3.

29. Ibid, 166–9, 178–9. A contrasting view is presented, e.g., in Stanley Trapido, 'Reflections on Land, Office and Wealth in the South African Republic, 1850–1900' in Marks and Atmore, *Economy and Society in Pre-Industrial South Africa*, 350–68.

30. Fredrickson, *White Supremacy*, 4–5, 85, 93, 220, 238 and *passim*. The 'slaveholding mentality' which Fredrickson invokes several times is ambiguous, but the book as a whole suggests that he regards the frontier, rather than the slave-based society of the southwestern Cape, as the wellspring of white-supremacist ideology in South Africa.

In *Children of Bondage: A Social History of the Slave Society at the Cape of Good Hope, 1652–1838* (Hanover, NH, 1994), Robert Shell's position is that the twentieth-century apartheid order grew out of the slave relationship, and the institution of serfdom into which Shell sees it having evolved, specifically at the private level of the slave-owning household. Thus apartheid can be seen as the slave relationship writ large, having its origin in the hierarchy of the family. It was at this level, rather than the level of the state, that the racial order had its origins. Interpersonal relations in the household were the central element in the social order, much more so than inter-class or inter-group relations. The family as metaphor is the central motif of South African history in Shell's analysis. Shell, unlike Fredrickson, explicitly downplays the importance of frontiers and 'settler-autochthonous' relations; but in both formulations, the slave–servant experience is presented as formative, and relations with the African majority are largely sidestepped or caricatured.

Thus Shell sets the context in his preface by pointing to the similarities between the system of apartheid and the slave society of the past. He uses Orlando Patterson's concepts of 'natal alienation' and 'social death' to describe both social orders. Patterson, *Slavery and Social Death: A Comparative Study* (Cambridge, Mass., 1982). 'The systematic natal alienation of black men and the informal incorporation of black women in the white domestic arena are profoundly similar in both societies', writes Shell. 'With both groups [slaves and contemporary South African blacks], their mother tongues were stilled. Their political identities were effectively, even ruthlessly, eliminated.' (Shell, xix-xx, also 395–6.) The purpose of his book is to explain these essential continuities, as he sees them, in South African history, which he argues are not fortuitous but systemic. The problem, however, is that Shell is crudely misrepresenting South African history. Apartheid was a brutal form of racial supremacy, to be sure, but its shape was dictated by the need to accommodate historical realities that could not be changed, specifically the resilience of African political authority and culture. Whatever this was, it bore little resemblance to 'natal alienation' or 'social death'. Thus in democratic South Africa, nine indigenous African languages enjoy official status, and the chiefs and their law enjoy constitutional recognition and reverence.

Another recent book which assumes a simple evolution from the slaveholding past to the twentieth-century racial order is Elizabeth Eldredge and Fred Morton (eds.), *Slavery in South Africa: Captive Labour on the Dutch Frontier* (Pietermaritzburg, 1995), which conflates labour relations throughout the white-settled subcontinent under the general rubric of slavery (see especially Morton's conclusion, 'Slavery in South Africa').

31. Fredrickson, *White Supremacy*, 329, 139; Herbert Blumer, 'Industrialisation and Race Relations' in Guy Hunter (ed.), *Industrialisation and Race Relations: A Symposium* (1965).

32. Fredrickson, *White Supremacy*, 192–4, 196.

33. L.M. Thompson, *The Political Mythology of Apartheid* (New Haven, 1985), chs. 4, 5. Thompson particularly draws on Du Toit, 'No Chosen People'; Hermann Giliomee, 'The Burgher Rebellions in the Eastern Frontier, 1795–1815' in Richard Elphick and Giliomee (eds.), *The Shaping of South African Society, 1652–1820*, 1st ed. (1979), 338–56.

34. Thompson, *Political Mythology*, 80–1.

35. Macmillan, *Cape Colour Question*, VIII, 255–7; Macmillan, 'The Problem of the Coloured People, 1792–1842' in *Cambridge History*, VIII, 294.

36. See the insightful comments of Legassick in 'The State, Racism and the Rise of Capitalism in the Nineteenth-Century Cape Colony', *SAHJ*, 28 (1993), 329–68, a seminal article which prefigured the general approach of this book.

37. Clifton Crais, *The Making of the Colonial Order: White Supremacy and Black Resistance in the Eastern Cape, 1770–1865* (Johannesburg, 1992).

Chapter Two: Dutch Beginnings

1. Leonard Guelke, 'Freehold Farmers and Frontier Settlers, 1657–1780' in Richard Elphick and

Hermann Giliomee (eds.), *The Shaping of South African Society, 1652–1840*, 2nd ed. (Cape Town, 1989), 66–7; Robert Shell, *Children of Bondage: A Social History of the Slave Society at the Cape of Good Hope, 1652–1838* (Hanover, NH, 1984), 289–90.

2. Richard Elphick, *Kraal and Castle: Khoikhoi and the Founding of White South Africa* (New Haven, 1977; 2nd ed., Johannesburg, 1985); Elphick and V.C. Malherbe, 'The Khoisan to 1828' in *SSAS*; H.C. Bredekamp, *Van Veeverskaffers tot Veewagters: 'n Historiese Ondersoek na Betrekkinge Tussen die Khoikhoi en Europeërs aan die Kaap, 1662–1679* (Bellville, 1982); Shell, *Children of Bondage*, 26–8, 221, and 1–26 for a discussion of the failure of European wage labour; also Victor de Kock, *Those in Bondage: An Account of the Life of the Slave at the Cape in the Days of the Dutch East Indies Company* (Cape Town, 1950), 62–5.

3. The older slave historiography included De Kock, *Those in Bondage*; I.E. Edwards, *Towards Emancipation: A Study in South African Slavery* (Cardiff, 1942); A.F. Hattersley, 'Slavery at the Cape, 1652–1838' in *The Cambridge History of the British Empire*, VIII (Cambridge, 1936), 262–73. In reaction against this literature, Nigel Worden and Robert Ross stress the centrality of violence and brutality in the slave relationship. Worden, *Slavery in Dutch South Africa* (Cambridge, 1985), 101–18; Ross, *Cape of Torments: Slavery and Resistance in South Africa* (1983); also Lewis Greenstein, 'Slave and Citizen: The South African Case', *Race*, 15 (1973), 25–45. But Robert Shell stresses psychological means of control, and the importance of paternalism and family incorporation, criticising what he calls Worden's 'naive neo-abolitionist view' of the horrors of the institution. Crucial to the family mode of management in Shell's view was the fact that the individual slaveholdings at the Cape were relatively small and unconcentrated. Slavery thus is seen as analogous to gender and age relations, with women and children in slave-owning families being 'on almost the same low level as the slaves and servants'. Thus Shell's analysis places Cape slavery closer to the anthropological model of African slave societies, based on family or lineage incorporation, than does the New World slave historiography. The slave thus was a 'perpetual child'. Further, Shell argues that dislocation of family ties among slaves was not so massive as is often assumed. Cadastral transfers (slaves being sold as part of the physical property on which they lived and worked) ensured a high degree of residential and family continuity (particularly in matrifocal families). But Shell does not see this as benign slavery. Slaves never bought fully into the patriarchal ideology, and hence incorporation into the household was always a partial fiction. Consent was forthcoming as long as it allowed slaves to assert rights. The reality indeed was one of physical and ideological resistance and the threat of violent coercion. Nevertheless, the legal paternalism of the VOC and the constraints imposed by the 'moral community' of the slave-owners themselves tempered the treatment of slaves. (On this see ch. 2 n.93 below.) Shell, 'The Family and Slavery at the Cape, 1680–1808' in Wilmot James and Mary Simons (eds.), *The Angry Divide: Social and Economic History of the Western Cape* (Cape Town, 1989), 20–30; Shell, *Children of Bondage*; also John Mason, '"Fit for Freedom": The Slaves, Slavery and Emancipation in the Cape Colony, South Africa, 1806–1842' (Ph.D., Yale, 1992), 145–226, who takes up the conception of the *familia* as the basic unit of slave society. But Robert Ross questions the use of the concepts of 'patriarchy' and 'paternalism' in 'Paternalism, Patriarchy and Afrikaans', *SAHJ*, 32 (1995), 34–47, without taking the argument forward.

4. G.M. Theal, *History of South Africa*, 11 vols. (1892–1919, repr. Cape Town, 1964), III, 272.

5. I.D. MacCrone, *Race Attitudes in South Africa: Historical, Experimental and Psychological Studies* (Johannesburg, 1937), 6–10, 40–6, 70–88, 133–5; George Fredrickson, *White Supremacy: A Comparative Study in American and South African History* (New York, 1981), 70–85; Robert Ross with D. van Arkel and G.C. Quispel, 'Going beyond the Pale: On the Roots of White Supremacy in South Africa' in Ross, *Beyond the Pale: Essays on the History of Colonial South Africa* (Hanover, NH, 1993). MacCrone was concerned to contrast this metropolitan inheritance, as represented in the original Cape settlement, with the new society evolving on the isolated frontier.

6. Shell, *Children of Bondage*, ch. 11; H.P. Cruse, *Die Opheffing van die Kleurlingbevolking* (Stellenbosch, 1947), 224. In fact, the Synod of Dort was unclear on the obligations of slave-owners, and on the precise rights of baptised slaves. Thus it was not argued that emancipation should occur *immediately* after baptism.

7. Elphick and Shell, 'Intergroup Relations: Khoikhoi, Settlers, Slaves and Free Blacks, 1652–1795' in *SSAS*, 188; MacCrone, *Race Attitudes*, 77–8.

8. MacCrone, *Race Attitudes*, 76–7; Cruse, *Opheffing*, 90–101; Shell, *Children of Bondage*, 343–5, 374–7.

9. Elphick and Shell, 'Intergroup Relations', 185–91, Elphick and Giliomee, 'The Origins and Entrenchment of European Dominance at the Cape, 1652–c.1840', 535, and James Armstrong and Worden, 'The Slaves, 1652–1834', 129, all in *SSAS*; Shell, *Children of Bondage*, 346–8, 366–8,

and ch. 7 on the company's slave lodge; C.R. Boxer, *The Dutch Seaborne Empire, 1600–1800* (New York, 1965), 126–72, on Dutch religious practice in the colonies; Cruse, *Opheffing*, 76–116, on educational opportunities for slaves and Khoi. According to Shell, some 2543 slave baptisms took place between 1652 and 1795, and of these 1715 belonged to the company. The great majority of those baptised were children (*Children of Bondage*, 343.)

10. Shell, *Children of Bondage*, 340–2, 349–55, 358–9; Hermann Giliomee, 'Eighteenth-Century Cape Society and its Historiography: Culture, Race and Class', *Social Dynamics*, 9, 1 (1983), 20–1; Elphick and Shell in *SSAS*, 190; MacCrone, *Race Attitudes*, 135; Fredrickson, *White Supremacy*, 83–5; Ross et al., 'Going Beyond the Pale', 74–81, and Ross, 'The Rise of Afrikaner Calvinism', 183–91, both in Ross, *Beyond the Pale*; De Kock, *Those in Bondage*, 214–15.

Fredrickson argues that masters in South Africa in post-slavery times retained an aversion to non-white dependants practising the same religion as themselves: they craved a cultural as well as a racial distinction. The long delay in establishing the principle that Christians could still be slaves 'may therefore have been one factor making the South African white-supremacist tradition more dependent on cultural pluralism than the American'. But this is a dubious speculation. The coloured labouring class of the Cape, descended from slaves and Khoi, became as thoroughly Christianised and acculturated as American slaves; but the post-Great Trek African labouring class, ultimately much more numerous than the colonists, retained a degree of cultural distinction for the same reasons American Indians did: they belonged to viable and cohesive native societies that mostly retained their independence until late in the nineteenth century. Colonial masters at the Cape certainly were hostile to the humanitarianism of early British missionaries, but this did not mean that they were hostile to baptism among their servants once the slaves had been emancipated. Shell takes a similar position to Fredrickson's, in *Children of Bondage*, 362–5, 368–70.

11. Johannes du Plessis, *A History of Christian Missions in South Africa* (1911), 61–9, 91–8; Ross, 'Going Beyond the Pale', 78–9. On the absence of an anti-slavery, humanitarian impulse in Holland at the time, see Gert Oostindie (ed.), *Fifty Years Late: Capitalism and Antislavery in the Dutch Orbit* (Leiden, forthcoming).

12. Shell, *Children of Bondage*, 355–62; G.W. Eybers, *Select Constitutional Documents Illustrating South African History* (1918), 18, for the 1812 proclamation. By 1825 there were 2167 Muslim slaves and free blacks in Cape Town according to the census, and by 1842 there were 6435 Muslims in the town. See Robert Shell, 'Rites and Rebellion: Islamic Conversion at the Cape, 1808–1915' in *Studies in the Development of Cape Town*, 5 (Cape Town, 1984), 1–46; Elphick and Shell in *SSAS*, 191–4; R.L. Watson, *The Slave Question: Liberty and Property in South Africa* (Middletown, Conn., 1990), 172–6; Fredrickson, *White Supremacy*, 82–3; Armstrong and Worden in *SSAS*, 148–9; Kirsten McKenzie, *The Making of an English Slaveowner: Samuel Eusebius Hudson at the Cape of Good Hope, 1796–1807*, Communications 24, Centre for African Studies (Cape Town, 1993), 87–104.

13. De Kock, *Those in Bondage*, 198–223; Elphick and Shell in *SSAS*, 189–90, 204–14; Cruse, *Opheffing*, 245–73; appendices in Anna Böeseken, *Slaves and Free Blacks at the Cape, 1658–1700* (Cape Town, 1977). Only 108 company-owned slaves were ever freed, fewer than one per year (Shell, *Children of Bondage*, 374–7).

14. Elphick and Shell in *SSAS*, 206.

15. MacCrone, *Race Attitudes*, 79; Fredrickson, *White Supremacy*, 82; Elphick and Shell in *SSAS*, 204; Shell, *Children of Bondage*, 379–80.

16. Elphick and Shell in *SSAS*, 208, 212; Cruse, *Opheffing*, 266–7; Fredrickson, *White Supremacy*, 117, who suggests that somatic preference accounts for the imbalance, which presumably would have been the case when European men bought the freedom of slave women in order to marry them; Shell, *Children of Bondage*, 49–54, 158–60, 388–9, 392.

17. Andrew Bank, *The Decline of Urban Slavery at the Cape, 1806–1834*, Communications 22, Centre for African Studies (Cape Town, 1991).

18. Elphick and Shell in *SSAS*, 212, 208–9; Shell, *Children of Bondage*, 92, 105–6, 118–21, 293, 328, and ch. 12 on manumissions.

19. Fredrickson, *White Supremacy*, 85–6; Elphick and Shell in *SSAS*, 214. For comparative purposes, see David W. Cohen and Jack P. Greene, *Neither Slave Nor Free: The Freedmen of African Descent in the Slave Societies of the New World* (Baltimore, 1972); Ira Berlin, *Slaves Without Masters: The Free Negro in the Antebellum South* (New York, 1976).

20. On free blacks, Elphick and Shell in *SSAS*, 214–24; Worden, *Slavery*, 144–7; De Kock, *Those in Bondage*, 198–223; Böeseken, *Slaves and Free Blacks*; G.C. de Wet, *Die Vryliede en Vryswartes in die Kaapse Nedersetting, 1657–1707* (Cape Town, 1981); Sheila Patterson, 'Some Speculations on the Status and Role of the Free People of Colour in the Western Cape' in Meyer Fortes and S. Patterson (eds.), *Studies in African Social Anthropology* (1975), 159–205; Shirley

Judges, 'Poverty, Living Conditions and Social Relations: Aspects of Life in Cape Town in the 1830s' (MA, UCT, 1977). Some Muslim free blacks were in fact modestly well-off, some of them being slave-owners themselves.

21. MacCrone, *Race Attitudes*, 70–3; Fredrickson, *White Supremacy*, 87–8; Elphick and Shell in *SSAS*, 214–16; J.L. Hattingh, *Die Eerste Vryswartes van Stellenbosch, 1679–1720* (Bellville, 1981); Shell, *Children of Bondage*, 267, 293–4.

22. On miscegenation and race mixing, Elphick and Shell in *SSAS*, 194–204; Worden, *Slavery*, 147–50; J.A. Heese, *Die Herkoms van die Afrikaner, 1657–1867* (Cape Town, 1971); H.F. Heese, *Groep Sonder Grense* (Bellville, 1984); J.H. Hoge, 'Personalia of the Germans at the Cape, 1652–1804', *AYB* (1946), 1–495; Hoge, 'Miscegenation in South Africa in the Seventeenth and Eighteenth Centuries' in Marius F. Valkhoff (ed.), *New Light on Afrikaans and 'Malayo-Portuguese'* (Louvain, 1972), 99–118; Anon., 'The Origin and Incidence of Miscegenation at the Cape during the Dutch East Indies Company's Regime, 1652–1795', *Race Relations Journal* (Johannesburg), 20 (1953), 23–7; G.F.C. de Bruyn, 'Die Samestelling van die Afrikaner', *Tydskrif vir Geesteswetenskappe*, 16 (1976); Ken Jordaan, 'The Origins of the Afrikaners and their Language, 1652–1720: A Study in Miscegenation and Creole', *Race*, 15, 4 (1974), 461–95.

23. Shell, *Children of Bondage*, 285–9. See Hermanus Hoetink, *Slavery and Race Relations in the Americas: Comparative Notes on their Nature and Nexus* (New York, 1973) on the significance of the 'somatic norm'. The only Christian marriage recorded with a full-blood indigenous woman was that of Eva, brought up as a Christian Dutch-speaker in Van Riebeeck's household, with Pieter van Meerhoff, company surgeon, in 1662. The parallel with Pocahontas is striking. Elphick, *Kraal and Castle*, 106–8, 201–3; MacCrone, *Race Attitudes*, 43; V.C. Malherbe, *Krotoa, Called 'Eva', A Woman Between*, Communications 19, Centre for African Studies (Cape Town, 1990).

24. Worden, *Slavery*, 138–52; Ross, 'The Rise of the Cape Gentry', *JSAS*, 9, 2 (1983), 194–217; Guelke and Shell, 'An Early Colonial Landed Gentry: Land and Wealth in the Cape Colony, 1652–1731', *Journal of Historical Geography*, 9 (1983), 265–86; Guelke in *SSAS*, 73–84. Giliomee and Shell emphasise the role of burgher women in bolstering a sense of racial propriety and sexual morality; see Giliomee, 'Eighteenth-Century Cape Society', 26; Shell, *Children of Bondage*, 323–4.

25. Guelke in *SSAS*, 99–100.

26. Elphick and Shell in *SSAS*, 199–200; Shell, *Children of Bondage*, 319.

27. MacCrone, *Race Attitudes*, 40–2; Fredrickson, *White Supremacy*, 17–21, 94–135. In British North America people of mixed ancestry were rigidly differentiated from the European population, which included many lower-class non-slaveowners whom the dominant slaveholding class were determined to keep as unaffected as possible by social intercourse with the black underclasses. Intermarriage was prohibited in most colonies, and all those accounted 'black' were denied the right to vote, to bear arms, and to testify in court against whites. In Latin and Caribbean America, upward mobility for blacks was possible and mulattoes enjoyed many of the rights, privileges and opportunities of the colonisers in a three-tier system, but the European colonisers maintained a sense of their own racial superiority. Carl Degler, *Neither Black Nor White: Slavery and Race Relations in Brazil and the United States* (New York, 1971); Herbert Klein, *African Slavery in Latin America and the Caribbean* (New York, 1986). Hence the Dutch East Indian pattern was unusual. But Blakely provides much evidence that the Dutch were as prone to racial prejudice and discrimination as any. At an earlier date Boxer stressed the effect of Dutch Calvinism in predisposing them to aversive attitudes towards colonised peoples. He points out what Fredrickson ignores – that Dutch men could not bring their non-European wives back to the Netherlands with them. They were effectively permanent exiles. There was thus a double standard between the exclusive ideals of the home society, and what was conceded as necessary and practical in the trading diaspora. Allison Blakely, *Blacks in the Dutch World: The Evolution of Racial Imagery in a Modern Society* (Bloomington, Ind., 1993); Boxer, *Dutch Seaborne Empire*, 241–72; also Ernst van den Boogaart, 'Colour Prejudice and the Yardstick of Civility: The Initial Dutch Confrontation with Black Africans, 1590–1635' in R. Ross (ed.), *Racism and Colonialism: Essays on Ideology and Social Structure* (The Hague, 1982), 44–54. Guelke also stresses the heritage of an original Dutch racial consciousness in reference to the Cape: 'The Origin of White Supremacy in South Africa: An Interpretation', *Social Dynamics*, 15, 2 (1989), 40–5.

28. Fredrickson, *White Supremacy*, 110–20, 309–10 n.47; Heese, *Herkoms van die Afrikaner*, 21, 67–170. W.M. Freund, 'Race in the Social Structure of South Africa, 1652–1836', *Race and Class*, 17 (1976), 53–67, tends to the same conclusions as Fredrickson; also Freund, 'The Cape under the Transitional Governments, 1795–1814' in *SSAS*, 334–5. One estimate has it that 10 per cent of all marriages were 'mixed' (Anon., 'Origin and Incidence of Miscegenation', 27; Elphick

and Shell in *SSAS*, 198).

H.F. Heese, *Groep Sonder Grense*, based on close research, also presents a picture of an uncommonly open society in the Dutch period, in which colour consciousness was not well developed. Heese maintains that the offspring of marriages between European men and coloured women were absorbed into the European community as a matter of course. He disaggregates the 'free black' category, arguing that those born as free persons were not counted among the free blacks, and, provided they were Christian, of part-European parentage and acculturated, could assimilate into the European community. In the absence of any indication of the circumstances of the mixed marriages he enumerates (who, where, etc.), the conclusions on the racial openness of Cape society are open to doubt.

Ross puts forward a similar argument. He considers that 'free black' was not a racial category, but an indication of servile birth, and was not inheritable. The children of free blacks, according to Ross, merged unnoticed into the general burgher population. This was thus a genuinely colour-blind society. 'There is no indication of a taxonomy based on race, only of one based on descent.' This seems to me to be a point of view that is difficult to sustain. Ross argues that a racially defined order emerged in the first thirty years of the nineteenth century, deriving principally from the need for docile and exploitable labour in a developing economy (Ross et al., 'Going Beyond the Pale').

29. Elphick, 'A Comparative History of White Supremacy', *Journal of Interdisciplinary History*, 13, 3 (1983), 503–13; Heese, '"Die Herkoms van die Afrikaner": 'n Nabetragting', *Familia*, 17, 3/4 (1980), 56–9; Shell, *Children of Bondage*, 324; Giliomee, 'Eighteenth-Century Cape Society', 25; Ross, 'The "White" Population of the Cape Colony' in Ross, *Pale*, 136–7. Elphick and Giliomee in *SSAS*, 521–66, represent this point of view, arguing that a racial order was created by legal fiat in the first decade of colonisation, and that it survived intact through centuries of geographic expansion, economic development and demographic change. Once established, the coincidence of race and legal status was never seriously challenged, and even survived the crises and injections of British humanitarianism in the early nineteenth century. Elphick and Giliomee thus downplay the importance of the early nineteenth century. While their larger picture of the Dutch period is convincing, the assumption of unproblematical continuity into the nineteenth century is challenged by this book. Worden, *Slavery*, 138–52, persuasively stresses the economic foundations of racial stratification in the slave economy of the arable southwest, rather than the policies of the VOC.

30. Guelke, 'Origin of White Supremacy'.

31. Elphick and Shell in *SSAS*, 215; Shell, *Children of Bondage*, 323–4, 372–4; MacCrone, *Race Attitudes*, 133–5; Fredrickson, *White Supremacy*, 120–3; Elphick and Giliomee in *SSAS*, 546–7. Ross, 'Going Beyond the Pale', 73–4, provides a different interpretation of the Smook episode.

32. Elphick and Shell in *SSAS*, 215–16; Elphick and Giliomee in *SSAS*, 548; Fredrickson, *White Supremacy*, 129; Giliomee, *Die Kaap tydens die Eerste Britse Bewind* (Cape Town, 1975), 258–9; Giliomee, 'The Eastern Frontier, 1770–1812' in *SSAS*, 450–2; Elphick and Malherbe in *SSAS*, 40–1.

33. Worden, *Slavery*, 17, 139; André du Toit and Hermann Giliomee, *Afrikaner Political Thought, Analysis and Documents, I: 1780–1850* (Cape Town, 1983), 7, 48.

34. For a discussion see Mason, '"Fit for Freedom,"' 61–73.

35. See n.2 above.

36. P.J. van der Merwe, *Die Trekboer in die Geskiedenis van die Kaapkolonie, 1657–1842* (Cape Town, 1938), 63–132 and *passim*; Van der Merwe, *Die Noordwaartse Beweging van die Boere voor die Groot Trek, 1770–1842* (The Hague, 1937); Van der Merwe, *Trek: Studies oor die Mobiliteit van die Pioniersbevolking aan die Kaap* (Cape Town, 1945) (Van der Merwe's trilogy is currently being published in English by Ohio University Press, translated by Roger Beck; see Nigel Penn, 'Trekboers Revisited', *African Affairs*, 95, 378 (1996), 126–30); A.J.H. van der Walt, *Die Ausdehnung der Kolonie am Kap der Guten Hoffnung, 1770–1799* (Berlin, 1928); MacCrone, *Race Attitudes*, 89–97; S.D. Neumark, *Economic Influences on the South African Frontier, 1652–1836* (Stanford, 1957); Leonard Guelke in *SSAS*, 77–9, 84–102; Guelke, 'Frontier Settlement in Dutch South Africa', *Annals of the Association of American Geographers*, 66, 1 (1976), 25–42; William Norton, 'Frontier Agriculture: Subsistence or Commercial?' and Guelke, 'Comment in Reply', both in *Annals*, 67, 3 (1977), 463–7; Guelke, 'The Early European Settlement of South Africa' (Ph.D., Toronto, 1974); Guelke, 'The Anatomy of a Colonial Settler Population: Cape Colony, 1657–1750', *IJAHS*, 21, 3 (1988), 453–73; L.C. Duly, *British Land Policy at the Cape, 1795–1844: A Study of Administrative Procedures in the Empire* (Durham, NC, 1968); and more recently Susan Newton-King, 'The Enemy Within: The Struggle for Ascendancy on the Cape Eastern Frontier, 1760–1799' (Ph.D., London, 1992); Nigel Penn, 'The Northern Cape Frontier Zone, 1700–c.1815' (Ph.D., UCT, 1995); Ross, 'The Developmental Spiral of the White Family

and the Expansion of the Frontier' in *Pale*. The white population of the Cape was mainly native-born by the 1730s (Guelke in *SSAS*, 82).

37. Elphick and Malherbe in *SSAS*; Penn, 'The Frontier in the Western Cape, 1700–1740' in John Parkington and Martin Hall (eds.), *Papers in the Prehistory of the Western Cape, South Africa*, BAR International Series 322 (Oxford, 1987), 462–503; Giliomee in *SSAS*, 430–1; Shell, *Children of Bondage*, 26–31; Russell Viljoen, 'Khoisan Labour Relations in the Overberg Districts During the Latter Half of the Eighteenth Century, *c.*1755–1795' (MA, UWC, 1993); also Guelke and Shell, 'Landscape of Conquest: Frontier Water Alienation and Khoikhoi Strategies of Survival, 1652–1780', *JSAS*, 18, 4 (1992), 803–24, on the slow and 'non-catastrophic' processes of Khoi dispossession, emphasising alienation of sources of water in the dry interior.

As early as 1721, Stellenbosch farmers petitioned for the binding in service, for a stipulated number of years, of children born of slave fathers and Khoi mothers (so-called Bastaard-Hottentots), who because of their mothers' status were legally free. The first statutory recognition of the system dates from 1775, when registration of Khoi children as *inboekelinge* and their indenture to the age of 25 (for males) was provided for. The system was used to tie entire families to farms, and applied increasingly to child captives as well. V.C. Malherbe, 'Indentured and Unfree Labour in South Africa: Towards an Understanding', *SAHJ*, 24 (1991), 15–16; Worden *Slavery*, 36, 58; De Kock, *Those in Bondage*, 124.

38. Martin Legassick, 'The Frontier Tradition in South African Historiography' in Shula Marks and Anthony Atmore (eds.), *Economy and Society in Pre-Industrial South Africa* (1980), 44–79; also Legassick, 'The Griqua, the Sotho–Tswana and the Missionaries, 1780–1840: The Politics of a Frontier Zone' (Ph.D., UCLA, 1969), 2–18, 85–101. The 'frontier' is not a boundary line, nor is it a readily defined geographical area, for its physical contours change constantly. It is an area where colonisation is taking place. 'Here two or more ethnic communities co-exist with conflicting claims to the land, and no authority is recognised as legitimate by all the parties or is able to exercise undisputed control over the area.' The frontier zone is therefore a disputed area, in which resort is had to coercive power, but also one in which a new society is being forged, with both conflictual and cooperative elements. Giliomee in *SSAS*, 427; Giliomee, 'Processes in Development of the South African Frontier' in Howard Lamar and L.M. Thompson (eds.), *The Frontier in History: North America and Southern Africa Compared* (New Haven, 1981).

39. An extreme form of this interpretation was evident in the writings of some contemporaries. At the time, the theme of 'degeneration', of 'sinking to the level of the rude Hottentot', was widespread. The French traveller Le Vaillant was moved to remark that the trekboers differed from Khoi 'only in physiognomy and colour'. Fredrickson, *White Supremacy*, 36; also André du Toit, 'No Chosen People: The Myth of the Calvinist Origins of Afrikaner Nationalism and Racial Ideology', *American Historical Review*, 88, 4 (1983), 931–6, on the 'degeneracy paradigm'.

40. Giliomee in *SSAS*; Giliomee, 'Processes in Development'.

41. Guelke in *SSAS*, 93–4. P.J. van der Merwe in his trilogy (n.36 above) characterised trekboers as essentially nomads, an image that has been greatly reassessed.

42. Neumark, *Economic Influences*. Pieter van Duin and Robert Ross, 'The Economy of the Cape Colony in the Eighteenth Century', *Intercontinenta*, 7 (Leiden, 1987), also stress the dynamism and opportunities of the frontier economy.

43. Guelke in *SSAS*, 87–93.

44. Susan Newton-King, 'Commerce and Material Culture on the Eastern Cape Frontier, 1784–1812', *The Societies of Southern Africa in the Nineteenth and Twentieth Centuries*, no. 14, Collected Seminar Papers, Institute of Commonwealth Studies (London, 1988), 1–32; Newton-King, 'The Enemy Within', 39–42, 291–395.

45. Elphick and Shell in *SSAS*, 227–9, on the 'composite culture' of the frontier.

46. MacCrone, *Race Attitudes*, 114–18.

47. Newton-King, 'The Enemy Within', 25–49, 338–42, 371–2.

48. Giliomee in *SSAS*, 450, 455–6.

49. Guelke differentiates between frontiers of exclusion and inclusion, between the 'orthodox' community dedicated to the maintenance of an exclusivist European way of life and a 'pluralist' community, in which peoples and cultures interacted in a much more open and fluid way. Guelke, 'The Making of Two Frontier Communities: Cape Colony in the Eighteenth Century', *Historical Reflections*, 12, 3 (1985), 419–48. But there were not so much two distinct social groupings as different positions on a continuum along which people could move over time or, given the system of partible inheritance, between generations. This stratification was well described by George Thompson, *Travels and Adventures in Southern Africa*, 2nd ed., 2 vols., ed. V.S. Forbes, Van Riebeeck Society, 48, 49 (Cape Town, 1967–8), II, 97.

50. MacCrone, *Race Attitudes*, 101–6; Penn, 'Land, Labour and Livestock in the Western Cape

during the Eighteenth Century' in James and Simons, *The Angry Divide*, 2–19; George Tylden, 'The Development of the Commando System in South Africa, 1715–1792', *Africana Notes and News*, 12 (1959).

51. Giliomee in *SSAS*, 456–9; Elphick and Giliomee in *SSAS*, 540–1; Elphick and Shell in *SSAS*, 200–2; MacCrone, *Race Attitudes*, 120–1; Fredrickson, *White Supremacy*, 123–4.

52. Penn, 'Land, Labour and Livestock'; Penn, 'Pastoralists and Pastoralism in the Northern Cape Frontier Zone during the Eighteenth Century' in Martin Hall and Andrew Smith (eds.), *Prehistoric Pastoralism in Southern Africa*, South African Archaeological Society Goodwin Series 5 (1986), 62–8. Penn sees this juncture as the 'crucible' of South African race attitudes.

53. Legassick, 'The Griqua, the Sotho–Tswana and the Missionaries'; Robert Ross, *Adam Kok's Griquas: A Study in the Development of Stratification in South Africa* (Cambridge, 1976). Further exoduses of Bastaards were to follow as frontiers closed off elsewhere, especially from the northeastern reaches of the colony in the 1820s. See ch. 6 below.

54. Newton-King, 'The Enemy Within', 69–87; also Newton-King, 'The Enemy Within' in Nigel Worden and Clifton Crais (eds.), *Breaking the Chains: Slavery and its Legacy in the Nineteenth-Century Cape Colony* (Johannesburg, 1994); Penn, 'Northern Cape Frontier Zone', 179–86. The particular focus of Newton-King's research is the vast Graaff-Reinet district encompassing in the eighteenth century the eastern reaches of the colony.

55. Penn, 'Northern Cape Frontier Zone', 211–52; Newton-King, 'The Enemy Within', 152–77, 116–21; John Parkington, 'Soaqua and Bushmen: Hunters and Robbers' in Carmel Schrire (ed.), *Past and Present in Hunter–Gatherer Societies* (New York, 1984); Shula Marks, 'Khoisan Resistance to the Dutch in the Seventeenth and Eighteenth Centuries', *JAH*, 13 (1972), 55–80. Hunter–robbers in practice consisted of many dispossessed Khoi as well as Bushmen. But there is little doubt that the pastoralist Khoi and the hunter–collector Bushmen were distinct social and cultural categories, and were perceived as such by the colonists. Bushman (San) studies are a currently flourishing field of interdisciplinary scholarship, evidenced by a recent rich collection, Pippa Skotnes (ed.), *Miscast: Negotiating the Presence of the Bushmen* (Cape Town, 1996). A debate on Bushman identity has raged in the pages of *Current Anthropology* in recent years. See ch. 4 n.102 below on the contemporary debates on Bushman identity.

56. On the *schepsel* stereotype, see Du Toit, 'No Chosen People'; Michael Streak, *The Afrikaner as Viewed by the English, 1795–1854* (Cape Town, 1974), 17–22. The fierceness of Bushman resistance had much to do with their profound spiritual connection to the physical landscape, in Penn's analysis: '"Fated to Perish": The Destruction of the Cape San' in Skotnes, *Miscast*.

57. Newton-King, 'The Enemy Within', 226–90; Penn, 'Northern Cape Frontier Zone', 253–78. On the question of definition, see Malherbe, 'Indentured and Unfree Labour'. Much contemporary polemical literature focused on the 'slaving' aspect, e.g. John Philip, *Researches in South Africa*, 2 vols. (1838, repr. New York, 1969), II, chs. 1–3. Adult male Bushmen (unlike Khoi) were regarded as having little utility as servants.

58. J.S. Marais, *Maynier and the First Boer Republic* (Cape Town, 1944, repr. 1962); Giliomee in *SSAS*, 440–45; Giliomee, 'Democracy and the Frontier: A Comparative Study of Bacon's Rebellion (1676) and the Graaff-Reinet Rebellion (1795–1796)', *SAHJ*, 6 (1974), 30–51; Newton-King and V.C. Malherbe, *The Khoikhoi Rebellion in the Eastern Cape (1799–1803)*, Communications 5, Centre for African Studies (Cape Town, 1981); Shell, *Children of Bondage*, 31–2. One of the rebels' demands in 1795 was that they should be allowed to buy and sell captives and that they be bound for life, something the government disallowed.

59. MacCrone, *Race Attitudes*, 124–5; *The Autobiography of the Late Sir Andries Stockenström*, ed. C.W. Hutton, 2 vols. (1887, repr. Cape Town, 1974), I, 230, 382. Penn, 'Anarchy and Authority in the Koue Bokkeveld, 1739–1779: The Banishing of Karel Buijtendag', *Kleio*, 17 (1985), 24–43, provides evidence of the limits of local burghers' tolerance of mistreatment of servants.

60. Giliomee in *SSAS*; John Hopper, 'Xhosa–Colonial Relations, 1770–1803' (Ph.D., Yale, 1980); J.B. Peires, *The House of Phalo: A History of the Xhosa People in the Days of their Independence* (Johannesburg, 1981), 53–8.

61. See chs. 6 and 8 below.

62. Ben Maclennan, *A Proper Degree of Terror: John Graham and the Cape's Eastern Frontier* (Johannesburg, 1985).

63. See ch. 3 below.

64. *Autobiography of Sir Andries Stockenström*, I, 79. The phrase 'irreclaimable savages' was notoriously coined by Governor Sir Benjamin D'Urban in 1835.

Chapter Three: Imperial Renewal

1. T.H. Aston and C.H.E. Philpin (eds.), *The Brenner Debate: Agrarian Class Structure and Economic Development in Pre-Industrial Europe* (Cambridge, 1985) on the rural origins of capitalism in England; N. McKendrick, J. Brewer and J.H. Plumb (eds.), *The Birth of a Consumer Society: The Commercialisation of Eighteenth-Century England* (1982); Linda Colley, *Britons: Forging the Nation, 1707–1837* (New Haven, 1992) on the ideology of Protestantism and anti-Catholicism. Generally, John Rule, *The Vital Century: England's Developing Economy, 1714–1815* (1992) and Rule, *Albion's People: English Society, 1714–1815* (1992).

2. David Cannadine, *The Decline and Fall of the British Aristocracy* (New Haven, 1990), 8–23; Cannadine, *Aspects of Aristocracy* (New Haven, 1994); Lawrence Stone and J.C.F. Stone, *An Open Elite? England, 1540–1880* (Oxford, 1984); W.D. Rubinstein, *Elites and the Wealthy in Modern British History: Essays in Social and Economic History* (Brighton, 1987). Early formulations are to be found in the Nairn–Anderson debate published in the *New Left Review* in the mid-1960s, e.g. Perry Anderson, 'Origins of the Present Crisis' (originally 1964) in *English Questions* (1992); see also Tom Nairn, *The Enchanted Glass: Britain and Its Monarchy* (1988).

3. John Brewer, *The Sinews of Power: War, Money and the English State, 1688–1783* (1989) on the development of the 'fiscal military state' in the eighteenth century, which stimulated industrial sectors and supported institutions such as the London money market which were of long-term significance to the economy as a whole. The debate which Brewer engendered is to be found in Lawrence Stone (ed.), *An Imperial State at War: Britain from 1689–1815* (1993).

4. Charles Wilson, *England's Apprenticeship, 1603–1763* (1965); Jack P. Greene, *Peripheries and Center: Constitutional Development in the Extended Polities of the British Empire and the United States, 1607–1788* (New York, 1990).

5. N.F.R. Crafts, *British Economic Growth During the Industrial Revolution* (Oxford, 1985); Crafts, 'Managing Decline?', *History Today*, 44, 5 (June 1994), 37–42, emphasises the limitations and incompleteness of the industrial revolution. M.J. Weiner, *English Culture and the Decline of the Industrial Spirit, 1850–1980* (Cambridge, 1981) stresses the failure of industrialism in British culture with its 'entrenched pre-modern elements'. Anderson, *English Questions*, stresses political blockages which prevented a truly bourgeois industrial society from taking root. On the continuing dynamism and innovativeness of the non-factory manufacturing sector, see Raphael Samuel, 'The Workshop of the World: Steam Power and Hand Technology in Mid-Victorian Britain', *History Workshop Journal*, 3 (1977), which stresses the 'combined and uneven development' of British capitalism. David Cannadine, 'The Present and the Past in the English Industrial Revol-ution, 1880–1980', *Past and Present*, 103 (1984), 131–72, provides a historiographical survey. Pat Hudson, *The Industrial Revolution* (1992) provides a useful introduction to the issues. Maxine Bergh and Pat Hudson, 'Rehabilitating the Industrial Revolution', *Economic History Review*, 2nd series, 45, 1 (1992), 24–50, stresses the fundamental social and economic changes of the industrial revolution; also R.V. Jackson, 'Rates of Industrial Growth during the Industrial Revolution', *Economic History Review*, 45, 1 (1992), 1–23.

6. E.P. Thompson, *The Making of the English Working Class* (1963) remains a classic; see H.J. Kaye and K. McClelland (eds.), *E.P. Thompson: Critical Perspectives* (1990); P. Joyce, 'Work' in F.M.L. Thompson (ed.), *Cambridge Social History of Britain, 1750–1950*, vol. 2; Hudson, *Industrial Revolution*, ch. 7; N. Kirk, 'In Defence of Class: A Critique of Recent Revisionist Writing upon the Nineteenth-Century English Working Class', *International Review of Social History*, 32 (1987).

7. Colley, *Britons*, ch. 4.

8. Ibid, ch. 5; Cannadine, 'The Context, Performance and Meaning of Ritual: The British Monarchy and the "Invention of Tradition"' in Eric Hobsbawm and T.O. Ranger (eds.), *The Invention of Tradition* (Cambridge, 1983).

9. References in n.5 above; Geoffrey Ingham, *Capitalism Divided? The City and Industry in British Social Development* (1984).

10. Ellen Meiksins Wood, *The Pristine Culture of Capitalism: A Historical Essay on Old Regimes and Modern States* (1991); Alex Callinicos, 'Exception or Symptom? The British Crisis and the World System', *New Left Review*, 169 (1988); Colin Mooers, *The Making of Bourgeois Europe: Absolutism, Revolution, and the Rise of Capitalism in England, France and Germany* (1991), 171–6; A. Mayer, *The Persistence of the Old Regime: Europe to the Great War* (New York, 1981).

11. References in n.2 above; also Rubinstein, *Capitalism, Culture and Decline in Britain, 1750–1990* (1994).

12. P.J. Cain and A.G. Hopkins, *British Imperialism*, vol. 1, *Innovation and Expansion*,

1688–1914, vol. 2, *Crisis and Deconstruction, 1914–1990* (1993).

13. For criticisms of the 'gentlemanly capitalism' thesis, see A.N. Porter, 'Gentlemanly Capitalism and Empire: The British Experience since 1750', *Journal of Imperial and Commonwealth History*, 18 (1990), 265–95; M.J. Daunton, '"Gentlemanly Capitalism" and British Industry, 1820–1914', *Past and Present*, 122 (1989), 119–58; Daunton, *Poverty and Progress: The Political Economy of Britain, 1700–1850* (Oxford, 1995); M. Barratt Brown, 'Away with All the Great Arches: Anderson's History of British Capitalism', *New Left Review*, 167 (1988); also Colin Barker and David Nicholls (eds.), *The Development of British Capitalist Society* (Manchester, 1989); Hudson, *Industrial Revolution*, 218–25. An earlier critique is to be found in E.P. Thompson, 'The Peculiarities of the English' (originally 1965) in *The Poverty of Theory and Other Essays* (1978). On Tory post-war economic policies, see Boyd Hilton, *Corn, Cash and Commerce: The Economic Policies of the Tory Governments, 1815–1830* (Oxford, 1977).

14. Hudson, *Industrial Revolution*, 182–3; Crafts, *British Economic Growth*, 143.

15. D.C.M. Platt, *Latin America and British Trade, 1806–1914* (1968); L.H. Jenks, *The Migration of British Capital to 1875* (1963).

16. J.R. Ward, 'The Industrial Revolution and British Imperialism, 1750–1850', *Economic History Review*, 47, 1 (1994), 44–65; Daunton, 'The Entrepreneurial State, 1700–1914', *History Today*, 44, 5 (1994), 11–16.

17. Eric Hobsbawm, *The Age of Revolution: Europe, 1789–1848* (1962), 48–51.

18. Vincent Harlow, 'The New Imperial System, 1783–1815' in *The Cambridge History of the British Empire*, vol. 2 (Cambridge, 1940); D.K. Fieldhouse, *The Colonial Empires: A Comparative Survey from the Eighteenth Century* (1966), 72–83; H.T. Manning, *British Colonial Government after the American Revolution, 1782–1820* (1933), 393–6; Frederick Madden and David Fieldhouse (eds.), *Imperial Reconstruction, 1763–1840* (1987); L.C.F. Turner, 'The Cape of Good Hope and the Anglo-French Conflict, 1797–1806', *Historical Studies of Australia and New Zealand*, 9 (1961). So tenuous was the British commitment to the Cape that in 1803, by the Treaty of Amiens, it handed the colony back to the Dutch Batavian Republic, only to retake it in 1806. It was not until 1814 that British control over the Cape was confirmed, with the Dutch withdrawing all claims.

19. Gerald S. Graham, *Great Britain in the Indian Ocean: A Study of Maritime Enterprise, 1810–1850* (Oxford, 1967), 36–40.

20. Lady Anne Barnard, *South Africa a Century Ago: Letters Written from the Cape of Good Hope (1797–1801)* (1901), 53–4.

21. Fieldhouse, *Colonial Empires*, 78–83; Manning, *Colonial Government*, 399–400. The humanitarian movement is examined in ch. 4 below.

22. C.A. Bayly, *Imperial Meridian: The British Empire and the World, 1780–1830* (1989), 133–5. On Somerset, *DSAB*, II, 685–91; A.K. Millar, *Plantagenet in Africa: Lord Charles Somerset* (Cape Town, 1965); Michael Roberts, 'Lord Charles Somerset and the Beaufort Influence', *AYB* (1951); M.C. Hughes, 'Lord Charles Somerset, Governor of the Cape, 1814–1827: A Reassessment' (Ph.D., Liverpool, 1964).

23. Bayly, *Imperial Meridian*, 193–216.

24. Greene, *Peripheries and Center*.

25. D.M. Young, *The Colonial Office in the Early Nineteenth Century* (1961); John Cell, *British Colonial Administration in the Mid-Nineteenth Century: The Policy-Making Process* (New Haven, 1970); John S. Galbraith, *Reluctant Empire: British Policy on the South African Frontier, 1834–1854* (Berkeley, 1963); Tony Kirk, 'Self-Government and Self-Defence in South Africa: The Interrelations between British and Cape Politics, 1846–1854' (D.Phil., Oxford, 1972), 81–119, for a discussion of the Colonial Office.

26. Paul Knaplund, *James Stephen and the British Colonial System, 1813–1847* (Madison, Iowa, 1953).

27. Fieldhouse, *Colonial Empires*, 248–9.

28. The older view is represented, e.g., by R.L. Schuyler, *The Fall of the Old Colonial System* (Oxford, 1945); C.A. Bodelson, *Studies in Mid-Victorian Imperialism* (1924, repr. 1960); K.E. Knorr, *British Colonial Theories, 1750–1850* (Toronto, 1944). The seminal challenge to this older orthodoxy came from J. Gallagher and R. Robinson, 'The Imperialism of Free Trade, 1815–1914', *Economic History Review*, 6, 1 (1953), 1–15. Also Wm Roger Louis (ed.), *Imperialism: The Robinson and Gallagher Controversy* (New York, 1976); Paul Kennedy, 'Continuity and Discontinuity in British Imperialism, 1815–1914' in C.C. Eldridge (ed.), *British Imperialism in the Nineteenth Century* (1984); Ged Martin, 'Anti-Imperialism in the Mid-Nineteenth Century and the Nature of the British Empire, 1820–1870' in R. Hyam and G. Martin (eds.), *Reappraisals in British Imperial History* (1975); B.A. Knox, 'Reconsidering Mid-Victorian Imperialism', *Journal*

of Imperial and Commonwealth History, 1 (1972).

The Gallagher and Robinson thesis was that the generally lukewarm attitude towards imperial expansion which predominated in official circles right up to the last few decades of the century derived from the evident fact that British pre-eminence and power were such that informal means of control over much of the non-European world were as efficacious and profitable, and much cheaper and safer, than formal rule. Informal, free-trade imperialism was still imperialism, but an imperialism that reduced cumbersome and expensive political responsibilities to a minimum. The use of military muscle or the threat thereof was always the sanction behind which free trade flourished. However, more recent critics argue that British political or economic influence was not always as efficacious as this formulation suggests. Certainly in West Africa, the British presence was too slight, and the African economies too self-sufficient, for any political hegemony or economic dependence to be meaningfully forged before the 1870s, when military technology and medical advance permitted real dominance to be asserted. Even the rise of 'legitimate commerce' in place of the slave trade cannot be laid primarily at the door of British intervention. See Martin Lynn, 'The "Imperialism of Free Trade" and the Case of West Africa, *ca* 1830–1870', *Journal of Imperial and Commonwealth History*, 15, 1 (1986), 22–40; Anthony Hopkins, 'Property Rights and Empire Building: Britain's Annexation of Lagos, 1861', *Journal of Economic History*, 40 (1980), 777–98.

29. This we shall return to in the next chapter.

30. H.J.M. Johnstone, *British Emigration Policy, 1815–1830: 'Shovelling out Paupers'* (Oxford, 1972); chapters by J.S. Galbraith, E.R. Kittrell, Bernard Semmel, D.N. Winch and R.N. Ghosh in A.G.L. Shaw (ed.), *Great Britain and the Colonies, 1815–1865* (1970); Shaw, 'British Attitudes to the Colonies, 1820–1850', *Journal of British Studies*, 9 (1969); Bernard Semmel, *The Rise of Free Trade Imperialism: Classical Political Economy: The Empire of Free Trade and Imperialism, 1750–1850* (Cambridge, 1970).

31. Johnstone, *Emigration Policy*, 2.

32. Ibid, 57–64; Semmel, 'The Philosophic Radicals and Colonisation' in Shaw, *Great Britain and the Colonies*.

33. Johnstone, *Emigration Policy*, 2–7.

34. On Horton's ideas, see L.C. Duly, *British Land Policy at the Cape, 1795–1844: A Study of Administrative Procedures in the Empire* (Durham, NC, 1968), 142–3; Douglas Pike, 'Wilmot Horton and the National Colonisation Society', *Historical Studies of Australia and New Zealand*, 7 (1956).

35. Johnstone, *Emigration Policy*, 9–10, 57; I.E. Edwards, *The 1820 Settlers in South Africa* (1934), 34–8; Fieldhouse, *Colonial Empires*, 251–2.

36. Johnstone, *Emigration Policy*, 1.

37. Fieldhouse, *Colonial Empires*, 250–4; Shaw, *Great Britain and the Colonies*. On Wakefield, see Johnstone, *Emigration Policy*, 109–10, 166, 170–3; Peter Burroughs, *Britain and Australia, 1831–1855: A Study in Imperial Relations and Crown Lands Administration* (Oxford, 1967), 12–34; D.N. Winch, *Classical Political Economy and the Colonies* (1965), 73–104; Paul Bloomfield, *Edward Gibbon Wakefield, Builder of the British Commonwealth* (1961).

38. T.R.H. Davenport, 'The Consolidation of a New Society: The Cape Colony' in *The Oxford History of South Africa*, eds. Monica Wilson and Leonard Thompson, I (Oxford, 1971), *passim*; Isobel Edwards, *Towards Emancipation: A Study in South African Slavery* (Cardiff, 1942), 19–20; L.M. Thompson, *Political Mythology of Apartheid* (New Haven, 1985), 107; W.M. Macmillan, *The Cape Colour Question: A Historical Survey* (1927, repr. Cape Town, 1968), 184–5, 189; George Cory, *The Rise of South Africa* (1910–1940, repr. Cape Town, 1965), II, 299–300.

39. J.B. Peires, 'The British and the Cape, 1814–1834' in Richard Elphick and Hermann Giliomee (eds.), *The Shaping of South African Society, 1652–1840*, 2nd ed. (Cape Town, 1989), 491–3.

40. Pieter van Duin and Robert Ross, 'The Economy of the Cape Colony in the 18th Century' *Intercontinenta*, 7 (Leiden, 1987); Ross, 'The Cape of Good Hope and the World Economy' in *SSAS*.

41. W.M. Freund, 'The Cape under the Transitional Governments' in *SSAS*, 328; Hermann Giliomee, *Die Kaap tydens die Eerste Britse Bewind* (Cape Town, 1975), 202. On the struggles against the VOC in the late eighteenth century, see Coenraad Beyers, *Die Kaapse Patriotte Gedurende die Laaste Kwart van die Agtiende Eeu* (Pretoria, 1967), 26–30 and *passim*; Davenport in *OHSA*, 287–8, 311–12.

42. Marcus Arkin, 'John Company at the Cape: A History of the Agency under Pringle, 1794–1815, Based on a Study of the "Cape of Good Hope Factory Records,"' *AYB* (1960, II); Arkin, 'Supplies for Napoleon's Gaolers: John Company and the Cape–St Helena Trade during the

Captivity, 1815–1821', *AYB* (1964, I).

43. Manning, *Colonial Government*, 429–35.

44. *DSAB*, II, 212–13, II, 606–7, V, 120; Peter Philip, *British Residents at the Cape, 1795–1819* (Cape Town, 1981), 66; Kirk, 'Self-Government', 47.

45. Robert Ross, 'Structure and Culture in Pre-Industrial Cape Town: A Survey of Knowledge and Ignorance' in Wilmot James and Mary Simons (eds.), *The Angry Divide: Social and Economic History of the Western Cape* (Cape Town, 1989).

46. *DSAB*, III, 80–1, II, 745–6, IV, 462, III, 168–9, IV, 90–1, 652–3, V, 544–5.

47. C.A. Jones, *International Business in the Nineteenth Century: The Rise and Fall of a Cosmopolitan Bourgeoisie* (Brighton, 1987); P.L. Cottrell, 'Commercial Enterprise' in R.A. Church (ed.), *The Dynamics of Victorian Business* (1980); Lalou Meltzer, 'The Growth of Cape Town Commerce and the Role of John Fairbairn's *Advertiser*, 1835–1859' (MA, UCT, 1989), 101–6.

48. R.F.M. Immelman, *Men of Good Hope: The Romantic Story of the Cape Town Chamber of Commerce, 1804–1954* (Cape Town, 1955), 29–42; Marian George, 'John Bardwell Ebden, His Business and Political Career at the Cape, 1806–1849', *AYB* (1986, I), 13–14; Digby Warren, 'Merchants, Municipal Commissioners and Wardmasters: Municipal Politics in Cape Town' (MA, UCT, 1986), 54; Meltzer, 'Cape Town Commerce', 29–31; Kirsten McKenzie, 'The South African Commercial Advertiser and the Making of Middle-Class Identity in Early Nineteenth-Century Cape Town' (MA, UCT, 1993), 67–70.

49. Immelman, *Men of Good Hope*, 58–70; Meltzer, 'Cape Town Commerce', 31–3; Warren, 'Municipal Politics', 55; George, 'Ebden', 15.

50. Meltzer, 'Cape Town Commerce', 98–100, 110–13; Kirk, 'Self-Government', 103–6, 308–10.

51. Mary Rayner, 'Wine and Slaves: The Failure of an Export Economy and the Ending of Slavery in the Cape Colony, South Africa, 1806–1834' (Ph.D., Duke, 1986), 89–94.

52. Van Ryneveld played a crucial early role in shaping British perceptions. See André du Toit and Hermann Giliomee, *Afrikaner Political Thought, Analysis and Documents, I: 1780–1850* (Cape Town, 1983), 50–3, 95–8; on Truter, see *DSAB*, I, 805–6. At one time Truter owned some fifty slaves.

53. Rayner, 'Wine and Slaves', 94–8; Robert Ross, 'The Rise of the Cape Gentry', *JSAS*, 9, 2 (1983), 206–8; Robert Ross, *Beyond the Pale: Essays on the History of Colonial South Africa* (Johannesburg, 1994), ch. 1 and 91–2; Leonard Guelke and Robert Shell, 'An Early Colonial Landed Gentry: Land and Wealth in the Cape Colony, 1682–1731', *Journal of Historical Geography*, 9 (1983), 265–86. Wayne Dooling describes a 'moral community' of slave-owners, never egalitarian, but one in which a high premium was placed on upholding standards of behaviour and respectability. A very high degree of family intermarriage resulted from the small pool of a few hundred original (pre-1717) female settlers, who comprised the genetic pool from which European settler society emerged. The rapid growth of that society resulted from the very young age of marriage (by European standards), and the extraordinary rate of fertility (by any standards), of European women. Widowhood seldom lasted for long, for single women, especially of childbearing age, were in great demand, and consequently were able to marry into higher social strata very commonly. Because of the system of partible inheritance, widows and daughters often were the conduit of wealth from one family to another. Dooling, '"The Good Opinion of Others": Law, Slavery and Community in the Cape Colony, *c.*1760–1830' in Nigel Worden and Clifton Crais (eds.), *Breaking the Chains: Slavery and its Legacy in the Nineteenth-Century Cape Colony* (Johannesburg, 1994), 31–6; Dooling, *Law and Community in a Slave Society: Stellenbosch District, South Africa, c.1760–1820*, Centre for African Studies, Communications no. 23 (Cape Town 1992), 6–28; Robert Shell, *Children of Bondage: A Social History of the Slave Society at the Cape of Good Hope, 1652–1838* (Hanover, NH, 1994), 289–90, 298–304, 319, 327; Leonard Guelke, 'The Anatomy of a Colonial Settler Population: Cape Colony, 1657–1750', *IJAHS*, 21, 3 (1988), 453–73; Ross, 'The "White" Population of the Cape Colony in the Eighteenth Century' and 'The Development Spiral of the White Family and the Expansion of the Frontier', both in Ross, *Beyond the Pale*.

54. James C. Armstrong and Nigel Worden, 'The Slaves, 1652–1834' in *SSAS*, 134–7, on the distribution of slaveholdings. The Cape was characterised by the fact that slave-ownership was very widespread, but relatively small-scale slaveholdings predominated, compared with plantation regimes in the Americas. At the start of the nineteenth century, 66 per cent of all white farmers owned at least one slave, and over 90 per cent of arable farmers were slave-owners. Nigel Worden, *Slavery in Dutch South Africa* (Cambridge, 1985), 27–31; Rayner, 'Wine and Slaves', 4; John Mason, '"Fit for Freedom": The Slaves, Slavery and Emancipation in the Cape Colony, South Africa, 1806–1842' (Ph.D., Yale, 1992), 42–3, 164.

55. Robert Shell, 'A Family Matter: The Sale and Transfer of Human Beings at the Cape, 1658–1830', *IJAHS*, 25, 2 (1992), 333–6; Shell, *Children of Bondage*, 100–1, 115–17, 132–4.

56. D.J. van Zyl, *Kaapse Wyn en Brandewyn, 1795–1860* (Cape Town, 1975), 103–13; Rayner, 'Wine and Slaves', 20.

57. Van Zyl, *Wyn en Brandewyn*, 114–21.

58. George, 'Ebden', 4–13.

59. Van Zyl, *Wyn en Brandewyn*, 122–8; Rayner, 'Wine and Slaves', 14–15.

60. Van Zyl, *Wyn en Brandewyn*, 51–7; Mason, '"Fit for Freedom,"' 91–3; Rayner, 'Wine and Slaves', 12–14; Duly, *British Land Policy*, 44.

61. Van Zyl, *Wyn en Brandewyn*, 127–31; George, 'Ebden', 11–13.

62. Rayner, 'Wine and Slaves', 14–16; Immelman, *Men of Good Hope*, 72; Van Zyl, *Wyn en Brandewyn*, 125.

63. Van Zyl, *Wyn en Brandewyn*, 159–70; Rayner, 'Wine and Slaves', 20–2.

64. Rayner, 'Wine and Slaves', 23–36.

65. Mason, '"Fit for Freedom,"' 89–90.

66. The sex ratio among slaves peaked at 650 males to 100 females early in the eighteenth century, and declined thereafter to 180:100 by 1833. Most privately owned slaves were locally born from about 1770 onward. By the early 1800s, the slave population was younger and included many more young women than before, and creolisation was accelerated perhaps as a result of the new importance in the nineteenth century of 'slave breeding' for owners after the abolition of the import trade in slaves, which meant that they now encouraged slave women to have children. Low slave fertility, Shell contends, had in the eighteenth century been due in part to the practice of wet-nursing, which lowered slave fertility while increasing the fertility of white women. Shell suggests that wet-nursing was largely abandoned after 1808, as slave women's child-bearing potential became paramount. Shell, *Children of Bondage*, 46–8, 58, 67–77, 304–12; Worden, *Slavery*, 52–63.

67. In consequence, manumissions dropped after 1808, but seem to have taken off in the late 1820s again (when depression struck and the slave economy stagnated), mainly owing to amelioration legislation (as we shall see), which facilitated the process. Shell, *Children of Bondage*, 328, 384–5, 388, 94, 101, 105–6, 118–21, 132–4; Andrew Bank, *The Decline of Urban Slavery at the Cape, 1806–1834*, Communications no. 22, Centre for African Studies, University of Cape Town (1991), 185–8; Armstrong and Worden in *SSAS*, 132–3; Rayner, 'Wine and Slaves', 38–42.

68. Shell, *Children of Bondage*, 32–3; Armstrong and Worden in *SSAS*, 140; Rayner, 'Wine and Slaves', 58, 208. But prices also seem to have dropped again in the 1820s owing to economic stagnation.

69. Bank, *Decline of Urban Slavery*.

70. Mason, '"Fit for Freedom,"' 44; Shell, *Children of Bondage*, 34–7. See ch. 6 below.

71. Rayner, 'Wine and Slaves', 60, 66–7.

72. About 2000 'prize negroes', almost all from Madagascar and Mozambique, were landed at the Cape in the decade after the abolition of the oceanic slave trade in 1808. They were apprenticed for fourteen years, becoming effectively part of the unfree labouring population of the colony, indistinguishable in practice from the slaves. The extensive racket that was involved in the illegal selling of such new arrivals resulted in the introduction of slave registration in 1816. C.C. Saunders, 'Liberated Africans in the Cape Colony in the First Half of the Nineteenth Century', *IJAHS*, 18, 2 (1985), 223–39; Saunders, '"Free Yet Slaves": Prize Negroes at the Cape Revisited' in Worden and Crais, *Breaking the Chains*; Rayner, 'Wine and Slaves', 42–56; Armstrong and Worden in *SSAS*, 120; Shell, *Children of Bondage*, 146–8.

73. Worden, *Slavery*, 20–6; Robert Ross, *Cape of Torments: Slavery and Resistance in South Africa* (1983), 25–6.

74. Mason, '"Fit for Freedom,"' 438–9.

75. Rayner, 'Wine and Slaves', 71–2.

76. P.J. Venter, 'Landdros en Heemrade, 1682–1827', *AYB* (1940, II); Ross, 'Gentry', 196–7; Rayner, 'Wine and Slaves', 99–101; Peires in *SSAS*, 493.

77. Hermann Giliomee, 'The Eastern Frontier, 1770–1812' in *SSAS*, 1st ed. (1979), 348–54, 2nd ed., 450; Thompson, *Political Mythology*, ch. 4 and 206–12; J.A. Heese, *Slagtersnek en sy Mense* (Cape Town, 1973), *passim*.

78. E.P. Thompson, *Whigs and Hunters: The Origins of the Black Act* (1975); Douglas Hay et al., *Albion's Fatal Tree: Crime and Society in Eighteenth-Century England* (1975).

79. See ch. 4 on missionaries; Susan Newton-King, 'The Labour Market of the Cape Colony, 1807–1828' in Shula Marks and Anthony Atmore (eds.), *Economy and Society in Pre-Industrial South Africa* (1980), 174–7, on Collins, whose report is in Donald Moodie, *The Record* (1838,

1842, repr. Cape Town, 1960), Part 5. The role of Khoi labour at the time is examined in V.C. Malherbe, 'Diversification and Mobility of Khoikhoi Labour in the Eastern Districts of the Cape Colony Prior to the Labour Law of 1 November 1809' (MA, UCT, 1978).

80. On the 1809 proclamation, see Newton-King, 'Labour Market', 174–7; Macmillan, *Cape Colour Question*, 156–70; J.S. Marais, *The Cape Coloured People, 1652–1937* (Johannesburg, 1957), 116–19; Hermann Giliomee, 'Die Administrasietydperk van Lord Caledon, 1807–1811', *AYB* (1966, II), 272–80; Richard Elphick and V.C. Malherbe, 'The Khoisan to 1828' in *SSAS*, 40–2; Nigel Penn, 'The Northern Cape Frontier Zone, 1700–*c*.1815' (Ph.D., UCT, 1995), 461–4; Elizabeth Elbourne, '"To Colonise the Mind": Evangelical Missionaries in Britain and the Eastern Cape, 1790–1837' (D.Phil., Oxford, 1992), 170–2; Elizabeth Elbourne, 'Freedom at Issue: Vagrancy Legislation and the Meaning of Freedom in Britain and the Cape Colony, 1799 to 1842', *Slavery and Abolition*, 15, 2 (1994), 120–3; Davenport in *OHSA*, 303–4; Robert Ross, 'The Origins of Capitalist Agriculture in the Cape Colony: A Survey' in W. Beinart, P. Delius and S. Trapido (eds.), *Putting a Plough to the Ground: Accumulation and Dispossession in Rural South Africa, 1850–1930* (Johannesburg, 1986), 77–9; Ross, *Beyond the Pale*, 94–6; John Philip, *Researches in South Africa*, 2 vols. (1828, repr. New York, 1969), I, ch. 8, II, 373–8. The proclamation is to be found in G.W. Eybers (ed.), *Select Constitutional Documents Illustrating South African History* (1918), 17–18.

81. Andrew Ross, *John Philip (1775–1851): Missions, Race and Politics in South Africa* (Aberdeen, 1986), 44–7; Elbourne, '"To Colonise the Mind,"' 172–88; Giliomee, 'Caledon', 298–305; Macmillan, CCQ, 157–8, on the background to the black circuit.

82. Thompson, *Political Mythology* (see n.77 above).

83. John Campbell, *Travels in South Africa undertaken at the Request of the Missionary Society* (1815, repr. Cape Town, 1974), 344–5; Ross, 'The Changing Legal Position of the Khoikhoi in the Cape Colony, 1652–1795' in *Beyond the Pale*, on the issue of Khoi testimony and its status in courts. See n.93 below.

84. Macmillan, CCQ, 88–90; Elbourne, '"To Colonise the Mind,"' 189–94.

85. Macmillan, CCQ, 161–2, 168; Marais, Cape Coloured People, 118–19, 127–9; Elbourne, '"To Colonise the Mind,"' 185–6; Philip, *Researches*, I, ch. 9, II, 378–80; Ross, *Pale*, 100–1.

86. On British paternalist ideology, see Rayner, 'Wine and Slaves', 118–24, 81–91; for discussions of the rule of law and race perceptions among Afrikaner colonists, see Du Toit and Giliomee, *Afrikaner Political Thought*, 35–9, 78–89.

87. Duly, *British Land Policy*, 44–9; Freund in *SSAS*, 331; Peires in *SSAS*, 502–3; Davenport in *OHSA*, 288.

88. Hermann Giliomee, 'Processes in Development of the Southern African Frontier' in Howard Lamar and L.M. Thompson (eds.), *The Frontier in History: North America and Southern Africa Compared* (New Haven, 1981), 98; Du Toit and Giliomee, *Afrikaner Political Thought*, 48–9.

89. Duly, *British Land Policy*, 56–79.

90. P.J. van der Merwe, *Die Noordwaartse Beweging van die Boere voor die Groot Trek, 1770–1842* (The Hague, 1937).

91. Rayner, 'Wine and Slaves', 121–4; Ross, 'The Rule of Law in the Cape Colony in the Eighteenth Century' in Ross, *Pale*. According to Albie Sachs, *Justice in South Africa* (Berkeley, 1973), 31, abolition of torture alarmed Cape judges who predicted an increase in capital offences, arguing that 'the distinction of persons is one of the essential points by which the degree of punishment is measured in most civilised nations'. Death by torture could be abolished without ill effects in the case of free people, but to abolish it generally would only encourage revolt among slaves. This was the voice of the eighteenth century arguing against the rising tides of liberalism, which were to arrive at the Cape in the 1820s.

92. Robin Blackburn, *The Overthrow of Colonial Slavery, 1776–1848* (1988); Eugene Genovese, *From Rebellion to Revolution: African-American Slave Revolts in the Making of the Modern World* (Baton Rouge, 1979); Michael Craton, *Testing the Chains: Resistance to Slavery in the British West Indies* (Ithaca, 1982); Craton, 'Slave Culture, Resistance and the Achievement of Emancipation in the British West Indies, 1783–1846' in James Walvin (ed.), *Slavery and British Society, 1776–1846* (1982).

93. Rayner, 'Wine and Slaves', 81–91. Legal paternalism is part and parcel of all slave systems, and under the Dutch there were also constraints on owners' treatment of slaves, flogging and other severe forms of punishment being the preserve of the authorities (who sometimes applied extreme forms of torture). The best study of the hegemonic functions of the law is Dooling, *Law and Community* and '"The Good Opinion of Others"' (n.53 above); also Victor de Kock, *Those in Bondage*, 146–97; Sachs, *Justice in South Africa*, 60–1; Ross, *Pale*, 98–9; Worden, *Slavery*, 110–18. Dooling argues that the moral community of slaveholders had great influence over the

workings of the legal system at a local level. The courts were used to assert codes of acceptable behaviour within the slave-owning community. Those known to be respectable and upright were protected against the charges of slaves, who could be punished for bringing false charges. But those masters who indulged in excessively brutal treatment and who were thus contravening the code of behaviour, were condemned, and more likely to be made an example of in court. Hence the question of masters' reputation dictated in large degree which slaves were able to get their complaints to court (or dared to try), who was believed in court, and the nature of sentences. In extreme cases, banishment of slave-owners from the colony was resorted to. British rule, though it came to stress an impartial 'rule of law', did not ultimately displace the influence of community will and community sentiment in the local judicial system (although for a period in the 1820s and 1830s the legitimacy of the law in colonists' eyes was seriously eroded by humanitarian reformism regarding labour relations).

94. Rayner, 'Wine and Slaves', 73–6; R.L. Watson, *The Slave Question: Liberty and Property in South Africa* (Johannesburg, 1990), 25–6. A contemporary pamphleteer wrote: 'This execution was not so much intended to repress cruelty to the slaves as to support the slave system. The death of the slave happened at an unfortunate time for his master, just as the news of the proceedings of the British Parliament in relation to slavery ... reached the colony, and when the abettors of slavery ... were trembling for its safety.' Watson (235) speculates that Thomas Pringle was the author.

95. See pp. 95–6 below.

96. On the proclamation, see Edwards, *Towards Emancipation*, 91–5, 221–6; Mason, '"Fit for Freedom,"' 101–2; Mason, 'The Slaves and their Protectors: Reforming Resistance in a Slave Society, the Cape Colony, 1826–1834', *JSAS*, 17, 1 (1991), 106–7; Rayner, 'Wine and Slaves', 160–3; Watson, *Slave Question*, 26–7; Armstrong and Worden in *SSAS*, 154–5; Margaret Donaldson, 'The Council of Advice at the Cape of Good Hope, 1825–1834: A Study in Colonial Government' (Ph.D., Rhodes, 1974), 215–18; Shell, *Children of Bondage*, 320–1. There were far more Islamic marriages than Christian, but they were not officially recognised.

97. Edwards, *Towards Emancipation*, 91; Watson, *Slave Question*, 24–9.

98. Rayner, 'Wine and Slaves', 164–6; Watson, *Slave Question*, 32–5.

99. A. Brady, *William Huskisson and Liberal Reform* (1928).

100. Immelman, *Men of Good Hope*, 58–62; Van Zyl, *Wyn en Brandewyn*, 132–8; George, 'Ebden', 31–3, 74–7; Rayner, 'Wine and Slaves', 208, 190–3; Donaldson, 'Council of Advice', 272–6.

101. On the 1825 rebellion, see Rayner, 'Wine and Slaves', 130–2, 174–89; Ross, *Cape of Torments*, 105–16; Watson, *Slave Question*, 50–9; Armstrong and Worden in *SSAS*, 161; B.J.I. Rutherford, 'The Galant Rebellion of 1825: A Study of Labour Relations within the Worcester District, between the Years 1820–1830' (BA Hons. thesis, UCT, 1990); P.G. Warnick, 'Die Toepassing en Invloed van Slawewetgewing in die Landdrosdistrik Tulbagh/Worcester, 1816–1830' (MA, Stellenbosch, 1988). André Brink's novel *A Chain of Voices* (1982) is a fictional account of Galant's rising.

102. On Denyssen's views, see Du Toit and Giliomee, *Afrikaner Political Thought*, 56–61. Denyssen, born in Amsterdam, received a doctorate from Leiden, and served on the Cape Court of Justice under the Batavian administration, staying on under British rule.

103. Watson, *Slave Question*, 22–3; Donaldson, 'Council of Advice', 222–4. An earlier slave rebellion in 1808 was an indication to local slave-owners of how dangerous abolitionist rumours were: the abolition of the slave trade in that year was regarded by local notables as the cause of this particular insurrection. Watson, *Slave Question*, 49–50; Rayner, 'Wine and Slaves', 151–6; Ross, *Cape of Torments*, 97–105; Karen Harris, 'The Slave "Rebellion" of 1808', *Kleio*, 20 (1988), 54–65; P.B. Borcherds, *An Autobiographical Memoir* (Cape Town, 1861), 291–7.

104. Rayner, 'Wine and Slaves', 193–203; Van Zyl, *Wyn en Brandewyn*, 138–52, 168–9; George, 'Ebden', 33–6; Hazel King, *Richard Bourke* (Melbourne, 1971), 79–80. Sequestrations accounted for a growing number of slave transfers in the 1820s, due to the depression and the growing practice of mortgaging slaves. Shell, *Children of Bondage*, 100–1, 105, 109–10, 117–18.

105. George Thompson, *Travels and Adventures in Southern Africa* (1827, repr. Cape Town, 1967–8), II, 92. Cf. the rates of return on slave investments in the eighteenth century, in Worden, *Slavery*, 64–85. John Philip wrote at the same time (1827) that 'the only class of people ... who of late years have been making money, are the cattle boors in the Bushman country'. In 1825 he had met a farmer near Genadendal who intended selling his slaves and farm and moving, as 'the interest which he would receive for the money he might obtain by the sale ... would be more than the return he now had by the produce of his farm; and that, he could get Bushmen, and other natives, for nothing in the Bushman country' (*Researches*, II, 44–5).

106. Donaldson, 'Council of Advice', 129–210; H.C. Botha, *John Fairbairn in South Africa*

(Cape Town, 1984), 77–80.

107. L. Bryer and K.S. Hunt, *The 1820 Settlers* (Cape Town, 1984), 13.

108. Edmund H. Burrows, *The Moodies of Melsetter* (Cape Town, 1954); Newton-King, 'Labour Market', 183–6.

109. M.D. Nash, *Bailie's Party of 1820 Settlers: A Collective Experience in Emigration* (Cape Town, 1982), 6–8; Bryer and Hunt, *1820 Settlers*, 15.

110. Guy Butler (ed.), *The 1820 Settlers: An Illustrated Commentary* (Cape Town, 1974) is an exemplar.

111. Isobel Edwards, *The 1820 Settlers in South Africa* (1934), 30–1, 40; Bryer and Hunt, *1820 Settlers*, 11.

112. Peires in *SSAS*, 481–2; A.C.M. Webb, 'The Agricultural Development of the 1820 Settlement down to 1846' (MA, Rhodes, 1975), 13–14.

113. Bryer and Hunt, *1820 Settlers*, 10–13; Nash, *Bailie's Party*, 5–6; Edwards, *1820 Settlers*, 29–30, 43.

114. Bryer and Hunt, *1820 Settlers*, 17–20; Nash, *Bailie's Party*, 8.

115. Johnstone, *Emigration Policy*, 35–6.

116. Ibid, 30–7, 48, 56; Edwards, *1820 Settlers*, 42, 46–7. The view of Edwards and others that frontier defence was the prime motive behind such official interest in the Cape is unconvincing. The supposed Xhosa threat to the cattle of a few Boers was hardly a concern in London.

117. Nash, *Bailie's Party*, 11–12.

118. Thompson, *Travels*, II, 102.

119. Bryer and Hunt, *1820 Settlers*, 16–17, 24–5, 41–2; Nash, *Bailie's Party*, 20, 24–6; Edwards, *1820 Settlers*, 54–6. Of the settlers 36 per cent were adult men, 20 per cent women, 44 per cent children.

120. Bryer and Hunt, *1820 Settlers*, 24–5.

121. Cory, *Rise of South Africa*, II, chs. 2–3, on the tribulations of the settlement; Nash, *Bailie's Party*, 38–9; Clifton Crais, *The Making of the Colonial Order: White Supremacy and Black Resistance in the Eastern Cape, 1770–1865* (Johannesburg, 1992), 87–95; H.E. Hockly, *The Story of the British Settlers of 1820 in South Africa* (Johannesburg, 1966); Edwards, *1820 Settlers*; Peires in *SSAS*, 474–80; Davenport in *OHSA*, 278–80; Thomas Pringle, *Narrative of a Residence in South Africa* (1835), *passim*; Thompson, *Travels*, II, 101–15; M.D. Nash, *The Settler Handbook: A New List of the 1820 Settlers* (Cape Town, 1987). A great many settler memoirs, collections of letters, etc., have been preserved and published, for example in the Graham's Town Series (Rhodes University).

122. B.A. le Cordeur, *The Politics of Eastern Cape Separatism, 1820–1854* (Cape Town, 1981), 3–6; Nash, *Bailie's Party*, 40–2, 51–60; Cory, *Rise of SA*, II, ch. 4; Bryer and Hunt, *1820 Settlers*, 47–54.

123. Nash, *Bailie's Party*, 69–76; Macmillan, *CCQ*, 113–21.

124. Crais, *Colonial Order*, 92–5; Newton-King, 'Labour Market', 182–92, on white worker immigration schemes.

125. Newton-King, 'Labour Market', 188–91.

126. Rayner, 'Wine and Slaves', 303–4.

127. Nash, *Bailie's Party*, 38–9; Edwards, *1820 Settlers*, 81.

128. Thompson, *Making of the English Working Class*, 40–58, 385–440; Eric Hobsbawm, 'Methodism and the Threat of Revolution in Britain' in Hobsbawm, *Labouring Men: Studies in the History of Labour* (1964); Élie Halévy, *The Birth of Methodism in England* (Chicago, 1971); Bernard Semmel, *The Methodist Revolution* (1974); Stuart Piggin, 'Halévy Revisited: The Origins of the Wesleyan Methodist Missionary Society: An Examination of Semmel's Thesis', *Journal of Imperial and Commonwealth History*, 9, 1 (1980), 17–37.

129. A.E. Makin, *The 1820 Settlers of Salem* (Wynberg, 1971); Pringle, *Narrative*, 18; John Stone, *Colonist or Uitlander? A Study of the British Immigrant in South Africa* (Oxford, 1973), 98–9.

130. P.H. Lyness, 'The Life and Influence of William Shaw, 1820–1856' (MA, Rhodes, 1982); also see ch. 5 n.8 below.

131. W. Eveleigh, *The Settlers and Methodism, 1820–1920* (Cape Town, 1920); Le Cordeur, *Eastern Cape Separatism*, 67–8; A.T.C. Slee, 'Some Aspects of Wesleyan Methodism in the Albany District between 1830 and 1844' (MA, Unisa, 1946); B.E. Seton, 'Wesleyan Missions and the Sixth Frontier War, 1834–1835' (Ph.D., UCT, 1962), 15–18; Jane Sales, *Mission Stations and the Coloured Communities of the Eastern Cape, 1800–1852* (Cape Town, 1975), 116; Johannes du Plessis, *A History of Christian Missions in South Africa* (1911), 165–81.

132. Le Cordeur, *Separatism*, 38–43; K.W. Smith, *From Frontier to Midlands: A History of the*

Graaff-Reinet District, 1786–1910, Occasional Paper no. 20, Institute of Social and Economic Research, Rhodes University (1976), 51; Andrew Steedman, *Wanderings and Adventures in the Interior of Southern Africa*, 2 vols. (1835, repr. Cape Town, 1966), I, 123–4; Thompson, *Travels*, I, 42–3.

133. K.S. Hunt, 'The Development of Municipal Government in the Eastern Province of the Cape of Good Hope, with Special Reference to Grahamstown, 1827–1862', *AYB* (1961), 152–3; Le Cordeur, *Separatism*, 39–40.

134. J.W.D. Moodie, *Ten Years in South Africa*, 2 vols. (1835), II, 305. See also John Montgomery's story, *The Reminiscences of John Montgomery*, ed. A. Giffard, Graham's Town Series no. 6 (Cape Town, 1981).

135. Le Cordeur, *Separatism*, 38, 58; Crais, *Colonial Order*, 106–7.

136. Moodie, *Ten Years*, II, 305.

137. Monica Wilson, 'Co-operation and Conflict: The Eastern Cape Frontier' in *OHSA*, 234–8; Roger Beck, 'The Legalisation and Development of Trade on the Cape Frontier' (Ph.D., Indiana, 1987), 45–6, 29–30; Les Switzer, *Power and Resistance in an African Society: The Ciskei Xhosa and the Making of South Africa* (Madison, Wis., 1993), 46–8; H.M. Robertson, '150 Years of Economic Contact between Black and White', *South African Journal of Economics*, 2 (1934), 403–25, 3 (1935), 3–25.

138. Roger Beck, 'Bibles and Beads: Missionaries as Traders in Southern Africa in the Early Nineteenth Century', *JAH*, 30, 2 (1989), 211–55.

139. Beck, 'Legalisation', 105–9.

140. Donaldson, 'Council of Advice', 309–32; Crais, *Colonial Order*, 108–12; Beck, 'Legalisation', 123–4, 144–6, 149, 171; J.B. Peires, *The House of Phalo: A History of the Xhosa People in the Days of their Independence* (Johannesburg, 1981), 82, 98–102; Saxe Bannister, *Humane Policy: or Justice to the Aborigines of New Settlements* (1830, repr. 1968), 116–17, 127–30; Steedman, *Wanderings*, I, 4–10; Stephen Kay, *Travels and Researches in Caffraria* (1833), 448–50; Henry Dugmore, *Reminiscences of an Albany Settler*, eds. F.G. van der Riet and L.A. Hewson (Graham's Town, 1958), 34–6; Robert Godlonton, *Introductory Remarks to a Narrative of the Irruption of the Kaffir Hordes into the Eastern Province of the Cape of Good Hope* (1836, repr. Cape Town, 1965), 138–44.

141. Beck, 'Legalisation', 333–4.

142. On Wood, see Makin, *1820 Settlers*, 82–5; *The Reminiscences of Thomas Stubbs*, eds. W.A. Maxwell and R.T. McGeogh, Graham's Town Series, 4 (Cape Town, 1978), 205–7, 284–5 n.383.

143. Peires, *Phalo*, 82, 95–8; Wilson in *OHSA*, 241–2; Beck, 'Legalisation', 157; Crais, *Colonial Order*, 110–12.

144. Beck, 'Legalisation', 175–6.

145. Cory, *Rise of SA*, II, 174–80; S.D. Neumark, *Economic Influences on the South African Frontier, 1652–1836* (Stanford, 1957), 66–8, 137–44, 152–8, 180–3; Kay, *Travels*, 450–7; Bannister, *Humane Policy*, 109–48.

146. Beck, 'Legalisation', 179, 70–2, 92.

147. Ibid, 238–9, 245–7, 289–97, 302–4.

148. Peires in *SSAS*, 485–6; Godlonton, *Introductory Remarks*, 109–10, 149.

149. Peires, *Phalo*, 102–3, 107–8, 156; Donaldson, 'Council of Advice', 330–2; Colin Bundy, *The Rise and Fall of the South African Peasantry* (1979), 29–32.

150. Nash, *Bailie's Party*, 87–90.

151. Donaldson, 'Council of Advice', 277–8; Beck, 'Legalisation', 20–1, 10–11; Godlonton, *Introductory Remarks*, 150–2, 198–9.

152. Edwards, *1820 Settlers*, 186; Smith, *Frontier to Midlands*, 51; King, *Bourke*, 80; Neumark, *Economic Influences*, 61–2.

153. Le Cordeur, *Separatism*, 42–3; Makin, *1820 Settlers*, 82–5; Hunt, 'Municipal Government', 152–3; Webb, 'Agricultural Development', 116–37; H.B. Thom, *Die Geskiedenis van die Skaapboerdery in Suid-Afrika* (Amsterdam, 1936); Giliomee, 'Processes in Development', 99–100; Davenport in *OHSA*, 290–1.

154. Bryer and Hunt, *1820 Settlers*, 66; Thom, *Skaapboerdery*, 305–12; Thompson, *Travels*, I, 15; C.J.F. Bunbury, *Journal of a Residence at the Cape of Good Hope* (1848, repr. New York, 1969), 128; A.L. Harington, 'The *Graham's Town Journal* and the Great Trek, 1834–1843', *AYB* (1969, II), 15.

155. Bryer and Hunt, *1820 Settlers*, 66–8; Thom, *Skaapboerdery*, 66–7, 170–2, 304–8; Harington, '*Graham's Town Journal*', 7; Godlonton, *Introductory Remarks*, 186–90. Between 1830 and 1835, the amount of wool shipped from Port Elizabeth increased in these years from

4500 lb to 79 848 lb.

156. L.H. Meurant, *Sixty Years Ago* (1885, repr. Cape Town, 1963), 76–101; on Godlonton, *DSAB*, II, 263–6; Harington, '*Graham's Town Journal*', 20–1; Le Cordeur, *Separatism*, 43, 64–5; see Bryer and Hunt, *1820 Settlers*, 61, 66–7; Butler, *1820 Settlers*, 217–19; Hockly, *British Settlers*.

157. Kirk, 'Self-Government', 61–2; Harington, '*Graham's Town Journal*'; Harington, 'The *Graham's Town Journal*: Its Founding, Early History and Influence', *SAHJ*, 1 (1969).

158. See McKenzie, 'Making of Middle-Class Identity', for a discussion of these issues with reference to the *Commercial Advertiser* of Cape Town. See also ch. 4 nn.81, 87 below.

159. See n.156 above.

160. Le Cordeur, *Separatism*, 51–5.

161. Ibid, 54–5.

162. Ibid, 57.

163. Hunt, 'Municipal Government', 142, 151.

164. H. Merivale, *Lectures on Colonization and Colonies* (1860), 460.

Chapter Four: Liberal Reform and the Humanitarian Movement

1. W. Reginald Ward, *The Protestant Evangelical Awakening* (Cambridge, 1992); John Walsh, '"Methodism" and the Origins of English-Speaking Evangelicalism', David Hempton, 'Evangelicalism in English and Irish Society, 1780–1840', and Mark A. Noll, 'Revolution and the Rise of Evangelical Social Influence in North Atlantic Societies', all in Noll, David W. Bebbington and George A. Rawlyk (eds.), *Evangelicalism: Comparative Studies of Popular Protestantism in North America, the British Isles, and Beyond, 1700–1990* (Oxford, 1994); D.W. Bebbington, *Evangelicalism in Modern Britain: A History from the 1730s to the 1980s* (1989); A.D. Gilbert, *Religion and Society in Industrial England: Church, Chapel and Social Change, 1740–1914* (1976); Doreen Rosman, *Evangelicals and Culture* (1984); Elizabeth Elbourne, '"To Colonise the Mind": Evangelical Missionaries in Britain and the Eastern Cape, 1790–1837' (D.Phil., Oxford, 1992), 35–8.

2. Elbourne, '"To Colonise the Mind,"' 45–9; Michael J. Crawford, 'Origins of the Eighteenth Century Evangelical Revival: England and New England Compared', *Journal of British Studies*, 26, 4 (1987); David Hempton, *Methodism and Politics in British Society, 1750–1850* (1984), ch. 14.

3. Elbourne, '"To Colonise the Mind,"' 85–6.

4. Ibid, 87.

5. See pp. 65–7 above on Bunting and Methodism. See Noll, 'Rise of Evangelical Social Influence', 120–3, on the relation between revolution and the advancement of evangelical thinking into mainstream British life, as a substitute for, and a reaction against, the revolutionary gospels of liberation and brotherhood.

6. This is the theme of Boyd Hilton's *The Age of Atonement: The Influence of Evangelicalism on Social and Economic Thought, 1795–1865* (Oxford, 1988).

7. See, e.g., Michel Foucault, *Discipline and Punish: The Birth of the Prison* (1979); John Beattie, *Crime and the Courts, 1660–1815* (Princeton, 1985); Michael Ignatieff, *A Just Measure of Pain: The Penitentiary in the Industrial Revolution, 1750–1850* (1978); C. Emsley, *Crime and Society in England, 1750–1900* (1987); M. Sanderson, *Education, Economic Change and Society in England, 1780–1870* (1983); Thomas Laqueur, *Religion and Respectability: Sunday Schools and Working Class Culture, 1780–1850* (New Haven, 1976); J.R. Poynter, *Society and Pauperism in England: Ideas on Poor Relief, 1795–1834* (1969); Andrew Scull, *Museums of Madness: The Social Organisation of Insanity in Nineteenth Century England* (Harmondsworth, 1982). Generally on the alliance between reform and humanitarianism, see Élie Halévy, *The Triumph of Reform* (1950); more recently, David Turley, *The Culture of English Antislavery, 1780–1860* (1991), 108–54; John Roach, *Social Reform in England, 1770–1880* (1978); Ian Bradley, *The Call to Seriousness: The Evangelical Impact on the Victorians* (1976).

8. The Clapham sect was so called as many middle-class Anglican evangelicals lived in Clapham and gathered at Rev. John Venn's church there. Ernest M. Howse, *Saints in Politics: The Clapham Sect and the Growth of Freedom* (Toronto, 1952, 2nd ed. 1971).

9. W.M. Macmillan, *The Cape Colour Question: A Historical Survey* (1927, repr. Cape Town, 1968), 51. See n.172 below on the reasons for the humanitarians' apparent lack of concern for the domestic poor.

10. Seymour Drescher, *Econocide: British Slavery in the Era of Abolition* (Pittsburgh, 1977), 27–30.

11. Eric Williams, *Capitalism and Slavery* (1944) provides the classic economic explanation for the rise of anti-slavery, stressing overproduction and decline in the sugar economy from the 1770s.

His thesis has been called into doubt in its specifics; but he was one of the first historians to consider abolitionism as more than mere moral idealism, and much of his work has survived the onslaught of more conservative critics. Roger Anstey, *The Atlantic Slave Trade and British Abolition, 1760–1810* (1975); Drescher, *Econocide*; Drescher, *Capitalism and Antislavery: British Mobilization in Comparative Perspective* (New York, 1986); Drescher, 'The Decline Thesis since *Econocide*', *Slavery and Abolition*, 7, 1 (1986), 3–23; David Eltis, *Economic Growth and the Ending of the Transatlantic Slave Trade* (Oxford, 1987); Christine Bolt and Seymour Drescher (eds.), *Anti-Slavery, Religion and Reform: Essays in Honour of Roger Anstey* (Folkestone, 1980); Eltis and Walvin (eds.), *The Abolition of the Atlantic Slave Trade: Origins and Effects in Europe, Africa and the Americas* (Madison, Wis., 1981); James Walvin (ed.), *Slavery and British Society, 1776–1846* (1982); Walvin, *England, Slaves and Freedom, 1776–1838* (1986). On Williams's legacy, see Barbara L. Solow and Stanley L. Engerman (eds.), *British Capitalism and Caribbean Slavery: The Legacy of Eric Williams* (New York, 1987); also Cedric J. Robinson, 'Capitalism, Slavery and Bourgeois Historiography (or Takin' on Ol' Massa)', *History Workshop Journal*, 23 (1987); and Selwyn Carrington, 'The State of the Debate on the Role of Capitalism in the Ending of the Slave System', *Journal of Caribbean History*, 22, 1–2 (1988), 20–41, for defences of Williams. David Brion Davis took up the connections between capitalist development and abolitionism in reinforcing the hegemony of capitalist values: see *The Problem of Slavery in Western Culture* (Ithaca, 1966, rev. ed. 1988); Davis, *The Problem of Slavery in the Age of Revolution, 1770–1823* (1975); Davis, *Slavery and Human Progress* (Oxford, 1984). Debates arising from Davis's work are to be found in Thomas Bender (ed.), *The Antislavery Debate: Capitalism and Abolitionism as a Problem in Historical Interpretation* (Berkeley, 1992). Robin Blackburn, *The Overthrow of Colonial Slavery, 1776–1848* (1988) extends the line of argument by illustrating the ways in which abolitionism appealed to various classes of Britons caught in the psychic and material dislocations of early industrialism. The rise of anti-slavery as a humanitarian cause and then as a mass movement from the 1780s is a different issue from that of why in the nineteenth century it became public policy at the level of the governing elite. The former issue created an ideological climate that made emancipation possible; the latter grew out of specific social and political relations of the time. Blackburn in particular, following Genovese, furthermore stresses the role played by slave rebelliousness, especially in the Haitian revolution, arising out of the collapse of absolutism in France, Spain and Portugal, and the spread of Jacobin and egalitarian ideas through the slave regimes, including Britain's (especially the creole slave elite influenced by evangelical mission activity) from the 1790s. See ch. 3 n.92 above.

12. G.R. Mellor, *British Imperial Trusteeship, 1783–1850* (1951).

13. Philip Curtin, *The Image of Africa: British Ideas in Action, 1780–1850* (Madison, Wis., 1964); P.J. Marshall and Glyndwr Williams, *The Great Map of Mankind: Perceptions of New Worlds in the Age of Enlightenment* (Cambridge, Mass., 1982); Robin Hallett, 'Changing European Attitudes to Africa' in J. Flint (ed.), *Cambridge History of Africa, c.1790–1870*, vol. 5 (Cambridge, 1976), 458–96.

14. Elbourne, '"To Colonise the Mind,"' 61–96, on the foundation of the missionary societies.

15. Roger H. Martin, *Evangelicals United: Ecumenical Stirrings in Pre-Victorian Britain, 1795–1830* (1983); Elbourne, '"To Colonise the Mind,"' 49–60.

16. Stuart Piggin, *Making Evangelical Missionaries, 1789–1858* (Abingdon, Oxfordshire, 1984); Sarah Potter, 'The Social Origins and Recruitment of English Protestant Missionaries in the Nineteenth Century' (Ph.D., London, 1974); Jean and John Comaroff, *Of Revelation and Revolution: Christianity, Colonialism, and Consciousness in South Africa* (Chicago, 1991), 80–2; Richard Elphick, 'Africans and the Christian Campaign in Southern Africa' in Howard Lamar and L.M. Thompson (eds.), *The Frontier in History: North America and Southern Africa Compared* (New Haven, 1981), 279–80; Elbourne, 'Concerning Missionaries: The Case of Van der Kemp', *JSAS*, 17, 1 (1991), 153–64; Donovan Williams, 'The Missionary Personality in Caffraria, 1799–1853: A Study in the Context of Biography', *Historia*, 34, 1 (1989), 15–35.

17. Andrew Ross, *John Philip (1775–1851): Missions, Race and Politics in South Africa* (Aberdeen, 1986), 36–7.

18. Elbourne, 'The Foundation of the Church Missionary Society: The Anglican Missionary Impulse' in J.D. Walsh, C.M. Haydon and S. Taylor (eds.), *The Church of England, ca 1689–1833: From Toleration to Tractarianism* (Cambridge, 1992); Elbourne, '"To Colonise the Mind,"' 80–96.

19. Penelope Carson, 'An Imperial Dilemma: The Propagation of Christianity in Early Colonial India', *Journal of Imperial and Commonwealth History*, 18, 2 (1990), 169–90.

20. Elbourne, 'A Question of Identity: Evangelical Culture and Khoisan Politics in the Early Nineteenth-Century Eastern Cape', *Societies of Southern Africa in the Nineteenth and Twentieth*

Centuries, vol. 18, Collected Seminar Papers no. 44, Institute of Commonwealth Studies, London (1992), 22–3.

21. Richard Brent, *Liberal Anglican Politics: Whiggery, Religion and Reform, 1830–1841* (Oxford, 1987) on the dominance of evangelicals in the corridors of power and the alliance with Nonconformism during the Whig ascendancy.

22. Bernard Kruger, *The Pear Tree Blossoms: A History of the Moravian Mission Stations in South Africa* (Genadendal, 1966); J.S. Marais, *The Cape Coloured People, 1652–1937* (Johannesburg, 1957), 34–40; *The Genadendal Diaries: Diaries of the Herrnhut Missionaries*, eds. H.C. Bredekamp and H.E.F. Plüddemann (Bellville, 1992).

23. Jane Sales, *Mission Stations and the Coloured Communities of the Eastern Cape, 1800–1852* (Cape Town, 1975), 7–20; Richard Lovett, *The History of the London Missionary Society, 1795–1895*, 2 vols. (1899), I, 498–517; Johannes du Plessis, *A History of Christian Missions in South Africa* (1911), 120–8; Susan Newton-King and V.C. Malherbe, *The Khoikhoi Rebellion in the Eastern Cape, 1799–1803*, Communications no. 5, Centre for African Studies (Cape Town, 1981); Elbourne, '"To Colonise the Mind,"' 143–58. The first formal corps for Khoi–Bastaard allies had been established in 1781–2. The Cape Regiment was re-established by the British in 1806 as a light infantry corps of 500–800 men, to be internally funded. From 1811 it was based at Graham's Town, and after the 1811–12 war it was augmented by 800 men for frontier defence. It was disbanded in 1817 owing to financial constraints; but Khoi–Bastaard regiments continued to serve Cape governments for many years thereafter when needed. See J. de Villiers, 'Die Cape Regiment, 1806–1817, 'n Koloniale Regiment in Britse Diens', *AYB* (1989, I); George Tylden, 'The Cape Coloured Regiments, 1793–1870', *Africana Notes and News*, 7, 2 (1950); Richard Elphick and V.C. Malherbe, 'The Khoisan to 1828' in Elphick and Hermann Giliomee (eds.), *The Shaping of South African Society, 1652–1840*, 2nd ed. (Cape Town, 1989), 35–8, 59–60 n.90; Marais, *Cape Coloured People*, 131–4; Giliomee, 'Die Administrasietydperk van Lord Caledon, 1807–1811', *AYB* (1966, II), 281–6.

24. On Van der Kemp, see W.M. Freund, 'The Career of Johannes Theodorus van der Kemp and his Role in the History of South Africa', *Tijdschrift voor Geschiedenis*, 86 (1973); Ido H. Enklaar, *The Life and Work of Dr J. Th. van der Kemp, 1747–1811: Missionary Pioneer and Protagonist of Racial Equality in South Africa* (Rotterdam, 1988); Elbourne, 'Concerning Missionaries'; Elbourne, '"To Colonise the Mind,"' 104–11; A.D. Martin, *Doctor Vanderkemp* (1931); *DSAB*, II, 774–8.

25. Elbourne, '"To Colonise the Mind,"' 195–209.

26. Cf. Somerset to Bathurst in June 1819: 'The establishment of a Theocracy entirely independent of the Civil Government was Brother van der Kemp's favourite and avowed plan.' Donovan Williams, *When Races Meet: The Life and Times of William Ritchie Thomson, Glasgow Society Missionary, Government Agent and Dutch Reformed Church Minister* (Johannesburg, 1981), 29.

27. We should not overemphasise this point; Boer employers quickly reconciled themselves to the spread of Christianity among servants when it occurred, provided it reinforced rather than undermined the hierarchy of discipline and deference. Elbourne, '"To Colonise the Mind,"' 141–3. See ch. 2 n.10 above.

28. Elphick and Malherbe in *SSAS*, 39–40; Elbourne, '"To Colonise the Mind"', 228–33.

29. Elbourne, 'A Question of Identity'; Elbourne, '"To Colonise the Mind,"' 122–31, on Khoisan religion and interaction with Christianity, and 254–61 on the uses of Christianity for the Khoi.

30. Elbourne, '"To Colonise the Mind,"' 211–14.

31. Martin Legassick, 'The Griqua, the Sotho–Tswana and the Missionaries, 1780–1840: The Politics of a Frontier Zone' (Ph.D., UCLA, 1969), 191–4, on the 'native agency'; Elbourne, '"To Colonise the Mind,"' 243–65, on the mission elite; V.C. Malherbe, 'The Life and Times of Cupido Kakkerlak', *JAH*, 20, 3 (1979), 365–78; Elphick and Malherbe in *SSAS*, 40. On the Griqua and developments north of the Orange, see ch. 6 below.

32. See, e.g., Timothy Keegan, 'Dispossession and Accumulation in the South African Interior: The Boers and the Tlhaping of Bethulie, 1833–1861', *JAH*, 28 (1987), 191–207.

33. Margaret Kinsman, 'Populists and Patriarchs: The Transformation of the Captaincy at Griqua Town, 1804–1822' in Alan Mabin (ed.), *Organisation and Economic Change* (Johannesburg, 1989).

34. Stanley Trapido, 'The Emergence of Liberalism and the Making of "Hottentot Nationalism", 1815–1834', *Societies of Southern Africa in the Nineteenth and Twentieth Centuries*, vol. 17, Collected Seminar Papers no. 42, Institute of Commonwealth Studies (London, 1992).

35. Elbourne, '"To Colonise the Mind,"' 159–66; Macmillan, *Cape Colour Question*, 88–9; William M. Freund, 'The Cape under the Transitional Governments, 1795–1814' in *SSAS*, 339–43;

A. Ross, *Philip*, 42–3; C.E.G. Schutte, 'Dr John Philip's Observations regarding the Hottentots', *AYB* (1940, I), 186.

36. Sales, *Mission Stations*, 21, 27, 29–33, 51–2.

37. Giliomee, 'Lord Caledon', 288–94, 298–305; Elbourne, '"To Colonise the Mind,"' 168–70, 228–9.

38. S. Newton-King, 'The Labour Market of the Cape Colony, 1807–1828' in S. Marks and A. Atmore (eds.), *Economy and Society in Pre-Industrial South Africa* (1980), 174–7; Richard Collins in Donald Moodie (ed.), *The Record* (1838, 1842, repr. Cape Town, 1960), Part V.

39. See pp. 54–6 above.

40. Elbourne, '"To Colonise the Mind,"' 172–82; Legassick, 'The Griqua', 159–63; Sales, *Mission Stations*, 51–7; Desmond Clinton, *The South African Melting Pot: A Vindication of Missionary Policy, 1799–1836* (1937), 52–63; Marais, *Cape Coloured People*, 134–54; Harry A. Gailey, 'The LMS and the Cape Government, 1799–1828' (Ph.D., UCLA, 1957); John Campbell, *Travels in South Africa, Undertaken at the Request of the Missionary Society* (1815, repr. Cape Town, 1974).

41. Legassick, 'The Griqua', 151–9, 163–8; De Villiers, 'Cape Regiment', 147–66.

42. Clinton, *Melting Pot*, 73–8, 100–3; John Philip, *Researches in South Africa, Illustrating the Civil, Moral and Religious Condition of the Native Tribes*, 2 vols. (1828, repr. New York, 1969), II, 61–4, 66–7.

43. Basil Holt, *Joseph Williams and the Pioneer Mission to the South-Eastern Bantu* (Lovedale, 1954); Williams, *When Races Meet*, 11–19; Sales, *Mission Stations*, 56, 63–4; Macmillan, *CCQ*, 128.

44. Legassick, 'Griqua', 281–5; Comaroffs, *Of Revelation and Revolution*, 45–6; Du Plessis, *Christian Missions*, 154–5; Macmillan, *CCQ*, 128–33; Clinton, *Melting Pot*, 103–6; Williams, *When Races Meet*, 29; Sales, *Mission Stations*, 58–63; Karel Schoeman, 'Die Londense Sendinggenootskap en die San: Die Stasies Toornberg en Hephzibah, 1814–1818', *SAHJ*, 28 (1993), 221–34. See ch. 5 n.25 below.

45. Thom used Lichtenstein's very unflattering picture of Bethelsdorp to sustain his charges. Sales, *Mission Stations*, 69–70. On the LMS crisis, see A. Ross, *Philip*, 48–51; Legassick, 'Griqua', 285–90; Lovett, *LMS*, I, 534–6; Doug Stuart, 'The Wicked Christians and the Children of the Mist: Missionary and Khoi Interactions at the Cape in the Early Nineteenth Century', *Societies of Southern Africa in the Nineteenth and Twentieth Centuries*, vol. 18, Collected Seminar Papers no. 44, Institute of Commonwealth Studies (London, 1992); Sales, *Mission Stations*, 56–7; Elbourne, '"To Colonise the Mind,"' 214–17; Macmillan, *CCQ*, 92–4. The prevalence of venereal disease entered much public discourse on Bethelsdorp. Race mixing and sexual immorality were conflated (Elbourne, '"To Colonise the Mind,"' 209–11).

46. Williams, *When Races Meet*, 20–2, 33–8, 54–7, 103–4 and *passim*; Macmillan, *CCQ*, 125; Philip, *Researches*, II, chs. 9, 10.

47. Philip looms very large in the historiography. But see Macmillan, *Bantu, Boer and Briton*, 2nd ed. (1963); Macmillan, *CCQ*; A. Ross, *Philip*; J.S. Galbraith, *Reluctant Empire: British Policy on the South African Frontier, 1834–1854* (Berkeley, 1963), 81–5; P.H. Kapp, 'Dr John Philip se Werksaamhede in Suid-Afrika, 1819–1828', *AYB* (1985, II), 1–310; Schutte, 'John Philip's Observations'; Julius Lewin, 'The Nineteenth-Century Reformer: Dr John Philip' in Lewin, *Politics and Law in South Africa: Essays on Race Relations* (1963).

48. Legassick, 'Griqua', 436–49; Robert and Mary Moffat, *Apprenticeship at Kuruman: Being the Journals and Letters of Robert and Mary Moffat, 1820–1828*, ed. Isaac Schapera (1951), 193–207; Lovett, *LMS*, I, 591–2.

49. Legassick, 'Griqua', 440–2.

50. Comaroffs, *Of Revelation and Revolution*, 252–4, 266–73; Moffat, *Missionary Labours and Scenes in Southern Africa* (1842), 206–9, where he warned against political involvements by missionaries.

51. Comaroffs, *Of Revelation and Revolution*, 84–5.

52. Linda Colley, *Britons: Forging the Nation, 1707–1837* (New Haven, 1992), 117–32; Gordon Donaldson, *The Scots Overseas* (1966), 181–93; T.C. Smout, *A History of the Scottish People, 1560–1830* (Glasgow, 1972); Bruce Lenman, *Integration, Enlightenment, and Industrialisation: Scotland, 1746–1832* (1981); Istvan Hout and Michael Ignatieff (eds.), *Wealth and Virtue: The Shaping of Political Economy in the Scottish Enlightenment* (Cambridge, 1983); A. Ross, *Philip*, 52–8.

53. A.L. Drummond and J. Bullock, *The Scottish Church, 1688–1843* (Edinburgh, 1973); A. Ross, *Philip*, 58–63.

54. Ross, *Philip*, 52–76; Macmillan, *CCQ*, 95–102. Robert Moffat's background was very

similar, as were those of later Scots missionaries. On Moffat, see Comaroffs, *Of Revelation and Revolution*, 82–3; John S. Moffat, *The Lives of Robert and Mary Moffat* (New York, 1886); Cecil Northcott, *Robert Moffat: Pioneer in South Africa, 1817–1870* (New York, 1961); *DSAB*, I, 546–50.

55. John MacInnes, *The Evangelical Movement in the Highlands of Scotland, 1688–1800* (Aberdeen, 1951) on the dramatic nature of the evangelisation of the Highlanders; also Noll, 'Revolution and the Rise of Evangelical Social Influence', 115–16, 120–2.

56. On this conversionist, assimilationist ideology, see Curtin, *Image of Africa*; Hallett, 'Changing European Attitudes'. The 1797 edition of the *Encyclopaedia Britannica* represented this spirit of the age when it asserted in the entry on 'Negro' that any apparent inferiority was due solely to the effects of slavery. Paul Johnson, *The Birth of the Modern: World Society, 1815–1830* (1991), 243–4. The missionary, wrote Philip, 'sees in every man a partaker of his own nature, and a brother of his own species' (*Researches*, I, xxxiii).

57. Andrew Bank, 'Liberals and their Enemies: Racial Ideology at the Cape of Good Hope, 1820 to 1850' (Ph.D., Cambridge, 1995), 89–100; George Stocking, *Victorian Anthropology* (1987), ch. 1.

58. A. Ross, *Philip*, 94–7, 66–7, 81.

59. Macmillan, *CCQ*, 109–10.

60. Ross, *Philip*, 97–9; Elphick and Malherbe in *SSAS*, 45–6; Elbourne, '"To Colonise the Mind,"' 267–8, 275–6; Sales, *Mission Stations*, 80–1; *The Kitchingman Papers*, eds. B.A. le Cordeur and C.C. Saunders (Johannesburg, 1976), 68; Philip, *Researches*, I, 209–15.

61. Williams, *When Races Meet*, 28.

62. Ibid, 30–1; Macmillan, *CCQ*, 124–5. On Philip's condescending attitude to Van der Kemp, see Philip, *Researches*, I, 133–41, in which he praises his predecessor, but regrets his too easy intimacy with his charges, and particularly his marriage to a slave woman. Also Du Plessis, *Christian Missions*, 140–1.

63. Macmillan, *CCQ*, 139.

64. Ibid, 134–9; Ross, *Philip*, 89–93; Du Plessis, *Christian Missions*, 143–5.

65. Macmillan, *CCQ*, 141–2; Ross, *Philip*, 98, 103.

66. Ross, *Philip*, 85–8.

67. Macmillan, *CCQ*, 187.

68. Ibid, 105–6.

69. Michael Streak, *The Afrikaner as Viewed by the English, 1795–1854* (Cape Town, 1974), *passim*.

70. Macmillan, *CCQ*, 113–14, 117–21.

71. Mary Rayner, 'Wine and Slaves: The Failure of an Export Economy and the Ending of Slavery in the Cape Colony, South Africa, 1806–1834' (Ph.D., Duke, 1986), 222–3.

72. Of course, this was a temporary and functional alliance; later, mercantile interests came to see the huge potential in the expansion of frontiers by conquest to incorporate the land (and labour) of independent African peoples, and in the expansion of settler capitalism.

73. Macmillan, *CCQ*, 183–6; Margaret Donaldson, 'The Council of Advice at the Cape of Good Hope, 1825–1834: A Study in Colonial Government' (Ph.D., Rhodes, 1974), 24–6; Ross, *Philip*, 101.

74. Donaldson, 'Council of Advice', 110.

75. Ibid, 92–128; J.B. Peires, 'The British at the Cape, 1814–1834' in *SSAS*, 494–503; George Theal (ed.), *Records of the Cape Colony*, 36 vols. (1895–1906), vol. 27, contains the commissioners' reports.

76. Elbourne, '"To Colonise the Mind,"' 275–7; Macmillan, *CCQ*, 190–1.

77. On Pringle, see Jane Meiring, *Thomas Pringle, His Life and Times* (Cape Town, 1968); Pringle, *Narrative of a Residence in South Africa* (1835), 188–213, for his period in Cape Town; H.E. Hockly, *The Story of the British Settlers of 1820 in South Africa* (Johannesburg, 1966), 95–9; Macmillan, *CCQ*, 115–16; D. Klopper, 'Politics of the Pastoral: The Poetry of Thomas Pringle', *English in Africa*, 17, 1 (1990), 21–60; David Bunn, '"Our Wattled Cot": Mercantile and Domestic Space in Thomas Pringle's African Landscapes' in W. Mitchell (ed.), *Landscape and Power* (Chicago, 1994).

78. H.C. Botha, *John Fairbairn in South Africa* (Cape Town, 1984), 1–14.

79. Hockly, *British Settlers*, 94–5; Botha, *Fairbairn*, 15–34; A.M.L. Robinson, *None Daring to Make Us Afraid: A Study of English Periodical Literature in the Cape Colony from its Beginnings in 1824 to 1835* (Cape Town, 1962), 17–18.

80. Botha, *Fairbairn*, 26–8; Macmillan, *CCQ*, 193–4, 198.

81. Cory, *The Rise of South Africa* (1910–40, repr. Cape Town, 1965), II, 282–95, 331–5;

Botha, *Fairbairn*, 35–62; Donaldson, 'Council of Advice', 436–68; Robinson, *None Daring*; Macmillan, *CCQ*, 205–7; Hazel King, *Richard Bourke* (Melbourne, 1971), 102–8. Colonial newspapers in these years probably had a circulation of no more than 500–700. However, newspaper reading was a more public activity then than now, and the impact in the public sphere was greater than the circulation figures suggest. In Cape Town, for example, the Commercial Exchange served as a reading room where gentlemen gathered to digest the news of the day, as in the clubs and coffee houses of European cities. Among the educated Khoi of the Kat River Settlement in 1835, it was the practice for individuals to attend 'reading societies' where the contents of the latest colonial newspapers were disseminated (*Kitchingman Papers*, 159). On the history of reading in general, see Robert Darnton, 'First Steps Towards a History of Reading' in Darnton, *The Kiss of Lamourette: Reflections in Cultural History* (New York, 1990).

82. Macmillan, *CCQ*, 115–16; J.G. Pretorius, 'The British Humanitarians and the Cape Eastern Frontier, 1834–1836', *AYB* (1988, I), 51–2.

83. Macmillan, *CCQ*, 112–13; Botha, *Fairbairn*, 135–45; Kirsten McKenzie, 'The *South African Commercial Advertiser* and the Making of Middle-Class Identity in Early Nineteenth-Century Cape Town' (MA, UCT, 1993), 216–17.

84. Pretorius, 'British Humanitarians', 21.

85. Lalou Meltzer, 'The Growth of Cape Town Commerce and the Role of John Fairbairn's *Advertiser* (1835–1859)' (MA, UCT, 1989), 35; Botha, *Fairbairn*, 49 n.97.

86. Botha, *Fairbairn*, 163–72; Meltzer, 'Cape Town Commerce'.

87. Kirsten McKenzie in a textual analysis of the *Advertiser* in its early years examines the role of the paper in the creation of a 'rational public sphere' in which a distinctive middle-class identity was formed ('Making of Middle-Class Identity'). The 'rational public sphere' was a bourgeois creation in contemporary Europe, and represented the enlargement of political life to incorporate newly emergent civil society. The public sphere had a spatial dimension in the recreation of the social geography of the city, and in the pages of the *Advertiser* the streets of Cape Town were presented as terrains of struggle, where the battle was joined against contamination, moral and material. While 'the public' was a nominally inclusive concept, it was defined in *de facto* exclusive ways. Thus 'the public' was clearly not the same thing as 'the mob', or Fairbairn's 'debased and debasing crowd' (160), and clearly excluded women and blacks. See Benedict Anderson, *Imagined Communities: Reflections on the Origin and Spread of Nationalism* (1983), on the role of 'print capitalism' in the rise of 'imagined communities'; also Bank, 'Liberals and their Enemies', 19–22.

88. Marcus Arkin, *Storm in a Teacup: The Later Years of John Company at the Cape, 1815–1836* (Cape Town, 1973), 49–61; Meltzer, 'Cape Town Commerce', 35–7; Marian George, 'John Bardwell Ebden: His Business and Political Career at the Cape, 1806–1849', *AYB* (1986, I), 44–5.

89. Arkin, *Storm*, 67–106.

90. Ibid, 107–26.

91. Donaldson, 'Council of Advice', 1–91; A.K. Fryer, 'The Government of the Cape of Good Hope, 1825–1854: The Age of Imperial Reform', *AYB* (1964, I).

92. Macmillan, *CCQ*, 204, 207.

93. King, *Bourke*, 87–100; Donaldson, 'Council of Advice', 397–8.

94. Donaldson, 'Council of Advice', 279–87.

95. L.C. Duly, *British Land Policy at the Cape, 1795–1844: A Study of Administrative Procedures in the Empire* (Durham, NC, 1968), 96–100; King, *Bourke*, 77–9.

96. Peires in *SSAS*, 496; Donaldson, 'Council of Advice', 123–6; K.S. Hunt, *Sir Lowry Cole: A Study in Colonial Administration* (Durban, 1974), 153–67; King, *Bourke*, 89–93; Albie Sachs, *Justice in South Africa* (Berkeley, 1973), 38–9; Macmillan, *CCQ*, 208–9; H.B. Fine, 'The Administration of Criminal Justice at the Cape of Good Hope, 1795–1828' (Ph.D., UCT, 1991).

97. Donaldson, 'Council of Advice', 110–12.

98. Ibid, 234–53; King, *Bourke*, 97–100; R.L. Watson, *The Slave Question: Liberty and Property in South Africa* (Johannesburg, 1990), 21.

99. Macmillan, *CCQ*, 203; Ross, *Philip*, 101–2.

100. Ross, *Philip*, 103–5.

101. Bank, 'Liberals and their Enemies', 117–22, 239–44, and 72–5 (on Barrow); Robert Ross, 'James Cropper, John Philip and the *Researches*' in Hugh Macmillan and Shula Marks (eds.), *Africa and Empire: W.M. Macmillan, Historian and Social Critic* (1989); Elbourne, '"To Colonise the Mind,"' 281–91; A. Ross, *Philip*, 105–9, 77–9; R. Ross, 'Donald Moodie and the Origins of South African Historiography' in Ross, *Beyond the Pale*, 196–201. The contrast with India, where settler demands for labour and land were not a major factor, is striking. There humanitarians presented a uniformly negative image of Hindu society, whereas it was their enemies, the

Orientalists, who developed a romanticised picture of an unchanging and unassimilable Indian civilisation (Eric Stokes, *The English Utilitarians and India* (Oxford, 1963), ch. 1; Bank, 'Liberals and their Enemies', 145–9).

102. See, e.g., Philip, *Researches*, I, ix-x.

103. Ross, *Philip*, 102–11; Macmillan, *CCQ*, 213–19; *Kitchingman Papers*, 97; *Memoirs of Sir T.F. Buxton* (1849), 208–12; Pringle, *Narrative*, 263–4; Elizabeth Elbourne, 'Freedom at Issue: Vagrancy Legislation and the Meaning of Freedom in Britain and the Cape Colony', *Slavery and Abolition*, 15, 2 (1994), 132.

104. Donaldson, 'Council of Advice', 375–87; King, *Bourke*, 119–22; Stockenström, *Autobiography*, I, 243–8, 286–91; Harry A. Gailey, 'John Philip's Role in Hottentot Emancipation', *JAH*, 3, 4 (1961), 419–33; Elbourne, '"To Colonise the Mind,"' 291–8; Elphick and Malherbe in *SSAS*, 47–8; Marais, *Cape Coloured People*, 155–9; Macmillan, *CCQ*, 211–12; L.C. Duly, 'A Revisit with the Cape's Hottentot Ordinance of 1828' in Marcelle Kooy (ed.), *Studies in Economics and Economic History* (1972); Les Switzer, *Power and Resistance in an African Society: The Ciskei Xhosa and the Making of South Africa* (Madison, Wis., 1993), 83–5; Elbourne, 'Freedom at Issue', 128–33; Pringle, *Narrative*, 227–9. The ordinance is contained in G.W. Eybers (ed.), *Select Constitutional Documents Illustrating South African History* (1911), 2–8.

105. Thus Fairbairn in November 1828: 'The propriety of recognising two distinct nations within the Colony as this Ordinance does, is very questionable. There should be one law for all free persons' (Botha, *Fairbairn*, 64).

106. Duly, 'Cape's Hottentot Ordinance'.

107. Newton-King, 'Labour Market'.

108. Newton-King ('Labour Market') errs in ascribing too much consistency and continuity to colonial decision-making, and in consigning more political clout to the British settler elite of the eastern Cape than they in fact possessed. But her speculative study, in contrast to Macmillan, did try to position liberal reform in a more complex and closer relationship to colonial economic developments. Trapido, 'Emergence of Liberalism', 42–5, supports the contention that the purpose of Ordinance 50 was to free the labour supply and thus to benefit more productive (English-·speaking) farmers. Cf. Robert Ross, 'The Origins of Capitalist Agriculture in the Cape Colony: A Survey' in W. Beinart, P. Delius and S. Trapido (eds.), *Putting a Plough to the Ground: Accumulation and Dispossession in Rural South Africa* (Johannesburg, 1986), 80, 97 n.135; see Ross, *Beyond the Pale*, 225 n.176, for an alternative view.

109. Donaldson, 'Council of Advice', 382–3.

110. King, *Bourke*, 113–18; C.F.J. Muller, *Die Oorsprong van die Groot Trek* (Cape Town, 1974), 105–35; Donaldson, 'Council of Advice', 344–76; Newton-King, 'Labour Market', 192–6; Trapido, 'Emergence of Liberalism', 42–5; Elphick and Malherbe in *SSAS*, 47; Sheila van der Horst, *Native Labour in South Africa* (Cape Town, 1942), 12–13; Philip, *Researches*, II, 84–9, 323–6.

Julian Cobbing, in his determination to prove that the primary motive of colonial policy towards independent African peoples was to secure a captive labour force, has argued that Ordinance 49 was intended to give Governor Bourke the opportunity and the cover to launch a military expedition across the Kei with the specific intention of securing labour. News of a 'Zulu' invasion south towards Xhosaland in 1828 provided the immediate pretext. A colonial invading force entered Xhosaland, and their actions there ended with the battle of Mbholompo against the Ngwane, a northern Nguni group which by 1828 had moved south into Thembu territory, causing a considerable degree of disruption. The battle ended with the capture of a number of refugees by Colonel Somerset – which Cobbing uses as the basis of his thesis that colonial labour raiding was at the core of the entire enterprise. Cobbing, 'The Mfecane as Alibi: Thoughts on Dithakong and Mbolompo', *JAH*, 29 (1988), 487–519; also Cobbing's disciple Alan Webster, 'Land Expropriation and Labour Extraction under Cape Colonial Rule: The War of 1835 and the "Emancipation" of the Fingo' (MA, Rhodes, 1991), 29–30, 48–50; and Timothy J. Stapleton, *Maqoma: Xhosa Resistance to Colonial Advance, 1798–1873* (Johannesburg, 1994), 15–16, 49–50, 55–6, in which he accepts uncritically the Cobbing interpretation of frontier history. In contrast, Jeff Peires, 'Matiwane's Road to Mbholompo: A Reprieve for the Mfecane?' in Carolyn Hamilton (ed.), *The Mfecane Aftermath: Reconstructive Debates in Southern African History* (Johannesburg, 1995) responds in a convincing critique to this whole line of argument. Peires rightly points out that Bourke's governorship was liberal and reformist, and he was an ally of the humanitarian–mercantile nexus at the Cape. When 3000 Thembu entered the colony in 1827 as a result of the initial arrival of the Ngwane, Bourke compelled them to depart again, rather than sought the opportunity to secure their labour. Indeed, virtually all British magistrates in frontier districts were opposed to any use of coercion to secure African labour from beyond colonial boundaries. Furthermore, Peires points out, there was no shortage of Africans wishing to enter the colony to labour in the aftermath of the disruptions in the interior, and such was the influx after Ordinance 49 legalised it (with passes issued on a large scale by missionaries) that the ordinance had to be suspended little more than a year after its promulgation. Godlonton claimed that the ordinance had been used by chiefs to infiltrate armed men into the colony, and that its suspension was necessary to prevent the outbreak of war (Godlonton, *Introductory Remarks*, 78–81). As for the campaign of 1828 itself, Peires shows that the capture of refugees was a by-product and not a cause of the battle of Mbholompo. The taking of captives was in fact a direct contradiction of official policy at the time. In short, Cobbing's and Webster's argument that forcibly securing labour was uppermost in the official mind at the time cannot be sustained. See ch. 5 n.85 and ch. 6 n.27 below for further discussion on the larger significance of this debate.

111. Newton-King, 'Labour Market', 195.

112. The humanitarians' indifference to this provision reveals something of the limitations of their vision. After all, Africans from beyond the borders were culturally alien, were not Christian, and, unlike the Khoi, could not be held up as the creatures of the mission. So they were not considered potential recipients of the same rights as colonial Khoi.

113. Stockenström, *Autobiography*, I, 289; Donaldson, 'Council of Advice', 376, 379, 382, 400.

114. *Kitchingman Papers*, 100–2, on the antagonism towards Philip. In 1830 Philip was sued by one McKay, deputy magistrate in Somerset East, for charges of mistreatment published in *Researches*, for which he was awarded £200 damages and £900 costs by three judges of the High Court. It became a *cause célèbre*, McKay being egged on furiously by colonists. Ultimately the money was paid by Philip's friends in London and Manchester. Botha, *Fairbairn*, 71–2; Macmillan, *CCQ*, 224–5, 219–20, 231–2; Ross, *Philip*, 111–12, 116–17.

115. Botha, *Fairbairn*, 65–70; Ross, *Philip*, 113–14; Macmillan, *CCQ*, 221.

116. See ch. 9 n.14 below on the consistencies in Fairbairn's career.

117. John Mason, '"Fit for Freedom": The Slaves, Slavery and Emancipation in the Cape Colony, South Africa, 1806–1842' (Ph.D., Yale, 1992); Mason, 'Paternalism under Siege: Slavery in Theory and Practice during the Era of Reform, *c*.1825 through Emancipation' in Nigel Worden and Clifton Crais (eds.), *Breaking the Chains: Slavery and its Legacy in the Nineteenth-Century Cape Colony* (Johannesburg, 1994); Rayner, 'Wine and Slaves', 246–8; Macmillan, *CCQ*, 72–5; Donaldson, 'Council of Advice', 253–63.

118. Mason, '"Fit for Freedom,"' 96–103. On Somerset's proclamation see pp. 58–9.

119. Bank, 'Liberals and their Enemies', 154–61; André du Toit and Hermann Giliomee, *Afrikaner Political Thought. Analysis and Documents, I: 1780–1850* (Cape Town, 1983), 61–4; Donaldson, 'Council of Advice', 228–33; Watson, *Slave Question*, 35–6, 65–6; Rayner, 'Wine and Slaves', 260–1; King, *Bourke*, 84–6. Bourke was responsible in 1827 for freeing the government's slaves, with the apprenticing of slave children. The slave lodge was turned into a charity hospital.

120. Isobel Edwards, *Towards Emancipation: A Study in South African Slavery* (Cardiff, 1942), 91–137; Mason, 'The Slaves and their Protectors: Reforming Resistance in a Slave Society, the Cape Colony, 1826–1834', *JSAS*, 17, 1 (1991), 106–9; Mason, '"Fit for Freedom,"' 103–10; Rayner, 'Wine and Slaves', 252–60, 274–94.

121. Hunt, *Cole*, 114–25; E. Hengherr, 'Emancipation and After: A Study of Cape Slavery and the Issues Arising from It, 1830–1843' (MA, UCT, 1953), 24–33. Cole had fallen under planter influence in his previous job as governor of Mauritius.

122. McKenzie, 'Making of Middle-Class Identity', 118–22.

123. Mason, '"Fit for Freedom,"' 110–24; Wayne Dooling, 'Slavery and Amelioration in the Graaff-Reinet District, 1823–1830', *SAHJ*, 27 (1992), 75–94; Mason, 'Hendrik Albertus and his Ex-Slave Mey: A Drama in Three Acts', *JAH*, 31, 3 (1990), 423–45, for a revealing vignette of the changing slave regime under amelioration. See Mason, '"Fit for Freedom,"' 425–526, on slave families in the age of amelioration. It is commonly assumed that stable slave families were rare in the eighteenth century, although this would depend on one's definition of family. Worden, *Slavery in Dutch South Africa* (Cambridge, 1985), 95. Amelioration facilitated family formation. Most slave families continued to be matrifocal, single-parent institutions; but two-parent families also appeared more frequently by the 1820s and 1830s, as the sex ratio among slaves evened out. Officially recognised marriages remained negligible, however, despite the amelioration legislation. Patricia van der Spuy questions assumptions about growing family stability among slaves in the nineteenth century, arguing that slave women continued to be closely enmeshed in the control of their owners. Van der Spuy, 'A Collection of Discrete Essays with the Common Theme of Gender and Slavery at the Cape of Good Hope with a Focus on the 1820s' (MA, UCT, 1993); Van der Spuy, 'Slave Women and the Family in Nineteenth-Century Cape Town', *SAHJ*, 27 (1992), 50–74; also R.E. van der Voort, 'Daughters of Bondage: Paternalism and Slave Women in the Cape

Colony, 1830–1834' (BA thesis, Princeton, 1993); Mason, '"Fit for Freedom,"' 202–25, on sexual exploitation of slave women.

124. The slave population of Cape Town dropped from 9367 in 1806 to 5583 in 1834. Andrew Bank, *The Decline of Urban Slavery at the Cape, 1806–1834*, Communications no. 22, Centre for African Studies, University of Cape Town (1991), 9, 21–2; Bank, 'The Erosion of Urban Slavery at the Cape' in Worden and Crais, *Breaking the Chains*; Armstrong and Worden in *SSAS*, 138–9. Robert Shell, *Children of Bondage: A Social History of the Slave Society at the Cape of Good Hope, 1652–1838* (Hanover, NH, 1994), 105, 143–6, disagrees that urban slavery was disintegrating, but Bank, who has done the research, is quite convincing on the point. Nowhere does Shell consider the effects of amelioration measures.

125. Bank, *Urban Slavery*, 20–45; Mason, '"Fit for Freedom,"' 261–92; Shell, *Children of Bondage*, 144.

126. Bank, *Urban Slavery*, 98–170; Mohamed Adhikari, 'The Sons of Ham: Slavery and the Making of Coloured Identity', *SAHJ*, 27 (1992), 95–113; Armstrong and Worden in *SSAS*, 148–9; Robert Shell, 'The Establishment and Spread of Islam at the Cape, 1652–1838' (BA Hons. thesis, UCT, 1974); Shell, 'Rites and Rebellion: Islamic Conversion at the Cape, 1808–1915' in *Studies in the History of Cape Town*, 5 (Cape Town, 1984); Katherine Elks, 'Crime, Community and Police in Cape Town, 1825–1850' (MA, UCT, 1986); Shirley Judges, 'Poverty, Living Conditions and Social Relations: Aspects of Life in Cape Town in the 1830s' (MA, UCT, 1977).

127. Bank, *Urban Slavery*, 171–207; Mason, '"Fit for Freedom,"' 506–16.

128. At the same time, there were few 'prize negroes' under indenture left by the 1830s, as their periods drew to an end, and also as their usefulness (like that of the slaves) eroded. However, being first-generation inhabitants, they continued to languish at the lowest level of society once freed. See ch. 3 n.72 above.

129. Turley, *Culture of English Antislavery*, 39–43.

130. Hunt, *Cole*, 118–19; McKenzie, 'Middle-Class Identity', 172–81; Watson, *Slave Question*, 135–47.

131. Donaldson, 'Council of Advice', 259, 262; Rayner, 'Wine and Slaves', 298–9.

132. Rayner, 'Wine and Slaves', 299–300; Watson, *Slave Question*, 116; Bank, 'Liberals and their Enemies', 141–5, 164–6.

133. H.C. Botha, 'Die Rol van Christoffel J. Brand in Suid-Afrika, 1820–1854', *AYB* (1977), 3–25; Bank, 'Liberals and their Enemies', 162–4.

134. Botha, 'Brand', 29–33.

135. Bank, 'Liberals and their Enemies', 244–54; Rayner, 'Wine and Slaves', 300; Watson, *Slave Question*, 145. C.E. Boniface, the first editor of *De Zuid-Afrikaan*, wrote a very popular play, *De Temperatisten*, in the early 1830s, a vicious satire of the morality of the humanitarians and the character and sobriety of the Khoi (Bank, 'Liberals and their Enemies', 173–80).

136. Du Toit and Giliomee, *Afrikaner Political Thought*, 31–5; Watson, *Slave Question*, 116–34.

137. Bank, 'Liberals and their Enemies', 166–70, for defences of slavery. The Cape was unusual among British slave colonies in the lukewarmness of the defence of slavery, although slave regimes were under political and economic strain everywhere. Worden provides a revealing comparative study of emancipation at the Cape and Mauritius in 'Diverging Histories: Slavery and its Aftermath in the Cape Colony and Mauritius', *SAHJ*, 27 (1992), 3–25. Mauritian slave-owners were thriving on the basis of sugar production, and in consequence the abolition of the slave trade was very ineffectively enforced on that island, and slaves from Madagascar continued to arrive by the thousand. An essential difference was that the sugar regime on Mauritius was given a big boost by the removal of tariffs protecting Caribbean sugar, at the same time as the wine regime at the Cape was being subverted. Thus emancipation was fought far more vigorously on Mauritius, where the slave-owners were a far more powerful lobby than the arable farmers of the Cape. From this comparative perspective, slave-owner resistance to emancipation at the Cape seems to have been relatively apathetic, given its declining profitability.

138. Watson, *Slave Question*, 59–66; Du Toit and Giliomee, *Afrikaner Political Thought*, 65–8; Stockenström, *Autobiography*, I, 258–66.

139. Watson, *Slave Question*, 127. In a memorial of March 1828, Truter, Stoll and Stockenström wrote: 'we think nothing more pernicious than to render the slave worthless to his master whilst the latter is left in the predicament of being unable to part with the former' (ibid, 37).

140. Botha, 'Brand', 30; Botha, *Fairbairn*, 86; Du Toit and Giliomee, *Afrikaner Political Thought*, 275–82; Bank, 'Liberals and their Enemies', 162–4.

141. Watson, *Slave Question*, 176–9; Philip, *Researches*, I, 151–2, 159–61; Robert Ross, *Cape*

of Torments, 51–2.

142. Watson, *Slave Question*, 178. Philip wrote in 1827 that 'the food of the Hottentot is generally of an inferior quality, and less in quantity than that allowed the slave ... he seldom has any medical assistance afforded him when he is sick ... the punishments inflicted upon him are in general more frequent and more severe than those inflicted upon the slave, the master sustaining no loss of property should his constitution sink under his hardships' (*Researches*, I, 160). Andrew Ross's image of Philip as a radical abolitionist is a misrepresentation (*Philip*, 3–4, 216–17).

143. Botha, *Fairbairn*, 28, 172–4; Edwards, *Towards Emancipation*, 160–4; Macmillan, CCQ, 249; Tony Kirk, 'Self-Government and Self-Defence in South Africa: The Interrelations between British and Cape Politics, 1846–1854' (D.Phil., Oxford, 1972), 155–6; Botha, 'Brand', 77; Trapido, 'The Origins of the Cape Franchise Qualifications of 1853', *JAH*, 5, 1 (1964), 46–7; McKenzie, 'Middle-Class Identity', 218–23.

144. Botha, *Fairbairn*, 172–3 and 163–94 generally on Fairbairn's role in the struggle for representative government from the 1820s to the 1840s.

145. Watson, *Slave Question*, 106–15; Botha, *Fairbairn*, 80–91; Meltzer, 'Cape Town Commerce', 43–7; McKenzie, 'Middle-Class Identity', 144–6; Bank, 'Liberals and their Enemies', 101–15, on the shifting basis of anti-slavery thought at the Cape. Fairbairn set out his position in *Five Papers on the Slave Question* (Cape Town, 1831). The radical argument that freedom from slavery was a basic human right superseding property rights, and attacking the basic moral legitimacy of slavery, was most notably elaborated in a pamphlet of 1831 by an obscure civil servant, Thomas Miller. J.C. Chase issued a pamphlet rebutting Miller's arguments (Watson, *Slave Question*, 95–106, 114–15).

146. Rayner, 'Wine and Slaves', 210.

147. Watson, *Slave Question*, 73–92; Botha, *Fairbairn*, 83–4; Edwards, *Towards Emancipation*, 157–9; Mason, '"Fit for Freedom,"' 516–24; C. Iannini, 'Slavery, Philanthropy and Hegemony: A History of the Cape of Good Hope Philanthropic Society, 1828–1833' (BA Hons. thesis, UCT, 1993).

148. Botha, *Fairbairn*, 83.

149. William H. Green, *British Slave Emancipation: The Sugar Colonies and the Great Experiment, 1830–1865* (Oxford, 1976), 99–161; Thomas Holt, *The Problem of Freedom: Race, Labour and Politics in Jamaica and Britain, 1832–1938* (Baltimore, 1992), 42–112 (21 for Goderich quote).

150. Rayner, 'Wine and Slaves', 308; Meltzer, 'Cape Town Commerce', 55; B.J.L. Liebenberg, 'Die Vrystelling van die Slawe in die Kaapkolonie en die Implikasies Daarvan' (MA, UOFS, 1959); Hengherr, 'Emancipation and After', 51–8.

151. Meltzer, 'Cape Town Commerce', 47.

152. Rayner, 'Wine and Slaves', 190, 245, 302.

153. Macmillan, CCQ, 78–9.

154. Edwards, *Towards Emancipation*, 187–95; Rayner, 'Wine and Slaves', 308–9; Hengherr, 'Emancipation', 58–65; Digby Warren, 'Merchants, Municipal Commissioners and Wardmasters: Municipal Politics in Cape Town, 1840–1854' (MA, UCT, 1986), 54–5; Meltzer, 'Cape Town Commerce', 47–55, 64–9; Meltzer, 'Emancipation, Commerce and the Role of John Fairbairn's *Advertiser*' in Worden and Crais, *Breaking the Chains*; Marais, *Cape Coloured People*, 189–90.

155. Macmillan, CCQ, 79–80. The best recent account of the economic impact of compensation and its beneficiaries is Kathleen Mary Butler, *The Economics of Emancipation: Jamaica and Barbados, 1823–1843* (Chapel Hill, NC, 1995).

156. Meltzer, 'Cape Town Commerce', 56–8, 60–1; Meltzer, 'Emancipation', 181–5; Hengherr, 'Emancipation', 65–71; Rayner, 'Wine and Slaves', 310; Tony Kirk, 'The Cape Economy and the Expropriation of the Kat River Settlement, 1846–1853' in Marks and Atmore, *Economy and Society*, 229; Switzer, *Power and Resistance*, 379 n.8.

157. George, 'Ebden', 49–50; D.J. van Zyl, *Kaapse Wyn en Brandewyn, 1795–1860* (Cape Town, 1974), 165.

158. Macmillan, CCQ. An alternative vision is provided by Ross, 'Origins of Capitalist Agriculture', 79–87. Ross exaggerates somewhat in describing the emancipations between 1828 and 1838 as 'non-events', but the larger point is a sound one; also Ross, *Beyond the Pale*, 44–9. Elphick and Giliomee, *SSAS*, follow the same line of argument. The difference is that Ross sees the racial order as being a recent development, only emerging since the advent of British rule, whereas Elphick and Giliomee see it originating in the seventeenth century. See ch. 2 nn.28, 29 above.

159. Elphick and Malherbe in *SSAS*, 48; *Kitchingman Papers*, 98. On the need for land, see William B. Boyce, *Notes on South African Affairs* (1838, repr. Cape Town, 1971), 126–32.

160. Elbourne, '"To Colonise the Mind,"' 269–72.

161. Ibid, 299–301.
162. On the decline of opportunities in artisanal work, transport riding and wood-cutting for mission Khoi in the eastern Cape through the 1820s, see ibid, 234–41; Sales, *Mission Stations*, 79–100; Philip, *Researches*, I, chs. 15–18.
163. Elbourne, '"To Colonise the Mind,"' 301–4; Stockenström, *Autobiography*, I, 341–51, 366–71, II, 350–8; J.L. Dracopoli, *Sir Andries Stockenström, 1792–1864* (Cape Town, 1969), 17–18; Sales, *Mission Stations*, 101; Hunt, *Cole*, 100–1.
164. J.C. Visagie, 'Die Katriviernedersetting, 1828–1839' (D.Litt. et Phil., Unisa, 1978), 73–88; Williams, *When Races Meet*, 113–214; Ross, *Philip*, 119–21; Sales, *Mission Stations*, 102–5; Elbourne, '"To Colonise the Mind,"' 304–5; *Kitchingman Papers*, 129–34.
165. C.C. Saunders, 'James Read: Towards a Reassessment', *Societies of Southern Africa in the Nineteenth and Twentieth Centuries*, vol. 7, Collected Seminar Papers, Institute of Commonwealth Studies (London, 1977); *DSAB*, I, 666–8; J.T. du Bruyn, 'James Read en die Tlhaping, 1816–1820', *Historia*, 35, 1 (1990), 22–37.
166. Elbourne, '"To Colonise the Mind,"' 308–10; Sales, *Mission Stations*, 105–7.
167. See, e.g., Pringle, *Narrative*, 264–80; Elbourne, '"To Colonise the Mind,"' 311–13; *Kitchingman Papers*, 138–45, 156–9; *Memoirs of Sir T.F. Buxton*, 213–19. On a visit to Kat River Khoi in 1830, Philip described the settlement as an experiment of the greatest importance in determining 'whether they were fit for freedom, whether they would work except under the lash of a Master' (Botha, *Fairbairn*, 66).
168. Donaldson, 'Council of Advice', 387–93; J.C.S. Lancaster, 'The Governorship of Sir Benjamin D'Urban at the Cape of Good Hope', *AYB* (1991, II), 64–70; Mason, '"Fit for Freedom,"' 580–5; Edwards, *Towards Emancipation*, 171–5; Ross, *Philip*, 113–15; Marais, *Cape Coloured People*, 180–3; Macmillan, *CCQ*, 233–46; Rayner, 'Wine and Slaves', 311–13; Elphick and Malherbe in *SSAS*, 48–9; Nigel Worden, 'Adjusting to Emancipation: Freed Slaves and Farmers in the Mid-Nineteenth-Century South-Western Cape' in James and Simons, *The Angry Divide*, 33-4.
169. Elbourne, 'Freedom at Issue', 136–7; Bank, 'Liberals and their Enemies', 208–11.
170. Elks, 'Crime, Community and Police', 93–129; Bank, 'Liberals and their Enemies', 180–8.
171. Lancaster, 'D'Urban', 65.
172. In the same year, 1834, the New Poor Law was being debated and passed at Westminster. Humanitarians supported it on the grounds that it dismantled the paternalist structure of outdoor relief and 'freed' labourers to fend for themselves. What was revealed in the debates of the time was the two-edged nature of the 'freedom' envisaged. Freedom from constraint and coercion was combined (in the New Poor Law) with the freedom to chose destitution as the penalty to be paid for indolence. The humanitarian insistence on the morally uplifting quality of self-motivated labour was combined with the utilitarian principle that any incentive to idleness must be removed. Thus the workhouse was designed as a punitive institution whose awfulness should serve as a further incentive to labour, rather than as an indiscriminate source of relief. The laws of political economy had it that poverty was caused, not by systemic factors, but by moral failing. Any succour for the poor was bound to be morally corrupting, and contrary to the laws of the market. Hostile and harsh attitudes towards the poor were a universal trait among the liberal reformers of the day; and it is true that in all the campaigns of the humanitarians at the Cape, there was little concern shown for the lot of the mass of impoverished Khoi and ex-slaves once legal emancipation had been achieved. Anthony Arblaster, *The Rise and Decline of Western Liberalism* (Oxford, 1984), 254–7; Peter Mandler, 'The Making of the New Poor Law Redivivus', *Past and Present*, 117 (1987), 130–57, argues that a modernised landed gentry, having imbibed utilitarian ideas, were the primary force behind the law.
173. Botha, *Fairbairn*, 97–103; Sales, *Mission Stations*, 110–12, 114; Edna Bradlow, 'The Khoi and the Proposed Vagrancy Legislation of 1834', *Quarterly Bulletin of the South African Library*, 39, 3 (1985); John Frye, 'The *South African Commercial Advertiser* and the Eastern Frontier, 1834–1847' (MA, Rhodes, 1968), 46; *Kitchingman Papers*, 121–3; Justus [MacKenzie Beverley], *The Wrongs of the Caffre Nation* (1837), 239–67, for contemporary humanitarian perceptions in Britain.
174. Trapido, 'Emergence of Liberalism', 50–3; Elbourne, 'Question of Identity', 23–5; Elbourne, '"To Colonise the Mind,"' 313–18; Williams, *When Races Meet*, 123–4; Elbourne, 'Freedom at Issue', 138–42.
175. Newton-King and Malherbe, *Khoikhoi Rebellion*; Elbourne, '"To Colonise the Mind,"' 156–8.
176. V.C. Malherbe, 'David Stuurman: "Last Chief of the Hottentots,"' *African Studies*, 39 (1980); Malherbe, 'Hermanus and his Sons: Khoi Bandits and Conspirators in the Post-Rebellion

324 References to pp. 120–125

Period, 1803–1818', *African Studies*, 41 (1982).

177. Webster, 'Land Expropriation', 89.

178. Trapido, 'Emergence of Liberalism', 52–3; Elbourne, 'Freedom at Issue', 135, 149 n.55. Thomson's pro-government congregation of 'Bastaards' who regarded themselves as a cut above common Hottentots petitioned in favour of the vagrancy law (although it was alleged that they were ignorant of what they were signing). The embrace of 'Hottentot' identity, and its paradoxical rootedness in mission notions of Christian universalism, were revealed by Esau Prins, speaking at a meeting at Philipton on the Kat River in 1834: 'I am a Boor's child, although I had to sit behind the chairs and stools, as my mother was a Hottentot woman, and therefore I consider myself a Hottentot also. Men say I have Christian blood in me, but I know only of one blood that God has made. The so-called "Christeman" steals the name!' (Elbourne, '"To Colonise the Mind,"' 248).

179. On Stoffels, see *DSAB*, IV, 623–5; Sales, *Mission Stations*, 156–7.

180. Botha, 'Brand', 33–4.

181. On the purposes of apprenticeship see David Eltis, 'Abolitionist Perceptions of Society after Slavery' in James Walvin (ed.), *Slavery and British Society, 1776–1846* (1982). On splits among humanitarians on the issue, see Howard Temperley, *British Antislavery, 1833–1870* (1972), ch. 2; also A. Tyrrell, 'The "Moral Radical Party" and the Anglo–Jamaican Campaign for the Abolition of the Negro Apprenticeship System', *Economic History Review*, 392 (1984), 481–504.

182. Lancaster, 'D'Urban', 60–4; Edwards, *Towards Emancipation*, 177–87; Nigel Worden, 'Between Slavery and Freedom: The Apprenticeship Period, 1834–8' and Pamela Scully, 'Private and Public Worlds of Emancipation in the Rural Western Cape, c.1830–1842', both in Worden and Crais, *Breaking the Chains*; Mason, '"Fit for Freedom,"' 124–34; Worden, 'Slave Apprenticeship in Cape Town, 1834–1838' in *Studies in the History of Cape Town*, 7 (Cape Town, 1994), 32–44.

183. Judges, 'Poverty, Living Conditions and Social Relations', 39–47, 70–84; Hengherr, 'Emancipation', 72–82, 86–93; Warren, 'Municipal Politics', 29; Meltzer, 'Cape Town Commerce', 71–2; Meltzer, 'Emancipation', 185–7.

184. Ross, 'Origins of Capitalist Agriculture', 83–4; Ross, '"Rather Mental than Physical": Emancipations and the Cape Economy' in Worden and Crais, *Breaking the Chains*, 153–5; John Marincowitz, 'Rural Production and Labour in the Western Cape, 1838–1888, with Special Reference to the Wheat-Growing Districts' (Ph.D., London, 1985), 29–31.

185. Mason, '"Fit for Freedom,"' 538–51, on the immediate aftermath of emancipation. Also, Marincowitz, 'Rural Production', 28–54; Elizabeth Host, 'Capitalisation and Proletarianisation on a Western Cape Farm: Klaver Valley, 1812–1898' (MA, UCT, 1992); Helen Ludlow, 'Missions and Emancipation in the South-Western Cape: A Case Study of Groenekloof (Mamre), 1838–1852' (MA, UCT, 1992); Edna Bradlow, 'Capitalists and Labourers in the Post-Emancipation Rural Cape', *Historia*, 30, 2 (1985), 49–62, and 31, 1 (1986), 57–68; Bradlow, 'Emancipation and Race Perceptions at the Cape', *SAHJ*, 15 (1983), 10–33; Sales, *Mission Stations*, 123–4; Marais, *Cape Coloured People*, 183–6, 190–5; Louise Whittaker, 'In the Shadow of Slavery: Masters and Servants in the Worcester District, 1839–1845' (BA Hons. thesis, UCT, 1992).

186. Mason, '"Fit for Freedom,"' 529–31; Marincowitz, 'Rural Production', 53; Scully, 'Private and Public Worlds', 215–17.

187. Mason, '"Fit for Freedom,"' 551–70; Scully, 'Private and Public Worlds'; Scully, 'Liberating the Family? Gender, Labour and Sexuality in the Rural Western Cape, South Africa, 1823–1853' (Ph.D., Michigan, 1993); Scully, 'Rape, Race, and Colonial Culture: The Sexual Politics of Identity in the Nineteenth-Century Cape Colony, South Africa', *American Historical Review*, 100, 2 (1995), 335–59, on the way in which the search for control and hierarchy in the post-emancipation world was reflected in attitudes towards gender and sexuality.

188. Marincowitz, 'Rural Production', 37, 46–7.

189. Ibid, 36–7, 39; Worden, 'Adjusting to Emancipation', 34–7; Ludlow, 'Missions and Emancipation'. The mission station population doubled in the decade after emancipation from 6000 to 12 000. In 1838 Groenekloof was the only station in the western Cape. In 1841–6 four new stations were established on the perimeter of the western Cape's commercial farming heartland (Marincowitz, 38–41, 48–9).

190. Worden, 'Adjusting to Emancipation', 36; Rayner, 'Wine and Slaves', 319–20; Mason, '"Fit for Freedom,"' 570–80, on the search for alternative land.

191. Marincowitz, 'Rural Production', 49–52.

192. Ross, '"Rather Mental than Physical,"' 161–7.

193. Edna Bradlow, 'The Children's Friend Society at the Cape of Good Hope', *Victorian Studies*, 27, 2 (1984), 155–77.

194. George, 'Ebden', 66–8; Botha, 'Brand', 58–60; J.J. Breitenbach, 'The Development of the Secretaryship to the Government at the Cape of Good Hope under John Montagu, 1845–1852',

AYB (1959, II), 214; H.M. Robertson, 'The Cape of Good Hope and "Systematic Colonisation,"' *South African Journal of Economics*, 5, 4 (1937), 367–411. Apart from labour from Britain, captured slave ships were again taken by the British navy to Cape Town from 1839, and over 4000 freed captives had been landed and indentured at Cape Town by 1846. Their bonded state was little different from the earlier 'prize negroes', revealing again the limited meaning of emancipation. Saunders, 'Liberated Africans', 230–9; Hengherr, 'Emancipation', 98–109.

195. Green, *British Slave Emancipation*, 170–7.

196. Marincowitz, 'Rural Production', 57–64; Mason, '"Fit for Freedom,"' 586–90, 535–6; Donaldson, 'Council of Advice', 293–4; Hengherr, 'Emancipation', 94–7; Marais, *Cape Coloured People*, 199–204; Worden, 'Adjusting to Emancipation', 37–8; Robert Ross, 'Pre-Industrial and Industrial Racial Stratification in South Africa' in Ross (ed.), *Racism and Colonialism: Essays on Ideology and Social Structure* (Leiden, 1982), 85–7; Rayner, 'Wine and Slaves', 321–2; Sheila van der Horst, *Native Labour in South Africa* (Cape Town, 1942), 34–8; Colin Bundy, 'The Abolition of the Masters and Servants Act', *South African Labour Bulletin*, 2, 1 (1975), 37–46, puts the legislation in long-term perspective.

197. Macmillan, *CCQ*, 255–7. Cf. Marais, *Cape Coloured People*, 157–8.

198. This last point is stressed by George Fredrickson, 'White Responses to Emancipation: The American South, Jamaica, and the Cape of Good Hope' in Fredrickson, *The Arrogance of Race: Historical Perspectives on Slavery, Racism, and Social Inequality* (Middletown, Conn., 1988). Fredrickson stresses the contrast with the American South, where a tradition of *herrenvolk* racism was manifested in a vicious post-reconstruction backlash. But the contrast is more apparent than real; for when Jim Crow was biting in the American South, the new ideology of segregationism was taking off in British colonies, including South Africa.

199. Fredrickson, *White Supremacy*, 258–9, 262–8; Elphick and Giliomee in *SSAS*, 557–9; Judges, 'Aspects of Life in Cape Town', 133–47, 162–3, 165–6; Bradlow, 'Race Perceptions'. Particularly in Cape Town, church and humanitarian organisations continued to try to Christianise and 'civilise' the underclasses – ex-slaves, free blacks, poor whites – and to wean them from Islam. Thus infant schools were set up in the 1830s for the children of 'slaves and poorer classes' up to the age of 6, but to little effect. By 1875, 69 per cent of coloured Capetonians over the age of 15 were illiterate (McKenzie, 'Middle-Class Identity', 154–9; Vivian Bickford-Smith, 'Meanings of Freedom: Social Position and Identity among Ex-Slaves and their Descendants in Cape Town, 1875–1910' in Worden and Crais, *Breaking the Chains*, 293).

200. See ch. 7 below. On Kat River, see Tony Kirk, 'Progress and Decline in the Kat River Settlement, 1829–1854', *JAH*, 14, 3 (1973); Kirk, 'Expropriation of the Kat River Settlement'.

201. Sales, *Mission Stations*, 115, 119–20, 146; Kirk, 'Self-Government', 177–8; Du Plessis, *Christian Missions*, 281–3; Lovett, *History of the LMS*, I, 572–6; *Kitchingman Papers*, 191–4. In the Caribbean colonies, by the end of the 1840s, the missions were in severe decline, and were being replaced by Afro-creole churches. The ex-slaves simply refused to conform to the ideal model of the redeemed mission product. The fragmentation and ineffectuality of the humanitarian lobby was graphically demonstrated by the removal of preferential tariffs on West Indian sugar in 1847. Decline in sugar production and rising sugar prices, leading to severe shortages in Britain, eroded prejudice against slave-grown sugar, despite the protests of last-ditch humanitarian elements. The interests of the British sugar colonies and their freed inhabitants were jettisoned. Free-trade ideology had triumphed over humanitarianism. The result was havoc for the British sugar colonies, particularly Jamaica, where bankruptcy and extensive abandonment of plantations followed, despite importations of indentured labourers. Extensive backcountry regions provided a refuge for ex-slaves. Attempts to forge a formally non-racial form of local class rule came to naught, when the colonial assembly disbanded in 1865 after the Morant Bay rebellion had shaken settler confidence in their capacity to maintain hegemony, and in 1866 the island reverted to direct imperial rule as a crown colony. Trinidad and Guiana, where the plantation economy was new and expanding, recovered by the 1850s, owing only to the importation of indentured Indian labourers. In Barbados and Antigua, in contrast, the absence of excess land meant that the peasant option did not exist for freed slaves, and the plantation economy was not affected to the same extent, the ex-slaves remaining bonded to the land (Green, *British Slave Emancipation*; Holt, *Problem of Freedom*). In Mauritius, slaves were quickly replaced by indentured Indian labour too, and the ex-slaves became a marginalised peasantry (see n.137 above). The peasant option did not exist at the Cape. The reliance on indentured labour in large parts of the British empire in the nineteenth century is in itself a telling indication of the limits of economic liberalism as it affected the civic freedoms of workers. Hugh Tinker, *A New System of Slavery: The Export of Indian Labour Overseas, 1830–1920* (1974); Robert A. Huttenback, *Racism and Empire: White Settlers and Coloured Immigrants in the British Self-Governing Colonies, 1830–1910* (Ithaca, NY, 1976); Kay

Saunders (ed.), *Indentured Labour in the British Empire, 1834–1920* (1984). All in all, the experience of emancipation gave the lie to the abolitionist claim that free labour was more productive and efficient than bound. The failure of the free-labour system to sustain the Caribbean export economies, if anything, vindicated rather than challenged the slave-owners of Brazil, Cuba and the United States. See W.A. Green, 'Was British Emancipation a Success? The Abolitionist Perspective' in David Richardson (ed.), *Abolition and its Aftermath: The Historical Context, 1790–1916* (1985); Temperley, *British Antislavery*, on the later history of the humanitarian movement in its decline. The literature on the aftermath of emancipation is growing rapidly: see, e.g., Frank McGlynn and Seymour Drescher (eds.), *The Meaning of Freedom: Economics, Politics and Culture after Slavery* (Pittsburgh, 1992); Michael Craton, 'The Transition from Slavery to Free Wage Labour in the Caribbean, 1780–1890: A Survey with Particular Reference to Recent Scholarship', *Slavery and Abolition*, 13, 2 (1992), 37–63; Kevin D. Smith, 'A Fragmented Freedom: The Historiography of Emancipation and its Aftermath in the British West Indies', *Slavery and Abolition*, 16, 1 (1995), 101–30.

Chapter Five: Colonial Initiatives and the Dynamics of Accumulation
   1. John Hopper, 'Xhosa–Colony Relations, 1770–1803' (Ph.D., Yale, 1980); J.B. Peires, 'A History of the Xhosa, ca 1700–1835' (MA, Rhodes, 1976); Peires, *The House of Phalo: A History of the Xhosa People in the Days of their Independence* (Johannesburg, 1981), 45–63; Hermann Giliomee, 'The Eastern Frontier, 1770–1812' in Richard Elphick and Giliomee (eds.), *The Shaping of South African Society, 1652–1840*, 2nd ed. (Cape Town, 1989); Les Switzer, *Power and Resistance in an African Society: The Ciskei Xhosa and the Making of South Africa* (Madison, Wis., 1993), 43–9.
   2. Donald Moodie (comp.), *The Record, or A Series of Official Papers Relative to the Condition and Treatment of the Native Tribes of South Africa* (1838, 1842, repr. Cape Town, 1960), Part V for Collins's report; Giliomee, 'Die Administrasietydperk van Lord Caledon, 1807–1811', *AYB* (1966, II), chs. 10–12; Giliomee, 'The Eastern Frontier, 1770–1812' in *SSAS*, 439–49; Switzer, *Power and Resistance*, 48–52; Peires, *Phalo*; Ben Maclennan, *A Proper Degree of Terror: John Graham and the Cape's Eastern Frontier* (Johannesburg, 1986). The nineteenth-century conflicts between colony and Xhosa chiefdoms continue to attract attention, of very variable quality. See, e.g., A.J. Smithers, *The Kaffir Wars, 1779–1877* (1973); John Milton, *The Edges of War* (Cape Town, 1983); J.S. Bergh and J.C. Visagie, *The Eastern Cape Frontier Zone, 1660–1980: A Cartographic Guide for Historical Research* (Durban, 1985); C.C. Saunders, 'The Hundred Years War: Some Reflections on African Resistance on the Cape–Xhosa Frontier' in D. Chanaiwa (ed.), *Profiles of Self-Determination: African Responses to European Colonialism in Southern Africa, 1652–Present* (Northridge, CA, 1976); Clifton Crais, *The Making of the Colonial Order: White Supremacy and Black Resistance in the Eastern Cape, 1770–1865* (Johannesburg, 1992); Timothy J. Stapleton, *Maqoma: Xhosa Resistance to Colonial Advance, 1798–1873* (Johannesburg, 1994); and, most impressively, Noël Mostert's classic, *Frontiers: The Epic of South Africa's Creation and the Tragedy of the Xhosa People* (1992).
   3. Imperial troop strength at the Cape was reduced from 4032 to 2400 at this time. C.F.J. Muller, *Die Oorsprong van die Groot Trek* (Cape Town, 1974), 177–8.
   4. W.D. Hammond-Tooke, 'Segmentation and Fission in Cape Nguni Political Units', *Africa*, 35 (1965), 143–66; Hammond-Tooke, 'Descent Groups, Chiefdoms and South African Historiography', *JSAS*, 11, 2 (1985), 305–19; Peires, 'The Rise of the Right-Hand House in the History and Historiography of the Xhosa', *History in Africa*, 2 (1975), 155–75; Peires, *Phalo*, 27–31.
   5. Peires, 'The British and the Cape, 1814–1834' in *SSAS*, 480–4; Peires, *Phalo*, 58–63, 78–80; Maclennan, *Proper Degree of Terror*, chs. 23–5; Crais, *Colonial Order*, 100; Switzer, *Power and Resistance*, 52–6. On Ngqika see Peires, 'Ngqika, ca 1779–1829' in C.C. Saunders (ed.), *Black Leaders in Southern African History* (1979), 15–30; on Nxele, see Peires, 'Nxele, Ntsikana and the Origins of the Xhosa Religious Reaction', *JAH*, 20, 1 (1979), 51–61.
   6. Pp. 68–71 above.
   7. Monica Wilson, 'Co-operation and Conflict: The Eastern Cape Frontier' in Wilson and Leonard Thompson (eds.), *Oxford History of South Africa*, vol. 2 (Oxford, 1971), 238–40; Peires in *SSAS*, 486–8; Jean and John Comaroff, *Of Revelation and Revolution: Christianity, Colonialism and Consciousness in South Africa* (Chicago, 1991), 46–8; Johannes du Plessis, *A History of Christian Missions in South Africa* (1911), 165–81.
   8. P.H. Lyness, 'The Life and Influence of William Shaw, 1820–1856' (MA, Rhodes, 1982); William Shaw, *The Story of my Mission in South-Eastern Africa* (1860); *The Journal of William Shaw*, ed. W.D. Hammond-Tooke, Graham's Town Series 2 (Cape Town, 1972); William B. Boyce, *Notes on South African Affairs* (1838, repr. Cape Town, 1971); Boyce, *Memoir of the Rev. William*

Shaw (1874).

9. Donovan Williams, *When Races Meet: The Life and Times of William Ritchie Thomson, 1794–1891* (Johannesburg, 1961), 54–5.

10. J.G. Galbraith, *Reluctant Empire: British Policy on the South African Frontier, 1834–1854* (Berkeley, 1963), 86–7; W.M. Macmillan, *Cape Colour Question* (1927, repr. Cape Town, 1969), 87–8; A.E.G. Duff, 'An Analysis of Wesleyan Missionary Strategy in the Eastern Districts of the Cape Colony and "Caffreland", 1823–1838' (MA, Rhodes, 1969); D.G.L. Cragg, 'The Relations of the AmaPondo and the Colonial Authorities (1830–1886) with Special Reference to the Role of the Wesleyan Missionaries' (D.Phil., Oxford, 1959); B.E. Seton, 'Wesleyan Missions and the Sixth Frontier War, 1834–1835' (Ph.D., UCT, 1962).

11. Comaroffs, *Of Revelation*, 195–7, 252–65 and *passim*; Richard Elphick, 'Africans and the Christian Campaign in Southern Africa' in Howard Lamar and L.M. Thompson (eds.), *The Frontier in History: North America and Southern Africa Compared* (New Haven, 1981); Crais, *Colonial Order*, 100–5; Peires, *Phalo*; Gabriel M. Setiloane, *The Image of God among the Sotho–Tswana* (Rotterdam, 1976), 89–157; Jean Comaroff, *Body of Power, Spirit of Resistance: The Culture and History of a South African People* (Chicago, 1985); Norman Etherington, *Preachers, Peasants and Politics in South-East Africa, 1835–1880: African Christian Communities in Natal, Pondoland and Zululand* (1978); Colin Bundy, *The Rise and Fall of the South African Peasantry* (1979); Nosipho Majeke [Dora Taylor], *The Role of the Missionaries in Conquest* (1952, repr. Cape Town, 1986); Donovan Williams, 'Social and Economic Aspects of Christian Missions in Caffraria, 1816–1854', *Historia*, 30, 2 (1985), 33–48, and 31, 1 (1986), 25–56.

12. Comaroffs, *Of Revelation*, 4, 199, and 198–251 on 'the long conversation' between the mission and the Africans.

13. Such as Phatho's Ngqunukhwebe and the Mfengu (Williams, *When Races Meet*, 45).

14. B.A. le Cordeur, *The Politics of Eastern Cape Separatism, 1820–1854* (Cape Town, 1981), 104–5; Galbraith, *Reluctant Empire*, 152–4; L.M. Thompson, *Survival in Two Worlds: Moshoeshoe of Lesotho, 1786–1870* (Oxford, 1975), 126–30.

15. Roger Beck, 'Bibles and Beads: Missionaries as Traders in Southern Africa in the Early Nineteenth Century', *JAH*, 30, 2 (1989), 211–55; Beck, 'The Legalisation and Development of Trade on the Cape Frontier, 1817–1830' (Ph.D., Indiana, 1987), 53–102.

16. Comaroffs, *Of Revelation*, 190; Martin Legassick, 'The Griqua, the Sotho–Tswana and the Missionaries, 1780–1840: The Politics of a Frontier Zone' (Ph.D., UCLA, 1969), 235–6.

17. Beck, 'Legalisation', 57–65. Thus as early as 1801 William Edwards, lay missionary of the LMS, was dismissed from the society for private trading, though he claimed that his trips to Tswana territory for ivory were an effective means of spreading the gospel. Subsequently he bought a wine farm near Tulbagh. Jane Sales, *Mission Stations and the Coloured Communities of the Eastern Cape, 1800–1852* (Cape Town, 1975), 13.

18. Beck, 'Legalisation', 65–79.

19. Ibid, 84–5; Richard Elphick and V.C. Malherbe, 'The Khoisan to 1828' in *SSAS*, 45.

20. Beck, 'Legalisation', 98; Williams, *When Races Meet*, 57–8.

21. Beck, 'Legalisation', 88–91.

22. J.G. Pretorius, 'The British Humanitarians and the Cape Eastern Frontier, 1834–1836', *AYB* (1988, I), 21–2.

23. Ibid, 22.

24. Ibid.

25. J.C.S. Lancaster, 'The Governorship of Sir Benjamin D'Urban at the Cape of Good Hope', *AYB* (1991, II), 186–9; Pretorius, 'Humanitarians', 22–3; J.L. Dracopoli, *Sir Andries Stockenström, 1792–1864* (Cape Town, 1969), 116; *The Porter Speeches* (Cape Town, 1886), 427–8.

26. One Ganya, counsellor to Chief Ngqika, in a deposition in Graham's Town in January 1836, stated: 'The Caffres got muskets from the shops in the Kat River, giving bullocks for them, sometimes one, sometimes two' (Lancaster, 'D'Urban', 188–9). John Green, *The Kat River Settlement in 1851, Containing the Substance of Evidence Given before the Commission for Investigating the Rebellion* (Graham's Town, 1853), Appendix, 53–85, on the alleged role of Kat River Khoi in instigating Xhosa and arming them; *The Kitchingman Papers*, eds. B.A. le Cordeur and C.C. Saunders (Johannesburg, 1976), 146, 156, on suspicions of Read's involvement. Read was expelled by D'Urban to Bethelsdorp during the 1835 war.

27. Pretorius, 'Humanitarians', 23; Sales, *Mission Stations*, 114; Dracopoli, *Stockenström*, 116–17; *The Journal of Charles Lennox Stretch*, ed. B.A. le Cordeur, Graham's Town Series 8 (Cape Town, 1988), 120–1, 126; Alan Webster, 'Land Expropriation and Labour Extraction under Cape Colonial Rule: The War of 1835 and the "Emancipation" of the Fingo' (MA, Rhodes, 1991), 95–6, 108, 170; George Cory, *The Rise of South Africa* (1910–1940, repr. 1965), IV, 336–40;

Commandant Holden Bowker, ed. I. Mitford-Barberton (Cape Town, 1970), 106.
28. Peires, *Phalo*, 155–7.
29. *David Livingstone, Family Letters*, ed. Isaac Schapera (1959), II, 161.
30. Webster, 'Land Expropriation', 84–5; Peires, *Phalo*, 102–3, 107–8, 156; Margaret Donaldson, 'The Council of Advice at the Cape of Good Hope, 1825–1834: A Study in Colonial Government' (Ph.D., Rhodes, 1974), 330–2; M. Wilson, 'Co-operation and Conflict' in *OHSA*, 241–2; Bundy, *Rise and Fall*, 29–32; Godlonton, *Introductory Remarks to a Narrative of the Irruption of the Kaffir Hordes into the Eastern Province of the Cape of Good Hope* (1836, repr. Cape Town 1965), 109–10, 149–50; Cory, *Rise of South Africa*, III, 73–4.
31. Pretorius, 'Humanitarians', 24–5; Peires, *Phalo*, 91–2; W.M. Macmillan, *Bantu, Boer and Briton: The Making of the South African Native Problem*, 2nd ed. (1963), 77–9; Andrew Ross, *John Philip (1775–1851): Missions, Race and Politics in South Africa* (Aberdeen, 1986), 123–6; Lancaster, 'D'Urban', 74–80; Dracopoli, *Stockenström*, 77; Hazel King, *Richard Bourke* (Melbourne, 1971), 110–18; Keith S. Hunt, *Sir Lowry Cole: A Study in Colonial Administration* (Durban, 1974), 100–2, 106–7. On Henry Somerset, see Dorothy Rivett-Carnac, *Hawk's Eye: Colonel Henry Somerset* (Cape Town, 1966).
32. P.J. van der Merwe, *Die Noordwaartse Beweging van die Boere voor die Groot Trek* (The Hague, 1937), 223–5, 231.
33. See ch. 4 n.110 above. Also Saxe Bannister, *Humane Policy: or Justice to the Aborigines of New Settlements* (1830, repr. 1968), 149–58; Stephen Kay, *Travels and Researches in Caffraria* (1833), 328–32; Godlonton, *Introductory Remarks*, 49–74.
34. Switzer, *Power and Resistance*, 56; Crais, *Colonial Order*, 113–15; Macmillan, *BBB*, 89–94; Ross, *Philip*, 126–7; J.S. Marais, *The Cape Coloured People, 1652–1937* (1939, repr. Johannesburg, 1957), 216–17; Peires, *Phalo*, 89; Lancaster, 'D'Urban', 78–9; Kay, *Travels*, 493–8; *The Autobiography of the Late Sir Andries Stockenström*, ed. C.W. Hutton (1887, repr. Cape Town, 1964), I, 292–9, ch. 14, 340–51; Dracopoli, *Stockenström*, 73–5; Peires in *SSAS*, 483–4; E.J.C. Wagenaar, 'A Forgotten Frontier Zone: Settlements and Reactions in the Stormberg Area between 1820–1860', *AYB* (1982, II), 117–21.
35. Thomas Pringle, *Narrative of a Residence in South Africa* (1835), 269–70; Jane Meiring, *Thomas Pringle, His Life and Times* (Cape Town, 1968), 121; Ross, *Philip*, 119, 126–7; Sales, *Mission Stations*, 101; *Kitchingman Papers*, 129–34. On the origins of the Kat River Settlement, see Elizabeth Elbourne, '"To Colonise the Mind": Evangelical Missionaries in Britain and the Eastern Cape, 1790–1837' (D.Phil., Oxford, 1992), 301–4; Stockenström, *Autobiography*, I, 366–71, II, 350–8; Dracopoli, *Stockenström*, 17–18; Justus [MacKenzie Beverley], *The Wrongs of the Caffre Nation* (1837), 102, 113–45. On the Kat River Settlement, see pp. 117–18 above.
36. Stockenström, *Autobiography*, I, 298, 365–6; on the reprisal system generally, ibid, I, 99–106, 251–7, 341–51, 393–407; J.D. Pitman, 'The Commissioner-Generalship of Andries Stockenström' (MA, UCT, 1939).
37. Dracopoli, *Stockenström*, 41–3.
38. Stockenström, *Autobiography*, I, 407, II, 15–16.
39. John Frye, 'The *South African Commercial Advertiser* and the Eastern Frontier, 1834–1847' (MA, Rhodes, 1968), 42–3; Pretorius, 'Humanitarians', 34; H.C. Botha, *John Fairbairn in South Africa* (Cape Town, 1984), 104–8.
40. Macmillan, *BBB*, 96–100; Le Cordeur, *Separatism*, 66–7; Botha, *Fairbairn*, 68–70; Frye, 'Eastern Frontier', 21–5; Ross, *Philip*, 121–3.
41. Macmillan, *BBB*, 100.
42. Ross, *Philip*, 128–9.
43. Ibid, 122–3; Pretorius, 'Humanitarians', 157.
44. Sales, *Mission Stations*, 63–4, 112–13; Elbourne, '"To Colonise the Mind,"' 245–6, 319–20.
45. Ross, *Philip*, 121, 125, 126, 127; *Rev. F.G. Kayser: Journal and Letters*, ed. Chris Hummel, Graham's Town Series 11 (Cape Town, 1990), *passim*.
46. Williams, *When Races Meet*, *passim*.
47. Pretorius, 'Humanitarians', 16–21; Macmillan, *BBB*, 93.
48. Ross, *Philip*, 128; Crais, *Colonial Order*, 115. On the build-up of tensions leading to war, see Pringle, *Narrative*, 319–38; Justus, *Wrongs of the Caffre Nation*, 146–95.
49. Hunt, *Cole*, 102–7; Pretorius, 'Humanitarians', 26–32; Galbraith, *Reluctant Empire*, 101; Macmillan, *BBB*, 103–5; Ross, *Philip*, 129–31; Muller, *Oorsprong*, 193–4; Lancaster, 'D'Urban', 80, 85; Godlonton, *Introductory Remarks*, 99–103.
50. Elbourne, '"To Colonise the Mind,"' 320–4; Macmillan, *BBB*, 102–5; Pretorius, 'Humanitarians', 12–13, 29–33; *Memoirs of Sir Thomas Fowell Buxton* (1849), 359–71.
51. Galbraith, *Reluctant Empire*, 102, 104–5; Pretorius, 'Humanitarians', 32.

52. Macmillan, *BBB*, 106–28; Pretorius, 'Humanitarians', 41–5; Ross, *Philip*, 131–3.

53. In his memorandum on frontier problems to D'Urban in March 1834, Philip foresaw the extension of British control to Delagoa Bay 'on the plan adopted by the ancient Romans which led them to spread themselves and their institutions over the countries which submitted to their government'. In this way the indigenous people would benefit and prosper, and not suffer the 'progressive extension of the colonial boundary by the extermination of the natives of the country'. Galbraith, *Reluctant Empire*, 105; Lancaster, 'D'Urban', 85–92, 103–9.

54. Macmillan, *BBB*, 119–20; Frye, 'Eastern Frontier', 34–45.

55. Webster, 'Land Expropriation', 53–7, 64–71.

56. On the war, see Peires, *Phalo*, 109–15; Webster, 'Land Expropriation', 72–123, 181–90; Switzer, *Power and Resistance*, 56–8; Mostert, *Frontiers*, 650–750.

57. Pretorius, 'Humanitarians', 52.

58. Frye, 'Eastern Frontier', 59; Godlonton, *A Narrative of the Irruption of the Kaffir Hordes* (1836, repr. Cape Town, 1965), 49–52. The most outlandish charge put forward by the conspiracy theorists of Graham's Town was that Thomas Pringle's innocent poem about the conflict of 1819, 'Makanna's Gathering', was responsible for the uprising (Pretorius, 'Humanitarians', 51–2). 'We have all manner of stories', wrote Philip, 'about the missionaries being the cause of the war, and how they got out whole boxes of assegais from Austin Friars [LMS headquarters] to distribute among the Caffres before war commenced' (Macmillan, *BBB*, 140). Yet Philip insisted that coloured men attached to LMS missions obey instructions to serve in the British military (Sales, *Mission Stations*, 116).

59. Frye, 'Eastern Frontier', 55–8; Pretorius, 'Humanitarians', 49–50; Macmillan, *BBB*, 136–7; Godlonton, *Introductory Remarks*, 114–19. On Fairbairn's reaction to the war, see Botha, *Fairbairn*, 109–12.

60. Godlonton, *Introductory Remarks*, 1–128, and Part III, 'Sketch of Kaffraria', on the issue of land rights; Andrew Bank, 'Liberals and their Enemies: Racial Ideology at the Cape of Good Hope, 1820–1850' (Ph.D., Cambridge, 1995), 217–25, 266–71; Clifton Crais, 'The Vacant Land: The Mythology of British Expansion in the Eastern Cape, South Africa', *Journal of Social History*, 25, 2 (1991), 255–75.

61. Boyce, *Notes on South African Affairs*, 14, Appendix p. 1; Shaw, *Story of my Mission*, 157–69, 181–3; [Shaw], *A Defence of the Wesleyan Missionaries in South Africa: Comprising Copies of a Correspondence with the Rev. John Philip, DD* (1839); Ross, *Philip*, 139; Sales, *Mission Stations*, 115–16; *Rev. F.G. Kayser*, 118–20. Read's comment was that the Methodists' role was 'quite a scandal to civil society and withal to the sacred name of missionary' (*Kitchingman Papers*, 154). The eminent Methodist missionary Boyce, who owned a farm in the 'ceded territory' which he began stocking with sheep in 1835, was described by Harry Smith as 'more full of dragooning our new subjects [the Xhosa] than a hundred soldiers ... The Man of the Gospel is, after all, a worldly fellow.' Webster, 'Land Expropriation', 196; Macmillan, *BBB*, 151.

62. Lancaster, 'D'Urban', 89, 103–9.

63. Le Cordeur, *Separatism*, 69–70; Pretorius, 'Humanitarians', 53; Macmillan, *BBB*, 127–8, 130.

64. Cory, *Rise of SA*, III, 183.

65. Lancaster, 'D'Urban', 177; Henry H. Dugmore, *Reminiscences of an Albany Settler*, eds. F.G. van der Riet and L.A. Hewson (Graham's Town, 1958), 52–3; Frye, 'Eastern Frontier', 59; Seton, 'Wesleyan Missions', 208–15, 221–6, 384–96; H.E. Hockly, *The Story of the British Settlers of 1820 in South Africa* (Johannesburg, 1966), 128.

66. Pretorius, 'Humanitarians', 50; Lancaster, 'D'Urban', 72.

67. Pretorius, 'Humanitarians', 53, 57.

68. Galbraith, *Reluctant Empire*, 104, 111; Pretorius, 'Humanitarians', 78; Macmillan, *BBB*, 130–1.

69. Lancaster, 'D'Urban', 112–14; Pretorius, 'Humanitarians', 59–73; Macmillan, *BBB*, 130–3.

70. Elbourne, '"To Colonise the Mind,"' 324–8.

71. On the inquiry into Hintsa's death and the repercussions, see Pretorius, 'Humanitarians', 178–258; Lancaster, 'D'Urban', 136–8. This episode's pivotal significance for the Xhosa is evidenced in the present day (1996), when the chieftaincy is seeking to define its role in the democratic order, in the highly publicised campaign by one of Hintsa's descendants to recover the king's skull, which it is believed was taken to Britain (although there is no historical evidence to support this).

72. Pretorius, 'Humanitarians', 74–82; Galbraith, *Reluctant Empire*, 112–13; Lancaster, 'D'Urban', 114. The proclamation is in K.N. Bell and W.P. Morrell (eds.), *Select Documents on British Colonial Policy, 1830–1860* (Oxford, 1928), 455–8.

73. Pretorius, 'Humanitarians', 126; Macmillan, *BBB*, 140–1. Harry Smith wrote to his sister that the 'magnificent territory' that had been annexed provided 'every faculty on earth for emigration' (Pretorius, 79).

74. *Commandant Holden Bowker*, 115–16; Le Cordeur, *Separatism*, 71; Pretorius, 'Humanitarians', 95.

75. Una Long, *Index to Authors of Unofficial, Privately Owned MSS, 1812–1920* (London, 1947), 184.

76. Galbraith, *Reluctant Empire*, 122; Le Cordeur, *Separatism*, 71–2; A.C.M. Webb, 'The Agricultural Development of the 1820 Settlement down to 1846' (MA, Rhodes, 1975), 172–3.

77. On war profiteering, see Le Cordeur, *Separatism*, 70–1; Webster, 'Land Expropriation', 188–9; A.H. Duminy, 'The Role of Sir Andries Stockenström in Cape Politics, 1848–1856', *AYB* (1960, II), 85 n.26; Webb, 'Agricultural Development', 194–5; Macmillan, *BBB*, 169–70, 270, 178; *The Reminiscences of Thomas Stubbs*, eds. W.A. Maxwell and R.T. McGeogh, Graham's Town Series 4 (Cape Town, 1978), 135–6, 211, 214; Tony Kirk, 'Self-Government and Self-Defence in South Africa: The Interrelations between British and Cape Politics, 1846–1854' (D.Phil., Oxford, 1972), 186; Stockenström, *Autobiography*, II, 97.

78. On Wood, see A.E. Makin, *The 1820 Settlers of Salem* (Wynberg, 1971), 82–4; *Reminiscences of Thomas Stubbs*, 106–7; *Journal of Charles Lennox Stretch*, 141, 196 n.68; Webster, 'Land Expropriation', 188–9.

79. James Backhouse, *Narrative of a Visit to the Mauritius and South Africa* (1844), 301–2.

80. Stretch, *Journal*, 196 n.68.

81. Godlonton, *Narrative of the Irruption*, 89–93; Le Cordeur, *Separatism*, 72.

82. A.C.M. Webb, 'The Immediate Consequences of the Sixth Frontier War on the Farming Community of Albany', *SAHJ*, 10 (1978), 38–48.

83. John Ayliff and J. Whiteside, *History of the Abambo, Generally Known as the Fingos* (Butterworth, 1912); R.A. Moyer, 'A History of the Mfengu of the Eastern Cape' (Ph.D., London, 1976); Peires, *Phalo*, 86–9; Webster, 'Land Expropriation', *passim*; Switzer, *Power and Resistance*, 58–60; Macmillan, *BBB*, 133–5; Pretorius, 'Humanitarians', 82–95; Crais, *Colonial Order*, 99.

84. For a critique of the historiography, from Ayliff on, see Webster, 'Land Expropriation', 15–19, 162–4, 219–22.

85. Peires, *Phalo*, 110–11; Switzer, *Power and Resistance*, 58–60; Pretorius, 'Humanitarians', 87–9; Crais, *Colonial Order*, 117–18; Lancaster, 'D'Urban', 72–3.

Webster presents an alternative view to that presented here. Webster, 'Land Expropriation' (n.27 above); Webster, 'Unmasking the Fingo: The War of 1835 Revisited' in Carolyn Hamilton (ed.), *The Mfecane Aftermath: Reconstructive Debates in Southern African History* (Johannesburg, 1995). Webster is closely followed by Timothy Stapleton, *Maqoma: Xhosa Resistance to Colonial Advance, 1798–1873* (Johannesburg, 1994), 49–50, 90–1, 101–2, 107, 235. Webster argues that Mfengu identity and history were essentially a colonial construct. Following Cobbing, he argues that the 'Mfecane', the disruptions and mass migrations that characterised the 1820s, was not so much the result of the rise of Zulu power among the northern Nguni, as conventional historiography has it, as the result in the first instance of the pincer movement of colonial 'plunder systems' emanating from the Cape and from the Portuguese settlements of the Mozambican coast. (See n.110 of ch. 4 above.) Webster uses the old colonial term 'Fingo' on the grounds that they were a colonial creation. But as there were many people in the 1830s (as today) who called themselves by this name, whatever their origins, declining to grace them with an African orthography is surely perverse.

According to Webster, D'Urban's campaigns beyond the Kei in 1835 were simply the culmination of a single-minded purpose that had been grimly pursued ever since the first meeting of the races – the enslavement of African labour. The evidence he provides of a 'large-scale secret slave trade' in the east of the colony over many years is very thin, incidental and anecdotal. Webster suggests that evidence was destroyed to cover up the practice. So monolithic and single-minded is the colonial enterprise supposed to be in this scenario that humanitarians such as James Read, who was not inclined to cover anything up, simply disappear as historical actors. Webster wishes to show that the war of 1834–5 was instigated in order to ensure the removal of thousands of people (the Mfengu) as a labour source.   The war was thus planned to create a labour supply, with D'Urban and Godlonton held up as the masterminds. The creation of 'Fingo' identity (mainly by the missionary Ayliff, 'probably with the aid of D'Urban and Godlonton') was part of a grand cover-up of what was really happening, used to disguise the forced removal of Xhosa as the voluntary exodus of an alien and oppressed refugee people. Now, one can accept that providing colonial employers with labour was a fortunate consequence of war, and that labour coercion was ubiquitous in the circumstances. But this conspiracy theory is without foundation. If the Xhosa could not be conquered and dispossessed (as they patently could not be in 1835), then how could so many of them have been forcibly removed as forced labourers, settled near the Keiskamma or on farms or in towns within walking distance of their homes, and kept there permanently? Far from being the all-powerful state that is presented here, the colonial state had very limited resources, despite brief and unsuccessful moments of military imperialism such as characterised 1835. And how does one explain the fact that the Mfengu were enthusiastic and unfailing armed allies of colonial forces in subsequent conflicts with the Xhosa? It is true that Mfengu identity was malleable and manipulated by different actors for their own purposes. There were clear advantages in Mfengu identity for those who had become closely entwined in the colonial society and economy; and in colonial terms, 'Fingo' became a blanket term for Nguni-speaking refugee labourers arriving in the colony. But the notion that 'Fingo' was an imposed identity as part of an elaborate colonial stratagem is untenable.

86. Pretorius, 'Humanitarians', 83; Lancaster, 'D'Urban', 114–15.

87. Bundy, *Rise and Fall*; Jack Lewis, 'An Economic History of the Ciskei, 1848–1900' (Ph.D., UCT, 1984).

88. Webster, 'Land Expropriation', 145–8.

89. Sales, *Mission Stations*, 118, 136, 140; Webster, 'Land Expropriation', 149.

90. Lancaster, 'D'Urban', 16–18, 133; Galbraith, *Reluctant Empire*, 115–18; Le Cordeur, *Separatism*, 75–6; Pretorius, 'Humanitarians', 100–21; Macmillan, *BBB*, 135–6, 148–51, 155; Webster, 'Land Expropriation', 165–74.

91. Lancaster, 'D'Urban', 117–18.

92. Macmillan, *BBB*, 150, 155–6; *The Autobiography of Lieutenant-General Sir Harry Smith*, ed. G.C. Moore Smith (1902), 420–51; A.L. Harington, *Sir Harry Smith: Bungling Hero* (Cape Town, 1980), 52–79.

93. Pretorius, 'Humanitarians', 127–59; Macmillan, *BBB*, 142–6, 160–1; Galbraith, *Reluctant Empire*, 126–7; Ross, *Philip*, 139; Lancaster, 'D'Urban', 121–3; Elbourne, '"To Colonise the Mind,"' 328–32; Robert Ross, 'Donald Moodie and the Origins of South African Historiography' in Ross, *Beyond the Pale: Essays on the History of Colonial South Africa* (Johannesburg, 1993), 201–4; *Kitchingman Papers*, 161–78.

94. J.M. Urie, 'A Critical Study of the Evidence of Andries Stockenström before the Aborigines Committee in 1835, Viewed in the Light of his Statements and Policies before 1835' (MA, Rhodes, 1953); Pretorius, 'Humanitarians', 142–4; Galbraith, *Reluctant Empire*, 132–3; Crais, *Colonial Order*, 119–20; Cory, *Rise of SA*, III, 286–9.

95. Ross, *Philip*, 140–2; Pretorius, 'Humanitarians', 97, 158; Macmillan, *BBB*, 146, 232. But before the aborigines committee in London in 1836, Philip said, 'Had I been consulted before the Caffre War on the propriety of annexing the country between the Keiskamma and the Kye to the colony, I should have said, let the Caffres alone, the work of civilisation is going forward among them, and in a little time what you wish for will come about by itself' (Bank, 'Liberals and their Enemies', 136–7).

96. Lancaster, 'D'Urban', 124–32; Pretorius, 'Humanitarians', 159–77; Macmillan, *BBB*, 173–7; Bell and Morrell, *Select Documents*, 463–77; Galbraith, *Reluctant Empire*, 129–31; J.E. Holloway, 'The Glenelg–D'Urban Dispute', *Historia*, 18, 2 (1973), 88–92.

97. Webster, 'Land Expropriation', 191–200; Pretorius, 'Humanitarians', 172.

98. Pretorius, 'Humanitarians', 174.

99. Stockenström, *Autobiography*, II, 30–40; André du Toit and Hermann Giliomee, *Afrikaner Political Thought, Analysis and Documents, I: 1780–1850* (Cape Town, 1983), 173–5.

100. Pretorius, 'Humanitarians', 171–2; Lancaster, 'D'Urban', 141.

101. Ross, *Philip*, 142; Galbraith, *Reluctant Empire*, 138; Macmillan, *BBB*, 180–1; Le Cordeur, *Separatism*, 76, 84; Lancaster, 'D'Urban', 166–7; Stockenström, *Autobiography*, II, 51–64.

102. Marian George, 'John Bardwell Ebden: His Business and Political Career at the Cape, 1806–1849', *AYB* (1986, I), 65–6; H.C. Botha, 'Die Rol van Christoffel J. Brand in Suid-Afrika, 1820–1854', *AYB* (1977), 36, 64–6; Botha, *Fairbairn*, 114; Donald Moodie, *The Record* (see n.2 above). On Moodie see *DSAB*, II, 488–91. The circumstances and import of Moodie's labours are examined in Ross, 'Donald Moodie' (n.93 above); Bank, 'Liberals and their Enemies', 261–6. Moodie conceived of this work as a response in part to the charges contained in Philip's *Researches*, and to this end included material going back to the earliest dealings with the Khoi in the seventeenth century. Although in the end his compilation did not extend beyond 1809, Moodie, like Godlonton, was a major force in launching a colonial historiographical tradition. Philip had asserted, for example, that the Bushmen were a colonial creation, that they were 'Hottentots' who had been dispossessed and had fled from enslavement. (This view was echoed by Pringle, *Narrative*, 235–44.) Moodie refuted this, arguing that the Bushmen were a distinct people, whose

evil designs on colonial livestock justified their suppression by commandos in the eighteenth century. This, of course, is a debate that still has relevance today. See [Moodie], *Remarks upon Some of the Results Developed by the Publication of a Portion of the Cape Records Relative to the Treatment of the Native Tribes of South Africa* (Cape Town, [1841]).

103. George, 'Ebden', 66; Botha, *Fairbairn*, 116, 134.

104. Duminy, 'Stockenström', 84–5; *Journals of Andrew Geddes Bain: Trader, Explorer, Soldier, Road Engineer and Geologist*, ed. M.H. Lister, Van Riebeeck Society, 30 (Cape Town, 1949), xxiv.

105. Duminy, 'Stockenström', 85; Lancaster, 'D'Urban', 167–9; Le Cordeur, *Separatism*, 84–90, 94–5, 97–8; Galbraith, *Reluctant Empire*, 138–41; Macmillan, *BBB*, 179–80, 184–5, 191; Peires, *Phalo*, 124–5; P.J. Smuts, 'The Lieutenant Governorship of Andries Stockenström' (MA, UCT, 1940), 41–52; Stockenström, *Autobiography*, II, 51–64, 130–82; Dracopoli, *Stockenström*, 115–17, 128–9; Ross, 'Moodie', 204–5; Urie, 'Aborigines Committee', 12; Bank, 'Liberals and their Enemies', 225–6. On Stockenström's lieutenant-governorship generally, see Lancaster, 'D'Urban', 146–58, 166–72.

106. G.B. Crankshaw, 'The Diary of C.L. Stretch: A Critical Edition and Appraisal' (MA, Rhodes, 1960), 13–58, 96–108; Duminy, 'Stockenström', 82–6, 145–7, 157–60; Stockenström, *Autobiography*, II, 94–131; Du Toit and Giliomee, *Afrikaner Political Thought*, 175–7; Wagenaar, 'Forgotten Frontier Zone', 137–48.

107. A.C. Wilmot and J.C. Chase, *History of the Colony of the Cape of Good Hope* (Cape Town, 1869), 330–45 (written by Chase), for the judgement of a colleague of Godlonton.

108. Lancaster, 'D'Urban', 155–8.

109. Duminy, 'Stockenström', 84, 158–60.

110. Long, *Index to Authors*, 252; Lancaster, 'D'Urban', 169–71; Galbraith, *Reluctant Empire*, 142–3; Peires, *Phalo*, 124; Stretch's memo. in Crankshaw, 'Stretch', n.p., para. 5; Stockenström, *Autobiography*, II, 122–8.

111. Peires, *Phalo*, 125–6; Galbraith, *Reluctant Empire*, 144–50; Le Cordeur, *Separatism*, 93, 96; Macmillan, *BBB*, 192.

112. Crankshaw, 'Stretch', 134–7.

113. Duminy, 'Stockenström', 146, 157. In 1851 a letter by Stockenström to an unknown friend was published as *Brief Notice of the Causes of the Kaffir War*, which best summarised his conception of frontier policy. Also Du Toit and Giliomee, *Afrikaner Political Thought*, 181–2.

114. See pp. 103–5 above on Stockenström and the Khoi.

115. Le Cordeur, *Separatism*, 135–6; Boyce, *Notes on South African Affairs*, 116–18.

116. Godlonton, *Introductory Remarks*, 75–6.

117. K.S. Hunt, 'The Development of Municipal Government in the Eastern Province of the Cape of Good Hope, with Special Reference to Graham's Town, 1827–1862', *AYB* (1961), 142–5; L.P. Green, *History of Local Government in South Africa: An Introduction* (Cape Town, 1957), 16–21. Ordinance 9 of 1836 is in G.W. Eybers (ed.), *Select Constitutional Documents Illustrating South African History* (1918), 78–81.

118. B. Keith-Lucas, *English Local Government in the Nineteenth and Twentieth Centuries* (1977).

119. Lancaster, 'D'Urban', 173–9. A separate ordinance was drawn up for the establishment of municipal government in Cape Town in 1840, delayed owing to its more complicated circumstances. Digby Warren, 'Merchants, Municipal Commissioners and Wardmasters: Municipal Politics in Cape Town, 1840–1854' (MA, UCT, 1986), 5–10.

120. Crais, *Colonial Order*, 151–2.

121. H.M. Robertson, 'The Cape of Good Hope and "Systematic Colonisation,"' *South African Journal of Economics*, 5, 4 (1937), 367–411.

122. Godlonton, *Sketches of the Eastern Districts of the Cape of Good Hope As They Are in 1842* (Graham's Town, 1842); Chase, *The Cape of Good Hope and the Eastern Province of Albany Bay* (1843, repr. Cape Town, 1967). On Chase see M.J. McGinn, 'J.C. Chase: 1820 Settler and Servant of the Colony' (MA, Rhodes, 1975), 72–5 and *passim*; Le Cordeur, *Separatism*, 126–7.

123. Kirk, 'Self-Government and Self-Defence', 293–4.

124. Godlonton, *Memorials of the British Settlers of South Africa* (Graham's Town, 1844); McGinn, 'Chase', 56, sees the celebrations as the 'self-conscious beginnings of the cult of the 1820 settlers'.

125. Le Cordeur, *Separatism*, 127.

126. Tony Kirk, 'The Cape Economy and the Expropriation of the Kat River Settlement, 1846–1853' in Shula Marks and Anthony Atmore (eds.), *Economy and Society in Pre-Industrial South Africa* (1980), 239–40; Kirk, 'Self-Government', 294–6.

127. *Reminiscences of Thomas Stubbs*, 136.

128. Peires, *Phalo*, 241 n.129 gives some examples; Stockenström, *Autobiography*, II, 129.

129. Crankshaw, 'Stretch', 117–18; 'Petition of Municipal Commissioners', Graham's Town, August 1843, in Bell and Morrell, *Select Documents*, 499–500; J.M. Bowker, *Speeches, Letters and Selections from Important Papers (1836–1847)* (1864, repr. Cape Town, 1962), 124–5, 191–3, 235–8 and *passim*; Bank, 'Liberals and their Enemies', 228–34.

130. Crankshaw, 'Stretch', 342.

131. Macmillan, *BBB*, 270; Crankshaw, 'Stretch', 121–3, 102.

132. Peires, *Phalo*, 156; Le Cordeur, *Separatism*, 102.

133. Le Cordeur, *Separatism*, 102.

134. The prevailing ethos of settler politics was quickly apprehended by the Quaker traveller Backhouse: 'Some of this class of persons, and some who long for a possession in the better land inhabited by the Caffres, appear at all times ready to fan any little spark of disturbance, between these people and the neighbouring colonists, into a flame of discord.' Backhouse, *Narrative of a Visit*, 301.

135. *Porter Speeches*, 433, 421–36, for the full speech. An extreme form of racial stereotyping was employed by settler propagandists, and was reflected in frontier art and in the settler interest in the rising racial science of phrenology. See Bank, 'Liberals and their Enemies', chs. 6 and 7 for fascinating discussions on these topics; also Crais, 'Vacant Land'.

136. H.B. Thom, *Die Geskiedenis van die Skaapboerdery in Suid-Afrika* (Amsterdam, 1936), 78–89, 178–80, 195–9; K.W. Smith, *From Frontier to Midlands: A History of the Graaff-Reinet District, 1786–1910* (Graham's Town, 1976), 58–9; Kirk, 'Cape Economy', 227–32; Mary Rayner, 'Wine and Slaves: The Failure of an Export Economy and the Ending of Slavery in the Cape Colony, South Africa, 1806–1834' (Ph.D., Duke, 1986), 241–5; Saul Dubow, *Land, Labour and Merchant Capital: The Experience of the Graaff-Reinet District in the Pre-Industrial Rural Economy of the Cape, 1852–1872*, Communications no. 6, Centre for African Studies (Cape Town, 1982); Webb, 'Agricultural Development', 116–37, 176–93; Crais, *Colonial Order*, 134; Lalou Meltzer, 'The Growth of Cape Town Commerce and the Role of John Fairbairn's *Advertiser*, 1835–1859' (MA, UCT, 1989), 90.

137. Webster, 'Land Expropriation', 204–5.

138. Crais, *Colonial Order*, 150–64; Kirk, 'Cape Economy', 233–5; Macmillan, *BBB*, 278–81; Sheila van der Horst, *Native Labour in South Africa* (Cape Town, 1942), 25–9; Godlonton, *Sketches*, 110–11.

139. Gustav Preller, *Voortrekkermense* (Cape Town, 1920, 1938), I, 10, 116; Henry Cloete, *Five Lectures on the Emigration of the Dutch Farmers from the Colony of the Cape of Good Hope* (1856, repr. Pretoria, 1968), 87.

140. H.M. Robertson, '"Systematic Colonisation,"' 375; H.B. Thom, *Die Lewe van Gert Maritz* (Cape Town, 1947), 80–2, on Maritz's land sales; John Noble, *Handbook of the Cape Colony* (1875), 149.

141. Crais, *Colonial Order*, 134–5; Smith, *Frontier to Midlands*, 53–4; C.F.J. Muller, *Die Britse Owerheid en die Groot Trek*, 3rd ed. (Pretoria, 1969), 63–4; Webb, 'Agricultural Development', 182–3; *Commandant Holden Bowker*, 67–8; Long, *Index to Authors*, 246; Noble, *Handbook*, 148–9.

142. Muller, *Oorsprong van die Groot Trek*, 184–5; Backhouse, *Narrative of a Visit*, 303; Peires, *Phalo*, 122–3; Le Cordeur, *Separatism*, 89, 147; Cory, *Rise of SA*, IV, 357n.

143. Elizabeth Anderson, *A History of the Xhosa of the Northern Cape, 1795–1879*, Communications 12, Centre for African Studies (Cape Town, 1987), 48–50, 61–3; Meltzer, 'Cape Town Commerce', 117–18.

144. Macmillan, *BBB*, 267–8, 270; Le Cordeur, *Separatism*, 88–9.

145. Macmillan, *CCQ*, 79–80; Dracopoli, *Stockenström*, 154–5. Attorney-General Porter also noted this contradiction: see *Porter Speeches*, 422–5.

146. J.J. Breitenbach, 'The Development of the Secretaryship to the Government at the Cape of Good Hope under John Montagu, 1845–1852', *AYB* (1959, II), 221–3, 244; Le Cordeur, *Separatism*, 219–20, 139–41; McGinn, 'Chase', 53–61; Alan Mabin, 'The Rise and Decline of Port Elizabeth, 1850–1900', *IJAHS*, 19 (1986), 275–303. On Paterson, see J.L. Stead, 'The Development and Failure of the Eastern Cape Separatist Movement', *AYB* (1982, II); Pamela ffolliot and E.L.H. Croft, *One Titan at a Time* (Cape Town, 1960).

147. Breitenbach, 'Montagu', 221; Le Cordeur, *Separatism*, 140, 196–7.

148. Le Cordeur, *Separatism*, 240 n.159.

149. Meltzer, 'Cape Town Commerce', 91; Le Cordeur, *Separatism*, 128–9. On Cape Town's predominance generally in the pre-mineral era, see Alan Mabin, 'The Making of Colonial

Capitalism: Intensification and Expansion in the Economic Geography of the Cape Colony, South Africa, 1854–1899' (Ph.D., Simon Fraser, 1984), ch. 3.

150. Le Cordeur, *Separatism*, 187.

151. Ibid, 129.

152. Meltzer, 'Cape Town Commerce', 119–21; Kirk, 'Cape Economy', 230–1.

153. Dubow, *Land, Labour and Merchant Capital*, 23; Le Cordeur, *Separatism*, 123–4; Boyce, *Notes on South African Affairs*, 57–8; R.F.M. Immelman, *Men of Good Hope: The Romantic Story of the Cape Town Chamber of Commerce, 1804–1954* (Cape Town, 1955), 80–1; Kirk, 'Self-Government and Self-Defence', 65; Warren, 'Municipal Politics', 54–5; Long, *Index to Authors*, 246–7.

154. Kirk, 'Cape Economy', 231; Gustav Saron and Louis Hotz (eds.), *The Jews in South Africa: A History* (Cape Town, 1955), 313, 349–51; D. Fleischer and D. Caccia, *Merchant Pioneers: The House of Mosenthal* (Johannesburg, 1983), 45, 78–84 and *passim*; Smith, *Frontier to Midlands*, 65; Louis Herrman, *A History of the Jews in South Africa* (Johannesburg, 1935), 208–16, who writes: 'the Mosenthals and their industrial and commercial activities were the means of introducing into South Africa nearly half the Jewish families who came to this land between 1845 and 1870'.

155. Edmund H. Burrows, *Overberg Outspan: A Chronicle of People and Places in the South Western Districts of the Cape* (Cape Town, 1952); A.P. Buirski, 'The Barrys and the Overberg' (MA, Stellenbosch, 1952); Meltzer, 'Cape Town Commerce', 118–19.

156. Thom, *Skaapboerdery*, 187–93.

157. Meltzer, 'Cape Town Commerce', 99–100, 113–14; Le Cordeur, *Separatism*, 124; Botha, *Fairbairn*, 147–8; George, 'Ebden', 50; Immelman, *Men of Good Hope*, 86–100.

158. Le Cordeur, *Separatism*, 124–5; E.H.D. Arndt, *Banking and Currency Development in South Africa, 1652–1927* (Cape Town, 1928), 197–238; Kirk, 'Self-Government', 69, 310; Immelman, *Men of Good Hope*, 112–21; George, 'Ebden', 17–18, 21–30; Botha, *Fairbairn*, 79–80; Warren, 'Municipal Politics', 47; Meltzer, 'Cape Town Commerce', 100–2.

159. Meltzer, 'Cape Town Commerce', 76–81; Warren, 'Municipal Politics', 46–8; Arndt, *Banking*, 238–9; E. Hengherr, 'Emancipation and After: A Study of Cape Slavery and the Issues Arising from It, 1830–1843' (MA, UCT, 1953), 65–71.

160. Meltzer, 'Cape Town Commerce', 88–90, 114–16, 119; Arndt, *Banking*, 239–44.

161. E.g. J.J.L. Smuts earned £2900 in compensation for his slaves, P.M. Brink £1165 (Meltzer 'Cape Town Commerce', 74–5, 78–80).

162. Kirk, 'Self-Government', 140–50, 310–20; Le Cordeur, *Separatism*, 213–14; Warren, 'Municipal Politics', 46, 255–6 and *passim*.

163. Botha, *Fairbairn*, 179–82; Botha, 'Brand', 78; Green, *History of Local Government*, 22–6.

164. Warren, 'Municipal Politics', 43–4, 47, 75; Botha, 'Brand', 79.

165. Meltzer, 'Cape Town Commerce', 73–4; Warren, 'Municipal Politics', 51–3, 62–6, 165, 253; Warren, 'Property, Profit and Power: The Rise of a Landlord Class in Cape Town in the 1840s' in *Studies in the History of Cape Town*, vol. 6, Centre for African Studies (Cape Town, 1988), 46–7, 54–5; Warren, 'The Early Years of "District 6": District Twelve in the 1840s', *Cabo* (1985); R.W. Murray, *South African Reminiscences* (Cape Town, 1894), 223–5, who records that 'some of the houses of the lower classes of the coloured poor were pictures of wretchedness and misery, ghastliness and unhealthiness'; Shirley Judges, 'Poverty, Living Conditions and Social Relations: Aspects of Life in Cape Town in the 1830s' (MA, UCT, 1977), 70–84, on overcrowding and living conditions in Cape Town slums at the time.

The most prominent commissioner at the time was H.C. Jarvis, member from 1840 to 1859 and chairman from 1848 to 1859. He was a wine merchant, a slum landlord in the Waterfront area of town, and a director of several banks and insurance companies. He was a director of the Cape Town Tramway Co., Railway and Dock Co., and Wellington and Wynberg Railways. He established a distillery at Wellington and a manganese mine near Paarl, and mined unsuccessfully for coal on the slopes of Table Mountain (Warren, 'Municipal Politics', 51; *DSAB*, IV, 259).

166. Meltzer, 'Cape Town Commerce', 61–4, 74, 197; Robert Ross, 'Cape Town, 1750–1850: Synthesis in the Dialectic of Continents' in Ross and G.J. Telkamp (eds.), *Colonial Cities: Essays on Urbanisation in a Colonial Context* (Dordrecht, 1985), 116; Andrew Bank, *The Decline of Urban Slavery at the Cape, 1806–1834*, Communications no. 22, Centre for African Studies (Cape Town, 1991); Warren, 'Municipal Politics', 29; Hengherr, 'Emancipation', 79–82.

167. Warren, 'Municipal Politics', 13, 72–3; Warren, 'Rise of a Landlord Class', 44.

168. Warren, 'Municipal Politics', 18, 77–117, 137–42; Hymen W.J. Picard, *Grand Parade: The Birth of Greater Cape Town, 1850–1913* (Cape Town, 1969), 70–1; Warren, 'Rise of a Landlord Class', 48–9, 52, 58 n.36.

169. Warren, 'Municipal Politics', 118–20; Immelman, *Men of Good Hope*, 174–80.

170. Kirk tends to overemphasise the economic basis of the factionalism within the bourgeoisie, describing a divide between the merchant elite and the newer bourgeoisie centred on the municipality, which was not always apparent in terms of economic interest or political behaviour. Cf. Digby Warren, 'Class Rivalry and Cape Politics in the Mid-Nineteenth Century: A Reappraisal of the Kirk Thesis', *SAHJ*, 24 (1991), 112–27.

171. Warren, 'Rise of a Landlord Class', 46–7.

172. Warren, 'Municipal Politics', 69–74, 226–32; Robert Ross, 'Structure and Culture in Pre-Industrial Cape Town: A Survey of Knowledge and Ignorance' in Wilmot James and Mary Simons (eds.), *The Angry Divide: Social and Economic History of the Western Cape* (Cape Town, 1989).

173. Warren, 'Class Rivalry', 118–19; Botha, 'Brand', 48–9, 58–9, 79; Michael Streak, *The Afrikaner as Viewed by the English, 1795–1854* (Cape Town, 1974).

174. See p. 113 above.

175. Du Toit and Giliomee, *Afrikaner Political Thought*, 247–50; Du Toit, 'The Cape Afrikaners' Failed Liberal Moment, 1850–1870' in Jeffrey Butler, Richard Elphick and David Welsh (eds.), *Democratic Liberalism in South Africa: Its History and Prospect* (Middletown, Conn., 1987), 40–3.

176. Botha, 'Brand', 75; George, 'Ebden', 71; Eybers, *Select Constitutional Documents*, 30–8, for the debate in the House of Commons in 1830; T.R.H. Davenport, 'The Cape Liberal Tradition to 1910' in Butler, Elphick and Welsh, *Democratic Liberalism*.

177. Botha, *Fairbairn*, 182–90; Botha, 'Brand', 80–2; George, 'Ebden', 72; Kirk, 'Self-Government', 156–9; Warren, 'Municipal Politics', 39, 129–34; Marais, *Cape Coloured People*, 209; Warren, 'Landlord Class', 55–6; Du Toit and Giliomee, *Afrikaner Political Thought*, 288–91; Eybers, *Select Constitutional Documents*, 41–3, for the municipal petition; Bell and Morrell, *Select Documents*, 47–53, for Stanley's response to the petition.

178. Botha, 'Brand', 82–3.

179. Kirk, 'Self-Government', 312–16; George, 'Ebden', 124–9.

180. Meltzer, 'Cape Town Commerce', 96–100, 104–8, 110–13.

181. Breitenbach, 'Montagu', 218–21; Warren, 'Municipal Politics', 197–9, 237–9.

Chapter Six: Expanding Frontiers: The Great Leap Forward

1. On the origins of the Griqua, see Martin Legassick, 'The Griqua, the Sotho–Tswana and the Missionaries, 1780–1840: The Politics of a Frontier Zone' (Ph.D., UCLA, 1969), 101–22; Legassick, 'The Northern Frontier to *c.*1840: The Rise and Decline of the Griqua People' in Richard Elphick and Hermann Giliomee (eds.), *The Shaping of South African Society, 1652–1840s* (Cape Town, 1989), 368–76; J.S. Marais, *The Cape Coloured People, 1652–1937* (1939, repr. Johannesburg, 1968), 32–3; Robert Ross, *Adam Kok's Griquas: A Study in the Development of Stratification in South Africa* (Cambridge, 1976), 12–21; George W. Stow, *The Native Races of South Africa* (1905), chs. 17–19; John Campbell, *Travels in South Africa, Undertaken at the Request of the LMS, Being a Narrative of a Second Journey in the Interior of that Country* (1822, repr. New York, 1967), II, 259–70; Henry Lichtenstein, *Travels in Southern Africa*, 2 vols. (1812, 1815, repr. Cape Town, 1928, 1930), II, 301–6.

2. Nigel Penn, 'Land, Labour and Livestock in the Western Cape during the Eighteenth Century' in Wilmot James and Mary Simons (ed.), *The Angry Divide: Social and Economic History of the Western Cape* (Cape Town, 1989), 13–19. The definition of 'Bastaard' was not very precise, denoting as much an intermediate social status as a genetic one; hence Christianised Khoi who enjoyed a degree of economic independence could perhaps be so classified. Legassick, 'Griqua', 93–9; Ross, *Adam Kok's Griquas*, 13.

3. Legassick, 'Griqua', 126–41.

4. Ibid, 130–1.

5. In the northern frontier zone too, white men who had turned their back on the dominant mores of the more settled colonial community participated in the local raiding economy, married local women, and established their own political communities. Legassick, 'Griqua', 133–41.

6. Legassick, 'Griqua', 169–200; Legassick in *SSAS*, 376–81; Marais, *Cape Coloured People*, 33–7; Margaret Kinsman, 'Populists and Patriarchs: The Transformation of the Captaincy at Griqua Town, 1804–1822' in Alan Mabin (ed.), *Organisation and Economic Change* (Johannesburg, 1989); Ross, *Adam Kok's Griquas*, 14–21.

7. Ross, *Adam Kok's Griquas*, 10, 144 n.28.

8. John Philip, *Researches in South Africa*, 2 vols. (1828, repr. New York, 1969), II, 56–61, painted a picture of Griqua savagery before their 'capture' by the missionaries.

9. Ross, *Adam Kok's Griquas*, 15–16; Kinsman, 'Populists and Patriarchs', 2–3; Legassick,

'Griqua', 181–4.
10. Legassick, 'Griqua', 236–7; William J. Burchell, *Travels into the Interior of South Africa* (1822, repr. 1953), I, 112, 261–2, 232–3, 259, 303, II, 154, 329–38.
11. Roger Beck, 'The Legalisation and Development of Trade on the Cape Frontier, 1817–1830' (Ph.D., Indiana, 1987), 32–45; Legassick, 'Griqua', 225–38; Jean and John Comaroff, *Of Revelation and Revolution: Christianity, Colonialism, and Consciousness in South Africa* (Chicago, 1991), 161–6. The extent of profit is indicated by the fact that a sheep purchased in the colony for 2 rix-dollars could be bartered for 100 lb of ivory, which fetched 1–2 rix-dollars per lb in the colony. Legassick, 'Griqua', 235.
12. Legassick, 'Griqua', 189–95; Legassick in *SSAS*, 381–4; Campbell, *Travels in South Africa* (1815, repr. Cape Town, 1974), 252–8; V.C. Malherbe, 'The Life and Times of Cupido Kakkerlak', *JAH*, 20, 3 (1979), 365–78.
13. Kinsman, 'Populists and Patriarchs', 4–6.
14. Legassick, 'Griqua', 281–5; W.M. Macmillan, *The Cape Colour Question: A Historical Survey* (1927, repr. Cape Town, 1968), 128–32; Desmond Clinton, *The South African Melting Pot: A Vindication of Missionary Policy, 1799–1836* (1937), 103–6; Marais, *Cape Coloured People*, 36–7; Philip, *Researches*, II, 62–8.
15. Kinsman, 'Populists and Patriarchs', 6–10; Legassick, 'Griqua', 200–24.
16. Legassick, 'Griqua', 208, 244–8.
17. Beck, 'Legalisation', 181–214; Legassick, 'Griqua', 238–40; Saxe Bannister, *Humane Policy, or Justice to the Inhabitants of New Settlements* (1830, repr. 1968), 117–26; Philip, *Researches*, II, 68–77; *The Autobiography of the Late Sir Andries Stockenström*, ed. C.W. Hutton, 2 vols. (1887, repr. Cape Town, 1964), I, 176–91.
18. Legassick, 'Griqua', 221–4, 290–7; Kinsman, 'Populists and Patriarchs', 10–12; Marais, *Cape Coloured People*, 38–9; W.M. Macmillan, *Bantu, Boer and Briton: The Making of the South African Native Problem*, 2nd ed. (Oxford, 1963), 55–9; Philip, *Researches*, II, 78–9.
19. D.F. Ellenberger and J.C. MacGregor, *History of the Basuto, Ancient and Modern* (1912), 117–236; MacGregor, *Basuto Traditions* (Cape Town, 1905); J.D. Omer-Cooper, *The Zulu Aftermath* (Evanston, Ill., 1966); William F. Lye, 'The Sotho Wars of the Interior of South Africa, 1822–1837' (Ph.D., UCLA, 1969); Lye, 'The Difaqane: The Mfecane in the Southern Sotho Area', *JAH*, 8 (1967), 107–31; Lye and Colin Murray, *Transformations on the Highveld: The Tswana and Southern Sotho* (Cape Town, 1980), 28–39; L.M. Thompson, *Survival in Two Worlds: Moshoeshoe of Lesotho, 1786–1870* (Oxford, 1975), 32–58; Thompson, 'Co-operation and Conflict: The High Veld' in Monica Wilson and Leonard Thompson (eds.), *Oxford History of South Africa*, I (Oxford, 1969), 391–405. Recently there has been much debate about the nature and significance of the 'Mfecane', and the traditional picture evoked in this literature on the disruptions on the highveld in the 1820s has been radically challenged. This debate is examined in n.27 below.
20. Legassick, 'Griqua', 349–51.
21. Ibid, 346–7.
22. Ibid.
23. P.J. van der Merwe, *Die Noordwaartse Beweging van die Boere voor die Groot Trek* (1937, repr. Pretoria, 1988), 205–40, 282–4, 312–13, 342–50; Macmillan, *BBB*, 60–5; Legassick, 'Griqua', 347–60; C.F.J. Muller, *Die Oorsprong van die Groot Trek* (Cape Town, 1974), 228–32.
24. Van der Merwe, *Noordwaartse Beweging*, 260–2.
25. Legassick, 'Griqua', 348–9, 355–8; Philip, *Researches*, II, 293–4, 298–9, 332–45; Muller, *Oorsprong*, 140 n.14; Lye and Murray, *Transformations*, 39–44. On the Kora, see Stow, *Native Races*, chs. 15, 16; Ross, *Adam Kok's Griquas*, 25–6; J.A. Engelbrecht, *The Korana: An Account of their Customs and their History* (Cape Town, 1936); L.F. Maingard, 'Studies in Korana History, Customs and Language', *Bantu Studies*, 6 (1932), 103–62. On Bergenaar–Kora raiding, see *Apprenticeship at Kuruman, Being the Journals and Letters of Robert and Mary Moffat*, ed. Isaac Schapera (1951), 161, 269, 277–9; T. Arbousset and F. Daumas, *Narrative of an Exploratory Tour to the North-East of the Colony of the Cape of Good Hope* (1846, repr. Cape Town, 1968), 310–12; Ellenberger and MacGregor, *History of the Basuto*, 212–16; *Reminiscences of John Montgomery*, ed. A. Giffard, Graham's Town Series 6 (Cape Town, 1981), 93–7; Stow, *Native Races*, 271, 279, 337.
26. Stockenström envisaged the territory north of the Orange as a Bushman reserve, where they could be converted into settled herders under missionaries. But his efforts were doomed, as were the independent Bushmen. Van der Merwe, *Noordwaartse Beweging*, 136–75, 241–62; Stockenström, *Autobiography*, I, 222–32, 372–90; J.L. Dracopoli, *Sir Andries Stockenström, 1792–1864* (Cape Town, 1969), 63–5, 78–9, 114. The closing of the Bushman frontier just south

of the Orange in the 1810s and 1820s was described vividly by Philip in *Researches*, II, 269; also chs. 14, 15 on commandos in the 1810s and 1820s.

27. Legassick, 'Griqua', 353–5; *The Journals of the Rev. T.L. Hodgson, Missionary to the Seleka–Rolong and the Griquas, 1821–1831*, ed. Richard Cope (Johannesburg, 1977), 69–70, 150–1, 173; Moffat, *Apprenticeship*, 131; *Andrew Smith's Journal of his Expedition into the Interior of South Africa, 1834–1836*, ed. William Lye (Cape Town, 1975), 140, 284; *The Diary of Dr Andrew Smith, Director of the Expedition for Exploring Central Africa, 1834–1836*, ed. Percival R. Kirby, 2 vols., Van Riebeeck Society, 20, 21 (Cape Town, 1939, 1940), I, 192–3; Samuel Broadbent, *A Narrative of the First Introduction of Christianity Amongst the Barolong Tribe of Bechuanas, South Africa* (1865), 97–8, 107–8; Philip, *Researches*, II, 79–84, 90–7; Arbousset and Daumas, *Narrative*, 227–9, 252–3; Stow, *Native Races*, 47–8, 163, 216–17; Bannister, *Humane Policy*, 225–9, who wrote: 'Amongst the Griquas and Bergenaars, who are ... in considerable connection with the Cape, slaves obtained by barter, or by capture from Bootchuanas or Bushmen, are a common article of saleable property ... They sell some of them into the Colony at a low price' (228). Bain remarked on the extent to which Griqua made use of Tswana and Bushman 'slaves', which they procured 'on hunting and predatory excursions in the interior'. *Journals of Andrew Geddes Bain, Trader, Explorer, Soldier, Road Engineer and Geologist*, ed. M.H. Lister, Van Riebeeck Society, 30 (Cape Town, 1949), 136. On the historical role of captives in Sotho–Tswana societies, see Comaroffs, *Of Revelation*, 164–5.

The trade in captives has evoked much controversy among historians. Julian Cobbing argues that colonial-inspired slaving was the primary motive force behind violence in the subcontinent. Cobbing wishes to do away with the 'Mfecane' paradigm altogether, arguing that the rise of militarised state systems (Zulu, Swazi, Ndebele, etc.) was itself a defensive reaction to the penetration of external forces derived ultimately from the rise of industrial capitalism in Western Europe. The 'transcontinental cross-fire of interrelated European plunder systems' took the form in the east of the trade in slaves for the Americas through the Portuguese port of Delagoa Bay, with the European 'conquistadores' established at Port Natal from 1824 as a subsidiary factor. And to the west of the Drakensberg, on the highveld, conflict was directly the result of an insatiable colonial demand for captive labourers and cattle originating in the Cape, in the pursuit of which Griqua and Kora surrogates were used, and not the result of 'Zulu expansionism'. Cobbing writes: 'Even where ... Sotho groups came simultaneously under pressure from invaders from the east during the period c.1818–1826, these incursions did not derive from the "Zulu revolution" but from an expansion in the European demand for sugar' – increasing the demand for African slaves in Brazil and the sugar islands of the Caribbean. Cobbing concludes that 'the dominant flow of violence in the west [i.e. the Sotho–Tswana region] was not from east to west, as Theal claimed, but rather from ... south-west to north-east ... Given the overwhelming disparity of force between the Griqua and even the more powerful of the black states north of the Orange in the 1820s this was inevitable.' A particular debate has raged around the famous Battle of Dithakong in June 1823. In the traditional interpretation, that battle pitted Waterboer's Griqua and Mothibi's Tlhaping against an invading horde of 'Mantatees', one of the migrating groupings set in motion by the rise of Zulu power below the Drakensberg escarpment. The LMS missionary Robert Moffat and the government agent at Griquatown, Melvill, were much involved in facilitating this defensive alliance against the invaders, who were defeated, and Kuruman was thereby saved. Cobbing's version has it that Dithakong was nothing but a slave raid organised by Moffat and Melvill. The 'Mantatee horde' was nothing but an alibi, and the victims were the hapless inhabitants of Dithakong. Cobbing, 'The Mfecane as Alibi: Thoughts on Dithakong and Mbolompo', *JAH*, 29 (1988), 487–519; also J. Richner, 'The Withering Away of the "Lifaqane": or a Change of Paradigm' (BA Hons. thesis, Rhodes, 1988); J.B. Gewald, '"Mountaineers" as Mantatees: A Critical Reassessment of Events Leading up to the Battle of Dithakong' (MA, Rijksuniversiteit, Leiden, 1990). Guy Hartley, on the basis of much more thorough research, systematically refutes this entire line of argument as a delusion. The idea that Moffat in particular, whose career has been fully documented, was involved in slave raiding is preposterous. Hartley argues that Griqua–Kora raids upon the Sotho–Tswana were not the 'initial motors of violence' in the region, a role he ascribes to the arrival in 1822 of Nguni invaders from the Zulu area. Hartley, 'Dithakong and the "Mfecane": A Historiographical and Methodological Analysis' (MA, UCT, 1992); Hartley, 'The Battle of Dithakong and "Mfecane" Theory' in Carolyn Hamilton (ed.), *The Mfecane Aftermath: Reconstructive Debates in Southern African History* (Johannesburg, 1995). Cobbing and his disciples tend to overestimate the strength, the homogeneity, and the fixity of purpose of the colonial state and its surrogates; and they indulge in elaborate conspiracy theories, accusing virtually all literate observers of the time, including even humanitarian missionaries, of elaborate efforts to cover up slaving activities, even while mining their writings for evidence to back up their theories. (Cf. ch. 4 n.110 and ch. 5 n.85 above.) Ultimately, whether frontier raiders acting as the outriders of a rapacious colonial economy were primarily responsible for the destabilisation of the region north of the Orange stretching far beyond the Vaal, or whether the process was initially set in train by invaders from east of the Drakensberg, is not really germane. The most that can be said is that indigenous and external historical forces were converging and interacting to produce a situation of great disruption and deprivation over large swaths of the subcontinent. The literature spawned by the 'Mfecane' debate is now voluminous. A conference on the subject was held at the University of the Witwatersrand in September 1991, which resulted in Hamilton's important volume, *Mfecane Aftermath*. Also Elizabeth Eldredge, 'Sources of Conflict in Southern Africa, *ca* 1800–1830: The "Mfecane" Reconsidered', *JAH*, 33, 1 (1992), 1–35; Eldredge, 'Slave Raiding Across the Cape Frontier' in Eldredge and Fred Morton (eds.), *Slavery in South Africa: Captive Labour on the Dutch Frontier* (Pietermaritzburg, 1995), 106–14; Comaroffs, *Of Revelation*, 167–9, 331 n.48; T.R.H. Davenport, *South Africa: A Modern History*, 4th ed. (1991), 12–18.

28. Legassick, 'Griqua', 360–78; Kevin Shillington, *The Colonisation of the Southern Tswana, 1870–1900* (Johannesburg, 1985), 12–13; Comaroffs, *Of Revelation*, 266–7.

29. Moffat, *Apprenticeship*, 274, and 224, 232, 235, 277, on the spread of arms to the Tswana. Also Bain, *Journals*, 14–15, 21–2; Hodgson, *Journals*, 110, 178, 361, etc.; Comaroffs, *Of Revelation*, 275; *Andrew Smith's Journal*, 113.

30. Legassick, 'Griqua', 373–5; Moffat, *Apprenticeship*, 232, 256, for opposition to arms sales. But Moffat was not entirely typical; LMS missionaries to the Tswana were often implicated in the supply of arms to their charges, especially as the white presence on either side of the Vaal River increased. Thus David Livingstone supplied occasional arms and ammunition, and supported the supply of guns by traders such as Gordon Cumming. Comaroffs, *Of Revelation*, 274–9; *David Livingstone, South African Papers*, ed. Isaac Schapera, Van Riebeeck Society, 2nd series, 5 (Cape Town, 1974), 40–5. On the early missionary impact on the Tlhaping, see J.T. du Bruyn, 'Die Aanvangsjare van die Christelike Sending onder die Tlhaping, 1800–1825', *AYB* (1989, II).

31. Margaret Kinsman, '"Beasts of Burden": The Subordination of Southern Tswana Women, *ca* 1800–1840', *JSAS*, 10, 1 (1983), 39–54; Comaroffs, *Of Revelation*, 169; Shillington, *Southern Tswana*, 16–21.

32. Beck, 'Legalisation', 215–37, 250–67; Muller, *Oorsprong van die Groot Trek*, 237.

33. Beck, 'Legalisation', 256–8, 316–17; Bannister, *Humane Policy*, 134–8; C.F.J. Muller, 'Robert Scoon, Vriend van die Afrikaner en die Matabele' in Muller, *Leiers na die Noorde: Studies oor die Groot Trek* (Cape Town, 1976), 22–49; Legassick, 'Griqua', 240–1; R. Kent Rasmussen, *Migrant Kingdom: Mzilikazi's Ndebele in South Africa* (1978), 67–70; *Diary of Dr Andrew Smith*, I, 250–1; Moffat, *Missionary Labours and Scenes in South Africa* (1842), 605; Andrew Steedman, *Wanderings and Adventures in the Interior of Southern Africa*, (1835, repr. Cape Town, 1966), 225–53; Robert Godlonton, *Introductory Remarks to a Narrative of the Irruption of the Kaffir Hordes into the Eastern Province of the Cape of Good Hope* (1836, repr. Cape Town, 1965), 178–86.

34. Thompson, *Survival in Two Worlds*; Peter Sanders, *Moshoeshoe, Chief of the Sotho* (1975); Sanders, 'Sekonyela and Moshweshwe: Failure and Success in the Aftermath of the Difaqane', *JAH*, 10 (1969), 439–55; Judy Kimble, 'Towards an Understanding of the Political Economy of Lesotho: The Origins of Commodity Production and Migrant Labour, 1830–*ca* 1885' (MA, National University of Lesotho, 1978); Elizabeth Eldredge, *A South African Kingdom: The Pursuit of Security in Nineteenth-Century Lesotho* (Cambridge, 1993); Timothy Keegan, 'The Dynamics of a South African Kingdom: Nineteenth-Century Lesotho Reassessed', *SAHJ*, 30 (1994), 109–20; E.T. Maloka, 'Missionary Historiography and Ethnography: Casalis, Arbousset and Ellenberger, and the History of Nineteenth-Century Lesotho' (BA Hons. thesis, UCT, 1988). Earlier reconstructions include Ellenberger and MacGregor, *History of the Basuto*; Godfrey Lagden, *The Basutos*, 2 vols. (1909); George Tylden, *The Rise of the Basuto* (Cape Town, 1950); Robert C. Germond (comp.), *Chronicles of Basutoland* (Morija, Lesotho, 1967).

35. Jean Casalis, *My Life in Basutoland* (1889, repr. Cape Town, 1971); V. Ellenberger, *A Century of Mission Work in Basutoland, 1833–1933* (Morija, 1938); Johannes du Plessis, *A History of Christian Missions in South Africa* (1911), 189–99.

36. Philip, *Researches*, II, 56.

37. Legassick, 'Griqua', 465–6. Generally on the ideal of the 'Christian Griqua Republic', see ibid, 449–79; Legassick in *SSAS*, 397–404.

38. Legassick, 'Griqua', 452, 457; Macmillan, *BBB*, 58, 64–5; Van der Merwe, *Noordwaartse Beweging*, 247–51; John S. Galbraith, *Reluctant Empire: British Policy on the South African Frontier, 1834–1854* (Berkeley, 1963), 56–7.

39. Legassick, 'Griqua', 458–60; Macmillan, *BBB*, 65; Van der Merwe, *Noordwaartse*

Beweging, 275.

40. Legassick, 'Griqua', 461–4; Macmillan, *BBB*, 65–8; Comaroffs, *Of Revelation*, 269–70.

41. Galbraith, *Reluctant Empire*, 107; Marais, *Cape Coloured People*, 41–2; Macmillan, *BBB*, 69. In a letter of May 1833 to J.B. Purney, a student at Princeton Seminary desirous of labouring in southern Africa, Philip spelled out his vision of the native agency as the cutting edge of mission enterprise. D.J. Kotze (ed.), *Letters of the American Missionaries, 1835–1838*, Van Riebeeck Society, 31 (Cape Town, 1950), 35–45; Legassick, 'Griqua', 470–7. This vision of Griqua expansionism led to enormous hostility between the Griqua mission and the missionaries to the Tswana, notably Moffat. Comaroffs, *Of Revelation*, 267–73; Legassick, 'Griqua', chs. 10, 11.

42. Legassick, 'Griqua', 502–11; Galbraith, *Reluctant Empire*, 90–1.

43. Ross, *Adam Kok's Griquas*, 23–5; Marais, *Cape Coloured People*, 40–1.

44. Van der Merwe, *Noordwaartse Beweging*, 262–70; Ross, *Adam Kok's Griquas*, 30–40; Legassick, 'Griqua', 395–6; Stockenström, *Autobiography*, I, 372–90. In 1834, the magistrate in Graaff-Reinet complained that Kok was reluctant to cooperate in controlling the arms trade (Macmillan, *BBB*, 69).

45. Van der Merwe, *Noordwaartse Beweging*, 309–11.

46. Ross, *Adam Kok's Griquas*, 30–3; Marais, *Cape Coloured People*, 52–3; Van der Merwe, *Noordwaartse Beweging*, 316–21, 351–3; Macmillan, *BBB*, 61–5, 221; *Journals of Andrew Geddes Bain*, 136. The history of the Griqua is taken up again in ch. 8 below.

47. Legassick, 'Griqua', 521–9; Van der Merwe, *Noordwaartse Beweging*, 319–20; Galbraith, *Reluctant Empire*, 197–8.

48. F.A. van Jaarsveld, *Die Beeld van die Groot Trek in die Suid-Afrikaanse Geskiedskrywing, 1843–1899*, Communications of Unisa, C42 (Pretoria, 1963).

49. Isobel Edwards, *Towards Emancipation: A Study in South African Slavery* (Cardiff, 1942), 201–4; Van der Merwe, *Noordwaartse Beweging*, 291–4; Chris Venter, 'Die Voortrekkers en die Ingeboekte Slawe wat die Groot Trek Meegemaak het', *Historia*, 36, 1 (1991), 14–29.

50. Van der Merwe, *Noordwaartse Beweging*, 366–84; M.C.E van Schoor, 'Die Nasionale en Politieke Bewuswording van die Afrikaner en sy Ontluiking in Transgariep tot 1854', *AYB* (1963, II), ch. 24; André du Toit and Hermann Giliomee, *Afrikaner Political Thought: Analysis and Documents, vol. 1, 1780–1850* (Cape Town, 1983), 114–15, 170–1.

51. Ken Smith, *The Changing Past: Trends in South African Historical Writing* (Johannesburg, 1988), 65–76.

52. J.A. Heese, *Slagtersnek en sy Mense* (Cape Town, 1973); Leonard Thompson, 'The Strange Career of Slagtersnek' in *The Political Mythology of Apartheid* (New Haven, 1985).

53. André du Toit, 'No Chosen People: The Myth of the Calvinist Origins of Afrikaner Nationalism and Racial Ideology', *American Historical Review*, 88, 4 (1983), 920–52; Du Toit, 'Captive to the Nationalist Paradigm: Prof. F.A. van Jaarsveld and the Historical Evidence for the Afrikaner's Ideas on his Calling and Mission', *SAHJ*, 16 (1984), 49–80; Carli Coetzee, 'Individual and Collective Notions of the "Promised Land": The "Private" Writings of the Boer Emigrants', *SAHJ*, 32 (1995), 48–65; Thompson, *Political Mythology*, 144–88, on the myth of the trekkers' 'covenant' and its development through time; also B.J. Liebenberg, 'Bloedrivier en Gods Hand', *SAHJ*, 12 (1980), 1–12; Liebenberg, 'Mites rondom Bloedrivier en die Gelofte', *SAHJ*, 20 (1988), 17–32. Changing twentieth-century uses of the myth of the trek are analysed in A.M. Grundlingh and Hilary Sapire, 'From Feverish Festival to Repetitive Ritual: The Changing Fortunes of Great Trek Mythology in an Industrialising South Africa, 1938–1988', *SAHJ*, 21 (1989), 19–37.

54. F.A. van Jaarsveld, *The Afrikaner's Interpretation of South African History* (Cape Town, 1964); Van Jaarsveld, *Geskiedkundige Verkenninge* (Pretoria, 1974). Examples of the genre include Coenraad Beyers, 'Die Groot Trek met Betrekking tot ons Nasiegroei', *AYB* (1941, I); Van Schoor, 'Nasionale en Politieke Bewuswording'; Van Schoor, 'Politieke Groepering in Transgariep', *AYB* (1950, II); J. du P. Scholtz, *Die Afrikaner en sy Taal, 1806–1875* (Cape Town, 1939); F.A. van Jaarsveld, *Die Eenheidstrewe van die Republikeinse Afrikaners, Deel 1: Pioniershartstogte, 1836–1864* (Johannesburg, 1951); G.D. Scholtz, *Die Politieke Denke van die Afrikaner*, 2 vols. (Johannesburg, 1967, 1970).

55. Muller, *Oorsprong van die Groot Trek*, 20–4; Muller, *Waarom die Groot Trek Geslaag het*, Communications of Unisa, B12 (Pretoria, 1960).

56. Stockenström, *Autobiography*, I, 249–50, 292, 390–1, II, 62; Du Toit and Giliomee, *Afrikaner Political Thought*, 297–9; Muller, *Oorsprong van die Groot Trek*, 181–3, 192–3; J.B. Peires, 'The British and the Cape, 1814–1834' in *SSAS*, 499–511, stresses the 'revolution in government' of the late 1820s as the origin of the trek. The old system is discussed in P.J. Venter, 'Landdros en Heemrade, 1682–1827', *AYB* (1940, II).

57. Muller, *Oorsprong van die Groot Trek*, 178–9; G.D.J. Duvenage, *Van die Tarka na die*

Transgariep: Die Emigrasie uit die Noordoosgrensdele van die Kaapkolonie, 1835–1840 (Pretoria, 1981), 97–9; Hermann Giliomee, 'Processes in Development of the Southern African Frontier' in Howard Lamar and Leonard Thompson (eds.), *The Frontier in History: North America and Southern Africa Compared* (New Haven, 1981), 115–16; Stockenström, *Autobiography*, II, 73–4.

58. Duvenage, *Tarka na die Transgariep*, 105–9; Muller, *Oorsprong*, 183–5; Muller, *Die Britse Owerheid en die Groot Trek*, 2nd ed. (Johannesburg, 1963), 64–5; Van der Merwe, *Noordwaartse Beweging*, 381–4; J.C. Visagie, 'Willem Fredrik Hertzog, 1792–1847', *AYB* (1974), 89–108. Giliomee, 'Processes in Development', sees the trek primarily as a response to the closing of the land frontier.

59. L.C. Duly, *British Land Policy at the Cape, 1795–1844: A Study of Administrative Procedures in the Empire* (Durham, NC, 1968), chs. 6, 7.

60. Visagie, 'Hertzog', 94–102.

61. Ibid, 103–4.

62. Muller, *Britse Owerheid*, 69–72; Muller, *Oorsprong*, 189–91; Clifton Crais, *The Making of the Colonial Order: White Supremacy and Black Resistance in the Eastern Cape, 1770–1865* (Johannesburg, 1992), 55–63; Peires in *SSAS*, 500–2; Du Toit and Giliomee, *Afrikaner Political Thought*, 16–18.

63. Crais, *Colonial Order*, 65–70; Crais, 'Slavery and Freedom along a Frontier: The Eastern Cape, South Africa, 1770–1838', *Slavery and Abolition*, 11, 2 (1990), 190–215; R.L. Watson, *The Slave Question: Liberty and Property in South Africa* (Johannesburg, 1990), 153–8; H.B. Thom, *Die Lewe van Gert Maritz* (Cape Town, 1947), 60–1. According to census figures, the number of slaves in the eastern districts rose from 4192 in 1813 to 6598 in 1828 – although British settlers were not allowed to own slaves. Mary Rayner, 'Wine and Slaves: The Failure of an Export Economy and the Ending of Slavery in the Cape Colony, South Africa, 1806–1834' (Ph.D., Duke, 1986), 58; Peires in *SSAS*, 500. On the prohibition on slaveholding among the settlers, and generally beyond the Fish River, see Edwards, *Towards Emancipation*, 65–77.

64. Crais, 'Slavery and Freedom', 198; Alan Webster, 'Land Expropriation and Labour Extraction under Cape Colonial Rule: The War of 1835 and the "Emancipation" of the Fingo' (MA, Rhodes, 1991), 51; Robert Shell, *Children of Bondage: A Social History of the Slave Society at the Cape of Good Hope, 1652–1838* (Hanover, NH, 1994), 34–7; Philip, *Researches*, II, 260. Slave registration was apparently a pretty haphazard affair, allowing for much abuse.

65. John Mason, '"Fit for Freedom": The Slaves, Slavery and Emancipation in the Cape Colony, South Africa, 1806–1842' (Ph.D., Yale, 1992), 316–50.

66. Rayner, 'Wine and Slaves', 296; Duvenage, *Tarka na die Transgariep*, 99–102.

67. Muller, *Oorsprong van die Groot Trek*, 186–7; Rayner, 'Wine and Slaves', 309; E. Hengherr, 'Emancipation and After: A Study of Cape Slavery and the Issues Arising from It' (MA, UCT, 1953), 58–65, Appendix, i–vii; Thom, *Maritz*, 62–70.

68. Susan Newton-King, 'Commerce and Material Culture on the Eastern Cape Frontier', *Societies of Southern Africa in the Nineteenth and Twentieth Centuries*, vol. 14, Collected Seminar Papers, Institute of Commonwealth Studies (London, 1988) deals with the indebtedness trap at an earlier date, before the arrival of the British settlers of 1820. Nothing comparable has been done on the economic consequences of their arrival for the Boers. But on settler commercial enterprise, see Beck, 'Legalisation and Development of Trade'; L. Bryer and K.S. Hunt, *The 1820 Settlers* (Cape Town, 1984), 42. John Montgomery was one trader who set out itinerating among the Boer farms of the eastern Cape in the 1820s. *Reminiscences of John Montgomery*; also H.H. Dugmore, *Reminiscences of an Albany Settler*, eds. F.G. van der Riet and L.A. Hewson (Graham's Town, 1958), 33–4.

69. *Reminiscences of John Montgomery*, 117.

70. Muller, *Oorsprong*, 312–68; Visagie, 'Hertzog', 90–1, 104; Visagie, 'Louis Tregardt se Plaas in Gqalekaland', *Historia*, 32, 1 (1987), 84–95; Visagie, *Die Trek uit Oos-Rietrivier: Studies oor die Groot Trek* (Stellenbosch, 1977); Peires in *SSAS*, 506–8; Macmillan, *BBB*, 196–7; Van der Merwe, *Noordwaartse Beweging*, 291–4.

71. Muller, *Oorsprong*, 347–52.

72. Eric Walker, *The Great Trek*, 5th ed. (1965), 107–13; W.H.J. Punt, *Louis Trichardt se Laaste Skof* (Pretoria, 1953); *Die Dagboek van Louis Trigardt*, ed. T.H. le Roux (Pretoria, 1977); M. Nathan, *Die Epos van Trichardt en Van Rensburg* (Pretoria, 1938). A similar fate befell Hans van Rensburg's small group, which moved north in close contact with Tregardt.

73. Muller, *Oorsprong*, 370–7; C.S. Potgieter and N.H. Theunissen, *Kommandant-Generaal Hendrik Potgieter* (Johannesburg, n.d.); Duvenage, *Tarka na die Transgariep*, 139–53.

74. S.D. Neumark, *Economic Influences on the South African Frontier, 1652–1836* (Stanford, 1957), 168–70, 184–6, and *passim*, stressed rational economic motives, particularly the spread of

wool farming. Also Norman Etherington, 'The Great Trek in Relation to the Mfecane: A Reassessment', *SAHJ*, 25 (1991), 3–21, for a somewhat simplistic view, which sees the trek as a 'pre-emptive strike' by Boers to get there first before the British; also Etherington, 'Old Wine in New Bottles: The Persistence of Narrative Structures in the Historiography of the Mfecane and the Great Trek' in Hamilton, *Mfecane Aftermath*.

75. A.E. Cubbin, 'Origins of the British Settlement at Port Natal, May 1824 to July 1842' (Ph.D., UOFS, 1983); Charles Ballard, 'Natal, 1824–1844: The Frontier Interregnum', *Journal of Natal and Zulu History*, 5 (1982), 49–64; Ballard, 'Traders, Trekkers and Colonists' in Andrew Duminy and Bill Guest (eds.), *Natal and Zululand from Earliest Times to 1910* (Pietermaritzburg, 1989), 116–45; John Wright, 'Political Mythology and the Making of Natal's Mfecane', *Canadian Journal of African Studies*, 23 (1989), 272–91, which tends to present the image of the Mfecane rather too starkly as a conspiracy of mercantile interests. Those responsible for spreading the 'devastation stereotype', however, included men of very diverse interests and with very different views of the proper role of the British in the subcontinent. Certainly Godlonton, for one, pushed hard for British intervention in Natal. For him, the image of the war-like Zulu, situated ominously beyond the Xhosa of the Cape's eastern frontier, lent itself well to the scare tactics about African intentions which were used to goad the British to a more resolute military policy in the eastern Cape. Godlonton, *Introductory Remarks*, 157–78; Percival Kirby, *Sir Andrew Smith: His Life and Works* (Cape Town, 1965), 106–7; Muller, *Oorsprong*, 175–6; A.L. Harington, 'The *Graham's Town Journal* and the Great Trek, 1834–1843', *AYB* (1969, II), 8; George Thompson, *Travels and Adventures in Southern Africa*, 2nd ed., 2 vols. (Cape Town, 1967, 1968), I, 172–5, II, 243–52; Kay, *Travels*, 394–419; Bannister, *Humane Policy*, Appendices I, VI and VII, i–cvi, ccxlv–ccliv, for the mix of mercenary and humanitarian motives of much missionary propaganda. See S.J.R. Martin, 'British Images of the Zulu, ca 1820–1879' (Ph.D., Cambridge, 1982), on how these images permeated popular consciousness in Britain.

76. Muller, *Oorsprong*, 289–90; Godlonton, *Introductory Remarks*, 174–5, 200a–200d.

77. *Andrew Smith and Natal*, ed. Percival Kirby, Van Riebeeck Society, 36 (Cape Town, 1955); Kirby, *Andrew Smith*, 89–112; Kirby, 'John Centlivres Chase: Geographer and Cartographer', *Africana Notes and News*, 18 (1968); Kirby's introduction to *Diary of Dr Andrew Smith*, 9–56.

78. *Smith and Natal*, 145–77; Muller, *Oorsprong*, 234–5; R.F.M. Immelman, *Men of Good Hope: The Romantic Story of the Cape Town Chamber of Commerce, 1804–1954* (Cape Town, 1955), 128–31; Marian George, 'John Bardwell Ebden: His Business and Political Career at the Cape, 1806–1849', *AYB* (1986, I), 48–9; J.C.S. Lancaster, 'The Governorship of Sir Benjamin D'Urban at the Cape of Good Hope', *AYB* (1991, II), 166; Galbraith, *Reluctant Empire*, 182; Kirby, *Andrew Smith*, 113–14; John Bird, *The Annals of Natal, 1495–1845*, 2 vols. (n.d., repr. Cape Town, 1965), I, 252–73, for the petition.

79. Muller, *Oorsprong*, 249–51; *Smith and Natal*, 5.

80. Muller, *Leiers na die Noorde*, 108–29; Muller, *Oorsprong*, 272–311 and 246–55, on other hunting and trading journeys by Boers in the early 1830s, evidence of which is scanty.

81. Muller, *Oorsprong*, 289–90, 292–4, 298. Muller uncritically accepts Theal's fantastical figures of the extent of the Mfecane slaughter, and suggests that the hunters' paradise that reigned in the aftermath of the alleged human depopulation of the territory was an important factor in the expansion of hunting and trading opportunities. Muller, *Oorsprong*, 82–3, 254.

82. Muller, *Oorsprong*, 284–5.

83. Ibid, 276–7.

84. H.M. Robertson, 'The Cape of Good Hope and "Systematic Colonisation,"' *South African Journal of Economics*, 5, 4 (1937), 374–5.

85. Harington, '*Graham's Town Journal*', 39, 52; B.A. le Cordeur, *The Politics of Eastern Cape Separatism, 1820–1854* (Cape Town, 1981), 127; Backhouse, *Narrative of a Visit to the Mauritius and South Africa* (1844), 327.

86. Stockenström, *Autobiography*, II, 56–64, 73; Macmillan, *BBB*, 225.

87. Macmillan, *BBB*, 232n.

88. Muller, *Britse Owerheid*, 98; H.C. Botha, *John Fairbairn in South Africa* (Cape Town, 1984), 118.

89. Thom, *Maritz*, 68; Lalou Meltzer, 'The Growth of Cape Town Commerce and the Role of John Fairbairn's *Advertiser*, 1835–1859' (MA, UCT, 1989), 58; Muller, *Oorsprong*, 186–7; Muller, *Britse Owerheid*, 147–8.

90. Beck, 'Legalisation', 326–7; *Reminiscences of John Montgomery*, 113; C. Venter, *The Great Trek* (Cape Town, 1985), 30–1.

91. *Reminiscences of John Montgomery*, 117–32.

92. Beck, 'Legalisation', 325–6; Muller, *Oorsprong*, 240–5, on the extent of cartographic

knowledge already available on the subcontinent. Steedman, *Wanderings*, 169–224, contains Chase's account of the progress of discovery in the subcontinent in previous years.

93. Harington, 'Graham's Town Journal', 47–68; B.A. le Cordeur, *The Politics of Eastern Cape Separatism, 1820–1854* (Cape Town, 1981), 90–1; Michael Streak, *The Afrikaner as Viewed by the English, 1795–1854* (Cape Town, 1974), 160; F.A. van Jaarsveld, 'Die Tydgenootlike Beoordeling van die Groot Trek' in Van Jaarsveld, *Geskiedkundige Verkenninge* (Pretoria, 1974), 10–11, 30–1. Recently George Fredrickson, *White Supremacy: A Comparative Study in American and South African History* (New York, 1981), 48, has repeated this argument.

94. Lancaster, 'Governorship of Sir Benjamin D'Urban', 116, 161–3; Macmillan, *BBB*, 198; Galbraith, *Reluctant Empire*, 176.

95. *The Autobiography of Lieutenant-General Sir Harry Smith*, ed. G.C. Moore Smith (1902), 463–4: 'Had my system been persisted in, and the order of things so firmly planted and rapidly growing into maturity been allowed to continue, not a Boer would have migrated.' See Henry Cloete, *Five Lectures on the Emigration of the Dutch Farmers from the Colony of the Cape of Good Hope* (1856, repr. Pretoria, 1968), 72–5, for another early expression of this view by the British commissioner in Natal in 1843–4.

96. Harington, 'Graham's Town Journal', 50–3, 55–7; also J.M. Bowker, *Speeches, Letters and Selections from Important Papers (1836–1847)* (1864, repr. Cape Town, 1962), 143, 192.

97. George, 'Ebden', 65.

98. Muller, 'Tydgenootlike Beoordeling'; Du Toit and Giliomee, *Afrikaner Political Thought*, 213–15.

99. J.L.M. Franken, *Piet Retief se Lewe in die Kolonie* (Pretoria, 1949); Eily and Jack Gledhill, *In the Steps of Piet Retief* (Cape Town, 1980), largely based on Franken's compendious study; Peires in *SSAS*, 508–10, provides a summary.

100. Harington, 'Graham's Town Journal', 39–40, 52–3; Franken, *Retief*, 429–30, 432. The manifesto is to be found in Franken, 432–4, and G.W. Eybers (ed.), *Select Constitutional Documents Illustrating South African History* (1918), 143–5. It is significant that when the Uys party moved through Graham's Town on their way northward, they were presented with an inscribed Bible by the English townsfolk. Walker, *The Great Trek*, 139.

101. Harington, 'Graham's Town Journal', 30–2.

102. Stockenström, *Autobiography*, I, 392, II, 57–8, 61, 62–3; A.H. Duminy, 'The Role of Sir Andries Stockenström in Cape Politics, 1848–1856', *AYB* (1960, II), 158.

103. Duminy, 'Stockenström', 79–81, 95, 147–56; Stockenström, *Autobiography*, II, 49–51, 58–61, 296; K.W. Smith, *From Frontier to Midlands: A History of the Graaff-Reinet District, 1786–1910* (Graham's Town, 1976), 246–7; Andrew Ross, *John Philip, 1775–1851: Missions, Race and Politics in South Africa* (Aberdeen, 1986), 125–6, 144; Le Cordeur, *Separatism*, 143.

104. Lancaster, 'D'Urban', 163–4; Gledhills, *Retief*, 132–41; Du Toit and Giliomee, *Afrikaner Political Thought*, 111–14.

105. Duminy, 'Stockenström', 158; Stockenström, *Autobiography*, I, 349–50.

106. In September 1835 D'Urban instructed all field cornets in the colony to produce lists of the men under them between the ages of 16 and 55 with details of horses and firearms for the purpose of forming a militia to make up for shortages of regular troops. But this order met with universal resistance: only one list (from Beaufort) was forthcoming. Lancaster, 'D'Urban', 191; J.C. Visagie, 'Verset teen die Burgermilisieplan van 1835', *Historia*, 38, 2 (1993), 77–85.

107. Peires in *SSAS*, 506–8; Peires, *The House of Phalo: A History of the Xhosa People in the Days of their Independence* (Johannesburg, 1981), 94, 118, 156; J.G. Pretorius, 'The British Humanitarians and the Cape Eastern Frontier, 1834–1836', *AYB* (1988, I), 86; Macmillan, *BBB*, 143.

108. Peires, *Phalo*, 118.

109. Pretorius, 'Humanitarians', 60; Muller, *Oorsprong*, 300–2; Webster, 'Land Expropriation and Labour Extraction', 109.

110. Walker, *Great Trek, passim*; Macmillan, *BBB*, 202. On trade with Africans, see Bird, *Annals of Natal*, I, 521; George Theal (ed.), *Basutoland Records*, 4 vols. (1883, repr. Cape Town, 1964), I, 35; Backhouse, *Narrative*, 430.

111. Peter Delius, *The Land Belongs to Us: The Pedi Polity, the Boers and the British in the Nineteenth-Century Transvaal* (Johannesburg, 1983), 30–40; Philip Bonner, *Kings, Commoners and Concessionaires: The Evolution and Dissolution of the Nineteenth-Century Swazi State* (Cambridge, 1983), chs. 4, 5; Roger Wagner, 'Zoutpansberg: The Dynamics of a Hunting Frontier, 1848–1867' in Shula Marks and Anthony Atmore (eds.), *Economy and Society in Pre-Industrial South Africa* (1980); Stanley Trapido, 'Reflections on Land, Office and Wealth in the South African Republic, 1850–1900' in Marks and Atmore, *Economy and Society*; Jan Boeyens, '"Zwart

Ivoor": Inboekelinge in Zoutpansberg, 1848–1869', *SAHJ*, 24 (1991), 31–66; Boeyens, '"Black Ivory": The Indenture System and Slavery in Zoutpansberg, 1848–1869' in Eldredge and Morton, *Slavery in South Africa*; Legassick, 'The Frontier Tradition in South African Historiography' in Marks and Atmore, *Economy and Society*, 66–7; Andrew Manson, 'The Hurutshe in the Marico District of the Transvaal, 1848–1914' (Ph.D., UCT, 1990); Manson, 'The Hurutshe and the Formation of the Transvaal State, 1835–1875', *IJAHS*, 25, 1 (1992), 85–98; Fred Morton, 'Captive Labour in the Western Transvaal after the Sand River Convention' in Eldredge and Morton, *Slavery in South Africa*. Earlier treatments include J.A.I. Agar-Hamilton, *The Native Policy of the Voortrekkers: An Essay in the History of the Interior of South Africa, 1836–1858* (Cape Town, 1928); F.J. Potgieter, 'Die Vestiging van die Blankes in Transvaal (1837–1886) met Spesiale Verwysing na die Verhouding tussen die Mens en die Omgewing', *AYB* (1958, II), 1–208; B.H. Dicke, 'The Northern Transvaal Voortrekkers', *AYB* (1941), 67–170.

112. B.J. Liebenberg, *Andries Pretorius in Natal* (Pretoria, 1977); Walker, *Great Trek*, 241–6; A.J. du Plessis, 'Die Republiek Natalia', *AYB* (1942, I), 149–51.

113. See references in n.111.

114. Harington, '*Graham's Town Journal*', 61–2, 65–6, 69–75; Muller, *Britse Owerheid*, 104–10, 146–60; Van Jaarsveld, 'Tydgenootlike Beoordeling', 30–3; Streak, *Afrikaner as Viewed by the English*, 164–70; Botha, *Fairbairn*, 116–26; Botha, 'Die Rol van Christoffel J. Brand in Suid-Afrika, 1820–1854', *AYB* (1977), 71–2. Brand's *De Zuid-Afrikaan*, while sympathetic to the trekkers, urged them to accept British sovereignty.

115. Walker, *Great Trek*, 201–5; Du Plessis, 'Republiek Natalia', 141–9; Galbraith, *Reluctant Empire*, 184. For example, a thousand Zulu children were reportedly carried off in February 1840 during the 'cattle commando' when the Zulu king Dingane was overthrown and replaced by his half-brother and Boer ally, Mpande, evoking much outrage in humanitarian circles. The Volksraad sought to regulate the use of 'apprentices' (*inboekelinge*), as such children were called in accordance with time-honoured colonial euphemistic tradition, providing for their freedom from obligations at the age of 25 for men, 21 for women; but they clearly were regarded as an indispensable source of labour, and for many Boers their acquisition was an explicit goal of armed operations. Muller, *Britse Owerheid*, 230–9, 242–54; Du Plessis, 'Natalia', 153–61; Henry Slater, 'The Changing Pattern of Economic Relationships in Rural Natal, 1838–1914' in Marks and Atmore, *Economy and Society*, 150–1; Agar-Hamilton, *Native Policy*, 27–48; Peter Delius and Stanley Trapido, '*Inboekselings* and *Oorlams*: The Creation and Transformation of a Servile Class' in Belinda Bozzoli (ed.), *Town and Countryside in the Transvaal* (Johannesburg, 1983), for the larger significance of this form of labour procurement.

Fears of destabilisation grew out of the evident fact that the trekkers had settled in territory that was inhabited by large numbers of Africans, despite the self-serving myth that it was an empty land. It is true that Africans who had been conquered and incorporated into the Zulu state began to return to the proclaimed Boer republic of Natal south of the Tugela River in large numbers after the defeat of Dingane. Ballard, 'Traders, Trekkers and Colonists', 122–3, has it that 60 000 African refugees arrived after the Boer republic was proclaimed; E.H. Brookes and Colin Webb, *A History of Natal*, 2nd ed. (Pietermaritzburg, 1987), 49–50, has this influx happening within a few days in 1840 to escape Mpande's cruelty. Macmillan in the 1920s (*BBB*, 206–8) rejected the idea that Natal south of the Tugela was ever an empty land, although African groups had probably moved their settlements away from exposed upland plains to escape the predations of the Zulu. Also Shula Marks, 'The Myth of the Empty Land', *History Today*, 30 (1980), 7–12; Keletso E. Atkins, *The Moon is Dead! Give Us our Money! The Cultural Origins of an African Work Ethic, Natal, South Africa, 1843–1900* (1993), 9–25. The Natal Raad tried to provide land reserves for dependent chiefs under republican control, and prohibited excessive 'squatting' on land claimed by the burghers by setting a limit of five African 'families' (a problematical and unworkable concept) on each burgher landholding. Segregation of unwanted Africans became the prescription. But the republic had few resources to impose its will on the African groups, small-scale and fractured though they were.

116. Muller, *Britse Owerheid*, 149–51, 153–5, 161–2, 198–204; Du Plessis, 'Republiek Natalia', 191.

117. Muller, *Britse Owerheid*, 146–8, 155–6; Botha, 'Brand', 67; Walker, *Great Trek*, 256–8.

118. A force was sent to occupy Port Natal when, in 1841, news arrived of a wildly impractical Volksraad decision to resettle 'surplus' Africans in a reserve to the south, threatening instability to the rear of the Cape frontier. Walker, *Great Trek*, 250–3, 260–1; Du Plessis, 'Natalia', 187–9; Galbraith, *Reluctant Empire*, 182–94; Alan Hattersley, *The British Settlement of Natal: A Study in Imperial Migration* (Cambridge, 1950), 44–8; C.J. Uys, *In the Era of Shepstone* (Lovedale, 1933), 10; Brookes and Webb, *History of Natal*, 37–46; Macmillan, *BBB*, 212–14; Leonard

Thompson, 'Co-operation and Conflict: The Zulu Kingdom and Natal' in *OHSA*, 364–73; T.C. Rautenbach, 'Sir George Napier en die Groot Trek' (MA, Unisa, 1978); Rautenbach, 'Sir George Napier en die Natalse Voortrekkers', *Historia*, 34, 2 (1989), 22–31; Bird, *Annals*, I, 618–66. The initial resistance of the Boers to the arrival of the British force and its siege at Congella resulted in a crescendo of expansionist and militarist fervour among British settler and commercial interests in the Cape. Harington, '*Graham's Town Journal*', 85–92; Streak, *Afrikaner as Viewed by the English*, 174–8.

119. Walker, *Great Trek*, 267–70; Muller, *Britse Owerheid*, 162–5; Galbraith, *Reluctant Empire*, 195–6; B.J. Liebenberg, *Nederland en die Voortrekkers van Natal*, Communications of Unisa, C51 (Pretoria, 1962).

120. Du Plessis, 'Natalia', 190–4; Muller, *Britse Owerheid*, 166–7; Hattersley, *British Settlement*, 61–2, 67–8, 75–8, 84–8; George, 'Ebden', 51–3.

121. Walker, *Great Trek*, 300–5, 339; Hattersley, *British Settlement*, 61–2; Du Plessis, 'Natalia', 209–16; Slater, 'Changing Pattern', 151–3. The importance of this factor in alienating the Natal Boers in the same way as had occurred in the Cape was described by the government secretary in 1849: 'The numerous grants given to a few individuals on the ground of purchase, contrasted with the rejection of applications for single farms by actual farmers, presented to the mass of the inhabitants an appearance of partiality; and the sanction which land-jobbing appeared to have received ... led the way to that monopoly by purchasers which has done more to denude the country of its [Boer] inhabitants than the rejection of claims and the political causes all put together' (Du Plessis, 'Natalia', 214).

122. Hattersley, *British Settlement, passim*; H.M. Robertson, 'The 1849 Settlers in Natal', *South African Journal of Economics* (1949); R.E. Ralls, 'Early Immigration Schemes in Natal, 1846–1853' (MA, Natal, 1938).

123. Slater, 'Changing Pattern', 153–6; Ballard, 'Traders, Trekkers and Colonists', 126–9; Le Cordeur, *Separatism*, 185; Le Cordeur, 'The Relations between the Cape and Natal, 1846–1879', *AYB* (1965, I), 23–41.

124. W.B. Boyce, *Notes on South African Affairs* (1838, repr. Cape Town, 1971), 165–95.

125. Reprinted Cape Town, 1963.

126. Muller, *Britse Owerheid*, 151–2, 231, 246–51; Hattersley, *British Settlement*, 88–91.

127. This is a subject which enjoys a huge literature. On Natal, see Slater, 'Changing Pattern'; Slater, 'Land, Labour and Capital in Natal: The Natal Land and Colonisation Company, 1860–1948', *JAH*, 16, 2 (1975), 257–83; Norman Etherington, *Preachers, Peasants and Politics in South-East Africa, 1835–1880: African Christian Communities in Natal, Pondoland and Zululand* (1978); Colin Bundy, *The Rise and Fall of the South African Peasantry* (1979); William Beinart, Peter Delius and Stanley Trapido (eds.), *Putting a Plough to the Ground: Accumulation and Dispossession in Rural South Africa, 1850–1930* (Johannesburg, 1986), especially editors' Introduction; John Lambert, *Betrayed Trust: Africans and the State in Colonial Natal* (Pietermaritzburg, 1995); Atkins, *The Moon Is Dead*.

128. Edgar Brookes, *The History of Native Policy in South Africa from 1830 to the Present Day* (Cape Town, 1924), 41–64; Hattersley, *British Settlement*, 71–5; Brookes and Webb, *History of Natal*, 56–61, 68–71; David Welsh, *The Roots of Segregation: Native Policy in Colonial Natal, 1845–1910* (Cape Town, 1971); Etherington, 'The "Shepstone System" in the Colony of Natal and Beyond the Borders' in Duminy and Guest, *Natal and Zululand*; Benjamin Kline, *Genesis of Apartheid: British African Policy in the Colony of Natal, 1845–1893* (1988).

129. Slater, 'Changing Pattern', 158–61; Brookes and Webb, *History of Natal*, 69–70.

Chapter Seven: Colonial Crises, Imperial Resolutions

1. W.P. Morrell, *British Colonial Policy in the Age of Peel and Russell* (Oxford, 1930); Earl Grey, *The Colonial Policy of Lord John Russell's Administration*, 2 vols. (1853); D.K. Fieldhouse, *The Colonial Empires from the Eighteenth Century* (New York, 1966), 250–64; John M. Ward, *Colonial Self-Government: The British Experience, 1759–1856* (1976); Peter Burroughs, 'The Determinants of Local Self-Government', *Journal of Imperial and Commonwealth History*, 6 (1978); Burroughs, 'Colonial Self-Government' in C.C. Eldridge (ed), *British Imperialism in the Nineteenth Century* (1984); P.J. Cain and A.G. Hopkins, *British Imperialism: Innovation and Expansion, 1688–1914* (1993), 234–43; Stanley R. Stembridge, *Parliament, the Press and the Colonies, 1846–1880* (1982); Tony Kirk, 'Self-Government and Self-Defence in South Africa: The Interrelations between British and Cape Politics, 1846–1854' (D.Phil., Oxford, 1972), *passim*, and 110–15, 379–83, on colonial reformers.

2. Peter Burroughs, *The Canadian Crisis and British Colonial Policy, 1828–1841* (1971); Ged Martin, *The Durham Report and British Policy* (Cambridge, 1972); Philip A. Buckner, *The*

Transition to Responsible Government: British Policy in British North America (Westport, Conn., 1985).

3. Peter Adams, *Fatal Necessity: British Intervention in New Zealand, 1830–1847* (Auckland, 1977).

4. Kirk, 'Self-Government', 167.

5. K.N. Bell and W.P. Morrell (eds.), *Select Documents on British Colonial Policy, 1830–1860* (Oxford, 1928), 108.

6. J.J. Breitenbach, 'The Development of the Secretaryship to the Government of the Cape of Good Hope under John Montagu, 1845–1852', *AYB* (1959), II, 183–9.

7. Kirk, 'Self-Government', 146–50. On Montagu generally, see Breitenbach, 'Montagu'; W.A. Newman, *Biographical Memoir of John Montagu* (1855); B.A. le Cordeur, *The Politics of Eastern Cape Separatism, 1820–1854* (Cape Town, 1981), 129–35; Alan Hattersley, *The Convict Crisis and the Growth of Unity: Resistance to Transportation in South Africa and Australia, 1848–1853* (Pietermaritzburg, 1965), 13–15; *DSAB*, I, 553–6.

8. Breitenbach, 'Montagu', 237–8.

9. Ibid, 231–49; Newman, *Montagu*, chs. 6, 7.

10. Breitenbach, 'Montagu', 223–4.

11. Ibid, 218–21.

12. Ibid, 226–7, 238, 247. See Michel Foucault, *Discipline and Punish: The Birth of the Prison* (Harmondsworth, 1979) for the ideological background.

13. Breitenbach, 'Montagu', 192–215; Newman, *Montagu*, 28–61; Kirk, 'Self-Government', 280–3; C.F.J. Muller, *Die Britse Owerheid en die Groot Trek*, 2nd ed. (Johannesburg, 1963), 83.

14. This included funding immigration. See pp. 125 above.

15. Kirk, 'Self-Government', 456.

16. Breitenbach, 'Montagu', 201–3. See ch. 5 above on the municipal party.

17. H.C. Botha, *John Fairbairn in South Africa* (Cape Town, 1984), 149–50; Digby Warren, 'Property, Profit and Power: The Rise of a Landlord Class in Cape Town in the 1840s' in *Studies in the History of Cape Town*, vol. 6, Centre for African Studies (Cape Town, 1988), 49–52; *The Porter Speeches* (Cape Town, 1886), 137–76.

18. Warren, 'Merchants, Municipal Commissioners and Wardmasters: Municipal Politics in Cape Town, 1840–1854' (MA, UCT, 1986), 168–76; Breitenbach, 'Montagu', 207–11; Marian George, 'John Bardwell Ebden: His Business and Political Career at the Cape, 1806–1849', *AYB* (1986, I), 62; H.C. Botha, 'Die Rol van Christoffel J. Brand in Suid-Afrika, 1820–1854', *AYB* (1977), 61–2; Botha, *Fairbairn*, 152–3.

19. Breitenbach, 'Montagu', 211.

20. Ibid, 203–7; Warren, 'Municipal Politics', 176–87.

21. Breitenbach, 'Montagu', 204.

22. Warren, 'Municipal Politics', 186–7.

23. J.B. Peires, *The House of Phalo: A History of the Xhosa People in the Days of their Independence* (Johannesburg, 1981), 119–34; Le Cordeur, *Separatism*, 109–11; J.S. Galbraith, *Reluctant Empire: British Policy on the South African Frontier, 1834–1854* (Berkeley, 1963), 168–75; W.M. Macmillan, *Bantu, Boer and Briton: The Making of the South African Native Policy*, 2nd ed. (1963), 281–3; Clifton Crais, *The Making of the Colonial Order: White Supremacy and Black Resistance in the Eastern Cape, 1770–1865* (Johannesburg, 1992), 141–3; A.E. du Toit, 'The Cape Frontier: A Study of Native Policy with Special Reference to the Years 1847–1866', *AYB* (1954, I), 13–17.

24. Le Cordeur, *Separatism*, 151–3.

25. G.B. Crankshaw, 'The Diary of C.L. Stretch: A Critical Edition and Appraisal' (MA, Rhodes, 1960), 124–5; Macmillan, *BBB*, 285–6.

26. Noël Mostert, *Frontiers: The Epic of South Africa's Creation and the Tragedy of the Xhosa People* (1992), 868–928; Peires, *Phalo*, 150–5; Jane Sales, *Mission Stations and the Coloured Communities of the Eastern Cape, 1800–1852* (Cape Town, 1975), 143–4; Macmillan, *BBB*, 292; Harriet Ward, *The Cape and the Kaffirs* (1851); *The Kitchingman Papers*, eds. B.A. le Cordeur and C.C. Saunders (Johannesburg, 1981), 259–73.

27. Le Cordeur, *Separatism*, 154; Kirk, 'Self-Government', 175–6.

28. A.H. Duminy, 'The Role of Sir Andries Stockenström in Cape Politics, 1848–1856', *AYB* (1960, II), 86–9; Kirk, 'Self-Government', 130–4; Macmillan, *BBB*, 294–5; J.L. Dracopoli, *Sir Andries Stockenström, 1792–1864* (Cape Town, 1969), 159–60; *The Autobiography of the Late Sir Andries Stockenström*, ed. C.W. Hutton, 2 vols. (1887, repr. Cape Town, 1964), II, ch. 26.

29. B.A. le Cordeur and C.C. Saunders, *The War of the Axe, 1847: Correspondence between the Governor of the Cape Colony, Sir Henry Pottinger, and the Commander of the British Forces*

at the Cape, Sir George Berkeley, and Others (Johannesburg, 1981), 143–5. In 1848 Stockenström published a pamphlet setting out his side of the growing rift between the burghers and the military authorities. *Narrative of Transactions Connected with the Kaffir War of 1846 and 1847* (Graham's Town, 1848). Cf. R. Godlonton, *The Case of the Colonists of the Eastern Frontier* (Graham's Town, 1847), which attempted to justify the military's treatment of Stockenström.

30. John Frye, 'The *South African Commercial Advertiser* and the Eastern Frontier, 1834–1847' (MA, Rhodes, 1968), 119–21, 99–101; Macmillan, *BBB*, 290–1; Phillida Brooke Simons, *Old Mutual, 1845–1995* (Cape Town, 1995), 18; Andrew Bank, 'Liberals and their Enemies: Racial Ideology at the Cape of Good Hope, 1820 to 1850' (Ph.D., Cambridge, 1995), 350–2.

31. Du Toit, 'Cape Frontier', 20–7; Kirk, 'Self-Government', 166–70; Macmillan, *BBB*, 295–6; Le Cordeur, *Separatism*, 157, 168; John Benyon, *Proconsul and Paramountcy in South Africa* (Pietermaritzburg, 1980), 20–6; Bell and Morrell, *Select Documents*, 502–6, for Grey's instructions to Pottinger.

32. Kirk, 'Self-Government', 176–9; Le Cordeur, *Separatism*, 168–9, 188.

33. Le Cordeur and Saunders, *War of the Axe*, 74; Le Cordeur, *Separatism*, 185–6; Macmillan, *BBB*, 298–9; Duminy, 'Stockenström', 90.

34. Le Cordeur and Saunders, *War of the Axe*, 93–118; Kirk, 'Self-Government', 186–90, 313; *The Reminiscences of Thomas Stubbs*, eds. W.A. Maxwell and R.T. McGeogh, Graham's Town Series 4 (Cape Town, 1978), 135–6. Stubbs provides examples of corruption, concluding, 'It appeared to me – that nearly everybody's eyes were on the Commissariat Chest. I have often stated in public in Graham's Town, that I wished the government would remove it – as then people would turn out and fight and put an end to the war ... the people on this frontier liked a Caffer war better than peace.' Compensation claims for services rendered and goods employed in the war of 1846–7 amounted to £66 393, quite apart from the £405 902 claimed for general war losses, claims which the government in London refused to entertain. Kirk, 'Self-Government', 134–6, 183–4, 302–4.

35. Le Cordeur, *Separatism*, 184–6, and 169–85 on the simultaneous drive for separate government in the eastern Cape, which was now firmly linked to the issue of territorial expansion in the propaganda coming out of Graham's Town. An enquiry was instituted by Pottinger in June 1847 into the feasibility of separation.

36. Kirk, 'Self-Government', 187.

37. A.L. Harington, *Sir Harry Smith: Bungling Hero* (Cape Town, 1980), 88–92; Kirk, 'Self-Government', 189–91.

38. Stockenström had written to D'Urban in 1836 that nobody except Smith 'believed it possible to undermine the power of the Kaffir chiefs and at the same time keep the nation in subjection and order, without a force far beyond what even now we have at our disposal'. Stockenström, *Autobiography*, II, 100.

39. A.L. Harington, 'The *Graham's Town Journal* and the Great Trek, 1834–1843', *AYB* (1969, II), 95, 100.

40. Kirk, 'Self-Government', 214–15, 190; M.J. McGinn, 'J.C. Chase, 1820 Settler and Servant of the Colony' (MA, Rhodes, 1975), 88; Le Cordeur, *Separatism*, 218; Alex Wilmot, *The Life and Times of Richard Southey* (1904), 11–21, 26, 29; on Southey, see *DSAB*, II, 695–6.

41. Harington, *Smith*, 98–109; Peires, *Phalo*, 165–6; Peires, *The Dead Will Arise: Nongqawuse and the Great Xhosa Cattle-Killing Movement of 1856–7* (1989), 4–7; Macmillan, *BBB*, 299–301; Galbraith, *Reluctant Empire*; Kirk, 'Self-Government', 202–7; Du Toit, 'Cape Frontier', 28–46; Benyon, *Proconsul and Paramountcy*, 53–6; Crais, *Colonial Order*, 144–6; Mostert, *Frontiers*, 930–7; *The Autobiography of Lieutenant-General Sir Harry Smith*, ed. G.C. Moore Smith (1902), 427–8, for similar behaviour in 1835.

42. Peires, *Phalo*, 165–9; Kirk, 'Self-Government', 204.

43. Kirk, 'Self-Government', 200–1, 301; Macmillan, *BBB*, 303.

44. Kirk, 'Self-Government', 204, 213–14, 302; Macmillan, *BBB*, 302.

45. Tony Kirk, 'The Cape Economy and the Expropriation of the Kat River Settlement, 1846–1853' in Shula Marks and Anthony Atmore (eds.), *Economy and Society in Pre-Industrial South Africa* (1980), 236–7; Kirk, 'Self-Government', 362; Le Cordeur, *Separatism*, 216–17; Duminy, 'Stockenström', 108–10.

46. Du Toit, 'Cape Frontier', 52–3; Wilmot, *Southey*, 54, 62; Kirk, 'Self-Government', 228–30; Le Cordeur, *Separatism*, 215.

47. Duminy, 'Stockenström', 93–6; Kirk, 'Self-Government', 207, 132; Du Toit, 'Cape Frontier', 53–4.

48. Du Toit, 'Cape Frontier', 54; Le Cordeur, *Separatism*, 217; Duminy, 'Stockenström', 102.

49. On Boomplaats, see pp. 258–9.

50. Kirk, 'Self-Government', 234–7; Duminy, 'Stockenström', 97–8.

51. Kirk, 'Self-Government', 143, 212–13; Duminy, 'Stockenström', 96 n.32; Le Cordeur, *Separatism*, 215; Hattersley, *Convict Crisis*, 74–5.

52. Warren, 'Municipal Politics', 190–4.

53. Duminy, 'Stockenström', 98–101; Kirk, 'Self-Government', 217–18; Hattersley, *Convict Crisis*, 33; K.W. Smith, *From Frontier to Midlands: A History of the Graaff-Reinet District, 1786–1910* (Graham's Town, 1976), 246–7; Stockenström, *Autobiography*, II, 294–5; Digby Warren, 'Class Rivalry and Cape Politics in the Mid-Nineteenth Century: A Reappraisal of the Kirk Thesis', *SAHJ*, 24 (1991), 118–19; Michael Streak, *The Afrikaner as Viewed by the English* (Cape Town, 1974), 194–5, 212–14; André du Toit and Hermann Giliomee, *Afrikaner Political Thought, Analysis and Documents, I: 1780–1850* (Cape Town, 1983), 247–50.

54. Le Cordeur, *Separatism*, 208–12.

55. Breitenbach, 'Montagu', 252–4; Newman, *Montagu*, 347–96.

56. Audrey Brooke, *Robert Gray, First Bishop of Cape Town* (Cape Town, 1947); *Life of Robert Gray, Bishop of Cape Town*, 2 vols., ed. Charles Gray (1876).

57. *Life of Robert Gray*, 232–3; Kirk, 'Self-Government', 215–16, 305–6; Newman, *Montagu*, 280–308. The municipal commissioners petitioned the Queen against the discriminatory grants to the Anglican Church in the colonial estimates for 1849. Warren, 'Municipal Politics', 194–5.

58. Warren, 'Municipal Politics', 134–6; Botha, 'Brand', 59–60; George, 'Ebden', 74–5; *Porter Speeches*, 104–19.

59. George, 'Ebden', 75–6.

60. A.G.L. Shaw, *Convicts and the Colonies: A Study of Penal Transportation from Great Britain and Ireland to Australia and Other Parts of the British Empire* (1966).

61. On the convict crisis in general, see Shaw, *Convicts and the Colonies*, 312–28; Harington, *Smith*, 147–57; Hattersley, *Convict Crisis*; Kirk, 'Self-Government', 252–78; Le Cordeur, *Separatism*, 212–23; George, 'Ebden', 76–90; J.F. Gobrechts, 'Die Anti-Bandiete Agitasie aan die Kaap' (MA, Stellenbosch, 1937).

62. Hattersley, *Convict Crisis*, 11–12, 15–16, 41.

63. George, 'Ebden', 77–8; Warren, 'Municipal Politics', 200–1.

64. Hattersley, *Convict Crisis*, 41–2, 47, 49; George, 'Ebden', 78–80; Warren, 'Municipal Politics', 201–3; Botha, 'Brand', 136; Lalou Meltzer, 'The Growth of Cape Town Commerce and the Role of John Fairbairn's *Advertiser*, 1835–1859' (MA, UCT, 1989), 136.

65. Kirk, 'Self-Government', 259.

66. Hattersley, *Convict Crisis*, 42–3; George, 'Ebden', 81–2.

67. George, 'Ebden', 82–4; Hattersley, *Convict Crisis*, 51–6; Warren 'Municipal Politics', 205–6; Botha, 'Brand', 85; Botha, *Fairbairn*, 210–11.

68. Hattersley, *Convict Crisis*, 50, 52–3, 55; Le Cordeur, *Separatism*, 218–19.

69. Hattersley, *Convict Crisis*, 58–65, 68–73; George, 'Ebden', 86–9; Le Cordeur, *Separatism*, 216; Warren, 'Municipal Politics', 207–10; Warren, 'Class Rivalry and Cape Politics', 124–5; Botha, *Fairbairn*, 214–15; Meltzer, 'Cape Town Commerce', 143–4. Adderley's efforts included publication of a polemical pamphlet, *Statement of the Present Cape Case* (1851). Cape Town's main commercial thoroughfare has to this day been named Adderley Street.

70. Smith, *Frontier to Midlands*, 248–50.

71. Hattersley, *Convict Crisis*, 79.

72. Wilmot, *Southey*, 85–6. Montagu's role is discussed in Newman, *Montagu*, 324–46.

73. Duminy, 'Stockenström', 120 n.22; Trapido, 'The Origins of the Cape Franchise Qualifications of 1853', *JAH*, 5, 1 (1964), 47–8.

74. Hattersley, *Convict Crisis*, 65; George, 'Ebden', 83–4; Kirk, 'Self-Government', 272–4; Le Cordeur, *Separatism*, 216; *Life of Robert Gray*, I, 233–4, 275; Le Cordeur, 'Robert Godlonton as Architect of Frontier Opinion, 1850–1857', *AYB* (1960, II), 18–19, 76. *The Cape of Good Hope* (1850), an anonymous pamphlet, warned that Boers and coloureds, who greatly outnumbered the British at the Cape, had 'no feelings of English patriotism or nationality', and would have to be 'swamped' by 'inundations' of British immigrants, state-supervised education, and government aid to the Anglican Church. James Adamson, *Notes on Cape Affairs* (1853) was another polemic by a leading conservative, a professor at the South African College.

75. Le Cordeur, *Separatism*, 218–23; Duminy, 'Stockenström', 101–3.

76. Kirk, 'Self-Government', 259.

77. Duminy, 'Stockenström', 98–9; Trapido, 'Cape Franchise', 45; Hattersley, *Convict Crisis*, 45; Du Toit and Giliomee, *Afrikaner Political Thought*, 291–3.

78. On Porter and his proposals, see Warren, 'Municipal Politics', 10–19, 211–15; Botha, 'Brand', 84; Le Cordeur, *Separatism*, 205–7; Trapido, 'Cape Franchise', 38, 49–50; J.R. Putzel, 'William Porter and Constitutional Issues at the Cape, 1839–1873' (MA, UCT, 1942); J.L.

McCracken, *New Light at the Cape of Good Hope: William Porter, the Father of Cape Liberalism* (Belfast, 1993), 105–7, 119–20.

79. Warren, 'Municipal Politics', 216–17; Kirk, 'Self-Government', 333–5.

80. Le Cordeur, *Separatism*, 224–7; Hattersley, *Convict Crisis*, 86–7; Duminy, 'Stockenström', 106–8; Kirk, 'Self-Government', 336–7; Stockenström, *Autobiography*, II, 297.

81. Kirk, 'Self-Government', 344–6, 348, 350–1; Breitenbach, 'Montagu', 261; Le Cordeur, *Separatism*, 229–34; Hattersley, *Convict Crisis*, 87, 95; Warren, 'Municipal Politics', 218–20; Meltzer, 'Cape Town Commerce', 139–40; Botha, *Fairbairn*, 241–60; Du Toit and Giliomee, *Afrikaner Political Thought*, 293–4; Wilmot, *Southey*, 92.

82. Botha, *Fairbairn*, 258–77; Kirk, 'Self-Government', 347; Hattersley, *Convict Crisis*, 95; Stockenström, *Autobiography*, II, 297, 330–1.

83. Le Cordeur, *Separatism*, 227–34, 246, 251. The conservatives in Cape Town set up a newspaper in October 1850, the *Cape Monitor*, backed by a group of the big merchants such as R.W. Eaton; and Montagu, Bishop Gray, Godlonton, Southey, and Adamson of the South African College were all implicated in its launching. Kirk, 'Self-Government', 349–50; Le Cordeur, 'Godlonton', 93; Hattersley, *Convict Crisis*, 95–6.

84. Kirk, 'Self-Government', 355, 390; Le Cordeur, *Separatism*, 235–6; Duminy, 'Stockenström', 113–15; Warren, 'Municipal Politics', 221–2; Meltzer, 'Cape Town Commerce', 140–1; W.M. Macmillan, *The Cape Colour Question: A Historical Survey* (1927, repr. Cape Town 1969), 261.

85. Le Cordeur, *Separatism*, 246; Hattersley, *Convict Crisis*, 94; Newman, *Montagu*, 385–8.

86. Kirk, 'Self-Government', 360–4; Duminy, 'Stockenström', 137; Peires, *Dead Will Arise*, 1–4, 7, 9–11.

87. Peires, *Dead Will Arise*, 8–11.

88. Ibid, 12–30; Mostert, *Frontiers*, 1014–156; Du Toit, 'Cape Frontier', 47–68; Crais, *Colonial Order*, 173–88; Harington, *Smith*, 180–203.

89. Le Cordeur, *Separatism*, 250, 270.

90. Le Cordeur, 'Godlonton', 51–2.

91. Duminy, 'Stockenström', 118, 123; Kirk, 'Self-Government', 405; Stockenström, *Brief Notice of the Causes of the Kaffir War* (1851); Smith, *Frontier to Midlands*, 251–3; Du Toit, 'Cape Frontier', 53–4.

92. R. Godlonton and E. Irving, *A Narrative of the Kaffir War of 1850–1852* (Graham's Town, 1852); Duminy, 'Stockenström', 119–23; Le Cordeur, 'Godlonton', 29–46; Stockenström, *Autobiography*, II, 304–8.

93. Kirk, 'Self-Government', 374–5.

94. Kirk, 'Self-Government', 395–8; Duminy, 'Stockenström', 126–7, 146, 157–8.

95. Kirk, 'Self-Government', 397.

96. Kirk, 'Expropriation of the Kat River Settlement'; J.S. Marais, *The Cape Coloured People, 1652–1937* (1939, repr. Johannesburg, 1968), 225–6; Kirk, 'Progress and Decline in the Kat River Settlement', *JAH*, 14, 3 (1973), 416–17; Le Cordeur, *Separatism*, 89; Sales, *Mission Stations*, 146; Macmillan, *CCQ*, 271–9; Richard Lovett, *The History of the London Missionary Society, 1795–1895*, 2 vols. (1899), I, 572–6; Du Plessis, *Christian Missions*, 281–3.

97. Kirk, 'Progress and Decline', 418–19; Marais, *Cape Coloured People*, 231–4; Crais, *Colonial Order*, 164–5; Le Cordeur, *Separatism*, 188–9; Kirk, 'Self-Government', 179–81; Macmillan, *BBB*, 296–7; Sales, *Mission Stations*, 145; Stockenström, *Autobiography*, II, 373, 377–9.

98. Kirk, 'Self-Government', 225–8.

99. Marais, *Cape Coloured People*, 234–9; Kirk, 'Progress and Decline', 420–3; Crais, *Colonial Order*, 165–72; Le Cordeur, 'Godlonton', 29–46; Godlonton, *Separatism*, 189.

100. Kirk, 'Expropriation', 235; Marais, *Cape Coloured People*, 238–9; Stockenström, *Autobiography*, II, 427–32; Sales, *Mission Stations*, 151–2.

101. Crais, *Colonial Order*, 177–88; Sales, *Mission Stations*, 149–53; Macmillan, *Cape Colour Question*, 279–82; Marais, *Cape Coloured People*, 239–45; Elizabeth Elbourne, '"To Colonise the Mind": Evangelical Missionaries in Britain and the Eastern Cape, 1790–1837' (D.Phil., Oxford, 1992), 335–6; Kirk, 'Progress and Decline', 424–5; Kirk, 'Self-Government', 406; Peires, *Dead Will Arise*, 19; James Read Jnr, *The Kat River Settlement in 1851, Described in a Series of Letters Published in the South African Commercial Advertiser* (Cape Town, 1852).

102. Read, Jnr, who was careful to declare himself a loyalist and was publicly critical of the rebels, wrote in a letter to the *Commercial Advertiser* in 1851 that 'The rebels have an indelible impression (wrong, of course, it is) that the Queen's authority was about to cease in this country, and consequently that the coming South African Parliament would be detrimental to their liberties

and civil rights as a people. Strange, however, that they have greater dread of the English than of the Dutch community! ... It is certain that the colonial natives look on the *Graham's Town Journal* as the exponent of the views of what they term "English settlers"; and remembering the principles of this paper ... it is no wonder that they have identified the English with class laws and oppressive legislation ... the coloured people have the idea that the English community incite the Government to wars.' In contrast, they looked on the British government as their 'natural protectors'. Read, *Kat River Settlement*, 113–14. Read's distancing of himself from the rebels, while representing their thoughts, reveals something of his ambiguous position between colonial and 'coloured' society. Also Martin Legassick, 'The State, Racism and the Rise of Capitalism in the Nineteenth-Century Cape Colony', *SAHJ*, 28 (1993), 348–54, on the significance of the events of 1851.

103. Marais, *Cape Coloured People*, 243–5 (quote from 243); Sales, *Mission Stations*, 153; Duminy, 'Stockenström', 83, 91; Kirk, 'Progress and Decline', 427; Anon., *The Trial of Andries Botha, Field Cornet of the Upper Blinkwater in the Kat River Settlement, for High Treason in the Supreme Court of the Colony of the Cape of Good Hope* (Cape Town, 1852). Godlonton set out to justify the break-up of the settlement in *Review of the Condition of the Frontier Hottentots from 1799 to 1851, and of the Incipient Stages of the Rebellion of the Latter Year* (Graham's Town, 1851). Stockenström did not let the matter rest, but his was a lone voice. Duminy, 'Stockenström', 134–6; Stockenström, *Light and Shade as Shown in the Character of the Hottentots of the Kat River Settlement, Being the Substance of a Speech by the Honourable Sir Andries Stockenström in the Legislative Council of the Cape of Good Hope* (Cape Town, 1854); Stockenström, *Autobiography*, II, 352–444. Some coloured landholders survived at the Kat River into the twentieth century. Jeffrey Peires, 'The Legend of Fenner Solomon' in Belinda Bozzoli (ed.), *Class, Community and Conflict: South African Perspectives* (Johannesburg, 1987).

104. Duminy, 'Stockenström', 115–16, 122–6; Kirk, 'Self-Government', 384, 394, 397–9; Du Toit and Giliomee, *Afrikaner Political Thought*, 294–6. In London, Fairbairn published a pamphlet detailing the popular position, *Papers Relative to the Establishment of a Representative Legislature at the Cape of Good Hope* (1851); also [Stockenström and Fairbairn], *Copies of Correspondence with Lord John Russell on Representative Government at the Cape of Good Hope* (1851).

105. Kirk, 'Self-Government', 388–9; Warren, 'Municipal Politics', 222; Le Cordeur, *Separatism*, 252–3.

106. Kirk, 'Self-Government', 417–21.

107. Ibid, 406, 421–32; Le Cordeur, *Separatism*, 251–2, 255–67; Breitenbach, 'Montagu', 265–6; P.B. Borcherds, *An Autobiographical Memoir* (Cape Town, 1861), 347–56; Edna Bradlow, '"The Great Fear" at the Cape of Good Hope, 1851–2', *IJAHS*, 22, 2 (1989), 401–22; John Marincowitz, 'From "Colour Question" to "Agrarian Problem" at the Cape: Reflections on the Interim' in Hugh Macmillan and Shula Marks (eds.), *Africa and Empire: W.M. Macmillan, Historian and Social Critic* (1989), 156–60; Robert Ross, '"Rather Mental than Physical": Emancipations and the Cape Economy' in Nigel Worden and Clifton Crais (eds.), *Breaking the Chains: Slavery and its Legacy in the Nineteenth-Century Cape Colony* (Johannesburg, 1994), 163–4.

108. Harington, *Smith*, 204–18; Le Cordeur, *Separatism*, 261–2.

109. Kirk, 'Self-Government', 406–9, 414–16, 455; Le Cordeur, *Separatism*, 263–4; Breitenbach, 'Montagu', 270; Duminy, 'Stockenström', 129.

110. Kirk, 'Self-Government', 452–4; Le Cordeur, *Separatism*, 262–3; R.W. Murray, *South African Reminiscences* (Cape Town, 1894), 4–5.

111. Kirk, 'Self-Government', 448–9, 456–73; Le Cordeur, *Separatism*, 268; Wilmot, *Southey*, 98–111.

112. Kirk, 'Self-Government', 467.

113. Kirk, 'Self-Government', 473–9; Peires, *Dead Will Arise*, 27–8; Du Toit, 'Cape Frontier', 69–85; *Correspondence of Sir George Cathcart KCB Relative to his Military Operations in Kaffraria* (1856, repr. New York, 1969), *passim*.

114. *Correspondence of Sir George Cathcart*, 347–51; Le Cordeur, 'Godlonton', 53; Kirk, 'Self-Government', 473.

115. *Correspondence of Sir George Cathcart*, 347, 349.

116. Kirk, 'Self-Government', 449–50, 498–9; Le Cordeur, *Separatism*, 268–70. The constitutional ordinance is in G.W. Eybers (ed.), *Select Constitutional Documents Illustrating South African History* (1918), 45–55.

117. Trapido, 'Cape Franchise', 38; McCracken, *New Light*, 105–7, 119–21. On Montagu's initial positive response to Porter's draft, see Bell and Morrell, *Select Documents*, 108–13. Porter regarded the non-racial franchise as a 'safety valve', and likened the Cape franchise to the

emancipation of the Catholics in Ireland: 'no privileges are so sure to be abused as privileges wrung from reluctant hands'. McCracken, *New Light*, 119, 121.
    118. Duminy, 'Stockenström', 154–5.
    119. Peires, *Dead Will Arise*. It is possible that the change in attitude among the Cape Town bourgeoisie towards frontier warfare between the outbreak of the war of 1846 and Mlanjeni's War in 1850 was also facilitated by the fact that by 1850 more immediate prospects for investment and profit than those held out by speculation in Xhosa land were apparently closer at hand, in railway construction and copper mining in Namaqualand for instance.
    120. Trapido, 'Cape Franchise', 37–9.
    121. Macmillan, *CCQ*, 249. See p. 113 above.
    122. Botha, *Fairbairn*, ch. 4; Meltzer, 'Cape Town Commerce', 133, 150; Du Toit and Giliomee, *Afrikaner Political Thought*, 247–50.
    123. Meltzer, 'Cape Town Commerce', 170–4; Stockenström, *Autobiography*, II, 294–5.
    124. Duminy, 'Stockenström', 151.
    125. Kirk, 'Self-Government', 471–2; Murray, *Reminiscences*, 17–19.

Chapter Eight: Colonial Advances, Imperial Retreat

    1. See ch. 6 above on the Griqua and early Transorangia. On Philip's campaign of 1841–2, see Martin Legassick, 'The Griqua, the Sotho–Tswana and the Missionaries, 1780–1840: The Politics of a Frontier Zone' (Ph.D., UCLA, 1969), 576–83; W.M. Macmillan, *Bantu, Boer and Briton: The Making of the South African Native Problem*, 2nd ed. (1963), 222–30; John S. Galbraith, *Reluctant Empire: British Policy on the South African Frontier, 1834–1854* (Berkeley, 1963), 197–200; Andrew Ross, *John Philip, 1775–1851: Missions, Race and Politics in South Africa* (Aberdeen, 1986), 159–71.
    2. Macmillan, *Bantu, Boer and Briton*, 222–3, 226. On annexation of the Griqua territory Philip wrote, 'I would be contented to die to see this object accomplished.' In 1845 he wrote that 'The simplest and only method is to take the Griquas into the Colony, and to get Moshesh to agree to have a fort in his territory to keep the way to Natal open.' Galbraith, *Reluctant Empire*, 198; Macmillan, *Bantu, Boer and Briton*, 240; C.F.J. Muller, *Die Britse Owerheid en die Groot Trek* (Cape Town, 1948), 229–33. Godlonton, who in the early 1840s was leading a vociferous campaign to secure British annexation of Natal, urged the extension of British rule in Transorangia too, but for reasons very different from Philip's. A.L. Harington, 'The *Graham's Town Journal* and the Great Trek, 1834–1843', *AYB* (1969, II), 96–105; Michael Streak, *The Afrikaner as Viewed by the English, 1795–1854* (Cape Town, 1974), 182–4.
    3. Philip–Hare, 12 July 1842, *Basutoland Records*, 4 vols. (1883, repr. Cape Town, 1964), I, 44–6; Galbraith, *Reluctant Empire*, 199.
    4. Casalis–Hare, 30 May 1842, *BR*, I, 42–3; French missionaries–Hare, 30 May 1842, *BR*, I, 43–4.
    5. Macmillan, *Bantu, Boer and Briton*, 234–5; Galbraith, *Reluctant Empire*, 199–200.
    6. Napier–Stanley, 15 Sept. 1842, *BR*, I, 49; 'Proclamation', 7 Sept. 1842, *BR*, I, 48.
    7. P.J. van der Merwe, *Die Noordwaartse Beweging van die Boere voor die Groot Trek, 1770–1842* (The Hague, 1937), 353–7; Muller, *Britse Owerheid*, 131–2, 137, 186–7; Macmillan, *Bantu, Boer and Briton*, 236–8; A. Ross, *Philip*, 171–4; Galbraith, *Reluctant Empire*, 202–4; Robert Ross, *Adam Kok's Griquas: A Study in the Development of Stratification in South Africa* (Cambridge, 1976), 49–53. Histories in the Afrikaner nationalist tradition dealing with political developments in Transorangia in the 1840s include J.H. Malan, *Die Opkoms van 'n Republiek, of die Geskiedenis van die Oranje-Vrystaat tot 1863* (Bloemfontein, 1929), chs. 4–6; F.A. van Jaarsveld, *Die Eenheidstrewe van die Republikeinse Afrikaners. Deel I: Pioniershartstogte, 1836–1864* (Johannesburg, 1951), ch. 2; M.C.E. van Schoor, 'Politieke Groeperinge in Transgariep', *AYB* (1950, II), chs. 1, 2; Van Schoor, 'Die Nasionale en Politieke Bewuswording van die Afrikaner en sy Ontluiking in Transgariep tot 1854', *AYB* (1963, II), ch. 1; G.D.J. Duvenage, 'Willem Hendrik Jacobs' se Rol in die Onafhanklikheid en Eenheidstrewe van die Voortrekkers op die Hoëveld, 1847–1852', *AYB* (1956, I), ch. 1.
    8. Macmillan, *Bantu, Boer and Briton*, 247; Muller, *Britse Owerheid*, 138, 204–9; Galbraith, *Reluctant Empire*, 204; R. Ross, *Adam Kok's Griquas*, 53–5; L.M. Thompson, *Survival in Two Worlds: Moshoeshoe of Lesotho, 1786–1870* (Oxford, 1975), 120–5; J.S. Marais, *The Cape Coloured People, 1652–1937* (1939, repr. Johannesburg, 1968), 53–4; 'Articles of Treaty', 5 Oct. 1843, *BR*, I, 55–6.
    9. Thompson, *Survival in Two Worlds*, 109–14, 124–32; Peter Sanders, *Moshoeshoe, Chief of the Sotho* (1975), 61–8, 102–3; Galbraith, *Reluctant Empire*, 91–7, 205; A. Ross, *Philip*, 175–7; Legassick, 'Griqua', 561–3, 588–9; Shaw–H. Hudson, 15 Dec. 1843, *BR*, I, 57–60; Casalis–

Rawstorne, 19 March 1844, *BR*, I, 65–8, etc. On the Rolong of Thaba Nchu, see Colin Murray, *Black Mountain: Land, Class and Power in the Eastern Orange Free State, 1880s–1980s* (Edinburgh, 1992), 13–15.

10. A. Ross, *Philip*, 178–9; Legassick, 'Griqua', 607–8; Macmillan, *Bantu, Boer and Briton*, 242.

11. Macmillan, *Bantu, Boer and Briton*, 250–2; Galbraith, *Reluctant Empire*, 206.

12. Moshesh–Montagu, 15 May 1845, *BR*, I, 87.

13. Eugène Casalis, *My Life in Basutoland* (1889, repr. Cape Town, 1971); Casalis, *The Basutos, or Twenty-Three Years in South Africa* (1861, repr. Cape Town, 1965).

14. It would be wrong to imagine two distinct communities, one of British loyalists and the other of rebels. W.Y. Thompson, missionary at Philippolis, was correct when he wrote in 1842 that the 'firm adherents' of either party were 'extremely few'. 'With the great mass of the emigrants it is a matter of indifference whether they belong to [the British] Government or to the "Modder River Republic" and they will assuredly adhere to the strongest party.' Macmillan, *Bantu, Boer and Briton*, 244.

15. Casalis–Hare, 16 Oct. 1844, *BR*, I, 80–1; Casalis–Pottinger, 14 April 1847, *BR*, I, 131–2; Casalis, *The Basutos*, 118. In 1839 Moshoeshoe had sent a circular informing Boers that he had no objection to their grazing their flocks on Sotho land until they were able to proceed further, on condition that they lived at peace with his people and recognised his (Moshoeshoe's) authority. Moshesh–Stockenström, 26 Nov. 1839, *BR*, I, 36.

16. Deposition of J. de Winnaar, 11 September 1858, *BR*, II, 430. Several such depositions are contained in *BR*, II, 424–38.

17. Moshesh, 'Bekendmaking', 29 Oct. 1844, *BR*, I, 81; also Moshoeshoe–Maitland, 15 May 1845, *BR*, I, 86.

18. Galbraith, *Reluctant Empire*, 206–9; Macmillan, *Bantu, Boer and Briton*, 252–7; Thompson, *Survival in Two Worlds*, 133–6; A. Ross, *Philip*, 179–84; R. Ross, *Adam Kok's Griquas*, 56– 62; *The Touwfontein Letters of William Porter, May–July 1845*, ed. Karel Schoeman (Cape Town, 1992); 'Terms of Treaty', 30 June 1845, *BR*, I, 88–91.

19. Eighty-four Boers in the lower Caledon petitioned Governor Maitland in August 1845 objecting to the drawing of a boundary line, clearly implying that they had no objection to living in an area over which Moshoeshoe's political authority was recognised, or in which African subjects of the paramount lived interspersed with Boer farms. Free State Archives, OSB 1/1, 215–18, 84 emigrant British subjects–Maitland, 19 August 1845.

20. Walker, *Great Trek*, 344–5; Sanders, *Moshoeshoe*, 91–2; Van Schoor, 'Politieke Groeperinge', 9–11.

21. OSB 1/3, 543–5, 547–50, 'Deposition of C.R. Eberhardt', Smithfield, 27 and 28 May 1852, 4 June 1852.

22. OSB 1/3, 193–5, H.J. Halse–Warden, 11 August 1847. Halse, like so many settler accumulators of the eastern Cape, had profited from British military expenditure in the war of 1834–5, making a profit of £150 in a week by selling horses to the army. Alan Webster, 'Land Expropriation and Labour Extraction under Cape Colonial Rule: The War of 1835 and the "Emancipation" of the Fingo' (MA, Rhodes, 1991), 188–9.

23. A.L. Harington, *Sir Harry Smith: Bungling Hero* (Cape Town, 1980), 111–17. This period of British intervention in Transorangia is analysed in Timothy Keegan, 'The Making of the Orange Free State, 1846–1854: Sub-Imperialism, Primitive Accumulation and State Formation', *Journal of Imperial and Commonwealth History*, 17, 1 (1988), 26–54. Parts of this chapter are drawn from that study. On Warden, see B.J. Barnard, 'Lewensbeskrywing van Majoor Henry Douglas Warden', *AYB* (1948, I). The Sovereignty period is dealt with in J.F. Midgley, 'The Orange River Sovereignty, 1848–1854', *AYB* (1949, II).

24. R. Ross, *Adam Kok's Griquas*, 62–5; Harington, *Smith*, 113–14; J.J. Freeman, *A Tour in South Africa* (1851), 242–57 (quote from 254).

25. 'Conference between Governor Sir H.G. Smith and Chief Moshesh', 27 Jan. 1848, *BR*, I, 158–9; Casalis–Rolland, 14 Feb. 1848, *BR*, III, 98–102; Sanders, *Moshoeshoe*, 98–101.

26. Sanders, *Moshoeshoe*, 99.

27. Casalis–Rolland, 14 Feb. 1848, *BR*, III, 100–1; Moshesh–Smith, 28 April 1848, *BR*, I, 171.

28. B.J. Liebenberg, *Andries Pretorius in Natal* (Pretoria, 1977), 266–80; Harington, *Smith*, 117–27; Galbraith, *Reluctant Empire*, 227–32; proclamation in *British Parliamentary Papers*, Irish University Press edn, vol. 22, 233–4.

29. *BPP*, vol. 22, 229–32, Smith–Grey, 3 Feb. 1848; *BPP*, 237–8, Grey–Smith, 21 June 1848.

30. *BPP*, vol. 22, 235–6, Proclamation of Sir H.G. Smith, 8 March 1848.

31. Pretorius–Moshesh, 20 April 1848, *BR*, I, 169. On the insurrection, see Liebenberg,

Pretorius, 282–96; Harington, *Smith*, 130–41; Malan, *Opkoms*, ch. 10; Van Schoor, 'Politieke Groeperinge', chs. 5–8. Pretorius wrote to Smith that the British 'have brought the Colonial Native Chiefs into an unavoidable state of enmity against the Emigrant Boers; whereas we formerly lived with them in a peaceable and friendly manner'. He charged that the extension of British rule north of the Orange would similarly turn black peoples with whom they had previously lived in 'peace and security' into their 'enemies and persecutors'. Free State Archives, OSH 1/9, 329–31, 361–5, Pretorius–Smith, 18 Feb. and 22 April 1848. This view of British imperialism as a destabilising factor in race relations and Boer emigrants as benevolently disposed towards African peoples among whom they lived, was clearly very different from the view propagated by humanitarian-minded contemporaries and by subsequent historians.

32. Moshesh–Pretorius, 28 April 1848, *BR*, I, 170.

33. Cape Archives, GH 10/2 and 10/3, *passim*; BPP, vol. 28, 258–63, 266–8, 271–7, Smith–Grey, various; proclamation in *BPP*, 309–10.

34. *BPP*, vol. 28, 305–6, Smith–Grey, 10 Sept. 1848; *BPP*, 316–19, Smith–Grey, 18 Sept. 1848.

35. Gustav Baumann and E. Bright, *The Lost Republic: The Biography of a Land Surveyor* (1940), 239–55; GH 10/3, 240– 3, Vowe–Southey, 28 Sept. 1848, on the complexities of the land claims the commissions had to deal with. For example, the *maatschappy* landdrosts in Winburg had apparently issued *uittreksels* or claims to a particular farm for some 2s 6d each, one of the few sources of income available to the unpaid and part-time Boer officials elected to this post. When the British land commission set to work in 1848, they discovered that two or three such claims were sometimes issued for the same piece of land, and that those who applied for them were often aware that there were other claims for the same land in the hands of others. It was even alleged that clerks to the landdrosts had issued these *uittreksels* for a bottle of brandy apiece. Indeed, such documents became common currency, and at least one enterprising man was a large-scale dealer in them. The British land commission invalidated and destroyed dozens of such claims; and magistrate Biddulph reported that hundreds were still in circulation north of the Vaal, fetching 5s each. GH 10/3, 253, Biddulph–Southey, 31 Oct. 1848; OSH 1/2, 11–12, Biddulph's memorandum attached to R. van Rooyen–Smith, 2 Aug. 1848.

36. George Clerk, special commissioner, reported after inspecting the land registers in 1853 that of 1265 farms inspected and to which titles had been issued since the Sovereignty had been established, 264 were registered in the names of 139 English-speakers, of whom the majority had never occupied their land. Of the 11 million acres that had been granted to white landowners, the British settlers and speculators owned nearly 2 million (22.4 per cent), or an average of 17 750 acres per landowner, while each Boer held an average of about 8500 acres. Among the worst offenders, he reported, were the officials. The leading government employees owned some 310 500 acres between them. *BPP*, vol. 36, 291–2, Clerk–Newcastle, 25 Aug. 1853; *BPP*, 303, Clerk–Newcastle, 8 Oct. 1853; *BPP*, 317, Table of acreages owned by several officials. The British Resident, Major Warden, himself acquired a 13 000-acre farm, Douglas Valley, adjoining the Bloemfontein town lands. 'Notice', *Friend*, 4 March 1854. See also Elizabeth Eldredge, *A South African Kingdom: The Pursuit of Security in Nineteenth-Century Lesotho* (Cambridge, 1993), 53–7; J.M. Orpen, *Reminiscences of Life in South Africa from 1846 to the Present Day* (1908, repr. Cape Town, 1964), 221–2.

37. J. Haasbroek, *Die Rol van die Engelse Gemeenskap in die Oranje-Vrystaat, 1848–1859*, Memoirs van die Nasionale Museum, 15 (Bloemfontein, 1980), 11–14; Galbraith, *Reluctant Empire*, 271; B.A. le Cordeur, *The Politics of Eastern Cape Separatism, 1820–1854* (Cape Town, 1981), 217; Editorial, *Friend*, 24 March 1851, 19 Nov. 1853.

38. GH 10/2, 378, Warden–Southey, 3 June 1849; GH 10/2, 253–4, Vaal River District, July 1849; Editorial, *Friend*, 24 March 1851. On the history of this region see Timothy Keegan, 'White Settlement and Black Subjugation on the South African Highveld: The Tlokoa Heartland in the North Eastern Orange Free State, *ca* 1850–1914' in W. Beinart, P. Delius and S. Trapido (eds.), *Putting a Plough to the Ground: Accumulation and Dispossession in Rural South Africa, 1850–1930* (Johannesburg, 1986), 218–58.

39. OSB 1/1, 141–2, Garvock–Warden, 13 June 1850.

40. 'Postscript', *Friend*, 10 June 1850; 'Farms in the Vaal River District', *Friend*, 17 June 1850; 'Extensive Sale of Landed Property', *Friend*, 24 Dec. 1853; Arthur R. Orpen, Advert., *Friend*, 14 August 1852; Henry Slater, 'Land, Labour and Capital in Natal: The Natal Land and Colonisation Company, 1860–1948', *JAH*, 16, 2 (1975), 267; F.A. Steytler, *Die Geskiedenis van Harrismith* (Bloemfontein, c.1933), 139–43; Orpen, *Reminiscences*, 64–5. The land surveyor De Kok remembered the commission inspecting 250 farms in 32 days, being followed by 'swarms of applicants and land agents'. K.J. de Kok, *Empires of the Veld* (Durban, 1904), 46, 205.

41. 'Explorator' to ed., *Friend*, 26 Jan. 1852; 'Veritas' to ed., *Friend*, 13 March 1852.

42. Steytler, *Harrismith*, 84; Orpen, *Reminiscences*, 58.

43. GH 20/2, J. Russell–G. Clerk, 2 March 1855; GH 10/2, 509–11, Warden–Southey, 10 Dec. 1849; OSB 1/1, 69–70, Southey–Warden, 31 Jan. 1850; OSB 1/1, 145–6, Garvock–Warden, 20 June 1850.

44. Edit., *Friend*, 4 Sept. 1850, 24 March 1851, 26 May 1851, 4 August 1851; Advert., *Friend*, 24 April 1852; GH 10/2, 461–3, Warden–Southey, 30 Sept. 1849.

45. 'Caledon Riviers Landbouwkundige Tentoonstelling', *Friend*, 21 April 1853; Edit., *Friend*, 17 Feb. 1853.

46. Haasbroek, *Engelse Gemeenskap*, 18–22; Le Cordeur, *Eastern Cape Separatism*, 218; Karel Schoeman, 'The Friend through the Formative Years', *Africana Notes and News*, 25, 2 (1982), 63–6. Godlonton, like so many of his colleagues, was involved in the land grab north of the Orange just as in the eastern Cape, owning five farms in the Sovereignty. He foresaw the incorporation of the Orange River Sovereignty into the separatist regime he was agitating for in the eastern Cape, firmly under the control of Graham's Town settler interests. Le Cordeur, *Separatism*, 258; Tony Kirk, 'The Cape Economy and the Expropriation of the Kat River Settlement, 1846–53' in Shula Marks and Anthony Atmore (eds.), *Economy and Society in Pre-Industrial South Africa* (1980), 241.

47. Edit., *Friend*, 14 August 1852.

48. OSH 1/2, 77–92, Vowe–Garvock, 12 March 1850; GH 10/2, 250, 26 landed proprietors and householders of Bloemfontein–Legislative Council, 19 July 1849; GH 20/2, Green–Government Clerk, 1 Nov. 1855; 'Interior Commerce', *Friend*, 8 May 1852; OSB 1/4, 443–50, Petition from Inhabitants of Harrismith, n.d. On the commercial class of the towns, see Haasbroek, *Engelse Gemeenskap*.

49. OSB 1/4, 55–6, Biddulph–Warden, 30 March 1851; GH 10/2, 252, Draft of a Bill, 21 July 1849.

50. 'An English Farmer' to ed., *Friend*, 31 March 1851; 'Postscript', *Friend*, 10 March 1851; Edit., *Friend*, 14 Oct. 1850, 25 August 1851, 10 July 1852. A good deal of information on such trading networks is contained in Martha Kirk's memoirs in *The Early Days of the Orange Free State*, ed. Karel Schoeman, Vrijstatia series 10 (Cape Town, 1989), 47–88. Kirk was settled during the Sovereignty period at Platberg, and later at Thaba Bosiu under Moshoeshoe's direct patronage. She travelled north across the Vaal River with Sotho grain to barter with the Transvaal Boers, and south to Burghersdorp in the colony to buy goods such as clothing to sell to Moshoeshoe and his chiefs. Governor Cathcart wrote that Moshoeshoe's people 'grow almost all the corn that is used in the Sovereignty, where the burghers only rear cattle, which they exchange for his grain'. *Correspondence of Lt.-Gen. Sir George Cathcart, KCB* (1856, repr. New York, 1969), 345.

51. GH 10/3, 284–90, Biddulph–Southey, 10 Nov. 1848.

52. Shaw–Montagu, 4 May 1848, *BR*, I, 173; GH 22/3, Chase–Southey, 10 April 1848; Haasbroek, *Engelse Gemeenskap*, 52.

53. Warden–Moshesh, 5 Feb. 1848, Moshesh–Warden, 15 Feb. 1848, *BR*, I, 166–7; correspondence in *BR*, I, 180–97; Peter Sanders, 'Sekonyela and Moshweshwe: Failure and Success in the Aftermath of the Difaqane', *JAH*, 10 (1969), 439–55.

54. Warden–Smith, 9 June 1848, *BR*, I, 175; Proceedings of the Land Commission, 8 Nov. 1848, *BR*, I, 191–7; Warden–Smith, 18 Nov. 1848, *BR*, I, 205–6.

55. Sanders, *Moshoeshoe*, 151–3; Southey–Casalis, 3 Dec. 1848, *BR*, I, 208; Moshesh–Rolland, 9 Dec. 1848, *BR*, I, 209–10; Southey–Moshesh, 11 Dec. 1848, *BR*, I, 210–11; Alex Wilmot, *The Life and Times of Sir Richard Southey* (1904), 57–9.

56. Moshesh–Warden, 17 Jan. 1849, *BR*, I, 217–18.

57. OSH 1/3, 375–85, Hoffman–family, 1 Jan. 1849. Hoffman had the previous month been prosecuted by Vowe and fined £50 for trading at Beersheba without a licence. Testimony was that it was well known in the vicinity that Hoffman kept a 'regular store' at his house. GH 10/3, 326–8, Report of proceedings in the court of RM Caledon River, 16 Dec. 1848.

58. Casalis–Smith, 28 Dec. 1848, *BR*, I, 211–14.

59. GH 10/3, 476–7, Vowe–Southey, 22 Jan. 1849; GH 10/3, 413–14, Vowe–Southey, 12 April 1849; GH 10/2, 291–4, Warden–Smith, 25 Feb. 1849.

60. Wessels–Vowe, 15 Jan. 1849, *BR*, I, 214–15.

61. Correspondence in *BR*, I, 232–8, 246–8; also Freeman, *Tour in South Africa*, 316–26.

62. Vowe–Warden, 30 June 1849, *BR*, I, 248–9; OSB 1/3, 239, Halse–Vowe, 1 August 1849; OSB 1/3, 233–6, H.J. Wessels–Warden, 29 July 1849; Warden–Southey, 2 Sept. 1849, *BR*, I, 276.

63. Warden–Smith, 5 August 1849, *BR*, I, 259–61; Warden–Southey, 5 August 1849, *BR*, I, 261.

64. Warden–Smith, 23 June 1849, *BR*, I, 245; Smith–Warden, 16 August 1849, *BR*, I, 265–6; Minutes of Meeting of Native Chiefs at Bloemfontein, 27 August 1849, *BR*, I, 270–3;

Warden–Smith, 26 August 1849, *BR*, I, 268–70.
65. OSB 1/3, 241–3, Smit–Warden, 15 Dec. 1849.
66. Moshesh–Warden, 21 Sept. 1849, *BR*, I, 283.
67. GH 10/3, 74, J. O'Reilly–Southey, 18 May 1848; GH 10/3, 138, O'Reilly–Southey, 24 June 1848; GH 10/3, 143–5, O'Reilly–Southey, 27 June 1848; GH 10/3, 146–51, O'Reilly–Southey, 29 June 1848; GH 10/3, 281–3, Vowe–Southey, 25 Oct. 1848; GH 10/3, 102, C.S. Halse–O'Reilly, 7 June 1848; GH 10/3, 312–15, proceedings in the court of the RM, 23 Oct. 1848.
68. GH 10/3, 156–7, Rex–Southey, 24 June 1848; OSH 1/7, 175–81, Robertson–Smith, 14 March 1849; GH 10/3, 429–33, Vowe–Southey, 7 May 1849; GH 10/2, 374–6, Warden–Southey, 27 May 1849.
69. Moshesh–Snyman, 13 Sept. 1849, *BR*, I, 278; OSH 1/3, 387–8, Snyman–Smith, 2 Nov. 1849; OSH 1/2, 93–113, Anon.–Smith, n.d.; GH 10/2, 506–8, Warden–Southey, 25 Nov. 1849.
70. Warden–Snyman, 22 Sept. 1849, *BR*, I, 285; OSH 1/2, 77–92, Vowe–Garvock, 12 March 1850.
71. Warden–Moshesh, 2 Oct. 1850, *BR*, I, 333–4; Warden–Garvock, 5 Oct. 1850, *BR*, I, 337–8; Warden–Garvock, 10 Nov. 1850, *BR*, I, 348–9; Warden–Garvock, 18 Nov. 1850, *BR*, I, 349–50.
72. Warden–Moshesh, 27 Dec. 1850, *BR*, I, 351–2.
73. E.g., OSB 1/4, 101–2, Biddulph–Warden, 4 June 1851; OSB 1/4, 133–7, Biddulph–Warden, 12 July 1851; OSB 1/4, 231–4, Biddulph–Warden, 13 Sept. 1851.
74. Warden–Garvock, 9, 16 and 27 June 1851, *BR*, I, 409–11, 414–15.
75. Warden–Smith, 6 July 1851, *BR*, I, 421–2; Van Schoor, 'Politieke Groeperinge', ch. 11; Malan, *Opkoms*, ch. 12; Midgley, 'Orange River Sovereignty', ch. 9.
76. 'Postscript', *Friend*, 14 July 1851; Edit., *Friend*, 28 July 1851.
77. Warden–Smith, 6 July 1851, *BR*, I, 421–2; Warden–Garvock, 3 August 1851, *BR*, I, 432–3.
78. Smith–Warden, 22 July 1851, *BR*, I, 429–30; Smith–Warden, 2 Sept. 1851, *BR*, I, 440–1.
79. OSB 1/3, 361–6, Vowe–Warden, 13 July 1851; OSB 1/3, 391–3, 395–8, Vowe–Warden, 9 August 1851; A.H. Brown to ed., *Friend*, 25 August 1851.
80. Warden–Garvock, 14 and 27 July 1851, *BR*, I, 428, 431.
81. 'Postscript', *Friend*, 14 July 1851; OSB 1/3, 377–9, C.S. Halse–Warden, 6 August 1851; OSB 1/3, 381–3, Deposition of H.J. Halse, 2 August 1851; H.J. Halse to ed., *Friend*, 29 Sept. 1851; C.S. Halse to ed., *Friend*, 8 Dec. 1851; OSB 1/3, Declaration of G.W. Voesee, Thaba Bosiu, 8 Sept. 1851; G.W. Voesee to ed., *Friend*, 27 Oct. 1851; OSB 1/3, 487–94, Vowe–Warden, 3 Oct. 1851.
82. OSB 1/3, 385–6, 487, Vowe–Warden, 8 August and 3 Oct. 1851.
83. 'A Farmer' to ed., *Friend*, 18 August 1851.
84. 'Amicus' to ed., *Friend*, 18 August 1851; also OSB 1/3, 547–50, Deposition of C.R. Eberhardt, Smithfield, 28 May 1852.
85. OSB 1/3, 487–94, Vowe–Warden, 3 Oct. 1851; Wm Holder to ed., *Friend*, 13 Oct. 1851; 'Public Meeting', *Friend*, 27 Oct. 1851; memorial in *BR*, I, 451. The meeting also condemned the capture and distribution among certain farmers in 1850 of some 200 'Bushmen' living on farms belonging to absentee speculators, including Charles Halse and other leading British settlers. Halse pointed out that J.T. Snyman, at the time still commandant of the district, had participated in the raid, and had himself received seven of the captives as his booty. C. Halse to ed., *Friend*, 8 Dec. 1851.
86. OSB 1/4, 157–62, Biddulph–Warden, 29 July 1851.
87. Edit., *Friend*, 8 Dec. 1851.
88. OSH 1/5, 539–42, Petition from 64 loyal inhabitants of Winburg district, 31 July 1851; OSB 1/4, 199–201, Extracts from J. Fick–Biddulph, 12 and 15 August 1851; OSH 1/5, 569–70, M.H. Wessels–Smith, 16 August 1851; OSH 1/5, 563–4, G.H. Meyer–Smith, 16 August 1851; OSB 1/4, 247–8, J. Fick–Warden, 13 Nov. 1851; Edit., *Friend*, 20 Oct. 1851; 'Communicated', *Friend*, 27 Oct. 1851.
89. OSB 1/4, 167–77, 179–86, Biddulph–Warden, 7 and 16 August 1851.
90. OSB 1/4, 219–28, Petitions from Winburg district to A.W.J. Pretorius; Edit., *Friend*, 27 Oct., 10 and 24 Nov. 1851.
91. Edit., *Friend*, 7 and 14 July 1851.
92. Grey–Smith, 15 Sept. 1851, *BR*, I, 445–8; also Grey–Smith, 21 Oct. 1851, *BR*, I, 463.
93. F.A.F. Wichmann, 'Die Wordingsgeskiedenis van die Zuid-Afrikaansche Republiek, 1838–1860' in *AYB* (1941, II), 110–17; Galbraith, *Reluctant Empire*, 256–60; the Convention is contained in G.W. Eybers (ed.), *Select Constitutional Documents Illustrating South African History, 1795–1910* (1918), 358–9.
94. 'Rough Notes of a Tourist', *Friend*, 18 Nov. 1854; report in *Graham's Town Journal*, 6 Jan. 1849; Muller, *Britse Owerheid*, 135–6, 173–9, 194–8, 216.

95. OSB 1/6, 505–6, Pretorius–Warden, 4 Oct. 1851.

96. The route to the ivory-rich Lake Ngami region was pioneered in 1850. The Potchefstroom Boers sought to monopolise it, requiring that all traders and hunters pass through the town. The trader J. McCabe was prosecuted in Potchefstroom for publicising the route in a Cape newspaper. OSB 1/1, 159–65, J. Montagu–Warden, 11 July 1850; OSH 1/9, 425–7, Pretorius–Assistant Commissioners, 22 Oct. 1852; 'Transvaal Boers', *Friend*, 17 June 1850.

97. *BPP*, vol. 36, 204–7, Cathcart–Secretary of State, 14 Nov. 1852; *Correspondence of Sir George Cathcart*, 137–44, 154–6, 164–82, 230–3; Edit., *Friend*, 18 Nov. 1852.

98. 'By Authority', *Friend*, 30 Dec. 1852; Edit., *Friend*, 2 Dec. 1852, 16 Dec. 1852, 6 Jan. 1853: '*Fear* is not inculcated by leniency. Yet ... fear – *through dread* – is the only reliable hold which a white man can calculate on maintaining over a native.'

99. OSB 1/3, 551–7, 38 Loyal Subjects–Cathcart, n.d.; OSB 1/3, 559–61, Resolutions at a Public Meeting, Smithfield, 24 Dec. 1852; 'A Farmer' to ed., *Friend*, 6 Jan. 1853; 'Petition', *Friend*, 20 Jan. 1853. Cathcart reported to the secretary of state that 'false expectations appear to have arisen on the part of those whom Government influence had hitherto favoured, that I should unscrupulously continue to exercise, to their peculiar benefit, might irrespective of right'. *Correspondence of Sir George Cathcart*, 20.

100. *BPP*, vol. 36, 228, Cathcart–Secretary of State, 13 Jan. 1853; 'Cathcart's Reply', *Friend*, 13 Jan. 1853. Cathcart wrote in September 1853 that the Sovereignty was for the British speculators 'a great gaming-table' which was 'out of the reach of the police' as many colonial debtors owned land there. *Correspondence of Sir George Cathcart*, 376.

101. Petitions are to be found in *BPP*, vol. 36, 272–82, 285, 297. Godlonton contributed in no small measure to the hysteria: see Le Cordeur, 'Robert Godlonton as Architect of Frontier Opinion, 1850–1857', *AYB* (1960, II), 58–63.

102. De Kiewiet, *British Colonial Policy*, 78; also *BPP*, vol. 36, 303, Clerk–Newcastle, 8 Oct. 1853. Clerk considered that speculative land grabbing had been the main cause of conflict with the Sotho; the settlers' 'rapacity ... could not have been expected to promote a good understanding between a tribe of natives who at that time were unoffending, and Europeans'. Significantly he reported after a meeting that Moshoeshoe was not apprehensive about the abandonment, and felt that 'no danger could now result from allowing his relations with the boers to revert to the understanding that generally prevailed between the boers and himself before the British government interfered with them'. Nor were the Boers who resided on his borders apprehensive either, and they had no fears regarding that 'security of their just rights, when not required by authority to place themselves in a position of antagonism towards a chief possessing a considerable degree of moderation and discretion'. *BPP*, vol. 36, 313–14, 336–7, Clerk–Newcastle, 10 Nov. 1853, 14 Jan. 1854. On Clerk's background in Indian administration, and his preference for informal and indirect forms of rule, see Donovan Williams, 'Sir George Russell Clerk and the Abandonment of the Orange River Sovereignty, 1853–54: Room for Another View', *Historia*, 36, 1 (1991), 30–42.

103. *BPP*, vol. 36, 298–9, Clerk–Newcastle, 10 Sept. 1853; *BPP*, 307–9, Proceedings of the Assembly of Delegates, 5–8 Sept. 1853. A memorial from Smithfield signed by 109 accused Clerk of 'cajolery, flattery, private canvassing and ... in some instances bribery' to secure support for his plans. Edit., *Friend*, 4 Feb. 1854.

104. *BPP*, vol. 36, 325–8, 332–4, for memorials from those willing to take over the government. Reports in *Friend*, Dec.–Jan. 1853–4. For reminiscences relating to these events, see W.W. Collins, *Free Statia, or Reminiscences of a Lifetime in the Orange Free State* (1907, repr. Cape Town, 1965), chs. 3, 4; Orpen, *Reminiscences*, chs. 34–41; *A Voice from Bloemfontein: The Reminiscences of Gustav Adolph Fichardt*, ed. D.A. van der Bank, Memoirs van die Nasionale Museum, 19 (Bloemfontein, 1984), ch. 1. On the constitutional history of the republic, see G.D. Scholtz, *Die Konstitusie en Staatsinstellings van die Oranje-Vrystaat, 1854–1902* (Amsterdam, 1937). Also W.P. Morrell, *British Colonial Policy in the Mid-Victorian Age* (Oxford, 1969), 299–304; Tony Kirk, 'Self-Government and Self-Defence in South Africa: The Interrelations between British and Cape Politics, 1846–1854' (D.Phil., Oxford, 1972), 479–86; Galbraith, *Reluctant Empire*, 242–76.

105. 'Gold', *Friend*, 11 Feb. 1854; H. Halse and 7 others–Clerk, 14 Feb. 1854 in *Friend*, 25 Feb. 1854; 'Public Meeting at Smithfield', *Friend*, 11 March 1854.

106. *South African Archival Records: Orange Free State*, vol. 1, *Notule van die Volksraad van die Oranje-Vrystaat, 1854–5* (Parow, 1952), 83 and *passim*.

107. 'A Political Squall', *Friend*, 16 Sept. 1854; H. Struys to ed., *Friend*, 28 Oct. 1854; petitions in *South African Archival Records: Orange Free State*, vol. 1, *passim*.

108. Keegan, 'Boers and Tlhaping of Bethulie'.

109. C.C. Eloff, 'Die Verhouding tussen die Oranje-Vrystaat en Basoetoeland, 1878–1884', *AYB* (1980, II), 125–9; Keegan, 'Tlokoa Heartland'; A.N. Grundlingh, *Die 'Hensoppers' en 'Joiners': Die Rasionaal en Verskynsel van Verraad* (Pretoria, 1979).

Chapter Nine: Conclusion: The Stabilisation of Contradictions

1. On the European predisposition to racial stereotyping, see Winthrop D. Jordan, *White over Black: American Attitudes toward the Negro, 1550–1812* (Chapel Hill, NC, 1968); George Fredrickson, 'Social Origins of American Racism' in Fredrickson, *The Arrogance of Race: Historical Perspectives on Slavery, Racism, and Social Inequality* (Middletown, Conn., 1988).

2. The concept of 'colonial capitalism' has been the subject of much polemical debate, much of it fairly vacuous and pointless. For a theoretical exegesis, see Timothy Keegan, 'The Origins of Agrarian Capitalism in South Africa: A Reply', *JSAS*, 15, 3 (1989), 666–84; also Helen Bradford, 'Highways, Byways and Cul-de-Sacs: The Transition to Agrarian Capitalism in Revisionist South African History', *Radical History Review*, 46/7 (1990), 59–88.

3. Nancy Stepan, *The Idea of Race in Science in Great Britain, 1800–1960* (1982); Christine Bolt, *Victorian Attitudes to Race* (1971); Douglas Lorimer, *Colour, Class and the Victorians: English Attitudes to the Negro in the Mid-Nineteenth Century* (New York, 1978); Patrick Brantlinger, 'Victorians and Africans: The Genealogy of the Myth of the Dark Continent' in Henry L. Gates (ed.), *'Race', Writing and Difference* (Chicago, 1986). Thomas Holt's brilliant *The Problem of Freedom: Race, Labour and Politics in Jamaica and Britain, 1832–1938* (Baltimore, 1992) deals with changing racial ideology in the context of the seminal colony of Jamaica; also Holt, '"An Empire of the Mind": Emancipation, Race and Ideology in the British West Indies and the American South' in J. Morgan Kousser and James McPherson (eds.), *Religion, Race and Reconstruction: Essays in Honour of C. Vann Woodward* (New York, 1982).

4. Richard Elphick and Hermann Giliomee, 'The Origins and Entrenchment of European Dominance at the Cape, 1652–c.1840' in *The Shaping of South African Society, 1652–1840* (Cape Town, 1989), 557–9 and *passim*.

5. Martin Legassick, 'The Griqua, the Sotho–Tswana and the Missionaries, 1780–1840' (Ph.D., UCLA, 1969), 467, 476–7. Also Nosipho Majeke [Dora Taylor], *The Role of the Missionaries in Conquest* (1952, repr. Cape Town, 1986) for a highly polemical and idiosyncratic, and yet thought-provoking, study.

6. Elizabeth Elbourne, '"To Colonise the Mind": Evangelical Missionaries in Britain and the Eastern Cape, 1790–1837' (D.Phil., Oxford, 1992), 340–2.

7. Edgar Brookes, *The History of Native Policy in South Africa from 1830 to the Present Day* (Cape Town, 1924), 91–8.

8. Legassick, 'Griqua', 611–18; J.S. Marais, *The Cape Coloured People, 1652–1937* (1939, repr. Johannesburg, 1968), 42–50.

9. Robert Ross, *Adam Kok's Griquas: A Study in the Development of Stratification in South Africa* (Cambridge, 1976), chs. 7–9; Marais, *Cape Coloured People*, 59–62, 71–3; Timothy Keegan, 'Dispossession and Accumulation in the South African Interior: The Boers and the Tlhaping of Bethulie, 1833–1861', *JAH*, 28, 2 (1987), 191–207.

10. Leonard Thompson, *Survival in Two Worlds: Moshoeshoe of Lesotho, 1786–1870* (Oxford, 1975), chs. 6, 7; Anthony Atmore, 'The Passing of Sotho Independence, 1865–1870' in Leonard Thompson (ed.), *African Societies in Southern Africa: Historical Studies* (1969), 282–301.

11. Saul Dubow, *Land, Labour and Merchant Capital: The Experience of the Graaff-Reinet District in the Pre-Industrial Rural Economy of the Cape, 1852–1872*, Communications 6, Centre for African Studies (Cape Town, 1982); Robert Ross, 'The Origins of Capitalist Agriculture in the Cape Colony: A Survey' in W. Beinart, P. Delius and S. Trapido (eds.), *Putting a Plough to the Ground: Accumulation and Dispossession in Rural South Africa, 1850–1930* (Johannesburg, 1986), 75–6; Alan Mabin, 'The Making of Colonial Capitalism: Intensification and Expansion in the Economic Geography of the Cape Colony, South Africa, 1854–1899' (Ph.D., Simon Fraser, 1984).

12. J.B. Peires, *The Dead Will Arise: Nongqawuse and the Great Xhosa Cattle-Killing Movement of 1856–7* (1989), 45–52, 218–21 and *passim*. On Grey, see J. Rutherford, *Sir George Grey, KCB* (1961); A.E du Toit, 'The Cape Frontier: A Study of Native Policy with Special Reference to the years 1847–1866', *AYB* (1954, I), 86–110. The cattle killing has become a major debating point among historians since Peires's book. See reviews in *SAHJ*, 25 (1991), 227–68, especially the essay by Jack Lewis; also Martin Legassick, 'The State, Racism and the Rise of Capitalism in the Nineteenth Century Cape Colony', *SAHJ*, 28 (1993), 359–65, for an acute analysis. Timothy Stapleton, '"They are Depriving Us of our Chieftainship": The Decline and Fall of the Traditional Xhosa Aristocracy, 1846–1857', *Historia*, 38, 2 (1993), 86–99, provides a

different interpretation.

13. Peires, *Dead Will Arise*, 250–61, 277–86; Peires, 'Sir George Grey versus the Kaffir Relief Committee', *JAH*, 10, 2 (1982), 145–69.

14. Lalou Meltzer, 'The Growth of Cape Town Commerce and the Role of John Fairbairn's *Advertiser*, 1835–1859' (MA, UCT, 1989), 180–2; Sheila van der Horst, *Native Labour in South Africa* (Cape Town, 1942), 30–2. There was no necessary inconsistency in Fairbairn's position here, which he did not substantially alter throughout his public life. He always distinguished between 'civilised' and 'barbarian', just as Philip did, and these Africans simply did not fit in with the ideal of the Christian and civilised native of his imagining, reshaped in the mould of the mission, and therefore they were simply not fit candidates for liberal consideration. See Meltzer, 'Cape Town Commerce', 183–8.

Another prominent liberal, the attorney-general William Porter was a firm supporter of the idea of non-racialism in constitution making. He was shocked at the racial sentiments of British settlers, supported the treaty system and opposed land grabbing, and insisted that coloureds with the necessary qualifications be eligible for jury duty. But after the war of 1846–7, he supported the subjugation of the Xhosa as the only possible response to what he saw as African savagery. In the aftermath of the cattle killing, Porter supported Grey's suppression of the relief committee, as its endeavours merely encouraged Xhosa 'idleness'. Porter, in short, represented the way in which even the most liberal of men could melt into racial hostility when confronted with the unassimilated African masses. J.L. McCracken, *New Light at the Cape of Good Hope: William Porter, The Father of Cape Liberalism* (Belfast, 1993), 95–112; Andrew Bank, 'Liberals and their Enemies: Racial Ideology at the Cape of Good Hope, 1820–1850' (Ph.D., Cambridge, 1995), 362–9; *William Porter, The Touwfontein Letters*, ed. Karel Schoeman (Cape Town, 1992), 38 and *passim*.

15. Colin Bundy, *The Rise and Fall of the South African Peasantry*, 2nd ed. (Cape Town, 1988), ch. 3; Jack Lewis, 'An Economic History of the Ciskei, 1848–1900' (Ph.D., UCT, 1984).

16. Stanley Trapido, '"The Friends of the Natives": Merchants, Peasants and the Political and Ideological Structure of Liberalism in the Cape, 1854–1910' in Shula Marks and Anthony Atmore (eds.), *Economy and Society in Pre-Industrial South Africa* (1980), 247–74; Trapido, 'White Conflict and Non-White Participation in the Politics of the Cape of Good Hope, 1853–1910' (Ph.D., London, 1970); Les Switzer, *Power and Resistance in an African Society: The Ciskei Xhosa and the Making of South Africa* (Madison, Wis., 1993), chs. 3–5; Arthur Keppel-Jones, 'A Case of Minority Rule: The Cape Colony, 1854–1898', in Canadian Historical Association, *Historical Papers* (1966); Phyllis Lewsen, 'The Cape Liberal Tradition: Myth or Reality?', *Race*, 13 (1971), 67–80; Rodney Davenport, 'The Cape Liberal Tradition to 1910' and André du Toit, 'The Cape Afrikaners' Failed Liberal Moment, 1850–1870', both in J. Butler, R. Elphick and D. Welsh (eds.), *Democratic Liberalism in South Africa: Its History and Prospect* (Middletown, Conn., 1987). Lewsen, *John X. Merriman: Paradoxical South African Statesman* (New Haven, 1982) provides an example of a Cape liberal in action.

17. A. Purkis, 'The Politics, Capital and Labour of Railway Building in the Cape Colony, 1870–1885' (D.Phil., Oxford, 1978); Robert Turrell, *Capital and Labour on the Kimberley Diamond Fields, 1871–1890* (Cambridge, 1987); William Worger, *South Africa's City of Diamonds: Mine Workers and Monopoly Capitalism in Kimberley, 1867–1895* (New Haven, 1987).

18. Among a large literature, see Jeff Guy, *The Destruction of the Zulu Kingdom: The Civil War in Zululand, 1879–1884* (1979); William Beinart, *The Political Economy of Pondoland, 1860–1930* (Cambridge, 1982); Peter Delius, *The Land Belongs to Us: The Pedi Polity, the Boers and the British in the Nineteenth-Century Transvaal* (Johannesburg, 1983), chs. 8, 9; Kevin Shillington, *The Colonisation of the Southern Tswana, 1870–1900* (Johannesburg, 1985); Shula Marks and Richard Rathbone (eds.), *Industrialisation and Social Change in South Africa: African Class Formation, Culture and Consciousness, 1870–1930* (1982).

19. Bundy, *South African Peasantry*, ch. 4.

20. There is a large literature on the Natal origins of segregationism: see Brookes, *Native Policy*; David Welsh, *The Roots of Segregation: Native Policy in Colonial Natal, 1845–1910* (Cape Town, 1971); Benjamin Kline, *Genesis of Apartheid: British African Policy in the Colony of Natal, 1845–1893* (1988); Shula Marks, *The Ambiguities of Dependence in South Africa: Class, Nationalism and the State in Twentieth-Century Natal* (Johannesburg, 1986); Nicholas Cope, *To Bind the Nation: Solomon kaDinuzulu and Zulu Nationalism, 1913–1933* (Pietermaritzburg, 1993).

21. Saul Dubow, *Racial Segregation and the Origins of Apartheid in South Africa, 1919–1936* (1989); Dubow, *Illicit Union: Scientific Racism in Modern South Africa* (Johannesburg, 1995).

Index